PHILIP'S

GW00697493

COMPLETE ROAD ATLAS

Britain

and Ireland

www.philips-maps.co.uk

First published in 2009 by Philip's
a division of Octopus Publishing Group Ltd
www.octopusbooks.co.uk
2–4 Heron Quays
London E14 4JP
An Hachette UK Company
www.hachettelivre.co.uk

First edition 2009
First impression 2009

ISBN 978-1-84907-024-9 (spiral)
ISBN 978-1-84907-025-6 (hardback)

Cartography by Philip's
Copyright © 2009 Philip's

This product includes mapping data licensed from Ordnance Survey®, with the permission of the Controller of Her Majesty's Stationery Office. © Crown copyright 2009. All rights reserved. Licence number 100011710

The map of Ireland on pages XVIII–XIX is based on Ordnance Survey Ireland by permission of the Government Permit Number 8525 © Ordnance Survey Ireland and Government of Ireland and

Ordnance Survey Northern Ireland on behalf of the Controller of Her Majesty's Stationery Office © Crown copyright 2009 Permit Number 90005.

Data for the speed cameras provided by **PocketGPSWorld.com Ltd**.

Information for National Parks, Areas of Outstanding Natural Beauty, National Trails and Country Parks in Wales supplied by the Countryside Council for Wales.

Information for National Parks, Areas of Outstanding Natural Beauty, National Trails and Country Parks in England supplied by Natural England. Data for Regional Parks, Long Distance Footpaths and Country Parks in Scotland provided by Scottish Natural Heritage.

Gaelic name forms used in the Western Isles provided by Comhairle nan Eilean.

Data for the National Nature Reserves in England provided by Natural England. Data for the National Nature Reserves in Wales provided by Countryside Council for Wales. Darparwyd data'n ymwneud â Gwarchodfeydd Natur Cenedlaethol Cymru gan Gyngor Cefn Gwlad Cymru.

Information on the location of National Nature Reserves in Scotland was provided by Scottish Natural Heritage.

Data for National Scenic Areas in Scotland provided by the Scottish Executive Office. Crown copyright material is reproduced with the permission of the Controller of HMSO and the Queen's Printer for Scotland. Licence number C02W0003960.

Printed in China

*Independent research survey, from research carried out by Outlook Research Limited, 2005/06.

**Estimated sales of all Philip's UK road atlases since launch.

Road map symbols

Motorway, toll motorway
Motorway junction – full, restricted access
Motorway service area – full, restricted access
Motorway under construction

Primary route – dual, single carriageway
Service area, roundabout, multi-level junction
Numbered junction – full, restricted access
Primary route under construction
Narrow primary route

Derby Primary destination

A road – dual, single carriageway
A road under construction, narrow A road

B road – dual, single carriageway
B road under construction, narrow B road

Minor road – over 4 metres, under 4 metres wide
Minor road with restricted access

Distance in miles
Scenic route
Speed camera – single, multiple
Toll, steep gradient – arrow points downhill
Tunnel

National trail – England and Wales
Long distance footpath – Scotland

Railway with station
Level crossing, tunnel
Preserved railway with station

National boundary
County / unitary authority boundary

Car ferry, catamaran
Passenger ferry, catamaran
Hovercraft
Ferry destination, journey time – hrs : mins
Car ferry – river crossing
Principal airport, other airport

National park
Area of Outstanding Natural Beauty – England and Wales National Scenic Area – Scotland
forest park / regional park / national forest
Woodland

Beach
Linear antiquity
Roman road

Hillfort, battlefield – with date
Viewpoint, nature reserve, spot height – in metres
Golf course, youth hostel, sporting venue
Camp site, caravan site, camping and caravan site
Shopping village, park and ride

29 Adjoining page number – road maps

Road map scale 1: 200 000 or 3·15 miles to 1 inch

0   1   2   3 miles
0   1   2   3   4   5 km

Approach map symbols

Motorway
Toll motorway
Motorway junction – full, restricted access
Service area
Under construction
Primary route – dual, single carriageway
Service area
Multi-level junction
roundabout
Under construction
A road – dual, single carriageway

B road – dual, single carriageway
Minor road – dual, single carriageway
Ring road
Distance in miles
Railway with station
Tramway with station
Underground or metro station
Congestion charge area
Uncharged road in congestion charge area

Town plan symbols

Motorway
Primary route – dual, single carriageway
A road – dual, single carriageway
B road – dual, single carriageway
Minor through road
one-way street
Pedestrian roads
Shopping streets
Railway with station
Tramway with station

Bus or railway station building
Shopping precinct or retail park
Park
Building of public interest
Theatre, cinema
Parking, shopmobility
Underground station
Metro station
Hospital, Police station
Post office

Tourist information

☨ Abbey, cathedral or priory
🏛 Ancient monument
Aquarium
Art gallery
Bird collection or aviary
Castle
Church
Country park
England and Wales
Scotland

Farm park
Garden
Historic ship
House
House and garden
Motor racing circuit
Museum
Picnic area
Preserved railway
Race course

Roman antiquity
Safari park
Theme park
Tourist information centre
  open all year
  open seasonally
Zoo
Other place of interest

Relief

Feet	metres
3000	914
2600	792
2200	671
1800	549
1400	427
1000	305
0	0

Speed Cameras

Fixed camera locations are shown using the 40 symbol.

In congested areas the 40 symbol is used to show that there are two or more cameras on the road indicated.

Due to the restrictions of scale the camera locations are only approximate and cannot indicate the operating direction of the camera. Mobile camera sites, and cameras located on roads not included on the mapping are not shown. Where two or more cameras are shown on the same road, drivers are warned that this may indicate that a SPEC system is in operation. These cameras use the time taken to drive between the two camera positions to calculate the speed of the vehicle.

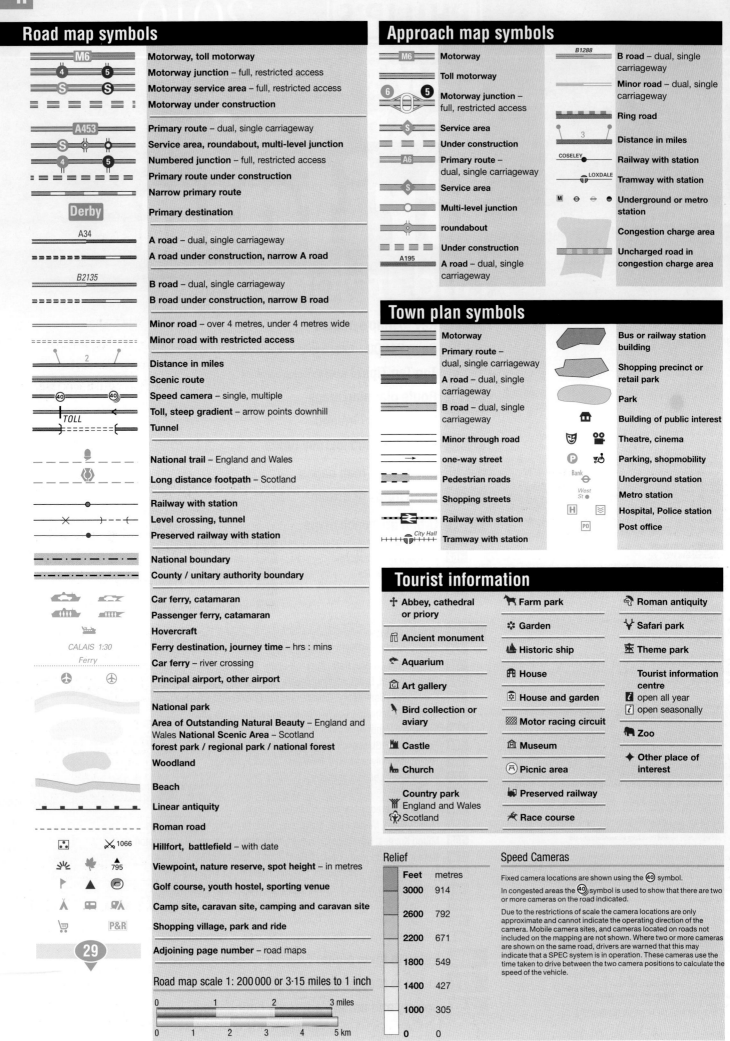

Jonathan Maddock / iStockphoto.com

Save £1000 off your annual motoring costs

Seven Top Tips from motoring journalist Andrew Charman

In today's cost-conscious motoring environment, is it possible to slice serious money from the cost of running a car? With the right preparation, it could well be.

Ask any motorist whether they get good value from their driving and most will likely say no – many argue that motoring has never been more expensive. Drivers fight a constant battle against many enemies including fluctuating fuel prices, aggressive tax rates and an ever-expanding epidemic of safety cameras that many believe are present to generate revenue from fines first, and slow speeds second.

Some 60% of the drivers questioned for the 2008 Annual Report on Motoring compiled by the RAC believed that rising costs were the biggest minus of running a car in Britain today. Those drivers will be surprised to hear that, in fact, motoring is getting cheaper – the report concluded that even rocketing fuel prices have not stopped the overall cost of motoring falling in the past two decades.

The RAC research concluded that such factors as cheaper purchase and maintainance prices for cars have resulted in motoring costs decreasing in real terms by 18% since 1988, despite fuel costs rising 210%. Take those fuel price rises out of the equation and motoring today is 28% cheaper than 20 years ago.

This little bit of good news, however, does not mean that you can't save money on your motoring – and I intend to show you how some simple moves could put significant cash back into your pocket each year – possibly more than £1000.

Different cars, different homes

Saving big money on your motoring costs starts even before you buy the car. The vehicle you choose and how you buy it can make a difference of thousands of pounds, as shown in the panel on page V. But have no fear, because whether you've just bought a brand-new car or have used the same vehicle for many years, you can still save a packet on your motoring costs.

Of course, I can't say exactly what you will save by following the advice in these pages – so many varying factors affect one's motoring expenses. For example, I used to live in commuter-belt Surrey. Every morning I drove my children 8 miles to school, a journey of around half an hour on congested roads. Now I live in Mid-Wales and drive my wife to work, coincidentally also around 8 miles; it takes less than 15 minutes and I use 10–15% less fuel.

Similarly, potential savings in such areas as tyre life will be affected by your car, the way you drive and the roads you drive on. What I can confidently predict, however, is that by following even some of the advice on these pages, you will leave a noticeable amount of cash in your pocket.

In order to calculate these savings, we've devised 'Mr Average Motorist'. He drives a petrol-powered car – because, despite diesel soaring in popularity in recent times, the majority of cars on today's roads still run on petrol. Our man owns a Ford Mondeo family car, which is regularly one of the UK's top ten most popular buys and averages 35mpg in fuel consumption. So, if he clocks up the national average of around 12,000 miles a year, he will use 1558 litres of fuel costing, at current prices, around £1402.

Preparation is everything

Fuel prices are the most visible and most obvious indicator of the cost of motoring today. As I write, the price of a litre of unleaded has plummeted to around 90p, having spent months steadily rising to over £1.20. But by the time you read this, prices could be soaring again and generally they are on the rise – remember that 210% figure within 20 years? We can't change fuel prices – but we can make the best use of every litre we buy.

You might think, then, that the first obvious move is to buy fuel from the cheapest source – but it's not. Before you put any fuel in your tank, you need to check that your car is in the best condition, both mechanically and otherwise, to stretch those litres. Skimping on servicing is NOT a way to save money on motoring. If your engine is not correctly tuned, it uses more fuel. In particular, clean fresh oil not only helps reduce fuel consumption but also wear caused by the friction of moving engine parts. Allow such parts to keep wearing and you could end up with a failure – and all your savings will be wiped out by an expensive repair bill. Ideally, on a petrol car you should change the oil at least once a year, and a diesel engine benefits from a change every six months.

But by far the biggest mechanical influence on fuel economy comes courtesy of what the car stands on – its tyres. Incorrectly inflated tyres, particularly containing too little pressure, leads to less mpg – and, incredibly, research by the tyre industry suggests that half of all tyres running on today's roads are under-inflated. Tyre manufacturers have calculated that for every 6psi a tyre is under-inflated, an extra 1% is added to consumption, and in road-side checks many cars have been found to have tyres under-inflated by as much as 20%.

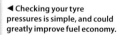

◄ **Checking your tyre pressures is simple, and could greatly improve fuel economy.**

▼ **Under-inflated or damaged tyres could end up costing you more than a bigger fuel bill.**
Photographs courtesy of TyreSafe

Seven Top Tips to save money

1 SLOWING DOWN
average annual saving: up to £532

The first, most obvious area to watch is speed. We are always being told to slow down, but apart from the risk of paying out big money in fines having been caught by a safety camera, there's a far more obvious reason to ease back on that right-hand pedal – it saves money!

The effect is most noticeable on motorways. The national speed limit in Britain is 70mph, but on many a motorway that seems to be treated as a minimum, with traffic charging along at 80mph-plus. However, above 70mph aerodynamic drag becomes a serious issue, really eating into your fuel. If you adopt a more radical attitude, though, cruising along at 50mph instead of 70mph, your fuel costs will plummet, by an astonishing 38% in the average car.

Of course, many drivers will consider slowing down that much, particularly on a clear motorway, as a step too far, but even keeping firmly within speed limits will greatly influence your fuel costs. And there is much more you can do.

Smooth is good – don't, for example, floor the throttle the moment you see a clear stretch of road open up ahead of you. Harsh acceleration, and the resultant equally harsh braking, burns up those litres. Keep a good distance back from the car in front, so you can slow down gently when they do.

Powering around to the red line on your rev counter is another no-no – today's engines work most efficiently at speeds between 1500–2000rpm, and on modern petrol cars changing up a gear at around 2500rpm (2000rpm on a diesel) is both safe, smooth and fuel-friendly.

2 FUEL'S GOLD
average annual saving: up to £420

Find a bargain. Fuel prices charged by garages vary enormously – within a 20-mile radius of my home the differences add up to 5p per litre. And at the time of writing prices are changing almost daily. Clearly the trick is to buy from the cheapest source, but don't drive around looking for cheap prices – you could use as much as you save. Online resources, such as www.petrolprices.com, are a good way of finding out where fuel costs the least in your area, and while prices change constantly, the cheapest garages tend to remain cheapest.

When you've found your cheap supplier, try not to make a special trip to fill up – it's an unnecessary journey that uses fuel. Plan your motoring, factoring in a visit to the garage on the way to or from somewhere else. It's also prudent to visit the garage more often and only run on half a tank instead of a full one, if doing so suits your schedule, because all that extra liquid in a full tank is extra weight.

Myth buster

A few motoring savings that are not always true....

? **Buy your fuel from a busy garage** because the fuel is used quicker, so has no time to age and lose quality

Not necessarily so – The big issue affecting fuel quality is water getting into the tanks through, for example, condensation. Garages periodically remove this water and busier garages may have less chance to do so compared to quieter rural outlets. Fuel quality depends on an individual garage's 'housekeeping' standards and there is no general standard. Also, by going to a busy garage you may lose any potential tiny saving from better-quality fuel while sitting in the queue with your engine running.

? **When buying fuel in the early morning or evening,** you get more for your money because in cooler conditions each litre of liquid becomes denser

False – Most garages keep their fuel in underground tanks, where temperature changes throughout the day are miniscule.

? **Coasting down hills** with the car in neutral saves fuel

False – At least with modern cars. Modern fuel systems cut off the supply to the engine the moment you come off the accelerator, but whether you are in gear or not a tiny amount is still used to ensure the engine does not stall. And without a gear, you have no engine braking, and less control.

? **It's cheaper to** get your car serviced at an independent

Not necessarily so – While independents might appear cheaper than a franchised dealer, because they don't specialize in a particular brand they don't know that brand so well, and crucially often don't possess the same level of diagnostic equipment as a franchised dealer. Therefore, tracing any faults can take significantly longer, which will be charged in service hours.

? **A fast-fit supplier** is the cheapest place to buy new tyres

Not necessarily so – Many franchised dealers are actively price-matching tyres to fast-fit opposition, and if you are told new tyres are needed during a service at the dealer, driving to a fast-fit supplier to find what you expect to be cheaper tyres can be an unnecessary, fuel-using journey.

▲ Nice luggage, but leave the bags in the boot when you don't need them and you are simply adding fuel-using weight.
Photo courtesy Volkswagen UK

▶ Roof racks are useful, but left atop the car when not in use, they simply ruin the aerodynamics, and the fuel economy.
Photo courtesy GM UK

3 CUTTING DRAG
average annual saving: up to £140

Surely we can't change a car's aerodynamics? Oh yes, we can. Did you fit a roof rack to take all the extras for the family holiday last summer? Is it still bolted to the roof? The extra drag from such a large, anything-but-aerodynamic item could be costing you as much as 30% in fuel consumption.

The same goes for bike racks hung on the back of a car – they don't have the same dramatic effect as a roof rack, but they will unsettle the air ahead of them, thus affecting the aerodynamics of the rear end. Even running with your windows open harms the aerodynamics, interrupting the flow along the sides of the car. Do you tow a caravan and use those wing-mirror extensions to see around it? Well, if you haven't got the van hitched behind, take them off – they act like a couple of airbrakes.

4 AVOID THE CON
average annual saving: up to £140

Remember how it was advised to keep your windows closed for the best aerodynamics? Well, this next tip will go against the grain. Most modern cars have air-conditioning and many drivers leave it permanently switched on. But in doing so they can use up to 10% more fuel. Use the fans on cool without the system switched on, or have the window open just a little. If it's really hot, use the air-con for short periods instead of leaving it switched on and forgetting about it.

5 CLEVER FUELLING
average annual saving: up to £78

Planning ahead saves fuel and first you need to ask, 'Do I really need to make this trip?' Cars take a while to warm up during which they use the most fuel, which is why you should drive gently, avoiding stressing the engine, for the first few miles of any journey. But if said trip is merely nipping down to the shops for, say, a pint of milk, the car never has a chance to warm up, and your fuel economy suffers greatly. So for such short journeys consider walking, or perhaps cycling – it will benefit your health, as well as your car and

your wallet. Alternatively, why not combine a number of short journeys in the week – visiting the family one night and doing the shopping on another – into one longer trip, perhaps popping into the garage for fuel at the same time.

Planning ahead comes into its own on longer journeys, especially if travelling to somewhere unfamiliar – you need to know exactly where you are going, to avoid driving around trying to find a destination and eating up extra miles in the process.

Try to avoid congestion hotspots, because sitting in traffic queues not only wastes fuel but also tries one's patience, and when the jam clears we then drive more aggressively, and less fuel-efficiently, to try and make up time. Check where the problems are likely to be – Traffic England, the Highways Agency's website (www.trafficengland.com), carries constantly updated information on traffic issues and even has a facility where one can look at the view from the roadside CCTV cameras to see how heavy the traffic is. Once in the car, listen out for traffic reports on the radio so you can plan ahead and avoid the hot spots. Don't forget to take this road atlas with you so you can use it to detour around problems.

6 PRESSURE POINTS
average annual saving: up to £42

Under-inflated tyres cause increased wear, which as well as becoming dangerous (a bald tyre will harm grip in anything but totally dry conditions, as well as further increasing fuel consumption) reduces the life of the tyre by as much as 30%. You should also check the alignment of your wheels – simply hitting a pothole or a kerb can knock the alignment out, which again will increase tyre wear.

A recent advance in tyre technology, used extensively on the new breed of 'eco' cars, is to cut the tyre's rolling resistance, which is basically the force required to move the rubber over the road. Lower-rolling-resistance tyres require less force and so aid fuel economy, by around 2.5%. Now, less rolling resistance would suggest less grip, which is not very desirable, but these tyres use silica in their construction which effectively puts the grip back. And, surprisingly, such tyres do not generally carry a big price premium over traditional counterparts.

7 CAR WEIGHTWATCHERS
average annual saving: up to £35

Of all the battles fought by motorsport car designers, two areas stand out – reducing the weight of their cars by as much as possible, and making them as smooth as possible, so they slice more efficiently through the air. Exactly the same principles apply to road cars, not for speed, but for economy, and while we would not advocate slicing bits from your car, or trying to add wings and things to a body shape honed over many hours in a wind tunnel by professionals, there are distinct steps one can take that will have major effects on efficiency.

Have you looked in the back of your car recently? Do you know what is in there? Carrying around a lot of unnecessary weight greatly affects fuel economy, and thus your motoring costs – in some cases by as much as 10%. So if you play golf and your clubs and bag live in the boot, or you've been for a day out and left the deckchairs in the car, along with the picnic basket, that weight is squeezing your wallet. Go through the car looking for those pounds that can be shed. You might not think, for example, that a glovebox full of CDs weighs very much, but it all adds up.

Out on the road
There are still big savings to be made, but the onus is now firmly on you and the way you drive the car. So, if you are a bit of a speed merchant, like to use your throttle and brakes, can't remember the last time you checked your tyre pressures, and throw your cases on the roof rack because there's no room left in the boot, following the economy regime above could save you at least £1000 in a year! But even if you are a conscientious motorist who only needs to follow a couple of these Top Tips, you could still save significant money.

▲ Recent on the scene are low-rolling-resistance tyres that extend fuel economy by causing less drag on the road surface.
Photo courtesy Mercedes-Benz

▼ Neglecting servicing is not a way to save money – in fact it will end up exactly the opposite. Photo courtesy ATA

◀ Whether filling up with petrol, diesel or the latest biofuels, a little preparation will make the most of your visit to the garage.
Photo courtesy GM UK

▼ These graphs show how much extra you could be adding to your annual motoring costs, depending on the type of car you drive and the mileage you do. Admittedly this is a 'worst case scenario', assuming that you need to use every part of the advice in this feature, and savings will vary depending on the individual characteristics of your car and your driving environment. However even following some of the advice will save you money. (Chart based on fuel prices of 90p per litre unleaded, 99p per litre diesel)

Road warrior approximately 40,000 miles per year

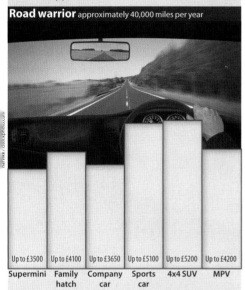

Up to £3500	Up to £4100	Up to £3650	Up to £5100	Up to £5200	Up to £4200
Supermini	Family hatch	Company car	Sports car	4x4 SUV	MPV

Professional driver approximately 22,000 miles per year

Up to £2000	Up to £2270	Up to £2000	Up to £2800	Up to £2900	Up to £2300
Supermini	Family hatch	Company car	Sports car	4x4 SUV	MPV

Family runabout approximately 12,000 miles per year

Up to £1150	Up to £1200	Up to £1100	Up to £1500	Up to £1500	Up to £1300
Supermini	Family hatch	Company car	Sports car	4x4 SUV	MPV

Just for shopping approximately 6000 miles per year

Up to £560	Up to £620	Up to £540	Up to £750	Up to £780	Up to £630
Supermini	Family hatch	Company car	Sports car	4x4 SUV	MPV

Buying a car

Most of us don't buy a new car every year, but when we do, there are thousands of pounds we can potentially save, as long as we do our homework first. Recent research by the AA found that a person spending up to £10,000 on a car could end up with a vehicle returning anything from 33 to almost 70mpg. Over a year, the difference in fuel costs for our average driver would add up to more than £700. When the AA compared the mpg figures for cars costing between £20,000 and £30000, the potential fuel savings came close to £2000! In addition, smaller, greener cars attract lower insurance premiums, and cheaper annual road tax – depending on your model, the cost of a tax disc can vary from £0 to £400 a year.

- **Think carefully before making your choice.** Do you really need a seven-seat people carrier? It might be useful on the few occasions your children bring friends home from school, but most of the time you will be carrying around extra, fuel-burning weight. Do you really want that sporty convertible? Folding roof mechanisms add weight, and as well as being less mpg-friendly to start with, performance engines encourage 'performance' driving, which gobble up those litres.
- **Many manufacturers are now producing new 'eco' versions** of their most popular models, with such refinements as low-rolling-resistance tyres, remapped engine electronics and reshaped aerodynamics to further stretch that fuel economy, and slash CO_2 emissions to levels that qualify for free road tax. But they can sometimes cost significantly more to buy than traditional counterparts.
- **The most economical cars will generally be diesel-powered.** Diesel engines travel a lot further on each litre of fuel and they produce less CO_2. But diesel fuel costs on average around 12p per litre more than the equivalent unleaded petrol – and the majority of diesel-powered cars come with a price premium over their petrol counterparts.
- **Spend time working out your annual mileage** and how far you will need to drive a diesel before you start saving money. Used-car specialist Parkers Guide recently launched a very useful fuel-cost calculator on its website (www.parkers.co.uk), which enables an instant check on how much individual car models will cost you in a year, and it can throw up surprises – for example, at current fuel prices and car list prices, a BMW 318d diesel would take close to 300,000 miles to recoup the £2790 more that it costs over the 318i petrol version.
- **Consider depreciation** when buying. Be sure to check the 'residual value' – which is an industry-quoted figure, easily found on internet sites such as Parkers, predicting how much the car will be worth after three years' use. Many factors influence such values – the make of car, its reliability, additional equipment installed, even in some cases the colour – so it's worth checking carefully to save money down the line.
- **Do you need to buy new?** New cars lose a significant amount of their value – sometimes 20-25% – the moment they are driven off the showroom forecourt. Yet there are many buyers who change their car every year, which adds excellent vehicles to a dealer's nearly-new selection. Many have at least a year of the manufacturer's warranty remaining – some substantially more with several makers moving to five-year and, in the case of Hyundai, seven-year warranties.
- **If you do buy used,** it's crucial to spend a little money, usually no more than £30–£40, on a vehicle data check, which will show up any irregularities in the car's history – whether it has outstanding finance owing on it, for example. This could avoid costing you a big bill, or even your car, later on.
- **Whether you buy new or used,** never accept the price stated at face value. With car sales having plummeted in the second half of 2008, dealers are desperate to sell – which puts the buyer in a very strong position to haggle over the price. Even persuading the dealer to fill the car with a tank of fuel is a significant saving at today's prices. And if you have hard cash available, this can encourage the dealer to offer you savings.
- **Shopping around for car insurance is essential,** and made easier these days thanks to a number of well-advertised internet price-comparison sites, but don't take these at face value – do your own research too. The choice of car is crucial to how much it will cost you in premiums, but insurers also like cars that are kept off the road, even better if you have a garage available. So if you have a garage full of junk with the car parked outside, why not have a clear out?
- **Also, think beyond the obvious.** If your eldest offspring has reached 17, passed their test and bought themselves an old banger to run around in, do they really need to be on the family car insurance too? If they are, it will send the premium rocketing. You might also consider taking an advanced driving course. While this will cost you money in the first place, insurers tend to give discounts to drivers with advanced qualifications, and along the way you learn driving techniques that will also help your overall economy.
- **Keeping your licence clean** can make a big difference to your insurance costs. You don't want penalty points, so don't use a handheld mobile phone at the wheel, and keep within speed limits – doing so offers a potential double saving, in fuel and insurance costs.

▲ All new cars on display in showrooms now include this chart giving the potential buyer a guide to their annual motoring cost.

Fuel Economy

Wasted fuel...

You could be using more than double the amount of fuel you need to! This chart shows how much cash you could be wasting by not attending to basic economy measures. Excess speed, for example, can increase fuel use by more than a third.

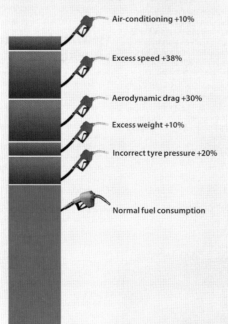

Air-conditioning +10%

Excess speed +38%

Aerodynamic drag +30%

Excess weight +10%

Incorrect tyre pressure +20%

Normal fuel consumption

▼ Careful driving really does save fuel. In the annual MPG challenge 400-mile endurance marathon, this Toyota Yaris diesel recorded 84.66mpg, almost 35% higher than its official combined fuel consumption figure.
Photo courtesy Toyota GB

Our Top 10 Tips
to avoid
speeding penalties

The good news for motorists is that, in the year ending March 2007, the money raised from speeding fines in England and Wales fell by 9%. But it's not all good news. The number of tickets sent out to motorists in that period fell by just 2% – most of the benefit for motorists came from the smaller chance of the fines actually being collected. At the same time, the responsibility for speed cameras has been devolved to a local level – which could make getting a ticket even more of a lottery. And there still remains the big question – is the time and money spent on speed cameras the best way to reduce road deaths?

We asked Stephen Mesquita, our speed camera expert, to give us an update on the whole thorny subject – and to give us his Top 10 Tips about what you can do to keep penalty points off your licence.

- It's three years since Philip's atlases first started its Speed Camera campaign. In that time, we've worked hard to bring to your attention the fact that speed camera fines are a regional lottery.
- I'm not a speed merchant. I don't regard it as the motorist's right to drive fast or to break the law. But the more research I've done on speed cameras, the less convinced I've become that this is an effective way to do what we all want to do – reduce the appalling total of nearly 3,000 killed on our roads every year.
- And in the past 12 months, there has been more sinister news on the future of speed cameras. Speed cameras have been 'devolved'. That means that each local authority decides its own policy (on what basis?) and runs its own camera bureaucracy. It can pretty much do what it wants both to raise the money and to spend it. This has had mixed results, including the much-publicised refusal of Swindon to pay for cameras.

- And there's another consequence of speed camera devolution. It's become almost impossible to collect consistent figures on fines from around the UK. It's as if central government has decided that speed cameras are too much trouble. The decision on whether they do or do not improve road safety is now to be taken at a local level.
- Nearly 1.75 million motorists had 3 points put on their licence in 2006/07 and paid a fixed penalty of £60. Here are my Top 10 Tips to avoid speeding fines in 2010.

1 Understand the system

If you are caught speeding, you can agree to pay a fixed £60 fine and get three points on your licence. The points normally stay on your licence for 4 years (11, if the conviction was drink or drug related or you failed to provide a specimen for analysis). In some cases, breaking a temporary speed limit where there are roadworks will only trigger the fine, not the points on your licence. If you get 12 points on your licence within a three-year period – or just 6 in your first two years as a driver – you will be banned from driving.

If you go over the speed limit by too much, you'll get an automatic summons. Then, at the discretion of the court, the fines will be higher and the points could go up to 6 or even a ban. You can challenge the penalty in court. But if you lose, it's likely to prove expensive.

2 Where you're most likely to get NIP-ped

When you're caught speeding on camera, you will be issued with a Notice of Impending Prosecution. In 2006/07, 3.02 million were sent out (2% down on 2005/06). Here were England and Wales' top 10 counties (with the number of NIP's sent out to motorists)

London	359 798
Mid and South Wales	242 473
Avon, Somerset	149 315
Thames Valley	143 525
Essex	137 802
Greater Manchester	108 533
Lancashire	103 872
West Yorkshire	90 008
Hertfordshire	84 835
Kent	84 774

Not surprisingly, these are some of the busiest parts of the country.

3 Will 'they' catch up with you?

Once you've received a Notice of Intended Prosecution, you can either accept it and agree to pay a Fixed Penalty Notice or contest it.

But, in 2006/07, 2.24 million Fixed Penalty Notices were sent out, compared with 3.02 million NIP's. That means that 28% of 'camera flashes' were not converted into requests for your £60. It's unlikely that nearly 840,000 people contested their NIP's – so you've immediately got a chance that the Fixed Penalty Notice will never even reach you.

Some counties claim 100% conversion from NIP to FPN – so here were the 10 worst conversion rates in England and Wales in 2006/07 (where, in theory, you're least likely to receive a Fixed Penalty Notice if you've been flashed):

Avon and Somerset	41%
London	44%
Essex	51%
Thames Valley	60%
Merseyside	61%
West Midlands	63%
Wiltshire	64%
Hampshire and Isle of Wight	65%
Derbyshire	66%
Warwickshire	67%

And then there's a further stage in the process – the collection of the money. And here, the record of the Safety Camera Partnerships seems to be getting worse. In 2006/07, only 80% of Fixed Penalty Notices issued were actually paid. That's compared with 85% in 2005/06. It seems that the authorities are finding it harder to collect your money.

 More Cash, less flash

Here are the 10 worst counties in England and Wales in 2006/07 at collecting the fixed penalty fines:

	%fixed penalties collected
West Yorkshire	48%
Lancashire	57%
Herts	59%
Mid and South Wales	59%
Leicestershire	63%
Northamptonshire	65%
Kent	72%
West Mercia	73%
Staffordshire	77%
Cheshire	77%

(All 2006/07 figures are taken from the Safety Camera Partnership Fixed Penalty Notice Hypothecation returns on the DfT website)

4 Understand the regional lottery

It is clear from all these figures why we are talking about the system as being a regional lottery. Just to prove the point finally, here are the Top 10 counties in England and Wales in 2006/07 for cash raised in speeding fines per person of population:

Beds	£5.18
North Wales	£4.88
Wiltshire	£4.78
Dorset	£4.00
Northamptonshire	£3.88
Warwickshire	£3.78
Cumbria	£3.73
Notts	£3.06
Suffolk	£2.74
Mid/North Wales	£2.59

You can't say we didn't warn you.

Speed limits (mph)	Built-up area	Single carriageway	Dual carriageway	Motorway
Cars and motorcycles	30	60	70	70
Cars towing caravans and trailers	30	50	60	60
Buses and Coaches	30	50	60	60
Goods vehicles under 7.5 tonnes	30	50	60	70 (60 if articulated or towing)

Top Gantry-mounted SPECS cameras in Cornwall
Above Truvelo camera
Below Mobile camera unit

5 Drive like a woman (it's safer)

More than 80% of all speeding penalties are given to men.

There are two types of speeder – the deliberate speeder and the accidental speeder.

If you are interested in the camera locations in this atlas so that you can break the speed limit between them, you're a deliberate speeder, and almost certainly a man. Read on. Our Top 10 Tips might make you more conscious of the chances – and consequences – of being caught.

Who are the accidental speeders? Almost everyone at some time. We've all done it. You're in an area that you're not familiar with. It's dark. You're quite alert but you're caught up in the rush hour and the traffic is moving fast. You've gone from a 40 zone to a 30 but you haven't seen the sign. Flash!

The truth is – most of us speed both deliberately and accidentally at some stage in our driving careers. The message is – cameras are widespread and they're not very forgiving.

So if you don't want the fine or the endorsement, you need to concentrate as much on your speed as you concentrate on not having an accident.

If you are a conscientious driver who feels the need to develop your skills of concentration in particular and defensive driving in general, then I'd recommend The Institute of Advanced Motorists (IAM) tel: 020 8996 9600.

6 Know your speed limit rules

Street lights = 30mph, unless it says otherwise. It's a horrible rule. Lots of people who should know about it don't. Lots of people who do know about it would like to see it changed.

Add to that the apparently arbitrary definition of 30mph and 40mph limits, and the frequency with which they change, and you have a recipe for confusion. Again, lots of inconsistencies to baffle the motorist.

> …done for speeding at 31mph in a 30mph zone

The round white sign with a black diagonal flash through it means 60mph max, except on dual carriageways and motorways.

How much leeway do you have? Is it zero tolerance? Is it the ACPO guidelines of +10%+2mph (that's the Association of Chief Police Officers, by the way)? Or is it somewhere in between? Well, the law is – you can be done for speeding at 31mph in a 30mph zone. As to the complicated equation, the police stress that guidelines are just that and they do not alter the law. But they probably would admit that they would be inundated

if they stopped every motorist who is driving a couple of mph over the limit.

You are probably getting a bit of help from your speedometer. It's the clever idea of the car makers to set our speedometers 2–3mph faster than we are actually going. Now that so many of us have GPS in the car, this is getting more widely known. Now you know, it might be wiser to use the extra mph as air between you and a ticket.

7 Learn to tell your Gatso from your Digital Specs

Here's a concise guide to cameras. There are loads of different species, so we're only going to describe the main families.

Gatso – the most common ones. Generally in yellow boxes, they flash you from the back and store your number plate on film. As the film only has 400 exposures, don't assume, if you see the flash in your rear-view mirror, that you've been done. In fact it's reckoned that you have a three in four chance that the one you've just passed is not working. And there's now a new type of digital Gatso called a Monitron that is starting to spring up in our cities. No film needed here. The data automatically creates a Notice of Intended Prosecution ready to post in 30 minutes.

Truvelo – pink-eyes. The pink eye gives you an infrared flash from the front, after sensors in the road have registered your speed. Unlike the GATSO, which can't identify the driver (worth remembering if you want to argue) the TRUVELO gets a mug-shot.

Digital Specs – pairs of video cameras set some distance apart to create a no-speeding zone between them. If your average speed over the distance exceeds the limit, you are snapped with an infrared flash. So they are much more testing for the driver. It's one thing slowing down when you see a camera, it's another thing maintaining an average speed over a distance of several miles. They are sprouting fast and likely to be used more and more.

DS2s – strips in the road detect your speed and pass the information to an innocent-looking post at the side of the road. Look out for the detector van nearby, because that's what does the business.

Red light cameras – the UK total is creeping up towards 1,000. If you drive through a traffic light when it's at red, sensors in the road tell the camera to flash you.

All of the above can be detected using GPS devices for fixed cameras but not these -

Lasers – most mobile cameras are Lasers. You normally see a tripod in a van with the backdoors open and facing you; or on a motorway bridge or handheld by the side of the road. They work – although rumour has it not in very bad weather – and they can't be detected by any of the GPS devices. If you happen to see a local villager touting a laser gun, you may get a letter asking you to drive more carefully but not a fine or penalty points.

8 Know where the cameras are

If you are serious about not getting caught speeding, there are some obvious precautions you can take before setting out.

- Check in this atlas whether there are fixed cameras on the route you are planning to take. They are marked on the map by the 40 symbol, with the figures inside the red circle indicating the

speed limit in mph (see the key to map symbols for further details).

- Check in the listings whether there are 'located' mobile sites on your route.
- Use a camera detector, such as those marketed by Road Angel, Road Pilot or Cyclops. These are perfectly legal, if expensive; they just tell you where the cameras are. Devices that detect and jam police laser detectors are about to be banned. Many sat-navs now include this information but you pay for updates.
- Use the websites for up-to-date information, including guidelines (but only guidelines) about where the police are locating their mobile vans each week. Each Safety Camera Partnership has a website (search for the county name followed by Safety Camera Partnership). Don't use the Department for Transport listings, which were 18 months out of date at the time we went to press.

9 Don't challenge a penalty without good reason

Check your ticket carefully: make sure it is your car and that you were driving it at the time and place recorded. The cameras aren't perfect and mistakes have been made. My favourite is the tractor caught speeding in Wales at 85mph. It turned out there was 'a confusion about the number plate' – the tractor had never been to Wales and could only do a max of 26mph.

Once you've checked the ticket, you have two choices. Pay the £60 and accept the three points. It's humiliating and irritating but then that's the idea. Or contest it.

If you do decide to fight, do as much research and get as much information about the circumstances as you can; and get as much case-study information as you can about the camera involved. The more witnesses and information you have, the more a good lawyer can build a case on your behalf.

Again, www.speed-trap.co.uk has some interesting case studies.

But don't expect success with a fabricated defence. The safety camera partnerships know the scams to look out for and lies can turn a simple speeding fine into something much more serious. In fact, you can be prosecuted for trying to pervert the course of justice. A criminal record can cost you much more than the £60 fixed penalty.

10 Avoid the points by going back to school

In a few areas, the police are giving drivers who are caught speeding another option. They can go on a Speed Awareness Scheme. These normally last half a day, you have to pay for them (probably more than £60) but you don't get the penalty points. So, if you like the sound of this as an option, it's worth considering.

Your alternative is to ask for your case to go forward for prosecution (see Top Tip No. 9)

And finally…

If you've got this far, you're obviously a bit of an aficionado on the subject of speeding, so I'm going to allow myself just one bit of preaching.

The 'Speed Kills' slogan has become much used. But here are three pieces of information that certainly make me think twice about letting the needle stray over the prescribed limit:

1 Every year we kill over 3,000 of our fellow-citizens on our roads and we seriously injure 35,000. If you happen to live in a reasonable-sized town, just work that out as a percentage of the population of where you live. Road deaths have not fallen substantially since the proliferation of speed cameras – but the evidence seems to be reasonably conclusive that speed cameras reduce the number of deaths and serious injuries at the sites themselves.

2 The argument rages about whether speed is the cause of accidents or not. But that's all rather academic (isn't it it?). A car that's not moving is not likely to injure someone. If the accident happens when the car is in motion, speed is at least part of the cause.

But here's the point. This is the 'if I hit a pedestrian, will I kill them?' chart ➤

Right The probability that a pedestrian will be killed when struck by a vehicle travelling between 20mph and 40mph

Websites for further information

Official

Safety Camera Partnerships (use Google and put in Safety Camera Partnership plus the area you want)

- www.safetycamera.org.uk • www.dvla.gov.uk
- www.thinkroadsafety.gov.uk • www.dft.gov.uk
- www.road-safe.org

Safety pressure groups
- www.rospa.com • www.transport2000.com
- www.roadpeace.org • www.brake.org.uk

Anti-camera pressure groups and websites
- www.speed-trap.co.uk • ukgatsos.com
- www.ukspeedcameras.co.uk
- www.abd.org.uk • www.ukspeedtraps.co.uk
- www.speedcam.co.uk
- www.speedcamerasuk.com

So if you hit a pedestrian in a 30mph area and you're doing just 35mph (just on the 10%+2mph leeway) you're more than twice as likely to kill them. Not a nice thought. Maybe I should have called that the 'if I am hit by a car while on foot, will I be killed by it?' chart.

3 Every death costs us, as taxpayers, £1.5m and every serious injury £100,000. And that's doesn't take into account the human cost.

So, at the end of all this, my 11th Top 10 Tip is

11 Don't press the pedal to the metal

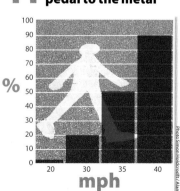

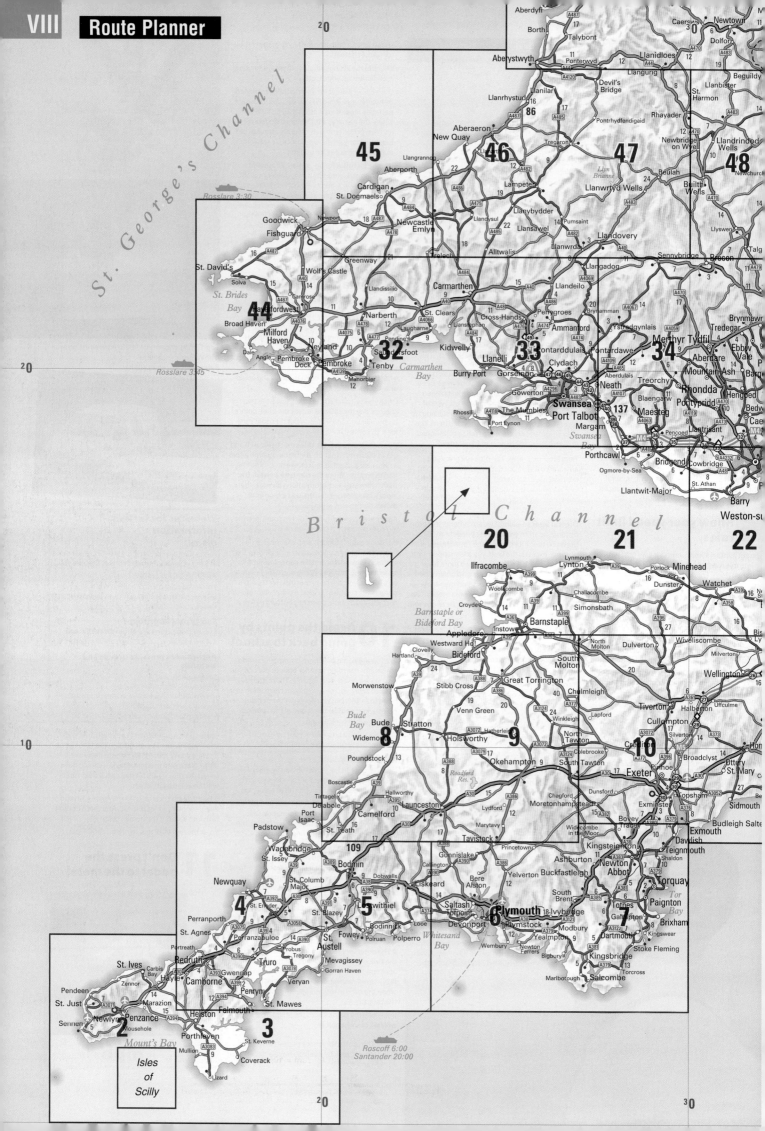

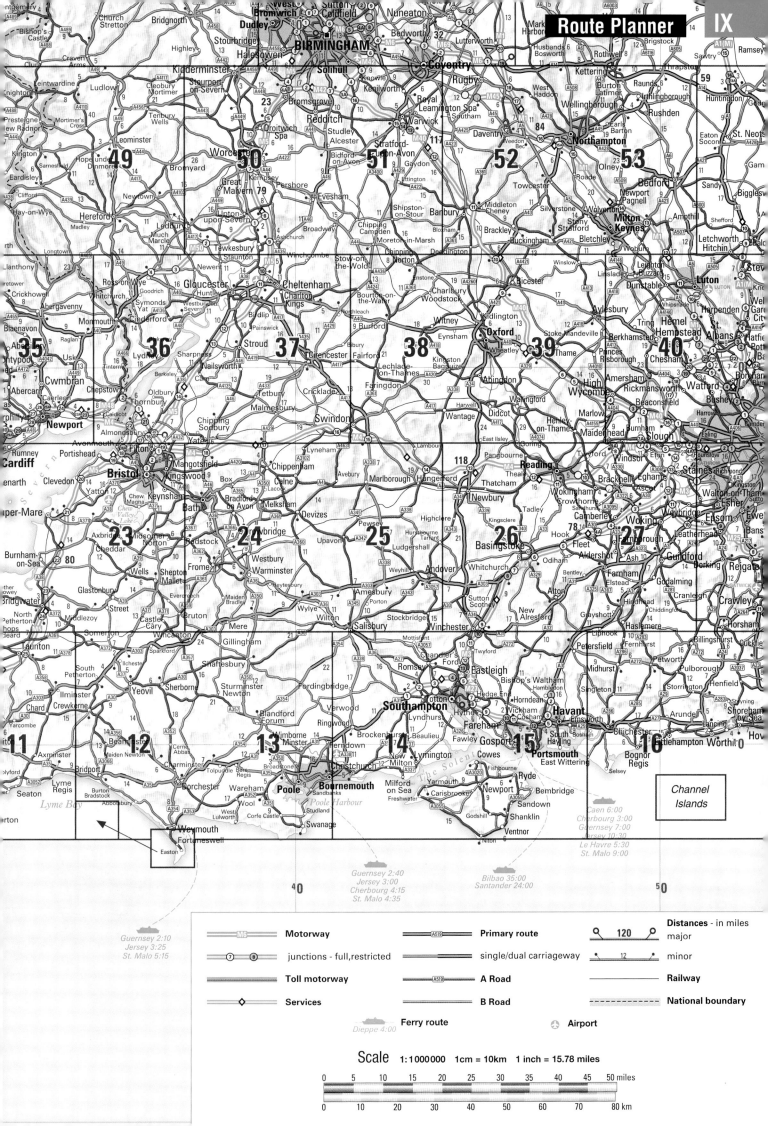

Channel Islands

Caen 6:00
Cherbourg 3:00
Guernsey 7:00
Jersey 10:30
Le Havre 5:30
St. Malo 9:00

Guernsey 2:40
Jersey 3:00
Cherbourg 4:15
St. Malo 4:35

Bilbao 35:00
Santander 24:00

Guernsey 2:10
Jersey 3:25
St. Malo 5:15

Dieppe 4:00

Motorway	Primary route	**Distances** - in miles
junctions - full, restricted	single/dual carriageway	major
Toll motorway	A Road	Railway
Services	B Road	National boundary
Ferry route	Airport	

Scale 1 : 1 000 000   1cm = 10km   1 inch = 15.78 miles

0 5 10 15 20 25 30 35 40 45 50 miles

0 10 20 30 40 50 60 70 80 km

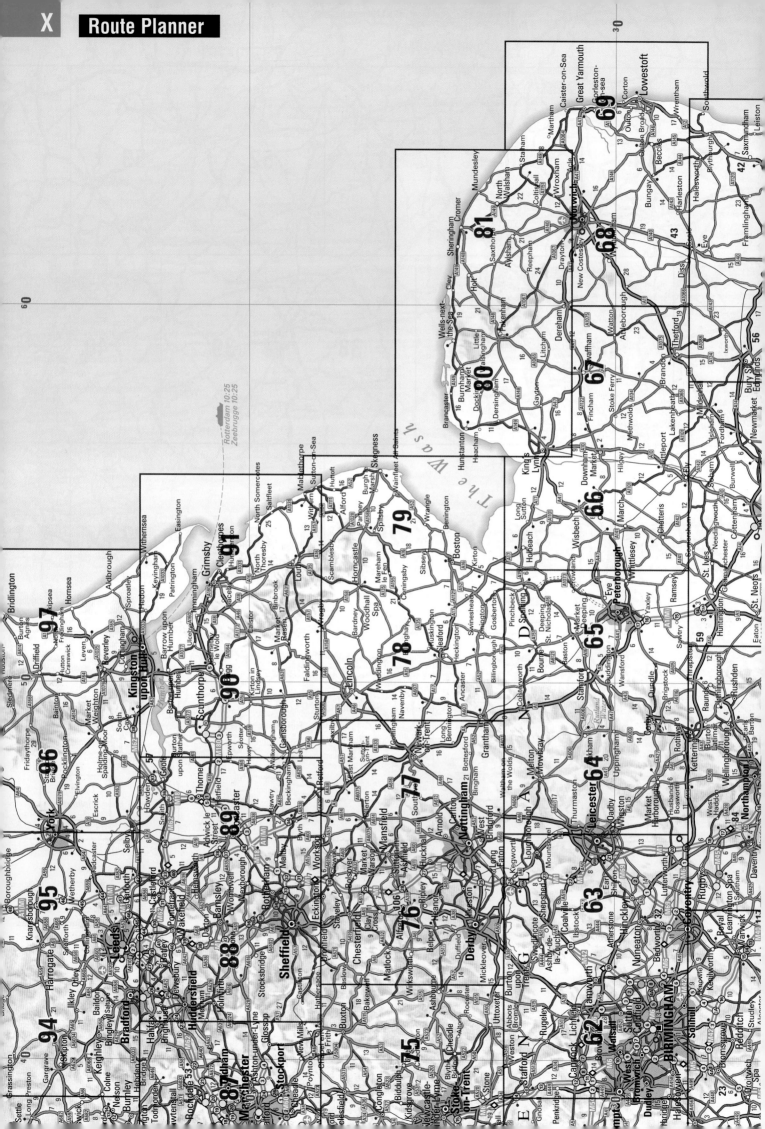

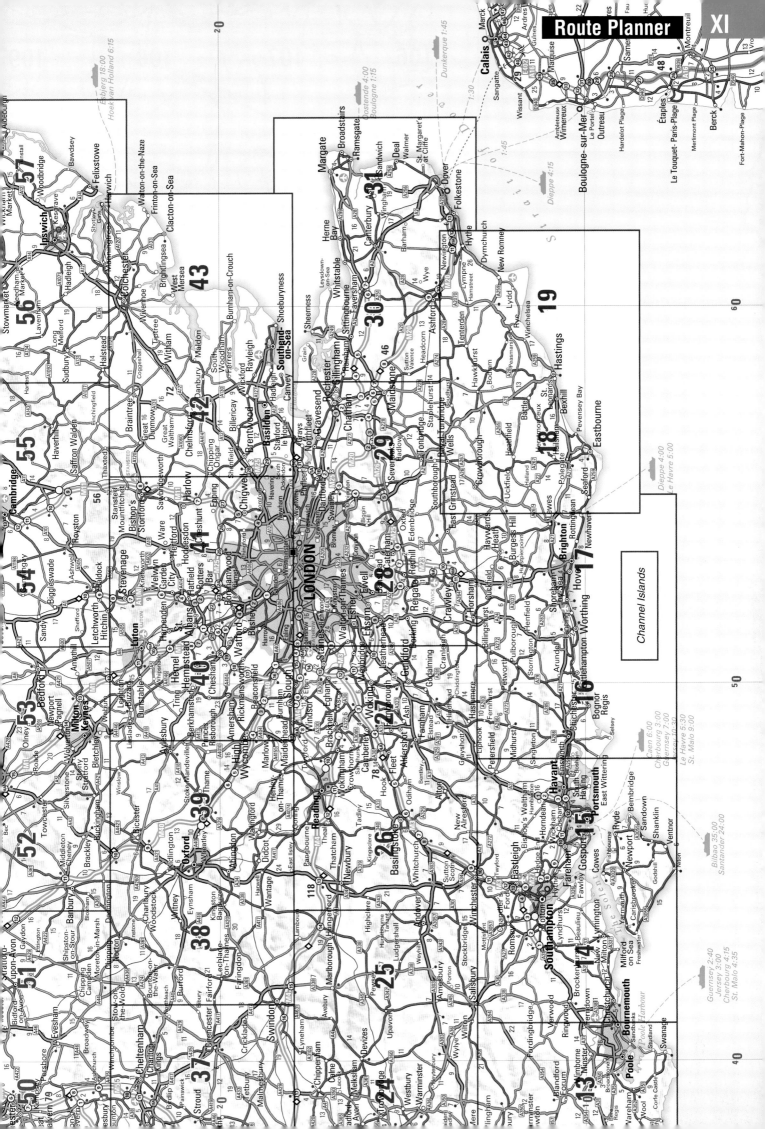

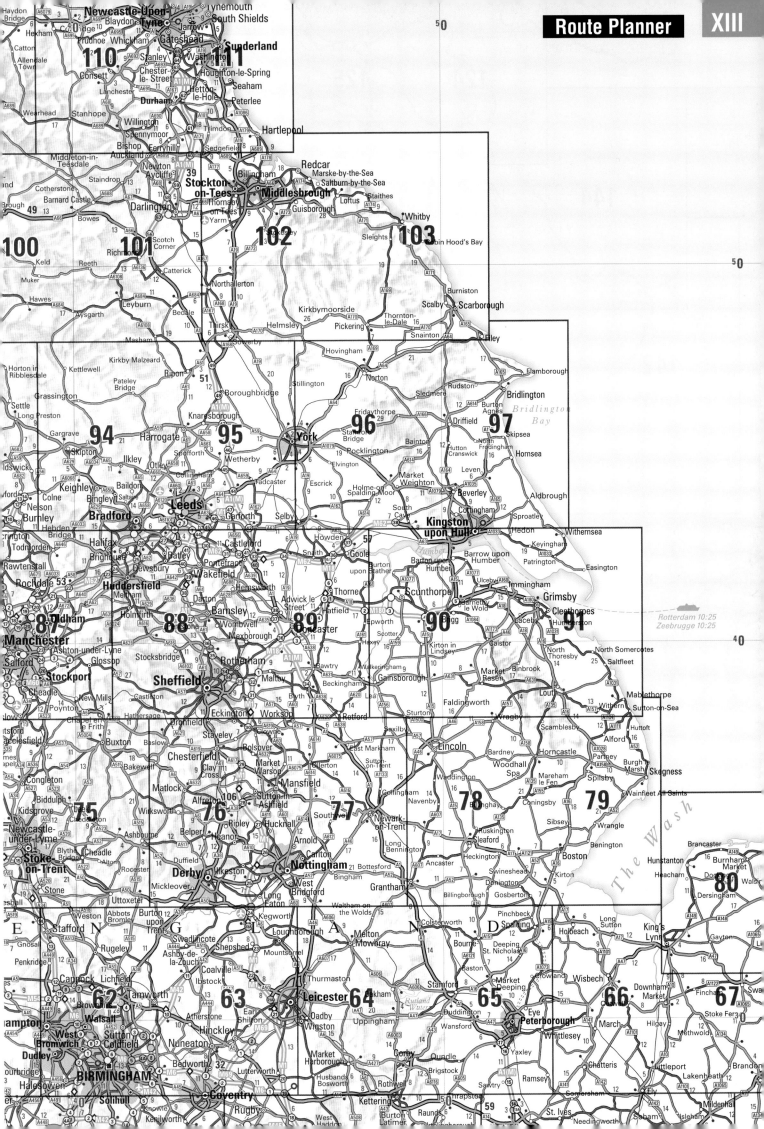

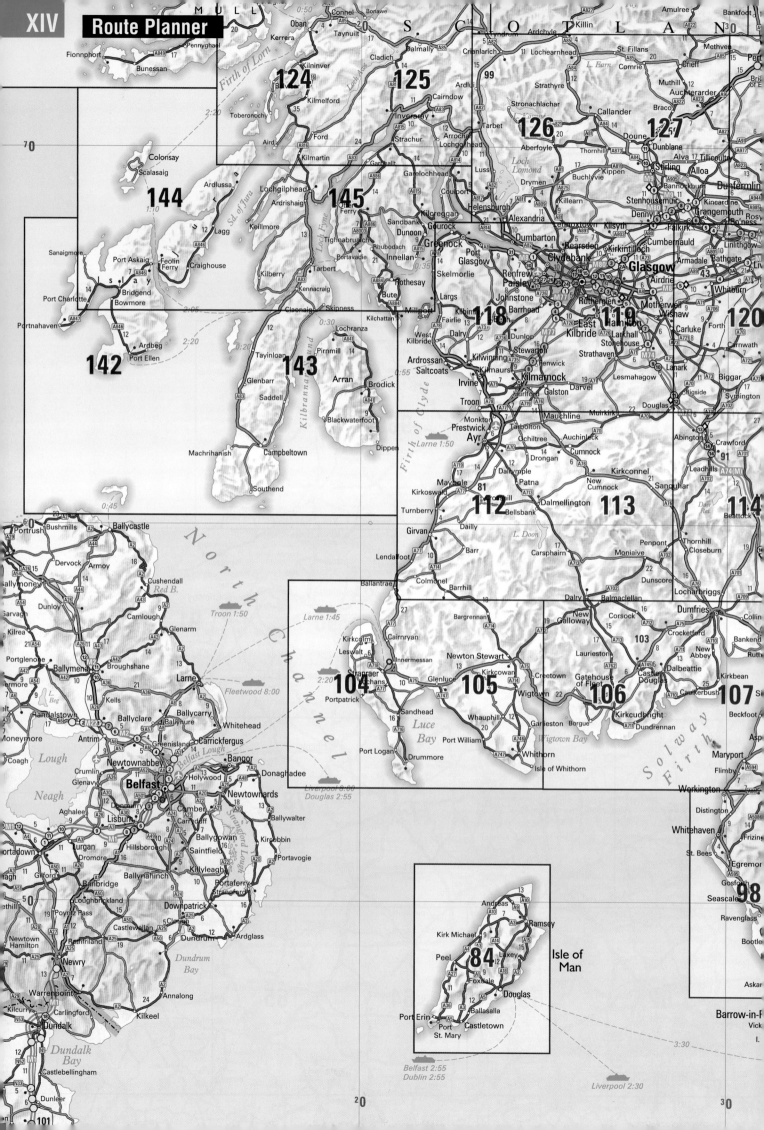

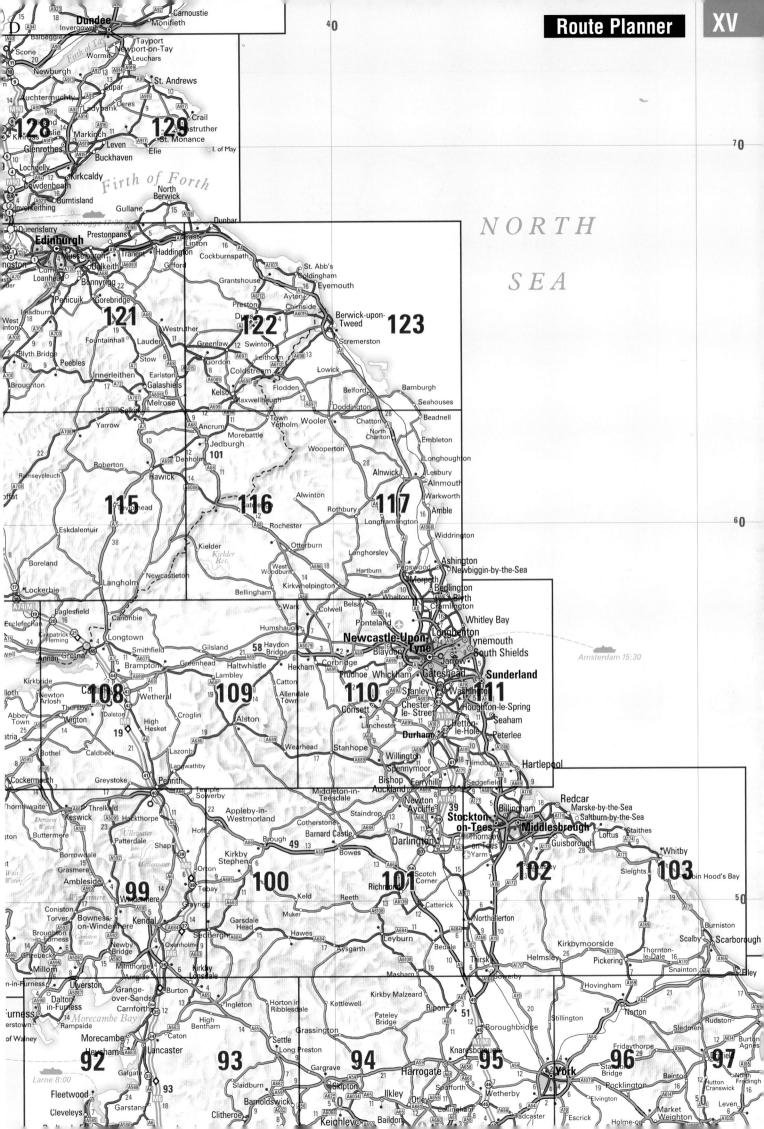

NORTH

SEA

128 129

121 122 123

115 116 117

108 109 110 111

99 100 101 102 103

92 93 94 95 96 97

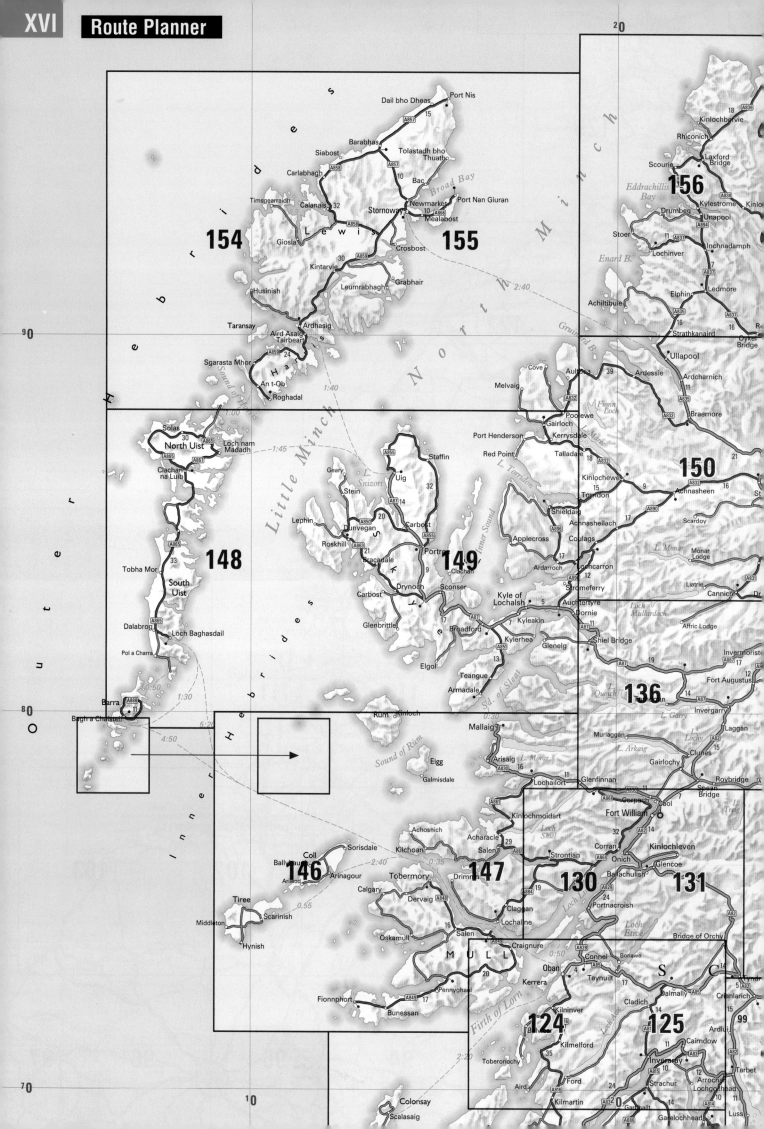

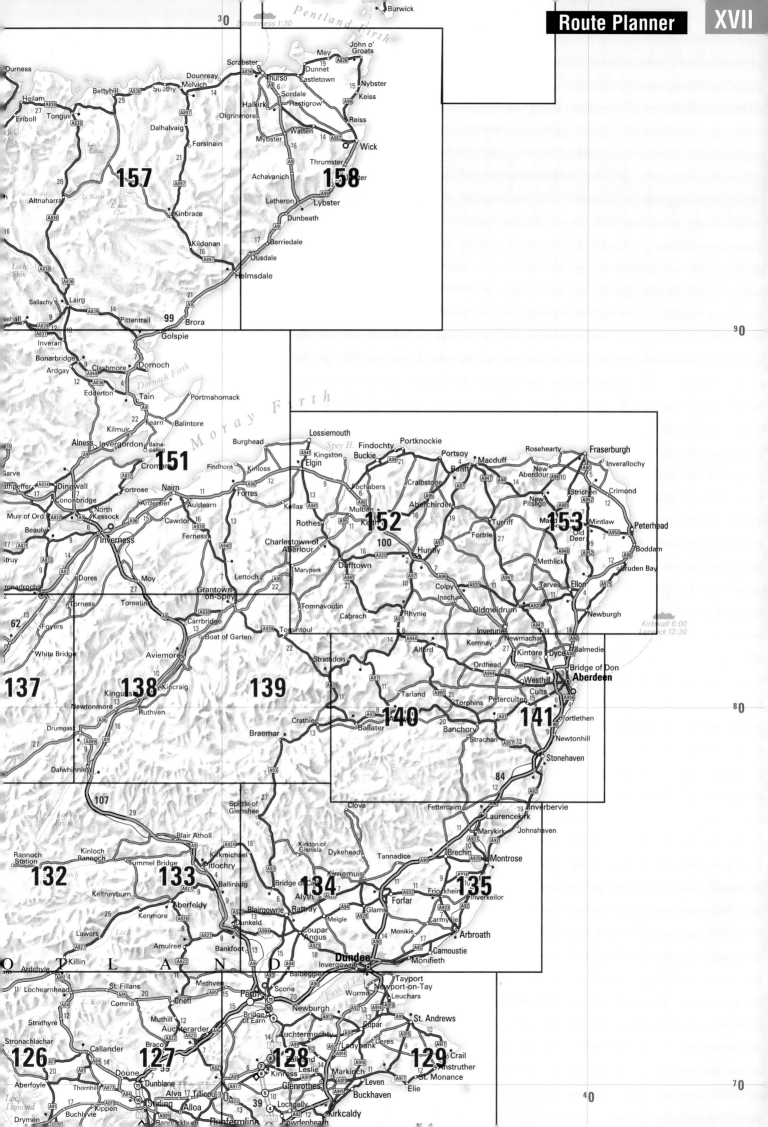

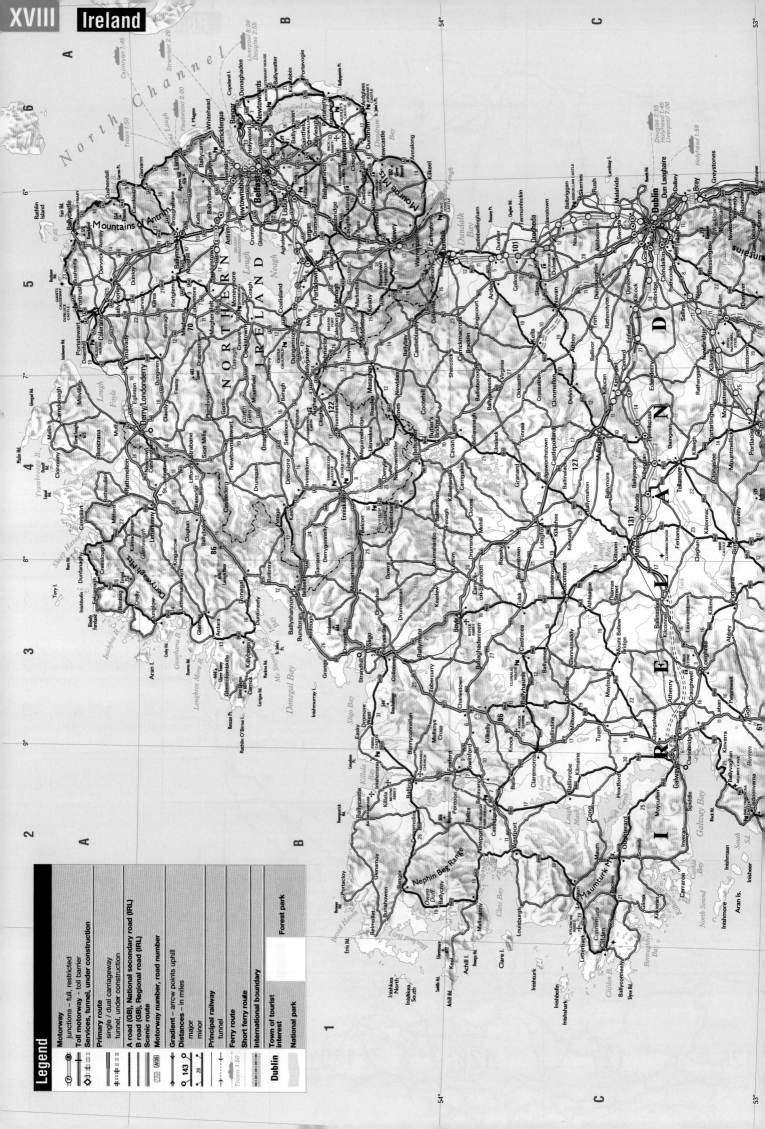

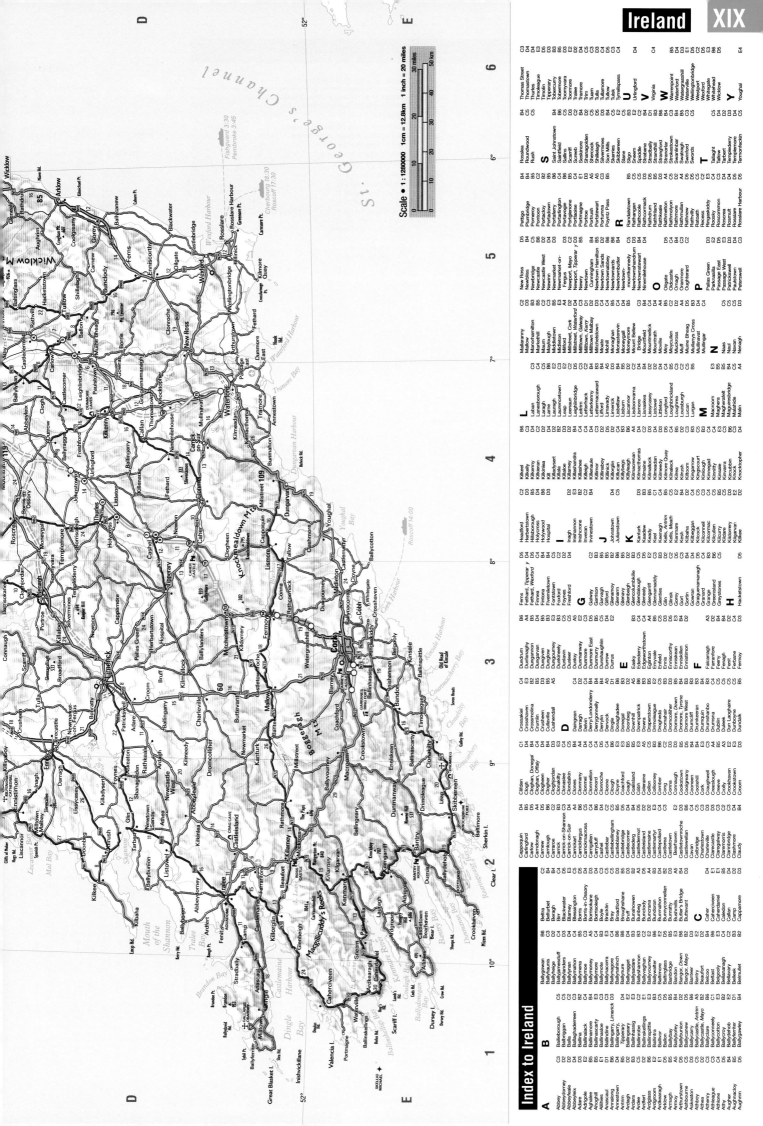

Distance table

How to use this table

Distances are shown in miles and kilometres with estimated journey times in hours and minutes.

For example: the distance between Dover and Fishguard is 331 miles or 533 kilometres with an estimated journey time of 6 hours, 20 minutes.

Estimated driving times are based on an average speed of 60mph on Motorways and 40mph on other roads. Drivers should allow extra time when driving at peak periods or through areas likely to be congested.

Supporting

THINK!

Travel safe –
Don't drive tired

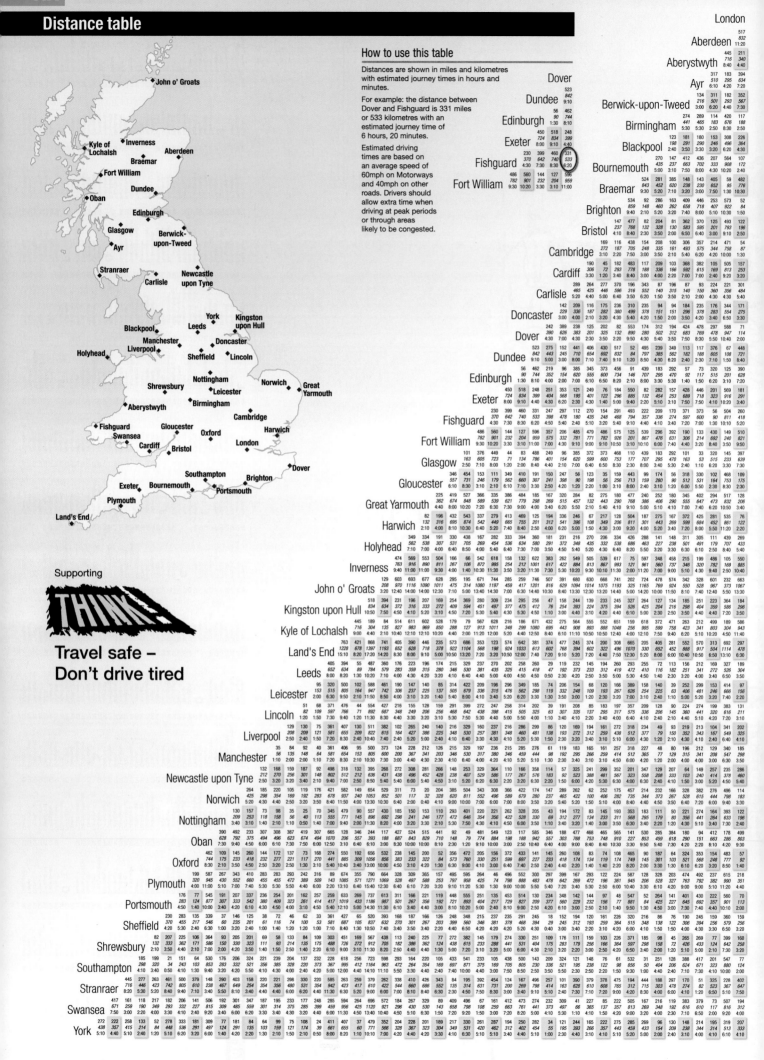

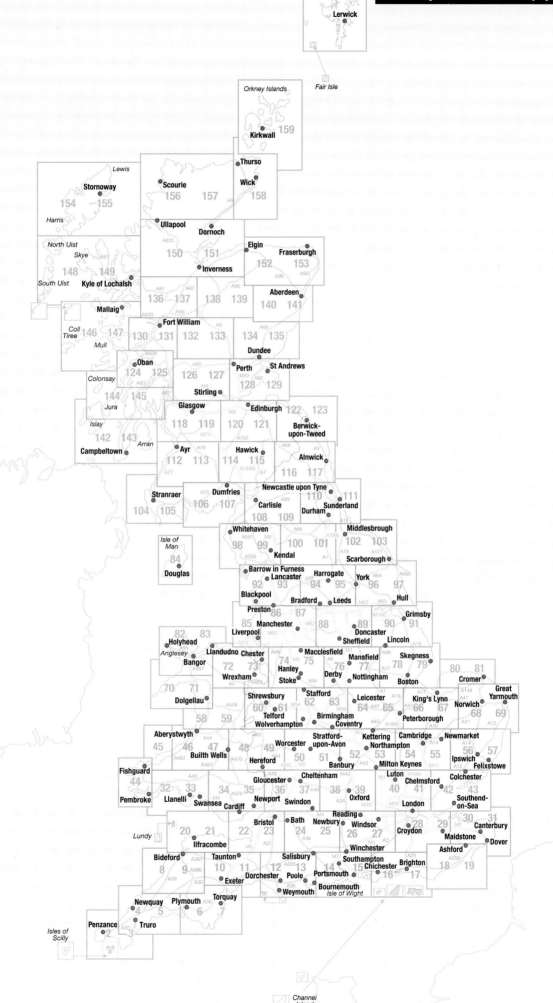

Shetland Islands 160
Lerwick

Fair Isle

Orkney Islands 159
Kirkwall

Lewis
Stornoway
154 155
Harris

Thurso
Scourie 157 Wick
156 158
A9

North Uist
Skye A87
148 149
South Uist Kyle of Lochalsh

Ullapool
Dornoch
150 151
A835

Elgin Fraserburgh
152 153
A96 A90

Inverness

Aberdeen
A87 A82 A95
136 137 138 139 140 141

Mallaig

A86
Coll A830 Fort William
Tiree 146 147 130 131 132 133 134 135
Mull A9 A90

Dundee
A828
Oban 124 125 126 127 Perth St Andrews
Colonsay A85 M90 A92
A83 Stirling 128 129
144 145 M9
Jura A82

Glasgow Edinburgh 122 123
Islay 118 119 120 121 Berwick-
M8 upon-Tweed
142 143 M74 A702
Arran Ayr A76 A68 Alnwick
Campbeltown 112 113 114 115
A77 Hawick A1
A74(M) A7 116 117

Newcastle upon Tyne
Stranraer A75 Dumfries 110 111
104 105 106 107 Carlisle A69 Sunderland
Durham
108 109

Whitehaven Middlesbrough
A1(M) M6 102 103
Isle of 98 99 100 101 A19
Man A595 Kendal A1 Scarborough
A66 A171
84
Douglas Barrow in Furness Harrogate York A64
Lancaster A165
92 93 94 95 96 97
Blackpool Bradford Leeds Hull
M62 A63
Preston 86 87 M180
85 Manchester 88 89 90 91
Liverpool M62 Doncaster Grimsby
M53 Sheffield Lincoln
Holyhead Macclesfield A16
Anglesey A55 Llandudno Chester 74 75 76 77 78 79 Skegness
Bangor A49 Mansfield A17 80 81
72 73 Hanley Derby A1 Cromer
70 71 Wrexham Stoke Nottingham Boston
A5 A483 A50 A148
Dolgellau Shrewsbury Stafford Leicester A16 King's Lynn Great
60 61 62 63 64 65 66 67 Yarmouth
58 59 Telford A47 Peterborough Norwich A47
Wolverhampton Birmingham M69 A1(M) 68 69
Coventry A43 A11 A12
Aberystwyth A44 Stratford- Kettering Cambridge Newmarket
45 46 47 48 49 upon-Avon 52 53 Northampton 54 55 A14 56 57
Builth Wells Worcester 50 51 Banbury M1 Milton Keynes Ipswich Felixstowe
A487 A483 Hereford A43 A12
M50 M5 A10
Fishguard A49 Cheltenham Luton Colchester
44 Gloucester M40 Chelmsford
Pembroke 32 33 34 35 36 37 38 39 40 41 42 43 Southend-
Llanelli Oxford London on-Sea
Swansea Newport Swindon A34 M25
Cardiff M4 M40
A4 Reading Bath Newbury Windsor Croydon 28 29 30 31
Lundy 20 21 22 23 24 25 26 27 Maidstone Canterbury Dover
Bristol M3 Ashford A259
Ilfracombe A37 Winchester A23 18 19
Salisbury Southampton
Bideford A361 Taunton 12 13 14 Chichester Brighton
8 9 10 11 Dorchester Poole Portsmouth 15 16 17
A39 A386 Exeter A303 *Isle of Wight*
A30 Weymouth Bournemouth
Newquay Torquay
4 5 6 7
Penzance Truro Plymouth
Isles of 2 3
Scilly

Channel Islands
Guernsey
Jersey

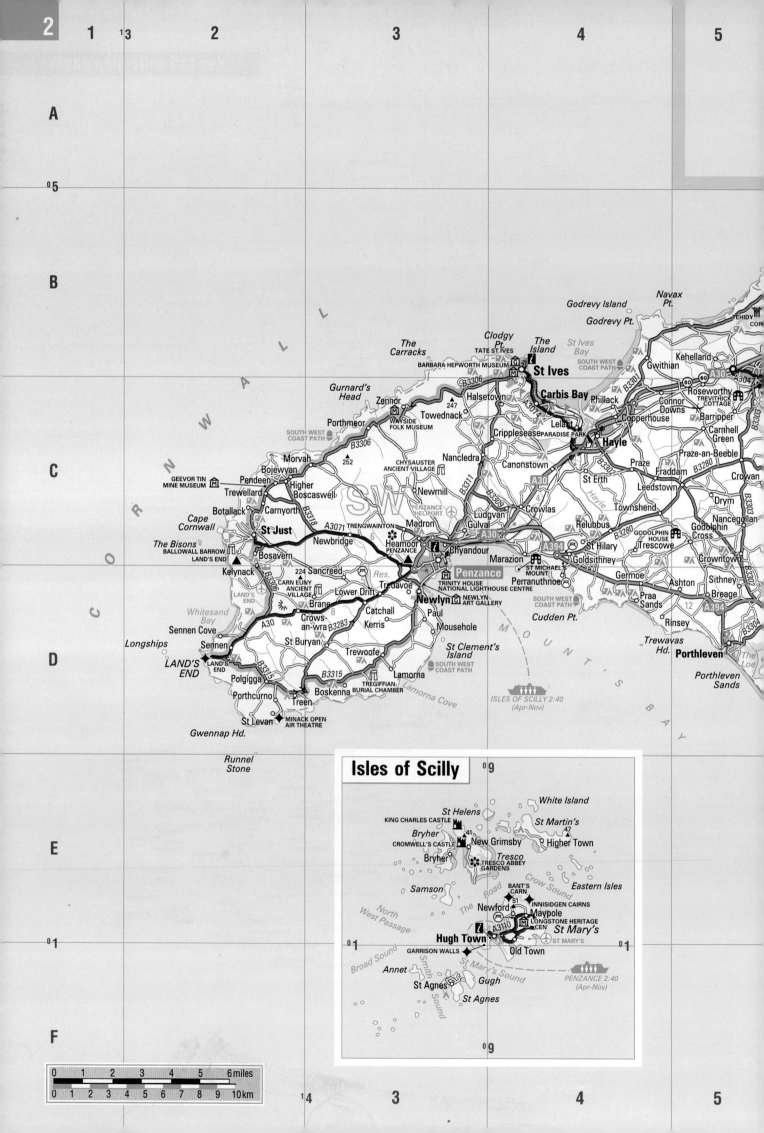

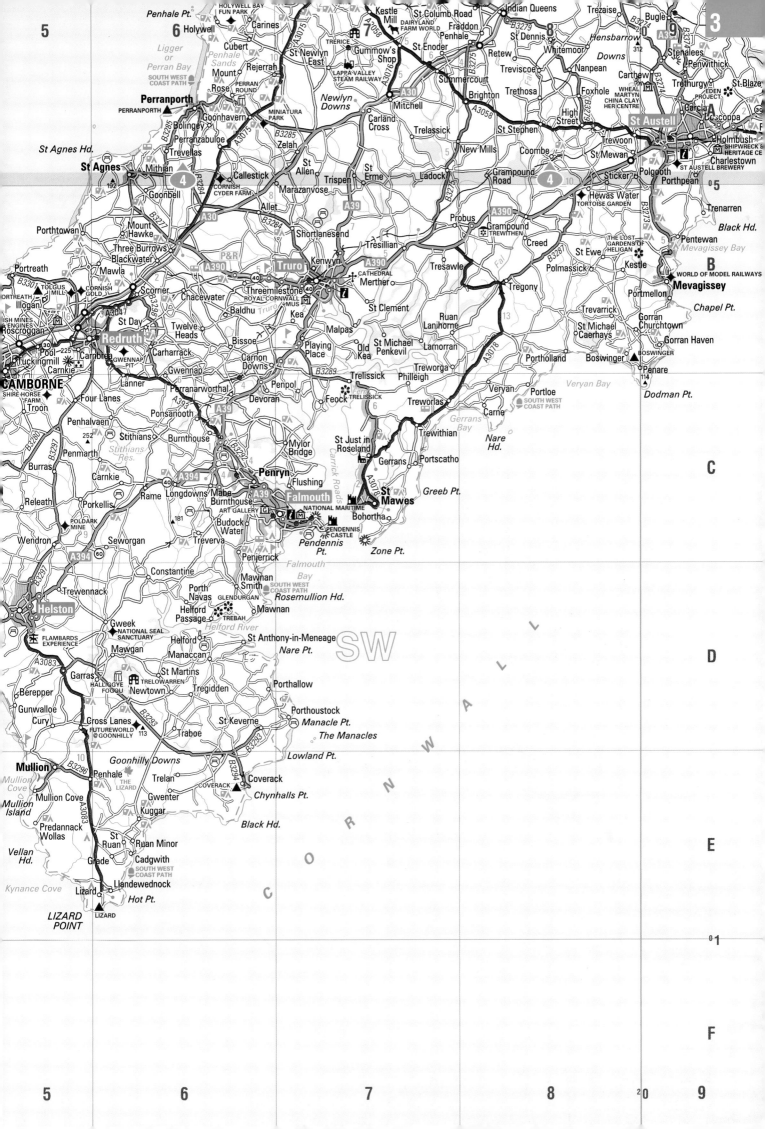

1   20   2   3   4   5

A

13

B

C

D

10

E

F

8

N O R T H   BIDEFORD

HARTLAND POINT

Titchberry   *Windbury Pt.*

CLOVELLY VILLAGE
Clovelly

HARTLAND ABBEY
Stoke   Higher Clovelly

Hartland Quay   Hartland

B3248

SOUTH WEST COAST PATH
Milford   DOCTON MILL   Philham   THE MILKY WAY ADVENTURE PARK   Buck's Cross

ELMSCOTT
Elmscott   Eddistone   Tosberry   Woolfardisworthy

South Hole   *Hartland Forest*   Alminstone Cross

Knaps Longpeak   Welcombe   235   Meddon   Ashmansworthy

Gooseham   Woolley   Youlstone

156   Eastcott

Morwenstow   Dinworthy

Higher Sharpnose Pt.   Shop   A39

Woodford   Bradworthy Cross

Lower Sharpnose Pt.   BROCKLANDS ADVENTURE PARK   14   Bradworthy

Coombe   Kilkhampton   Alfardisworthy   Sutcombe

Stibb   Soldon Cross

B U D E   DUNSDON

Poughill   Chilsworthy

Flexbury   Hersham   Grimscott

Bude Haven   1643   **Stratton**   Pancrasweek

BAY   **Bude**   A3072

Launcells   9   **Holsworthy**

Upton   Derril

Marhamchurch   Bridgerule   Pyworthy   162   Derriton

Widemouth Bay   B3254   Chasty

Widemouth Sand   Budd's Titson   Leworthy

Coppathorne

Millook   Whitstone

Dizzard Pt.   Poundstock   Treskinnick Cross   North Tamerton

SOUTH WEST COAST PATH   Tregole   9   Tetcott

St Genny's   Trewint   PENHALLAM   Week St Mary   Lana

Cambeak   Rosecare   Luffincott

Crackington Haven   Jacobstow

Wainhouse Corner   South Wheatley   West Curry   Northcott

Tresparrett Posts   B3263   Maxworthy   Boyton

Fire Beacon Pt.   260   Beeny   Bennacott

Marshgate   Canworthy Water   Brazacott   TAMAR OTTER & WILDLIFE CENTRE   Langdon

BOSCASTLE   Tresparrett   A39

Boscastle   Lesnewth   Otterham   256   Warbstow   North Petherwin   Bridgetown

Trevalga   Trelash   Tremaine   Werrington

CASTLE   *Tintagel Hd.*   B3266   B3262   Treneglos   Yeolmbridge

OLD POST OFFICE TINTAGEL   Bossiney   Hallworthy   Tresmeer   Egloskerry   Langore

Tintagel   308   13   Tregeare   St Stephen's

Treknow   Trewarmett   THE ARTHURIAN CENTRE   Davidstow   Dutson

Start Pt.   B3263   Trewassa   Tremail   HIDDEN VALLEY DISCOVERY PARK

Trebarwith   BRITISH CYCLING MUS   B3314   Cold Northcott   A395   Piper's Pool   **Launceston** CASTLE

Davidstow Moor

Treligga   Tregadillett

SOUTH WEST COAST PATH   Delabole   St Clether   Laneast   Trewen   Daw's House

Port Isaac Bay   Valley Truckle   **Camelford**   *Crowdy Res.*   TRETHORNE LEISURE FARM   A30

Helstone   Polyphant   70   South Petherwin

Port Isaac   *High Moor*   Altarnun   Lewannick   Lezant

Port Quin Bay   Port Quin   Port Gaverne   St Teath   400 ROUGH TOR   Trewint   Trekenner

LONG CROSS   Trelights   B3267   Pendoggett   veighan   5   5   B3257   Treburley

Polzeath   Michaelstow   *High Moor*   Codda   A30   Congdon's Shop   Coad's Gree

St Mi   Pityme   369   Trebartha   5

420 BROWN WILLY   331 GARROW TOR   MUSEUM OF SMUGGLING   Bolventor   North Hill

B O D M I N

St M   St Breward   Row   18   *M O O R*

Rock   Chapel Amble   St Kew   Bradford

0   1   2   3   4   5   6 miles
0   1   2   3   4   5   6   7   8   9   10km

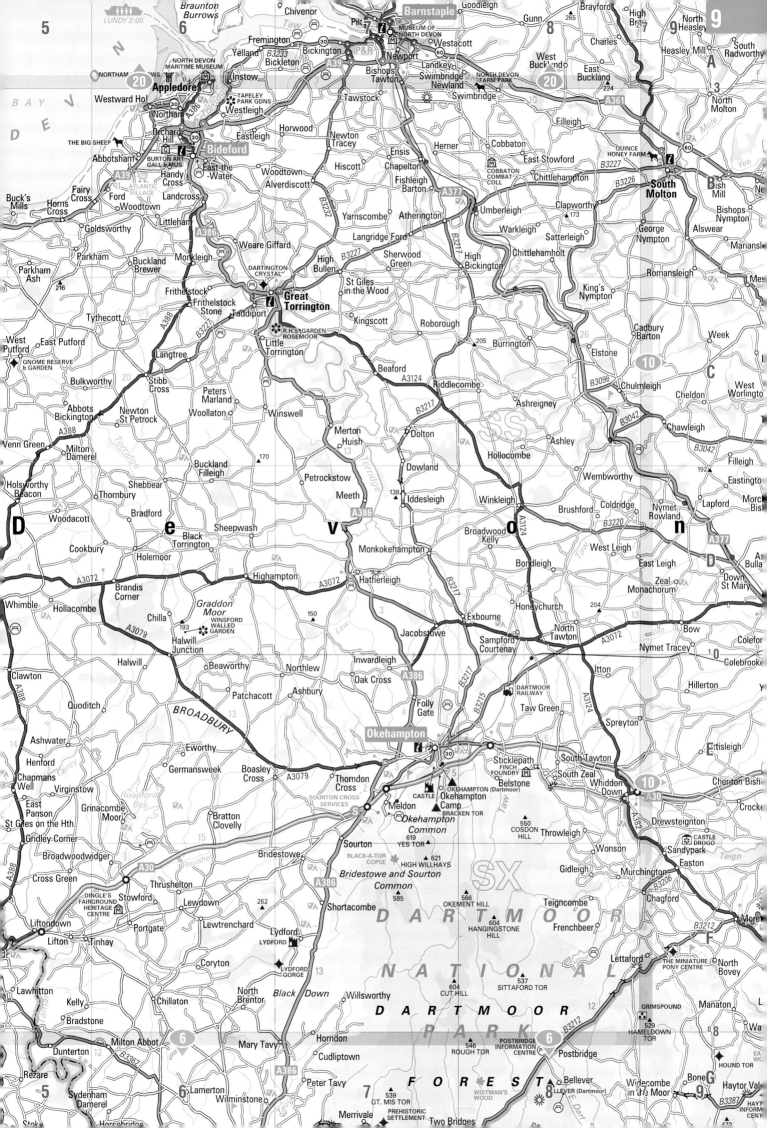

Fluckley Thorne
GODINTON HOUSE
Kennington
Brook
Hastingleigh
Elham
BUTTERFLY CENTRE
Swingfield Minnis
Alkh

HEADCORN
5
6
7
Great Chart
Hinxhill
Willesborough Lees
Brabourne
Lymbridge Green
Rhodes Minnis
Ottinge
Densole
Drellingore
A
4
West Hougham

Smarden Bell
Maltman's Hill
Ashford
Willesborough Lees
Stowting
KENT BATTLE OF BRITAIN MUSEUM
Paddlesworth
Hawkinge
Capel le Ferne

Smarden
Wissenden
Willesborough
Sevington
Mersham
Smeeth
Sellindge
Brabourne Lees
Lyminge
Etchinghill
Postling
CHANNEL TUNNEL

Haffenden Quarter
Bether
30
Kingsnorth
Cheeseman's Green
Sellindge Lees
Beachborough
Stanford
Newington
13
EAST WAR

Standen
Stubbs Cross
Shadoxhurst
Aldington Frith
Clap Hill
STOP 24 SERVICES
M20-S
Pedlinge
Newgreen
11A
12
Folkestone

Biddenden
Tanden
Henghurst
Bromley Green
Bonnington
Aldington
Court-at-Street
FOLKESTONE
Saltwood
ROTUNDA

High Halden
St Michael's
Shirkoak
Orlestone
Lympne
PORT LYMPNE WILD ANIMAL PARK AND GARDENS
Cheriton
Sandgate
CLIFF LIFT
B

Woodchurch
SOUTH OF ENGLAND RARE BREEDS CEN
Bilsington
West Hythe
Hythe
Palmarsh

Parkgate
Leigh Green
Ruckinge
Hamstreet
BROCKHILL
31

Tenterden
Brook Street
Kenardington
Warehorne
Burmarsh
ROMNEY, HYTHE AND DYMCHURCH LIGHT RAILWAY

COLONEL STEPHENS RAILWAY MUSEUM
Reading Street
Appledore Heath
Snave
Newchurch

Small Hythe
SMALLHYTHE PLACE
HORNE'S PLACE CHAPEL
ROMNEY MARSH
St Mary in the Marsh
Dymchurch
MARTELLO TOWER

Rolvenden Layne
ISLE OF OXNEY
Appledore
Snargate
Ivychurch
St Mary's Bay

Peening Quarter
Stone
Brenzett
AERONAUTICAL MUSEUM

Wittersham
Brookland
Old Romney
Littlestone on Sea
C

ROTHER LEVELS
Ham Green
The Stocks
New Romney
Romney Sands

FARM WORLD
Four Oaks
Iden
Houghton Green
Walland Marsh
Greatstone on Sea

Beckley
Peasmarsh
Rye Foreign
Playden
East Guldeford
Lydd
Lydd on Sea

Rye
RYE HERITAGE CENTRE
Camber
Denge Marsh

Udimore
Rye Harbour
LYDD

Winchelsea
CAMBER CASTLE
Rye Bay
DUNGENESS
Denge Beach
DUNGENESS

WINCHELSEA COURT HALL MUSEUM
Winchelsea Beach
DUNGENESS POWER STATION & INFORMATION CENTRE
THE OLD LIGHTHOUSE
D

Icklesham
Pett
Guestling Green
Cliff End
Fairlight
Fairlight Cove
HASTINGS
CAVES

ATER WORLD
E

ENGLISH CHANNEL
10
F
09

5
6
7
8
9
G

18

LUNDY

North West Point

North East Point

LUNDY MARINE NATURE RESERVE

142 ▲

ILFRACOMBE 2:00
BIDEFORD 2:00

South West Point

Surf Point

5

2 2

2 1

1 4

SS

N O R T H   D E V O N

LUNDY 2:00

OLD CORN MILL
Rillage Pt.
Combe Martin Bay
Trentishoe

Ilfracombe
ILFRACOMBE MUSEUM
WATERMOUTH CASTLE
Girt Down
Heale
349

Hele
Combe Martin
A10

Bull Pt.
Rockham Bay
Lee
Whitestone
Slade
206
Berrynarbor
Sterridge

WILDLIFE & DINOSAUR PARK

Morte Point
Mortehoe
A361
B3230
Berry Down Cross
Kentisbury

269 ▲
A3123
Kentisbury Ford

Woolacombe
MORTE BAY
Trimstone
Cheglinch
Berry Down
East Down
Patchole

Woolacombe Sand
SOUTH WEST COAST PATH
210
Dean
West Down
Bittadon
Churchill
Arlington
ARLINGTON COURT

Pickwell
North Buckland
B3230
Loxhore

Baggy Pt.
Putsborough
Nethercott
Halsinger
Milltown
Muddiford
A39
11
Shirwell
Bratton Fleming

Croyde Bay
Georgeham
Darracott
Knowle
Marwood
Guineaford
198 ▲
Shirwell Cross
Stoke Rivers

Croyde
158
Lobb
Pippacott
Kingsheanton
Prixford

B3231
Saunton
14
MARWOOD HILL GARDENS
BROOMHILL

Braunton
Heanton
Punchardon
Ashford
Burridge
Goodleigh
Gunn

ELLIOT GALLERY
Wrafton
TOLL
Chivenor
Pilton
Barnstaple
Westacott

Saunton Sands
Braunton Burrows
A361
40
MUSEUM OF NORTH DEVON

LUNDY 2:00
Taw
Newport
Landkey
NORTH DEVON FARM PARK

Fremington
Yelland
B3233
Bickington
P&R
Bishops Tawton
Swimbridge
Newland

BIDEFORD BAY
NORTH DEVON MARITIME MUSEUM
Instow
A39
Swimbridge

13
NORTHAM BURROWS
Bickleton

Appledore
Westward Ho!
TAPELEY PARK GDNS
Westleigh
Newton Tracey
Herner
Cobbaton
East Stowford

THE BIG SHEEP
Northam
A386
Westleigh
Horwood
A377
Ensis
Chapelton
COBBATON COMBAT COLL.
Chittlehampton

TLAND ABBEY
Orchard Hill
Bideford
Eastleigh
Ta
Hiscott

Abbotsham
BURTON ART GALL & MUS
East-the-Water
Woodtown
Handy

CLOVELLY VILLAGE
A39

9

0 1 2 3 4 5 6 miles
0 1 2 3 4 5 6 7 8 9 10km

9

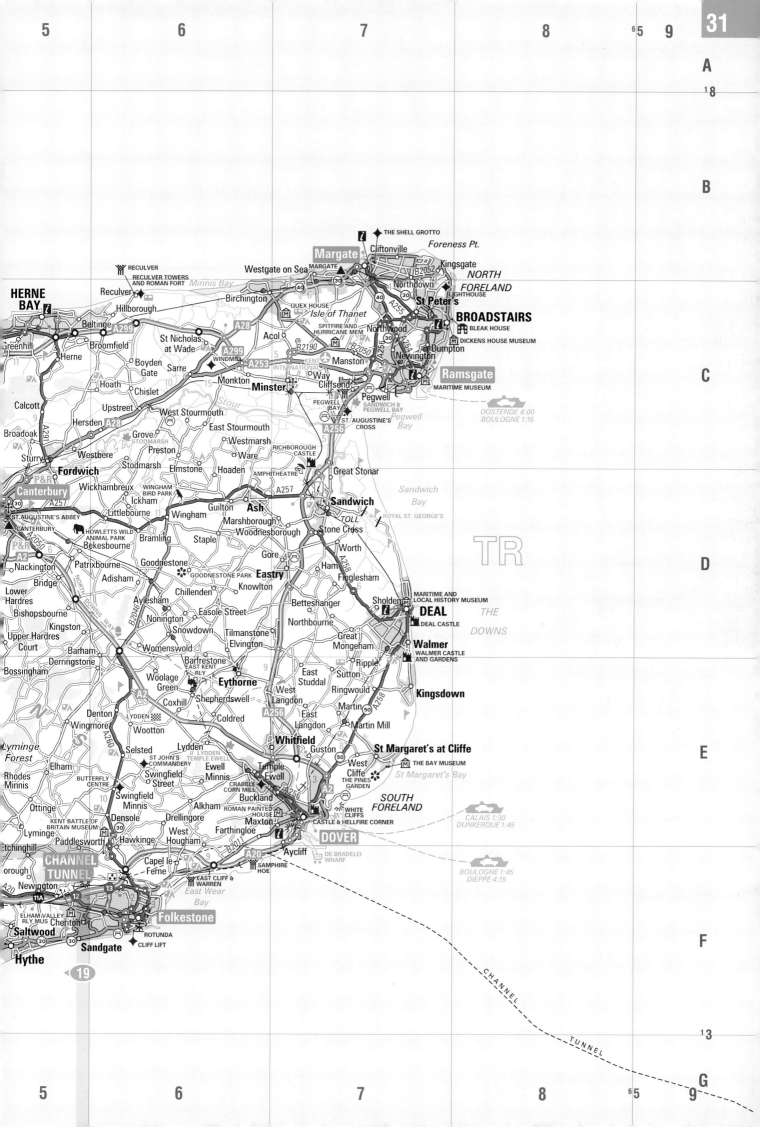

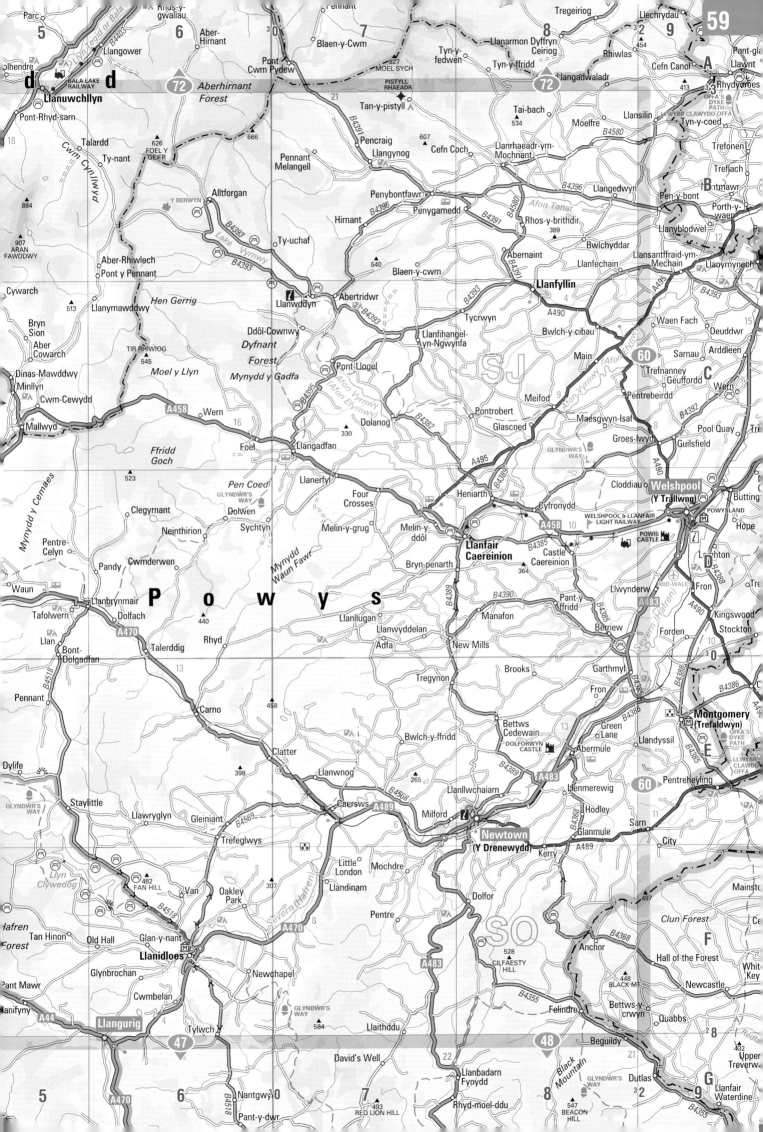

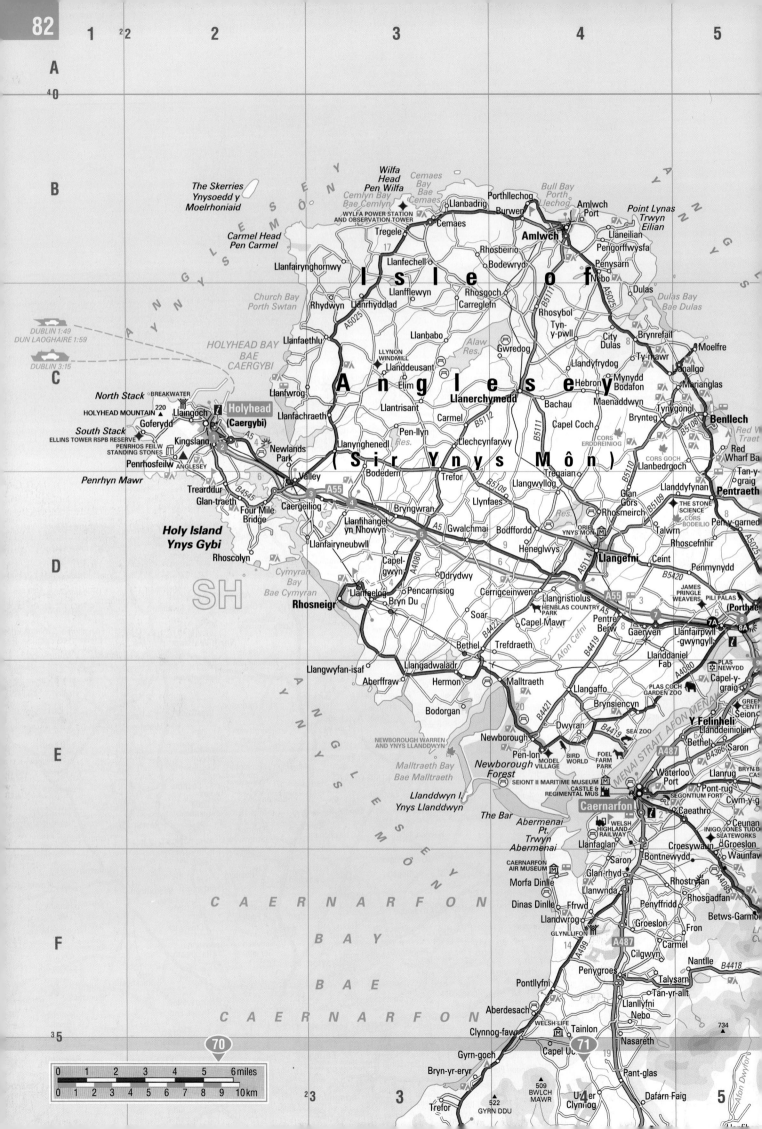

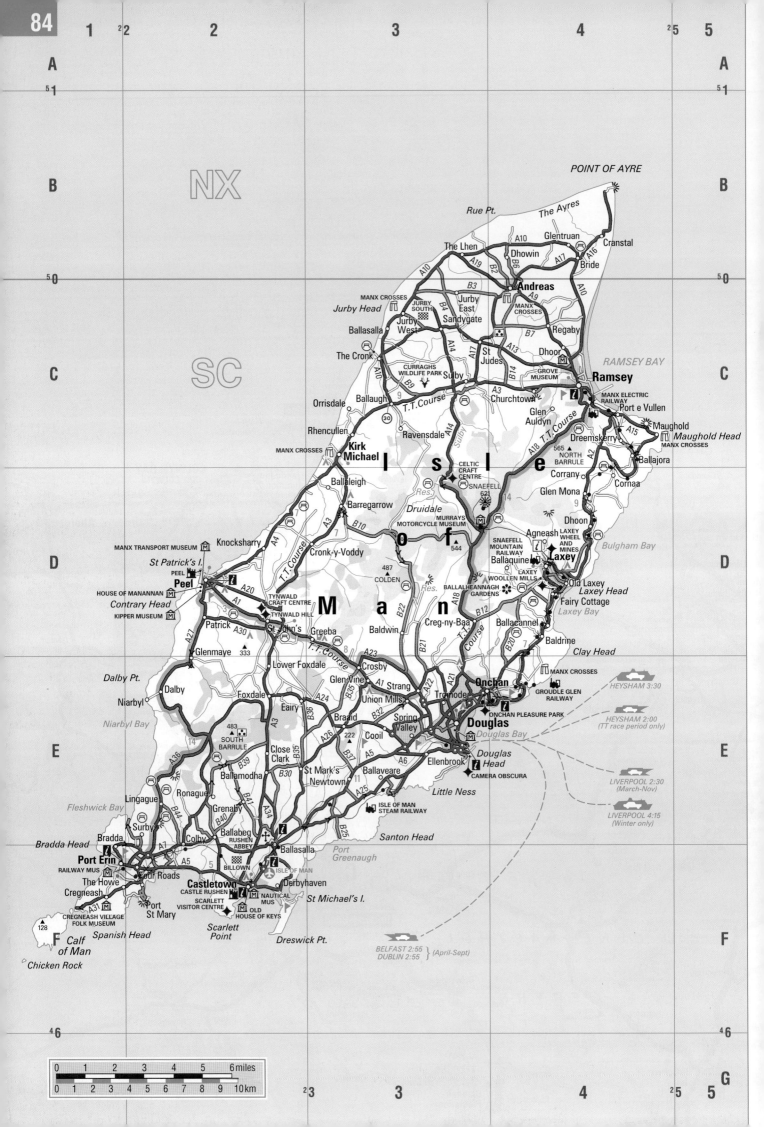

POINT OF AYRE

Rue Pt.

The Ayres

NX

SC

Glentruan
The Lhen
Dhowin
Cranstal
Bride

Andreas

Jurby Head
MANX CROSSES
JURBY SOUTH
Jurby East
Sandygate
Jurby West
Ballasalla
Regaby
MANX CROSSES
The Cronk
St Judes
Dhoor
RAMSEY BAY
Ballaugh
Orrisdale
Sulby
Churchtown
GROVE MUSEUM
Ramsey
CURRAGHS WILDLIFE PARK
T.T. Course
MANX ELECTRIC RAILWAY
Rhencullen
Port e Vullen
Ravensdale
Glen Auldyn
Maughold
Dreemskerry
Maughold Head
MANX CROSSES
Kirk Michael
CELTIC CRAFT CENTRE
NORTH BARRULE
MANX CROSSES
Ballaugh
Isle
Ballajora
Ballaleigh
SNAEFELL
Corrany
Cornaa
Barregarrow
Glen Mona
Druidale
MURRAYS MOTORCYCLE MUSEUM
Dhoon
MANX TRANSPORT MUSEUM
of
Agneash
LAXEY WHEEL AND MINES
Bulgham Bay
Knocksharry
Cronk-y-Voddy
SNAEFELL MOUNTAIN RAILWAY
St Patrick's I.
BALLALHEANNAGH GARDENS
Ballaquine
Laxey
PEEL
Peel
COLDEN
LAXEY WOOLLEN MILLS
HOUSE OF MANANNAN
Man
Old Laxey
Contrary Head
Laxey Head
KIPPER MUSEUM
Fairy Cottage
Patrick
TYNWALD CRAFT CENTRE
Baldwin
Creg-ny-Baa
Ballacannel
Laxey Bay
Glenmaye
TYNWALD HILL
St John's
Greeba
Baldrine
Clay Head
Dalby Pt.
Lower Foxdale
Crosby
MANX CROSSES
Dalby
Glen Vine
Strang
Onchan
Niarbyl
Foxdale
Union Mills
Tromode
GROUDLE GLEN RAILWAY
HEYSHAM 3:30
Niarbyl Bay
Eairy
Braaid
Spring Valley
ONCHAN PLEASURE PARK
HEYSHAM 2:00 (TT race period only)
SOUTH BARRULE
Cooil
Douglas
Close Clark
St Mark's Newtown
Ballaveare
Douglas Bay
Ronague
Ballamodha
A5
Ellenbrook
Douglas Head
LIVERPOOL 2:30 (March-Nov)
Lingague
Grenaby
ISLE OF MAN STEAM RAILWAY
CAMERA OBSCURA
Little Ness
LIVERPOOL 4:15 (Winter only)
Fleshwick Bay
Surby
Colby
Ballabeg
RUSHEN ABBEY
Bradda Head
Bradda
BILLOWN
Ballasalla
Santon Head
Port Greenaugh
Port Erin
Four Roads
Castletown
Derbyhaven
RAILWAY MUS
CASTLE RUSHEN
NAUTICAL MUS
St Michael's I.
The Howe
SCARLETT VISITOR CENTRE
OLD HOUSE OF KEYS
Cregneash
Port St Mary
Scarlett Point
BELFAST 2:55 DUBLIN 2:55 (April-Sept)
CREGNEASH VILLAGE FOLK MUSEUM
Spanish Head
Scarlett Point
Dreswick Pt.
Calf of Man
Chicken Rock

0 1 2 3 4 5 6 miles
0 1 2 3 4 5 6 7 8 9 10km

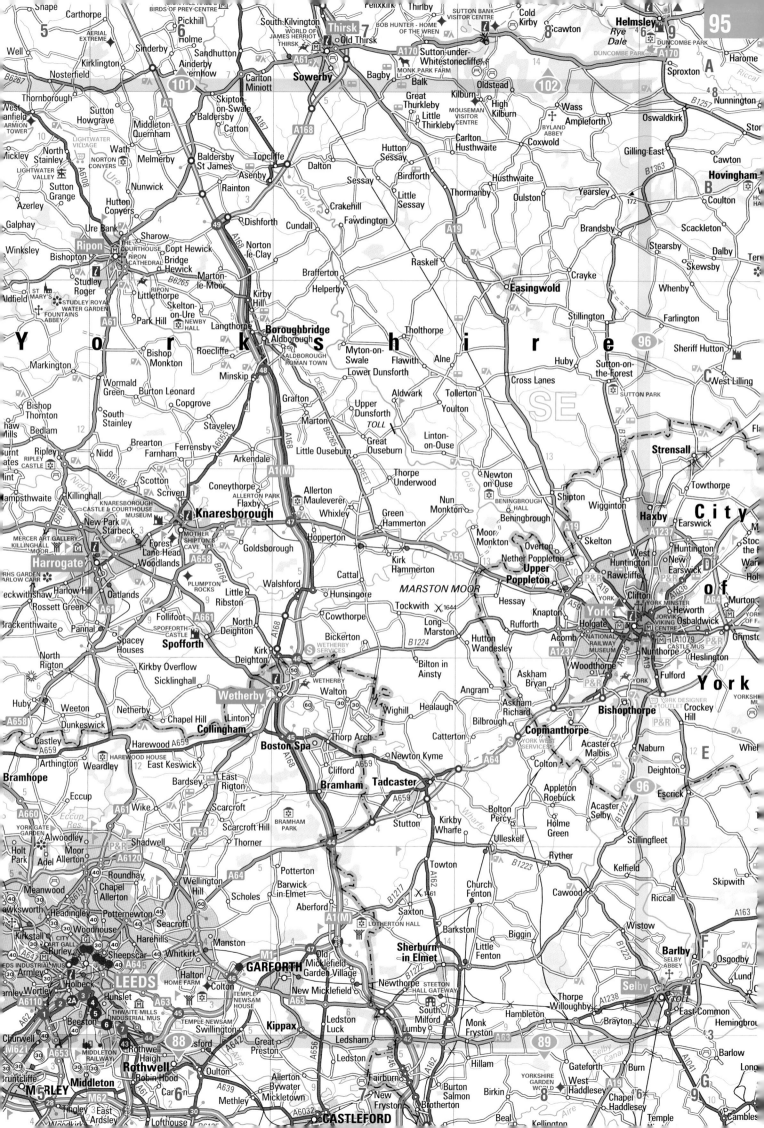

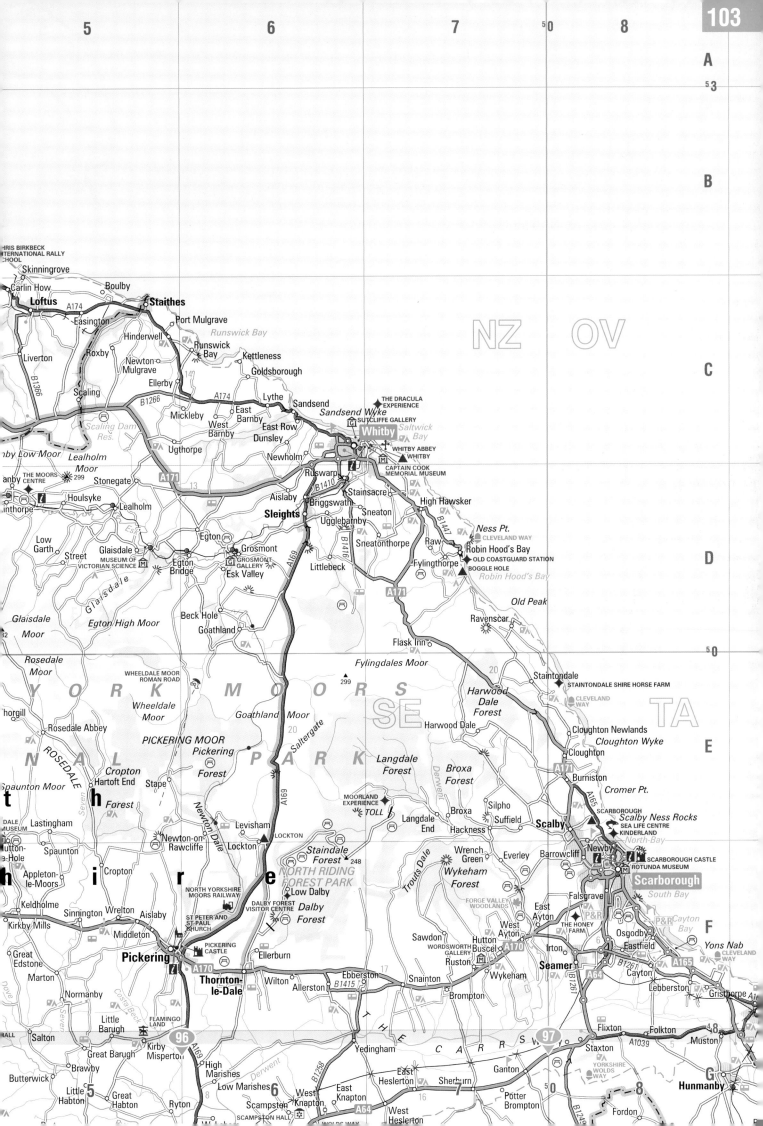

A

B

C

5   6   7   8

NZ OV

SE

TA

Skinningrove
Carlin How
Boulby
Loftus   A174   Staithes
Easington   Port Mulgrave
Hinderwell   Runswick Bay
Liverton   Roxby   Runswick Bay   Kettleness
Newton   Mulgrave   Goldsborough
Scaling   Ellerby   Lythe   Sandsend
Mickleby   East   Barnby   Sandsend Wyke   THE DRACULA EXPERIENCE
West Barnby   East Row   SUTCLIFFE GALLERY
Scaling Dam Res.   Ugthorpe   Dunsley   Newholm   Whitby   Saltwick Bay
Low Moor   Lealholm Moor   Ruswarp   WHITBY ABBEY   WHITBY
THE MOORS CENTRE   Stonegate   A171   B1410   CAPTAIN COOK MEMORIAL MUSEUM
Houlsyke   Aislaby   Briggswath   Stainsacre
Lealholm   Sleights   Sneaton   High Hawsker
Low Garth   Egton   Grosmont   Ugglebarnby   Ness Pt.   CLEVELAND WAY
Street   GROSMONT GALLERY   Sneatonthorpe   Raw   Robin Hood's Bay
MUSEUM OF VICTORIAN SCIENCE   Egton Bridge   Esk Valley   Littlebeck   Fylingthorpe   OLD COASTGUARD STATION
Glaisdale   BOGGLE HOLE
Beck Hole   Robin Hood's Bay
Glaisdale Moor   Egton High Moor   Goathland   Old Peak
Rosedale Moor   Ravenscar
YORKSHIRE   MOORS
Flask Inn
Rosedale Abbey   WHEELDALE MOOR ROMAN ROAD   Fylingdales Moor   Staintondale   STAINTONDALE SHIRE HORSE FARM
Wheeldale Moor   Goathland Moor   Harwood Dale Forest   CLEVELAND WAY
Spaunton Moor   PICKERING MOOR   Pickering Forest   Harwood Dale   Cloughton Newlands   Cloughton Wyke
Cropton   Saltergate   Langdale Forest   Cloughton
Hartoft End   Stape   Broxa Forest   Burniston   Cromer Pt.
ROSEDALE   NATIONAL   PARK   MOORLAND EXPERIENCE   TOLL   Broxa   Silpho   A165   Scarborough
Lastingham   Levisham   Langdale End   Suffield   Scalby   Scalby Ness Rocks   SEA LIFE CENTRE
Spaunton   Newton-on-Rawcliffe   LOCKTON   Hackness   KINDERLAND
Hutton-le-Hole   Lockton   Staindale Forest   Wrench Green   Everley   Barrowcliff   Newby   North Bay
Appleton-le-Moors   Cropton   NORTH YORKSHIRE MOORS RAILWAY   NORTH RIDING FOREST PARK   Wykeham Forest   SCARBOROUGH CASTLE   ROTUNDA MUSEUM
Keldholme   Low Dalby   FORGE VALLEY WOODLANDS   Scarborough
Sinnington   Wrelton   Aislaby   ST PETER AND ST PAUL CHURCH   DALBY FOREST VISITOR CENTRE   Dalby Forest   East Ayton   Falsgrave   South Bay
Kirkby Mills   Middleton   PICKERING CASTLE   Ellerburn   Sawdon   Hutton Buscel   West Ayton   THE HONEY FARM   Osgodby   Yons Nab
Great Edstone   Pickering   Ruston   Irton   Eastfield   CLEVELAND WAY
Marton   Thornton-le-Dale   Wilton   Allerston   Ebberston   Snainton   Wykeham   Seamer   Cayton   Cayton Bay
Normanby   B1415   Brompton   A64   Lebberston
FLAMINGO LAND   Snainton   Muston   Gristhorpe
Little Barugh   96   97   Flixton   Folkton   A1039
Salton   Kirby Misperton   Staxton   YORKSHIRE WOLDS WAY
Great Barugh   High Marishes   Yedingham   Ganton
Brawby   Low Marishes   East Heslerton   Sherburn   Potter   Fordon
Butterwick   West Knapton   East Knapton   Brompton
Little Habton   Great Habton   Ryton   West Heslerton   A64   Hunmanby
Scampston   SCAMPSTON HALL   WOLDS WAY

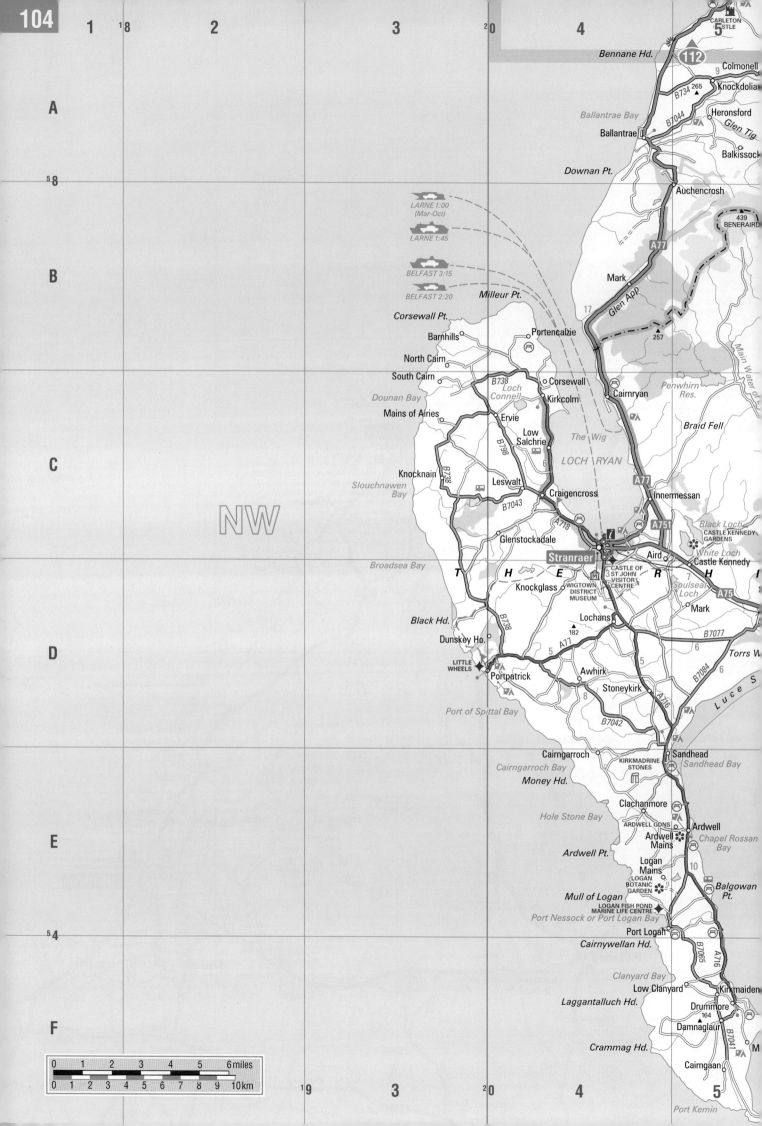

CARLETON CSTLE

Bennane Hd.

Colmonell

Knockdolia

B734 265

Heronsford

B7044

Glen Tig

Ballantrae Bay

Ballantrae

Balkissock

Downan Pt.

Auchencrosh

439 BENERAIRD

A77

Mark

Glen App

257

LARNE 1:00 (Mar-Oct)

LARNE 1:45

BELFAST 3:15

BELFAST 2:20

Milleur Pt.

Corsewall Pt.

Portencalzie

Barnhills

North Cairn

Corsewall

Penwhirn Res.

Cairnryan

B738

Loch Connell

Kirkcolm

South Cairn

Dounan Bay

Mains of Airies

Ervie

Braid Fell

The Wig

LOCH RYAN

Low Salchrie

B798

B738

A77

Knocknain

Leswalt

Slouchnawen Bay

Craigencross

Innermessan

B7043

Black Loch

CASTLE KENNEDY GARDENS

A718

A751

NW

Glenstockadale

White Loch

Stranraer

Aird

Castle Kennedy

Broadsea Bay

CASTLE OF ST JOHN VISITOR CENTRE

T H E

E

R H I

Knockglass

WIGTOWN DISTRICT MUSEUM

Soulseat Loch

Mark

Black Hd.

Lochans

A75

182

B7077

Dunskey Ho.

A77

Torrs W

LITTLE WHEELS

Portpatrick

Awhirk

B7084

6

Stoneykirk

A716

Luce S

Port of Spittal Bay

8

B7042

Cairngarroch

Sandhead

Cairngarroch Bay

KIRKMADRINE STONES

Sandhead Bay

Money Hd.

Clachanmore

Hole Stone Bay

ARDWELL GDNS

Ardwell

Ardwell Pt.

Ardwell Mains

Chapel Rossan Bay

Logan Mains

10

LOGAN BOTANIC GARDEN

Balgowan Pt.

Mull of Logan

LOGAN FISH POND MARINE LIFE CENTRE

Port Nessock or Port Logan Bay

Port Logan

Cairnywellan Hd.

B7065

A716

Clanyard Bay

Low Clanyard

Kirkmaiden

Laggantalluch Hd.

Drummore

164

Damnaglaur

B7041

Crammag Hd.

M

Cairngaan

0 1 2 3 4 5 6 miles

0 1 2 3 4 5 6 7 8 9 10km

Port Kemin

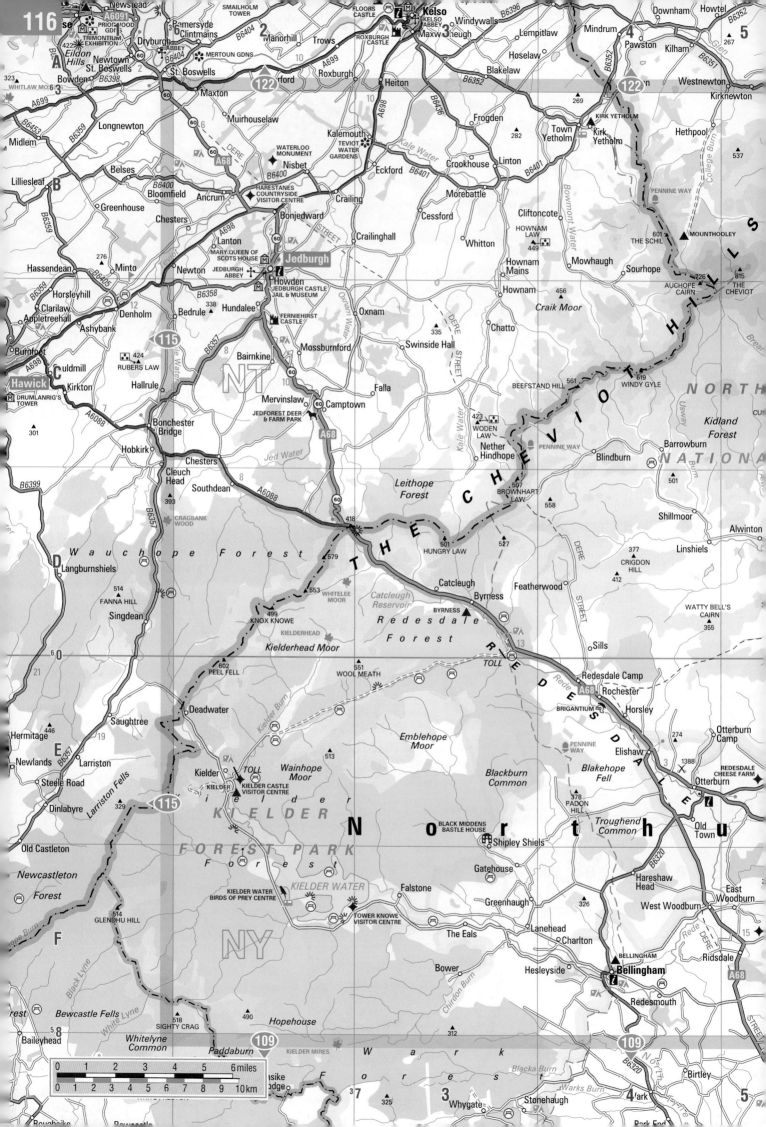

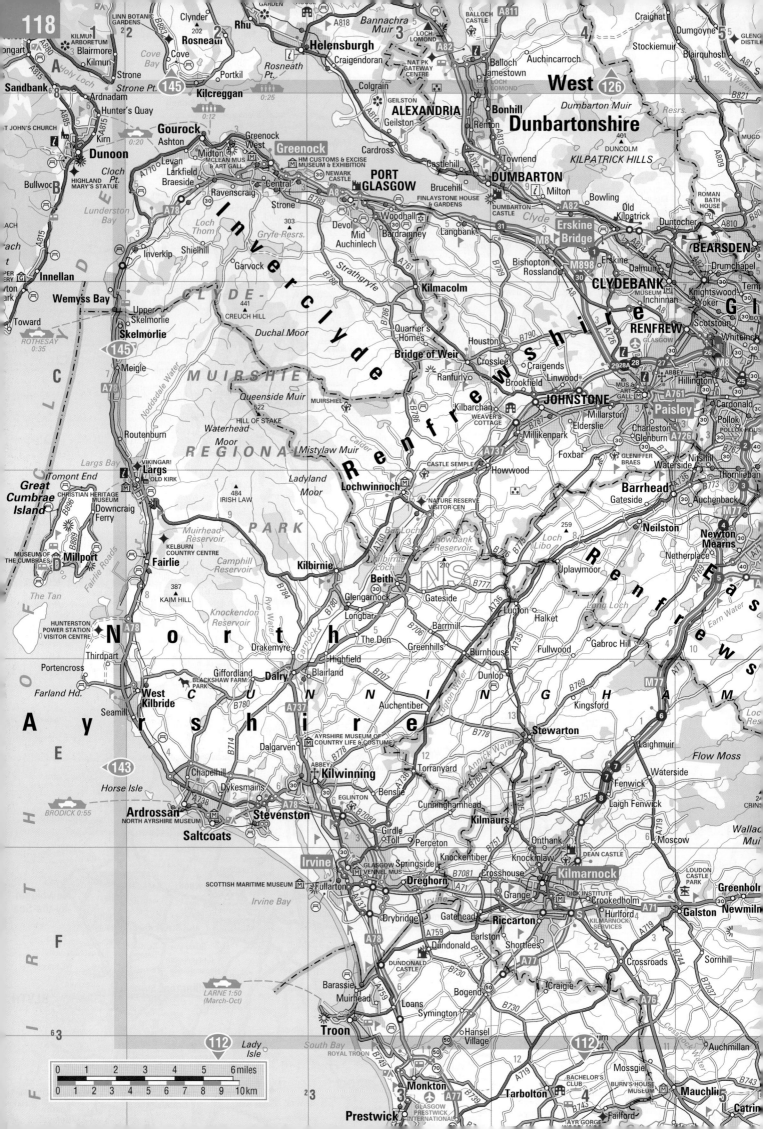

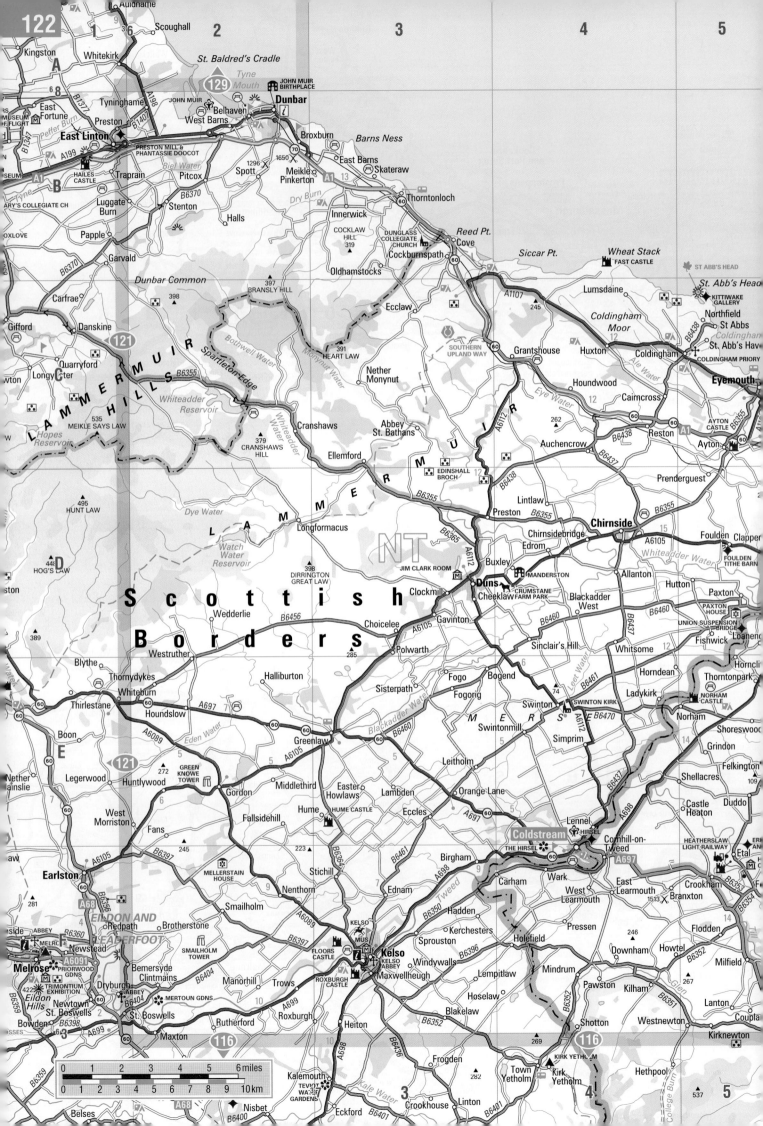

5   40   6   7   8   43   9

A

B

C

EYEMOUTH MUSEUM

Burnmouth

Lamberton Beach

Lamberton

NU

1333

Highfields

Berwick-upon-Tweed

BARRACKS MUSEUM & RAMPARTS

TOWER HOUSE POTTERY

East Ord

Tweedmouth

Spittal

B6461

Priory Park

Redshin Cove

A698

108

Murton

Thornton

Scremerston

West Allerdean

Shoresdean

Cheswick

Ancroft

North Low

Goswick

E

B6525

Berrington

Haggerston

South Low

Beal

Bowsden

82

B6353

12

Causeway Holy Island Sands

Holy Island

LINDISFARNE

Emmanuel Hd.

Holy Island (Lindisfarne)

LINDISFARNE CASTLE

Castle Pt.

LINDISFARNE PRIORY

HERITAGE CENTRE

Fenham

Guile Pt.

Barmoor Castle

Barmoor Lane End

West Kyloe

Fenwick

Lowick

Kyloe Hills

East Kyloe

Buckton

WATERFORD HALL

B6353

ST CUTHBERTS WAY

Elwick

Ross

Farne Islands

Budle Bay

Staple Sound

FARNE ISLANDS

157

Holburn

Detchant

Inner Sound

Kimmerston

Hetton Steads

Middleton

Budle

BAMBURGH CASTLE

Bamburgh

F

Fenton Town

Nesbit

North Hazelrigg

211

Belford

Easington

Waren Mill

Glororum

Burton

Doddington

200

South Hazelrigg

B6349

Mousen

Spindlestone

Bradford

B1341

Newtown

West Horton

East Horton

Bellshill

Clford

North Sunderland

Seahouses

Akeld

10

Warenton

Adderstone

Lucker

Beadnell Bay

A1402

B6325

B6348

117

60

Warenford

Newham Hall

Bea

117

43

G

Wooler

WOOLER

166

Chatton

Greendikes

A1

Warenford

Newham Hall

Swinhoe

Benthall

Humbleton

A697

Haugh Head

CHILLINGHAM CASTLE

Chillingham

WILD CATTLE OF CHILLINGHAM

Rosebrough

Newstead

Chathill

B1340

High Newton-by-the-Sea

Middleton Hall

Earle

Newtown

Ellingham

Preston

5   40   6   7   8   43   9

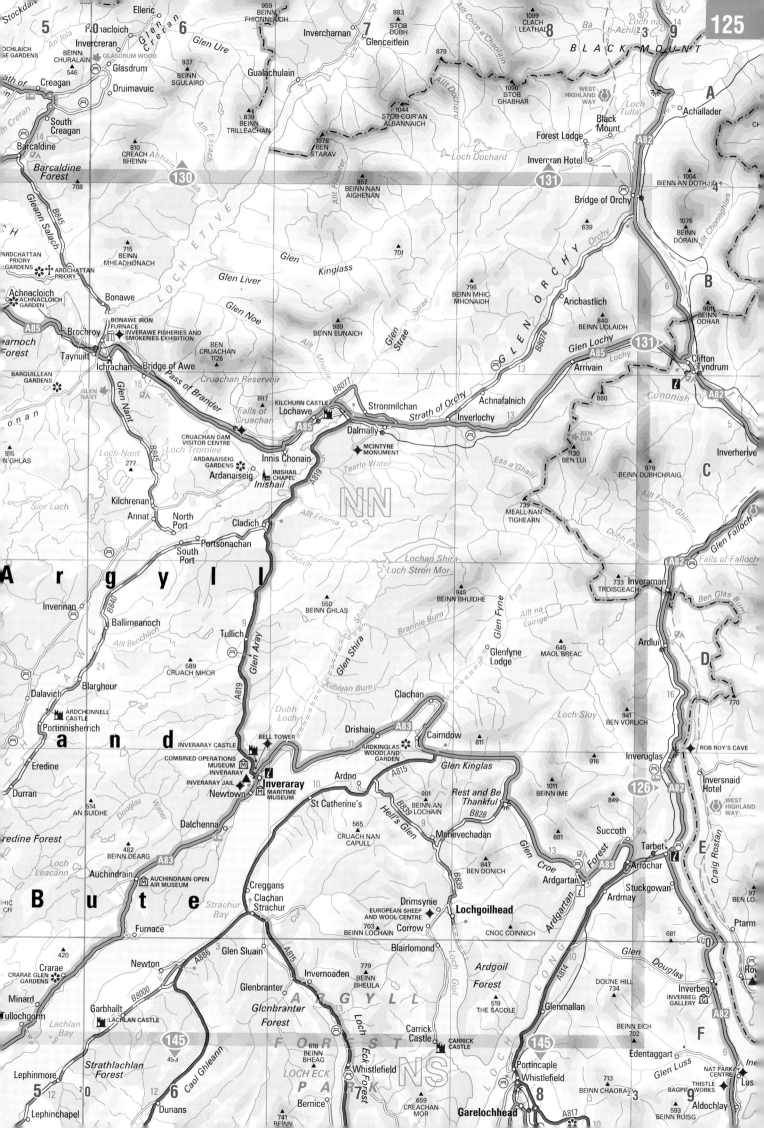

A

B

C

D

E

F

G

5 6 7 8

Glen Dye

Drumtochty Forest
464 Forest

525 MELUNCART

Mains of Dellavaird

Tannachie
Nev Hill Carmont

778 MOUNT BATOCK

5

6

7

8 90

Thornyhive Bay

Burns Family Memorials

Mains of Dellavaird

Drumlithie

141

Fiddes
Barras

Mill of Uras

10

THE RETREAT · GLEN ESK FOLK MUS

140

Cairn o' Mount

Glenfarquhar Lodge

Drumtochty Castle

Strath Finella

Glenbervie

Monboddo House

14

Pitforthie

Crawton

FOWLSHEUGH NATURE RESERVE

Roadside of Catterline

Catterline

Millden Lodge

Clatterin Bridge

Glensaugh

Auchenblae

Fordoun

70

Mondynes

Parkneuk

Arbuthnott

Roadside of Kinneff

Braidon Bay

Todhead Point

Auchmull

Mains of Balnakettle

Thainston

FASQUE HOUSE

East Cairnbeg

Brownmuir

70

B967

GRASSIC GIBBON CENTRE

Kinneff

Little John's Haven

FETTERCAIRN DISTILLERY VISITOR CENTRE

Fettercairn

Howe of the Mearns

Scotston

ARBUTHNOTT CHURCH

ARBUTHNOTT HOUSE GARDENS

Mains of Allardice

Inverbervie

678 HILL OF WIRREN

Dalbog

Meikle Strath

Mains of Thornton

Bent

B9120

A90

Laurencekirk

Garvock

Tulloch

Bervie Bay

Witton

Gannochy

Inch of Arnhall

Edzell

Sauchieburn

50

Dykelands

Garvock Hill

Redford

DAMSIDE GARDEN HERBS & ARBORETUM

Gourdon

EDZELL CASTLE AND GARDENS

Luthermuir

Benholm

Bridgend

Balfield

Dunlappie

North Water Bridge

Johnshaven

MILL OF BENHOLM

440

Ilyarblet

BROWN CATERTHUN

Inchbare

Pert

Marykirk

Ecclesgreig

13

WHITE CATERTHUN

Newtonmill

70

10

Craigo

Lochside

Morphie

St Cyrus

Milton Ness

Kirkton of Menmuir

Tigerton

Keithock

Logie Pert

Muirton of Ballochy

Logie

Pathhead

ST CYRUS

Mains of Balhall

Lochty

Belliehill

Little Brechin

Trinity

A937

Hillside

Kirkhill

Careston Castle

West Muir

BRECHIN CASTLE CENTRE

A935

Brechin

PICTAVIA

CATHEDRAL & ROUND TOWER

HOUSE OF DUN

Dun

A935

CALEDONIAN RAILWAY

Kirkhill

A92

70

A90

Aldbar Castle

Kinnaird Castle

Bridge of Dun

Barnhead

Montrose Basin

Montrose

MUSEUM AND ART GALLERY

Netherton Mains of Melgund

Middle Drums

A933

Farnell

Bonnyton

Inchbraoch

MONTROSE BASIN VISITOR CENTRE

Scurdie Ness

WILLIAM LAMB MEMORIAL STUDIO

ABERLEMNO SCULPTURED STONES

Aberlemno

A934

Carcary

Maryton

Ferryden

B9134

Pitkennedy

Montreathmont Forest

Dubton

Rossie Moor

Westerton

Dunninald

Kirkton of Craig

Long Craig

Fishtown of Usan

252

Turin

Montreathmont Moor

Bolshan

Braehead of Lunan

Boddin Pt.

NO

Rescobie

B9113

Glasterlaw

13

Lunan

Reswallie

9

A932

Balgavies

Milldens

Guthrie

Kinnell

A92

Redcastle

LUNAN BAY

Burnside

Pitmuies

Friockheim

Boysack

Inverkeilor

Dunnichen

Letham

HOUSE OF PITMUIES GARDEN

Chapelton

Lunan Water

B965

Lang Craig

Craichie

Idvies

Leysmill

Cauldcots

Ethie Mains

Red Head

Tulloes

B961

Colliston

Letham Grange

Ethie Castle

12

Mosston

Redford

Drunkendub

rkbuddo

B9128

Greystone

St Vigeans

Marywell

Auchmithie

Meg's Craig

B9127

B9127

Carmyllie

Denhead of Arbilot

ST VIGEANS MUSEUM

Hayshead

The Deil's Heid

Hayhillock

B961

Arbirlot

Cliffburn

ARBROATH ABBEY

CROMBIE

Res.

Kirkton of Monikie

Balmirmer

Elliot

Arbroath

SIGNAL TOWER MUSEUM

Craigton

A92

CARLUNGIE SOUTERRAIN

Muirdrum

East Haven

BARRY MILL

Panbride

Mains of Ardestie

Barry

A930

Carnoustie

CARNOUSTIE

Barry Links

Buddon Ness

129

Buddon Ness

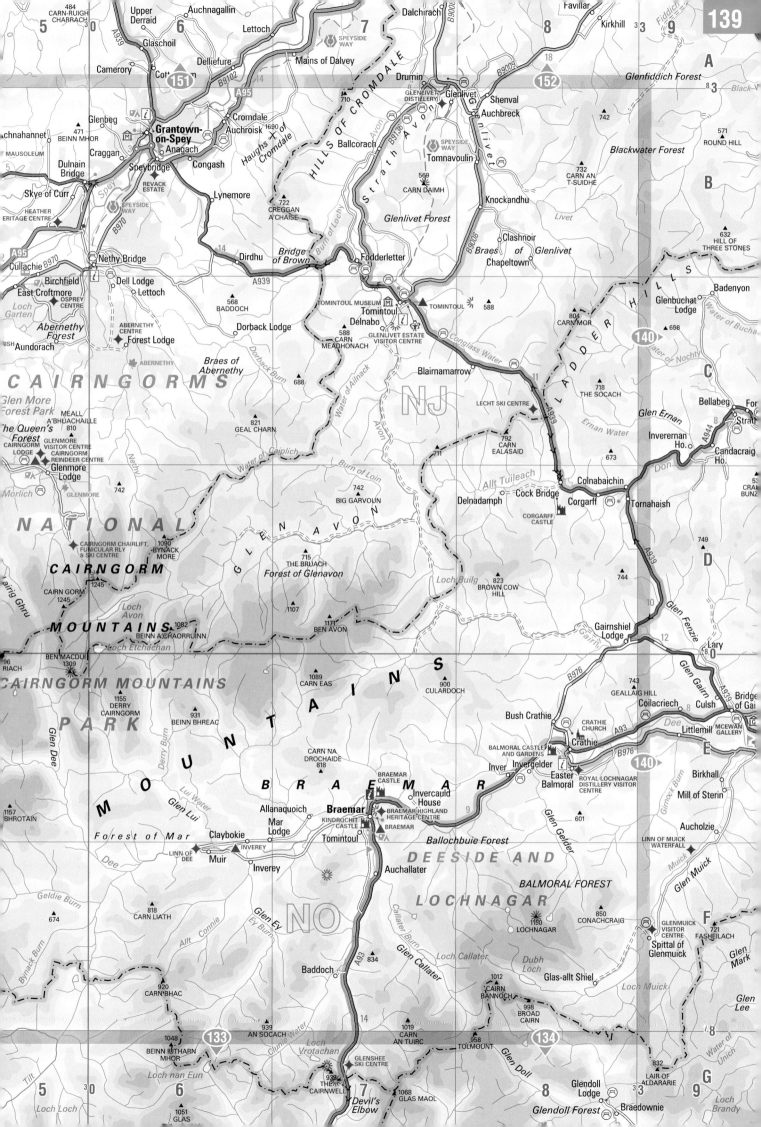

A

B

C

D

E

F

G

5   0   6   7   8   9

GLENFIDDICH FOREST

Favillar
Kirkhill
Black W

Dalchirach
B9009
18   152

Upper Derraid
Auchnagallin
Lettoch
Glaschoil
Delliefure
Mains of Dalvey
SPEYSIDE WAY
Drumin
GLENLIVET DISTILLERY   Glenlivet
Shenval
Auchbreck
742

Camerory
151   B9102   14
Cott

484 CARN-RUIGH CHARRACH
A939

571 ROUND HILL

Glenbeg
471 BEINN MHOR
Grantown-on-Spey
Cromdale
Auchroisk
Anagach   Ballcorach
Tomnavoulin
569 CARN DAIMH
Knockandhu
Blackwater Forest

chnahannet
MAUSOLEUM
Craggan
Speybridge
Congash
Lynemore
722 CREGGAN A'CHAISE
732 CARN AN T-SUIDHE
632 HILL OF THREE STONES

Dulnain Bridge
REVACK ESTATE
Glenlivet Forest
Clashnoir
Braes of Glenlivet
Chapeltown

Skye of Curr
HEATHER HERITAGE CENTRE
A95   B970
SPEYSIDE WAY
Nethy Bridge
Dirdhu
Bridge of Brown
Fodderletter
B9008
Badenyon
Glenbuchat Lodge

Cullachie   B970
Birchfield
Dell Lodge
Lettoch
568 BADDOCH
A939
Tomintoul Museum
TOMINTOUL
588
804 CARN'MOR
140   658
Water of Bucha

East Croftmore
OSPREY CENTRE
Dorback Lodge
Delnabo
GLENLIVET ESTATE VISITOR CENTRE
LADDER HILLS
Glen Ernan

Loch Garten
Abernethy Forest
ABERNETHY CENTRE
Forest Lodge
588 CARN MEADHONACH
718 THE SOCACH
Bellabeg
For Strath

IRISH
Aundorach
ABERNETHY
Braes of Abernethy
688
Blairnamarrow
11
Inverernan Ho.
A944   8

CAIRNGORMS
821 GEAL CHARN
Lecht Ski Centre
A939
673
Candacraig Ho.
CRA BUNZ

Glen More Forest Park
MEALL A'BHUACHAILLE 810
792 CARN EALASAID
711
Ernan Water

The Queen's Forest
CAIRNGORM LODGE
GLENMORE VISITOR CENTRE
CAIRNGORM REINDEER CENTRE
Glenmore Lodge
742
Colnabaichin
Tornahaish
Don

Morlich   GLENMORE
Cock Bridge
Corgarff
749

NATIONAL
CAIRNGORM CHAIRLIFT, FUNICULAR RLY & SKI CENTRE
1090 BYNACK MORE
715 THE BRUACH
Delnadamph
CORGARFF CASTLE

CAIRNGORM
742
BIG GARVOUN
Forest of Glenavon
744
A939

Cairn Ghru
CAIRN GORM 1245
1245
1082
1107
1171 BEN AVON
823 BROWN COW HILL
Gairnshiel Lodge
12
Lary

MOUNTAINS
BEINN A'CHAORRUINN
Loch Etchachan
Loch Builg
10

BEN MACDUI
1309
Loch Avon
GLEN AVON
B976

96 RIACH

CAIRNGORM MOUNTAINS
1089 CARN EAS
900 CULARDOCH
743 GEALLAIG HILL
Coilacriech
Culsh
Bridge of Gai

1155 DERRY CAIRNGORM
Bush Crathie
Glen Gairn
A939

PARK
931 BEINN BHREAC
CRATHIE CHURCH
Littlemill
MCEWAN GALLERY

Glen Dee
CARN NA DROCHAIDE 818
BALMORAL CASTLE AND GARDENS
Crathie
Dee
B976

1157 BHROTAIN
BRAEMAR
BRAEMAR CASTLE
Inver
Invergelder
140
Birkhall

M   **MOUNTAINS**
Lui Water
Glen Lui
Allanaquoich
Invercauld House
Easter Balmoral
ROYAL LOCHNAGAR DISTILLERY VISITOR CENTRE
Mill of Sterin

Forest of Mar
Claybokie
Mar Lodge
KINDROCHIT CASTLE
BRAEMAR
BRAEMAR HIGHLAND HERITAGE CENTRE
601
Aucholzie

LINN OF DEE
INVEREY
Muir
Tomintoul
Auchallater
DEESIDE AND
LINN OF MUICK WATERFALL
Glen Muick

Dee
Inverey
Ballochbuie Forest
LOCHNAGAR
BALMORAL FOREST
GLENMUICK VISITOR CENTRE

Geldie Burn
674
818 CARN LIATH
Glen Ey
NO
1150 LOCHNAGAR
850 CONACHCRAIG
721 FASHEILACH
Spittal of Glenmuick
Glen Mark

Bynack Burn
920 CARN'BHAC
Baddoch
A93
834
Loch Callater
1012 CAIRN BANNOCH
998 BROAD CAIRN
Glen Lee

133
939 AN SOCACH
1019 CARN AN TUIRC
Tolmount
134
832 LAIR OF ALDARARIE
Glen Doll
Water of Unich

BEINN IUTHARN MHOR
1048
Loch Vrotachan
GLENSHEE SKI CENTRE
958
1012
Glendoll Lodge
Glendoll Forest
Braedownie
Loch Brandy

1051 GLAS
THE CAIRNWELL
939
Devil's Elbow
1068 GLAS MAOL
Tilt
Loch Loch
Loch nan Eun

5   0   6   7   8   9

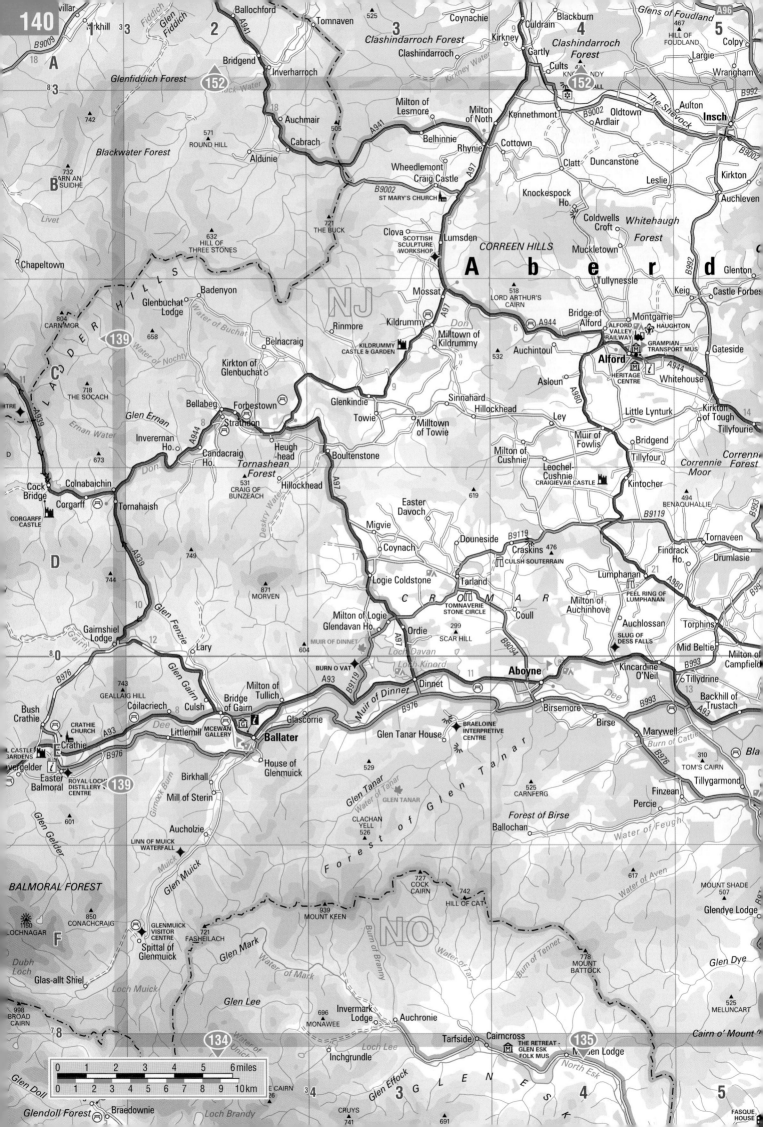

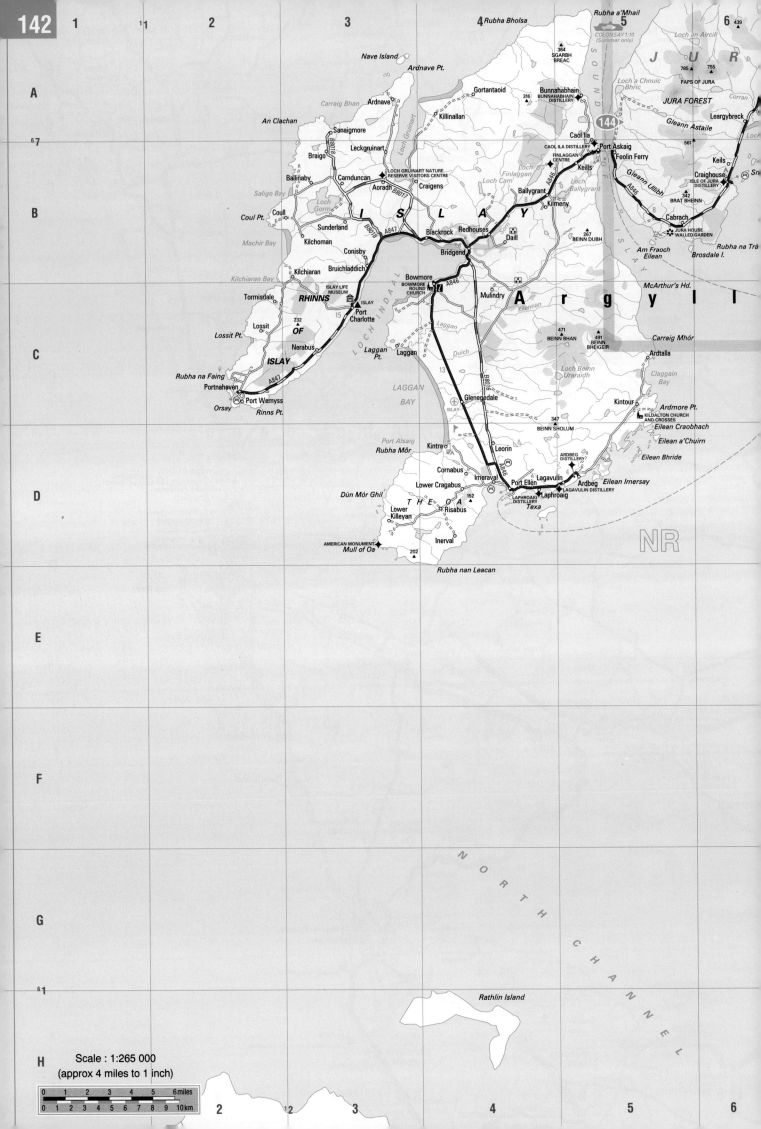

ARDMEANACH

Killiemore House
Aird of Kinloch
MACLEAN'S CROSS
Eilean Annraidh
STAFFA 0:45 (April-Oct)
Rubha nan Cearc
THE BURG
Ben Buie 717
Loch Airdeglais
Loch Spelve
Croggan
Rubha nan Sailthean
Bach I.
Ardmore
248
Loch Fuaron
CREACH BEINN 698
Kinlochspelve
Lochbuie
Barachandroman
Rubha Seanac
IONA ABBEY AND CATHEDRAL
Kintra
ST COLUMBA EXHIBITION & WELCOME CENTRE
Aridhglas
Eorabus
A849
Pennycross
503
BEINN NA CROISE
Torrans
Leidle
Loch Uisg
Loch Buie
IONA HERITAGE CENTRE
Iona
Beile Mor
Fionnphort
Fidden
Tiraghoil
Lee
Bunessan
18
376 CRUACHAN MIN
BROLASS
Carsaig
376
Laggan
405 DRUIM FADA
Deer Forest
LORD LOVAT'S CAVE
Insh I.
Clachan
CLACHAN BRIDGE
Erraid
ROSS OF MULL
Ardalanish
Uisken
Scoor
Ardchiavaig
125
Malcolm's Pt.
CARSAIG ARCHES
Rubha Dubh
Carsaig Bay
Frank Lockwood's Island
Seil
AN CALA GARDENS
Easdale
B844
Balvicar
Eilean a'Chalmain
Rubha nam Braithrean
Easdale
EASDALE ISLAND FOLK MUSEUM
Rubh Ardalanish
146
Dubh-fheith
Cuan
Torsa
Kilchoan
Torran Rocks
NM
Garbh Eileach
Cullipool
94
Luing
Garvellachs
SCARBA, Eilean Dubh Mor
Achafolla
ARDUAINE GARDEN
Arduain
Eileach an Naoimh
LUNGA AND
Toberonochy
Shuna
OBAN 2:20
124
THE GARVELLACHS
Lunga
Shuna Pt.
Lunga
CRUACH SCARBA 449
Scarba
Rubha Aird Luing
Shuna Sound
Gulf of Corryvreckan
Aird
Rèisa an t-Sruith
Rubh'a'Geadha
Balnahard
Kiloran Bay
Glengarrisdale Bay
Kinuachdrachd
296 CRUACH NA SEILCHEIG
Kinuachdrachd Harbour
Craignish Pt.
Island Macaskin
SCULPTURE
KILORAN GARDENS
Kiloran
Glendebadel Bay
124
Loch Crinan
COLONSAY
Kilchattan
Scalasaig
B8086
B8087
Crinan
Killmahumaig
Bellanoch
Garvard
B8085
Rubha Dubh
Loch Staosnaig
365 BEN GARRISDALE
265
KNAPD
PRIORY
Dubh Eilean
Oronsay
467 BEINN BHREAC
Lealt
Gallachoille
Carsaig
Tayvallich
Achanama
Eilean nan Ron
Shian Bay
453 RAINBERG MOR
Ardlussa
Ardlussa Bay
Inverlussa
Lussagiven
Kilmichael of Inverlussa
Rubh'an t-Sàilein
Loch Righ Mòr
318
Shian
Barrahormid
Taynish
466 CRUACH LUSA
Rubha Lang-aoinidh
1:10 (Summer Only)
Loch Tarbert
Tarbert
KEILLS CHAPEL
Keillmore
New Ulva
Dunrostan
Rubha a'Mhail
Lagg
Island of Danna
CASTLE SWEEN
Lochead
Rubha Bholsa
Loch Lesgamaill
St COLUMBA'S CAVE
Achahoish
364 SGARBH BREAC
439
Nave Island
Ardnave Pt.
Ardnave
Gortantaoid
785
755
JURA
Eilean Mòr
St CORMAC'S CHAPEL
CHAPEL
Kilmory
Ellary
Clachbreck
Loch a Chnuic Bhric
PAPS OF JURA
Corran
An Dùnan
Kilmory Bay
Pt. of Knap
Baile Boidheach
Killinallan
316
BUNNAHABHAIN DISTILLERY
Bunnahabhain
JURA FOREST
Knockrome
Lowlandman's Bay
Ormsary
Leckgruinart
Leargybreck
Gleann Astaile
Loch na Mile
Druimdrishaig
Caol Ila
561
Miller's Bay
Cretshengan
305
Loch nan Torran
CAOL ILA DISTILLERY
Port Askaig
Feolin Ferry
Keils
Small Isles
FINLAGGAN CENTRE
Keills
Gleann Ullibh
Craighouse
ISLE OF JURA DISTILLERY
CRUACH LAGAIN 264
Kilberry Hd.
Loch Gruinart
ISLAY
Ballygrant
Kilmeny
342 BRAT BHEINN
Cretshengan
Kilberry
SCULPTURED STONES
LOCH GRUINART NATURE RESERVE VISITORS CENTRE
Aoradh
Craigens
Loch Cam
Loch Finlaggan
Loch Ballygrant
JURA HOUSE WALLED GARDEN
Cabrach
NR
B8017
Craigens
8
GISLAY
Y
142
Rubha na Tràille
Kilberry Hd.
Blackrock
Redhouses
Daill
267 BEINN DUBH
Bridgend
Am Fraoch Eilean
Brosdale I.
Carse Ho.
Dunmore
Conisby
A847
Ardpatrick Ho.
Portachoillan
hladdich
A846
McArthur's Hd.
Ardpatrick
Bowmore
BOWMORE ROUND CHURCH
A846
Mulindry
Ardpatrick Pt.
Eilean Tràighe
Ronachan Pt.
A83
Clachan
Port Charlotte
Kilnennan
471 BEINN BHAN
491 BEINN BHEIGEIR
Carraig Mhòr
Loch Stornoway
143
Laggan Pt.
Laggan
Scale 1:265 000
(approx 4 miles to 1 inch)
Ardtalla
Loch Beinn Uraraidh
Claggain Bay
Eilean Garbh
West Tarbert Bay
East Tarbert Bay
Gigha Island
Tarbert
0 1 2 3 4 5 6 miles
0 1 2 3 4 5 6 7 8 9 10km
ISLAY
Kin ur
Ardmore Pt.
PORT ELLEN 2:20
KILDALTON CHURCH
Gigha Island
Balochroy
Loch Ciaran

NF

09 2 10 3 4 5 6 7

80 148 149

NL

Canna
Garrisdale Pt. A'Chill
Sanday
Canna Harbour
Rubha Shamhnan Insir
Kilmory
Guirdil Bay
Kilmory Glen
388
571 ORVAL
A'Bhrideanach
Schooner Pt.
RÙM
Kinloch Glen
Kinloch
Loch Scresort
Kinloch Castle
Rubha Port na Caranean
Rubha na Roinne
MALLAIG 2:30
0:55

Harris
Glen Harris
812 ASKIVAL
781 AINSHVAL
Rubha Sgorr an t-Snidhe
Rubha nam Meirleach
THE SMALL ISLES
SOUND OF RÙM
1:00
1:10

Bay of Laig
Cleadale
Rubha an Fhasaidh
Eigg
393 AN SGURR
Kildonnan
Galmisdale
Eilean
Eilean nan Each
SOUND OF EIGG
0:35

Muck
137
Port Mor

Oigh-sgeir

Inset box B–C, 2–3:
Bhatarsaigh (Vatersay)
Uidh
Bagh Bhatarsaigh
148
Bhatarsaigh
Caolas Shanndraigh
Flodaigh (Flodday)
207
Sanndraigh (Sandray)
79 79
Lingeigh (Lingay)
Greanamul
Theisgeir (Heiskers)
171
Pabaidh (Pabbay)
Caolas Phabaigh
Caolas Mhiui Laigh
273
Miùgh Laigh (Mingulay)
Bearnaraigh (Berneray)
Caolas Bhearnaraigh
78 78
Barra Hd.
06

Sanna Point
Sanna
Sanna Bay
Portuairk
Achnaha
Point of Ardnamurchan
ARDNAMURCHAN LIGHTHOUSE
Achosnich
Cairns of Coll
Ormsaigmore
An Acairseid
Ormsaigbeg
Kilchoan
Kilchoan Bay

Rubha Mor
Eilean Mor
Bousd
Sorisdale
Arnabost
Gallanach
Cliad Bay
Grishipoll
B8072
73
COLL
OBAN 2:40
Ballyhaugh
B8071
104
Loch Cliad
Hogh Bay
Totronald
Arinagour
Loch Eatharna
Ardmore Bay
Ardmore Pt.
Quinish Pt.
Glengorm Castle
MULL MUSEUM
Arileod
Acha
Caliach Pt.
Rubha an Aird
Sunipol
MISHNISH
'S AIRDE-BEINN
292
Feall Bay
Breachacha Castle
Friesland
Eilean Ornsay
Calgary Pt.
MORNISH
Penmore Mill
Dervaig
THE OLD BYRE HERITAGE CENTRE
SPE
Gunna
Crossapol Bay
Soa
Loch Breachacha
Calgary
Calgary Bay
Achnadrish
MULL LITTLE THEATRE

TIREE
Vaul Bay
Salum
Caolas
Rubha Dubh
Hough Skerries
Balephetrish Bay
Vaul
Ruaig
B8069
R. Chraiginis
Balevullin
Kenovay
B8068
Scarinish
Soa
Treshnish Pt.
342 CARN MOR
Ensay
Kilkenneth
Moss
TIREE
Heanish
Rubh a'Chaoil
Burg
Haunn
B8073
Kilninian
Achnacraig
Middleton
Heylipol
Crossapol
Rubha Traig an Duin
Gott Bay
424 BEINN NA DRISE
Fanmore
390
23
Lettermo
Port Mor
Barrapol
B8065
Balemartine
Hynish Bay
LOCH TUATH
Ballygown
EAS FORS WATERFALL
Laggan Bay
Lagganulva
Rinn Thorbhais
Balephuil
B8066
141
Mannal
Treshnish Isles
Fladda
Eilean Dioghlum
Gometra
Bearnus
313
ULVA
Ulva House
Oskamull
Killiemor
Balephuil Bay
Port Snoig
Hynish
Lunga
Bac Mor
Eorsa
LOCH NA KEAL
ISLE OF

Staffa
STAFFA
FINGAL'S CAVE
Little Colonsay
INCH KENNETH CHAPEL
Inch Kenneth
Derryguaig
Balnahard
MACKINNON'S CAVE
Erisgeir
519
GLEN SEILISDEIR
561
ARDMEANACH
BEINN NA SREINE
Killiemor House
THE BURG
LOCH SCRIDAIN

April-Oct 0:45
MACLEAN'S CROSS
Eilean Annraidh
Rubha nan Cearc
IONA ABBEY AND CATHEDRAL
100
ST COLUMBA EXHIBITION & WELCOME CENTRE
Kintra
IONA HERITAGE CENTRE
Iona
Baile Mor
Aridhglas
Eorabus
Fidden
Fionnphort
A849
Bunessan
Lee
376 CRUACHAN MIN
Stac an Aoineidh
Tiraghoil
Loch Assapol
Torra
Erraid
ROSS OF MULL
Uisken
Scoor
Malcolm's P
Ardalanish
Ardchiavaig
125
Soa I.
Eilean a'Chalmain
Rubh Ardalanish
144
Rubha nam Braithean
Torran Rocks

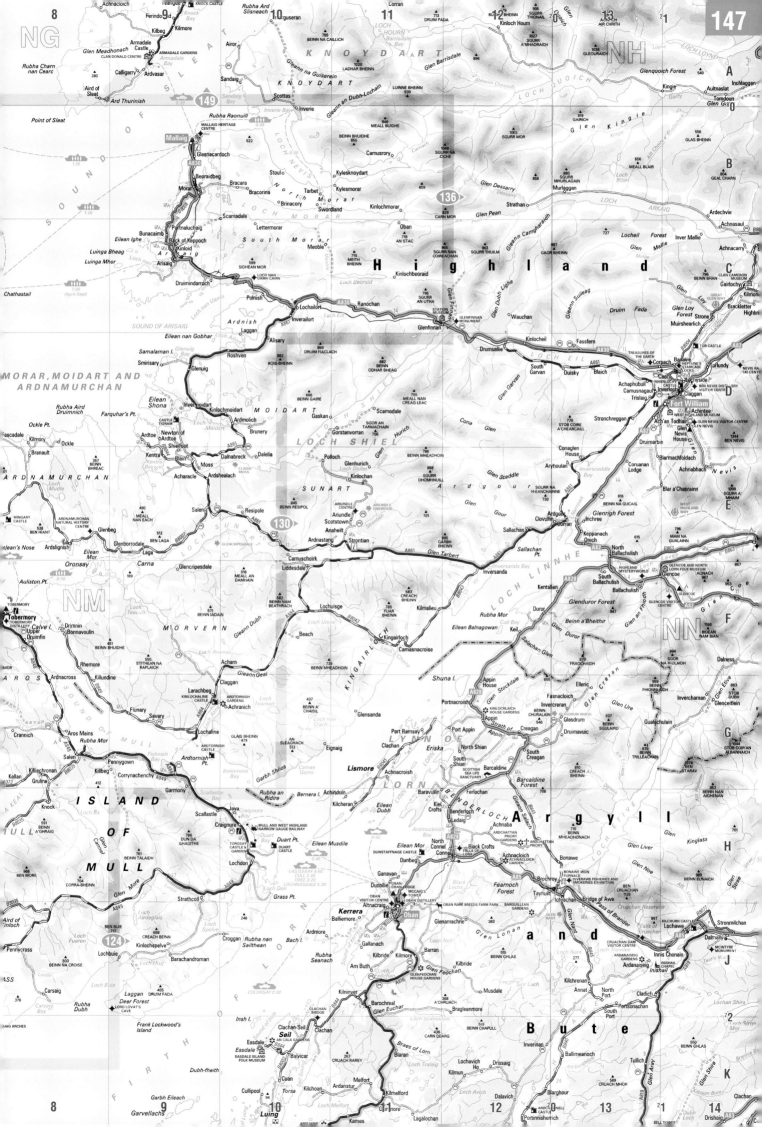

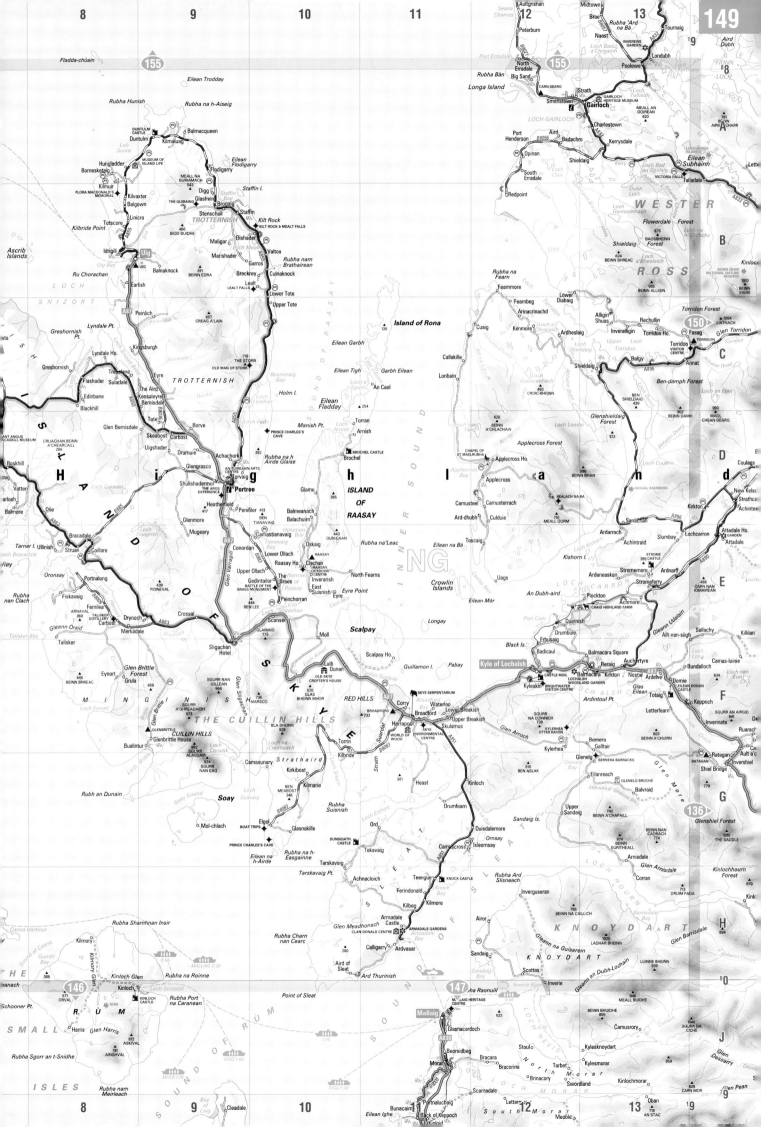

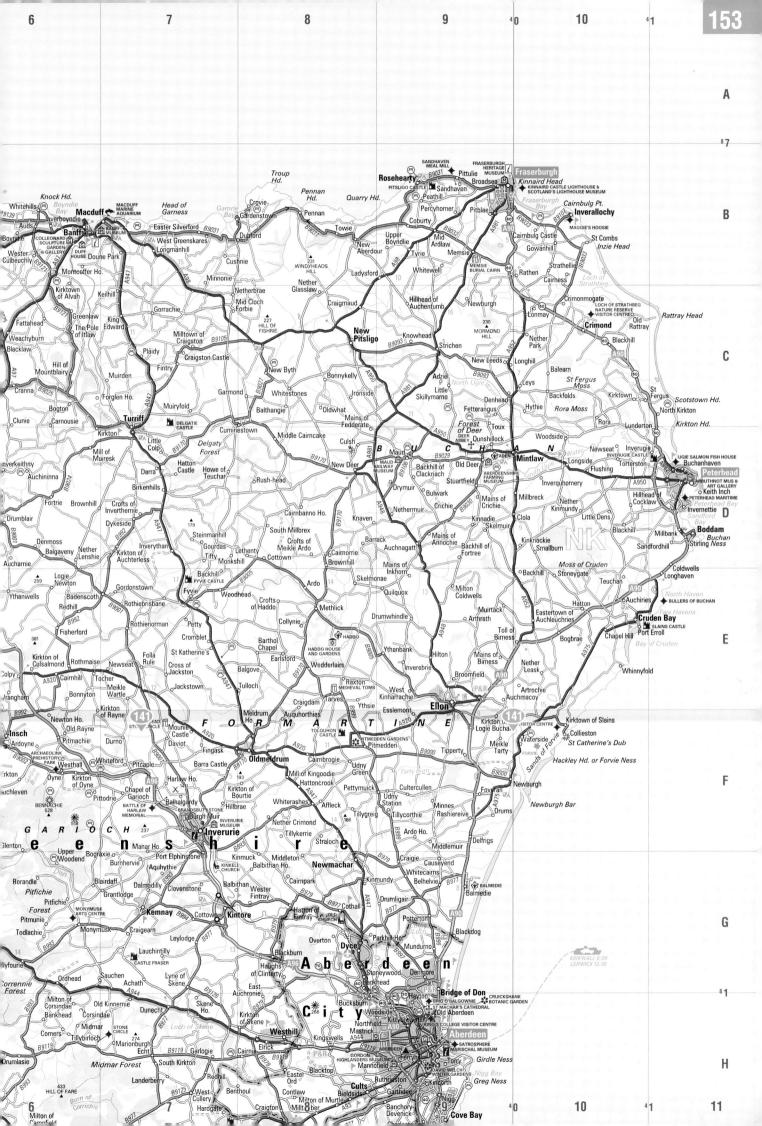

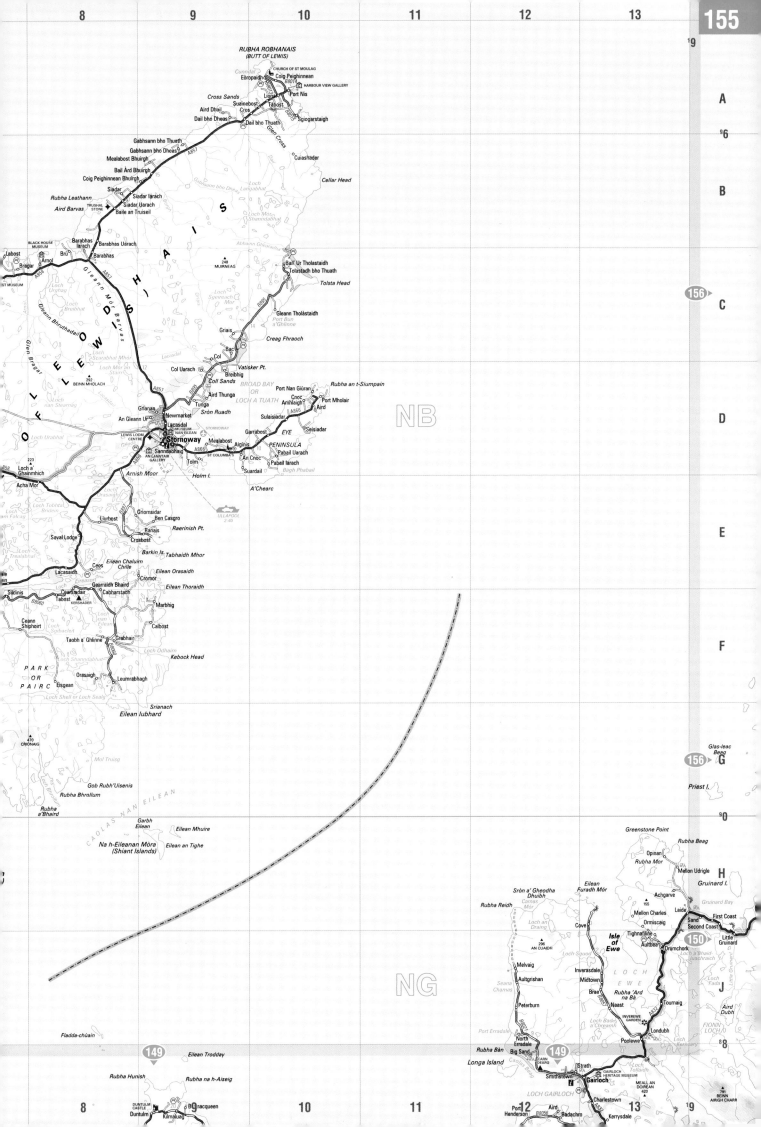

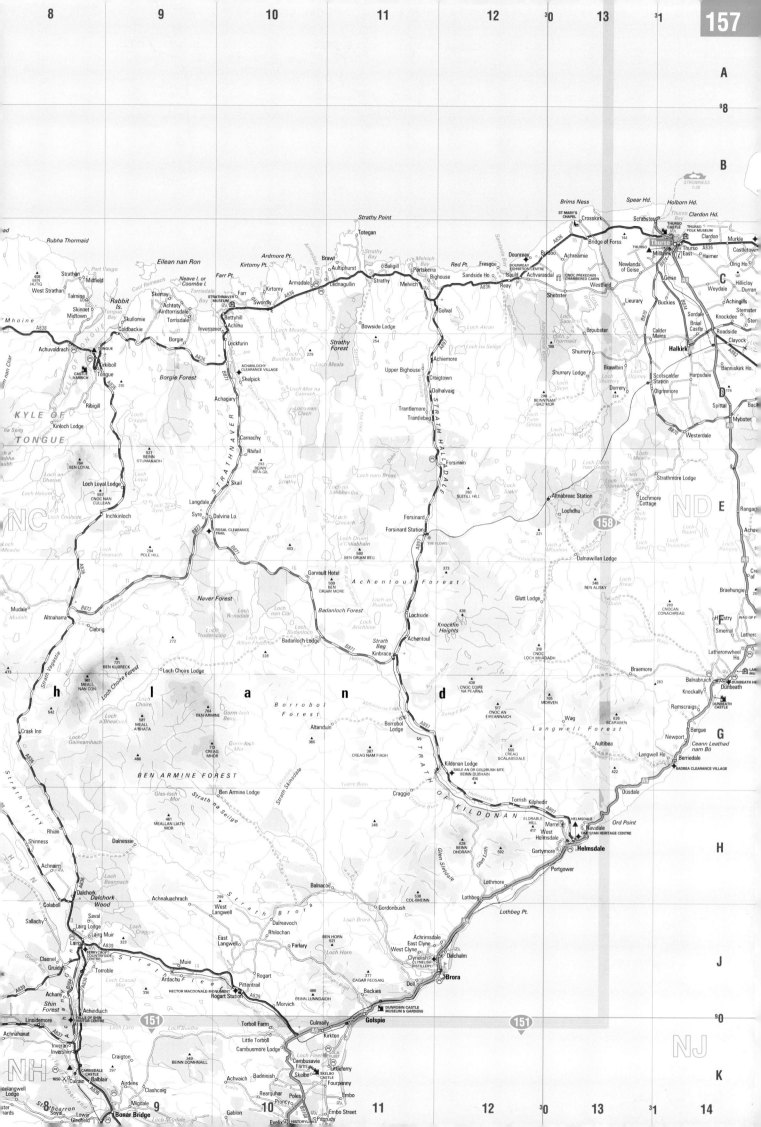

HOY

Rackwick
Pegal Burn
Rysa Little 5
Rose Ness 7
KNAP OF TROWIEGLEN
Fara
Calf of Flotta
Hunda
Burray
FOSSIL AND VINTAGE CENTRE
Hillside
Burray Village
Southtown
Burray Ness
Grimness

Rack Wick
236
Roan Hd.
Weddel Sd.
SCAPA FLOW VISITOR CENTRE
Lyness
Rinnigill
Bows
Flotta
Uppertown
St. Margaret's Hope
Quindry
Papley
Grim Ness

Sneuk Hd.
Heldale Water
Burn of Ora
Little Ayre
Crockness
Swiha Sound
Herston
Widewall
Aikers
Newark Bay

Little Rack Wick
Hoglinns Water
199
Longhope
Hackness
Wyng
Hoxa
Herston Hd.
Sandwick
Sand Wick
Lythes
SOUTH RONALDSAY

Tor Ness
Melsetter
Hurliness
Brims
MARTELLO TOWERS
SOUTH WALLS
Cantick Hd.
Suckquoy
Wind Wick

Brims Ness
Garth Hd.
North Hd.
Barth Hd.
Linklater
Halcro Hd.

PENTLAND FIRTH

Swona
Dundas Ho.
Burwick
Cleat
Old Hd.
TOMB OF THE EAGLES AND BRONZE AGE HOUSE
Brough Ness
Liddel

159

Langaton Point
Muckle Skerry
Red Head
Netherton
Island of Stroma
Pentland Skerries
Mell Head
Uppertown
(0:40 May-Sept)

DUNNET HEAD
Briga Hd.
Scarfskerry Pt.
Men of Mey
St John's Pt.
Boars of Duncansby
Scarfskerry
STROMNESS 1:30
The Thirl
Brough
Ham
Rattar
Mey
Gills Bay
Huna
DUNCANSBY HEAD

Brims Ness
Spear Hd.
Holborn Hd.
Hunspow
St John's
CASTLE OF MEY
Gills
Kirkstyle
JOHN O'GROATS
John o' Groats
Stacks of Duncansby

ST MARY'S CHAPEL
Crosskirk
Scrabster
NATURAL HISTORY DISPLAY
Corsback
Barrock
Canisbay

Bridge of Forss
144
THURSO CASTLE
THURSO FOLK MUSEUM
Dunnet
FLAGSTONE INTERPRETATIVE TRAIL
Castlehill
Brabster
124
Tofts
Skirza
Skirza Head

Buldoo
Achreamie
Newlands of Geise
Thurso
Clardon
Murkle
Castletown
Greenland
Freswick
Freswick Bay

DOUNREAY EXHIBITION CENTRE
Thurso East
Millbank
Haimer
Olrig Ho.
Tain
CASTLETOWN
Lochend
NORTHLANDS VIKING CENTRE
Ness Head

Fresgoe
Isauld
Achvarasdal
CNOC FREKEDAIN CHAMBERED CAIRN
Geise
Hilliclay
Durran
6
Reaster
Slickly
BUCHOLLY CASTLE
Nybster
Auckengill
Brough Head

Reay
Shebster
Westfield
Lieurary
Buckies
Weydale
Achingills
Bowermadden
Alterwall
LYTH ARTS CENTRE
Keiss

Loch Akran
Broubster
Shurrery
Sordale
Knockdee
Stemster
Bowertower
Lyth
Barrock Ho.
Sortat
Howe
Mireland
KEISS CASTLE

Loch na Seilge
198
Calder Mains
Brial Castle
Halcro
Hastigrow
Gillock
Kirk

NC
Loch Saorich
Shurrery Lodge
Loch Scye
Brawlbin
Dorrery
Loch Oigney
Scotscalder Station
Olgrinmore
Harpsdale
Halkirk
Roadside
Clayock
Loch Scarmclate
North Watten
Myrelandhorn
Killimster
CASTLE GIRNIGOE
Noss Head

ND

Loch Sletill
BEINN NAM BAD MOR
290
Shurrery
224
Spittal
Backlass
Watten
Loch Watten
Mains of Watten
Reiss
CASTLE SINCLAIR
Sealky Head

Loch Tuim Ghlais
Loch Calium
Westerdale
Mybster
Loch of Toftingall
Bilbster
Strath
Winless
Ackergill
Staxigoe
Papigoe
WICK HERITAGE CENTRE

Altnabreac Station
221
Loch Meadie
Strathmore Lodge
Rangag
Loch Ruard
Badlipster
Stirkoke Ho.
Wick
Broadhaven
Old Wick
South Hd.
CASTLE OF OLD WICK

157
Lochdhu
Lochmore Cottage
Loch More
Achavanich
HILL OF OLICLETT
141
Gansclet
Helman Hd.
Thrumster

Highland
Loch Sand
Loch Rangag
GREY CAIRNS OF CAMSTER
Camster
212
Ulbster
CAIRN OF GET
Sarclet
Sarclet Hd.

Dalnawillan Lodge
Loch Thulachan
248
STEMSTER HILL
Roster
HILL O' MANY STANES
Whaligoe

Glutt Lodge
BEN ALISKY
348
269
CNOCAN CONACHREAG
Braehungie
287
Crofts of Benachielt
RUMSTER FOREST
Upper Lybster
Mid Clyth
Bruan

Loch Breac
Loch Dubh
Houstry
Smerral
Forse Ho.
Swiney
West Clyth
LYBSTER ART GALLERY
Lybster

CNOC LOCH MHADADH
318
Latheron
WAG OF FORSE
Forse
CLAN GUNN HERITAGE CENTRE

Langwell Forest
438
CNOC COIRE NA PEARNA
517
CNOC AN EIREANNAICH
626
SCARABEN
Wag
Latheronwheel Ho.
Latheronwheel
LAIDHAY CROFT MUSEUM

705
MORVEN
283
Balnabruich
Knockally
DUNBEATH HERITAGE CENTRE
Dunbeath
Dunbeath Bay
DUNBEATH CASTLE

Newport
Borgue
Ramscraigs

Aultibea
Newport
Ceann Leathad nam Bò
19
Berriedale

Lodge
AN OR GOLDRUSH SITE
BEINN DUBHAIN
414
555
CREAG SCALABSDALE
422
Langwell Ho.
BADBEA CLEARANCE VILLAGE

Ousdale
Torrish
Kilphedir
Ord Point

ELDRABLE HILL
417
Marrel
Navidale
TIMESPAN HERITAGE CENTRE

West Helmsdale
Helmsdale

592
Gartymore
Portgower

Lothmore
Lothbeg
Lothbeg Pt.

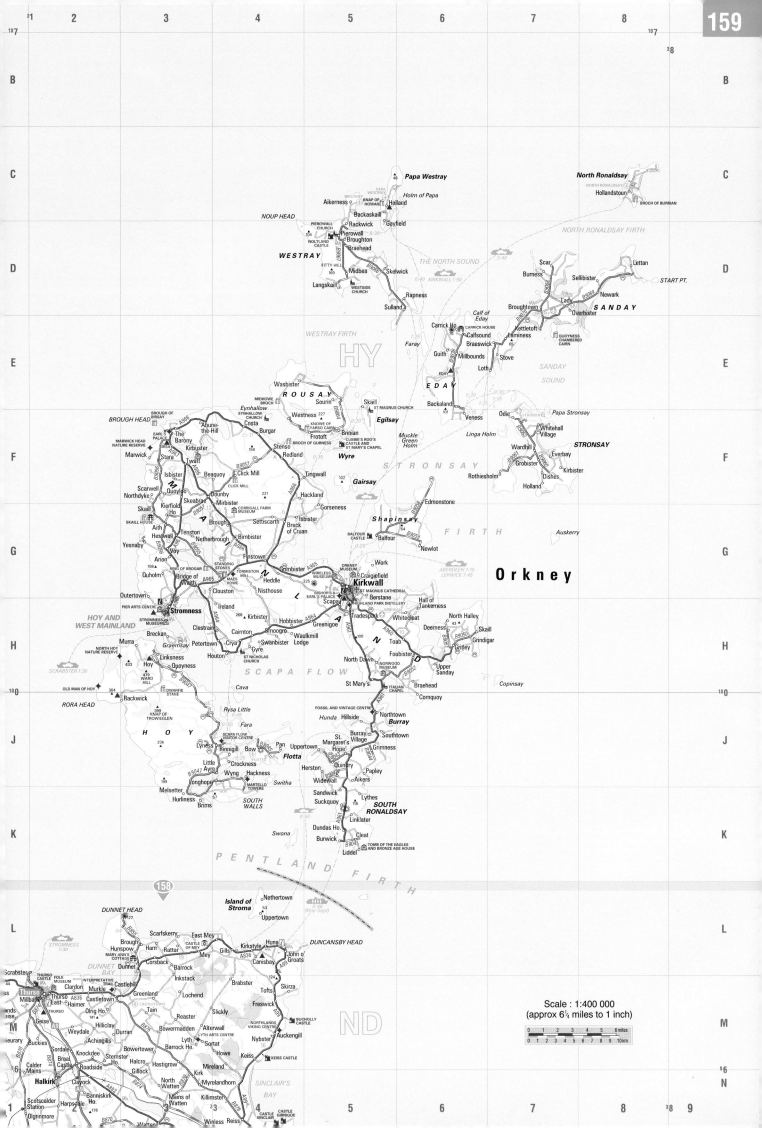

Scale : 1:400 000
(approx 6¼ miles to 1 inch)

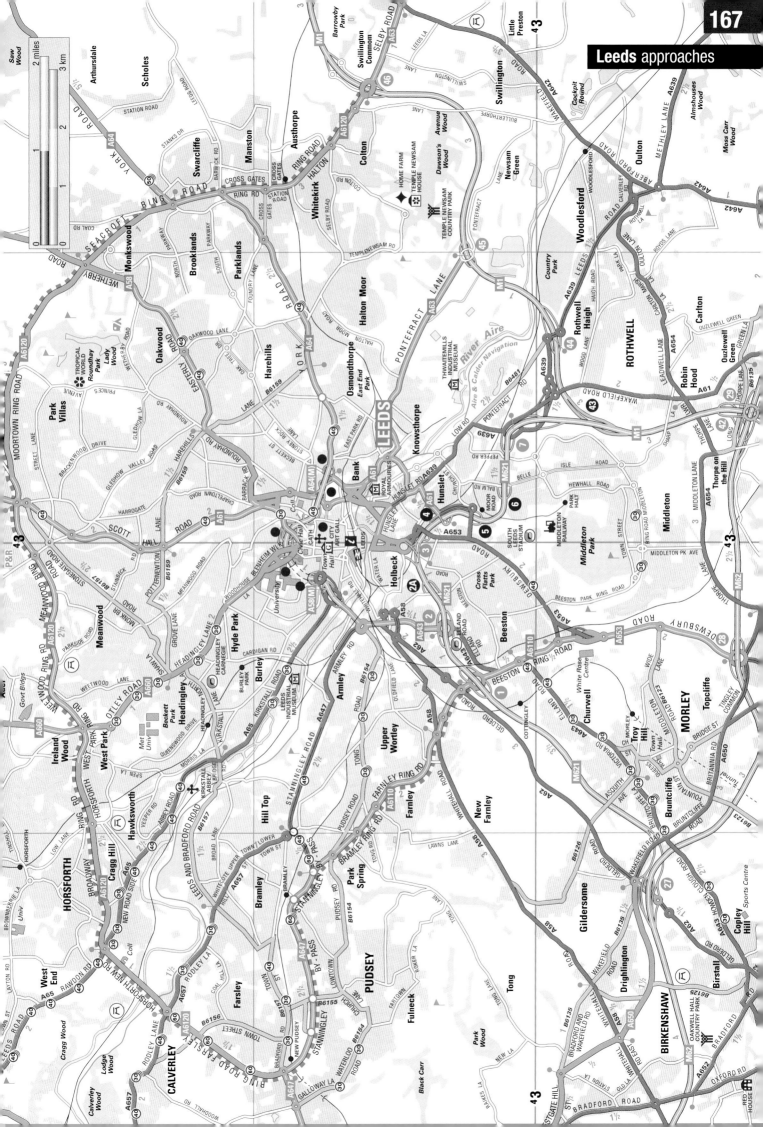

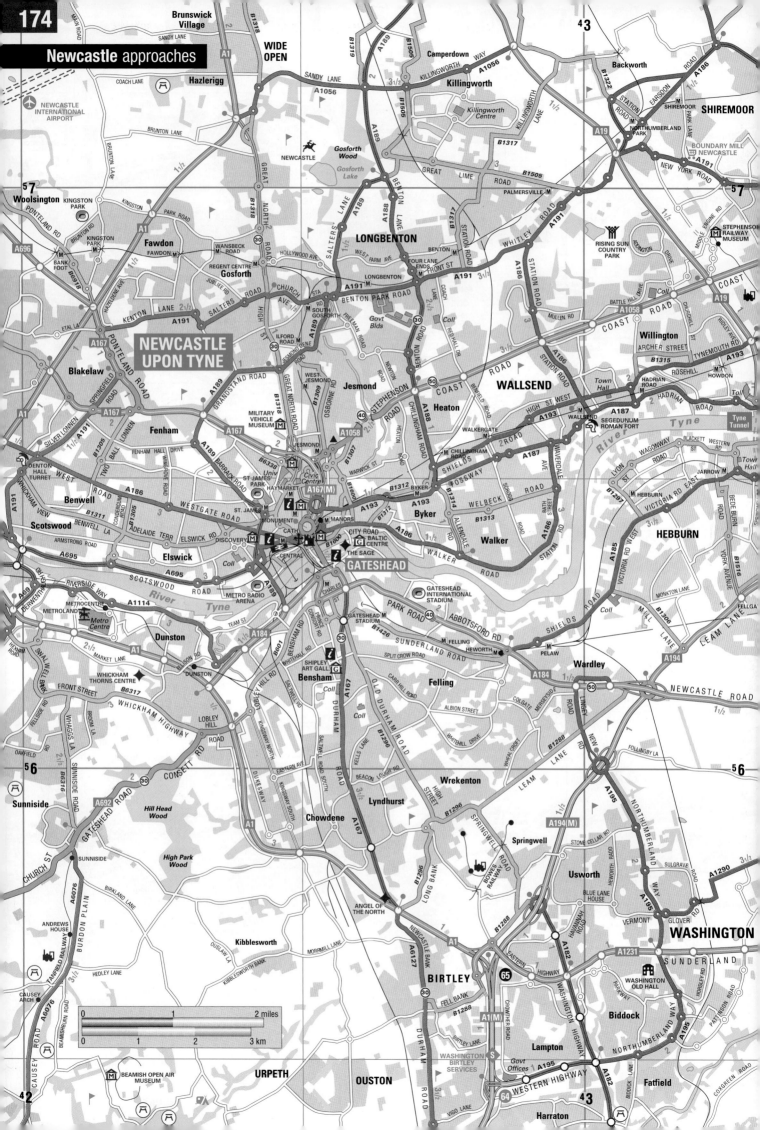

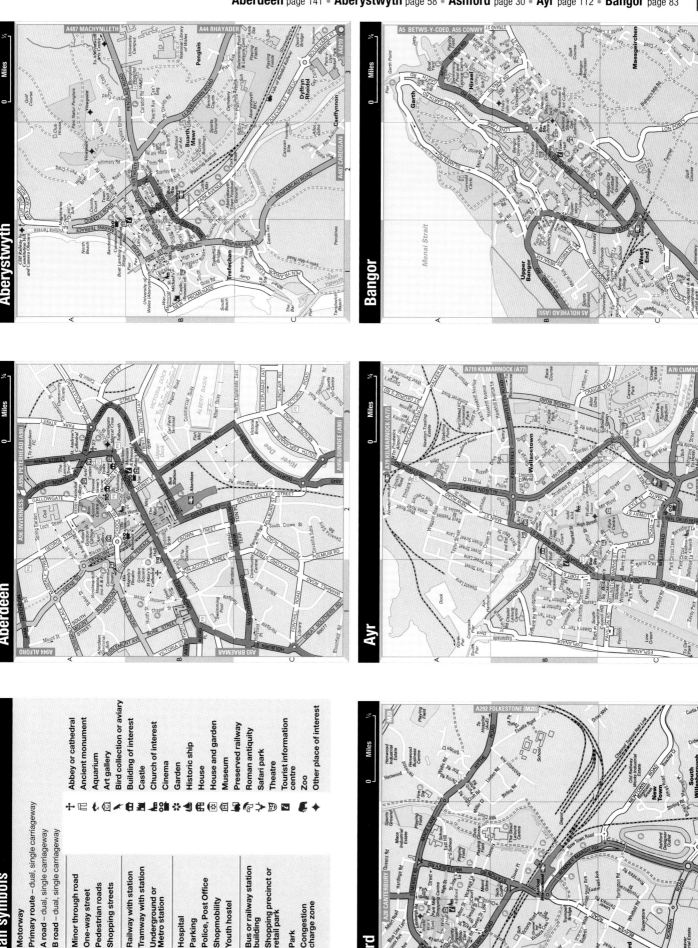

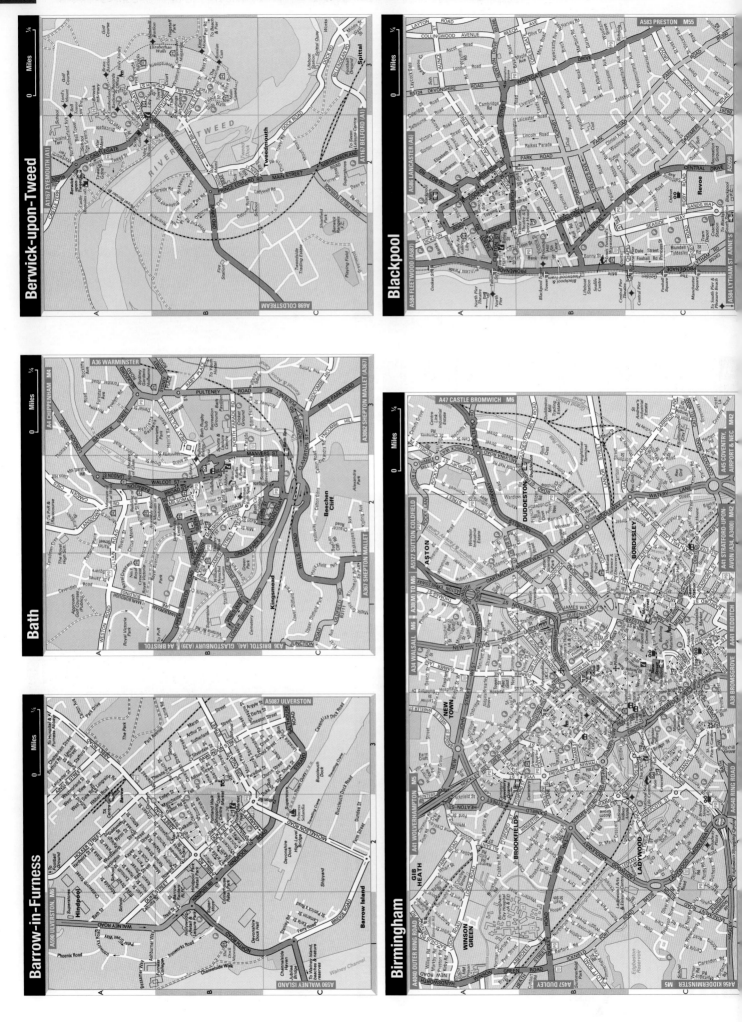

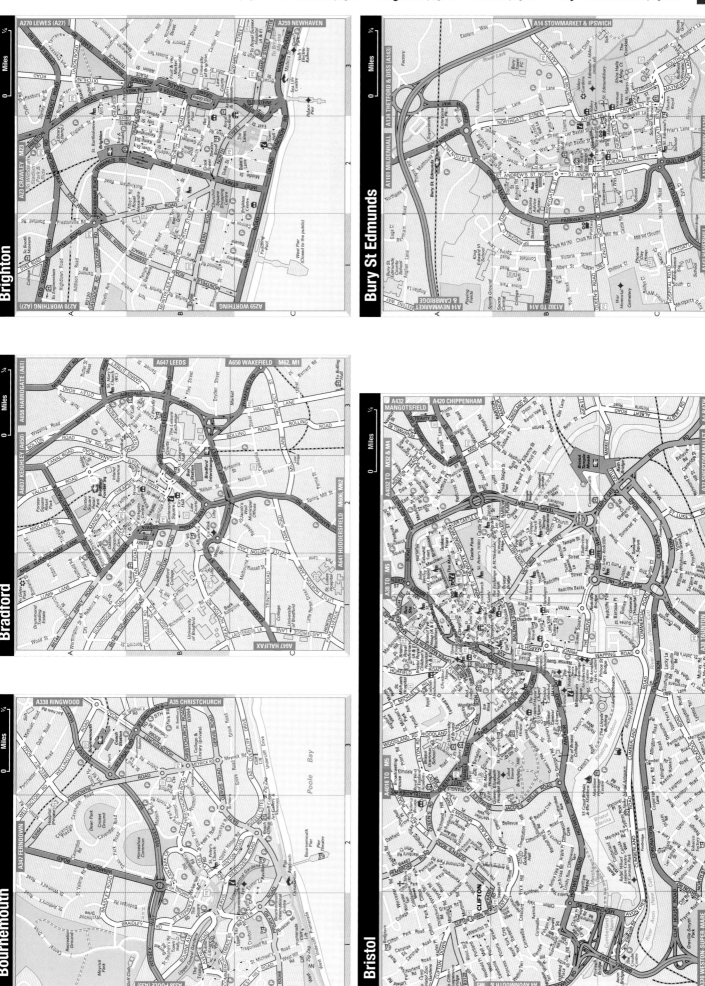

Brighton

Bury St Edmunds

Bradford

Bournemouth

Bristol

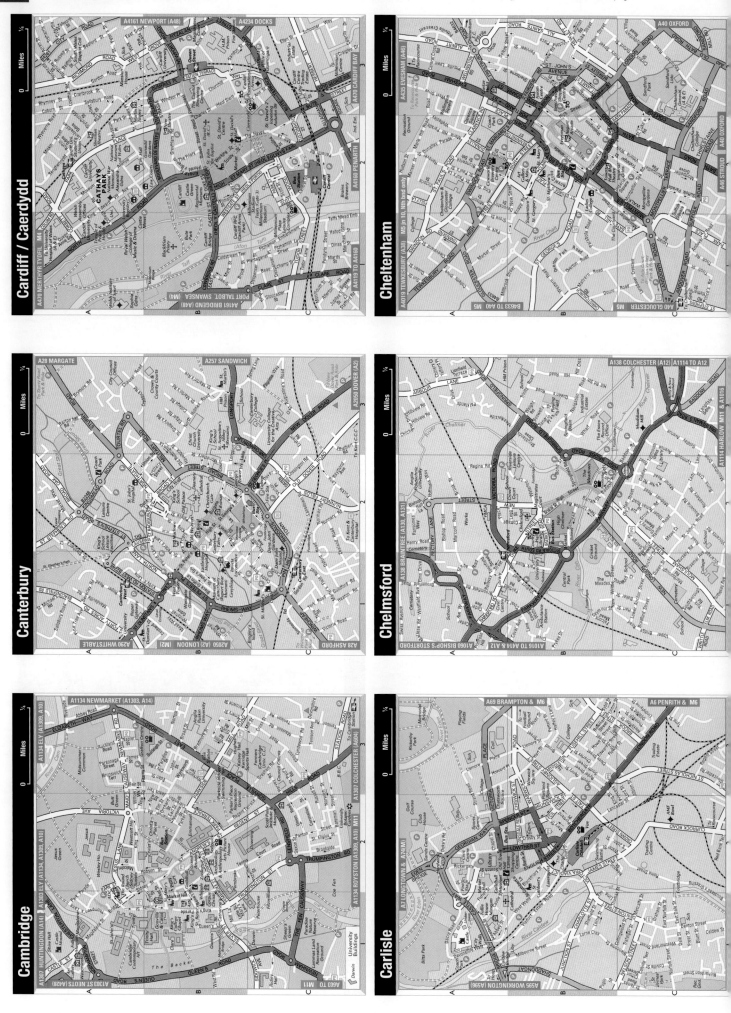

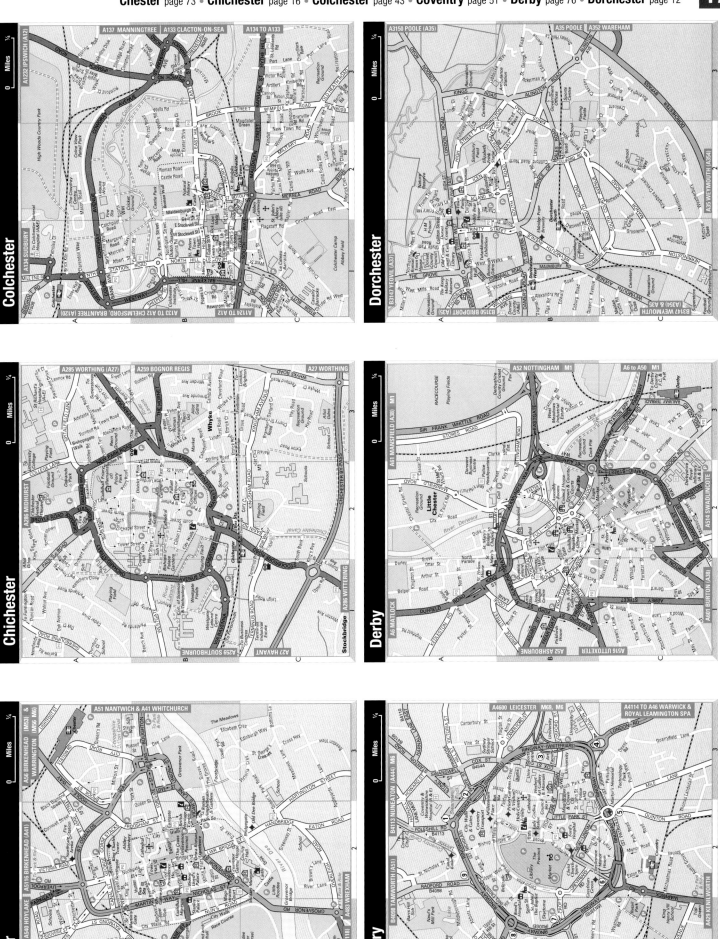

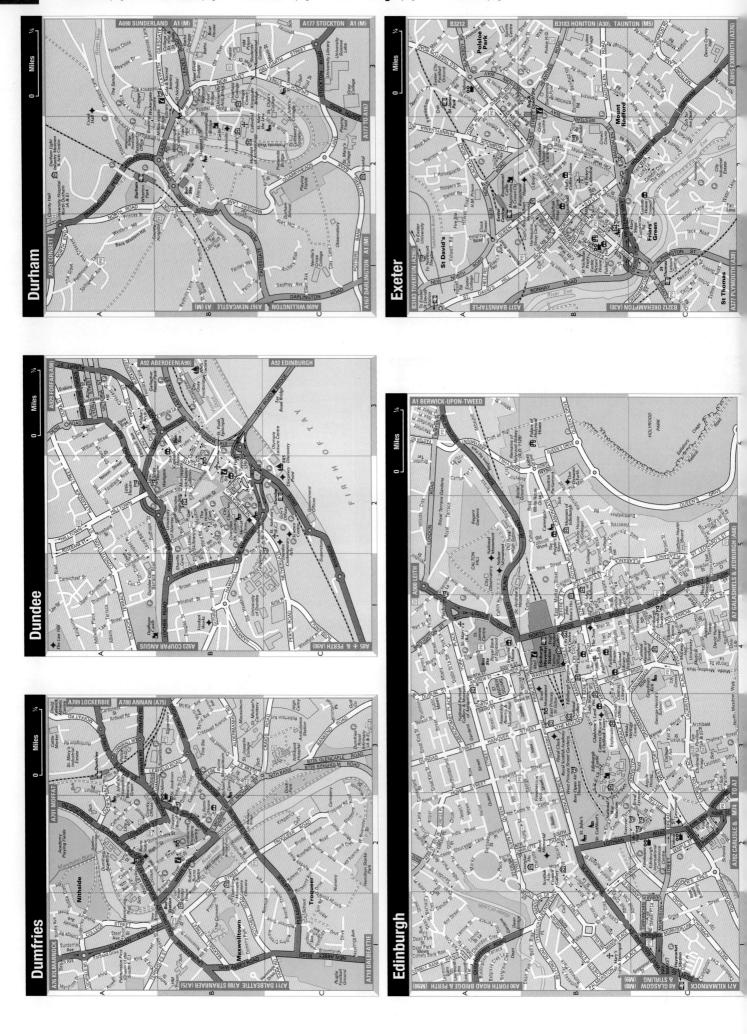

Fort William page 131 • **Glasgow** page 119 • **Gloucester** page 37 • **Grimsby** page 91 • **Hanley (Stoke-on-Trent)** page 75

181

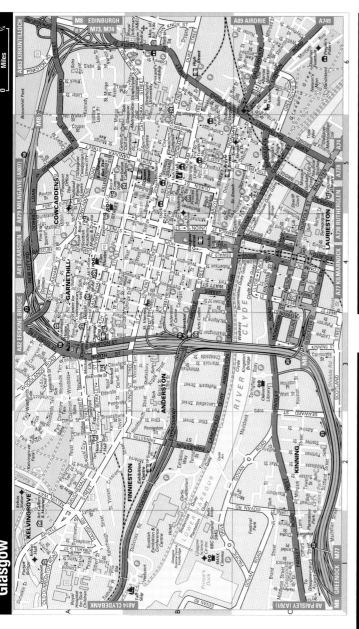

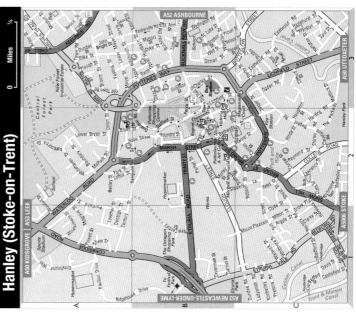

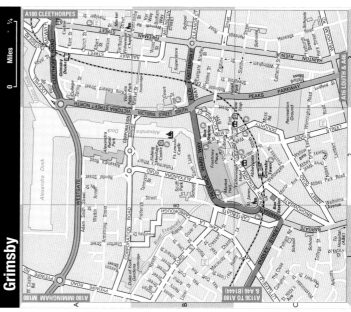

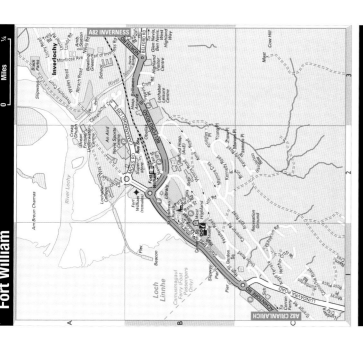

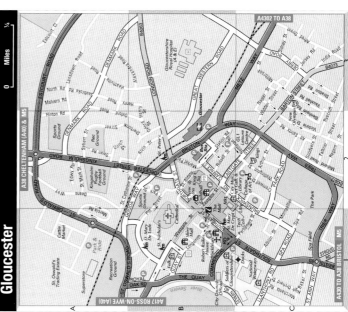

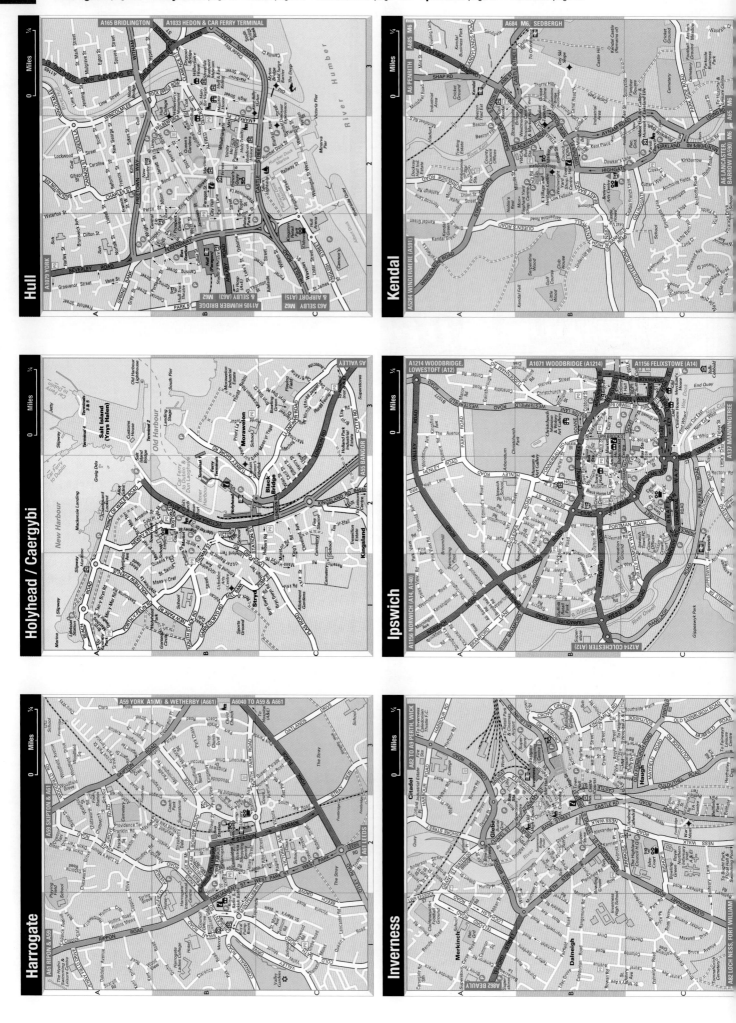

Leeds

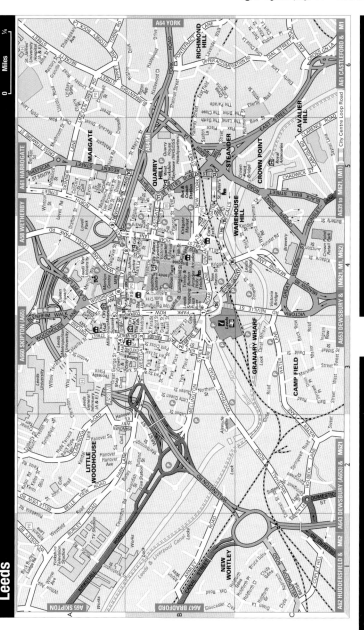

Lewes

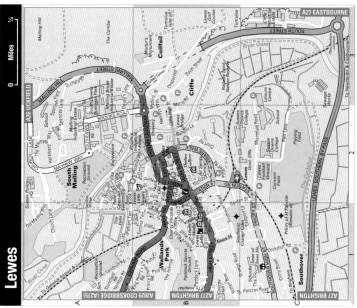

Leicester

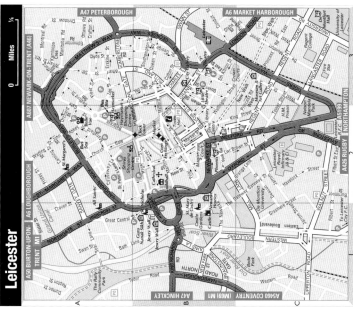

King's Lynn

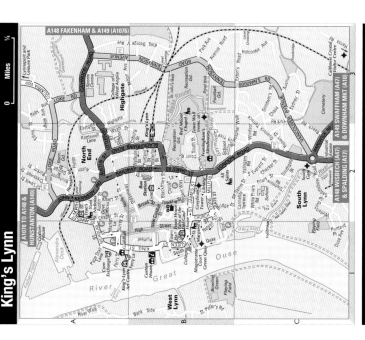

Lancaster

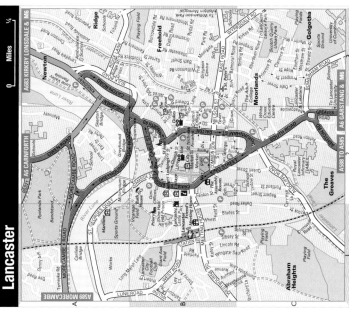

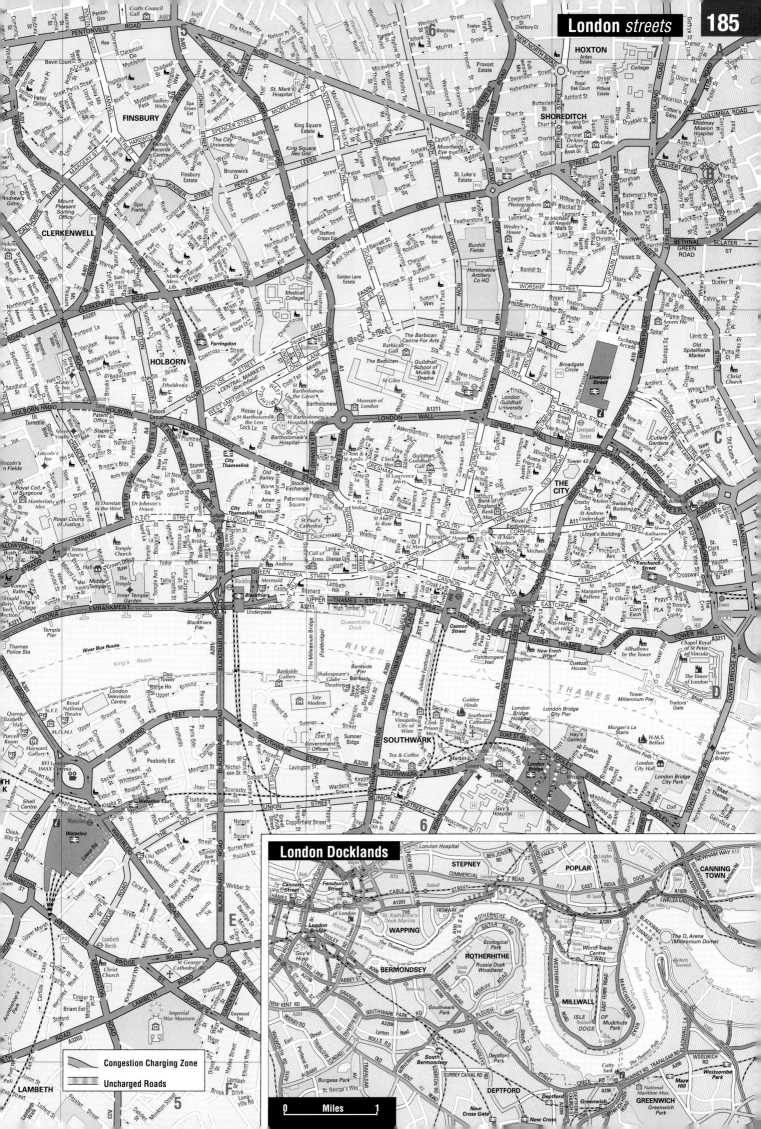

London Docklands

Congestion Charging Zone

Uncharged Roads

0 Miles 1

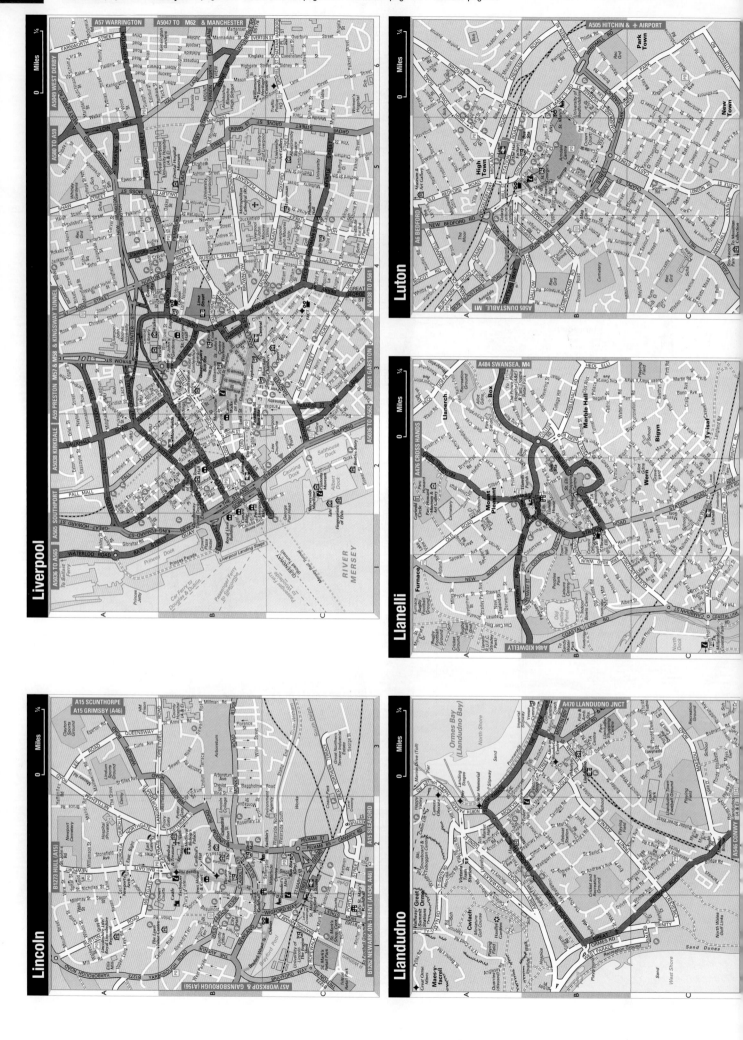

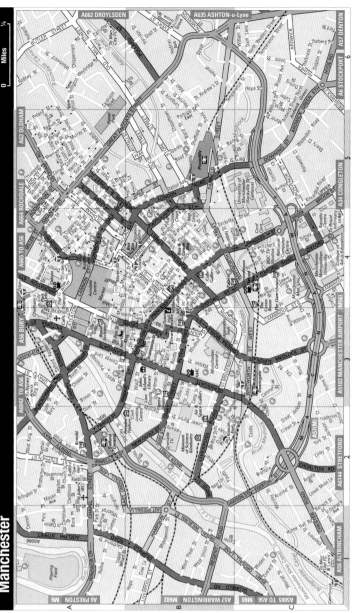

Manchester

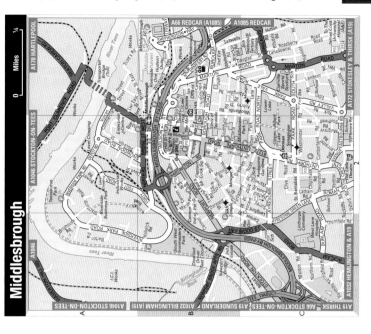

Middlesbrough

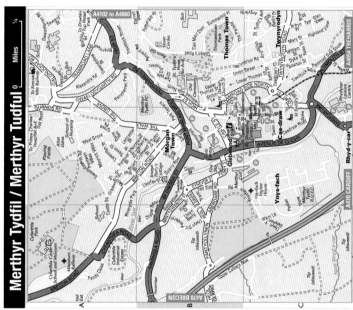

Merthyr Tydfil / Merthyr Tudful

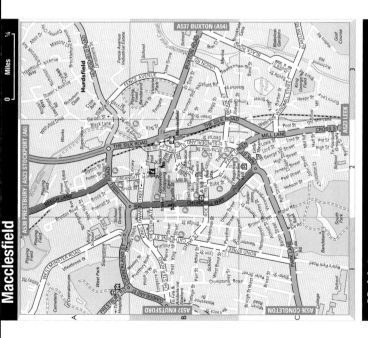

Macclesfield

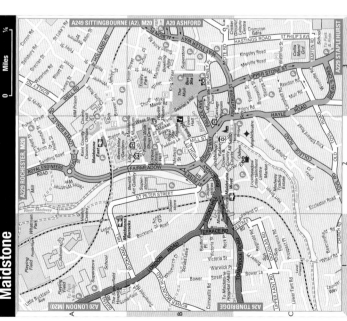

Maidstone

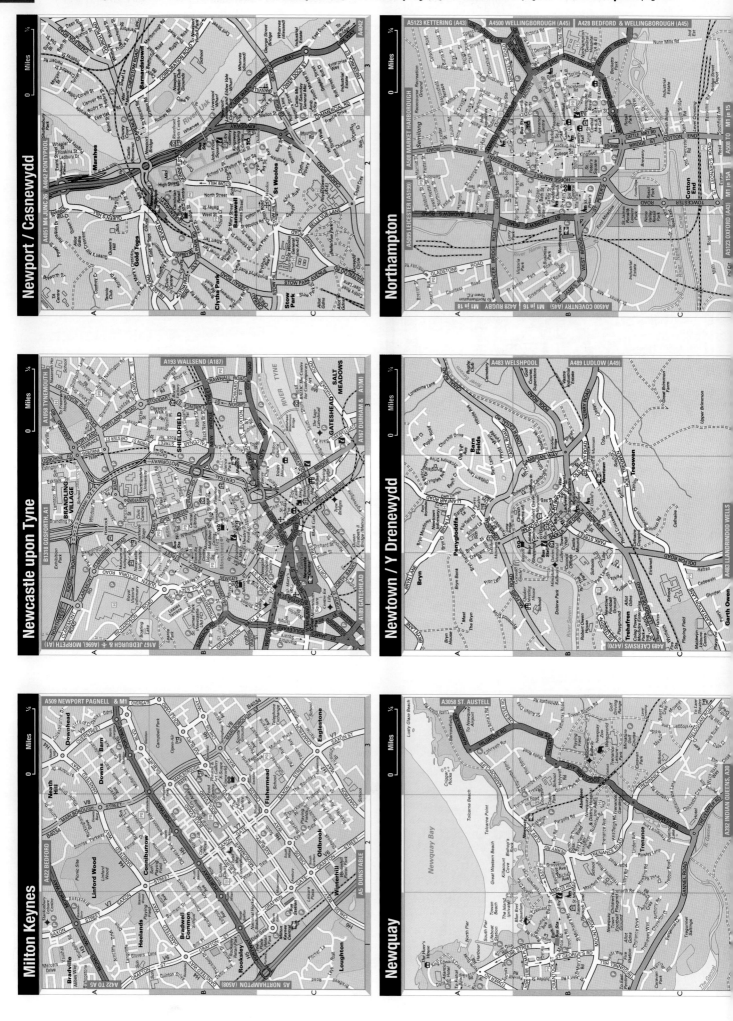

Norwich page 69 • **Nottingham** page 77 • **Oban** page 124 • **Oxford** page 39 • **Perth** page 128 • **Peterborough** page 65

189

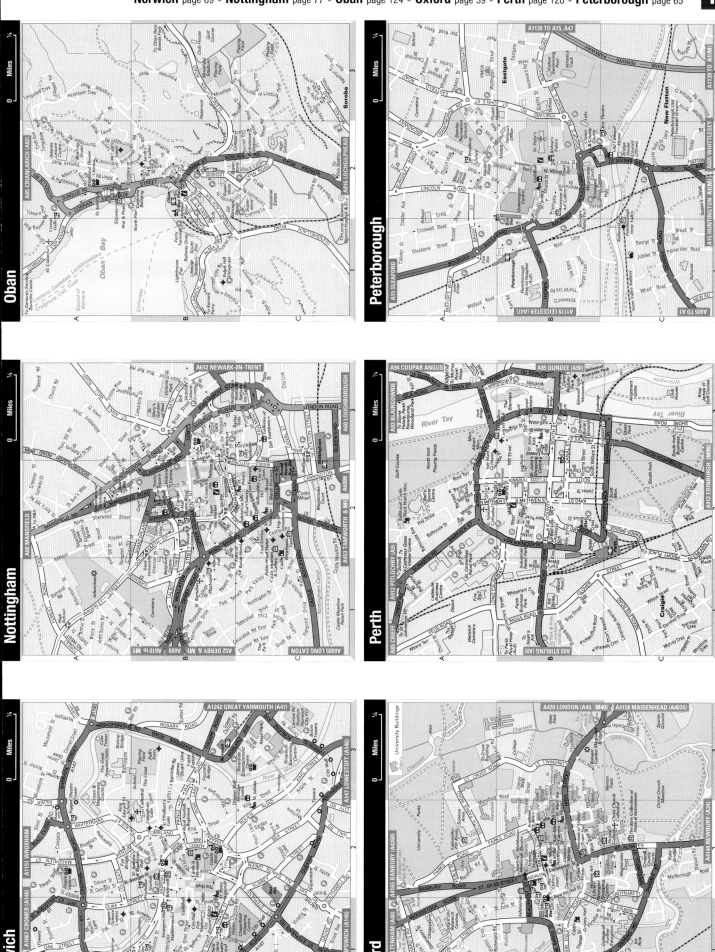

Oban

Peterborough

Nottingham

Perth

Norwich

Oxford

190

Plymouth page 6 • **Poole** page 13 • **Portsmouth** page 15 • **Preston** page 86 • **Reading** page 26 • **St Andrews** page 129

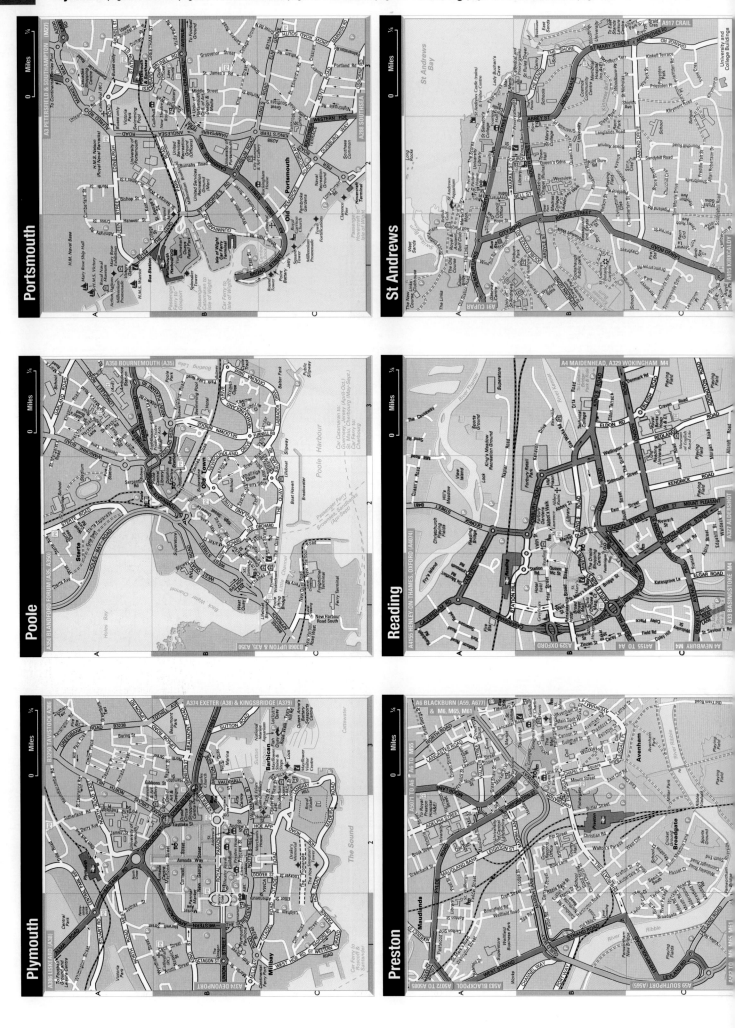

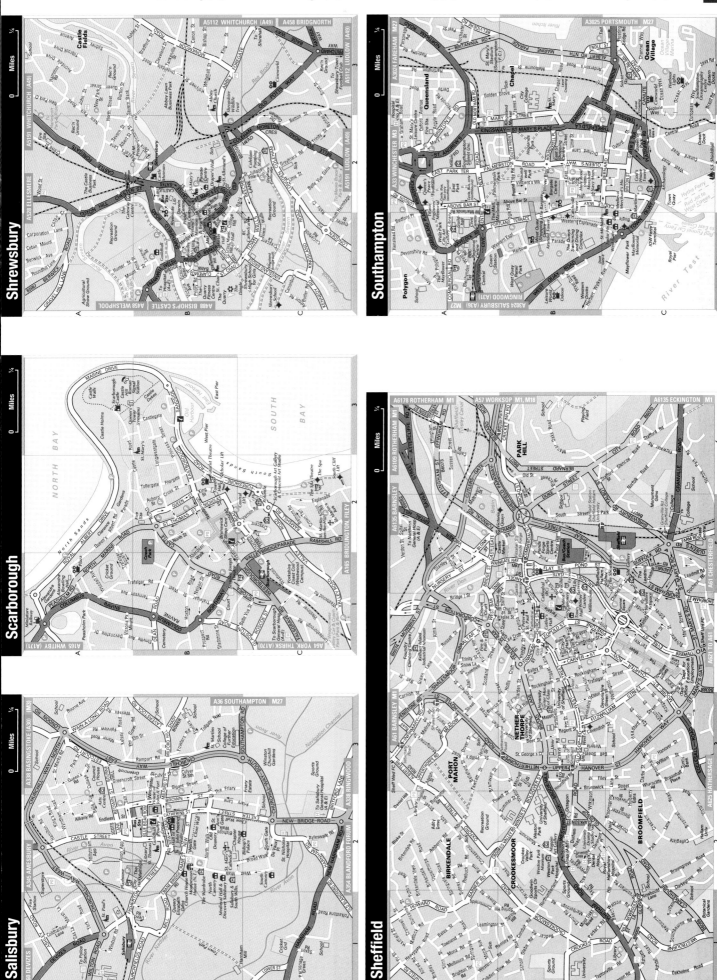

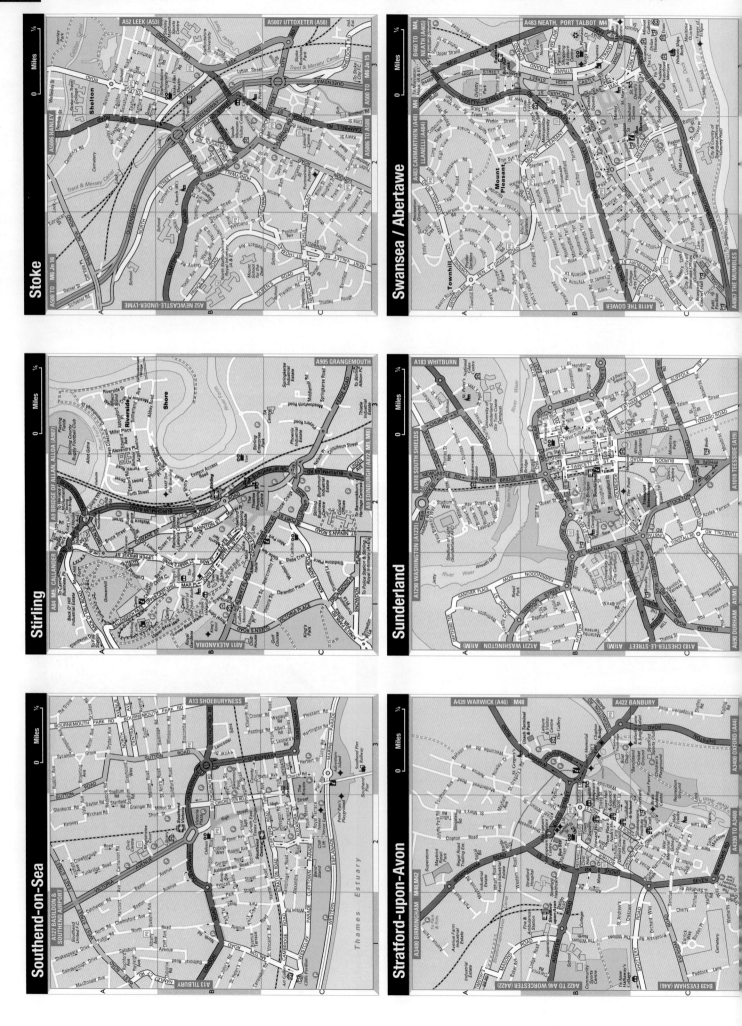

Swindon page 38 • **Taunton** page 11 • **Telford** page 61 • **Torquay** page 7 • **Truro** page 3 • **Wick** page 158

193

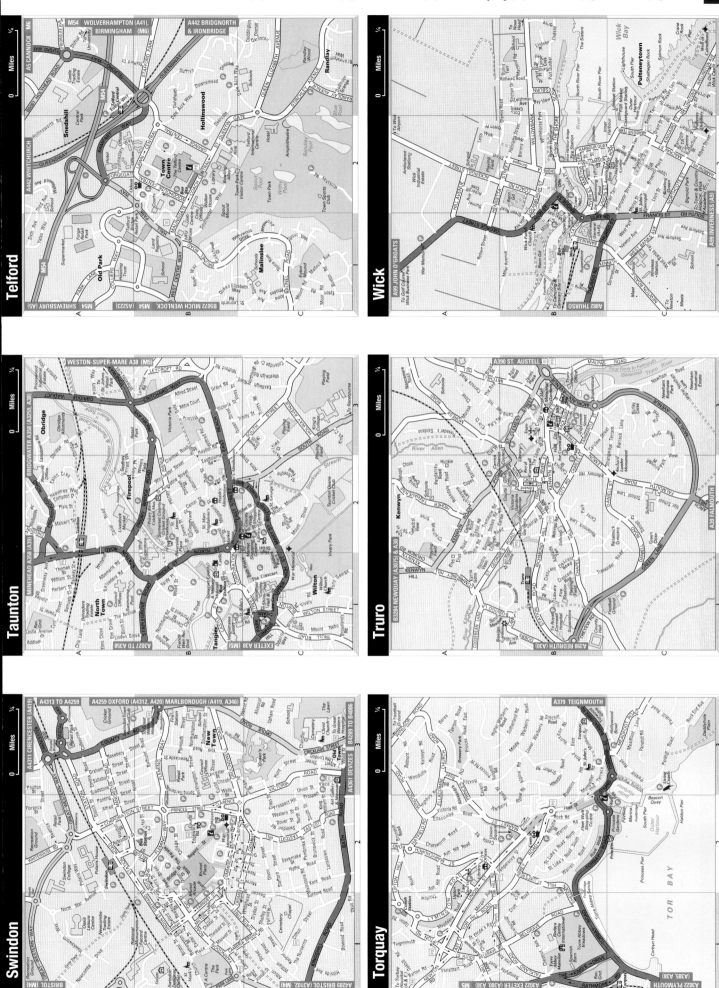

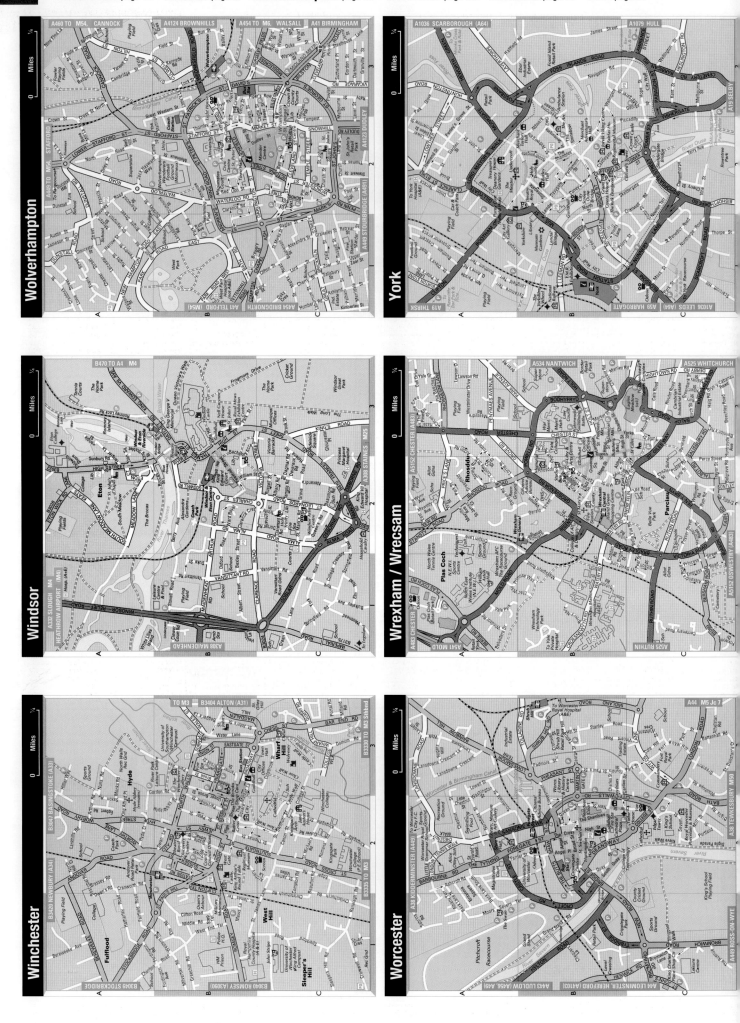

Arthur St C6
Assay Office B3
Aston Expressway A5
Aston Science Park B5
Aston St B4
Aston University B4/B5
Avenue Rd A5
BT Tower✦ B3
Bacchus Rd A1
Bagot St B4
Banbury St B5
Barford Rd B1
Barford St C4
Barn St C5
Barnwell Rd C6
Barr St A3
Barrack St B5
Bartholomew St C4
Barwick St B4
Bath Row C3
Beaufort Rd C1
Belmont Row B5
Benson Rd A1
Berkley St C3
Bexhill Gr C3
Birchall St C5
Birmingham City FC C6
Birmingham City Hospital (A&E) A1
Bishopsgate St C3
Blews St A4
Bloomsbury St A6
Blucher St C3
Bordesley St C4
Bowyer St C5
Bradburne Way A5
Bradford St C5
Branston St A3
Brearley St A4
Brewery St A4
Bridge St A3
Bridge St C3
Bridge St West A4
Brindley Dr B3
Broad St C3
Broad St UGC C2
Broadway Plaza✦ C2
Bromley St C5
Bromsgrove St C4
Brookfield Rd A2
Browning St C2
Bryant St A1
Buckingham St A3
Bullring C4
Bull St B4
Cambridge St C3
Camden Dr B3
Camden St B2
Cannon St C4
Cardigan St B5
Carlisle St A1
Carlyle Rd C1
Caroline St B3
Carver St B2
Cato St A6
Cattell Rd C6
Cattells Gr A6
Cawdor Cr C1
Cecil St B4
Cemetery A2/B2
Cemetery La A2
Centre Link Industrial Estate A6
Charlotte St B3
Cheapside C4
Chester St A5
Children's Hospital (A&E) B4
Church St B4
Claremont Rd A2
Clarendon Rd C1
Clark St C1
Clement St B3
Clissold St B2
Cliveland St B4
Coach Station C5
College St B2
Colmore Circus B4
Colmore Row B4
Commercial St C3
Constitution Hill B3
Convention Centre, The C3
Cope St B2
Coplow St B1
Corporation St B4
Council House B3
County Court B4
Coveley Gr A2
Coventry Rd C6
Coventry St C5
Cox St B3
Crabtree Rd A2
Cregoe St C3
Crescent Ave A2
Crescent Theatre C3
Cromwell St A6
Cromwell St B3
Curzon St B5
Cuthbert Rd B1
Dale End B4
Dart St C6
Dartmouth Circus A4
Dartmouth Middleway A5
Dental Hosp B4
Deritend C5
Devon St A6
Devonshire St A1
Digbeth Civic Hall C5
Digbeth High St C4
Dolman St B6
Dover St A1
Duchess Rd C2
Duddeston B6
Duddeston Manor Rd B5
Duddeston Mill Rd B6
Duddeston Mill Trading Estate B6
Dudley Rd B1
Edgbaston Shopping Centre C2
Edmund St B3
Edward St B3
Elkington St A4
Ellen St B2
Ellis St C3
Erskine St B6
Essex St C4
Eyre St B2
Farm Croft A3
Farm St A3
Fazeley St B4/C5
Felstead Way B5
Finstall Cl C6
Five Ways C2
Fleet St B3
Floodgate St C5
Ford St A2
Fore St C4
Forster St B5
Francis Rd C2
Francis St B5
Frankfort St A4
Frederick St B3
Freeth St C1
Freightliner Terminal B6
Garrison La C6
Garrison St B6
Gas St C3
Geach St A4
George St B3
George St West B2
Gibb St C5
Gillott Rd B1
Gilby Rd C2
Glover St C5
Goode Ave A2
Goodrick Way A6
Gordon St B6
Graham St B3
Granville St C3
Gray St C6
Great Barr St C5
Great Charles St B3
Great Francis St B6
Great Hampton Row A3
Great Hampton St A3
Great King St A3
Great Lister St A5
Great Tindal St C2
Green La C6
Green St C5
Greenway St C6
Grosvenor St West C2
Guest Gr A3
Guild Cl C2
Guildford Dr A4
Guthrie Cl A3
Hagley Rd C1
Hall St B3
Hampton St A3
Handsworth New Rd A1
Hanley St B4
Harford St A3
Harmer Rd A2
Harold Rd C1
Hatchett St A4
Heath Mill La C5
Heath St B1
Heath St South B1
Heaton St A2
Heneage St B5
Henrietta St B4
Herbert Rd C6
High St C4
High St C5
Hilden Rd B5
Hill St C3/C4
Hindlow Cl B6
Hingeston St B2
Hippodrome Theatre C4
HM Prison A1
Hockley Circus A2
Hockley Hill A3
Hockley St A3
Holliday St C3
Holloway Circus C4
Holloway Head C3
Holt St B5
Hooper St B1
Horse Fair C4
Hospital St A4
Howard St B3
Howe St B5
Hubert St A5
Hunters Rd A2
Hunters Vale A3
Huntly Rd C2
Hurst St C4
Icknield Port Rd B1
Icknield Sq B2
Icknield St A2/B2
Ikon Gallery C3
Information Ctr C4
Inge St C4
Irving St C3
Ivy La C5
James Watt Queensway B4
Jennens Rd B5
Jewellery Quarter A3
Jewellery Quarter Mus B3
John Bright St C4
Keeley St C6
Kellett Rd B5
Kent St C4
Kenyon St B3
Key Hill A3
Kilby Ave C2
King Edwards Rd B2
King Edwards Rd C3
Kingston Rd C6
Kirby Rd A1
Ladywood Arts & Leisure Centre B1
Ladywood Middleway C2/C3
Ladywood Rd C1
Lancaster St B4
Landor St B6
Law Courts B4
Lawford Cl B5
Lawley Middleway B5
Ledbury Cl C2
Ledsam St B2
Lees St A1
Legge La B3
Lennox St A3
Library A6/C3
Library Walk B2
Lighthorne Ave B2
Link Rd B1
Lionel St B3
Lister St B5
Little Ann St C5
Little Hall Rd A6
Liverpool St C5
Livery St B3/B4
Lodge Rd A1
Lord St A5
Love La A5
Loveday St B4
Lower Dartmouth St C6
Lower Loveday St B4
Lower Tower St A4
Lower Trinity St C5
Ludgate Hill B3
Mailbox Centre & BBC C3
Margaret St B3
Markby Rd A1
Marroway St B1
Maxstoke St C6
Melvina Rd A6
Meriden St C4
Metropolitan (RC)† B4
Midland St B6
Milk St C5
Mill St A5
Millennium Point B5
Miller St A4
Milton St A4
Moat La C4
Montague Rd C1
Montague St C5
Monument Rd C1
Moor Street C4
Moor St Queensway C4
Moorsom St A4
Morville St C2
Mosborough Cr A3
Moseley St C4
Mott St B3
Mus & Art Gallery B3
Musgrave Rd A1
National Indoor Arena✦ C2
National Sea Life Centre C3
Navigation St C3
Nechell's Park Rd A6
Nechells Parkway B5
Nechells Pl A6
New Bartholomew St C4
New Canal St C5
New John St West A3
New Spring St B2
New St C4
New Street C4
New Summer St A4
New Town Row A4
Newhall Hill B3
Newhall St B3
Newton St B4
Newtown A4
Noel Rd C1
Norman St A1
Northbrook St B1
Northwood St B3
Norton St A2
Old Crown House C5
Old Rep Theatre, The C4
Old Snow Hill B4
Oliver Rd C1
Oliver St A5
Osler St C1
Oxford St C5
Pallasades Centre C4
Palmer St C5
Paradise Circus C3
Paradise St C3
Park Rd A2
Park St C4
Pavilions Centre C4
Paxton Rd A2
Peel St A1
Penn St B5
Pershore St C4
Phillips St A4
Pickford St C5
Pinfold St C4
Pitsford St A2
Plough & Harrow Rd C1
Police Station A4/B1/B4/C2/C4
Pope St B2
Portland Rd C1
Post Office A3/A5/B1/B3/B4/B5/C2/C3/C5
Preston Rd A1
Price St B4
Princip St B4
Printing House St B4
Priory Queensway B4
Pritchett St A4
Proctor St A5
Queensway B3
Radnor St A2
Rea St C4
Regent Pl B3
Register Office C3
Repertory Theatre C3
Reservoir Rd C1
Richard St A5
River St C5
Rocky La A5/A6
Rodney Cl C2
Roseberry St B2
Rotton Park St B1
Rupert St A5
Ruston St C2
Ryland St C2
St Andrew's Industrial Estate C6
St Andrew's Rd C6
St Andrew's St C6
St Bolton St C6
St Chads Queensway B4
St Clements Rd A6
St George's St A3
St James Pl B5
St Marks Cr B2
St Martin's C4
St Paul's B3
St Paul's (Metro station) B3
St Paul's Sq B3
St Philip's† B4
St Stephen's St A4
St Thomas' Peace Garden C3
St Vincent St C2
Saltley Rd A6
Sand Pits Pde B3
Severn St C3
Shadwell St B4
Sheepcote St C2
Shefford Rd A4
Sherborne St C2
Shylton's Croft C2
Skipton Rd C2
Smallbrook Queensway C4
Smith St A3
Snow Hill B4
Snow Hill Queensway B4
Soho, Benson Rd (Metro station) A1
South Rd A2
Spencer St B3
Spring Hill B2
Staniforth St B4
Station St C4
Steelhouse La B4
Stephenson St C4
Steward St B2
Stirling Rd C1
Stour St B2
Suffolk St C3
Summer Hill Rd B2
Summer Hill St B2
Summer Hill Terr B2
Summer La A4
Summer Row B3
Summerfield Cr B1
Summerfield Park B1
Sutton St C3
Swallow St C3
Sydney Rd C6
Symphony Hall C3
Talbot St A1
Temple Row C4
Temple St C4
Templefield St C6
Tenby St B3
Tenby St North B2
Tennant St C2/C3
The Crescent A2
Thimble Mill La A6
Thinktank (Science & Discovery) B5
Thomas St A4
Thorpe St C4
Tilton Rd C6
Tower St A4
Town Hall C3
Trent St C5
Turner's Buildings A1
Unett St A3
Union Terr B5
Upper Trinity St C5
Uxbridge St A3
Vauxhall Gr B5
Vauxhall Rd B5
Vernon Rd C1
Vesey St B4
Viaduct St B5
Victoria Sq C3
Villa St A3
Vittoria St B3
Vyse St B3
Walter St A6
Wardlow Rd A5
Warstone La B2
Washington St C3
Water St B3
Waterworks Rd C1
Watery La C5
Well St A3
Western Rd B1
Wharf St A2
Wheeler St A3
Whitehouse St A5
Whitmore St A2
Whittall St B4
Wholesale Market C4
Wiggin St B1
Willes Rd A1
Windsor Industrial Estate A5
Windsor St A5
Windsor St B5
Winson Green Rd A1
Witton St C6
Wolseley St C6
Woodcock St B5

Blackpool 176

Abingdon St A1
Addison Cr A3
Adelaide St B1
Albert Rd B2
Alfred St B2
Ascot Rd A3
Ashton Rd C2
Auburn Gr C3
Bank Hey St B1
Banks St A1
Beech Ave A3
Bela Gr C2
Belmont Ct B2
Birley St A1
Blackpool & Fleetwood Tram B1
Blackpool FC C2
Blackpool North A2
Blackpool Tower✦ B1
Blundell St C1
Bonny St B1
Breck Rd B3
Bryan Rd A3
Buchanan St A2
Cambridge Rd A3
Caunce St A2/A3
Central Dr B1/C2
Central Pier✦ C1
Central Pier (Tram stop) C1
Central Pier Theatre C1
Chapel St C1
Charles St A2
Charnley Rd B2
Church St A1/A2
Clinton Ave B2
Coach Station A2/C1
Cocker St A1
Cocker St (Tram stop) A1
Coleridge Rd A3
Collingwood Ave A3
Condor Gr C3
Cookson St A2
Coronation St B1
Corporation St A1
Courts B1
Cumberland Ave B3
Cunliffe Rd C3
Dale St C1
Devonshire Rd A3
Devonshire Sq A3
Dickson Rd A1
Elizabeth St A2
Ferguson Rd C3
Forest Gate B3
Foxhall Rd C1
Foxhall Sq (Tram stop) C1
Freckleton St C2
George St A2
Gloucester Ave B3
Golden Mile, The C1
Gorse Rd B3
Gorton St A2
Granville Rd A2
Grasmere Rd C2
Grosvenor St A2
Grundy Art Gallery A1
Harvey Rd B3
Hornby Rd B2
Hounds Hill Shopping Centre B1
Hull Rd B1
Ibbison Ct C2
Information Ctr A1
Kent Rd C2
Keswick Rd C2
King St A2
Knox Gr C3
Laycock Gate A3
Layton Rd A3
Leamington Rd B2
Leeds Rd B3
Leicester Rd B2
Levens Gr C2
Library A1
Lifeboat Station B1
Lincoln Rd B2
Liverpool Rd B3
Livingstone Rd B2
London Rd A3
Louis Tussaud's Waxworks B1
Lune Gr C2
Lytham Rd C1
Manchester Sq (Tram stop) C1
Manor Rd B3
Maple Ave B3
Market St A1
Marlboro Rd B3
Mere Rd B3
Milbourne St A2
Newcastle Ave B3
Newton Dr A3
North Pier✦ A1
North Pier Theatre A1
Odeon C2
Olive Gr B3
Palatine Rd B2
Park Rd B2/C3
Peter St A2
Police Station B1
Post Office A1/A3/B1/B2/B3
Princess Pde A1
Princess St C1/C2
Promenade A1/C1
Queen St A1
Queen Victoria Rd C2
Raikes Pde B2
Read's Ave B2
Regent Rd B2
Ribble Rd B2
Rigby Rd C1/C2
Ripon Rd B3
St Albans Rd B3
St Ives Ave C3
St Vincent Ave C3
Salisbury Rd B3
Salthouse Ave C2
Sands Way C2
Sealife Centre B1
Seaside Way C1
Selbourne Rd A2
Sharrow Gr C3
Somerset Ave C3
Springfield Rd A1
South King St B2
Sutton Pl B2
Talbot Rd A1/A2
Talbot Sq (Tram stop) A1
Thornber Gr C2
Topping St A1
Tower (Tram stop) B1
Town Hall A1
Tram Depot C1
Tyldesley Rd C1
Vance Rd B1
Victoria St B1
Victory Rd A2
Wayman Rd A3
Westmorland Ave C2/C3
Whitegate Dr B3
Winter Gardens Theatre & Opera House B1
Woodland Gr B3
Woolman Rd B2

Bournemouth 177

Ascham Rd A3
Avenue Rd B1
Bath Rd C2
Beacon Rd C1
Beach Office C2
Beechey Rd A3
Bodorgan Rd B1
Bourne Ave B1
Bournemouth A3
Bournemouth Eye✦ C2
Bournemouth International Ctr C1
Bournemouth Pier C2
Bournemouth Station (r'about) B3
Braidley Rd A1
Cavendish Place A2
Cavendish Rd A2
Central Drive A1
Christchurch Rd B3
Cliff Lift C1/C3
Coach House Pl A3
Coach Station A3
College & Library (private) B3
Commercial Rd B1
Cotlands Rd B3
Courts B3
Cranborne Rd C1
Cricket Ground A2
Cumnor Rd B2
Dean Park A2
Dean Park Cr B2
Dean Park Rd A2
Durrant Rd B1
East Overcliff Dr C3
Exeter Cr C1
Exeter La C2
Exeter Rd C1
Gervis Place B1
Gervis Rd B3
Glen Fern Rd B2
Golf Club B1
Grove Rd B3
Hinton Rd C2
Holdenhurst Rd B3
Horseshoe Common B2
Hospital (Private) A2
Information Ctr B2
Lansdowne (r'about) B3
Lansdowne Rd A2
Lorne Park Rd B2
Lower Central Gdns B1/C2
Madeira Rd B2
Methuen Rd A3
Meyrick Park A1
Meyrick Rd B3
Milton Rd A2
Oceanarium C2
Old Christchurch Rd B2
Ophir Rd A3
Oxford Rd B3
Park Rd A3
Parsonage Rd B2
Pavilion C2
Pier Approach C2
Pier Theatre C2
Police Station A3/B3
Portchester Rd A3
Post Office B1/B3
Priory Rd C1
Recreation Ground A1
Richmond Hill Rd B1
Russell Cotes Art Gallery & Mus C2
Russell Cotes Rd C2
St Anthony's Rd A1
St Michael's Rd C1
St Paul's (r'about) A3
St Paul's La B3
St Paul's Rd A3
St Peter's B2
St Peter's (r'about) B2
St Peter's Rd B2
St Stephen's Rd B1/B2
St Swithun's (r'about) B3
St Swithun's Rd B3
St Swithun's Rd South B3
St Valerie Rd A2
St Winifred's Rd A2
Stafford Rd B3
Terrace Rd B1
The Square B1
The Triangle B1
Town Hall B1
Tregonwell Rd C1
Trinity Rd B2
Undercliff Drive C3
Upper Central Gdns B1
Upper Hinton Rd B2
Upper Terr Rd C1
Wellington Rd A2/A3
Wessex Way A3/B1/B2
West Cliff Promenade C1
West Hill Rd C1
West Undercliff Promenade C1
Westover Rd B2
Wimborne Rd A2
Wootton Mount B2
Wychwood Dr A1
Yelverton Rd B2
York Rd B3
Zig-Zag Walks C1/C3

Bradford 177

Alhambra B2
Back Ashgrove B1
Barkerend Rd A3
Barnard Rd C3
Barry St B2
Bolling Rd C3
Bolton Rd A3
Bowland St A1
Bradford College B1
Bradford Forster Sq A2
Bradford Interchange B3
Bridge St B2
Britannia St B2
Broadway B2
Burnett St B3
Bus Station B2
Butler St West A3
Caledonia St C2
Canal Rd A2
Carlton St B1
Cathedral† A3
Centenary Sq B2
Chapel St B3
Cheapside A2
Church Bank B3
City Hall B2
City Rd A1
Claremont B1
Colour Mus B1
Croft St B2
Darfield St A1
Darley St A2
Drewton Rd A1
Drummond Trading Estate A1
Dryden St B3
Dyson St A1
Easby Rd C1
East Parade B3
Eldon Pl A1
Filey St B3
Forster Square Retail Park A2
Gallery B3
Garnett St B3
Godwin St B2
Gracechurch St A1
Grattan Rd B1
Great Horton Rd B1/B2
Grove Terr B1
Hall Ings B2
Hall La C3
Hallfield Rd A1
Hammstrasse A2
Harris St B3
Holdsworth St A2
Ice Rink✦ B2
Information Ctr B2
Ivegate B2
Inland Revenue A2
Jacob's Well Municipal Offices B2
James St A2
John St A2
Kirkgate B2
Kirkgate Centre B2
Laisteridge La C1
Law Courts B2/B3
Leeds Rd B3
Library B1/B2
Listerhills Rd B1
Little Horton La C1
Little Horton Gn C1
Longside La B1
Lower Kirkgate B2
Lumb La A1
Manchester Rd C2
Manningham La A1
Manor Row A2
Market C3
Market St B2
Melbourne Place C1
Midland Rd A2
Mill La C2
Morley St B1
Nelson St B2/C2
Nesfield St A2
New Otley Rd A3
Norcroft St B1
North Parade A2
North St A3
North Wing A3
Oastler Shopping Centre A2
Otley Rd A3
Park Ave C1
Park La C1
Park Rd C2
Parma St C2
Peckover St B3
Piccadilly A2
Police Station B2/C2
Post Office A2/B1/B2/C3
Priestley B3
Princes Way B2
Prospect St C3
Radwell Drive C2
Rawson Rd A1
Rebecca St A1
Richmond Rd B1
Russell St C1
St George's Hall B2
St Lukes Hosp C1
St Mary's A3
Shipley Airedale Rd A3/B3
Simes St A1
Smith St B1
Spring Mill St C2
Stott Hill A3
Sunbridge Rd A1/B1/B2
The Leisure Exchange B3
Thornton Rd A1/B1
Trafalgar St A2
Trinity Rd C1
Tumbling Hill St B1
Tyrrel St B2
University of Bradford B1/C1
Usher St C3
Valley Rd A2
Vicar La B3
Wakefield Rd C3
Wapping Rd A3
Westgate A1
White Abbey Rd A1
Wigan Rd A1
Wilton St B1
Wood St A1
Wool Exchange B2
Worthington St A1

Brighton 177

Addison Rd A1
Albert Rd B2
Albion Hill B3
Albion St B3
Ann St A3
Art Gallery & Mus B3
Baker St A3
Brighton A2
Brighton Centre C2
Broad St C3
Buckingham Pl A2
Buckingham Rd B2
Cannon Pl C1
Carlton Hill B3
Chatham Pl A1
Cheapside A3
Church St B2
Churchill Square Shopping Centre B2
Clifton Hill B1
Clifton Pl B1
Clifton Rd B1
Clifton Terr B1
Clock Tower B2
Clyde Rd A3
Coach Park C3
Compton Ave A2
Davigdor Rd A1
Denmark Terr B1
Ditchling Rd A3
Dome, The B2
Duke St B2
Duke's La C2
Dyke Rd A1/B2
East St C2
Edward St B3
Elmore Rd B3
Frederick St B2
Fruit & Veg Market (wholesale) B3
Gardner St B2
Gloucester Pl B3
Gloucester Rd B2
Goldsmid Rd A1
Grand Junction Rd C2
Grand Pde B3
Hampton Pl B1
Hanover Terr A3
High St C3
Highdown Rd A1
Information Ctr C2
John St B3
Kemp St B2
Kensington Pl B2
Kings Rd C1
Law Courts B3
Lewes Rd A3
Library (temp) A2
London Rd A3
Madeira Dr C3
Marine Pde C3
Middle St C2
Montpelier Pl B1
Montpelier Rd B1
Montpelier St B1
New England Rd A2
New England St A2
New Rd B2
Newhaven St A3
Nizells Ave A1
Norfolk Rd B1
Norfolk Terr B1
North Rd B2
North St B2
Old Shoreham Rd A1
Old Steine C3
Osmond Rd A1
Over St B2
Oxford St A3
Paddling Pool C1
Palace Pier✦ C3
Park Crescent Terr A3
Police Station B3
Post Office A1/A2/A3/B1/B2/B3/C3
Preston Rd A2
Preston St B1
Prestonville Rd A1
Queen's Rd B2
Regency Sq C1
Regent St B2
Richmond Pl B3
Richmond St B3
Richmond Terr A3
Rose Hill Terr
Royal Alexandra Hosp
Royal Pavilion
St Bartholomew's
St James' St
St Nicholas'
St Peter's
Sea Life Centre
Shaftesbury Rd
Sillwood Rd
Sillwood St
Southover St
Spring Gdns
Stanford Rd
Stanley Rd
Sussex St
Sussex Terr
Swimming Pool
Sydney St
Temple Gdns
Terminus Rd
The Lanes
Theatre Royal
Tidy St
Town Hall
Toy & Model Mus
Trafalgar St
Union Rd
University of Brighton
Upper Lewes Rd
Upper North St
Viaduct Rd
Victoria Gdns
Victoria Rd
Volk's Electric Railway✦
West Pier (Closed to the Public)
West St
Western Rd
Whitecross St
York Ave
York Pl

Bristol

Acramans Rd
Albert Rd
Alfred Hill
All Saint's St
All Saints'
Allington Rd
Alpha Rd
Ambra Vale
Ambra Vale East
Ambrose Rd
Amphitheatre
Anchor Rd
Anvil St
Architecture Centre✦
Argyle Pl
Arlington Villas
Arnolfini Arts Centre, The✦
Art Gallery
Ashton Gate Rd
Ashton Rd
at-Bristol✦
Avon Bridge
Avon Cr
Avon St
Baldwin St
Baltic Wharf
Baltic Wharf Leisure Centre & Caravan Park✦
Barossa Pl
Barton Manor
Barton Rd
Barton Vale
Bath Rd
Bathurst Basin
Bathurst Parade
Beauley Rd
Bedminster Bridge
Bedminster Parade
Bellevue
Bellevue Cr
Bellevue Rd
Berkeley Pl
Berkeley Sq
Birch Rd
Blackfriars
Bond St
Braggs La
Brandon Hill
Brandon Steep
Bristol Bridge
Bristol Cathedral (CE)†
Bristol Central Library
Bristol Eye Hospital (A & E)
Bristol Grammar School
Bristol Harbour Railway
Bristol Marina
Bristol Royal Children's Hosp
Bristol Royal Infirmary (A & E)
Bristol Temple Meads Station
Broad Plain
Broad Quay
Broad St
Broad Weir
Broadcasting House
Broadmead
Brunel Way
Brunswick Sq
Burton Cl
Bus Station
Butts Rd
Cabot Tower✦
Caledonia Pl
Callowhill Ct

198 Chelmsford • Cheltenham • Chester • Chichester • Colchester • Coventry • Derby

Fusehill St B3
Georgian Way A2
Gloucester Rd C3
Golf Course A2
Graham St C1
Grey St B3
Guildhall Mus B3
Halfey's La B3
Hardwicke Circus A2
Hart St B3
Hewson St C2
Howard Pl A3
Howe St B3
Information Ctr A2
James St B2
Junction St B1
King St B2
Lancaster St B2
Lanes Shopping Centre B2
Laserquest B2
Library A2/B1
Lime St B1
Lindisfarne St C3
Linton St B3
Lismore Pl A3
Lismore St B3
London Rd C3
Lonsdale Rd B2
Lord St C3
Lorne Cres B1
Lorne St B1
Lowther St B2
Market Hall A2
Mary St B2
Memorial Bridge A3
Metcalfe St C1
Milbourne St B1
Myddleton St B3
Nelson St C1
Norfolk St C1
Old Town Hall A2
Oswald St C3
Peter St A2
Petteril St B3
Police Station A2
Portland Pl B2
Portland Sq B2
Post Office A2/B2/B3/C1/C3
Princess St C2
Pugin St B1
Red Bank Terr C2
Regent St C3
Richardson St C1
Rickerby Park A3
Rickergate A2
River St B3
Rome St C2
Rydal St B3
St Cuthbert's B2
St Cuthbert's La B2
St James' Park C1
St James' Rd C1
St Nicholas St C3
Sands Centre A2
Scotch St A2
Shaddongate B1
Sheffield St B1
South Henry St B3
South John St C2
South St B3
Spencer St B2
Sports Centre A2
Strand Rd A2
Swimming Baths B2
Sybil St B3
Tait St B2
Thomas St B1
Thomson St C3
Trafalgar St C1
Tullie House Mus A1
Tyne St C3
Viaduct Estate Rd B1
Victoria Pl A2
Victoria Viaduct B2
Vue B2
Warwick Rd B2
Warwick Sq B3
Water St B2
West Walls B1
Westmorland St C1

Chelmsford 178

Ambulance Station B1
Anchor St C1
Anglia Polytechnic University A2
Arbour La A3
Baddow Rd B2/C3
Baker St C1
Barrack Sq B2
Bellmead B2
Bishop Hall La A2
Bishop Rd A2
Bond St B2
Boswells Dr B3
Boudicca Mews C2
Bouverie Rd C2
Bradford St C1
Braemar Ave C1
Brook St A2
Broomfield Rd A1
Burns Cres C2
Bus Station B1
Can Bridge Way B2
Cedar Ave A1
Cedar Ave West A1
Cemetery A1
Cemetery A2
Cemetery C1
Central Park B1
Chelmsford B2
Chelmsford ≷ A1
Chichester Dr A3
Chinery Cl A3
Cinema B2
Civic Centre A1
College C1
Cottage Pl A2
County Hall B2
Coval Ave B1
Coval La B1
Coval Wells B1
Cricket Ground B2
Crown Court B2
Duke St B2
Elm Rd C1
Elms Dr A1
Essex Record Office, The B3
Fairfield Rd B1
Falcons Mead B1
George St C2
Glebe Rd A1
Godfrey's Mews C2
Goldlay Ave C3
Goldlay Rd C2
Grove Rd C2
HM Prison A3
Hall St C2
Hamlet Rd C2
Hart St C1
Henry Rd A2
High Bridge Rd B2
High Chelmer Shopping Centre B2
High St B2
Hill Cres B3
Hill Rd Sth B3
Hill Rd B3
Hillview Rd A3
Hoffmans Way A2
Hosp A2
Information Ctr B2
Lady La C2
Langdale Gdns C3
Legg St B2
Library A1
Library A2
Library C2
Lionfield Terr A3
Lower Anchor St C1
Lynmouth Ave C2
Lynmouth Gdns C3
Magistrates Court B2
Maltese Rd A1
Manor Rd C2
Marconi Rd A2
Market B2
Market Rd B2
Marlborough Rd C1
Meadows Shopping Centre, The B2
Meadowside A3
Mews Ct C2
Mildmay Rd C2
Moulsham Dr C2
Moulsham Mill C3
Moulsham St C1/C2
Navigation Rd B3
New London Rd B2/C1
New St A2/B2
New Writtle St C1
Nursery Rd C2
Orchard St C2
Park Rd B1
Parker Rd C2
Parklands Dr A3
Parkway A1/B1/B2
Police Station A2
Post Office A3/B2/C2
Primrose Hill A1
Prykes Dr B1
Queen St C1
Queen's Rd B3
Railway St A1
Rainsford Rd A1
Ransomes Way A2
Rectory La A2
Regina Rd A2
Riverside Leisure Centre B2
Rosebery Rd C2
Rothesay Ave C1
St John's Rd C2
Sandringham Pl B3
Seymour St B1
Shrublands Cl B3
Southborough Rd C1
Springfield Basin B3
Springfield Rd A3/B2/B3
Stapleford Cl C1
Swiss Ave A1
Telford Pl A3
The Meades B1
Tindal St B2
Townfield St A1
Trinity Rd B3
University B1
Upper Bridge Rd C1
Upper Roman Rd C2
Van Dieman's Rd C3
Viaduct Rd B1
Vicarage Rd C1
Victoria Rd A2
Victoria Rd South B2
Vincents Rd C2
Waterloo La B2
Weight Rd B3
Westfield Ave A1
Wharf Rd B3
Writtle Rd C1
YMCA A2
York Rd C1

Cheltenham 178

Albert Rd A3
Albion St B3
All Saints Rd B3
Andover Rd C1
Art Gallery & Mus B2
Axiom Centre B3
Bath Pde B2
Bath Rd C2
Bays Hill Rd C1
Beechwood Shopping Centre B3
Bennington St B2
Berkeley St B3
Brewery Centre A2
Brunswick St South A2
Bus Station B2
Carlton St B3
Central Cross Road A3
Cheltenham & Gloucester College A2
Cheltenham College C2
Cheltenham FC A3
Cheltenham General (A & E) C3
Christchurch Rd B1
Cineworld A2
Clarence Rd A2
Clarence Sq A2
Clarence St B2
Cleeveland St A1
Coach Park A2
College Rd C2
Colletts Dr A1
Corpus St C3
Devonshire St A2
Douro Rd B1
Duke St B3
Dunalley Pde A2
Dunalley St A2
Everyman B2
Evesham Rd A3
Fairview Rd B3
Fairview St B3
Folly La A2
Gloucester Rd A1
Grosvenor St B3
Grove St A1
Gustav Holst A3
Hanover St A2
Hatherley St C1
Henrietta St A2
Hewlett Rd B3
High St B2/B3
Hudson St A2
Imperial Gdns C2
Imperial La B2
Imperial Sq C2
Information Ctr B2
Keynsham Rd C3
King St A2
Knapp Rd B2
Ladies College B2
Lansdown Cr C1
Lansdown Rd C1
Leighton Rd B3
London Rd C3
Lypiatt Rd C1
Malvern Rd B1
Manser St A2
Market St A1
Marle Hill Pde A2
Marle Hill Rd A2
Millbrook St A1
Milsom St A2
Montpellier Gdns C2
Montpellier Gr C2
Montpellier Pde C2
Montpellier Spa Rd C2
Montpellier St C1
Montpellier Terr C2
Montpellier Walk C2
New St B2
North Pl B2
Old Bath Rd C3
Oriel Rd B2
Overton Park Rd B1
Overton Rd B1
Oxford St C3
Parabola Rd B1
Park Pl C1
Park St A1
Pittville Circus A3
Pittville Cr A3
Pittville Lawn A3
Playhouse B2
Police Station B1/C1
Portland St B3
Post Office B2/C1/C2
Prestbury Rd A3
Prince's Rd C1
Priory St B3
Promenade B2
Queen St A1
Recreation Ground A2
Regent Arcade B2
Regent St B2
Rodney Rd B2
Royal Cr B2
Royal Wells Rd B2
St George's Pl B2
St George's Rd B1
St Gregory's B2
St James St B3
St John's Ave B3
St Luke's Rd C2
St Margaret's Rd A2
St Mary's B2
St Matthew's B2
St Paul's La A2
St Paul's Rd A2
St Paul's St A2
St Stephen's Rd C1
Sandford Lido C3
Sandford Mill Road C3
Sandford Park C3
Sandford Rd C2
Selkirk St A3
Sherborne Pl B3
Sherborne St B3
Suffolk Pde C2
Suffolk Rd C1
Suffolk Sq C1
Sun St A1
Swindon Rd B2
Sydenham Villas Rd C3
Tewkesbury Rd A1
The Courtyard B1
Thirlstaine Rd C2
Tivoli Rd C1
Tivoli St C1
Town Hall & Theatre B2
Townsend St A1
Trafalgar St C2
Victoria Pl B3
Victoria St A2
Vittoria Walk C2
Wellesley Rd A2
Wellington Rd A3
Wellington Sq A3
Wellington St B2
West Drive A3
Western Rd B1
Winchcombe St B3

Chester 179

Abbey Gateway A2
Appleyards La C3
Bedward Row B1
Beeston View C3
Bishop Lloyd's Palace B2
Black Diamond St A2
Bottoms La C3
Boughton B3
Bouverie St A1
Bridge St B2
Bridgegate C2
British Heritage Centre B2
Brook St A3
Brown's La C2
Bus Station B2
Cambrian Rd A1
Canal St A2
Carrick Rd C1
Castle C2
Castle Dr C2
Cathedral B2
Catherine St A1
Chester ≷ A3
Cheyney Rd A1
Chichester St A1
City Rd A3
City Walls B1/B2
City Walls Rd B1
Cornwall St A2
County Hall C2
Cross Hey C3
Cuppin St B2
Curzon Park North C1
Curzon Park South C1
Dee Basin A1
Dee La B3
Delamere St A2
Dewa Roman Experience B2
Duke St B2
Eastgate B2
Eastgate St B2
Eaton Rd C2
Edinburgh Way C3
Elizabeth Cr B3
Fire Station A2
Foregate St B2
Frodsham St B2
Gamul House B2
Garden La A1
Gateway Theatre B2
George St A2
Gladstone Ave A1
God's Providence House B2
Gorse Stacks A2
Greenway St C2
Grosvenor Bridge C1
Grosvenor Mus B2
Grosvenor Park B3
Grosvenor Precinct B2
Grosvenor Rd C1
Grosvenor St B2
Groves Rd B3
Guildhall Mus B1
Handbridge C2
Hartington St C3
Hoole Way A2
Hunter St B2
Information Ctr B2
King Charles' Tower A2
King St A2
Library B2
Lightfoot St A3
Little Roodee C2
Liverpool Rd A2
Love St B3
Lower Bridge St B2
Lower Park Rd B3
Lyon St A2
Magistrates Court B2
Meadows La C3
Military Mus C2
Milton St A3
New Crane St B1
Nicholas St B2
Northgate A2
Northgate Arena A2
Northgate St A2
Nun's Rd B1
Old Dee Bridge C2
Overleigh Rd C2
Park St B2
Police Station B2
Post Office A2/A3/B2/C2
Princess St B2
Queen St B2
Queen's Park Rd C3
Queen's Rd A3
Race Course B1
Raymond St A1
River La C2
Roman Amphitheatre & Gardens B2
Roodee, The (Chester Racecourse) B1
Russell St A3
St Anne St A2
St George's Cr C3
St Martin's Gate A1
St Martin's Way B1
St Oswalds Way A2
Saughall Rd A1
Sealand Rd A1
South View Rd A1
Stanley Palace B1
Station Rd A3
Steven St A3
The Bars B3
The Cross B2
The Groves B2
The Meadows B3
Tower Rd B1
Town Hall B2
Union St B3
Vicar's La B2
Victoria Cr C3
Victoria Rd A2
Walpole St A1
Water Tower St A1
Watergate B1
Watergate St B2
Whipcord La A1
White Friars B2
York St B3

Chichester 179

Adelaide Rd A3
Alexandra Rd A3
Arts Centre B2
Ave de Chartres B1/B2
Barlow Rd A1
Basin Rd C2
Beech Ave B1
Bishops Palace Gardens B2
Bishopsgate Walk A3
Bramber Rd C3
Broyle Rd A2
Bus Station B2
Caledonian Rd B3
Cambrai Ave B3
Canal Wharf C2
Canon La B2
Cathedral B2
Cavendish St A1
Cawley Rd B2
Cedar Dr A1
Chapel St A2
Cherry Orchard Rd C3
Chichester By-Pass C2/C3
Chichester Festival A2
Chichester ≷ B2
Churchside A2
Cinema B3/C1
City Walls B2
Cleveland Rd B3
College La A2
Coll of Science & Technology B1
Cory Cl C2
Council Offices B2
County Hall B2
Courts B2
District B2
Duncan Rd A1
Durnford Cl A1
East Pallant B2
East Row B2
East St B2
East Walls B3
Eastland Rd C3
Ettrick Cl B1
Ettrick Rd B1
Exton Rd C3
Fire Station A2
Football Ground A2
Franklin Pl A2
Friary (Rems of) A2
Garland Cl C3
Green La A3
Grove Rd C3
Guilden Rd B3
Guildhall A2
Hawthorn Cl A1
Hay Rd C3
Henty Gdns B1
Herald Dr C3
Information Ctr B2
John's St B2
Joys Croft A3
Jubilee Pk A3
Jubilee Rd A3
Juxon Cl B1
Kent Rd A3
King George Gdns A2
King's Ave C2
Kingsham Ave C3
Kingsham Rd C2
Laburnum Gr B2
Leigh Rd C1
Lennox Rd A3
Lewis Rd A3
Library B2
Lion St B2
Litten Terr A3
Little London B2
Lyndhurst Rd B3
Market B3
Market Ave B2
Market Cross B2
Market Rd B3
Martlet Cl C2
Melbourne Rd A3
Mount La B1
New Park Rd A3
Newlands La A1
North Pallant B2
North St A2
North Walls A2
Northgate A2
Oak Ave A1
Oak Cl A1
Oaklands Park A2
Oaklands Way A2
Orchard Ave A1
Orchard St A1
Ormonde Ave B3
Pallant House B2
Parchment St A1
Parklands Rd A1/B1
Peter Weston Pl B3
Police Station C2
Post Office A1/B2/B3
Priory La A2
Priory Park A2
Priory Rd A2
Queen's Ave C1
Riverside A3
Roman Amphitheatre B3
St Cyriacs A2
St Pancras A3
St Paul's Rd A2
St Richard's Hospital (A + E) A3
Shamrock Cl A3
Sherbourne Rd A1
Somerstown A2
South Bank C2
South Pallant B2
South St B2
Southgate B2
Spitalfield La A3
Stirling Rd B3
Stockbridge Rd C1/C2
Swanfield Dr A3
Terminus Industrial Estate C1
Terminus Rd C1
The Hornet B3
The Litten A3
Tower St A2
Tozer Way A3
Turnbull Rd A3
Upton Rd C1
Velyn Ave B3
Via Ravenna B1
Walnut Ave A1
West St B2
Westgate B1
Westgate Fields B1
Westgate Leisure Centre B1
Weston Ave C1
Whyke Cl C3
Whyke La B3
Whyke Rd C3
Winden Ave B3

Colchester 179

Abbey Gateway C2
Albert St A1
Albion Grove C2
Alexandra Rd C1
Artillery St C3
Arts Centre B1
Balkerne Hill B1
Barrack St C3
Beaconsfield Rd C1
Beche Rd C3
Bergholt Rd A1
Bourne Rd C3
Brick Kiln Rd A1
Bristol Rd B2
Broadlands Way A3
Brook St B3
Bury Cl B2
Butt Rd C1
Camp Folley North C2
Camp Folley South C2
Campion Rd C2
Cannon St C3
Canterbury Rd C2
Castle B2
Castle Park B2
Castle Rd B2
Catchpool Rd A1
Causton Rd B1
Cavalry Barracks C1
Chandlers Row C3
Circular Rd East C2
Circular Rd North C1
Circular Rd West C1
Clarendon Way A1
Claudius Rd C2
Clock B1
Colchester Camp Abbey Field C1
Colchester Institute B1
Colchester ≷ A1
Colchester Town ≷ C2
Colne Bank Ave A1
Colne View Retail Park A2
Compton Rd A3
Cowdray Ave A1/A2
Cowdray Centre, The A2
Crouch St B1
Crowhurst Rd B1
Culver Centre B1
Culver St East B2
Culver St West B1
Dilbridge Rd A3
East Hill B2
East St B3
East Stockwell St B1
Eld La B1
Essex Hall Rd A1
Exeter Dr B2
Fairfax Rd C2
Fire Station A2
Flagstaff Rd C1
George St B2
Gladstone Rd C2
Golden Noble Hill C2
Goring Rd A3
Granville Rd C3
Greenstead Rd B3
Guildford Rd B2
Harsnett Rd C3
Harwich Rd B3
Head St B1
High St B1/B2
High Woods Country Park A2
Hythe Hill C3
Information Ctr B2
Ipswich Rd A3
Kendall Rd C2
Kimberley Rd C3
King Stephen Rd C3
Le Cateau Barracks C1
Leisure World A2
Library B1
Lincoln Way B2
Lion Walk Shopping Centre B1
Lisle Rd C2
Lucas Rd C2
Magdalen Green C3
Magdalen St C2
Maidenburgh St B2
Maldon Rd C1
Manor Rd B1
Margaret Rd A1
Mason Rd A2
Mercers Way A1
Mercury B1
Mersea Rd C2
Meyrick Cr C2
Mile End Rd A1
Military Rd C2
Mill St C2
Minories B2
Moorside B3
Morant Rd C3
Napier Rd C2
Natural History B2
New Town Rd C2
Norfolk Cr A3
North Hill B1
North Station Rd A1
Northgate St B1
Nunns Rd B1
Odeon B1
Old Coach Rd B3
Old Heath Rd C3
Osborne St B2
Petrolea Cl A1
Police Station C1
Popes La B1
Port La C3
Post Office A1/B1/B2/C2/C3
Priory St B2
Queen St B2
Rawstorn Rd B1
Rebon St C3
Recreation Rd C3
Ripple Way A3
Roman Rd B2
Roman Wall B2
Romford Cl A3
Rosebery Ave B2
St Andrews Ave B3
St Andrews Gdns B3
St Botolph St B2
St Botolphs B2
St John's Abbey (site of) C2
St John's St B1
St John's Walk Shopping Centre B1
St Leonards Rd C3
St Marys Fields B1
St Peters B1
St Peter's St B1
Salisbury Ave C1
Serpentine Walk A1
Sheepen Pl B1
Sheepen Rd B1
Sir Isaac's Walk B1
Smythies Ave B2
South St C1
South Way C1
Sports Way A2
Suffolk Cl A3
Town Hall B1
Valentine Dr A3
Victor Rd C3
Wakefield Cl B2
Wellesley Rd C1
Wells Rd B2/B3
West St C1
West Stockwell St B1
Weston Rd C3
Westway A1
Wickham Rd C1
Wimpole Rd C3
Winchester Rd C2
Winnock Rd C2
Wolfe Ave C2
Worcester Rd B2

Coventry 179

Abbots La A1
Albany Rd B1
Alma St B3
Art Faculty B3
Asthill Grove C2
Bablake School A1
Barras La A1/B1
Barrs Hill School A1
Belgrade B2
Bishop Burges St A2
Bond's Hospital B1
Broad Gate B2
Broadway C1
Bus Station A3
Butts Radial B1
Canal Basin A2
Canterbury St A3
Cathedral B3
Chester St A1
Cheylesmore Manor House B2
Christ Church Spire B2
City Walls & Gates A2
Corporation St B2
Council House B2
Coundon Rd A1
Coventry & Warwickshire Hospital (A&E) A2
Coventry Station ≷ C2
Coventry Transport Mus A2
Cox St A3
Croft Rd B1
Dalton Rd C1
Deasy Rd C3
Earl St B2
Eaton Rd C2
Fairfax St B2
Foleshill Rd A2
Ford's Hospital B2
Fowler Rd A1
Friars Rd C2
Gordon St C1
Gosford St B3
Greyfriars Green B2
Greyfriars Rd B2
Gulson Rd B3
Hales St A2
Harnall Lane East A3
Harnall Lane West A2
Herbert Art Gallery & Mus B3
Hertford St B2
Hewitt Ave A1
High St B2
Hill St B1
Holy Trinity B2
Holyhead Rd A1
Howard St A3
Huntingdon Rd C1
Information Ctr B2
Jordan Well B3
King Henry VIII School C1
Lady Godiva Statue B2
Lamb St A2
Leicester Row A2
Library B2
Little Park St B2
London Rd C3
Lower Ford St B3
Magistrates & Crown Courts B2
Manor House Drive B2
Manor Rd C2
Market B2
Martyr's Memorial C2
Meadow St B1
Meriden St A1
Michaelmas Rd C2
Middleborough Rd A1
Mile La C3
Millennium Place A2
Much Park St B3
Naul's Mill Park A1
New Union B2
Park Rd C2
Parkside C3
Police HQ C2
Post Office B2
Primrose Hill St A3
Priory Gardens & Visitor Centre B2
Priory St B3
Puma Way C3
Quarryfield La C3
Queen's Rd B1
Quinton Rd C2
Radford Rd A2
Raglan St B3
Retail Park C1
Ringway (Hill Cross) A1
Ringway (Queens) B1
Ringway (Rudge) B1
Ringway (St Johns) B3
Ringway (St Nicholas) A2
Ringway (St Patricks) C2
Ringway (Swanswell) A2
Ringway (Whitefriars) B3
St John St B2
St John The Baptist B2
St Nicholas St A2
Skydome B1
Spencer Ave C1
Spencer Park C1
Spon St B1
Sports Centre B3
Stoney Rd C2
Stoney Stanton Rd A3
Swanswell Pool A3
Sydney Stringer School A3
Technical College B1
Technology Park C3
The Precinct B2
Theatre B1
Thomas Landsdail St C2
Tomson Ave A1
Top Green C1
Toy Mus B3
Trinity St B2
University B3
Upper Hill St A1
Upper Well St A2
Victoria St A3
Vine St A3
Warwick Rd C2
Waveley Rd B1
Westminster Rd C1
White St A3
Windsor St B1

Derby 179

Abbey St C1
Agard St B1
Albert St B2
Albion St B2
Ambulance Station B1
Arthur St A1
Ashlyn Rd B3
Assembly Rooms B2
Babington La C2
Becket St B1
Belper Rd A1
Bold La
Bradshaw Way
Bridge St
Brook St
Burrows Walk
Burton Rd
Bus Station
Caesar St
Canal St
Carrington St
Cathedral
Cathedral Rd
Charnwood St
Chester Green Rd
City Rd
Clarke St
Cock Pitt
Council House
Courts
Cranmer Rd
Crompton St
Crown & County Courts
Crown Walk
Curzon St
Darley Grove
Derby ≷
Derbyshire County Cricket Ground
Derbyshire Royal Infirmary (A&E)
Derwent Business Centre
Derwent St
Devonshire Walk
Drewry La
Duffield Rd
Duke St
Dunton Cl
Eagle Market
Eastgate
East St
Exeter St
Farm St
Ford St
Forester St
Fox St
Friar Gate
Friary St
Full St
Gerard St
Gower St
Green La
Grey St
Guildhall
Harcourt St
Highfield Rd
Hill La
Industrial
Information Ctr
Iron Gate
John St
Joseph Wright Centre
Kedleston Rd
Key St
King Alfred St
King St
Kingston St
Leopold St
Library
Liversage St
Lodge La
London Rd
Macklin St
Mansfield Rd
Market
Market Pl
May St
Meadow La
Melbourne St
Midland Rd
Monk St
Morledge
Mount St
Mus & Art Gallery
Noble St
North Parade
North St
Nottingham Rd
Osmaston Rd
Otter St
Park St
Parker St
Pickfords House
Playhouse
Police HQ
Police Station
Post Office A1/A2/B1/B2/C2/C3
Pride Parkway
Prime Parkway
Queens Leisure Centre
Racecourse
Railway Terr
Register Office
Sacheverel St
Sadler Gate
St Alkmund's Way B1/B
St Helens House
St Mary's
St Mary's Bridge
St Mary's Bridge Chapel
St Mary's Gate
St Paul's Rd
St Peter's
St Peter's St
Siddals Rd
Sir Frank Whittle Rd
Spa La
Spring St
Stafford St
Station Approach
Stockbrook St
Stores Rd
Traffic St
Wardwick
Werburgh St

Dorchester • Dumfries • Dundee • Durham • Edinburgh • Exeter 199

t Ave ... A1
tfield Centre ... C2
t Meadows
ustrial Estate ... B3
rf Rd ... A2
not St ... C2
on St ... C1
d's La ... C1

rchester 179

erman Rd ... B3
nd Rd ... A2
ert Rd ... A1
andra Rd ... B1
ed Place ... B3
ed Rd ... B2
gton Ave ... B3
gton Rd ... B3
pulance Station ... B3
ey Rd ... B1
noral Cres ... C3
nes Way ... B2/C2
ough Gdns ... A1
port Rd ... A1
kingham Way ... C3
ers Place ... A1
netery ... A3/C1
rles St ... A2
urg Rd ... B1
iton St ... A1
nwall Rd ... A1
mwell Rd ... B1
iford Rd ... B2
iford Rd North ... B2
mar Rd ... B1
ner's Rd ... B1
gory Cres ... C2
osaur Mus ... A2
chester Bypass ... C2
chester South ation ... B1
chester West ation ... B1
set County Council fices ... A1
set County +E) ... B1
set County Mus ... A1
chy Close ... C3
ke's Ave ... B2
ngate St ... A2
nover Court ... A3
lison Ave ... B3
vard Rd ... B1
lon Rd ... C2
ridge Pope ewery ✦ ... B1
zabeth Frink atue ✦ ... B2
frae Cres ... B2
ary Hill ... A2
ary Lane ... A2
me Terr ... A2
land Cres ... C3
de Path Rd ... A1
vernment Offices ... B3
Western Rd ... B1
osvenor Cres ... C1
osvenor Rd ... C1
M Prison ... A1
rrington Rd ... C1
h St East ... A2
h Street ordington ... A2
h Street West ... A1
lloway Rd ... A2
n Way ... A2
ep Military Mus, he ... A1
gs Rd ... A3/B3
gsbere Cres ... C2
ncaster Rd ... B2
rary ... C1
ne Cl ... C1
den Ave ... B2
ndon Cl ... A3
ndon Rd ... A2/A3
bbecke Way ... A3
cetta La ... B2
iden Castle Rd ... C1
nor Rd ... C2
umbury Rd ... B1
umbury Rings ... B1
llstock Ave ... C2
ll St ... A3
ller's Cl ... A1
stover Cl ... C1
onmouth Rd ... B1/B2
ture Reserve ... A2
rth Sq ... A2
rthernhay ... A1
d Crown Court & ells ... A1
ga Rd ... B1
chard St ... A2
lice Station ... B1
st Office ... A1/B1/B2
und Lane ... A2
undbury Rd ... A1
ince of Wales Rd ... B2
ince's St ... A1
ueen's Ave ... B1
man Town House ... A1
man Wall ... A1
thesay Rd ... C2
George's Rd ... B3
lisbury Field ... A2
aston Cres ... C2
nokey Hole La ... B3
uth Court Ave ... C1
uth St ... B1
uth Walks Rd ... B2
orts Centre ... B3
perstore ... C3
ddy Bear House ... A1
mple Cl ... C1
e Grove ... A1
wn Hall ... A2
Town Pump ✦ ... A2
Trinity St ... A1
Tutankhamun Exhibition ... A1
Victoria Rd ... A1
Weatherbury Way ... C2
Wellbridge Cl ... C1
West Mills Rd ... A1
West Walks Rd ... A1
Weymouth Ave ... B1
Williams Ave ... B1
Winterbourne Hosp ... C1
Wollaston Rd ... A2
York Rd ... B2

Dumfries 180

Academy St ... A2
Aldermanhill Rd ... B3
Ambulance Station ... C3
Annan Rd ... A3
Ardwall Rd ... A3
Ashfield Dr ... A1
Atkinson Rd ... C1
Averill Cres ... C1
Balliol Ave ... C1
Bank St ... B2
Bankend Rd ... C3
Barn Slaps ... B3
Barrie Ave ... B3
Beech Ave ... A1
Bowling Green ... A3
Brewery St ... B1
Bridge House ... B1
Brodie Ave ... C2
Brooke St ... B2
Broomlands Dr ... C1
Brooms Rd ... B3
Buccleuch St ... A2
Burns House ... B2
Burns Mausoleum ... B3
Burns St ... B2
Burns Statue ✦ ... A2
Bus Station ... B1
Cardoness St ... A3
Castle St ... A2
Catherine St ... A2
Cattle Market ... A3
Cemetery ... B3
Cemetery ... C2
Church Cres ... A2
Church St ... B2
College Rd ... A1
College St ... A1
Corbelly Hill ... B1
Convent, The ... B1
Corberry Park ... B1
Cornwall Mt ... A3
County Offices ... A2
Court ... A2
Craigs Rd ... C3
Cresswell Ave ... B3
Cresswell Hill ... B3
Cumberland St ... B3
David Keswick Athletic Centre ... A3
David St ... B1
Dock Park ... C3
Dockhead ... B2
Dumfries ... A3
Dumfries Academy ... A2
Dumfries Mus & Camera Obscura ... B2
Dumfries Royal Infirmary (A & E) ... C3
East Riverside Dr ... C3
Edinburgh Rd ... A2
English St ... B2
Fire Station ... B3
Friar's Vennel ... A2
Galloway St ... B1
George Douglas Dr ... C1
George St ... A2
Gladstone Rd ... C2
Glasgow St ... A1
Glebe St ... B3
Glencaple Rd ... C3
Goldie Ave ... A1
Goldie Cres ... A1
Golf Course ... C3
Greyfriars ... A2
Grierson Ave ... B3
HM Prison ... B1
Hamilton Ave ... C1
Hamilton Starke Park ... C2
Hazelrigg Ave ... C1
Henry St ... B3
Hermitage Dr ... C1
High Cemetery ... C3
High St ... A2
Hill Ave ... C2
Hill St ... B1
Holm Ave ... C2
Hoods Loaning ... A3
Howgate St ... B1
Huntingdon Rd ... A3
Information Ctr ... B2
Irish St ... B2
Irving St ... A2
King St ... A1
Kingholm Rd ... C3
Kirkpatrick Ct ... C2
Laurieknowe ... B1
Leafield Rd ... B3
Library ... A2
Lochfield Rd ... A1
Loreburn Pk ... A3
Loreburn St ... A2
Loreburne Shopping Centre ... B2
Lover's Walk ... A2
Martin Ave ... B3
Maryholm Dr ... A1
Mausoleum ... B3
Maxwell St ... B1
McKie Ave ... B3
Mews La ... A2
Mill Green ... B2
Mill Rd ... B1
Moat Rd ... C2
Moffat Rd ... A3
Mountainhall Pk ... C3
Nelson St ... B1
New Abbey Rd ... B1/C1
New Bridge ... B1
Newall Terr ... A2
Nith Ave ... A2
Nith Bank ... C3
Nithbank Hosp ... C3
Nithside Ave ... A1
Odeon ... B2
Old Bridge ... B1
Palmerston Park (Queen of the South FC) ... A1
Park Rd ... C1
Pleasance Ave ... C1
Police HQ ... A3
Police Station ... A2
Portland Dr ... A1
Post Office ... A2/B1/B2/B3/B3
Priestlands Dr ... C1
Primrose St ... B1
Queen St ... B3
Queensberry St ... A2
Rae St ... A2
Richmond Ave ... C2
Robert Burns Centre ... B2
Roberts Cres ... C1
Robertson Ave ... C3
Robinson Dr ... C1
Rosefield Rd ... C2
Rosemount St ... B1
Rotchell Park ... C1
Rotchell Rd ... B1
Rugby Football Ground ... C1
Ryedale Rd ... C2
St Andrews ... B2
St John the Evangelist ... A2
St Josephs College ... B3
St Mary's Industrial Estate ... A3
St Mary's St ... A3
St Michael St ... B2
St Michael's ... B2
St Michael's Bridge ... B2
St Michael's Bridge Rd ... B2
St Michael's Cemetery ... B3
Shakespeare St ... B2
Solway Dr ... C2
Stakeford St ... A1
Stark Cres ... C2
Station Rd ... A3
Steel Ave ... A1
Sunderries Ave ... A1
Sunderries Rd ... A1
Suspension Brae ... B2
Swimming Pool ... A1
Terregles St ... B1
Theatre Royal ... B2
Troqueer Rd ... C2
Union St ... A1
Wallace St ... B3
Welldale ... B2
West Riverside Dr ... C2
White Sands ... B2

Dundee 180

Adelaide Pl ... A1
Airlie Pl ... C1
Albany Terr ... A1
Albert St ... A3
Alexander St ... A2
Ann St ... A2
Arthurstone Terr ... A3
Bank St ... B2
Barrack Rd ... A1
Barrack St ... B2
Bell St ... B2
Blackscroft ... A3
Blinshall St ... B1
Brown St ... B1
Bus Station ... B3
Caird Hall ... B2
Camperdown St ... B3
Candle La ... B3
Carmichael St ... A1
City Churches ... B2
City Quay ... B3
City Sq ... B2
Commercial St ... B2
Constable St ... A3
Constitution Ct ... A1
Constitution Cres ... A1
Constitution St ... A1/B2
Cotton Rd ... A3
Courthouse Sq ... B1
Cowgate ... A3
Crescent St ... A3
Crichton St ... B2
Dens Brae ... A3
Dens Rd ... A3
Discovery Point ✦ ... C2
Douglas St ... B1
Drummond St ... A1
Dudhope Castle ... A1
Dudhope St ... A2
Dudhope Terr ... A1
Dundee ... C2
Dundee College ... A1
Dundee Contemporary Arts ✦ ... C2
Dundee High School ... B2
Dura St ... A3
East Dock St ... B3
East Whale La ... B3
East Marketgait ... B3
Erskine St ... A3
Euclid Cr ... B2
Forebank Rd ... A2
Foundry La ... A3
Gallagher Retail Park ... B3
Gellatly St ... B3
Government Offices ... C2
Guthrie St ... B1
Hawkhill ... B1
Hilltown ... A2
HMS Unicorn ✦ ... B3
Howff Cemetery, The ... B2
Information Ctr ... B2
King St ... A3
Kinghorne Rd ... A1
Ladywell Ave ... A3
Laurel Bank ... A2
Law Hill, The ✦ ... A1
Law Rd ... A1
Law St ... A1
Library ... A2
Little Theatre ... A2
Lochee Rd ... B1
Lower Princes St ... A3
Lyon St ... A3
McManus Galleries ... B2
Meadow Side ... B2
Meadowside St Pauls ... B2
Mercat Cross ✦ ... B2
Murraygate ... B2
Nelson St ... A2
Nethergate ... B2/C1
North Marketgait ... B2
North Lindsay St ... B2
Old Hawkhill ... B1
Olympia Leisure Centre ... C3
Overgate Shopping Centre ... B2
Park Pl ... B1
Perth Rd ... C1
Police Station ... A2/B1
Post Office ... B2
Princes St ... A3
Prospect Pl ... A2
Reform St ... B2
Repertory ... C2
Riverside Dr ... C2
Roseangle ... C1
Rosebank St ... A2
RRS Discovery ... C2
St Andrew's ✝ ... C2
St Pauls Episcopal ✝ ... B3
Science Centre ✦ ... C2
Seagate ... B2
Sheriffs Court ... B1
South George St ... A2
South Marketgait ... B3
South Tay St ... B2
South Ward Rd ... B2
Steps ... A2
Tay Road Bridge ✦ ... C3
Tayside House ... B2
Trades La ... B3
Union St ... B2
Union Terr ... A1
University Library ... B2
University of Abertay ... B2
University of Dundee ... B1
Upper Constitution St ... A1
Verdant Works ✦ ... B1
Victoria Dock ... B3
Victoria Rd ... A2
Victoria St ... A3
West Marketgait ... B1/B2
Ward Rd ... B1
Wellgate ... B2
West Bell St ... B1
Westfield Pl ... C1
William St ... A3
Wishart Arch ✦ ... A3

Durham 180

Alexander Cr ... B2
Allergate ... B2
Archery Rise ... C1
Assize Courts ... B3
Back Western Hill ... A1
Bakehouse La ... A3
Baths ... B3
Baths Bridge ... B3
Boat House ... B3
Bowling ... A2
Boyd St ... C3
Bus Station ... B2
Castle ... B2
Castle Chare ... B2
Cathedral ✝ ... B2
Church St ... C3
Clay La ... C1
Claypath ... B3
College of St Hild & St Bede ... B3
County Hall ... A1
County Hosp ... A1
Crook Hall ... A3
Crossgate ... B2
Crossgate Peth ... C1
Darlington Rd ... C1
Durham ... A2
Durham Light Infantry Mus & Arts Centre ... A2
Durham School ... C2
Ellam Ave ... C1
Elvet Bridge ... B3
Elvet Court ... B3
Farnley Hey ... B1
Ferens Cl ... A3
Fieldhouse La ... A1
Flass St ... B1
Framwelgate ... A2
Framwelgate Bridge ... B2
Framwelgate Peth ... A2
Framwelgate Waterside ... A2
Frankland La ... A3
Freeman's Pl ... A3
Gala & Sacred Journey ... B3
Geoffrey Ave ... C1
Gilesgate ... B3
Grey College ... C3
Grove St ... C2
Hallgarth St ... C3
Hatfield College ... B3
Hawthorn Terr ... B1
Heritage Centre ... B3
HM Prison ... B3
Information Ctr ... B3
John St ... B1
Kingsgate Bridge ... B3
Laburnum Terr ... B1
Lawson Terr ... B1
Leazes Rd ... B2/B3
Library ... B2
Margery La ... B2
Mavin St ... C3
Millburngate ... B2
Millburngate Bridge ... B2
Millburngate Centre ... B2
Millennium Bridge (foot/cycle) ... A2
Mus of Archaeology ... B2
Neville's Cross College ... C1
Nevilledale Terr ... B1
New Elvet ... B3
New Elvet Bridge ... B3
North Bailey ... B3
North End ... A1
North Rd ... A1/B2
Observatory ... C1
Old Elvet ... B3
Oriental Mus ... C2
Passport Office ... A2
Percy Terr ... B1
Pimlico ... C2
Police Station ... B3
Post Office ... A1/B2
Potters Bank ... C1/C2
Prebends Bridge ... C2
Prebends Walk ... C2
Prince Bishops Shopping Centre ... B3
Princes St ... A1
Providence Row ... A3
Quarryheads La ... C2
Redhills La ... B1
Redhills Terr ... B1
Saddler St ... B3
St Chad's College ... C3
St Cuthbert's Society ... C2
St John's College ... C2
St Margaret's ... B2
St Mary The Less ... C2
St Mary's College ... C2
St Monica Grove ... B1
St Nicholas' ... B3
St Oswald's ... C3
Sidegate ... A2
Silver St ... B2
South Bailey ... C2
South Rd ... C3
South St ... B2
Springwell Ave ... A1
Stockton Rd ... C3
Students' Rec Centre ... B3
Sutton St ... B2
The Avenue ... B1
The Crescent ... A1
The Grove ... A1
The Sands ... A3
Town Hall ... B2
Treasury Mus ... B2
University ✦ ... B2
University Arts Block ... B3
University Library ... C3
University Science Labs ... C3
Walkergate Centre ... A3
Wearside Dr ... A3
Western Hill ... A1
Wharton Park ... A2
Whinney Hill ... C3

Edinburgh 180

Abbey Strand ... B6
Abbeyhill ... A6
Abbeyhill Cr ... B6
Abbeymount ... A6
Abercromby Pl ... A3
Adam St ... C5
Albany La ... A4
Albany St ... A4
Albert Memorial ✦ ... B2
Albyn Pl ... A2
Alva Pl ... A6
Alva St ... B1
Ann St ... A1
Appleton Tower ... C4
Archibald Pl ... C3
Argyle House ... C3
Assembly Rooms & Musical Hall ... A3
Atholl Cr ... B1
Atholl Crescent La ... C1
Bank St ... B4
Barony St ... A4
Beaumont Pl ... C5
Belford Rd ... B1
Belgrave Cr ... A1
Belgrave Crescent La ... A1
Bell's Brae ... B1
Blackfriars St ... B4
Blair St ... B4
Bread St ... C2
Bristo Pl ... C4
Bristo St ... C4
Brougham St ... C2
Broughton St ... A4
Brown St ... C5
Brunton Terr ... A6
Buckingham Terr ... A1
Burial Ground ... A6
Bus Station ... A4
Caledonian Cr ... C1
Caledonian Rd ... C1
Calton Hill ... A4
Calton Hill ... A5
Calton Rd ... B4
Camera Obscura & Outlook Tower ✦ ... B3
Candlemaker Row ... C4
Canning St ... B2
Canongate ... B5
Canongate ... B5
Carlton St ... A1
Carlton Terr ... A6
Carlton Terrace La ... A6
Castle St ... B2
Castle Terr ... B2
Castlehill ... B3
Central Library ... B4
Chalmers Hosp ... C3
Chalmers St ... C3
Chambers St ... C4
Chapel St ... C4
Charles St ... C4
Charlotte Sq ... B2
Chester St ... B1
Circus La ... A2
Circus Pl ... A2
City Art Centre ... B4
City Chambers ... B4
City Observatory ... A5
Clarendon Cr ... A1
Clerk St ... C5
Coates Cr ... B1
Cockburn St ... B4
College of Art ... C3
Comely Bank Ave ... A1
Comely Bank Row ... A1
Cornwall St ... C2
Cowans Cl ... C5
Cowgate ... B4
Cranston St ... B5
Crichton St ... C4
Croft-An-Righ ... A6
Cumberland St ... A2
Dalry Pl ... C1
Dalry Rd ... C1
Danube St ... A1
Darnawy St ... A2
David Hume Tower ... C4
Davie St ... C5
Dean Bridge ... A1
Dean Gdns ... A1
Dean Park Cr ... A1
Dean Park Mews ... A1
Dean Park St ... A1
Dean Path ... B1
Dean St ... A1
Dean Terr ... A1
Dewar Pl ... C1
Dewar Place La ... C1
Doune Terr ... A2
Drummond Pl ... A3
Drummond St ... C5
Drumsheugh Gdns ... B1
Dublin Mews ... A3
Dublin St ... A4
Dublin Street Lane South ... A4
Dumbiedykes Rd ... B5
Dundas St ... A3
Earl Grey St ... C2
East Crosscauseway ... C5
East Market St ... B4
East Norton Pl ... A6
East Princes St Gdns ... B3
Easter Rd ... A6
Edinburgh (Waverley) ... B4
Edinburgh Castle ... B3
Edinburgh Dungeon ✦ ... B4
Edinburgh Festival Theatre ... C4
Edinburgh International Conference Ctr ... C2
Elder St ... A4
Esplanade ... B3
Eton Terr ... A1
Eye Pavilion ... C3
Festival Office ... B3
Filmhouse ... C2
Fire Station ... C2
Floral Clock ✦ ... B3
Forres St ... A2
Forth St ... A4
Fountainbridge ... C2
Frederick St ... A3
Freemasons' Hall ... B3
Fruit Market ... B4
Gardner's Cr ... C2
George Heriot's School ... C3
George IV Bridge ... B4
George Sq ... C4
George Sq La ... C4
George St ... B3
Georgian House ... B2
Gladstone's Land ... B4
Glen St ... C3
Gloucester La ... A2
Gloucester Pl ... A2
Gloucester St ... A2
Graham St ... C3
Grassmarket ... C3
Great King St ... A3
Great Stuart ... B1
Greenside La ... A5
Greenside Row ... A5
Greyfriars Kirk ... C4
Grindlay St ... C2
Grosvenor St ... C1
Grove St ... C1
Gullan's Cl ... B5
Guthrie St ... B4
Hanover St ... A3
Hart St ... A4
Haymarket ... C1
Haymarket Station ... C1
Heriot Pl ... C3
Heriot Row ... A2
High School Yard ... B5
High St ... B4
Hill Pl ... C5
Hill St ... A2
Hillside Cr ... A5
Holyrood Park ... C6
Holyrood Rd ... B5
Home St ... C2
Hope St ... B2
Horse Wynd ... B6
Howden St ... C5
Howe St ... A2
India Pl ... A2
India St ... A2
Infirmary St ... B4
Information Ctr ... B4
Jamaica Mews ... A2
Jeffrey St ... B4
John Knox's House ... B4
Johnston Terr ... C3
Keir St ... C3
Kerr St ... A2
King's Stables Rd ... B2
Lady Lawson St ... C3
Lady Stair's House ... B4
Laserquest ✦ ... C2
Lauriston Gdns ... C3
Lauriston Park ... C3
Lauriston Pl ... C3
Lauriston St ... C3
Lawnmarket ... B3
Learmonth Gdns ... A1
Learmonth Terr ... A1
Leith St ... A4
Lennox St ... A1
Lennox St La ... A1
Leslie Pl ... A2
London Rd ... A5
Lothian Health Board ... C5
Lothian Rd ... B2
Lothian St ... C4
Lower Menz Pl ... A6
Lynedoch Pl ... B1
Manor Pl ... B1
Market St ... B4
Marshall St ... C4
Maryfield ... A6
Maryfield Pl ... A6
McEwan Hall ... C4
Medical School ... C4
Melville St ... B1
Meuse La ... B4
Middle Meadow Walk ... C4
Milton St ... A6
Montrose Terr ... A6
Moray House (college) ... B5
Moray Place ... A2
Morrison Link ... C1
Morrison St ... C1
Mound Pl ... B3
Mus of Childhood ... B5
Mus of Edinburgh ... B5
National Gallery ... B3
National Library of Scotland ... B4
National Monument ✦ ... A5
National Mus of Scotland ... C4
National Portrait Gallery & Mus of Antiquities ... A3
Nelson Monument ✦ ... A5
Nelson St ... A3
New St ... B5
Nicolson Sq ... C4
Nicolson St ... C4
Niddry St ... B4
North Bridge ... B4
North Meadow Walk ... C3
North Bank St ... B3
North Castle St ... A2
North Charlotte St ... A2
North St Andrew St ... A4
North St David St ... A3
North West Circus Pl ... A2
Northumberland St ... A3
Odeon ... C2
Old Royal High School ... A5
Old Tolbooth Wynd ... B5
Our Dynamic Earth ✦ ... B6
Oxford Terr ... A1
Palace of Holyrood House ... B6
Palmerston Pl ... B1
Panmure Pl ... C3
Parliament House ... B4
Parliament Sq ... B4
People's Story, The ... B5
Playhouse Theatre ... A4
Pleasance ... C5
Police Station ... A4
Ponton St ... C2
Post Office ... A3/A4/B5/C1/C2/C4/C5
Potterrow ... C4
Princes Mall ... B4
Princes St ... B3
Queen St ... A2
Queen Street Gdns ... A3
Queen's Dr ... B6/C6
Queensferry Rd ... A1
Queensferry St ... B1
Queensferry Street La ... B2
Radical Rd ... C6
Randolph Cr ... B1
Regent Gdns ... A5
Regent Rd ... B5
Regent Rd Park ... A6
Regent Terr ... A5
Register House ... A4
Remains of Holyrood Abbey (AD 1128) ... A6
Richmond La ... C5
Richmond Pl ... C5
Rose St ... B2
Rosemount Bldgs ... C1
Ross Open Air Theatre ... B3
Rothesay Pl ... B1
Rothesay Terr ... B1
Roxburgh Pl ... C5
Roxburgh St ... C5
Royal Bank of Scotland ... A4
Royal Circus ... A2
Royal Lyceum ... C2
Royal Scottish Academy ... B3
Royal Terr ... A5
Royal Terrace Gdns ... A5
Rutland Sq ... B2
Rutland St ... B2
St Andrew Sq ... A3
St Andrew's House ... A4
St Bernard's Cr ... A1
St Cecilia's Hall ... B4
St Colme St ... A2
St Cuthbert's ... B2
St Giles' ✝ ... B4
St James Centre ... A4
St John St ... B5
St John's ... B2
St John's Hill ... B5
St Leonard's Hill ... C5
St Leonard's La ... C5
St Leonard's St ... C5
St Mary's ... A4
St Mary's Scottish Episcopal ✝ ... B1
St Mary's St ... B5
St Stephen St ... A2
Salisbury Crags ... C6
Saunders St ... A2
Scott Monument ✦ ... B4
Scottish Arts Council Gallery ... B2
Scottish Parliament ... B6
Semple St ... C2
Shandwick Pl ... B2
South Bridge ... B4
South Charlotte St ... B2
South College St ... C4
South Learmonth Gdns ... A1
South St Andrew St ... A4
South St David St ... A3
Spittal St ... C2
Stafford St ... B1
Student Centre ... C4
TA Centre ... C4
Tattoo Office ... B4
Teviot Pl ... C4
The Mall ... B6
The Mound ... B3
The Royal Mile ... B5
Thistle St ... A3
Torphichen Pl ... C1
Torphichen St ... C1
Traverse Theatre ... B2
Tron Sq ... B4
Tron, The ✦ ... B4
Union St ... A4
University ... C4
University Library ... C4
Upper Grove Pl ... C1
Usher Hall ... C2
Vennel ... C3
Victoria St ... B3
Viewcraig Gdns ... B5
Viewcraig St ... B5
Walker St ... B1
Waterloo Pl ... A4
Waverley Bridge ... B4
Wemyss Pl ... A2
West Approach Rd ... C1
West Crosscauseway ... C5
West Maitland St ... C1
West of Nicholson St ... C4
West Port ... C3
West Princes Street Gdns ... B3
West Richmond St ... C5
West Tollcross ... C2
White Horse Cl ... B5
William St ... B1
Windsor St ... A5
York La ... A4
York Pl ... A4
Young St ... B2

Exeter 180

Alphington St ... C1
Athelstan Rd ... B3
Bampfylde St ... B2
Barnardo Rd ... C3
Barnfield Hill ... B3
Barnfield Rd ... B2/B3
Barnfield Theatre ... B2
Bartholomew St East ... B1
Bartholomew St West ... B1
Bear St ... B2
Beaufort Rd ... C1
Bedford St ... B2
Belgrave Rd ... A3
Belmont Rd ... A3
Blackall Rd ... A2
Blackboy Rd ... A3
Bonhay Rd ... B1
Bull Meadow Rd ... C2
Bus & Coach Sta ... B3
Castle St ... B2
Cecil Rd ... C1
Cheeke St ... A3
Church Rd ... C1
Chute St ... A3
City Industrial Estate ... C2
City Wall ... B1/B2
Civic Centre ... B2
Clifton Rd ... B3
Clifton St ... B3
Clock Tower ... A1
College Rd ... B3
Colleton Cr ... C2
Commercial Rd ... C1
Coombe St ... B2
Cowick St ... C1
Crown Courts ... B2
Custom House ... C2
Danes' Rd ... A2
Denmark Rd ... B3
Devon County Hall ... C3
Devonshire Pl ... A3
Dinham Rd ... B1
East Grove Rd ... C3
Edmund St ... C1
Elmgrove Rd ... A1
Exe St ... B1
Exeter Central Station ... A1
Exeter City Football Ground ... A3
Exeter College ... A1
Exeter Picture House ... B1
Fire Station ... A1
Fore St ... B1
Friars Walk ... C2
Guildhall ... B2
Guildhall Shopping Centre ... B2
Harlequins Shopping Centre ... B1
Haven Rd ... C2
Heavitree Rd ... B3
Hele Rd ... A1
High St ... B2
HM Prison ... A2
Holloway St ... C2
Hoopern St ... A2
Horseguards ... A2
Howell Rd ... A1
Information Ctr ... B3
Iron Bridge ... B1
Isca Rd ... C1
Jesmond Rd ... A3
King William St ... A2
King St ... B1
Larkbeare Rd ... C2
Leisure Centre ... C1
Library ... B2
Longbrook St ... A2
Longbrook Terr ... A2
Lower North St ... B1
Lucky La ... C2
Lyndhurst Rd ... C3
Magdalen Rd ... B3
Magdalen St ... B2
Magistrates & Crown Courts ... A2
Market ... B2
Market St ... B2
Marlborough Rd ... C3
Mary Arches St ... B1
Matford Ave ... C3
Matford La ... C3
Matford Rd ... C3
May St ... A3
Mol's Coffee House ... B2
New Bridge St ... B1
New North Rd ... A1/A2
North St ... B1
Northernhay St ... B1
Norwood Ave ... C3
Odeon ... A3
Okehampton St ... C1
Old Mill Cl ... C2
Old Tiverton Rd ... A3
Oxford Rd ... A3
Paris St ... B2
Parr St ... A3
Paul St ... B1
Pennsylvania Rd ... A2
Police HQ ... B3
Portland Street ... A3
Post Office ... A3/B1/B3/C1
Powderham Cr ... A3
Preston St ... B1
Princesshay Shopping Centre ... B2
Queen St ... A1
Queens Rd ... C1
Queen's Terr ... A1
Radford Rd ... C2
Richmond Rd ... A1
Roberts Rd ... C2
Rougemont Castle ... A2
Rougemont House ✦ ... B2
Royal Albert Memorial Mus ... B2
St David's Hill ... A1
St James' Park Station ... A3
St James' Rd ... A3
St Leonard's Rd ... C3
St Lukes College ... B3
St Mary Steps ... C1
St Nicholas Priory ... B1
St Peter's Cathedral ✝ ... B2
St Thomas Station ... C1
Sandford Walk ... B3
School for the Deaf ... C2
School Rd ... C1
Sidwell St ... A2
Smythen St ... B1
South St ... B2
Southernhay East ... B2
Southernhay West ... B2
Spacex Gallery ... B1
Spicer Rd ... B3
Sports Centre ... A3
Summerland St ... A3
Swimming Pool ... B3
Sydney Rd ... C1
Tan La ... C2
The Quay ... C2
Thornton Hill ... A2
Topsham Rd ... C3
Tucker's Hall ... B1
Tudor St ... B1
Velwell Rd ... A1
Verney St ... A3
Water La ... C1/C2
Weirfield Rd ... C2
Well St ... A3
West Ave ... A2
West Grove Rd ... C3
Western Way ... A3/B1/B2
Wonford Rd ... B3/C3
York Rd ... A2

200 Fort William • Glasgow • Gloucester • Grimsby • Hanley • Harrogate

Fort William 181

Abrach Rd A3
Achintore Rd C1
Alma Rd B2
Am Breun Chamas A2
Ambulance Station A3
An Aird A2
Argyll Rd C1
Argyll Terr C1
Bank St B2
Belford Hosp B2
Belford Rd B2/B3
Black Parks A3
Braemore Pl C2
Bruce Pl C2
Bus Station B2
Camanachd Cr A3/B2
Cameron Rd C1
Cameron Sq B1
Carmichael Way A2
Claggan Rd B3
Connochie Rd C1
Cow Hill C3
Creag Dhubh A2
Croft Rd B3
Douglas Pl B2
Dudley Rd B2
Dumbarton Rd C1
Earl of Inverness Rd A3
Fassifern Rd B1
Fort William B2
Fort William (Remains) ✦ B2
Glasdrum Rd C1
Glen Nevis Pl B3
Gordon Sq B1
Grange Rd C1
Heather Croft Rd C1
Henderson Row C2
High St B1
Highland Visitor Centre B3
Hill Rd B2
Hospital Belhaven Annexe B3
Information Ctr A3
Inverlochy Ct A3
Kennedy Rd B2/C2
Library B2
Linnhe Rd B1
Lochaber College A2
Lochaber Leisure Centre B3
Lochiel Rd A3
Lochy Rd A3
Lundavra Cres C1
Lundavra Rd C1
Lundy Rd A3
Mamore Cr B2
Mary St B2
Middle St B1
Montrose Ave A3
Moray Pl C1
Morven Pl C2
Moss Rd B2
Nairn Cres C1
Nevis Bridge B3
Nevis Rd A3
Nevis Sports Centre A2
Nevis Terr B2
North Rd B3
Obelisk B2
Ocean Frontier Underwater Centre A2
Parade Rd B2
Police Station A3/C1
Post Office A3/B2
Ross Pl C1
St Andrews B2
Shaw Pl B2
Station Brae B1
Studio B1
Treig Rd A3
Union Rd C1
Victoria Rd B2
Wades Rd A3
West Highland B2
Young Pl B2

Glasgow 181

Admiral St C2
Albert Bridge C5
Albion St B5
Anderston B3
Anderston Centre B3
Anderston Quay B3
Arches B4
Argyle St A1/A2/B3/B4/B5
Argyle Street B5
Argyll Arcade B5
Arlington St A3
Art Gallery & Mus A1
Arts Centre B3
Ashley St A3
Bain St C6
Baird St A6
Baliol St A3
Ballater St C5
Barras, The (Market) C6
Bath St A3
BBC Scotland/SMG B1
Bell St C6
Bell's Bridge B1
Bentinck St A2
Berkeley St A3
Bishop La B3
Black St A6
Blackburn St C2
Blackfriars St B6
Blantyre St A1
Blythswood Sq A4
Blythswood St B4
Bothwell St B4
Brand St C1
Breadalbane St A2
Bridge St C4
Bridge St (Metro Station) C4
Bridgegate C5
Briggait C5
Broomhill Park A6
Broomielaw B4
Broomielaw Quay Gdns B3
Brown St B4
Brunswick St B5
Buccleuch St A3
Buchanan Bus Station A5
Buchanan Galleries A5
Buchanan St B5
Buchanan St (Metro Station) B5
Cadogan St B4
Caledonian University A5
Calgary St A5
Cambridge St A4
Canal St A5
Candleriggs B5
Carlton Pl C4
Carnarvon St A3
Carnoustie St C3
Carrick St B4
Castle St B6
Cathedral Sq B6
Cathedral St B5
Central College of Commerce B5
Centre for Contemporary Arts A4
Centre St C4
Cessnock (Metro Station) C1
Cessnock St C1
Charing Cross A3
Charlotte St C6
Cheapside St B3
Citizens' Theatre C5
City Chambers Complex B5
City Halls B5
Clairmont Gdns A2
Claremont St A2
Claremont Terr A2
Claythorne St C6
Cleveland St A3
Clifford La C1
Clifford St C1
Clifton Pl A2
Clifton St A2
Clutha St C1
Clyde Arc B2
Clyde Auditorium B2
Clyde Pl C4
Clyde Place Quay C4
Clyde St C5
Clyde Walkway C3
Clydeside Expressway B2
Coburg St C4
Cochrane St B5
College of Nautical Studies C5
College St B6
Collins St B6
Commerce St C4
Cook St C4
Cornwall St C2
Couper St A5
Cowcaddens (Metro Station) A4
Cowcaddens Rd A4
Crimea St B4
Custom House C4
Custom House Quay Gdns C4
Dalhousie St A4
Dental Hosp A4
Derby St A2
Dobbie's Loan A4/A5
Dobbie's Loan Pl A5
Dorset St A3
Douglas St B4
Doulton Fountain ✦ C6
Dover St A2
Drury St B4
Drygate B6
Duke St B6
Dunaskin St A1
Dunblane St A4
Dundas St B5
Dunlop St C5
East Campbell St C6
Eastvale Pl A1
Eglinton St C4
Elderslie St A3
Elliot St B2
Elmbank St A3
Esmond St A1
Exhibition Centre B2
Exhibition Way B2
Eye Infirmary A2
Festival Park C1
Film Theatre A4
Finnieston Quay B2
Finnieston Sq B2
Finnieston St B2
Fitzroy Pl A2
Florence St C5
Fox St C5
Gallowgate C6
Garnet St A3
Garnethill St A4
Garscube Rd A4
George Sq B5
George St B5
George V Bridge C4
Gilbert St A1
Glasgow Bridge C4
Glasgow Cathedral ✝ B6
Glasgow Central B4
Glasgow Green C6
Glasgow Metropolitan College B5/C5
Glasgow Science Centre ✦ B1
Glasgow Science Centre Footbridge B1
Glassford St B5
Glebe St A6
Gloucester St C3
Gorbals Cross C5
Gorbals St C5
Gordon St B4
Govan Rd B1/C1/C2
Grace St B3
Grafton Pl A5
Grant St A3
Granville St A3
Gray St A2
Greendyke St C6
Harley St C1
Harvie St C1
Haugh Rd A1
Heliport B1
Henry Wood Hall A2
High Court C5
High St B6
High Street B6
Hill St A3
Holland St A3
Holm St B4
Hope St A5
Houldsworth St B2
Houston Pl C3
Houston St C3
Howard St C5
Hunter St C6
Hutcheson St B5
Hutchesons Hall B5
Hydepark St B3
Imax Cinema B1
India St A3
Information Ctr B5
Ingram St B5
Jamaica St B4
James Watt St B4
John Knox St B6
John St B5
Kelvin Hall ✦ A1
Kelvin Statue ✦ A2
Kelvin Way A2
Kelvingrove Park A2
Kelvingrove St A2
Kelvinhaugh St A1
Kennedy St A6
Kent Rd A2
Killermont St A5
King St B5
King's A3
Kingston Bridge C3
Kingston St C4
Kinning Park (Metro Station) C2
Kinning St C3
Kyle St A5
Laidlaw St C3
Lancefield Quay B2
Lancefield St B3
Langshot St C1
Lendel Pl C1
Lighthouse ✦ B4
Lister St A6
Little St B3
London Rd C6
Lorne St C1
Lower Harbour B1
Lumsden St A1
Lymburn St A1
Lyndoch Cr A3
Lynedoch Pl A3
Lynedoch St A3
Maclellan St C1
Mair St C2
Maitland St A4
Mavisbank Gdns C2
Mcalpine St B3
Mcaslin St A6
McLean Sq C2
McLellan Gallery A4
McPhater St A4
Merchants' House B5
Middlesex St C2
Middleton St C1
Midland St B4
Miller St B5
Millroad St C6
Milnpark St C2
Milton St A4
Minerva St B2
Mitchell Library A3
Mitchell St West B4
Mitchell Theatre A3
Modern Art Gallery B5
Moir St C6
Molendinar St C6
Moncur St C6
Montieth Row C6
Montrose St B5
Morrison St C3
Mosque C5
Mus of Religious Life B6
Nairn St A1
Nelson Mandela Sq B5
Nelson St C4
Nelson's Monument C6
New City Rd A4
Newton St A3
Newton Pl A3
Nicholson St C4
Nile St B5
Norfolk Court C4
Norfolk St C4
North Frederick St B5
North Hanover St B5
North Portland St B6
North St A3
North Wallace St A5
Odeon C3
Old Dumbarton Rd A1
Osborne St B5/C5
Oswald St B4
Overnewton St A1
Oxford St C4
Pacific Dr B1
Paisley Rd C3
Paisley Rd West C1
Park Circus A2
Park Gdns A2
Park St South A2
Park Terr A2
Parkgrove Terr A2
Parnie St C5
Parson St A6
Partick Bridge A1
Passport Office A5
Paterson St C3
Pavilion Theatre A4
Pembroke St A3
People's Palace C6
Pinkston Rd A6
Piping Centre, The National ✦ A5
Pitt St A4/B4
Plantation Park C1
Plantation Quay B1
Police Station A4/A6/B5
Port Dundas Rd A5
Port St B2
Portman St C2
Prince's Dock B1
Princes Sq B5
Provand's Lordship B6
Queen St B5
Queen Street B5
Regimental Mus A3
Renfrew St A3/A4
Renton St A5
Richmond St B5
Robertson St B4
Rose St A4
Rottenrow A5
Royal Concert Hall A5
Royal Cr A2
Royal Exchange Sq B5
Royal Hospital For Sick Children A1
Royal Infirmary B6
Royal Scottish Academy of Music & Drama A4
Royal Terr A2
Rutland Cr C2
St Kent St C6
St Andrew's (RC) ✝ C5
St Andrew's C6
St Andrew's St C5
St Enoch (Metro Station) B5
St Enoch Shopping Centre B5
St Enoch Sq B4
St George's Rd A3
St James Rd B6
St Mungo Ave A5/A6
St Mungo Pl A6
St Vincent Cr A2
St Vincent Pl B5
St Vincent St B3/B4
St Vincent Street Church B4
St Vincent Terr B3
Saltmarket C5
Sandyford Pl A3
Sauchiehall St A2/A4
School of Art A4
Scotland St C2/C3
Scott St A4
Scottish Exhibition & Conference Centre B1
Seaward St C2
Shaftesbury St B3
Sheriff Court C5
Shields Rd (Metro Station) C3
Shuttle St B6
Somerset Pl A2
South Portland St C4
Springburn Rd A6
Springfield Quay C3
Stanley St C2
Stevenson St C6
Stewart St A4
Stirling Rd B6
Stirling's Library B5
Stobcross Quay B1
Stobcross Rd B1
Stock Exchange B5
Stockwell Pl C5
Stockwell St B5
Stow College A4
Strathclyde University B6
Sussex St C2
Synagogues A3/C4
Tall Ship B1
Taylor Pl A6
Tenement House A3
Teviot St A1
Theatre Royal A4
Tolbooth Steeple & Mercat Cross ✦ C6
Tower St C2
Trades House B5
Tradeston St C4
Transport Mus A1
Tron Steeple & Theatre C5
Trongate B5
Tunnel St B2
Turnbull St C5
UGC B4
Union St B4
Victoria Bridge C5
Virginia St B5
West Greenhill Pl B2
West Regent St A4
Wallace St C3
Walls St B6
Walmer Cr C1
Warrock St B3
Washington St B3
Waterloo St B4
Watson St B6
Watt St C3
Wellington St B4
West Campbell St B4
West George St B4
West Graham St A4
West Regent St B4
West St C4
West St (Metro Station) C4
Westminster Terr A2
Whitehall St B3
Wilson St B5
Woodlands Gate A3
Woodlands Rd A3
Woodlands Terr A2
Woodside Cr A3
Woodside Pl A3
Woodside Terr A3
York St B4
Yorkhill Pde A1
Yorkhill St A1

Gloucester 181

Albion St C1
Alexandra Rd B3
Alfred St C3
All Saints Rd C2
Alvin St B2
Arthur St C2
Baker St C1
Barton St C2
Blackfriars ✝ B1
Blenheim Rd C2
Bristol Rd C1
Brunswick Rd C2
Bruton Way B2
Bus Station B2
Cattle Market A1
City Council Offices B1
City Mus, Art Gall & Library B2
Clarence St B2
College of Art C2
Commercial Rd B1
Cromwell St C2
Deans Way A2
Denmark Rd A3
Derby Rd C3
Docks ✦ C1
Eastgate St B2
Edwy Pde A2
Estcourt Cl A3
Estcourt Rd A3
Falkner St C2
Folk Mus B1
GL1 Leisure Centre C2
Gloucester Cathedral ✝ B1
Gloucester Station B2
Gloucestershire Royal Hospital (A & E) B3
Goodyere St C2
Gouda Way A1
Great Western Rd B3
Guildhall B2
Heathville Rd A3
Henry Rd B3
Henry St B2
High Orchard St C1
Hinton Rd A2
India Rd C3
Information Ctr B1
Jersey Rd C3
King's C2
King's Sq B2
Kingsholm Rd A2
Kingsholm Rugby Football Ground A2
Lansdown Rd A3
Library C2
Llanthony Rd C1
London Rd B3
Longsmith St B1
Malvern Rd A3
Market Pde B2
Merchants Rd C1
Mercia Rd A1
Metz Way C3
Midland Rd C2
Millbrook St C3
Market B2
Montpellier C1
Napier St C3
National Waterways C1
Nettleton Rd C2
New Inn B2
New Olympus C3
North Rd A3
Northgate St B2
Oxford Rd A2
Oxford St B2
Park & Ride Gloucester A1
Park Rd C2
Park St B2
Parliament St C1
Pitt St B1
Police Station B1
Post Office B2
Quay St B1
Recreation Gd A1/A2
Regent St C2
Robert Raikes House B1
Royal Oak Rd B1
Russell St B2
Ryecroft St C2
St Aldate St B2
St Ann Way C1
St Catherine St A2
St Mark St A2
St Mary De Crypt B1
St Mary De Lode B1
St Nicholas's B1
St Oswald's Rd A1
St Oswald's Trading Estate A1
St Peter's B2
Seabroke Rd A3
Sebert St A2
Severn Rd C1
Sherborne St B2
Shire Hall B1
Sidney St C3
Soldiers of Gloucestershire B1
Southgate St B1/C1
Spa Field C1
Spa Rd C1
Sports Ground A2/B2
Station Rd B2
Stratton Rd C3
Stroud Rd C1
Superstore A1
Swan Rd A2
Technical College C1
The Mall B2
The Park C2
The Quay B1
Trier Way C1/C2
Union St A2
Vauxhall Rd C3
Victoria St C2
Wellington St C2
Westgate St B1
Widden St C2
Worcester St B2

Grimsby 181

Abbey Drive East C2
Abbey Drive West C2
Abbey Park Rd C2
Abbey Rd C2
Abbey Walk C2
Abbeygate Shopping Centre C2
Abbotsway C2
Adam Smith St A1/A2
Ainslie St C2
Albert St A3
Alexandra Dock A2/B2
Alexandra Retail Park A2
Alexandra Rd A2/B2
Annesley St A2
Armstrong St A1
Arthur St B1
Augusta St C1
Bargate C1
Beeson St A1
Bethlehem St C2
Bodiam Way B3
Bradley St B3
Brighowgate C1/C2
Bus Station B2/C2
Canterbury Dr C1
Cartergate B1/C1
Catherine St C3
Caxton A3
Chantry La B1
Charlton St A1
Church La C2
Church St A3
Cleethorpe Rd A3
College A3
College St C1
Compton Dr C1
Corporation Bridge A2
Corporation Rd A1
Court B3
Crescent St B1
Deansgate C1
Doughty Rd C2
Dover St B1
Duchess St C2
Dudley St C1
Duke of York Gardens B1
Duncombe St B3
Earl La B1
East Marsh St B3
East St B2
Eastgate B3
Eastside Rd A3
Eaton Ct C1
Eleanor St B3
Ellis Way B3
Fisherman's Chapel A3
Fisherman's Wharf B2
Fishing Heritage Centre B2
Flour Sq A3
Frederick St B1
Frederick Ward Way B2
Freeman St A3/B3
Freshney Dr B1
Freshney Pl B2
Garden St C2
Garibaldi St A3
Garth La B2
Grime St B3
Grimsby Docks Station A3
Grimsby Town Station C2
Hainton Ave C3
Har Way B3
Hare St C3
Harrison St B1
Haven Ave B1
Hay Croft Ave B1
Hay Croft St B1
Heneage Rd B3/C3
Henry St B1
Holme St B3
Hume St C1
James St B1
Joseph St B1
Kent St A3
King Edward St A3
Lambert Rd C2
Library B2
Lime St B1
Lister St B1
Littlefield La C1
Lockhill A3
Lord St B1
Ludford St C3
Macaulay St B1
Mallard Mews C3
Manor Ave C2
Market A3
Market Hall B2
Market St B3
Moss Rd C2
Nelson St A3
New St B2
Osbourne St B2
Pasture St B3
Peaks Parkway C3
Pelham Rd C1
Police Station A3
Post Office B1/B2/C2
PS Lincoln Castle B2
Pyewipe Rd A1
Railway Pl A3
Railway St A3
Recreation Ground C2
Rendel St A2
Retail Park B3
Richard St B1
Ripon St B1
Robinson St East B3
Royal St A3
St Hilda's Ave C1
St James C2
Sheepfold St B3/C3
Sixhills St C3
South Park B2
Spring St A3
Superstore B3
Tasburgh St C3
Tennyson St B2
The Close C1
Thesiger St A3
Time Trap C2
Town Hall B2
Veal St B1
Victoria Retail Park A3
Victoria St North A2
Victoria St South B2
Victoria St West B2
Watkin St A1
Welholme Ave C2
Welholme Rd C3
Wellington St B3
Wellowgate C2
Werneth Rd B3
West Coates Rd A1
Westgate A2
Westminster Dr C1
Willingham St C3
Wintringham Rd C2
Wood St B3
Yarborough Dr B1
Yarborough Hotel C2

Hanley 181

Acton St A3
Albion St B2
Argyle St C1
Ashbourne Gr A2
Avoca St A3
Baskerville Rd B3
Bedford Rd C1
Bedford St C1
Bethesda St B2
Bexley St A2
Birches Head Rd A3
Botteslow St C3
Boundary St A2
Broad St C2
Broom St A3
Bryan St A2
Bucknall New Rd B3
Bucknall Old Rd B3
Bus Station B3
Cannon St C2
Castlefield St C1
Cavendish St B1
Central Forest Pk A2
Charles St B3
Cheapside B2
Chell St A3
Clarke St C1
Cleveland Rd C2
Clifford St C3
Clough St B2
Clyde St C1
College Rd C2
Cooper St C2
Corbridge Rd A1
Cutts St C2
Davis St C1
Denbigh St A1
Derby St C3
Dilke St A3
Dundas St A3
Dundee Rd C1
Dyke St B3
Eastwood Rd C3
Eaton St A3
Etruria Park B1
Etruria Rd B1
Etruria Vale Rd C1
Festing St A3
Fire Station C2
Foundry St B2
Franklyn St C3
Garnet St B1
Garth St B3
George St A3
Gilman St B3
Glass St B3
Goodson St B3
Greyhound Way A1
Grove Pl C1
Hampton St C3
Hanley Park C2
Harding Rd C2
Hassall St B3
Havelock Pl C1
Hazlehurst St C3
Hinde St C2
Hope St B2
Houghton St C2
Hulton St A3
Hypermarket A1/B2
Information Ctr B3
Jasper St C2
Jervis St A3
John Bright St A3
John St B2
Keelings Rd A3
Kimberley Rd C1
Ladysmith Rd C1
Lawrence St C2
Leek Rd C3
Library C2
Lichfield St C3
Linfield Rd B3
Loftus St A2
Lower Bedford St C1
Lower Bryan St A2
Lower Mayer St A3
Lowther St A1
Magistrates Court C2
Malham St A2
Marsh St B2
Matlock St C3
Mayer St A3
Milton St C1
Mitchell Memorial Theatre B2
Morley St B2
Moston St A3
Mount Pleasant C1
Mulgrave St A1
Mynors St B3
Nelson Pl B3
New Century St B1
New Forest Industrial Estate A3
Octagon, The Shopping Park B1
Ogden Rd C3
Old Hall St B3
Old Town Rd A3
Pall Mall B2
Palmerston St C3
Park and Ride C2
Parker St B2
Pavilion Dr A1
Pelham St C3
Percy St B2
Piccadilly B2
Picton St B3
Plough St A3
Police Station C2
Portland St A1
Post Office A3/B3/C3
Potteries Mus & Art Gallery B2
Potteries Shopping Centre B2
Potteries Way C2
Powell St A1
Pretoria Rd C1
Quadrant Rd B2
Ranelagh St C2
Raymond St C2
Rectory Rd C1
Regent Rd C2
Regent Theatre B2
Richmond Terr C2
Ridgehouse Dr A1
Robson St C2
St Ann St B3
St Luke St B3
Sampson St B2
Shaw St A1
Sheaf St C2
Shearer St C1
Shelton New Rd C1
Shirley Rd C2
Slippery La B2
Snow Hill C2
Sports Stadium A1
Spur St C3
Stafford St B2
Statham St B2
Stubbs La C3
Sun St C1
Talbot St C3
The Parkway C2
Town Hall B2
Town Rd A3
Trinity St B2
Union St A2
Upper Hillchurch St A3
Upper Huntbach St B3
Victoria Hall Theatre B3
Warner St C2
Warwick St C1
Waterloo Rd A1
Waterloo St B3
Well St B3
Wellesley St C2
Wellington Rd B3
Wellington St B3
Whitehaven Dr A2
Whitmore St C1
Windermere St A1
Woodall St A1
Yates St C2
York St A2

Harrogate 182

Albert St C2
Alexandra Rd B2
Arthington Ave B2
Ashfield Rd A2
Back Cheltenham Mount B2
Beech Grove C1
Belmont Rd C1
Bilton Dr A2
Bower Rd B2
Bower St B2
Bus Station B2
Cambridge Rd B2
Cambridge St B2
Cemetery A2
Chatsworth Pl
Chatsworth Grove
Chatsworth Rd
Chelmsford Rd
Cheltenham Cr
Cheltenham Mt
Cheltenham Pde
Christ Church
Christ Church Oval
Chudleigh Rd
Clarence Dr
Claro Rd
Claro Way
Coach Park
Coach Rd
Cold Bath Rd
Commercial St
Coppice Ave
Coppice Dr
Coppice Gate
Cornwall Rd
Council Offices
Court
Crescent Gdns
Crescent Rd
Dawson Terr
Devonshire Pl
Diamond Mews
Dixon Rd
Dixon Terr
Dragon Ave
Dragon Parade
Dragon Rd
Duchy Rd
East Parade
East Park Rd
Esplanade
Fire Station
Franklin Mount
Franklin Rd
Franklin Square
Glebe Rd
Grove Park Ct
Grove Park Terr
Grove Rd
Hampswaite Rd
Harcourt Dr
Harcourt Rd
Harrogate
Harrogate International Centre
Harrogate Ladies College
Harrogate Theatre
Heywood Rd
Hollins Cr
Hollins Mews
Hollins Rd
Homestead Rd
Hydro Leisure Centre, The
Information Ctr
James St
Jenny Field Dr
John St
Kent Dr
Kent Rd
Kings Rd
Kingsway
Kingsway Dr
Lancaster Rd
Leeds Rd
Lime Grove
Lime St
Mayfield Grove
Mayfield Pl
Mercer
Montpellier Hill
Mornington Cr
Mornington Terr
Mowbray Sq
North Park Rd
Nydd Vale Rd
Oakdale Ave
Oatlands Dr
Odeon
Osborne Rd
Otley Rd
Oxford St
Park Chase
Park Parade
Park View
Parliament St
Police Station
Post Office B2/
Providence Terr
Queen Parade
Queen's Rd
Raglan St
Regent Ave
Regent Grove
Regent Parade
Regent St
Regent Terr
Rippon Rd
Robert St
Royal Baths & Turkish Baths
Royal Pump Room
St Luke's Mount
St Mary's Ave
St Mary's Walk
Scargill Rd
Skipton Rd
Skipton St
Slingsby Walk
South Park Rd
Spring Grove
Springfield Ave
Station Ave
Station Parade
Strawberry Dale
Stray Rein
Studley Rd
Superstore
Swan Rd
The Parade
The Stray C2/
Tower St

Holyhead • Hull • Inverness • Ipswich • Kendal • King's Lynn • Lancaster • Leeds 201

ity Rd C2
on St B2
ey Dr C1
ey Gardens C1
ey Mount C1
oria Ave C2
oria Rd C1
oria Shopping
ntre B2
erloo St A2
st Park C2
st Park St C2
od View A1
odfield Ave A3
odfield Dr A3
odfield Grove A3
odfield Rd A3
odfield Square A3
odside B3
k Pl C3
k Rd B1

lyhead
ergybi 182

henia St A2
nur St C2
ach Rd A1
ton St B2
wling Green C3
n Erw Rd C3
n Glas Cl C3
n Glas Rd C3
n Gwyn Rd C1
n Marchog A1
n Mor Terr A2
ngoleu Ave A1
Braenar C3
nbria St B1
ptain Skinner's
belisk✦ B2
cil St C2
metery C1/C2
veland Ave C2
stguard Lookout A2
urt B2
stoms House A3
i Pl A2
tir Rd C3
mund St B1
pire B2
rry Terminals B2
rdd Beibio B3
rdd Feurig C3
rdd Hirnos C3
rdd Jasper C3
rdd Tudur B3
e Station C2
rreglwyd Rd B1
bert St C2
rsedd Circle B1
elfor Ave A1
rbour View B3
nry St C2
h Terr C1
l St B2
born Rd C2
land Park Industrial
tate C3
yhead Park B1
lyhead Station B2
ormation Ctr B2
g's Rd C2
gsland Rd C2
wascote C3
rary B2
eboat Station A1
nfawr Cl C3
nfawr Rd C3
gwy St C2
n Deg C3
ndon Rd C3
gford Rd B1
gford Terr B1
es Cybi B1
es Hedd A1
es-Hyfryd Rd C1
es-y-Dref B1
es-yr-Haf A2/B1
es-yr-Ysgol C3
rchog A1
rina A1
ritime Mus A1
rket B2
rket St B2
l Bank B1
n-y-Mor Rd A1
rawelon Industrial
state B3
rawelon Rd B3
rreton Rd B1
w Park Rd B1
wry St A2
d Harbour
ighthouse A3
s Rd C1
lice Station B2
st Office
. A1/B1/B2/B3/C2/C3
ince of Wales Rd A2
ory La B3
mp St B1
eens Park B1
seifion Rd C1
ck St B2
man Fort B2
Cybi St B1
Cybi's Church B2
Seiriol's Cl B1
t Island Bridge A2
abourne Rd A1
uth Stack Rd B1
orts Ground B1
anley St B2
ation St B2
n-y-Bryn Rd A1
n-yr-Efail C2
ra St C1
Thomas St B1
Town Hall A2
Treseifion Estate C2
Turkey Shore Rd B2
Ucheldre Arts
Centre✦ B1
Ucheldre Ave B1
Upper Baptist St B1
Victoria Rd B2
Victoria Terr B2
Vulcan St B1
Walthew Ave A1
Walthew La A1
Wian St C2

Hull 182

Adelaide St C1
Albert Dock C1
Albion St B2
Alfred Gelder St B2
Anlaby Rd B1
Beverley Rd A1
Blanket Row C2
Bond St B2
Bridlington Ave A2
Brook St B1
Brunswick Ave A1
Bus Station B1
Camilla Cl C3
Canning St B1
Cannon St A2
Cannon's C1
Caroline St A2
Carr La B2
Castle St C2
Central Library B1
Charles St A2
Citadel Way B3
City Hall B2
Clarence St B3
Cleveland St A3
Clifton St A1
Collier St B1
Colonial St B1
Court B2
Deep, The C3
Dock Office Row B3
Dock St B2
Drypool Bridge B3
Egton St A3
English St C1
Ferens Gallery B2
Ferensway B1
Francis St A2
Francis St West A2
Freehold St A1
Freetown Way A2
Garrison Rd B3
George St B2
Gibson St A2
Great Thornton St B1
Great Union St A3
Green La A2
Grey St A1
Grimston St B2
Grosvenor St A1
Guildhall B2
Guildhall Rd B2
Hands-on History B2
Harley St A1
Hessle Rd C1
High St B3
Holy Trinity B2
Hull & East Riding
Mus B3
Hull Arena C1
Hull College B3
Hull (Paragon)
Station B1
Hull Truck Theatre B1
Humber Dock Marina C2
Humber Dock St C2
Humber St C2
Hyperion St A3
Information Ctr B2
Jameson St B1
Jarratt St B2
Jenning St A3
King Billy Statue✦ C2
King Edward St B2
King St A2
Kingston Retail Park C1
Kingston St C2
Library Theatre B1
Liddell St A1
Lime St A3
Lister St C1
Lockwood St A2
Maister House B3
Maritime Mus B2
Market B2
Market Place B2
Minerva Pier C2
Mulgrave St A3
Myton Bridge C3
Myton St B1
Nelson St C2
New Cleveland St A3
New George St A2
New Theatre A2
Norfolk St A1
North Bridge A3
North St B1
Odeon C1
Old Harbour C3
Osborne St B1
Paragon St B2
Park St B1
Percy St A2
Pier St C2
Police Station B1
Post Office A1/B1/B2
Porter St C1
Portland St B1
Posterngate B2
Prince's Quay B2
Prospect Centre B1
Prospect St B1
Queen's Gdns B2
Railway Dock Marina C2
Railway St C2
Reform St A2
Retail Park B1
Riverside Quay C2
Roper St B2
St James St C1
St Luke's St B1
St Mark St A3
St Mary the Virgin B3
Scott St A2
South Bridge Rd B3
Spring Bank A1
Spring St A1
Spurn Lightship C2
Spyvee St A3
Streetlife Transport
Mus B3
Sykes St A2
Tidal Surge Barrier✦ C3
Tower St B3
Trinity House B2
University B2
Vane St A1
Victoria Pier C2
Waterhouse La B2
Waterloo St A1
Waverley St C1
Wellington St C2
Wellington St West C2
West St B1
Whitefriargate B2
Wilberforce Dr B2
Wilberforce House B3
Wilberforce
Monument✦ B3
William St C1
Wincolmlee A3
Witham A3
Wright St A1

Inverness 182

Abban St A1
Academy St B2
Alexander Pl B2
Anderson St A2
Annfield Rd C3
Ardconnel St B3
Ardconnel Terr B3
Ardross Pl B2
Ardross St B2
Argyle St B3
Argyle Terr B3
Attadale Rd B1
Ballifeary La C2
Ballifeary Rd C1/C2
Balnacraig La A1
Balnain St B2
Bank St B2
Bellfield Park C2
Bellfield Terr C3
Benula Rd A1
Birnie Terr A1
Bishop's Rd C2
Bowling Green A2
Bowling Green B2
Bowling Green C2
Bridge St B2
Brown St A2
Bruce Ave C1
Bruce Gdns C1
Bruce Pk C1
Burial Ground A2
Burnett Rd A3
Bus Station B3
Caledonian Rd B1
Cameron Rd A1
Cameron Sq A1
Carse Rd A1
Carsegate Rd Sth A1
Castle (Courts) B3
Castle Rd B2
Castle St B3
Celt St B2
Chapel St A2
Charles St B3
Church St B2
Clachnacuddin Football
Ground A1
College A3
Columba Rd B1/C1
Crown Ave B3
Crown Circus B3
Crown Dr B3
Crown Rd B3
Crown St B3
Culduthel Rd C3
Dalneigh Cres C1
Dalneigh Rd C1
Denny St B3
Dochfour Dr B1/C1
Douglas Row B2
Duffy Dr C3
Dunabban Rd A1
Dunain Rd B1
Duncraig St B2
Eastgate Shopping
Centre B3
Eden Court C2
Fairfield Rd B1
Falcon Sq B3
Fire Station A3
Fraser St B2
Fraser St C2
Friars' Bridge A2
Friars' La B2
Friars' St A2
George St A2
Gilbert St A2
Glebe St A2
Glendoe Terr A1
Glenurquhart Rd C1
Gordon Terr B3
Gordonville Rd C2
Grant St A2
Greig St B2
HM Prison B3
Harbour Rd A3
Harrowden Rd B1
Haugh Rd C2
Heatherley Cres C3
High St B3
Highland Council HQ,
The C2
Hill Park C3
Hill St B3
Huntly Pl A2
Huntly St B2
India St A2
Industrial Estate A3
Information Ctr B2
Innes St A2
Inverness B3
Inverness High School B1
Jamaica St A2
Kenneth St B2
Kilmuir Rd A1
King St B2
Kingsmills Rd B3
Laurel Ave B1/C1
Library A3
Lilac Gr B1
Lindsay Ave C1
Lochalsh Rd A1/B1
Longman Rd A3
Lotland Pl A2
Lower Kessock St A1
Madras St A2
Market Hall B3
Maxwell Dr C1
Mayfield Rd C3
Midmills College B3
Millburn Rd B3
Mitchell's La C3
Montague Row B2
Muirfield Rd C3
Muirtown St B1
Museum B2
Nelson St A2
Ness Bank C2
Ness Bridge B2
Ness Walk B2/C2
Old Edinburgh Rd C3
Old High Church B2
Park Rd C1
Paton St C2
Perceval Rd B1
Planefield Rd B2
Police Station A3
Porterfield Bank C3
Porterfield Rd C3
Portland Pl A2
Post Office
A2/B1/B2/B3
Queen St B2
Queensgate B2
Railway Terr A3
Rangemore Rd B1
Reay St B3
Riverside St A2
Rose St A2
Ross Ave B1
Rowan Rd B1
Royal Northern
Infirmary C2
St Andrew's
Cathedral✝ C2
St Columba B2
St John's Ave C1
St Mary's Ave C1
Shore St A2
Smith Ave C1
Southside Pl C3
Southside Rd C3
Spectrum Centre B2
Strothers La B3
Superstore B2
TA Centre C2
Telford Gdns B1
Telford Rd A1
Telford St A1
Tomnahurich
Cemetery C1
Tomnahurich St B2
Town Hall B3
Union Rd B3
Union St B3
Walker Pl A2
Walker Rd A3
War Memorial✦ C2
Waterloo Bridge A2
Wells St B1
Young St B2

Ipswich 182

Alderman Rd B2
All Saints' Rd A1
Alpe St B2
Ancaster Rd C1
Ancient House B3
Anglesea Rd B2
Ann St B2
Arboretum A2
Austin St C2
Belstead Rd C2
Berners St B2
Bibb Way B1
Birkfield Dr C1
Black Horse La B2
Bolton La B3
Bond St C3
Bowthorpe Cl B2
Bramford La A1
Bramford Rd A1
Bridge St C2
Brookfield Rd A1
Brooks Hall Rd A1
Broomhill A2
Broomhill Rd A1
Broughton Rd A2
Bulwer Rd B1
Burrell Rd C2
Bus Station B2/C3
Butter Market B2
Butter Market Centre B3
Carr St B3
Cecil Rd B2
Cecilia St C2
Chancery Rd C2
Charles St B2
Chevallier St A1
Christchurch Mansion &
Wolsey Art Gallery B3
Christchurch Park A3
Christchurch St B3
Civic Centre B2
Civic Dr B2
Clarkson St B1
Cobbold St B3
Commercial Rd C2
Constable Rd A3
Constantine Rd C1
Constitution Hill A2
Corder Rd A3
Corn Exchange B2
Cotswold Ave A2
Council Offices C2
County Hall B3
Crown Court C2
Crown St B2
Cullingham Rd B1
Cumberland St B2
Curriers La B2
Dale Hall La A2
Dales View Rd A1
Dalton Rd B2
Dillwyn St B1
Elliot St B1
Elm St B2
Elsmere Rd A3
End Quay C3
Falcon St C2
Felaw St C3
Flint Wharf C3
Fonnereau Rd B2
Fore St C3
Foundation St C3
Franciscan Way C2
Friars St C2
Gainsborough Rd A3
Gatacre Rd B1
Geneva Rd B2
Gippeswyk Ave C1
Gippeswyk Park C1
Grafton Way C2
Graham Rd A1
Grimwade St C3
Great Whip St C3
Handford Cut B1
Handford Rd B1
Henley Rd A2
Hervey St B3
High St B2
Holly Rd A2
Information Ctr B3
Ipswich School A2
Ipswich Station C2
Ipswich Town FC
(Portman Road) C2
Ivry St A2
Kensington Rd A1
Kesteven Rd C1
Key St C3
Kingsfield Ave A3
Kitchener Rd A1
Magistrates Court B2
Little's Cr C2
London Rd B1
Low Brook St C3
Lower Orwell St C3
Luther Rd C2
Manor Rd A3
Mornington Ave A1
Mus & Art Gallery B2
Museum St B2
Neale St B3
New Cardinal St C2
New Cut East C3
New Cut West C3
Newson St B2
Norwich Rd A1/B1
Oban St B2
Old Customs House C3
Old Foundry Rd B3
Old Merchant's
House C3
Orford St B2
Paget Rd A2
Park Rd A3
Park View Rd A2
Peter's St C2
Philip Rd C2
Pine Ave A2
Pine View Rd A2
Police Station B2
Portman Rd B2
Portman Walk C1
Post Office B2/B3
Princes St C2
Prospect St B1
Queen St B2
Ranelagh Rd C1
Recreation Ground B1
Rectory Rd C2
Regent Theatre B3
Richmond Rd A1
Rope Walk C3
Rose La C2
Russell Rd C2
St Edmund's Rd A2
St George's St B2
St Helen's St B3
Samuel Rd B3
Sherrington Rd A1
Silent St C2
Sir Alf Ramsey Way C1
Sirdar Rd B1
Soane St B3
Springfield La A1
Star La C3
Stevenson Rd B1
Suffolk College C3
Suffolk Retail Park B1
Superstore B1
Surrey Rd B1
Swimming Pool A1
Tacket St C3
Tavern St B3
The Avenue A3
Tolly Cobbold Mus C3
Tower Ramparts B2
Tower St B3
Town Hall B2
Tuddenham Rd A3
UGC C2
Upper Brook St B3
Upper Orwell St B3
Valley Rd A2
Vermont Cr B3
Vermont Rd B3
Vernon St C3
Warrington Rd A2
Waterloo Rd A1
Waterworks St C3
Wellington St B1
West End Rd B1
Westerfield Rd A3
Westgate St B2
Westholme Rd A1
Westwood Ave A1
Willoughby Rd C2
Withipoll St B3
Wolsey Theatre B2
Woodbridge Rd B3
Woodstone Ave A3
Yarmouth Rd B1

Kendal 182

Abbot Hall Art Gallery
& Mus of Lakeland
Life C2
Ambulance Station A2
Anchorite Fields C2
Anchorite Rd C2
Ann St A3
Appleby Rd A3
Archers Meadow C3
Ashleigh Rd A2
Aynam Rd B2
Bankfield Rd B1
Beast Banks B2
Beezon Fields A2
Beezon Rd A2
Beezon Trad Est A3
Belmont B2
Birchwood Cl C1
Blackhall Rd B2
Brewery Arts
Centre B2
Bridge St B2
Brigsteer Rd C1
Burneside Rd A2
Bus Station B2
Buttery Well La C2
Canal Head North B3
Captain French La C2
Caroline St A2
Castle Hill B3
Castle Howe B2
Castle Rd B3
Castle St A3/B3
Cedar Gr C1
Council Offices B2
County Council
Offices A2
Cricket Ground A3
Cricket Ground C3
Cross La C2
Dockray Hall Ind
Estate A2
Dowker's La B2
Dry Ski Slope✦ B3
East View B1
Echo Barn Hill C1
Elephant Yard Shopping
Centre B2
Fairfield La A1
Finkle St B2
Fire Station A2
Fletcher Square C3
Football Ground C3
Fowling La A3
Gillinggate C2
Glebe Rd C2
Golf Course B1
Goose Holme B3
Gooseholme Bridge B3
Green St A1
Greengate C2
Greengate La C1/C2
Greenside B1
Greenwood C1
Gulfs Rd B2
High Tenterfell B1
Highgate B2
Hillswood Ave C1
Horncop La A2
Information Ctr B2
K Village and Heritage
Centre✦ C3
Kendal Business Park A3
Kendal Castle
(Remains Of) B3
Kendal Fell B1
Kendal Green A1
Kendal A3
Kendal Station A3
Kent Pl B2
Kirkbarrow C2
Kirkland C2
Library B2
Library Rd B2
Little Aynam B3
Little Wood B1
Long Cl C1
Longpool A3
Lound Rd C3
Lound St C3
Low Fellside B2
Lowther St B2
Maple Dr C1
Market Pl B2
Maude St B2
Miller Bridge B2
Milnthorpe Rd C2
Mint St A3
Mintsfeet Rd A3
Mintsfeet Rd South A2
New Rd B2
Noble's Rest B2
Parish Church C2
Park Side Rd C3
Parkside Business
Park C3
Parr St B3
Police Station A2
Post Office A3/B2/C2
Quaker Tapestry✦ B2
Queen's Rd B1
Riverside Walk C2
Rydal Mount A2
Sandes Ave A2
Sandgate A3
Sandylands Rd A3
Serpentine Rd B1
Serpentine Wood B1
Shap Rd A3
South Rd C2
Stainbank Rd C1
Station Rd A3
Stramongate B2
Stramongate Bridge B2
Stricklandgate A2/B2
Sunnyside C3
Thorny Hills B3
Town Hall B2
Undercliff Rd B1
Underwood C1
Union St A2
Vicar's Fields C2
Vicarage Dr C1/C2
Wainwright Yard
Shopping Centre B2
Wasdale Cl C3
Well Ings C2
Westmorland Shopping
Ctr & Market Hall B2
Westwood Ave C1
Wildman St A3
Windermere Rd A1
YHA B2
YWCA B2

King's Lynn 183

Albert St A2
Albion St B2
All Saints B2
All Saints St B2
Austin Fields A2
Austin St A2
Avenue Rd B3
Bank Side B1
Beech Rd C2
Birch Tree Cl B2
Birchwood St A2
Blackfriars Rd B2
Blackfriars St B2
Boal St B1
Bridge St B2
Broad St B2
Broad Walk B3
Burkitt St A2
Bus Station A2
Carmelite Terr C2
Chapel St A2
Chase Ave C3
Checker St C2
Church St B2
Clough La B2
Coburg St B2
College of
West Anglia A3
Columbia Way A3
Corn Exchange A1
County Court Rd B2
Cresswell St A2
Custom House A1
Eastgate St A2
Edma St A2
Exton's Rd C3
Ferry La B1
Ferry St A1
Framingham's
Almshouses B2
Friars St C2
Gaywood Rd A3
George St A2
Gladstone Rd C2
Goodwin's Rd C3
Green Quay✦ B1
Greyfriars' Tower✦ B2
Guanock Terr C2
Guildhall A1
Hansa Rd C3
Hardwick Rd C2
Hextable Rd A2
High St B1
Holcombe Ave C3
Hospital Walk C2
Information Ctr B1
John Kennedy Rd A2
Kettlewell Lane A2
King George V Ave B3
King's Lynn Art
Centre A1
King's Lynn Station B2
King St B1
Library B2
Littleport St A2
Loke Rd A2
London Rd B2
Lynn Mus B2
Majestic B2
Magistrates Court B1
Market La A1
Millfleet B2
Milton Ave A3
Nar Valley Walk C2
Nelson St B1
New Conduit St B2
Norfolk St A2
North St A2
Oldsunway B2
Ouse Ave C1
Page Stair Lane A1
Park Ave B3
Police Station B2
Portland Pl C1
Portland St B2
Post Office A3/B2/C2
Purfleet B1
Queen St B1
Raby Ave A3
Railway Rd A2
Red Mount Chapel B3
Regent Way B2
River Walk A1
Robert St C2
Saddlebow Rd C2
St Ann's St A1
St James' Rd B2
St James St B2
St John's Walk B3
St Margaret's B1
St Nicholas A2
St Nicholas St A1
St Peter's Rd B1
Sir Lewis St A2
Smith Ave A3
South Everard St C2
South Gate✦ C2
South Quay B1
South St B2
Southgate St C2
Stonegate St B2
Surrey St A1
Sydney St C3
Tennyson Ave B3
Tennyson Rd B3
The Friars C2
Tower St B2
Town Hall B1
Town House & Tales
of The Old Gaol
House B1
Town Wall
(Remains)✦ B3
True's Yard Mus A2
Valingers Rd C2
Vancouver Ave C2
Waterloo St B2
Wellesley St B2
White Friars Rd C2
Windsor Rd C2
Winfarthing St C2
Wyatt St A2
York Rd C3

Lancaster 183

Aberdeen Rd C3
Adult College, The C3
Aldcliffe Rd C2
Alfred St B3
Ambleside Rd A3
Ambulance Sta A3
Ashfield Ave B1
Ashton Rd C2
Assembly Rooms,
The B2
Balmoral Rd B3
Bath House B2
Bath Mill La B3
Bath St B3
Blades St B1
Borrowdale Rd B3
Bowerham Rd C3
Brewery La B2
Bridge La B2
Brook St C1
Bulk Rd A3
Bulk St B2
Bus Station B2
Cable St B2
Carlisle Bridge A1
Carr House La C2
Castle B1
Castle Park B1
Caton Rd A3
China St B2
Church St B2
City Mus B2
Clarence St C3
Common Gdn St B2
Coniston Rd A3
Cottage Mus B2
Council Offices B2
Court B2
Cromwell Rd C1
Dale St C3
Dallas Rd B1/C1
Dalton Rd B3
Dalton Sq B2
Damside St B2
De Vitre St B3
Dee Rd A1
Denny Ave A1
Derby Rd A2
Dukes B2
Earl St B2
East Rd B3
Eastham St C3
Edward St B3
Fairfield Rd B1
Fenton St B2
Firbank Rd A3
Fire Station B2
Friend's Meeting
House B1
Garnet St B3
George St B2
Giant Axe Field B1
Gov Offices B2
Grand, The B2
Grasmere Rd B3
Greaves Rd C2
Green St A3
Gregson Centre, The B3
Gregson Rd C3
Greyhound Bridge A2
Greyhound Bridge Rd A2
High St B2
Hill Side B1
Hope St C3
Hubert Pl B1
Information Ctr B2
Judges Lodgings B2
Kelsy St B1
Kentmere Rd B3
King St B2
Kingsway A3
Kirkes Rd C3
Lancaster &
Lakeland C3
Lancaster City Football
Club B1
Lancaster Station B1
Langdale Rd A3
Ley Ct B1
Library B2
Lincoln Rd B1
Lindow St C2
Lodge St B2
Long Marsh La B1
Lune Rd A1
Lune St A2
Lune Valley Ramble A3
Mainway A2
Maritime Mus A1
Market St B2
Marketgate Shopping
Centre B2
Meadowside C2
Meeting House La B1
Millennium Bridge A2
Moor La B2
Moorgate B3
Morecambe Rd A1/A2
Nelson St B2
North Rd B2
Orchard La C1
Owen Rd A2
Park Rd B3
Parliament St A3
Patterdale Rd A3
Penny St B2
Police Station B2
Portland St C2
Post Office
A2/A3/B1/B2/B3/C3
Primrose St C3
Priory B1
Prospect St C3
Quarry Rd B3
Queen St C2
Regent St C2
Ridge La A3
Ridge St A3
Royal Lancaster
Infirmary (A&E) C2
Rydal Rd B3
Ryelands Park A1
St Georges Quay A1
St John's B2
St Leonard's Gate B2
St Martin's Rd C3
St Nicholas Arcades
Shopping Centre B2
St Oswald St C3
St Peter's✝ B3
St Peter's Rd B3
Salisbury Rd B1
Scotch Quarry
Urban Park C3
Shire Hall/HM Prison B1
Sibsey St B1
Skerton Bridge A2
South Rd C2
Station Rd B1
Stirling Rd C3
Storey Ave B1
Sunnyside La C1
Sylvester St C1
Tarnsyke Rd A1
Thurnham St C2
Town Hall B2
Troutbeck Rd B3
Ulleswater Rd B3
University of Cumbria C3
Vicarage Field B1
Vue B2
West Rd B1
Westbourne Dr C1
Westbourne Rd B1
Westham St C3
Wheatfield St B1
White Cross
Education Centre C2
Williamson Rd B3
Willow La B1
Windermere Rd B3
Wingate-Saul Rd B1
Wolseley St B3
Woodville St B3
Wyresdale Rd C3

Leeds 183

Aire St B3
Aireside Centre B2
Albion Pl B4
Albion St B4
Albion Way B1
Alma St A6
Arcades B4
Armley Rd B1
Back Burley Lodge Rd A1
Back Hyde Terr A2
Back Row C3
Bath Rd C3
Beckett St A6
Bedford St B3
Belgrave St A4
Belle View Rd A2
Benson St A5
Black Bull St C5
Blenheim Walk A3
Boar La B4

Stoney St D6
Strand C5
Stratton St D2
Sumner St D5
Sutton's Way B6
Swanfield St B7
Swinton St B4
Tabernacle St B6
Tate Modern🏛 D6
Tavistock Pl B4
Tavistock Sq B3
Tea & Coffee Mus🏛 D6
Temple⊖ D5
Temple Ave D5
Temple Pl D4
Terminus Pl E2
Thayer St C2
The Barbican Centre for Arts C6
The Cut E5
The Mall E3
Theobald's Rd C4
Thorney St F4
Threadneedle St C6
Throgmorton St C6
Tonbridge St B4
Tooley St D7
Torrington Pl B3
Tothill St E3
Tottenham Court Rd B3
Tottenham Court Rd⊖ C3
Tottenham St C3
Tower Bridge✦ D7
Tower Bridge App D7
Tower Bridge Rd E7
Tower Hill⊖ D7
Tower of London, The🏰 D7
Toynbee St C7
Trafalgar Square D3
Trinity Sq D7
Trocadero Centre D3
Tudor St D5
Turnmill St C5
Ufford St E5
Union St D5
University College Hosp⊞ B3
University of London C3
University of Westminster C2
University St B3
Upper Belgrave St E2
Upper Berkeley St C1
Upper Brook St D2
Upper Grosvenor St D2
Upper Ground D5
Upper Montague St C1
Upper St A5
Upper St Martin's La D4
Upper Thames St D6
Upper Wimpole St C2
Upper Woburn Pl B3
Vere St C2
Vernon Pl C4
Vestry St B6
Victoria⊖≋ E2
Victoria Embankment D4
Victoria Place Shopping Centre F2
Victoria St E3
Villiers St D4
Vincent Sq F3
Vinopolis City of Wine🏛 D6
Virginia Rd B7
Wakley St B5
Walbrook C6
Wallace Collection🏛 C2
Wardour St C3/D3
Warner St B5
Warren St⊖ B3
Warren St B3
Waterloo⊖≋ E4
Waterloo Bridge D4
Waterloo East≋ D5
Waterloo Rd E5
Watling St C6
Webber St E5
Welbeck St C2
Wellington Arch✦ E2
Wellington Mus🏛 E2
Wells St C3
Wenlock Rd A6
Wenlock St A6
Wentworth St C7
Werrington St A3
West Smithfield C5
West Sq E5
Westminster⊖ E4
Westminster Abbey✝ E4
Westminster Bridge E4
Westminster Bridge Rd E5
Westminster Cathedral (RC)✝ E3
Westminster City Hall E3
Westminster Hall🏛 E4
Weymouth St C2
Wharf Rd A6
Wharfdale Rd A4
Wharton St B4
Whitcomb St D3
White Cube🏛 B7
White Lion Hill D5
White Lion St A5
Whitecross St B6
Whitefriars St C5
Whitehall D4
Whitehall Pl D4
Wigmore Hall C2
Wigmore St C2
William IV St D4
Wilmington Sq B5
Wilson St C6
Wilton Cres E2
Wimpole St C2
Windmill Walk D5
Woburn Pl B4
Woburn Sq B3
Women's Hosp⊞ C3
Wood St C6
Woodbridge St B5
Wootton St D5
Wormwood St C7
Worship St B6
Wren St B4
Wynford Rd A4
Wynyatt St B5
York Rd E4
York St C1
York Terrace East B2
York Terrace West B2
York Way A4

Luton 186

Adelaide St B1
Albert Rd C2
Alma St B2
Alton Rd C3
Anthony Gdns C1
Arndale Centre B2
Arthur St C2
Ashburnham Rd B1
Ashton Rd C2
Avondale Rd A1
Back St A2
Bailey St C3
Baker St C2
Biscot Rd A1
Bolton Rd B3
Boyle Cl A2
Brantwood Rd B1
Bretts Mead C1
Bridge St B2
Brook St A1
Brunswick St A3
Burr St A3
Bury Park Rd A1
Bus Station B2
Bute St B2
Buxton Rd B2
Cambridge St C3
Cardiff Grove B1
Cardiff Rd B1
Cardigan St A2
Castle St B2/C2
Chapel St C2
Charles St A3
Chase St C2
Cheapside B2
Chequer St C3
Church St B2/B3
Cinema🎦 A2
Cobden St A3
Collingdon St A1
Concorde Ave A3
Corncastle Rd C1
Cowper St C2
Crawley Green Rd B3
Crawley Rd A1
Crescent Rise A3
Crescent Rd A3
Cromwell Rd A1
Cross St A2
Crown Court B2
Cumberland St B2
Cutenhoe Rd C3
Dallow Rd B1
Downs Rd B1
Dudley St A2
Duke St A2
Dumfries St B1
Dunstable Place B2
Dunstable Rd A1/B1
Edward St A3
Elizabeth St C2
Essex Cl C3
Farley Hill C1
Flowers Way B2
Francis St A1
Frederick St A2
Galaxy Leisure Complex A2
George St B2
George St West B2
Gillam St A2
Gordon St B2
Grove Rd B1
Guildford St A2
Haddon Rd A3
Harcourt St C2
Hart Hill Drive A3
Hart Hill Lane A3
Hartley Rd A3
Hastings St B2
Hat Factory, The🎭 B2
Hatters Way A1
Havelock Rd A2
Hibbert St C2
High Town Rd A3
Highbury Rd A1
Hillary Cres C1
Hillborough Rd C1
Hitchin Rd A3
Holly St C2
Holm C1
Hucklesby Way A2
Hunts Cl C1
Information Ctr ℹ B2
Inkerman St A2
John St B2
Jubilee St A3
Kelvin Cl C2
King St B2
Kingsland Rd C3
Latimer Rd C2
Lawn Gdns C2
Lea Rd B3
Library B2
Library Rd B2
Liverpool Rd B1
London Rd C2
Luton Station≋ A2
Lyndhurst Rd B1
Magistrates Court B2
Manchester St B2
Manor Rd B3
May St C3
Meyrick Ave C1
Midland Rd A2
Mill St A2
Milton Rd B1
Moor St A1
Moor, The A1
Moorland Gdns A2
Moulton Rise A3
Mus & Art Gallery🏛 A2
Napier Rd B1
New Bedford Rd A1
New Town St C2
North St A3
Old Bedford Rd A2
Old Orchard C2
Osbourne Rd C3
Oxen Rd A3
Park Sq B2
Park St B3/C3
Park St West B2
Park Viaduct B3
Parkland Drive C1
Police Station B1
Pomfret Ave A3
Pondwicks Rd B3
Post Office A1/A2/B2/C3
Power Court B3
Princess St B1
Red Rails C1
Regent St B2
Reginald St A2
Rothesay Rd B1
Russell Rise C1
Russell St C1
Ruthin Cl C1
St Ann's Rd B3
St George's🎭 B2
St Mary's⛪ B3
St Mary's Rd B3
St Paul's Rd C2
St Saviour's Cres C1
Salisbury Rd B1
Seymour Ave C3
Seymour Rd C3
Silver St B2
South Rd C2
Stanley St B1
Station Rd A2
Stockwood Cres C2
Stockwood Park C1
Strathmore Ave C2
Stuart St B2
Studley Rd A1
Surrey St C3
Sutherland Place C1
Tavistock St C2
Taylor St A3
Telford Way A1
Tennyson Rd C2
Tenzing Grove C1
The Cross Way C1
The Larches A2
Thistle Rd B3
Town Hall B2
Townsley Cl C2
Union St B2
University of Bedfordshire B3
Upper George St B2
Vicarage St B3
Villa Rd A2
Waldeck Rd A1
Wellington St B1/B2
Wenlock St A2
Whitby Rd A1
Whitehill Ave C1
William St A2
Wilsden Ave C1
Windmill Rd B3
Windsor St C2
Winsdon Rd B1
York St A3

Macclesfield 187

108 Steps B2
Abbey Rd A1
Alton Dr A3
Armett St C1
Athey St B1
Bank St C3
Barber St A3
Barton St C1
Beech La A2
Beswick St B1
Black La A2
Black Rd C3
Blakelow Gardens C3
Blakelow Rd C3
Bond St B1/C1
Bread St C1
Bridge St B1
Brock St A2
Brocklehurst Ave A3
Brook St B3
Brookfield La B3
Brough St West C1
Brown St C1
Brynton Rd A2
Buckley St C2
Bus Station B2
Buxton Rd B3
Byrons St C2
Canal St B3
Carlsbrook Ave A3
Castle St B2
Catherine St B1
Cemetery A1
Chadwick Terr A3
Chapel St C2
Charlotte St B2
Chester Rd B1
Chestergate B1
Churchill Way B2
Coare St A1
Commercial Rd B2
Conway Cres A3
Copper St C3
Cottage St B1
Court A2
Court B2
Crematorium A1
Crew Ave A3
Crompton Rd B1/C1
Cross St C2
Crossall St C1
Cumberland St A1/B1
Dale St B3
Duke St B2
Eastgate B3
Exchange St B2
Fence Ave B3
Fence Avenue Industrial Estate A3
Flint St B3
Foden St A2
Fountain St B3
Garden St A3
Gas Rd B2
George St B2
Glegg St B3
Golf Course C3
Goodall St B3
Grange Rd C1
Great King St B1
Green St B3
Grosvenor Shopping Centre B2
Gunco La C3
Half St C2
Hallefield Rd B3
Hatton St C1
Hawthorn Way A3
Heapy St C3
Henderson St B1
Heritage Centre & Silk Mus🏛 B2
Hibel Rd A2
High St C2
Hobson St C2
Hollins Rd C3
Hope St West B1
Horseshoe Dr B1
Hurdsfield Rd A3
Information Ctr ℹ C2
James St C2
Jodrell St B3
John St C2
Jordangate A2
King Edward St B2
King George's Field C3
King St B2
King's School A1
Knight Pool C3
Knight St C3
Lansdowne St A3
Library B2
Lime Gr B3
Little Theatre🎭 C2
Loney St B1
Longacre St B1
Lord St C2
Lowe St C2
Lowerfield Rd A3
Lyon St B1
Macclesfield Station≋ B2
Marina B3
Market B2
Market Pl B2
Masons La A3
Mill La C2
Mill Rd C2
Mill St B2
Moran Rd C1
New Hall St A2
Newton St C1
Nicholson Ave A3
Nicholson Cl A3
Northgate Ave A2
Old Mill La C2
Paradise Mill🏛 C2
Paradise St B1
Park Green B2
Park La C1
Park Rd C1
Park St C2
Park Vale Rd C1
Parr St B1
Peel St C2
Percyvale St A3
Peter St C1
Pickford St B2
Pierce St B1
Pinfold St B1
Pitt St C2
Police Station B2
Pool St C2
Poplar Rd C2
Post Office B1/B2/B3
Pownall St A2
Prestbury Rd A1/B1
Queen Victoria St B2
Queen's Ave A3
Registrar B2
Richmond Hill C3
Riseley St B1
Roan Ct B3
Roe St B2
Rowan Way A3
Ryle St C2
Ryle's Park Rd C1
St George's St C2
St Michael's⛪ B2
Samuel St B2
Saville St C3
Shaw St B1
Slater St C1
Snow Hill C3
South Park C1
Spring Gdns A2
Statham St C2
Station St A2
Steeple St A3
Sunderland St B2
Superstore A1/A2/C2
Swettenham St B3
The Silk Rd A2/B2
Thistleton Cl C2
Thorp St B2
Town Hall B2
Townley St B2
Turnock St C3
Union Rd B3
Union St B2
Victoria Park B3
Vincent St C2
Waters Green B2
Waterside C2
West Bond St B1
West Park A1
Westbrook Dr A1
Westminster Rd A1
Whalley Hayes B1
Windmill St C3
Withyfold Dr A2
York St B3

Maidstone 187

Albion Pl B3
All Saints⛪ B2
Allen St A3
Amphitheatre✦ C2
Archbishop's Palace🏰 B2
Bank St B2
Barker Rd C2
Barton Rd C3
Beaconsfield Rd C1
Bedford Pl B1
Bentlif Art Gallery🏛 B2
Bishops Way B2
Bluett St A3
Bower La C1
Bower Mount Rd B1
Bower Pl C1
Bower St B1
Bowling Alley B3
Boxley Rd A3
Brenchley Gardens A2
Brewer St A3
Broadway B2
Brunswick St C3
Buckland Hill A1
Buckland Rd B1
Bus Station B3
Campbell Rd C3
Carriage Mus🏛 B2
Church Rd C1
Church St B3
Cinema🎦 C2
College Ave C2
College Rd C2
Collis Memorial Garden C3
Cornwallis Rd B1
Corpus Christi Hall B2
County Hall A2
County Rd A3
Crompton Gdns C3
Crown & County Courts B2
Curzon Rd A3
Dixon Cl C2
Douglas Rd C1
Earl St B2
Eccleston Rd C2
Fairmeadow B2
Fisher St A2
Florence Rd C1
Foley St A3
Foster St C3
Fremlin Walk Shopping Centre B2
Gabriel's Hill B3
George St C3
Grecian St A3
Hardy St A3
Hart St C2
Hastings Rd C3
Hayle Rd C3
Hazlitt Theatre🎭 B2
Heathorn St A3
Hedley St A3
High St B2
HM Prison A3
Holland Rd A3
Hope St A2
Information Ctr ℹ B2
James St A3
James Whatman Way A2
Jeffrey St A3
Kent County Council Offices A2
King Edward Rd C2
King St B3
Kingsley Rd C3
Knightrider St B3
Launder Way C1
Lesley Pl A1
Library B2
Little Buckland Ave A1
Lockmeadow Leisure Complex C2
London Rd B1
Lower Boxley Rd A2
Lower Fant Rd C1
Magistrates Court B3
Maidstone Barracks Station≋ A1
Maidstone Borough Council Offices B1
Maidstone East Station≋ A2
Maidstone Mus🏛 B2
Maidstone West Station≋ B2
Market C2
Market Buildings B2
Marsham St B3
Medway St B2
Medway Trading Estate C2
Melville Rd C3
Mill St B2
Millennium Bridge C2
Mote Rd B3
Muir Rd C3
Old Tovil Rd C2
Palace Ave B3
Perryfield St A2
Police Station B3
Post Office A2/B2/B3/C3
Priory Rd C3
Prospect Pl C1
Pudding La B2
Queen Anne Rd B3
Queens Rd A1
Randall St A2
Rawdon Rd C3
Reginald Rd C1
Rock Pl B1
Rocky Hill B1
Romney Pl B3
Rose Yard B2
Rowland Cl C1
Royal Engineers' Rd A2
Royal Star Arcade B2
St Annes Ct B1
St Faith's St B2
St Luke's Rd A3
St Peter's Br B2
St Peter St B2
St Philip's Ave C3
Salisbury Rd A3
Sandling Rd A2
Scott St A2
Scrubs La B1
Sheal's Cres C3
Somerfield La B1
Somerfield Rd B1
Staceys St A2
Station Rd A2
Superstore A1/B2/B3
Terrace Rd B1
The Mall B3
The Somerfield Hosp⊞ A1
Tonbridge Rd C1
Tovil Rd C2
Town Hall B2
Trinity Park B3
Tufton St B3
Union St B3
Upper Fant Rd C1
Upper Stone St C3
Victoria St B1
Visitor Centre A1
Warwick Pl B1
Wat Tyler Way B3
Waterloo St C3
Waterlow Rd A3
Week St B2
Well Rd A3
Westree Rd C1
Wharf Rd C1
Whatman Park A1
Wheeler St A3
Whitchurch Cl B1
Woodville Rd C3
Wyatt St B3
Wyke Manor Rd B3

Manchester 187

Adair St B6
Addington St A5
Adelphi St A1
Air & Space Gallery🏛 B2
Albert Sq B3
Albion St C3
AMC Great Northern🎦 B3
Ancoats Gr B6
Ancoats Gr North B6
Angela St C2
Aquatic Centre C4
Ardwick Green C5
Ardwick Green North C5
Ardwick Green South C5
Arlington St A2
Arndale Centre A4
Artillery St B3
Arundel St C2
Atherton St B2
Atkinson St B3
Aytoun St B4
Back Piccadilly A4
Baird St B5
Balloon St A4
Bank Pl A1
Baring St B5
Barrack St C1
Barrow St A1
BBC TV Studios C4
Bendix St A5
Bengal St A5
Berry St C5
Blackfriars Rd A3
Blackfriars St A3
Blantyre St C2
Bloom St B4
Blossom St A5
Boad St B5
Bombay St B4
Booth St A3
Booth St B4
Bootle St B3
Brazennose St B3
Brewer St A5
Bridge St A3
Bridgewater Hall B3
Bridgewater Pl A4
Bridgewater St B2
Brook St C4
Brotherton Dr A2
Brown St A3
Brown St B4
Brunswick St C6
Brydon Ave C6
Buddhist Centre A4
Bury St A2
Bus & Coach Station B4
Bus Station B4
Butler St A6
Buxton St C5
Byrom St B3
Cable St A5
Calder St B1
Cambridge St C3/C4
Camp St B3
Canal St B4
Cannon St A1
Cannon St A4
Cardroom Rd A6
Carruthers St A6
Castle St C2
Cateaton St A3
Cathedral✝ A3
Cathedral St A3
Cavendish St C4
Chapel St A1/A3
Chapeltown St B5
Charles St C4
Charlotte St B4
Chatham St B4
Cheapside A3
Chepstow St B3
Chester Rd C1/C2
Chester St C4
Chetham's (Dept Store) A3
China La B5
Chippenham Rd A6
Chorlton Rd C2
Chorlton St B4
Church St A2
Church St A4
City Park A4
City Rd C3
Civil Justice Centre B2
Cleminson St A2
Clowes St A3
College Land A3
College of Adult Education C4
Collier St B2
Commercial St C3
Conference Centre C4
Cooper St B4
Copperas St A4
Cornbrook (Metro Station) C1
Cornell St A5
Cornerhouse🎦 C4
Corporation St A4
Cotter St C6
Cotton St A5
Cow La B1
Cross St B3
Crown Court B4
Crown St C2
Cube Gallery🏛 B4
Dalberg St C6
Dale St A4/B5
Dancehouse, The🎭 C4
Dantzic St A4
Dark La C6
Dawson St C2
Dean St A5
Deansgate A3/B3
Deansgate Station≋ C3
Dolphin St C6
Downing St C5
Ducie St B5
Duke Pl B2
Duke St B2
Durling St C6
East Ordsall La A2/B1
Edge St A4
Egerton St C2
Ellesmere St C1
Everard St C1
Every St B6
Fairfield St B5
Faulkner St B4
Fennel St A3
Ford St A2
Ford St C6
Fountain St B4
Frederick St A2
Gartside St B2
Gaythorne St A1
George Leigh St A5
George St A1
George St B4
G-Mex (Metro Station) C3
Goadsby St A4
Gore St A2
Goulden St A5
Granada TV Studios B2
Granby Row B4
Gravel St A3
Great Ancoats St A5
Great Bridgewater St B3
Great George St A1
Great Jackson St C2
Great Marlborough St C4
Greengate A3
Green Room, The🎭 C4
Grosvenor St C5
Gun St A5
Hadrian Ave B6
Hall St B3
Hampson St B1
Hanover St A4
Hanworth Cl C5
Hardman St B3
Harkness St C6
Harrison St B6
Hart St B4
Helmet St B6
Henry St A5
Heyrod St B6
High St A4
Higher Ardwick C6
Hilton St A4/A5
Holland St A6
Hood St A5
Hope St B1
Hope St B4
Houldsworth St A5
Hoyle St C6
Hulme Hall Rd C1
Hulme St A1
Hulme St C3
Hyde Rd C6
Information Ctr ℹ B3
Irwell St A2
Islington St A2
Jackson Cr C2
Jackson's Row B3
James St A1
Jenner Cl C2
Jersey St A5
John Dalton St A1
John Dalton St B3
John Ryland's Library🏛 B3
John St A3
Kennedy St B3
Kincardine Rd C5
King St A3
King St West A3
Law Courts B3
Laystall St B5
Lever St A5
Library B3
Library Theatre🎭 B3
Linby St C2
Little Lever St A4
Liverpool Rd B2
Liverpool St B1
Lloyd St B3
Lockton Cl C5
London Rd B5
Long Millgate A3
Longacre St B6
Loom St A5
Lower Byrom St B2
Lower Mosley St B3
Lower Moss La C2
Lower Ormond St C4
Loxford La C4
Luna St A5
Major St B4
Manchester Art Gallery🏛 B4
Manchester Central B3
Manchester Metropolitan University B4/C4
Mancunian Way C3
Manor St C5
Marble St A4
Market St A2
Market St A4
Market St (Metro Station) A4
Marsden St A3
Marshall St A5
Mayan Ave A2
Medlock St C3
Middlewood St B1
Miller St A4
Minshull St B4
Mosley St A4
Mosley St (Metro Station) B4
Mount St B3
Mulberry St B3
Murray St A5
Mus of Science & Technology🏛 B2
Nathan Dr A2
National Computer Centre C4
Naval St A5
New Bailey St A2
New Elm Rd B2
New Islington A6
New Quay St B2
New Union St A6
Newgate St A4
Newton St A5
Nicholas St B4
North Western St C6
Oak St A4
Odeon🎦 A4
Old Mill St A6
Oldfield Rd A1/C1
Oldham Rd A5
Oldham St A4
Opera House🎭 B3
Ordsall La C1
Oxford Rd C4
Oxford Rd≋ C4
Oxford St B4
Paddock St C6
Palace Theatre🎭 B4
Pall Mall A3
Palmerston St B6
Park St A1
Parker St B4
Peak St B5
Penfield Cl C5
Peoples' History Mus🏛 B2
Peru St A1
Peter St B3
Piccadilly A4
Piccadilly (Metro Station) B5
Piccadilly Gdns (Metro Station) B4
Piccadilly Station≋ B5
Piercy St A6
Poland St A5
Police Station B3/B5
Pollard St B6
Port St A5
Portland St B4
Portugal St East B5
Post Office A1/A4/A5/B3
Potato Wharf B2
Princess St B3/C4
Pritchard St
Quay St
Quay St
Queen St
Radium St
Redhill St
Regent Rd
Renold Theatre🎭
Retail Park
Rice St
Richmond St
River St
Roby St
Rodney St
Roman Fort✦
Rosamond St
Royal Exchange🎭
Sackville St
St Andrew's St
St Ann St
St Ann's⛪
St George's Ave
St James St
St John St
St John's Cathedral (RC)✝
St Mary's⛪
St Mary's Gate
St Mary's Parsonage
St Peter's Sq (Metro Station)
St Stephen St
Salford Approach
Salford Central≋
Sheffield St
Shepley St
Sherratt St
Shudehill
Shudehill (Metro Station)
Sidney St
Silk St
Silver St
Skerry Cl
Snell St
South King St
Sparkle St
Spear St
Spring Gdns
Stanley St A2
Station Approach
Store St
Swan St
Tariff St
Tatton St
Temperance St B6/
The Triangle
Thirsk St
Thomas St
Thompson St
Tib La
Tib St
Town Hall (Manchester)
Town Hall (Salford)
Trafford St
Travis St
Trinity Way
Turner St
Union St
University of Manchester (Sackvill Street Campus)
Upper Brook St
Upper Cleminson St
Upper Wharf St
Urbis Mus🏛
Vesta St
Victoria (Metro Station)
Victoria Station≋
Victoria St
Wadesdon Rd
Water St
Watson St
West Fleet St
West King St
West Mosley St
West Union St
Weybridge Rd
Whitworth St
Whitworth St West
Wilburn St
William St
William St
Wilmott St
Windmill St
Windsor Cr
Withy Gr
Woden St
Wood St
Woodward St
Worrall St
Worsley St
York St
York St
York St

Merthyr Tydfil
Merthyr Tudful 1

Aberdare Rd
Abermorlais Terr
Alexandra Rd
Alma St
Arfryn Pl
Argyle St
Avenue De Clichy
Bethesda St
Bishops Gr
Brecon Rd A1/
Briarmead
Bryn St
Bryntirion Rd B3/
Bus Station
Caedraw Rd
Cae Mari Dwn
Castle Sq
Castle St

206 Norwich • Nottingham • Oban • Oxford • Perth • Peterborough • Plymouth

Bailiff St A2
Barrack Rd A2
Beaconsfield Terr A3
Becketts Park C3
Bedford Rd B3
Billing Rd B3
Brecon St A1
Brewery C2
Bridge St C2
Bridge St Depot C3
Broad St B2
Burns St A3
Bus Station B2
Campbell St A2
Castle (Site of) B2
Castle St B2
Cattle Market Rd C2
Central Mus & Art Gallery B2
Charles St A3
Cheyne Walk B3
Church La A2
Clare St A3
Cloutsham St A3
College St B2
Colwyn Rd A3
Cotton End C2
Countess Rd A1
County Hall B2
Court A2
Craven St A3
Crown & County Courts B3
Denmark Rd B3
Derngate B3
Derngate & Royal Theatres B3
Doddridge Church B2
Duke St A3
Earl St A3
Euston Rd C2
Fire Station A3
Foot Meadow B2
Gladstone Rd A1
Gold St B2
Grafton St A2
Gray St A3
Greenwood Rd B1
Greyfriars B2
Grosvenor Centre B2
Grove Rd A3
Guildhall B2
Hampton St A2
Harding Terr A2
Hazelwood Rd B3
Herbert St B2
Hervey St A3
Hester St A2
Holy Sepulchre A2
Hood St A3
Horse Market B2
Hunter St A3
Information Ctr B1
Kettering Rd A3
Kingswell St B2
Lady's La B2
Leicester St A2
Leslie Rd A2
Library B3
Lorne Rd A2
Lorry Park A1
Louise Rd A2
Lower Harding St A2
Lower Hester St A2
Lower Mounts B3
Lower Priory St A2
Main Rd C1
Marefair B2
Market Sq B2
Marlboro Rd B1
Marriott St A2
Military Rd A3
Nene Valley Retail Park C1
New South Bridge Rd C2
Northampton General Hospital (A & E) B3
Northampton Station B1
Northcote St A2
Nunn Mills Rd C3
Old Towcester Rd C2
Overstone Rd A3
Peacock Pl B2
Pembroke Rd A1
Penn Court C2
Police Station B3
Post Office A1/A2/B3/C2
Quorn Way A2
Ransome Rd C3
Regent Sq A2
Retail Park C2
Robert St A2
St Andrew's Rd B1
St Andrew's St A2
St Edmund's Rd B3
St George's St A2
St Giles B3
St Giles St B3
St Giles' Terr B3
St James' Mill Rd B1
St James' Mill Rd East C1
St James Park Rd B1
St James Retail & Leisure Park C1
St James Rd B1
St Leonard's Rd C2
St Mary's St B2
St Michael's Rd A3
St Peter's B2
St Peter's Square Shopping Precinct B2
St Peter's Way B2
Salisbury St A2
Scarletwell St B2
Semilong Rd A2
Sheep St B2
Sol Central (Leisure Centre) B2
South Bridge C2
Southfield Ave C2
Spencer Bridge Rd A1
Spencer Rd A3
Spring Gdns B3
Spring La B2
Swan St B3
The Drapery B2
The Ridings B3
Tintern Ave A1
Towcester Rd C2
Upper Bath St B2
Upper Mounts A2
Victoria Park A1
Victoria Promenade B2
Victoria Rd B3
Victoria St A2
Wellingborough Rd B3
West Bridge B1
York Rd B3

Norwich 189

Albion Way C3
All Saints Green C2
Anchor Cl A3
Anchor St A3
Anglia Sq A2
Argyle St C3
Arts Centre B1
Ashby St C2
Assembly House B1
Bank Plain B2
Barker St A1
Barn Rd A1
Barrack St A3
Ber St C2
Bethel St B1
Bishop Bridge A3
Bishopbridge Rd A3
Bishopgate A3
Blackfriars St A2
Botolph St A2
Bracondale C3
Brazen Gate C2
Bridewell B2
Brunswick Rd C1
Bull Close Rd A2
Bus Station C2
Calvert St A2
Cannell Green A3
Carrow Rd C3
Castle Mall B2
Castle Meadow B2
Castle & Mus B2
Cathedral B2
Cattlemarket St B2
Chantry Rd C1
Chapel Loke C2
Chapelfield East B1
Chapelfield Gdns B1
Chapelfield North B1
Chapelfield Rd B1
Chapelfield Shopping Centre C1
City Hall B1
City Rd C2
City Wall C1/C3
Colegate A2
Coslany St B1
Cow Hill B1
Cow Tower A3
Cowgate A2
Crown & Magistrates Courts A2
Dragon Hall Heritage Centre C3
Duke St A1
Edward St A2
Elm Hill B2
Erpingham Gate B2
Fire Station B1
Fishergate A2
Foundry Bridge B3
Fye Bridge A2
Garden St C2
Gas Hill B3
Grapes Hill B1
Great Hospital Halls, The A3
Grove Ave C1
Grove Rd C1
Guildhall B1
Gurney Rd A3
Hall Rd C2
Heathgate A3
Heigham St A1
Horn's La C2
Information Ctr B1
Inspire (Science Centre) A1
Ipswich Rd C1
James Stuart Gdns B3
King Edward VI School B2
King St B2
King St C3
Koblenz Ave C3
Library B1
London St B2
Lower Clarence Rd B3
Lower Cl B3
Maddermarket B1
Magdalen St A2
Mariners La C2
Market B2
Market Ave B2
Mountergate B3
Mousehold St A3
Newmarket Rd C1
Norfolk Gallery B2
Norfolk St C1
Norwich City FC C3
Norwich Station B3
Oak St A1
Palace St A2
Pitt St A1
Playhouse B2
Post Office A2/B2/C2
Pottergate B1
Prince of Wales Rd B2
Princes St B2
Pull's Ferry B3
Puppet Theatre A2
Quebec Rd B3
Queen St B2
Queens Rd C2
Recorder Rd B3
Retail Park C3
Riverside Entertainment Centre C3
Riverside Swimming Centre C3
Riverside Rd B3
Rosary Rd B3
Rose La B2
Rouen Rd C2
Royal Norfolk Regiment Mus B2
St Andrew's & Blackfriars Hall B2
St Andrews St B2
St Augustines St A1
St Benedicts St B1
St Ethelbert's Gate B2
St Faiths La B3
St Georges St A2
St Giles St B1
St James Cl A3
St Julians C2
St Martin's La A1
St Peter Mancroft B2
St Peters St B1
St Stephens Rd C1
St Stephens St C1
Silver Rd A2
Silver St A2
Southwell Rd C2
Strangers Hall B1
Superstore C2
Surrey St C2
Sussex St A1
The Close B3
The Forum B1
The Walk B2
Theatre Royal B1
Theatre St B1
Thorn La C2
Thorpe Rd B3
Tombland B2
Union St C1
Vauxhall St B1
Victoria St C1
Walpole St B1
Wensum St A2
Wessex St C1
Westwick St A1
Wherry Rd C3
Whitefriars A2
Willow La B1
Yacht Station B3

Nottingham 189

Abbotsford Dr A3
Addison St A1
Albert Hall B1
Alfred St South A3
Alfreton Rd B1
All Saints Rd A1
Annesley Gr A2
Arboretum A1
Arboretum St A1
Arthur St A1
Arts Theatre B3
Ashforth St A3
Balmoral Rd A1
Barker Gate B3
Bath St B3
Belgrave Centre B1
Bellar Gate B3
Belward St B3
Blue Bell Hill Rd B3
Brewhouse Yard C2
Broad Marsh Bus Station C2
Broad Marsh Precinct C2
Broad St B3
Brook St B3
Burns St A1
Burton St B2
Bus Station A2
Canal St C2
Carlton St B3
Carrington St C2
Castle Blvd C1
Castle C2
Castle Gate C2
Castle Meadow Retail Park C1
Castle Meadow Rd C2
Castle Mus & Gallery C2
Castle Rd C2
Castle Wharf C2
Cavendish Rd East C1
Cemetery B1
Chaucer St B1
Cheapside B2
Church Rd A3
City Link C3
City of Caves C2
Clarendon St B1
Cliff Rd C3
Clumber Rd East C1
Clumber St B2
College St B1
Collin St C2
Conway Cl A2
Council House B2
Court B2
Cranbrook St B3
Cranmer St A2
Cromwell St B1
Curzon St B3
Derby Rd B1
Dryden St A2
Fishpond Dr C1
Fletcher Gate B3
Forest Rd East A1
Forest Rd West A1
Friar La C2
Galleries of Justice C3
Gedling Gr A1
Gedling St B3
George St B3
Gill St A2
Glasshouse St B2
Goldsmith St B2
Goose Gate B3
Great Freeman St A2
Guildhall B2
Hamilton Dr C1
Hampden St A1
Heathcote St B3
High Pavement C3
High School (tram stop) A1
Holles Cr C1
Hope Dr C1
Hungerhill Rd A3
Huntingdon Dr C1
Huntingdon St A2
Information Ctr B2
Instow Rise A3
International Community Centre A2
Kent St B3
King St B2
Lace Centre, The C2
Lace Market (tram stop) B3
Lace Market Theatre C3
Lamartine St B3
Lenton Rd C1
Lewis Cl A3
Lincoln St B2
London Rd C3
Long Row B2
Low Pavement C2
Lower Parliament St B3
Magistrates Court C2
Maid Marian Way B2
Mansfield Rd A2/B2
Middle Hill C2
Milton St B2
Mount St B2
National Ice Centre C3
Newcastle Dr B1
Newstead Gr A2
North Sherwood St A2
Nottingham Arena C3
Nottingham Station C3
Old Market Square (tram stop) B2
Oliver St A1
Park Dr C1
Park Row C1
Park Terr B1
Park Valley C1
Peas Hill Rd A3
Peel St A1
Pelham St B2
Peveril Dr C1
Plantagenet St A3
Playhouse Theatre B1
Plumptre St C3
Police Station B2
Poplar St C3
Portland Rd B1
Post Office B2
Queen's Rd C3
Raleigh St A1
Regent St B1
Rick St B3
Robin Hood Statue C2
Robin Hood St B3
Royal Centre (tram stop) B2
Royal Children Inn C2
Royal Concert Hall B2
St Ann's Hill Rd A2
St Ann's Way A2
St Ann's Well Rd A3
St Barnabas B1
St James' St B2
St Mark's St B3
St Mary's Garden of Rest B3
St Mary's Gate B3
St Nicholas C2
St Peter's C2
St Peter's Gate B2
Salutation Inn C2
Shakespeare St B2
Shelton St A2
South Pde B2
South Rd C1
South Sherwood St B2
Station St C3
Station Street (tram stop) C3
Stoney St B3
Talbot St B1
Tales of Robin Hood C2
Tattershall Dr C1
Tennis Dr B1
Tennyson St A1
The Park C1
The Ropewalk B1
Theatre Royal B2
Trent St C3
Trent University A2/B2
Trent University (tram stop) B2
Trinity Square Shopping Centre B2
Trip To Jerusalem Inn C2
Union Rd B3
Upper Parliament St B2
Victoria Centre B2
Victoria Leisure Centre B3
Victoria Park B3
Victoria St B2
Walter St A1
Warser Gate B3
Watkin St A2
Waverley St A1
Wheeler Gate B2
Wilford Rd C2
Wilford St C2
Willoughby House C2
Wollaton St B1
Woodborough Rd A2
Woolpack La B3
York St A2

Oban 189

Aird's Cres B2
Albany St B2
Albert La A2
Albert Rd A2
Alma Cres B1
Ambulance Station C2
Angus Terr C3
Ardconnel Rd A2
Ardconnel Terr B2
Argyll Sq B2
Argyll St B2
Atlantis Leisure Centre A2
Bayview Rd A1
Benvoulin Rd A2
Bowling Green A2
Breadalbane St A2
Bus Station B2
Campbell St B2
College B2
Colonsay Terr C3
Columba Building B2
Combie St B2
Corran Brae A1
Corran Esplanade A1/A2
Corran Halls A2
Court B2
Crannaig-a-Mhinisteir B1
Crannog La C2
Croft Ave A2
Dalintart Dr C3
Dalriach Rd A2
Drummore Rd C2
Duncraggan Rd A2
Dunollie Rd A2
Dunuaran Rd B1
Feochan Gr C3
Ferry Terminal B1
Gallanach Rd B1
George St A2
Glencruitten Dr C3
Glencruitten Rd B3
Glenmore Rd C1
Glenshellach Rd C1
Glenshellach Terr B2
Harbour Bowl B2
Hazeldean Cres A3
High St B2
Highland Theatre Cinema A2
Hill St B2
Industrial Estate C2
Information Ctr B2
Islay Rd C3
Jacob's Ladder B2
Jura Rd C3
Knipoch Pl C3
Laurel Cres A2
Laurel Rd A2/A3
Library B1
Lifeboat Station B1
Lighthouse Pier B1
Lismore Cres A2
Lochavullin Dr B2
Lochavullin Rd C2
Lochside St B2
Longsdale Cres A3
Longsdale Rd A2/A3
Longsdale Terr A3
Lunga Rd C3
Lynn Rd C2
Market St B2
McCaig Rd C3
McCaig's Tower A2
Mill La C2
Miller Rd C2
Millpark Ave C2
Millpark Rd C2
Mossfield Ave B3
Mossfield Dr B3
Mossfield Stadium B3
Nant Dr C3
Nelson Rd C2
North Pier B2
Nursery La A2
Oban B2
Police Station B2
Polvinister Rd B3
Post Office A2/B2
Pulpit Dr C1
Pulpit Hill C1
Pulpit Hill Viewpoint B1
Quarry Rd C2
Queen's Park Pl B2
Railway Quay B2
Rockfield Rd B2
St Columba's A1
St John's B2
Scalpay Terr C3
Shore St B1
Shuna Terr C3
Sinclair Dr C2
Soroba Rd B2/C2
South Pier B2
Stevenson St B2
Tweedale St B2
Ulva Rd C2
Villa Rd B1
War & Peace A2

Oxford 189

Adelaide St A1
Albert St A1
All Souls (Coll) B2
Ashmolean Mus B2
Balliol (Coll) B2
Banbury Rd A2
Bate Collection of Musical Instruments C2
Beaumont St B1
Becket St B1
Blackhall Rd A2
Blue Boar St B2
Bodleian Library B2
Botanic Garden B3
Brasenose (Coll) B2
Brewer St C2
Broad St B2
Burton-Taylor Theatre B2
Bus Station B1
Canal St A1
Cardigan St A1
Carfax Tower B2
Castle B1
Castle St B1
Catte St B2
Cemetery C1
Christ Church (Coll) B2
Christ Church Cathedral C2
Christ Church Meadow C2
Clarendon Centre B2
Coach & Lorry Park C1
College B3
College of Further Education C1
Cornmarket St B2
Corpus Christi (Coll) B2
County Hall B1
Covered Market B2
Cowley Pl C3
Cranham St A1
Cranham Terr A1
Cricket Ground B1
Crown & County Courts C2
Deer Park B3
Exeter (Coll) B2
Folly Bridge C2
George St B1
Great Clarendon St A1
Hart St A1
Hertford (Coll) B2
High St B3
Hollybush Row B1
Holywell St B2
Hythe Bridge St B1
Ice Rink C1
Information Ctr B2
Jericho St A1
Jesus (Coll) B2
Jowett Walk B3
Juxon St A1
Keble (Coll) A2
Keble Rd A2
Library B2
Linacre (Coll) A3
Lincoln (Coll) B2
Little Clarendon St A1
Longwall St B3
Magdalen (Coll) B3
Magdalen Bridge B2
Magdalen St B2
Magistrate's Court C2
Manchester (Coll) B2
Manor Rd B3
Mansfield (Coll) A2
Mansfield Rd A3
Market B1
Marlborough Rd C2
Martyrs' Memorial B2
Merton Field B3
Merton (Coll) B3
Merton St B2
Mus of Modern Art B2
Mus of Oxford B2
Museum Rd A2
New College (Coll) B3
New Inn Hall St B2
New Rd B1
New Theatre B2
Norfolk St C1
Nuffield (Coll) B1
Observatory A1
Observatory St A1
Odeon B1/B2
Old Fire Station B1
Old Greyfriars St C2
Oriel (Coll) B2
Oxford Station B1
Oxford Story, The B2
Oxford University Research Centres A1
Oxpens Rd C1
Paradise Sq C1
Paradise St B1
Park End St B1
Parks Rd A2/B2
Pembroke (Coll) C2
Phoenix A1
Picture Gallery C2
Plantation Rd A1
Playhouse B2
Police Station C2
Post Office A1/B2
Pusey St B1
Queen's La B3
Queen's (Coll) B3
Radcliffe Camera B2
Rewley Rd B1
Richmond Rd A1
Rose La B3
Ruskin (Coll) B1
Saïd Business School B1
St Aldates C2
St Anne's (Coll) A1
St Antony's (Coll) A1
St Bernard's Rd A1
St Catherine's (Coll) B3
St Cross Building A3
St Cross Rd A3
St Edmund Hall (Coll) B3
St Giles St A2
St Hilda's (Coll) C3
St John St B2
St John's (Coll) B2
St Mary the Virgin B2
St Michael at the Northgate B2
St Peter's (Coll) B1
St Thomas St B1
Science Area A2
Science Mus B2
Sheldonian Theatre B2
Somerville (Coll) A1
South Parks Rd A2
Speedwell St C2
Sports Ground C3
Thames St C2
Town Hall B2
Trinity (Coll) B2
Turl St B2
University College (Coll) B3
University Mus & Pitt Rivers Mus A2
University Parks A2
Wadham (Coll) B2
Walton Cr A1
Walton St A1
Western Rd C2
Westgate Shopping Centre B2
Woodstock Rd A1
Worcester (Coll) B1

Perth 189

A K Bell Library B2
Abbot Cres C1
Abbot St C1
Albany Terr A1
Albert Monument A3
Alexandra St B2
Art Gallery B3
Atholl St A2
Balhousie Ave A2
Balhousie Castle Black Watch Mus A2
Balhousie St A2
Ballantine Pl A1
Barossa Pl A2
Barossa St A2
Barrack St A2
Bell's Sports Centre A2
Bellwood B3
Blair St B1
Burn Park C1
Bus Station B2
Caledonian Rd B2
Canal Cres B2
Canal St B3
Cavendish Ave C1
Charles St B2
Charlotte Pl A2
Charlotte St A3
Church St A1
City Hall B3
Club House C3
Clyde Pl C1
Commercial St A3
Concert Hall B3
Council Chambers B3
County Pl B2
Court B3
Craigie Pl C2
Crieff Rd A1
Croft Park C2
Cross St B2
Darnhall Cres C1
Darnhall Dr C1
Dundee Rd B3
Dunkeld Rd A1
Earl's Dykes B1
Edinburgh Rd C3
Elibank St B1
Fair Maid's House A3
Fergusson B3
Feus Rd A1
Fire Station A1
Fitness Centre B3
Foundary La A2
Friar St C1
George St B3
Glamis Pl C1
Glasgow Rd B1
Glenearn Rd C2
Glover St B1/C1
Golf Course A2
Gowrie St A3
Gray St B1
Graybank Rd B1
Greyfriars Burial Grnd B3
Hay St A2
High St B2/B3
Hotel B2
Ice Rinks B1
Inchaffray St A1
Industrial/Retail Park B1
Information Ctr B2
Isla Rd A3
James St B2
Keir St A3
King Edward St B3
King James VI Golf Course C3
King St B2
Kings Pl C2
Kinnoull Causeway B2
Kinnoull Aisle 'Monument' B3
Kinnoull St B2
Knowelea Pl C1
Knowelea Terr C1
Ladeside Business Centre A1
Leisure Pool B1
Leonard St B2
Lickley St B2
Lochie Brae A3
Long Causeway A1
Low St A2
Main St A3
Marshall Pl C3
Melville St A2
Mill St B3
Milne St B2
Murray Cres C1
Murray St B2
Needless Rd C1
New Rd B2
North Inch A3
North Methven St A2
Park Pl C1
Perth B2
Perth Bridge A3
Perth Business Park B1
Perth Station C2
Pickletulllum Rd B1
Pitheavlis Cres C1
Playhouse B2
Police Station A2
Pomarium St B2
Post Office A3/B2/C2
Princes St B3
Priory Pl C2
Queen St C1
Queen's Bridge B3
Riggs Rd B1
Riverside B3
Riverside Park B3
Rodney Park B3
Rose Terr A2
St Catherines Retail Park A1
St Catherine's Rd A1/A2
St John St B3
St John's Kirk B3
St John's Shopping Centre B2
St Leonards Bridge C2
St Ninians Cathedral A2
Scott Monument C2
Scott St B2
Sheriff Court B3
Shore Rd C3
Skate Park C3
South Inch C2
South Inch Business Centre C3
South Inch Park C2
South Inch View C2
South Methven St B2
South St B3
South William St B2
Stormont St A2
Strathmore St A3
Stuart Ave C1
Tay St B3
The Stables A1
The Stanners B3
Union La A2
Victoria St B2
Watergate B3
Wellshill Cemetery A1
West Bridge St A3
West Mill St B2
Whitefriers Cres B1
Whitefriers St B1
Wilson St C1
Windsor Terr C1
Woodside Cres C1
York Pl B2
Young St C1

Peterborough 189

Bishop's Palace B2
Bishop's Rd B2/B3
Boongate A3
Bourges Boulevard A1
Bread St C1
Bourges Retail Park B1/B2
Bridge House (Council Offices) C2
Bridge St B2
Bright St A1
Broadway A2
Broadway A2
Brook St A2
Burghley Rd A2
Bus Station B2
Cavendish St A3
Charles St A3
Church St B2
Church Walk A2
Cobden Ave A1
Cobden St A1
Cowgate B2
Craig St A2
Crawthorne Rd A2
Cripple Sidings La C2
Cromwell Rd A1
Dickens St A3
Eastfield Rd A3
Eastgate B3
Fire Station A1
Fletton Ave C2
Frank Perkins Parkway C3
Geneva St A2
George St C1
Gladstone St A1
Glebe Rd C2
Gloucester Rd C3
Granby St B3
Grove St C1
Guildhall B2
Hadrians Ct C3
Henry St A2
Hereward Rd B3
Information Ctr B2
Jubilee St
Key Theatre
Kent Rd
Kirkwood Cl
Lea Gdns
Library
Lincoln Rd
London Rd
Long Causeway
Lower Bridge St
Magistrates Court
Manor House St
Mayor's Walk
Midland Rd
Monument St
Mus & Art Gallery
Nene Valley Railway
New Rd
New Rd
North Minster
Old Customs House
Oundle Rd
Padholme Rd
Palmerston Rd
Park Rd
Passport Office
Peterborough Distric[t] Hospital (A+E)
Peterborough Station
Peterborough Nene Valley
Peterborough United FC
Police Station
Post Office A3/B1/B2/B3
Priestgate
Queen's Walk
Queensgate Centre
Railworld
River La
Rivergate Shopping Centre
Riverside Mead
Russell St
St John's
St John's St
St Mark's St
St Peter's
St Peter's Rd
Saxon Rd
Spital Bridge
Stagshaw Dr
Star Rd
Thorpe Lea Rd
Thorpe Rd
Thorpe's Lea Rd
Town Hall
Viersen Platz
Vineyard Rd
Wake Rd
Wellington St
Wentworth St
Westgate
Whalley St
Wharf Rd
Whitsed St
YMCA

Plymouth

ABC
Alma Rd
Anstis St
Armada Centre
Armada St
Armada Way
Arts Centre
Athenaeum
Athenaeum St
Barbican
Barbican
Baring St
Bath St
Beaumont Park
Beaumont Rd
Black Friars Gin Distillery
Breton Side
Bus Station
Castle St
Cathedral (RC)
Cecil St
Central Park
Central Park Ave
Charles Church
Charles Cross (r'about)
Charles St
Citadel Rd
Citadel Rd East
Civic Centre
Cliff Rd
Clifton Pl
Cobourg St
College of Art & Design
Continental Ferry Po[rt]
Cornwall St
Dale Rd
Deptford Pl
Derry Ave
Derry's Cross (r'about)
Drake Circus
Drake Circus Shopp[ing] Centre
Drake's Memorial
Eastlake St
Ebrington St
Elizabethan House
Elliot St
Endsleigh Pl
Exeter St
Fire Station
Fish Quay
Gibbons St
Glen Park Ave

ffron Meadow C2
Andrew's Cr B1
Gregory's⛪ A3
Gregory's Rd A3
Mary's Rd A2
nctus Dr C2
nctus St C2
ndfield Rd C2
holars La B2
ven Meadows Rd C2
akespeare Centre✦ B2
akespeare Institute C2
akespeare St B2
akespeare's
irthplace✦ B2
eep St B2
elley Rd C3
ipston Rd C3
ottery Rd C1
ngates Rd A2
uthern La C2
ation Rd B1
atford
ealthcare🏥 B2
atford Hosp🏥 B2
atford Sports Club B1
atford-upon-Avon
ation⇌ B1
bot Rd A2
e Greenway C2
e Willows B1
e Willows North B1
dington Rd B3
nothy's Bridge Rd A1
wn Hall & Council
ffices B2
wn Sq B2
mway Bridge B3
nity St C2
er St B2
r Memorial Gdns B3
rwick Rd B3
terside B3
lcombe Rd A3
st St C2
stern Rd A2
arf Rd A2
od St B2

nderland 192

ion Pl C2
ance Pl B1
yle St C2
wood St C1
enaeum St B2
lea Terr C2
ach St A1
de Theatre🎭 C3
lford St B2
echwood Terr C1
vedere Rd C2
ndford St B2
rough Rd B3
dge Cr B2
dge St B2
oke St A2
ugham St B2
rdon Rd C2
n Park C1
n Park Rd C1
n Park Tech Park C1
ol St B1
arles St A3
ester Rd C1
ester Terr B1
urch St A3
eworld🎬 B3
ic Centre C2
k St B3
onation St B3
wan Terr C2
wtree Rd B2
ne Dorothy St A2
tford Rd B1
tford Terr A1
by St C2
went St C2
k St A3
ndas St A2
ham Rd C1
ington St A2
rton St C3
pire Theatre🎭 C2
ringdon Row B1
cett St B2
St C1
le St B3
derick St B3
Rd B2
over Pl A1
elock Terr C1
St A2
dworth Sq B3
don Rd B3
h St East B3
h St West B2/B3
meside B2
ton Rd B1
rmation Ctrℹ B2
n St B3
Hardie Way A2
nbton St B3
ra St C3
rence St B3
ure Centre B2
ary & Arts Centre B3
St B1
e St B1
ngstone Rd B2
Row B2
amba Terr B1
burn St B1
ennium Way A2
ster⛪ B2
nkwearmouth Station
us🏛 A2
wbray Park C3
wbray Rd C3
Murton St C3
Museum🏛 B3
National Glass
Centre✦ A3
New Durham Rd C1
Newcastle Rd A2
Nile St B3
Norfolk St B3
North Bridge St A2
Otto Terr C1
Park La C2
Park Lane
(metro station) C2
Park Rd C2
Paul's Rd B3
Peel St C3
Police Station🚓 B2
Post Office📮 B2
Priestly Cr A1
Queen St B2
Railway Row B1
Retail Park B1
Richmond St A2
Roker Ave A2
Royalty Theatre🎭 C1
Ryhope Rd C2
St Mary's Way B2
St Michael's Way B2
St Peter's⛪ A3
St Peter's
(metro station) A2
St Peter's Way A3
St Vincent St C3
Salem Rd C3
Salem St C3
Salisbury St C3
Sans St B3
Silkworth Row B1
Southwick Rd A2
Stadium of Light
(Sunderland AFC) A2
Stadium Way A2
Stobart St A2
Stockton Rd C2
Suffolk St C3
Sunderland
(metro station) B2
Sunderland Station⇌ B2
Sunderland St B3
Tatham St C3
Tavistock Pl B3
The Bridges B2
The Place B3
The Royalty C1
Thelma St C1
Thomas St North A2
Thornholme Rd C1
Toward Rd C3
Transport Interchange C2
Trimdon St Way B1
Tunstall Rd C2
University (metro sta-
tion) C1
University Library C1
University of Sunderland
(City Campus) B1
University of Sunderland
(Sir Tom Cowle
Campus) A3
Vaux Brewery Way A2
Villiers St B3
Villiers St South B3
Vine Pl C2
Violet St B1
Walton La B3
Waterworks Rd B1
Wearmouth Bridge B2
Wellington La A1
West Sunniside B3
West Wear St B3
Westbourne Rd B1
Western Hill C1
Wharncliffe B1
Whickham St A3
White House Rd C3
Wilson St North A2
Winter Gdns C3
Wreath Quay A1

Swansea
Abertawe 192

Adelaide St C3
Albert Row C3
Alexandra Rd B3
Argyle St C1
Baptist Well Pl A2
Beach St C1
Belle Vue Way B3
Berw Rd A1
Berwick Terr A2
Bond St C1
Brangwyn Concert
Hall🎭 C1
Bridge St A3
Brookands Terr B1
Brunswick St C1
Bryn-Syfi Terr A2
Bryn-y-Mor Rd C1
Bullins La B1
Burrows Rd C1
Bus/Rail link A3
Bus Station C2
Cadfan Rd A1
Cadrawd Rd A1
Caer St B3
Carig Cr A1
Carlton Terr B2
Carmarthen Rd A3
Castle Square B3
Castle St B3
Catherine St C1
City & County of
Swansea Offices
(County Hall) C2
City & County of
Swansea Offices
(Guildhall) C1
Clarence St C2
Colbourne Terr A2
Constitution Hill B1
Court B3
Creidiol Rd A2
Cromwell St B2
Duke St B1
Dunvant Pl C2
Dyfatty Park A3
Dyfatty St A3
Dyfed Ave A1
Dylan Thomas Ctr✦ B3
Dylan Thomas
Theatre🎭 C3
Eaton Cr C1
Eigen Cr A1
Elfed Rd A1
Emlyn Rd A1
Evans Terr A3
Fairfield Terr B1
Ffynone Dr B1
Ffynone Rd B1
Fire Station B3
Firm St A2
Fleet St C1
Francis St C1
Fullers Row B2
George St B2
Glamorgan St C2
Glyndwr Pl A1
Glynn Vivian🏛 B3
Graig Terr A3
Grand Theatre🎭 C2
Granogwen Rd A2
Guildhall Rd South C1
Gwent Rd A1
Gwynedd Ave A1
Hafod St A3
Hanover St B1
Harcourt St B2
Harries St A2
Heathfield B2
Henrietta St B1
Hewson St B2
High St A3/B3
High View A2
Hill St A2
Historic Ships Berth⚓ C3
HM Prison C2
Information Ctrℹ C2
Islwyn Rd A1
King Edward's Rd C1
Law Courts C1
Library B3
Long Ridge A2
Madoc St C2
Mansel St B2
Maritime Quarter C3
Market B3
Mayhill Gdns B1
Mayhill Rd A1
Mega Bowl✦🎬 B3
Milton Terr A2
Mission Gallery🏛 C3
Montpellier Terr B1
Morfa Rd A3
Mount Pleasant B2
National Waterfront
Mus🏛 C3
Nelson St C2
New Cut Rd A3
New St A3
Nicander Pde A2
Nicander Pl A2
Nicholl St B2
Norfolk St B2
North Hill Rd A2
Northampton La B2
Orchard St B3
Oxford St B2
Oystermouth Rd C1
Page St B2
Pant-y-Celyn Rd B1
Parc Tawe Link B3
Parc Tawe North B3
Parc Tawe Shopping &
Leisure Centre B3
Patti Pavilion🎭 C1
Paxton St C2
Penmaen Terr B1
Pen-y-Graig Rd A1
Phillips Pde C1
Picton Terr B2
Plantasia✿ B3
Police Station🚓 B2
Post Office
📮 A1/A2/B2/C1
Powys Ave A1
Primrose St B2
Princess Way B3
Promenade B2
Pryder Gdns A1
Quadrant Centre C2
Quay Park B3
Rhianfa La B1
Rhondda St B2
Richardson St C2
Rodney St C1
Rose Hill B1
Rosehill Terr B1
Russell St B1
St David's Sq C3
St Helen's Ave C1
St Helen's Cr C1
St Helen's Rd C1
St James Gdns B1
St James's Cr B1
St Mary's⛪ B3
Sea View Terr A3
Singleton St C2
South Dock C3
Stanley Pl B2
Strand B3
Swansea Castle🏰 B3
Swansea College Arts
Centre C1
Swansea Metropolitan
University B2
Swansea Mus🏛 C3
Swansea Station⇌ A3
Taliesyn Rd B1
Tan y Marian Rd A1
Tegid Rd A2
Teilo Cr A1
Terrace Rd B1/B2
The Kingsway B2
The LC C3
Tontine St A3
Tower of Eclipse✦ C3
Townhill Rd A1
Tram Mus🏛 C3
Trawler Rd C3
Union St B2
Upper Strand A3
Vernon St A3
Victoria Quay C3
Victoria Rd B3
Vincent St C1
Walter Rd B1
Watkin St A2
Waun-Wen Rd A2
Wellington St C2
Westbury St C1
Western St C1
Westway C2
William St C2
Wind St B3
Woodlands Terr B1
YMCA B2
York St C3

Swindon 193

Albert St C3
Albion St C1
Alfred St A2
Alvescot Rd C3
Art Gallery & Mus🏛 C3
Ashford Rd C1
Aylesbury St A2
Bath Rd C2
Bathampton St B1
Bathurst Rd B3
Beatrice St A2
Beckhampton St B3
Bowood Rd C1
Bristol St B1
Broad St A3
Brunel Arcade B2
Brunel Plaza B2
Brunswick St C2
Bus Station B2
Cambria Bridge Rd B1
Cambria Place B1
Canal Walk B2
Carfax St B2
Carr St B1
Cemetery C1/C3
Chandler Cl C3
Chapel C1
Chester St B1
Christ Church⛪ C3
Church Place B1
Cirencester Way A3
Clarence St B2
Clifton St C1
Cockleberry Rdbt A2
Colbourne Rdbt A3
Colbourne St A3
College St B2
Commercial Rd B2
Corporation St A2
Council Offices B3
County Rd A3
Courts B2
Cricket Ground A3
Cricklade Street C3
Crombey St B1/C2
Cross St C2
Curtis St B1
Deacon St C1
Designer Outlet (Great
Western) B1
Dixon St C2
Dover St C2
Dowling St C2
Drove Rd C3
Dryden St C1
Durham St C3
East St B1
Eastcott Hill C2
Eastcott Rd C2
Edgeware Rd B2
Elmina Rd A3
Emlyn Square B1
Euclid St B3
Exeter St B1
Fairview C1
Faringdon Rd B1
Farnsby St B1
Fire Station B3
Fleet St B2
Fleming Way B2/B3
Florence St A2
Gladstone St A3
Gooch St A2
Graham St A3
Great Western
Way A1/A2
Groundwell Rd B3
Hawksworth Way A1
Haydon St A2
Henry St B2
Hillside Ave C1
Holbrook Way B2
Hunt St C3
Hydro B1
Hythe Rd C2
Information Ctrℹ B2
Joseph St C1
Kent Rd C2
King William St C2
Kingshill Rd C1
Lansdown Rd C2
Leicester St B3
Library B2
Lincoln St B3
Little London C3
London St B1
Magic Rdbt B3
Maidstone Rd C2
Manchester Rd A3
Maxwell St B1
Milford St B2
Milton Rd B1
Morse St C2
National Monuments
Record Centre B1
Newcastle St B3
Newcombe Drive A1
Newcombe Trading
Estate A1
Newhall St C2
North St C2
North Star Ave A1
North Star Rdbt A1
Northampton St B3
Oasis Leisure Centre A1
Ocotal Way A3
Okus Rd C1
Old Town C3
Oxford St B1
Park Lane B1
Park Lane Rdbt B1
Pembroke St C2
Plymouth St B3
Polaris House A2
Polaris Way A2
Police Station🚓 B2
Ponting St A2
Post Office
📮 B1/B2/C1/C3
Poulton St A3
Princes St B2
Prospect Hill C2
Prospect Place C2
Queen St B2
Queen's Park C3
Radnor St C1
Read St C1
Reading St B1
Regent St B2
Retail Park A2/A3/B3
Rosebery St A3
St Mark's⛪ B1
Salisbury St A3
Savernake St C2
Shelley St C1
Sheppard St B1
South St C2
Southampton St B3
Spring Gardens B3
Stafford Street C2
Stanier St C2
Station Road A2
Steam🏛 B1
Swindon College A2
Swindon Rd C2
Swindon Station⇌ A2
Swindon Town Football
Club A3
T A Centre B1
Tennyson St B1
The Lawn C3
The Nurseries C1
The Parade B2
The Park B1
Theobald St B1
Town Hall B2
Transfer Bridges Rdbt A3
Union St C2
Upham Rd C3
Victoria Rd C3
Walcot Rd B3
War Memorial✦ B2
Wells St B3
Western St C2
Westmorland Rd B3
Whalebridge Rdbt B2
Whitehead St C1
Whitehouse Rd A2
William St C1
Wood St C3
Wyvern Theatre & Arts
Centre🎭🎬 B2
York Rd B3

Taunton 193

Addison Gr A1
Albemarle Rd A1
Alfred St B3
Alma St C2
Bath Pl C1
Belvedere Rd A1
Billet St B2
Billetfield C2
Birch Gr A1
Brewhouse Theatre🎭 B2
Bridge St B1
Bridgwater & Taunton
Canal A2
Broadlands Rd C1
Burton Pl C1
Bus Station B1
Canal Rd A2
Cann St C1
Canon St B2
Castle🏰 B1
Castle St B1
Cheddon Rd A2
Chip Lane A1
Clarence St B1
Cleveland St B1
Coleridge Cres C3
Compass Hill C1
Compton Cl A2
Corporation St B1
Council Offices A1
County Walk Shopping
Centre C2
Courtyard B2
Cranmer Rd B2
Critchard Way B3
Cyril St A1
Deller's Wharf B1
Duke St B2
East Reach B3
East St B3
Eastbourne Rd B2
Eastleigh Rd C3
Eaton Cres A2
Elm Gr A1
Elms Cl A1
Fons George C1
Fore St B2
Fowler St A1
French Weir
Recreation Grd B1
Geoffrey Farrant Wk A2
Gray's Almshouses⌂ B2
Grays Rd B3
Greenway Ave A1
Guildford Pl C1
Hammet St B2
Haydon Rd B3
Heavitree Way A2
Herbert St A1
High St C2
Holway Ave C3
Hugo St B3
Huish's
Almshouses⌂ B2
Hurdle Way C2
Information Ctrℹ C2
Jubilee St A1
King's College C3
Kings Cl C3
Laburnum St B2
Lambrook Rd B3
Lansdowne Rd A3
Leslie Ave A1
Leycroft Rd B3
Library C2
Linden Gr A1
Livestock Market A2
Magdalene St B2
Magistrates Court B1
Malvern Terr A2
Market House⌂ B2
Mary St C2
Middle St B2
Midford Rd B2
Mitre Court B3
Mount Nebo C1
Mount St C2
Mountway C2
North St B2
Northfield Ave B1
Northfield Rd B1
Northleigh Rd C3
Obridge Allotments A3
Obridge Lane A3
Obridge Rd A3
Obridge Viaduct A3
Old Market Shopping
Centre C2
Osborne Way C1
Park St C1
Paul St C2
Plais St A2
Playing Field C3
Police Station🚓 C1
Portland St B1
Post Office
📮 A1/B1/B2/C1
Priorswood Industrial
Estate A3
Priorswood Rd A2
Priory Ave B2
Priory Barn Cricket
Mus🏛 B2
Priory Bridge Rd B2
Priory Park A2
Priory Way A3
Queen St B3
Railway St A1
Records Office A2
Recreation Grd A1
Riverside Place B2
St Augustine St B2
St George's⛪ C2
St Georges Sq C2
St James⛪ B2
St James St B2
St John's⛪ C1
St John's Rd B1
St Josephs Field C2
St Mary
Magdalene's⛪ B2
Samuels Ct A1
Shire Hall & Law
Courts C1
Somerset County &
Military Mus🏛 B1
Somerset County
Cricket Ground B2
Somerset County Hall C1
South Rd C3
South St C3
Staplegrove Rd B1
Station Rd A1
Stephen St B2
Swimming Pool A1
Tancred St B2
Tauntfield Cl C3
Taunton Dean
Cricket Club C2
Taunton Station⇌ A2
The Avenue A1
The Crescent C1
The Mount C2
Thomas St A1
Toneway A3
Tower St B1
Trevor Smith Pl C3
Trinity Rd C3
Trinity St B3
Trull Rd C1
Tudor House⌂ B2
Upper High St C1
Venture Way A3
Victoria Gate B3
Victoria Park B3
Victoria St B3
Viney St B3
Vivary Park C2
Vivary Rd C1
War Memorial✦ C1
Wellesley St A2
Wheatley Cres A3
Whitehall A1
Wilfred Rd B3
William St A1
Wilton Church⛪ C1
Wilton Cl C1
Wilton Gr C1
Wilton St C1
Winchester St B2
Winters Field B2
Wood St B1
Yarde Pl B1

Telford 193

Alma Ave C1
Amphitheatre C2
Bowling Alley B2
Brandsfarm Way C3
Brunel Rd B1
Bus Station B2
Buxton Rd C1
Castle Trading Estate A3
Central Park A2
Civic Offices B2
Coach Central B2
Coachwell Cl B1
Colliers Way A1
Courts B2
Dale Acre Way B3
Darliston C3
Deepdale B3
Deercote B2
Dinthill C3
Doddington C3
Dodmoor Grange C3
Downemead B3
Duffryn B3
Dunsheath B3
Euston Way A3
Eyton Mound C1
Eyton Rd C1
Forge Retail Park A1
Forgegate A2
Grange Central B2
Hall Park Way B1
Hinkshay Rd C2
Hollinsworth Rd A2
Holyhead Rd A3
Housing Trust A1
Ice Rink B2
Information Ctrℹ B2
Ironmasters Way A2
Job Centre B1
Land Registry B1
Lawn Central B2
Lawnswood C1
Library B2
Malinsgate B1
Matlock Ave C1
Moor Rd C1
Mount Rd C1
NFU Offices B1
Odeon🎬 B2
Park Lane A1
Police Station🚓 B1
Post Office📮 B2
Priorslee Ave A3
Queen Elizabeth Ave C3
Queen Elizabeth Way B1
Queensway A2/B3
Rampart Way A2
Randlay Ave C3
Randlay Wood C3
Rhodes Ave C1
Royal Way B1
St Leonards Rd B1
St Quentin Gate B2
Shifnal Rd A3
Sixth Ave A1
Southwater Way B1
Spout Lane C1
Spout Mound B1
Spout Way C1
Stafford Court B3
Stafford Park B3
Stirchley Ave C3
Stone Row C1
Telford Bridge Retail
Park A1
Telford Central
Station⇌ A3
Telford Centre, The B2
Telford International
Centre C2
Telford Way A3
Third Ave A2
Town Park C2
Town Park Visitor
Centre B2
Town Sports Club C2
Walker House B2
Wellswood Ave A2
West Centre Way B1
Withywood Drive C1
Woodhouse Central B2
Yates Way A1

Torquay 193

Abbey Rd B2
Alexandra Rd A2
Alpine Rd B3
Ash Hill Rd A2
Babbacombe Rd B3
Bampfylde Rd B1
Barton Rd A1
Beacon Quay C2
Belgrave Rd A1/B1
Belmont Rd A3
Berea Rd A3
Braddons Hill Rd East B3
Brewery Park A3
Bronshill Rd A2
Castle Rd A2
Cavern Rd A3
Central🎬 B2
Chatsworth Rd A2
Chestnut Ave B1
Church St A1
Civic Offices⌂ A2
Coach Station A1
Corbyn Head C1
Croft Hill B1
Croft Rd B1
Daddyhole Plain C3
East St A1
Egerton Rd A3
Ellacombe Church Rd A3
Ellacombe Rd A2
Falkland Rd B1
Fleet St B2
Fleet Walk Shopping
Centre B2
Grafton Rd B3
Haldon Pier C2
Hatfield Rd A2
Highbury Rd A2
Higher Warberry Rd A3
Hillesdon Rd B3
Hollywood Bowl C3
Hoxton Rd A3
Hunsdon Rd B3
Information Ctrℹ B2
Inner Harbour C3
Kenwyn Rd A3
Laburnum St A1
Law Courts A2
Library A2
Lime Ave B1
Living Coasts🐧 C3
Lower Warberry Rd B3
Lucius St B1
Lymington Rd A1
Magdalene Rd A1
Marina C2
Market St B2
Meadfoot Lane C3
Meadfoot Rd C3
Melville St B2
Middle Warberry Rd B3
Mill Lane A1
Montpellier Rd B3
Morgan Ave A1
Museum Rd B3
Newton Rd A1
Oakhill Rd A1
Outer Harbour C2
Parkhill Rd C3
Pavilion C2
Pimlico B2
Police Station🚓 A1
Post Office📮 A1/B2
Princes Rd A3
Princes Rd East A3
Princes Rd West A3
Princess Gdns C2
Princess Pier C2
Princess Theatre🎭 C2
Rathmore Rd B1
Recreation Grd B1
Riviera Centre
International B1
Rock End Ave C3
Rock Rd B2
Rock Walk B2
Rosehill Rd A3
St Efride's Rd A1
St John's⛪ B3
St Luke's Rd B2
St Luke's Rd North B2
St Luke's Rd South B2
St Marychurch Rd A2
Scarborough Rd B1
Shedden Hill B2
South Pier C2
South St A1
Spanish Barn B1
Stitchill Rd B3
Strand B3
Sutherland Rd B3
Teignmouth Rd A1
Temperance St B2
The King's Drive B1
The Terrace B3
Thurlow Rd A1
Tor Bay B1
Tor Church Rd A1
Tor Hill Rd A1
Torbay Rd B2
Torquay Mus🏛 B3
Torquay Station⇌ C1
Torre Abbey
Mansion⌂ B1
Torre Abbey Meadows B1
Torre Abbey Sands B1
Torwood Gdns B3
Torwood St C3
Union Square A2
Union St A1
Upton Hill A2
Upton Park A1
Upton Rd A1
Vanehill Rd C3
Vansittart Rd A1
Vaughan Parade C2
Victoria Parade C3
Victoria Rd A2
Warberry Rd West B2
Warren Rd B2
Windsor Rd A2/A3
Woodville Rd A3

Truro 193

Adelaide Ter B1
Agar Rd B3
Arch Hill C2
Arundell Pl C2
Avondale Rd B1
Back Quay B3
Barrack La C3
Barton Meadow A1
Benson Rd A2
Bishops Cl A2
Bosvean Gdns B1
Bosvigo Gardens✿ B1
Bosvigo La A1
Bosvigo Rd B2
Broad St A3
Burley Cl C3
Bus Station B3
Calenick St B2
Campfield Hill B3
Carclew St B3
Carew Rd A2
Carey Park B2
Carlyon Rd A2
Carvoza Rd A3
Castle St B2
Cathedral View A2
Chainwalk Dr A2
Chapel Hill B1
Charles St B2
City Hall B3
City Rd B2
Coinage Hall⌂ B3
Comprigney Hill A1
Coosebean La A1
Copes Gdns A2
County Hall B1
Courtney Rd A2
Crescent Rd B1
Crescent Rise B1
Daniell Court C2
Daniell Rd C2
Daniell St C2
Daubuz Cl A2
Dobbs La B1
Edward St B2
Eliot Rd A2
Elm Court A3
Enys Cl A1
Enys Rd A1
Fairmantle St B3
Falmouth Rd C2
Ferris Town B2
Fire Station B1
Frances St B2
George St B2
Green Cl C2
Green La C1
Grenville Rd A2
Hall For Cornwall🎭 B3
Hendra Rd A2
Hendra Vean A1
High Cross B3
Higher Newham La C3
Higher Trehaverne A2
Hillcrest Ave B1
Hosp🏥 B2
Hunkin Cl A2
Hurland Rd C3
Infirmary Hill B2
James Pl B3
Kenwyn Church Rd A1
Kenwyn Hill A1
Kenwyn Rd A2
Kenwyn St B2
Kerris Gdns A1
King St B3
Lemon Quay B3
Lemon Street
Gallery🏛 B3
Library B1/B3
Malpas Rd B3
Market B3
Memorial Gdns B3
Merrifield Close B1
Mitchell Hill A3
Moresk Cl A3
Moresk Rd A3
Morlaix Ave C3
Nancemere Rd A3
Newham Business
Park C3
Newham Industrial
Estate C3
Newham Rd C3
Northfield Dr C3
Oak Way A3
Pal's Terr A3
Park View C2
Pendarves Rd A2
Plaza Cinema🎬 B3
Police Station🚓 B3
Post Office📮 B2/B3
Prince's St B3
Pydar St A2
Quay St B3
Redannick Cres C2
Redannick La B2
Richard Lander
Monument✦ C2
Richmond Hill B1
River St B2
Rosedale Rd A2
Royal Cornwall
Mus🏛 B2
St Clement St B3
St George's Rd A1
School La C2
Station Rd B1
Stokes Rd A2
Strangways Terr C3
Tabernacle St B3
The Avenue A3
The Crescent B1
The Leats B2
The Spires A2
Trehaverne La A2
Tremayne Rd A2
Treseder's Gdns A3
Treworder Rd B1
Treyew Rd B1
Truro Cathedral✝ B3
Truro Harbour Office B3
Truro Station⇌ B3
Union St B2
Upper School La C2
Victoria Gdns B2
Waterfall Gdns B2

Index to road maps of Britain

Abbreviations used in the index

Aberdeen	**Aberdeen City**	E Loth	**East Lothian**
Aberds	**Aberdeenshire**	E Renf	**East Renfrewshire**
Ald	**Alderney**	E Sus	**East Sussex**
Anglesey	**Isle of Anglesey**	E Yorks	**East Riding of**
Angus	**Angus**		**Yorkshire**
Argyll	**Argyll and Bute**	Edin	**City of Edinburgh**
Bath	**Bath and North East**	Essex	**Essex**
	Somerset	Falk	**Falkirk**
Bedford	**Bedford**	Fife	**Fife**
Bl Gwent	**Blaenau Gwent**	Flint	**Flintshire**
Blackburn	**Blackburn with**	Glasgow	**City of Glasgow**
	Darwen	Glos	**Gloucestershire**
Blackpool	**Blackpool**	Gtr Man	**Greater Manchester**
Bmouth	**Bournemouth**	Guern	**Guernsey**
Borders	**Scottish Borders**	Gwyn	**Gwynedd**
Brack	**Bracknell**	Halton	**Halton**
Bridgend	**Bridgend**	Hants	**Hampshire**
Brighton	**City of Brighton and**	Hereford	**Herefordshire**
	Hove	Herts	**Hertfordshire**
Bristol	**City and County of**	Highld	**Highland**
	Bristol	Hrtlpl	**Hartlepool**
Bucks	**Buckinghamshire**	Hull	**Hull**
C Beds	**Central Bedfordshire**	IoM	**Isle of Man**
Caerph	**Caerphilly**	IoW	**Isle of Wight**
Cambs	**Cambridgeshire**	Invclyd	**Inverclyde**
Cardiff	**Cardiff**	Jersey	**Jersey**
Carms	**Carmarthenshire**	Kent	**Kent**
Ceredig	**Ceredigion**	Lancs	**Lancashire**
Ches E	**Cheshire East**	Leicester	**City of Leicester**
Ches W	**Cheshire West and**	Leics	**Leicestershire**
	Chester	Lincs	**Lincolnshire**
Clack	**Clackmannanshire**	London	**Greater London**
Conwy	**Conwy**	Luton	**Luton**
Corn	**Cornwall**	M Keynes	**Milton Keynes**
Cumb	**Cumbria**	M Tydf	**Merthyr Tydfil**
Darl	**Darlington**	Mbro	**Middlesbrough**
Denb	**Denbighshire**	Medway	**Medway**
Derby	**City of Derby**	Mers	**Merseyside**
Derbys	**Derbyshire**	Midloth	**Midlothian**
Devon	**Devon**	Mon	**Monmouthshire**
Dorset	**Dorset**	Moray	**Moray**
Dumfries	**Dumfries and Galloway**	N Ayrs	**North Ayrshire**
Dundee	**Dundee City**	N Lincs	**North Lincolnshire**
Durham	**Durham**	N Lanark	**North Lanarkshire**
E Ayrs	**East Ayrshire**	N Som	**North Somerset**
E Dunb	**East Dunbartonshire**	N Yorks	**North Yorkshire**

NE Lincs	**North East Lincolnshire**	Soton	**Southampton**
Neath	**Neath Port Talbot**	Staffs	**Staffordshire**
Newport	**City and County of**	Southend	**Southend-on-Sea**
	Newport	Stirling	**Stirling**
Norf	**Norfolk**	Stockton	**Stockton-on-Tees**
Northants	**Northamptonshire**	Stoke	**Stoke-on-Trent**
Northumb	**Northumberland**	Suff	**Suffolk**
Nottingham	**City of Nottingham**	Sur	**Surrey**
Notts	**Nottinghamshire**	Swansea	**Swansea**
Orkney	**Orkney**	Swindon	**Swindon**
Oxon	**Oxfordshire**	T&W	**Tyne and Wear**
Pboro	**Peterborough**	Telford	**Telford and Wrekin**
Pembs	**Pembrokeshire**	Thurrock	**Thurrock**
Perth	**Perth and Kinross**	Torbay	**Torbay**
Plym	**Plymouth**	Torf	**Torfaen**
Poole	**Poole**	V Glam	**The Vale of Glamorgan**
Powys	**Powys**	W Berks	**West Berkshire**
Ptsmth	**Portsmouth**	W Dunb	**West Dunbartonshire**
Reading	**Reading**	W Isles	**Western Isles**
Redcar	**Redcar and Cleveland**	W Loth	**West Lothian**
Renfs	**Renfrewshire**	W Mid	**West Midlands**
Rhondda	**Rhondda Cynon Taff**	W Sus	**West Sussex**
Rutland	**Rutland**	W Yorks	**West Yorkshire**
S Ayrs	**South Ayrshire**	Warks	**Warwickshire**
S Glos	**South Gloucestershire**	Warr	**Warrington**
S Lanark	**South Lanarkshire**	Wilts	**Wiltshire**
S Yorks	**South Yorkshire**	Windsor	**Windsor and**
Scilly	**Scilly**		**Maidenhead**
Shetland	**Shetland**	Wokingham	**Wokingham**
Shrops	**Shropshire**	Worcs	**Worcestershire**
Slough	**Slough**	Wrex	**Wrexham**
Som	**Somerset**	York	**City of York**

How to use the index

Example

Trudoxhill Som   **24** E2

- grid square
- page number
- county or unitary authority

A

Ab Kettleby Leics 64 B4
Ab Lench Worcs 50 D5
Abbas Combe Som 12 B5
Abberley Worcs 50 C2
Abberton Essex 43 C6
Abberton Worcs 50 D4
Abberwick Northumb 117 C7
Abbess Roding Essex 42 C1
Abbey Devon 11 C6
Abbey-cwm-hir Powys 48 B2
Abbey Dore Hereford 49 F5
Abbey Field Essex 43 B5
Abbey Hulton Stoke 75 E6
Abbey St Bathans Borders 122 C3
Abbey Town Cumb 107 D8
Abbey Village Lancs 86 B4
Abbey Wood London 29 B5
Abbeydale S Yorks 88 F4
Abbeystead Lancs 93 D5
Abbots Bickington Devon 9 C5
Abbots Bromley Staffs 62 B4
Abbots Langley Herts 40 D3
Abbots Leigh N Som 23 B7
Abbots Morton Worcs 50 D5
Abbots Ripton Cambs 54 B3
Abbots Salford Warks 51 D5
Abbotsbury Dorset 12 F3
Abbotsham Devon 9 B6
Abbotskerswell Devon 7 C6
Abbotsley Cambs 54 D3
Abbotswood Hants 14 B4
Abbotts Ann Hants 25 E8
Abcott Shrops 49 B5
Abdon Shrops 61 F5
Aber Ceredig 46 E3
Aber-Arad Carms 46 F2
Aber-banc Ceredig 46 E2
Aber Cowarch Gwyn 59 C5
Aber-Giâr Carms 46 E4
Aber-gwynfi Neath 34 E2
Aber-Hirnant Gwyn 72 F3
Aber-nant Rhondda 34 D4
Aber-Rhiwlech Gwyn 59 B6
Aber-Village Powys 35 B5
Aberaeron Ceredig 46 C3
Aberaman Rhondda 34 D4
Aberangell Gwyn 58 C5
Aberarder Highld 137 F7
Aberarder House Highld 138 B2
Aberarder Lodge Highld 137 F8
Aberargie Perth 128 C3
Aberarth Ceredig 46 C3
Aberavon Neath 33 E8
Aberbeeg Bl Gwent 35 D6
Abercanaid M Tydf 34 D4
Abercarn Caerph 35 E6
Abercastle Pembs 44 B3
Abercegir Powys 58 D5
Aberchirder Aberds 152 C6
Abercraf Powys 34 C2
Abercrombie Fife 129 D7
Abercych Pembs 45 E4
Abercynafon Powys 34 C4
Aberdalgie Perth 128 B2
Aberdâr = Aberdare Rhondda 34 D3
Aberdare = Aberdâr Rhondda 34 D3
Aberdaron Gwyn 70 E2
Aberdaugleddau = Milford Haven Pembs 44 E4
Aberdeen Aberdeen 141 D8
Aberdesach Gwyn 82 F4
Aberdour Fife 128 F3
Aberdovey Gwyn 58 E3
Aberdulais Neath 34 D1
Aberedw Powys 48 E2
Abereiddy Pembs 44 B2
Abererch Gwyn 70 D4
Aberfan M Tydf 34 D4
Aberfeldy Perth 133 E5

Aberffraw Anglesey 82 E3
Aberffrwd Ceredig 47 B5
Aberford W Yorks 95 F7
Aberfoyle Stirling 126 D4
Abergavenny = Y Fenni Mon 35 C6
Abergele Conwy 72 B3
Abergorlech Carms 46 F4
Abergwaun = Fishguard Pembs 44 B4
Abergwesyn Powys 47 D7
Abergwili Carms 33 B5
Abergwynant Gwyn 58 C3
Abergwyngregyn Gwyn 83 D6
Abergynolwyn Gwyn 58 D3
Aberhonddu = Brecon Powys 34 B4
Aberhosan Powys 58 E5
Aberkenfig Bridgend 34 F2
Aberlady E Loth 129 F6
Aberlemno Angus 135 D5
Aberllefenni Gwyn 58 D4
Abermagwr Ceredig 47 B5
Abermaw = Barmouth Gwyn 58 C3
Abermeurig Ceredig 46 D4
Abermule Powys 59 E8
Abernaint Powys 59 B8
Abernant Carms 32 B4
Abernethy Perth 128 C3
Abernyte Perth 134 F2
Aberpennar = Mountain Ash Rhondda 34 E4
Aberporth Ceredig 45 D4
Abersoch Gwyn 70 E4
Abersychan Torf 35 D6
Abertawe = Swansea Swansea 33 E7
Aberteifi = Cardigan Ceredig 45 E3
Aberthin V Glam 22 B2
Abertillery = Abertyleri Bl Gwent 35 D6
Abertridwr Caerph 35 F5
Abertridwr Powys 59 C7
Abertyleri = Abertillery Bl Gwent 35 D6
Abertysswg Caerph 35 D5
Aberuthven Perth 127 C8
Aberyscir Powys 34 B3
Aberystwyth Ceredig 58 F2
Abhainn Suidhe W Isles 154 G5
Abingdon Oxon 38 E4
Abinger Common Sur 28 E2
Abinger Hammer Sur 27 E8
Abington S Lanark 114 B2
Abington Pigotts Cambs 54 E4
Ablington Glos 37 D8
Ablington Wilts 25 E6
Abney Derbys 75 B8
Aboyne Aberds 140 E4
Abram Gtr Man 86 D4
Abriachan Highld 151 H8
Abridge Essex 41 E7
Abronhill N Lanark 119 B7
Abson S Glos 24 B2
Abthorpe Northants 52 E4
Abune-the-Hill Orkney 159 F3
Aby Lincs 79 B7
Acaster Malbis York 95 E8
Acaster Selby N Yorks 95 E8
Accrington Lancs 87 B5
Acha Argyll 146 F4
Acha Mor W Isles 155 E8
Achabraid Argyll 145 E7
Achachork Highld 149 D9
Achafolla Argyll 124 D3
Achagary Highld 157 D10
Achahoish Argyll 144 F6
Achalader Perth 133 E8
Achallader Argyll 131 E7
Ach'an Todhair Highld 130 B4
Achanalt Highld 150 E5
Achanamara Argyll 144 E6

Achandunie Highld 151 D9
Achany Highld 157 J8
Achaphubuil Highld 130 B4
Acharacle Highld 147 E9
Acharn Highld 147 F10
Acharn Perth 132 E4
Acharole Highld 158 E4
Achath Aberds 141 C6
Achavanich Highld 158 F3
Achavraat Highld 151 G12
Achddu Carms 33 D5
Achduart Highld 156 J3
Achentoul Highld 157 F11
Achfary Highld 156 F5
Achgarve Highld 155 H13
Achiemore Highld 156 C6
Achiemore Highld 157 D11
A'Chill Highld 148 H7
Achiltibuie Highld 156 J3
Achina Highld 157 C10
Achinduich Highld 157 J8
Achinduin Argyll 124 B4
Achingills Highld 158 D3
Achintee Highld 131 B5
Achintee Highld 150 G2
Achintraid Highld 149 E13
Achlean Highld 138 E4
Achleck Argyll 146 G7
Achluachrach Highld 137 F5
Achlyness Highld 156 D5
Achmelvich Highld 156 G3
Achmore Highld 149 E13
Achmore Stirling 132 F2
Achnaba Argyll 124 D5
Achnaba Argyll 145 E8
Achnabat Highld 151 H8
Achnacarnin Highld 156 F3
Achnacarry Highld 136 F4
Achnacloich Argyll 125 B5
Achnacloich Highld 149 H10
Achnaconeran Highld 137 C7
Achnacraig Argyll 146 G7
Achnacroish Argyll 130 E2
Achnadrish Argyll 146 F7
Achnafalnich Argyll 125 C8
Achnagarron Highld 151 E9
Achnaha Highld 146 E7
Achnahanat Highld 151 B8
Achnahannet Highld 139 B5
Achnairn Highld 157 H8
Achnaluachrach Highld 157 J9
Achnasaul Highld 136 F4
Achnasheen Highld 150 F4
Achosnich Highld 146 E7
Achranich Highld 147 G10
Achreamie Highld 157 C13
Achriabhach Highld 131 C5
Achriesgill Highld 156 D5
Achrimsdale Highld 157 J12
Achtoty Highld 157 C9
Achurch Northants 65 F7
Achuvoldrach Highld 157 D8
Achvaich Highld 151 B10
Achvarasdal Highld 157 C12
Ackergill Highld 158 E5
Acklam Mbro 102 C2
Acklam N Yorks 96 C3
Ackleton Shrops 61 E7
Acklington Northumb 117 D8
Ackton W Yorks 88 B5
Ackworth Moor Top W Yorks 88 C5
Acle Norf 69 C7
Acock's Green W Mid 62 F5
Acol Kent 31 C7
Acomb Northumb 110 C2
Acomb York 95 D8
Aconbury Hereford 49 F7
Acre Lancs 87 B5
Acre Street W Sus 15 E8
Acrefair Wrex 73 E6
Acton Ches E 74 D3
Acton Dorset 13 G7
Acton London 41 F5
Acton Shrops 60 F3
Acton Suff 56 E2
Acton Wrex 73 D7

Acton Beauchamp Hereford 49 D8
Acton Bridge Ches W 74 B2
Acton Burnell Shrops 60 D5
Acton Green Hereford 49 D8
Acton Pigott Shrops 60 D5
Acton Round Shrops 61 E6
Acton Scott Shrops 60 F4
Acton Trussell Staffs 62 C3
Acton Turville S Glos 37 F5
Adbaston Staffs 61 B7
Adber Dorset 12 B3
Adderley Shrops 74 E3
Adderstone Northumb 123 F7
Addiewell W Loth 120 C2
Addingham W Yorks 94 E3
Addington Bucks 39 B7
Addington Kent 29 D7
Addington London 28 C4
Addinston Borders 121 D8
Addiscombe London 28 C4
Addlestone Sur 27 C8
Addlethorpe Lincs 79 C8
Adel W Yorks 95 F5
Adeney Telford 61 C7
Adfa Powys 59 D7
Adforton Hereford 49 B6
Adisham Kent 31 D6
Adlestrop Glos 38 B2
Adlingfleet E Yorks 90 B2
Adlington Lancs 86 C4
Admaston Staffs 62 B4
Admaston Telford 61 C6
Admington Warks 51 E7
Adstock Bucks 52 F5
Adstone Northants 52 D3
Adversane W Sus 16 B4
Advie Highld 152 E1
Adwalton W Yorks 88 B3
Adwell Oxon 39 E6
Adwick le Street S Yorks 89 D6
Adwick upon Dearne S Yorks 89 D5
Adziel Aberds 153 C9
Ae Village Dumfries 114 F2
Affleck Aberds 141 B7
Affpuddle Dorset 13 E6
Affric Lodge Highld 136 B4
Afon-wen Flint 72 B5
Afton IoW 14 F4
Agglethorpe N Yorks 101 F5
Agneash IoM 84 D4
Aigburth Mers 85 F4
Aiginis W Isles 155 D9
Aike E Yorks 97 E6
Aikerness Orkney 159 C5
Aikers Orkney 159 J5
Aiketgate Cumb 108 E4
Aikton Cumb 108 D2
Ailey Hereford 48 E5
Ailstone Warks 51 D7
Ailsworth Pboro 65 E8
Ainderby Quernhow N Yorks 102 F1
Ainderby Steeple N Yorks 101 E8
Aingers Green Essex 43 B7
Ainsdale Mers 85 C4
Ainsdale-on-Sea Mers 85 C4
Ainstable Cumb 108 E5
Ainsworth Gtr Man 87 C5
Ainthorpe N Yorks 103 D5
Aintree Mers 85 E4
Aird Argyll 124 E3
Aird Dumfries 104 D4
Aird Highld 149 A12
Aird W Isles 155 D10
Aird a Mhachair W Isles 148 D2
Aird a' Mhulaidh W Isles 154 F6
Aird Asaig W Isles 154 G6
Aird Dhail W Isles 155 A9
Aird Mhidhinis W Isles 148 H2
Aird Mhighe W Isles 154 H6
Aird Mhighe W Isles 154 J5
Aird Mhor W Isles 148 H2

Aird of Sleat Highld 149 H10
Aird Thunga W Isles 155 D9
Aird Uig W Isles 154 D5
Airdens Highld 151 B9
Airdrie N Lanark 119 C7
Airdtorrisdale Highld 157 C9
Airidh a Bhruaich W Isles 154 F7
Airieland Dumfries 106 D4
Airmyn E Yorks 89 B8
Airntully Perth 133 F7
Airor Highld 149 H12
Airth Falk 127 F7
Airton N Yorks 94 D2
Airyhassen Dumfries 105 E7
Aisby Lincs 78 F3
Aisby Lincs 90 E2
Aisgernis W Isles 148 F2
Aiskew N Yorks 101 F7
Aislaby N Yorks 103 D6
Aislaby N Yorks 103 F5
Aislaby Stockton 102 C2
Aisthorpe Lincs 78 A2
Aith Orkney 159 G3
Aith Shetland 160 D8
Aith Shetland 160 H5
Aithsetter Shetland 160 K6
Aitkenhead S Ayrs 112 D3
Aitnoch Highld 151 H12
Akeld Northumb 117 B5
Akeley Bucks 52 F5
Akenham Suff 57 E5
Albaston Corn 6 B2
Alberbury Shrops 60 C3
Albourne W Sus 17 C6
Albrighton Shrops 60 C4
Albrighton Shrops 62 D2
Alburgh Norf 69 F5
Albury Herts 41 B7
Albury Sur 27 E8
Albury End Herts 41 B7
Alby Hill Norf 81 D7
Alcaig Highld 151 F8
Alcaston Shrops 60 F4
Alcester Warks 51 D5
Alciston E Sus 18 E2
Alcombe Som 21 E8
Alcombe Wilts 24 C3
Alconbury Cambs 54 B2
Alconbury Weston Cambs 54 B2
Aldbar Castle Angus 135 D5
Aldborough N Yorks 95 C7
Aldborough Norf 81 D7
Aldbourne Wilts 25 B7
Aldbrough E Yorks 97 F8
Aldbrough St John N Yorks 101 C7
Aldbury Herts 40 C2
Aldcliffe Lancs 92 C4
Aldclune Perth 133 C6
Aldeburgh Suff 57 D8
Aldeby Norf 69 E7
Aldenham Herts 40 E4
Alderbury Wilts 14 B2
Aldercar Derbys 76 E4
Alderford Norf 68 C4
Alderholt Dorset 14 C2
Alderley Glos 36 E4
Alderley Edge Ches E 74 B5
Aldermaston W Berks 26 C3
Aldermaston Wharf W Berks 26 C4
Alderminster Warks 51 E7
Alder's End Hereford 49 E8
Aldersey Green Ches W 73 D8
Aldershot Hants 27 D6
Alderton Glos 50 F5
Alderton Northants 52 E5
Alderton Shrops 60 B4
Alderton Suff 57 E7
Alderton Wilts 37 F5
Alderwasley Derbys 76 D3
Aldfield N Yorks 95 C5
Aldford Ches W 73 D8
Aldham Essex 43 B5
Aldham Suff 56 E4
Aldie Highld 151 C10
Aldingbourne W Sus 16 D3

Aldingham Cumb 92 B2
Aldington Kent 19 B7
Aldington Worcs 51 E5
Aldington Frith Kent 19 B7
Aldochlay Argyll 126 E2
Aldreth Cambs 54 B5
Aldridge W Mid 62 D4
Aldringham Suff 57 C8
Aldsworth Glos 38 C1
Aldunie Moray 140 B2
Aldwark Derbys 76 D2
Aldwark N Yorks 95 C7
Aldwick W Sus 16 E3
Aldwincle Northants 65 F7
Aldworth W Berks 26 B3
Alexandria W Dunb 118 B3
Alfardisworthy Devon 8 C4
Alfington Devon 11 E6
Alfold Sur 27 F8
Alfold Bars W Sus 27 F8
Alfold Crossways Sur 27 F8
Alford Aberds 140 C4
Alford Lincs 79 B7
Alford Som 23 F8
Alfreton Derbys 76 D4
Alfrick Worcs 50 D2
Alfrick Pound Worcs 50 D2
Alfriston E Sus 18 E2
Algaltraig Argyll 145 F9
Algarkirk Lincs 79 F5
Alhampton Som 23 F8
Aline Lodge W Isles 154 F6
Alisary Highld 147 D10
Alkborough N Lincs 90 B2
Alkerton Oxon 51 E8
Alkham Kent 31 E6
Alkington Shrops 74 F2
Alkmonton Derbys 75 F8
All Cannings Wilts 25 C6
All Saints South Elmham Suff 69 F6
All Stretton Shrops 60 E4
Alladale Lodge Highld 150 C7
Allaleigh Devon 7 D6
Allanaquoich Aberds 139 E7
Allangrange Mains Highld 151 F9
Allanton Borders 122 D4
Allanton N Lanark 119 D8
Allathasdal W Isles 148 H1
Allendale Town Northumb 109 D8
Allenheads Northumb 109 E8
Allens Green Herts 41 C7
Allensford Durham 110 D3
Allensmore Hereford 49 F6
Allenton Derby 76 F3
Aller Som 12 B2
Allerby Cumb 107 F7
Allerford Som 21 E8
Allerston N Yorks 103 F6
Allerthorpe E Yorks 96 E3
Allerton Mers 86 F2
Allerton W Yorks 94 F4
Allerton Bywater W Yorks 88 B5
Allerton Mauleverer N Yorks 95 D7
Allesley W Mid 63 F7
Allestree Derby 76 F3
Allet Corn 3 B6
Allexton Leics 64 D5
Allgreave Ches E 75 C6
Allhallows Medway 30 B2
Allhallows-on-Sea Medway 30 B2
Alligin Shuas Highld 149 C13
Allimore Green Staffs 62 C2
Allington Lincs 77 E8
Allington Wilts 25 C5
Allington Wilts 25 F7
Allithwaite Cumb 92 B3
Alloa Clack 127 E7
Allonby Cumb 107 E7
Alloway S Ayrs 112 C3
Allt Carms 33 D6
Allt na h-Airbhe Highld 150 B4
Allt-nan-sùgh Highld 136 B2
Alltchaorunn Highld 131 D5

Alltforgan Powys 59 B6
Alltmawr Powys 48 E2
Alltnacaillich Highld 156 E7
Alltsigh Highld 137 C7
Alltwalis Carms 46 F3
Alltwen Neath 33 D8
Alltyblaca Ceredig 46 E4
Allwood Green Suff 56 B4
Almeley Hereford 48 D5
Almer Dorset 13 E7
Almholme S Yorks 89 D6
Almington Staffs 74 F4
Alminstone Cross Devon 8 B5
Almondbank Perth 128 B2
Almondbury W Yorks 88 C2
Almondsbury S Glos 36 F3
Alne N Yorks 95 C7
Alness Highld 151 E9
Alnham Northumb 117 C5
Alnmouth Northumb 117 C8
Alnwick Northumb 117 C7
Alperton London 40 F4
Alphamstone Essex 56 F2
Alpheton Suff 56 D2
Alphington Devon 10 E4
Alport Derbys 76 C2
Alpraham Ches E 74 D2
Alresford Essex 43 B6
Alrewas Staffs 63 C5
Alsager Ches E 74 D4
Alsagers Bank Staffs 74 E5
Alsop en le Dale Derbys 75 D8
Alston Cumb 109 E7
Alston Devon 11 D8
Alstone Glos 50 F4
Alstonefield Staffs 75 D8
Alswear Devon 10 B2
Altandhu Highld 156 H2
Altanduin Highld 157 G11
Altarnun Corn 8 F4
Altass Highld 156 J7
Alterwall Highld 158 D4
Altham Lancs 93 F7
Althorne Essex 43 E5
Althorpe N Lincs 90 D2
Alticry Dumfries 105 D6
Altnabreac Station Highld 157 E13
Altnacealgach Hotel Highld 156 H5
Altnacraig Argyll 124 C4
Altnafeadh Highld 131 D6
Altnaharra Highld 157 F8
Altofts W Yorks 88 B4
Alton Derbys 76 C3
Alton Hants 26 F5
Alton Staffs 75 E7
Alton Pancras Dorset 12 D5
Alton Priors Wilts 25 C6
Altrincham Gtr Man 87 F5
Altrua Highld 137 F5
Altskeith Stirling 126 D3
Altyre Ho. Moray 151 F13
Alva Clack 127 E7
Alvanley Ches W 73 B8
Alvaston Derby 76 F3
Alvechurch Worcs 50 B5
Alvecote Warks 63 D6
Alvediston Wilts 13 B7
Alveley Shrops 61 F7
Alverdiscott Devon 9 B7
Alverstoke Hants 15 E7
Alverstone IoW 15 F6
Alverton Notts 77 E7
Alves Moray 152 B1
Alvescot Oxon 38 D2
Alveston S Glos 36 F3
Alveston Warks 51 D7
Alvie Highld 138 D4
Alvingham Lincs 91 E7
Alvington Glos 36 D3
Alwalton Cambs 65 E8
Alweston Dorset 12 C4
Alwinton Northumb 116 D5
Alwoodley W Yorks 95 E5
Alyth Perth 134 E2

Amatnatua Highld 150 B7
Amber Hill Lincs 78 E5
Ambergate Derbys 76 D3
Amberley Glos 37 D5
Amberley W Sus 16 C4
Amble Northumb 117 D8
Amblecote W Mid 62 F2
Ambler Thorn W Yorks 87 B8
Ambleside Cumb 99 D5
Ambleston Pembs 44 C5
Ambrosden Oxon 39 C6
Amcotts N Lincs 90 C2
Amersham Bucks 40 E2
Amesbury Wilts 25 E6
Amington Staffs 63 D6
Amisfield Dumfries 114 F2
Amlwch Anglesey 82 B4
Amlwch Port Anglesey 82 B4
Ammanford = Rhydaman Carms 33 C7
Amod Argyll 143 E8
Amotherby N Yorks 96 B3
Ampfield Hants 14 B5
Ampleforth N Yorks 95 B8
Ampney Crucis Glos 37 D7
Ampney St Mary Glos 37 D7
Ampney St Peter Glos 37 D7
Amport Hants 25 E7
Ampthill C Beds 53 F8
Ampton Suff 56 B2
Amroth Pembs 32 D2
Amulree Perth 133 F5
An Caol Highld 149 C11
An Cnoc W Isles 155 D9
An Gleann Ur W Isles 155 D9
An t-Ob = Leverburgh W Isles 154 J5
Anagach Highld 139 B6
Anaheilt Highld 130 C2
Anancaun Highld 150 E3
Ancaster Lincs 78 E2
Anchor Shrops 59 F8
Anchorsholme Blackpool 92 E3
Ancroft Northumb 123 E5
Ancrum Borders 116 B2
Anderby Lincs 79 B8
Anderson Dorset 13 E6
Anderton Ches W 74 B3
Andover Hants 25 E8
Andover Down Hants 25 E8
Andoversford Glos 37 C7
Andreas IoM 84 C4
Anfield Mers 85 E4
Angarrack Corn 2 C4
Angersleigh Som 11 C6
Angle Pembs 44 E3
Angmering W Sus 16 D4
Angram N Yorks 95 E8
Angram N Yorks 100 E3
Anie Stirling 126 C4
Ankerville Highld 151 D11
Anlaby E Yorks 90 B4
Anmer Norf 80 E3
Anna Valley Hants 25 E8
Annan Dumfries 107 C8
Annat Argyll 125 C6
Annat Highld 149 C13
Annbank S Ayrs 112 B4
Annesley Notts 76 D5
Annesley Woodhouse Notts 76 D4
Annfield Plain Durham 110 D4
Annifirth Shetland 160 J3
Annitsford T&W 111 B5
Annscroft Shrops 60 D4
Ansdell Lancs 85 B4
Ansford Som 23 F8
Ansley Warks 63 E6
Anslow Staffs 63 B6
Anslow Gate Staffs 63 B5
Anstey Herts 54 F5
Anstey Leics 64 D2
Anstruther Easter Fife 129 D7
Anstruther Wester Fife 129 D7
Ansty Hants 26 E5
Ansty W Sus 17 B6
Ansty Warks 63 F7

Ansty Wilts 13 B7
Anthill Common Hants 15 C7
Anthorn Cumb 107 D8
Antingham Norf 81 D8
Anton's Gowt Lincs 79 E5
Antonshill Falk 127 F7
Antony Corn 5 D8
Anwick Lincs 78 D4
Anwoth Dumfries 106 D2
Aoradh Argyll 142 B3
Apes Hall Cambs 67 E5
Apethorpe Northants 65 E7
Apeton Staffs 62 C2
Apley Lincs 78 B4
Apperknowle Derbys 76 B3
Apperley Glos 37 B5
Apperley Bridge W Yorks 94 F4
Appersett N Yorks 100 E3
Appin Argyll 130 E3
Appin House Argyll 130 E3
Appleby N Lincs 90 C3
Appleby-in-Westmorland Cumb 100 B1
Appleby Magna Leics 63 D7
Appleby Parva Leics 63 D7
Applecross Highld 149 D12
Applecross Ho. Highld 149 D12
Appledore Devon 11 C5
Appledore Devon 20 F3
Appledore Kent 19 C6
Appledore Heath Kent 19 B6
Appleford Oxon 39 E5
Applegarthtown Dumfries 114 F4
Appleshaw Hants 25 E8
Applethwaite Cumb 98 B4
Appleton Halton 86 F3
Appleton Oxon 38 D4
Appleton-le-Moors N Yorks 103 F5
Appleton-le-Street N Yorks 96 B3
Appleton Roebuck N Yorks 95 E8
Appleton Thorn Warr 86 F4
Appleton Wiske N Yorks 102 D1
Appletreehall Borders 115 C8
Appletreewick N Yorks 94 C3
Appley Som 11 B5
Appley Bridge Lancs 86 D3
Apse Heath IoW 15 F6
Apsley End C Beds 54 F2
Apuldram W Sus 16 D2
Aquhythie Aberds 141 C6
Arabella Highld 151 D11
Arbeadie Aberds 141 E5
Arberth = Narberth Pembs 32 C2
Arbirlot Angus 135 E6
Arboll Highld 151 C11
Arborfield Wokingham 27 C5
Arborfield Cross Wokingham 27 C5
Arborfield Garrison Wokingham 27 C5
Arbour-thorne S Yorks 88 F4
Arbroath Angus 135 E6
Arbuthnott Aberds 135 B7
Archiestown Moray 152 D2
Arclid Ches E 74 C4
Ard-dhubh Highld 149 D12
Ardachu Highld 157 J9
Ardalanish Argyll 146 K6
Ardanaiseig Argyll 125 C6
Ardaneaskan Highld 149 E13
Ardanstur Argyll 124 D4
Ardargie House Hotel Perth 128 C2
Ardarroch Highld 149 E13
Ardbeg Argyll 142 D5
Ardbeg Argyll 145 E10
Ardcharnich Highld 150 C4
Ardchiavaig Argyll 146 K6
Ardchullarie More Stirling 126 C4
Ardchyle Stirling 126 B4
Arddleen Powys 60 C2
Ardechvie Highld 136 E4
Ardeley Herts 41 B6
Ardelve Highld 149 F13
Arden Argyll 126 F2
Ardens Grafton Warks 51 D6
Ardentinny Argyll 145 E10
Ardentraive Argyll 145 F9
Ardeonaig Stirling 132 F3
Ardersier Highld 151 F10
Ardessie Highld 150 C3
Ardfern Argyll 124 E4
Ardgartan Argyll 125 E8
Ardgay Highld 151 B8
Ardgour Highld 130 C4
Ardheslaig Highld 149 C12
Ardiecow Moray 152 B5
Ardindrean Highld 150 C4
Ardingly W Sus 17 B7
Ardington Oxon 38 F4
Ardlair Aberds 140 B4
Ardlamont Ho. Argyll 145 G8
Ardleigh Essex 43 B6
Ardler Perth 134 E2
Ardley Oxon 39 B5
Ardlui Argyll 126 C2
Ardlussa Argyll 144 E5
Ardmair Highld 150 B4
Ardmay Argyll 125 E8
Ardminish Argyll 143 D7
Ardmolich Highld 147 D10
Ardmore Argyll 124 C3
Ardmore Highld 151 C10
Ardmore Highld 156 D5
Ardnacross Argyll 147 G8
Ardnadam Argyll 145 F10
Ardnagrask Highld 151 G8
Ardnarff Highld 149 E13
Ardnastang Highld 130 C2
Ardnave Argyll 142 A3
Ardno Argyll 125 E7
Ardo Aberds 153 E8
Ardo Ho. Aberds 141 B8
Ardoch Perth 133 F7
Ardochy House Highld 136 D5
Ardoyne Aberds 141 B5
Ardpatrick Argyll 144 G6
Ardpatrick Ho. Argyll 144 H6
Ardpeaton Argyll 145 E11
Ardrishaig Argyll 145 E7
Ardross Fife 129 D7
Ardross Highld 151 D9
Ardross Castle Highld 151 D9
Ardrossan N Ayrs 118 E2
Ardshealach Highld 147 E9
Ardsley S Yorks 88 D4
Ardslignish Highld 147 E8
Ardtalla Argyll 142 C5
Ardtalnaig Perth 132 F4
Ardtoe Highld 147 D9
Ardtrostan Perth 127 B5
Arduaine Argyll 124 D3
Ardullie Highld 151 E8
Ardvasar Highld 149 H11
Ardvorlich Perth 126 B5
Ardwell Dumfries 104 E5
Ardwell Mains Dumfries 104 E5
Ardwick Gtr Man 87 E6
Areley Kings Worcs 50 B3
Arford Hants 27 F6
Argoed Caerph 35 E5
Argoed Mill Powys 47 C8
Arichamish Argyll 124 E5
Arichastlich Argyll 125 B8
Aridhglas Argyll 146 J6
Arileod Argyll 146 F4
Arinacrinachd Highld 149 C12
Arinagour Argyll 146 F5
Arion Orkney 159 G3
Arisaig Highld 147 C9
Ariundle Highld 130 C2
Arkendale N Yorks 95 C6
Arkesden Essex 55 F5
Arkholme Lancs 93 B5
Arkle Town N Yorks 101 D5
Arkleton Dumfries 115 E6
Arkley London 41 E5
Arksey S Yorks 89 D6
Arkwright Town Derbys 76 B4
Arle Glos 37 B6
Arlecdon Cumb 98 C2
Arlesey C Beds 54 F2
Arleston Telford 61 C6
Arley Ches E 86 F4
Arlingham Glos 36 C4
Arlington Devon 20 E5
Arlington E Sus 18 E2
Arlington Glos 37 D8
Armadale Highld 157 C10
Armadale W Loth 120 C2
Armadale Castle Highld 149 H11
Armathwaite Cumb 108 E5
Arminghall Norf 69 D5
Armitage Staffs 62 C4
Armley W Yorks 95 F5
Armscote Warks 51 E7
Armthorpe S Yorks 89 D7
Arnabost Argyll 146 F5
Arncliffe N Yorks 94 B2
Arncroach Fife 129 D7
Arne Dorset 13 F7
Arnesby Leics 64 E3
Arngask Perth 128 C3
Arnisdale Highld 149 G13
Arnish Highld 149 D10
Arniston Engine Midloth 121 C6
Arnol W Isles 155 C8
Arnold E Yorks 97 E7
Arnold Notts 77 E5
Arnprior Stirling 126 E5
Arnside Cumb 92 B4
Aros Mains Argyll 147 G8
Arowry Wrex 73 F8
Arpafeelie Highld 151 F9
Arrad Foot Cumb 99 F5
Arram E Yorks 97 E6
Arrathorne N Yorks 101 E7
Arreton IoW 15 F6
Arrington Cambs 54 D4
Arrivain Argyll 125 B8
Arrochar Argyll 125 E8
Arrow Warks 51 D5
Arthington W Yorks 95 E5
Arthingworth Northants 64 F4
Arthog Gwyn 58 C3
Arthrath Aberds 153 E9
Arthurstone Perth 134 E2
Artrochie Aberds 153 E10
Arundel W Sus 16 D4
Aryhoulan Highld 130 C4
Asby Cumb 98 B2
Ascog Argyll 145 G10
Ascot Windsor 27 C7
Ascott Warks 51 F8
Ascott-under-Wychwood Oxon 38 C3
Asenby N Yorks 95 B6
Asfordby Leics 64 C4
Asfordby Hill Leics 64 C4
Asgarby Lincs 78 E4
Asgarby Lincs 79 C6
Ash Kent 29 C6
Ash Kent 31 D6
Ash Som 12 B2
Ash Sur 27 D6
Ash Bullayne Devon 10 D2
Ash Green Warks 63 F7
Ash Magna Shrops 74 F2
Ash Mill Devon 10 B2
Ash Priors Som 11 B6
Ash Street Suff 56 E4
Ash Thomas Devon 10 C5
Ash Vale Sur 27 D6
Ashampstead W Berks 26 B3
Ashbocking Suff 57 D5
Ashbourne Derbys 75 E8
Ashbrittle Som 11 B5
Ashburton Devon 7 C5
Ashbury Devon 9 E7
Ashbury Oxon 38 F2
Ashby N Lincs 90 D3
Ashby by Partney Lincs 79 C7
Ashby cum Fenby NE Lincs 91 D6
Ashby de la Launde Lincs 78 D3
Ashby-de-la-Zouch Leics 63 C7
Ashby Folville Leics 64 C4
Ashby Magna Leics 64 E2
Ashby Parva Leics 64 F2
Ashby Puerorum Lincs 79 B6
Ashby St Ledgers Northants 52 C3
Ashby St Mary Norf 69 D6
Ashchurch Glos 50 F4
Ashcombe Devon 7 B7
Ashcott Som 23 F6
Ashdon Essex 55 E6
Ashe Hants 26 E3
Asheldham Essex 43 D5
Ashen Essex 55 E8
Ashendon Bucks 39 C7
Ashfield Carms 33 B7
Ashfield Stirling 127 D6
Ashfield Suff 57 C6
Ashfield Green Suff 57 B6
Ashfold Crossways W Sus 17 B6
Ashford Devon 20 F4
Ashford Hants 14 C2
Ashford Kent 30 E4
Ashford Sur 27 B8
Ashford Bowdler Shrops 49 B7
Ashford Carbonell Shrops 49 B7
Ashford Hill Hants 26 C3
Ashford in the Water Derbys 75 C8
Ashgill S Lanark 119 E7
Ashill Devon 11 C5
Ashill Norf 67 D8
Ashill Som 11 C8
Ashingdon Essex 42 E4
Ashington Northumb 117 F8
Ashington Som 12 B3
Ashington W Sus 16 C5
Ashintully Castle Perth 133 C8
Ashkirk Borders 115 B7
Ashlett Hants 15 D5
Ashleworth Glos 37 B5
Ashley Cambs 55 C7
Ashley Ches E 87 F5
Ashley Devon 9 C8
Ashley Dorset 14 D2
Ashley Glos 37 E6
Ashley Hants 14 E3
Ashley Hants 25 F8
Ashley Northants 64 E4
Ashley Staffs 74 F4
Ashley Green Bucks 40 D2
Ashley Heath Dorset 14 D2
Ashley Heath Staffs 74 F4
Ashmanhaugh Norf 69 B6
Ashmansworth Hants 26 D2
Ashmansworthy Devon 8 C5
Ashmore Dorset 13 C7
Ashorne Warks 51 D8
Ashover Derbys 76 C3
Ashow Warks 51 B8
Ashprington Devon 7 D6
Ashreigney Devon 9 C8
Ashtead Sur 28 D2
Ashton Ches W 74 C2
Ashton Corn 2 D5
Ashton Hants 15 C6
Ashton Hereford 49 C7
Ashton Involyd 118 B2
Ashton Northants 53 E5
Ashton Northants 65 F7
Ashton Common Wilts 24 D3
Ashton-In-Makerfield Gtr Man 86 E3
Ashton Keynes Wilts 37 E7
Ashton under Hill Worcs 50 F4
Ashton-under-Lyne Gtr Man 87 E7
Ashton upon Mersey Gtr Man 87 E5
Ashurst Hants 14 C4
Ashurst Kent 18 B2
Ashurst W Sus 17 C5
Ashurstwood W Sus 28 F5
Ashwater Devon 9 E5
Ashwell Herts 54 F3
Ashwell Rutland 65 C5
Ashwell Som 11 C8
Ashwellthorpe Norf 68 E4
Ashwick Som 23 E8
Ashwicken Norf 67 C7
Ashybank Borders 115 C8
Askam in Furness Cumb 92 B2
Askern S Yorks 89 C6
Askerswell Dorset 12 E3
Askett Bucks 39 D8
Askham Cumb 99 B7
Askham Notts 77 B7
Askham Bryan York 95 E8
Askham Richard York 95 E8
Asknish Argyll 145 D8
Askrigg N Yorks 100 E4
Askwith N Yorks 94 E4
Aslackby Lincs 78 F3
Aslacton Norf 68 E4
Aslockton Notts 77 F7
Asloun Aberds 140 C4
Aspatria Cumb 107 E8
Aspenden Herts 41 B6
Asperton Lincs 79 F5
Aspley Guise C Beds 53 F7
Aspley Heath C Beds 53 F7
Aspull Gtr Man 86 D4
Asselby E Yorks 89 B8
Asserby Lincs 79 B7
Assington Suff 56 F3
Assynt Ho. Highld 151 E8
Astbury Ches E 74 C5
Astcote Northants 52 D4
Asterley Shrops 60 D3
Asterton Shrops 60 E3
Asthall Oxon 38 C2
Asthall Leigh Oxon 38 C3
Astley Shrops 60 C5
Astley Warks 63 F7
Astley Worcs 50 C2
Astley Abbotts Shrops 61 E7
Astley Bridge Gtr Man 86 C5
Astley Cross Worcs 50 C3
Astley Green Gtr Man 86 E5
Aston Ches E 74 E3
Aston Ches W 74 B2
Aston Derbys 88 F2
Aston Hereford 49 B6
Aston Herts 41 B5
Aston Oxon 38 D3
Aston S Yorks 89 F5
Aston Shrops 60 B5
Aston Staffs 74 E4
Aston Telford 61 D6
Aston W Mid 62 F4
Aston Wokingham 39 F7
Aston Abbotts Bucks 39 B8
Aston Botterell Shrops 61 F6
Aston-By-Stone Staffs 75 F6
Aston Cantlow Warks 51 D6
Aston Clinton Bucks 40 C1
Aston Crews Hereford 36 B3
Aston Cross Glos 50 F4
Aston End Herts 41 B5
Aston Eyre Shrops 61 E6
Aston Fields Worcs 50 C4
Aston Flamville Leics 63 E8
Aston Ingham Hereford 36 B3
Aston juxta Mondrum Ches E 74 D3
Aston le Walls Northants 52 D2
Aston Magna Glos 51 F6
Aston Munslow Shrops 60 F5
Aston on Clun Shrops 60 F3
Aston-on-Trent Derbys 63 B8
Aston Rogers Shrops 60 D3
Aston Rowant Oxon 39 E7
Aston Sandford Bucks 39 D7
Aston Somerville Worcs 50 F5
Aston Subedge Glos 51 E6
Aston Tirrold Oxon 39 F5
Aston Upthorpe Oxon 39 F5
Astrop Northants 52 F3
Astwick C Beds 54 F3
Astwood M Keynes 53 E7
Astwood Worcs 50 D3
Astwood Bank Worcs 50 C5
Aswarby Lincs 78 F3
Aswardby Lincs 79 B6
Atch Lench Worcs 50 D5
Atcham Shrops 60 D5
Athelhampton Dorset 13 E5
Athelington Suff 57 B6
Athelney Som 11 B8
Athelstaneford E Loth 121 B8
Atherington Devon 9 B7
Atherstone Warks 63 E7
Atherstone on Stour Warks 51 D7
Atherton Gtr Man 86 D4
Atley Hill N Yorks 101 D7
Atlow Derbys 76 E2
Attadale Highld 150 H2
Attadale Ho. Highld 150 H2
Attenborough Notts 76 F5
Atterby Lincs 90 E3
Attercliffe S Yorks 88 F4
Attleborough Norf 68 E3
Attleborough Warks 63 E7
Attlebridge Norf 68 C4
Atwick E Yorks 97 D7
Atworth Wilts 24 C3
Aubourn Lincs 78 C2
Auchagallon N Ayrs 143 E9
Auchallater Aberds 139 F7
Aucharnie Aberds 153 D6
Auchattie Aberds 141 E5
Auchavan Angus 134 C1
Auchbreck Moray 139 B8
Auchenback E Renf 118 D5
Auchenbainzie Dumfries 113 E8
Auchenblae Aberds 135 B7
Auchenbrack Dumfries 113 E7
Auchenbreck Argyll 145 E9
Auchencairn Dumfries 106 D4
Auchencairn Dumfries 114 F2
Auchencairn N Ayrs 143 F11
Auchencrosh S Ayrs 104 B5
Auchencrow Borders 122 C4
Auchendinny Midloth 121 C5
Auchengray S Lanark 120 D2
Auchenhalrig Moray 152 B3
Auchenheath S Lanark 119 E8
Auchenlochan Argyll 145 F8
Auchenmalg Dumfries 105 D6
Auchensoul S Ayrs 112 E2
Auchentiber N Ayrs 118 E3
Auchertyre Highld 149 F13
Auchgourish Highld 138 C5
Auchincarroch W Dunb 126 F3
Auchindrain Argyll 125 E6
Auchindrean Highld 150 C4
Auchininna Aberds 153 D6
Auchinleck E Ayrs 113 B5
Auchinloch N Lanark 119 B6
Auchinroath Moray 152 C2
Auchintoul Aberds 140 C4
Auchiries Aberds 153 E10
Auchlee Aberds 141 E7
Auchleven Aberds 140 B5
Auchlochan S Lanark 119 F8
Auchlossan Aberds 140 D4
Auchlunies Aberds 141 E7
Auchlyne Stirling 126 B4
Auchmacoy Aberds 153 E9
Auchmair Moray 140 B2
Auchmantle Dumfries 105 C5
Auchmillan E Ayrs 112 B5
Auchmithie Angus 135 E6
Auchmuirbridge Fife 128 D4
Auchmull Angus 135 B5
Auchnacree Angus 134 C4
Auchnagallin Highld 151 H13
Auchnagatt Aberds 153 D9
Auchnaha Argyll 145 E8
Auchnashelloch Perth 127 C6
Aucholzie Aberds 140 E2
Auchrannie Angus 134 D2
Auchroisk Highld 139 B6
Auchronie Angus 140 F3
Auchterarder Perth 127 C8
Auchteraw Highld 137 D6
Auchterderran Fife 128 E4
Auchterhouse Angus 134 F3
Auchtermuchty Fife 128 C4
Auchterneed Highld 150 F7
Auchtertool Fife 128 E4
Auchtertyre Moray 152 C1
Auchtubh Stirling 126 B4
Auckengill Highld 158 D5
Auckley S Yorks 89 D7
Audenshaw Gtr Man 87 E7
Audlem Ches E 74 E3
Audley Staffs 74 D4
Audley End Essex 56 F2
Auds Aberds 153 B6
Aughton E Yorks 96 F3
Aughton Lancs 85 D4
Aughton Lancs 93 C5
Aughton S Yorks 89 F5
Aughton Wilts 25 D7
Aughton Park Lancs 86 D2
Auldearn Highld 151 F12
Aulden Hereford 49 D6
Auldgirth Dumfries 114 F2
Auldhame E Loth 129 F7
Auldhouse S Lanark 119 D6
Ault a'chruinn Highld 136 B2
Aultanrynie Highld 156 F6
Aultbea Highld 155 J13
Aultdearg Highld 150 E5
Aultgrishan Highld 155 J12
Aultguish Inn Highld 150 D6
Aultibea Highld 157 G13
Aultiphurst Highld 157 C11
Aultmore Moray 152 C4
Aultnagoire Highld 137 B8
Aultnamain Inn Highld 151 C9
Aultnaslat Highld 136 D4
Aulton Aberds 140 B5
Aundorach Highld 139 C5
Aunsby Lincs 78 F3
Auquhorthies Aberds 141 B7
Aust S Glos 36 F2
Austendike Lincs 66 B2
Austerfield S Yorks 89 E7
Austrey Warks 63 D6
Austwick N Yorks 93 C7
Authorpe Lincs 91 F8
Authorpe Row Lincs 79 B8
Avebury Wilts 25 C6
Aveley Thurrock 42 F1
Avening Glos 37 E5
Averham Notts 77 D7
Aveton Gifford Devon 6 E4
Avielochan Highld 138 C5
Aviemore Highld 138 C4
Avington Hants 26 F3
Avington W Berks 25 C8
Avoch Highld 151 F10
Avon Hants 14 E2
Avon Dassett Warks 52 E2
Avonbridge Falk 120 B2
Avonmouth Bristol 23 B7
Avonwick Devon 6 D5
Awbridge Hants 14 B4
Awhirk Dumfries 104 D4
Awkley S Glos 36 F2
Awliscombe Devon 11 D6
Awre Glos 36 D4
Awsworth Notts 76 E4
Axbridge Som 23 D6
Axford Hants 26 E4
Axford Wilts 25 B7
Axminster Devon 11 E7
Axmouth Devon 11 E7
Axton Flint 85 F2
Aycliff Kent 31 E7
Aycliffe Durham 101 B7
Aydon Northumb 110 C3
Aylburton Glos 36 D3
Ayle Northumb 109 E7
Aylesbeare Devon 10 E5
Aylesbury Bucks 39 C8
Aylesby NE Lincs 91 D6
Aylesford Kent 29 D8
Aylesham Kent 31 D6
Aylestone Leicester 64 D2
Aylmerton Norf 81 D7
Aylsham Norf 81 E7
Aylton Hereford 49 F8
Aymestrey Hereford 49 C6
Aynho Northants 52 F3
Ayot St Lawrence Herts 40 C4
Ayot St Peter Herts 41 C5
Ayr S Ayrs 112 B3
Aysgarth N Yorks 101 F5
Ayside Cumb 99 F5
Ayston Rutland 65 D5
Aythorpe Roding Essex 42 C1
Ayton Borders 122 C5
Aywick Shetland 160 E7
Azerley N Yorks 95 B5

B

Babbacombe Torbay 7 C7
Babbinswood Shrops 73 F7
Babcary Som 12 B3
Babel Carms 47 F7
Babell Flint 73 B5
Babraham Cambs 55 D6
Babworth Notts 89 F7
Bac W Isles 155 C9
Bachau Anglesey 82 C4
Back of Keppoch Highld 147 C9
Back Rogerton E Ayrs 113 B5
Backaland Orkney 159 E6
Backaskaill Orkney 159 C5
Backbarrow Cumb 99 F5
Backe Carms 32 C3
Backfolds Aberds 153 C10
Backford Ches W 73 B8
Backford Cross Ches W 73 B7
Backhill Aberds 153 E7
Backhill Aberds 153 E10
Backhill of Clackriach Aberds 153 D9
Backhill of Fortree Aberds 153 D9
Backhill of Trustach Aberds 140 E5
Backies Highld 157 J11
Backlass Highld 158 E4
Backwell N Som 23 C6
Backworth T&W 111 B6
Bacon End Essex 42 C2
Baconsthorpe Norf 81 D7
Bacton Hereford 49 F5
Bacton Norf 81 D9
Bacton Suff 56 C4
Bacton Green Suff 56 C4
Bacup Lancs 87 B6
Badachro Highld 149 A12
Badanloch Lodge Highld 157 F10
Badavanich Highld 150 F4
Badbury Swindon 38 F1
Badby Northants 52 D3
Badcall Highld 156 D5
Badcaul Highld 150 B3
Baddeley Green Stoke 75 D6
Baddesley Clinton Warks 51 B7
Baddesley Ensor Warks 63 E6
Baddidarach Highld 156 G3
Baddoch Aberds 139 F7
Baddock Highld 151 F10
Badenscoth Aberds 153 E7
Badenyon Aberds 140 C2
Badger Shrops 61 E7
Badger's Mount Kent 29 C5
Badgeworth Glos 37 C6
Badgworth Som 23 D5
Badicaul Highld 149 F12
Badingham Suff 57 C7
Badlesmere Kent 30 D4
Badlipster Highld 158 F4
Badluarach Highld 150 B2
Badminton S Glos 37 F5
Badnaban Highld 156 G3
Badninish Highld 151 B10
Badrallach Highld 150 B3
Badsey Worcs 51 E5
Badshot Lea Sur 27 E6
Badsworth W Yorks 89 C5
Badwell Ash Suff 56 C3
Bae Colwyn = Colwyn Bay Conwy 83 D8
Bag Enderby Lincs 79 B6
Bagby N Yorks 102 F2
Bagendon Glos 37 D7
Bagh a Chaisteil = Castlebay W Isles 148 J1
Bagh Mor W Isles 148 C3
Bagh Shiarabhagh W Isles 148 H2
Baghasdal W Isles 148 G2
Bagillt Flint 73 B6
Baginton Warks 51 B8
Baglan Neath 33 E8
Bagley Shrops 60 B4
Bagnall Staffs 75 D6
Bagnor W Berks 26 C2
Bagshot Sur 27 C7
Bagshot Wilts 25 C8
Bagthorpe Norf 80 D3
Bagthorpe Notts 76 D4
Bagworth Leics 63 D8
Bagwy Llydiart Hereford 35 B8
Bail Àrd Bhuirgh W Isles 155 B9
Bail Uachdraich W Isles 148 B3
Baildon W Yorks 94 F4
Baile W Isles 154 J4
Baile a Mhanaich W Isles 148 C2
Baile Ailein W Isles 155 E7
Baile an Truiseil W Isles 155 B8
Baile Boidheach Argyll 144 F6
Baile Glas W Isles 148 C3
Baile Mhartainn W Isles 148 A2
Baile Mhic Phail W Isles 148 A3
Baile Mor Argyll 146 J5
Baile Mor W Isles 148 B2
Baile na Creige W Isles 148 H1
Baile nan Cailleach W Isles 148 C2
Baile Raghaill W Isles 148 A2
Bailebeag Highld 137 C8
Baileyhead Cumb 108 B5
Bailiesward Aberds 152 E4
Baillieston Glasgow 119 C6
Bail'lochdrach W Isles 148 C3
Bail'Ur Tholastaidh W Isles 155 C10
Bainbridge N Yorks 100 E4
Bainsford Falk 127 F7
Bainshole Aberds 152 E6
Bainton E Yorks 97 D5
Bainton Pboro 65 D7
Bairnkine Borders 116 C2
Baker Street Thurrock 42 F2
Baker's End Herts 41 C6
Bakewell Derbys 76 C2
Bala = Y Bala Gwyn 72 F3
Balachuirn Highld 149 D10
Balavil Highld 138 D3
Balbeg Highld 137 B7
Balbeg Highld 150 H7
Balbeggie Perth 128 B3
Balbithan Aberds 141 C6
Balbithan Ho. Aberds 141 C7
Balblair Highld 151 B8
Balblair Highld 151 E10
Balby S Yorks 89 D6
Balchladich Highld 156 F3
Balchraggan Highld 151 G8
Balchraggan Highld 151 H8
Balchrick Highld 156 D4
Balchrystie Fife 129 D6
Balcladaich Highld 137 B5
Balcombe W Sus 28 F4
Balcombe Lane W Sus 28 F4
Balcomie Fife 129 C8
Balcurvie Fife 128 D5
Baldersby N Yorks 95 B6
Baldersby St James N Yorks 95 B6
Balderstone Lancs 93 F6
Balderton Ches W 73 C7
Balderton Notts 77 D8
Baldhu Corn 3 B6
Baldinnie Fife 129 C6
Baldock Herts 54 F3
Baldovie Dundee 134 F4
Baldrine IoM 84 D4
Baldslow E Sus 18 D4
Baldwin IoM 84 D3
Baldwinholme Cumb 108 D3
Baldwin's Gate Staffs 74 E4
Bale Norf 81 D6
Balearn Aberds 153 C10
Balemartine Argyll 146 G2
Balephuil Argyll 146 G2
Balerno Edin 120 C4
Balevullin Argyll 146 G2
Balfield Angus 135 C5
Balfour Orkney 159 G5
Balfron Stirling 126 F4
Balfron Station Stirling 126 F4
Balgaveny Aberds 153 D6
Balgavies Angus 135 D5
Balgonar Fife 128 E2
Balgove Aberds 153 E8
Balgowan Highld 138 E2
Balgown Highld 149 B8
Balgrochan E Dunb 119 B6
Balgy Highld 149 C13
Balhaldie Stirling 127 D7
Balhalgardy Aberds 141 B6
Balham London 28 B3
Balhary Perth 134 E2
Baliasta Shetland 160 C8
Baligill Highld 157 C11
Balintore Angus 134 D2
Balintore Highld 151 D11
Balintraid Highld 151 D10
Balk N Yorks 102 F2
Balkeerie Angus 134 E3
Balkemback Angus 134 F3
Balkholme E Yorks 89 B8
Balkissock S Ayrs 104 A5
Ball Shrops 60 B3
Ball Haye Green Staffs 75 D6
Ball Hill Hants 26 C2
Ballabeg IoM 84 E2
Ballacannel IoM 84 D4
Ballachulish Highld 130 D4
Ballajora IoM 84 C4
Ballaleigh IoM 84 D3
Ballamodha IoM 84 E2
Ballantrae S Ayrs 104 A4
Ballaquine IoM 84 D4
Ballards Gore Essex 43 E5
Ballasalla IoM 84 C3
Ballasalla IoM 84 E2
Ballater Aberds 140 E2
Ballaugh IoM 84 C3
Ballaveare IoM 84 E3
Ballcorach Moray 139 B7
Ballechin Perth 133 D6
Balleigh Highld 151 C10
Ballencrieff E Loth 121 B7
Ballentoul Perth 133 C5
Ballidon Derbys 76 D2
Balliemore Argyll 124 C4
Balliemore Argyll 145 E9
Ballikinrain Stirling 126 F4
Ballimeanoch Argyll 125 D6
Ballimore Argyll 145 E8
Ballimore Stirling 126 C4
Ballinaby Argyll 142 B3
Ballindean Perth 128 B4
Ballingdon Suff 56 E2
Ballinger Common Bucks 40 D2
Ballingham Hereford 49 F7
Ballingry Fife 128 E3
Ballinlick Perth 133 E6
Ballinluig Perth 133 D6
Ballintuim Perth 133 D8
Balloch Angus 134 D3
Balloch Highld 151 G10
Balloch N Lanark 119 B7
Balloch W Dunb 126 F2
Ballochan Aberds 140 E4
Ballochford Moray 152 E3
Ballochmorrie S Ayrs 112 F2
Balls Cross W Sus 16 B3
Balls Green Essex 43 B6
Ballygown Argyll 146 G7
Ballygrant Argyll 142 B4
Ballyhaugh Argyll 146 F4
Balmacara Highld 149 F13
Balmacara Square Highld 149 F13
Balmaclellan Dumfries 106 B3
Balmacneil Perth 133 D6
Balmacqueen Highld 149 A9
Balmae Dumfries 106 E3
Balmaha Stirling 126 E3
Balmalcolm Fife 128 D5
Balmeanach Highld 149 D10
Balmedie Aberds 141 C8
Balmer Heath Shrops 73 F8
Balmerino Fife 129 B5
Balmerlawn Hants 14 D4
Balmichael N Ayrs 143 E10
Balmirmer Angus 135 F5
Balmore Highld 149 D7
Balmore Highld 150 H6
Balmore Highld 151 G11
Balmore Perth 133 D6
Balmule Fife 128 F4
Balmullo Fife 129 B6
Balmungie Highld 151 F10
Balnaboth Angus 134 C3
Balnabruaich Highld 151 E10
Balnabruich Highld 158 H3
Balnacoil Highld 157 H11
Balnacra Highld 150 G2
Balnafoich Highld 151 H9
Balnagall Highld 151 C11
Balnaguard Perth 133 D6
Balnahard Argyll 144 D3
Balnahard Argyll 146 H7
Balnain Highld 150 H7
Balnakeil Highld 156 C6
Balnaknock Highld 149 B9
Balnapaling Highld 151 E10
Balne N Yorks 89 C6
Balochroy Argyll 143 C8
Balone Fife 129 C6
Balornock Glasgow 119 C6
Balquharn Perth 133 F7
Balquhidder Stirling 126 B4
Balsall W Mid 51 B7
Balsall Common W Mid 51 B7
Balsall Heath W Mid 62 F4
Balscott Oxon 51 E8
Balsham Cambs 55 D6
Baltasound Shetland 160 C8
Balterley Staffs 74 D4
Baltersan Dumfries 105 C8
Balthangie Aberds 153 C8
Baltonsborough Som 23 F7
Balvaird Highld 151 F8
Balvicar Argyll 124 D3
Balvraid Highld 149 G13
Balvraid Highld 151 H11
Bamber Bridge Lancs 86 B3
Bambers Green Essex 42 B1
Bamburgh Northumb 123 F7
Bamff Perth 134 D2
Bamford Derbys 88 F3
Bamford Gtr Man 87 C6
Bampton Cumb 99 C7
Bampton Devon 10 B4
Bampton Oxon 38 D3
Bampton Grange Cumb 99 C7
Banavie Highld 131 B5
Banbury Oxon 52 E2
Bancffosfelen Carms 33 C5
Banchory Aberds 141 E5
Banchory-Devenick Aberds 141 D8
Bancycapel Carms 33 C5
Bancyfelin Carms 32 C4
Bancyffordd Carms 46 F3
Bandirran Perth 134 F2
Banff Aberds 153 B6
Bangor Gwyn 83 D5
Bangor-is-y-coed Wrex 73 E7
Banham Norf 68 F3
Bank Hants 14 D3
Bank Newton N Yorks 94 D2
Bank Street Worcs 49 C8
Bankend Dumfries 107 C7
Bankfoot Perth 133 F7
Bankglen E Ayrs 113 C6
Bankhead Aberdeen 141 C7
Bankhead Aberds 141 D5
Banknock Falk 119 B7
Banks Cumb 109 C5
Banks Lancs 85 B4
Bankshill Dumfries 114 F4
Banningham Norf 81 E8
Banniskirk Ho. Highld 158 E3
Bannister Green Essex 42 B2
Bannockburn Stirling 127 E7
Banstead Sur 28 D3
Bantham Devon 6 E4
Banton N Lanark 119 B7
Banwell N Som 23 D5
Banyard's Green Suff 57 B6
Bapchild Kent 30 C3
Bar Hill Cambs 54 C4
Barabhas W Isles 155 C8
Barabhas Iarach W Isles 155 C8
Barabhas Uarach W Isles 155 B8
Barachandroman Argyll 124 C2
Barassie S Ayrs 118 F3
Baravullin Argyll 124 E4
Barbaraville Highld 151 D10
Barber Booth Derbys 88 F2
Barbieston S Ayrs 112 C4
Barbon Cumb 99 F8
Barbridge Ches E 74 D3
Barbrook Devon 21 E6
Barby Northants 52 B3
Barcaldine Argyll 130 E3
Barcheston Warks 51 F7
Barcombe E Sus 17 C8
Barcombe Cross E Sus 17 C8
Barden N Yorks 101 E6
Barden Scale N Yorks 94 D3
Bardennoch Dumfries 113 E5
Bardfield Saling Essex 42 B2
Bardister Shetland 160 F5
Bardney Lincs 78 C4
Bardon Leics 63 C8
Bardon Mill Northumb 109 C7
Bardowie E Dunb 119 B5
Bardrainney Involyd 118 B3
Bardsea Cumb 92 B3
Bardsey W Yorks 95 E6
Bardwell Suff 56 B3
Bare Lancs 92 C4
Barfad Argyll 145 G7
Barford Norf 68 D4
Barford Warks 51 C7
Barford St John Oxon 52 F2
Barford St Martin Wilts 25 F5
Barford St Michael Oxon 52 F2
Barfrestone Kent 31 D6
Bargod = Bargoed Caerph 35 E5
Bargoed = Bargod Caerph 35 E5
Bargrennan Dumfries 105 B7
Barham Cambs 54 B2
Barham Kent 31 D6
Barham Suff 56 D5
Barharrow Dumfries 106 D3
Barhill Dumfries 106 C5
Barholm Lincs 65 C7
Barkby Leics 64 D3
Barkestone-le-Vale Leics 77 F7
Barkham Wokingham 27 C5
Barking London 41 F7
Barking Suff 56 D4
Barking Tye Suff 56 D4
Barkingside London 41 F7
Barkisland W Yorks 87 C8
Barkston Lincs 78 E2
Barkston N Yorks 95 F7
Barkway Herts 54 F4
Barlaston Staffs 75 F5
Barlavington W Sus 16 C3
Barlborough Derbys 76 B4
Barlby N Yorks 96 F2
Barlestone Leics 63 D8
Barley Herts 54 F4
Barley Lancs 93 E8
Barley Mow T&W 111 D5
Barleythorpe Rutland 64 D5
Barling Essex 43 F5
Barlow Derbys 76 B3
Barlow N Yorks 89 B7
Barlow T&W 110 C4
Barmby Moor E Yorks 96 E3
Barmby on the Marsh E Yorks 89 B7
Barmer Norf 80 D4
Barmoor Castle Northumb 123 F5
Barmoor Lane End Northumb 123 F6
Barmouth = Abermaw Gwyn 58 C3
Barmpton Darl 101 C8
Barmston E Yorks 97 D7
Barnack Pboro 65 D7
Barnacle Warks 63 F7
Barnard Castle Durham 101 C5
Barnard Gate Oxon 38 C4
Barnardiston Suff 55 E8
Barnbarroch Dumfries 106 D5
Barnburgh S Yorks 89 D5
Barnby Suff 69 F7
Barnby Dun S Yorks 89 D7
Barnby in the Willows Notts 77 D8
Barnby Moor Notts 89 F7
Barnes Street Kent 29 E7
Barnet London 41 E5
Barnetby le Wold N Lincs 90 D4
Barney Norf 81 D5
Barnham Suff 56 B2
Barnham W Sus 16 D3
Barnham Broom Norf 68 D3
Barnhead Angus 135 D6
Barnhill Ches W 73 D8
Barnhill Dundee 134 F4
Barnhill Moray 152 C1
Barnhills Dumfries 104 B3
Barningham Durham 101 C5
Barningham Suff 56 B3
Barnoldby le Beck NE Lincs 91 D6
Barnoldswick Lancs 93 E8
Barns Green W Sus 16 B5
Barnsley Glos 37 D7
Barnsley S Yorks 88 D4
Barnstaple Devon 20 F4
Barnston Essex 42 C2
Barnston Mers 85 F3
Barnstone Notts 77 F7
Barnt Green Worcs 50 B5
Barnton Ches W 74 B3
Barnton Edin 120 B4
Barnwell All Saints Northants 65 F7
Barnwell St Andrew Northants 65 F7
Barnwood Glos 37 C5
Barochreal Argyll 124 C4
Barons Cross Hereford 49 D6
Barr S Ayrs 112 E2
Barra Castle Aberds 141 B6
Barrachan Dumfries 105 E7
Barrack Aberds 153 D8
Barraglom W Isles 154 D6
Barrahormid Argyll 144 E6
Barran Argyll 124 C4
Barrapol Argyll 146 G2
Barras Aberds 141 F7
Barras Cumb 100 C3
Barrasford Northumb 110 B2
Barravullin Argyll 124 E4
Barregarrow IoM 84 D3
Barrhead E Renf 118 D4
Barrhill S Ayrs 112 F2
Barrington Cambs 54 E4
Barrington Som 11 C8
Barripper Corn 2 C5
Barrmill N Ayrs 118 D3
Barrock Highld 158 C4
Barrock Ho. Highld 158 D4
Barrow Lancs 93 F7
Barrow Rutland 65 C5
Barrow Suff 55 C8
Barrow Green Kent 30 C3
Barrow Gurney N Som 23 C7
Barrow Haven N Lincs 90 B4
Barrow-in-Furness Cumb 92 C2
Barrow Island Cumb 92 C1
Barrow Nook Lancs 86 D2
Barrow Street Wilts 24 F3
Barrow upon Humber N Lincs 90 B4
Barrow upon Soar Leics 64 C2
Barrow upon Trent Derbys 63 B7
Barroway Drove Norf 67 D5
Barrowburn Northumb 116 C4
Barrowby Lincs 77 F8
Barrowcliff N Yorks 103 F8
Barrowden Rutland 65 D6
Barrowford Lancs 93 F8
Barrows Green Ches E 74 D3
Barrows Green Cumb 99 F7
Barrow's Green Mers 86 F3
Barry Angus 135 F5
Barry = Y Barri V Glam 22 C3
Barry Island V Glam 22 C3
Barsby Leics 64 C3
Barsham Suff 69 F6
Barston W Mid 51 B7
Bartestree Hereford 49 E7
Barthol Chapel Aberds 153 E8
Barthomley Ches E 74 D4
Bartley Hants 14 C4
Bartley Green W Mid 62 F4
Bartlow Cambs 55 E6
Barton Cambs 54 D5
Barton Ches W 73 D8
Barton Glos 37 B8
Barton Lancs 85 D4
Barton Lancs 92 F5
Barton N Yorks 101 D7
Barton Oxon 39 D5
Barton Torbay 7 C7
Barton Warks 51 D6
Barton Bendish Norf 67 D7
Barton Hartshorn Bucks 52 F4
Barton in Fabis Notts 76 F5
Barton in the Beans Leics 63 D7
Barton-le-Clay C Beds 53 F8
Barton-le-Street N Yorks 96 B3
Barton-le-Willows N Yorks 96 C3
Barton Mills Suff 55 B8
Barton on Sea Hants 14 E3
Barton on the Heath Warks 51 F7
Barton St David Som 23 F7
Barton Seagrave Northants 53 B6
Barton Stacey Hants 26 E2
Barton Turf Norf 69 B6
Barton-under-Needwood Staffs 63 C5
Barton-upon-Humber N Lincs 90 B4
Barton Waterside N Lincs 90 B4
Barugh S Yorks 88 D4
Barway Cambs 55 B6
Barwell Leics 63 E8
Barwick Herts 41 C6
Barwick Som 12 C3
Barwick in Elmet W Yorks 95 F6
Baschurch Shrops 60 B4
Bascote Warks 52 C2
Basford Green Staffs 75 D6
Bashall Eaves Lancs 93 E6
Bashley Hants 14 E3
Basildon Essex 42 F3
Basingstoke Hants 26 D4
Baslow Derbys 76 B2
Bason Bridge Som 22 E5
Bassaleg Newport 35 F6
Bassenthwaite Cumb 108 F2
Bassett Soton 14 C5
Bassingbourn Cambs 54 E4
Bassingfield Notts 77 F6
Bassingham Lincs 78 C2
Bassingthorpe Lincs 65 B6
Basta Shetland 160 D7
Baston Lincs 65 C8
Bastwick Norf 69 C7
Baswick Steer E Yorks 97 E6
Batchworth Heath Herts 40 E3
Batcombe Dorset 12 D4
Batcombe Som 23 F8
Bate Heath Ches E 74 B3
Batford Herts 40 C4
Bath Bath 24 C2
Bathampton Bath 24 C2
Bathealton Som 11 B5
Batheaston Bath 24 C2
Bathford Bath 24 C2
Bathgate W Loth 120 C2
Bathley Notts 77 D7
Bathpool Corn 5 B7
Bathpool Som 11 B7
Bathville W Loth 120 C2
Batley W Yorks 88 B3
Batsford Glos 51 F6
Battersby N Yorks 102 D3
Battersea London 28 B3
Battisborough Cross Devon 6 E3
Battisford Suff 56 D4
Battisford Tye Suff 56 D4
Battle E Sus 18 D4
Battle Powys 48 F2
Battledown Glos 37 B6
Battlefield Shrops 60 C5
Battlesbridge Essex 42 E3
Battlesden C Beds 40 B2
Battlesea Green Suff 57 B6
Battleton Som 10 B4
Battram Leics 63 D8
Battramsley Hants 14 E4
Baughton Worcs 50 E3
Baughurst Hants 26 D3

214 Bra – Bux

Braaid IoM 84 E3
Braal Castle Highld 158 D3
Brabling Green Suff 57 C6
Brabourne Kent 30 E4
Brabourne Lees Kent 30 E4
Brabster Highld 158 D5
Bracadale Highld 149 E8
Bracara Highld 147 B10
Braceborough Lincs 65 C7
Bracebridge Lincs 78 C2
Bracebridge Heath Lincs 78 C2
Bracebridge Low Fields Lincs 78 C2
Braceby Lincs 78 F3
Bracewell Lancs 93 E8
Brackenfield Derbys 76 D3
Brackenthwaite Cumb 108 E2
Brackenthwaite N Yorks 95 D5
Bracklesham W Sus 16 E2
Brackletter Highld 136 F4
Brackley Argyll 143 D8
Brackley Northants 52 F3
Brackloch Highld 156 G4
Bracknell Brack 27 C6
Braco Perth 127 D7
Bracobrae Moray 152 C5
Bracon Ash Norf 68 E4
Bracorina Highld 147 B10
Bradbourne Derbys 76 D2
Bradbury Durham 101 B8
Bradda IoM 84 F1
Bradden Northants 52 E4
Braddock Corn 5 C6
Bradeley Stoke 75 D5
Bradenham Bucks 39 E8
Bradenham Norf 68 D2
Bradenstoke Wilts 24 B5
Bradfield Essex 56 F5
Bradfield Norf 81 D8
Bradfield W Berks 26 B4
Bradfield Combust Suff 56 D2
Bradfield Green Ches E 74 D3
Bradfield Heath Essex 43 B7
Bradfield St Clare Suff 56 D3
Bradfield St George Suff 56 C3
Bradford Corn 5 B6
Bradford Derbys 76 C2
Bradford Devon 9 D6
Bradford Northumb 123 F7
Bradford W Yorks 94 F4
Bradford Abbas Dorset 12 C3
Bradford Leigh Wilts 24 C3
Bradford-on-Avon Wilts 24 C3
Bradford-on-Tone Som 11 B6
Bradford Peverell Dorset 12 E4
Brading IoW 15 F7
Bradley Derbys 76 E2
Bradley Hants 26 E4
Bradley NE Lincs 91 D6
Bradley Staffs 62 C2
Bradley W Mid 62 E3
Bradley W Yorks 88 B2
Bradley Green Worcs 50 C4
Bradley in the Moors Staffs 75 E7
Bradlow Hereford 50 F2
Bradmore Notts 77 F5
Bradmore W Mid 62 E2
Bradninch Devon 10 D5
Bradnop Staffs 75 D7
Bradpole Dorset 12 E2
Bradshaw Gtr Man 86 C5
Bradshaw W Yorks 87 C8
Bradstone Devon 9 F5
Bradwall Green Ches E 74 C4
Bradway S Yorks 88 F4
Bradwell Derbys 88 F2
Bradwell Essex 42 B4
Bradwell M Keynes 53 F6
Bradwell Norf 69 D8
Bradwell Staffs 74 E5
Bradwell Grove Oxon 38 D2
Bradwell on Sea Essex 43 D6
Bradwell Waterside Essex 43 D5
Bradworthy Devon 8 C5
Bradworthy Cross Devon 8 C5
Brae Dumfries 107 B5
Brae Highld 155 J13
Brae Highld 156 J7
Brae Shetland 160 G5
Brae of Achnahaird Highld 156 H3
Brae Roy Lodge Highld 137 E6
Braeantra Highld 151 D8
Braedownie Angus 134 B2
Braefield Highld 150 H7
Braegrum Perth 128 B2
Braehead Dumfries 105 D8
Braehead Orkney 159 D5
Braehead Orkney 159 H6
Braehead S Lanark 119 F8
Braehead S Lanark 120 D2
Braehead of Lunan Angus 135 D6
Braehoulland Shetland 160 F4
Braehungie Highld 158 G3
Braelangwell Lodge Highld 151 B8
Braemar Aberds 139 E7
Braemore Highld 150 D4
Braemore Highld 158 G2
Braes of Enzie Moray 152 C3
Braeside Invclyd 118 B2
Braeswick Orkney 159 E7
Braewick Shetland 160 H5
Brafferton Darl 101 B7
Brafferton N Yorks 95 B7
Brafield-on-the-Green Northants 53 D6
Bragar W Isles 155 C7
Bragbury End Herts 41 B5
Bragleenmore Argyll 124 C5
Braichmelyn Gwyn 83 E6
Braid Edin 120 C5
Braides Lancs 92 D4
Braidley N Yorks 101 F5
Braidwood S Lanark 119 E8
Braigo Argyll 142 B3
Brailsford Derbys 76 E2
Brainshaugh Northumb 117 D8
Braintree Essex 42 B3
Braiseworth Suff 56 B5
Braishfield Hants 14 B4
Braithwaite Cumb 98 B4
Braithwaite S Yorks 89 C7
Braithwaite W Yorks 94 E3
Braithwell S Yorks 89 E6
Bramber W Sus 17 C5
Bramcote Notts 76 F5
Bramcote Warks 63 F8
Bramdean Hants 15 B7
Bramerton Norf 69 D5
Bramfield Herts 41 C5
Bramfield Suff 57 B7
Bramford Suff 56 E5
Bramhall Gtr Man 87 F6
Bramham W Yorks 95 E7
Bramhope W Yorks 95 E5
Bramley Hants 26 D4
Bramley S Yorks 89 E5
Bramley Sur 27 E8
Bramley W Yorks 94 F5
Bramling Kent 31 D6
Brampford Speke Devon 10 E4
Brampton Cambs 54 B3
Brampton Cumb 100 B1
Brampton Cumb 108 C5
Brampton Derbys 76 B3
Brampton Hereford 49 F6
Brampton Lincs 77 B8
Brampton Norf 81 E8
Brampton S Yorks 88 D5
Brampton Suff 69 F7
Brampton Abbotts Hereford 36 B3
Brampton Ash Northants 64 F4
Brampton Bryan Hereford 49 B5
Brampton en le Morthen S Yorks 89 F5
Bramshall Staffs 75 F7
Bramshaw Hants 14 C3
Bramshill Hants 26 C5
Bramshott Hants 27 F6
Bran End Essex 42 B2
Branault Highld 147 E8
Brancaster Norf 80 C3
Brancaster Staithe Norf 80 C3
Brancepeth Durham 110 F5
Branch End Northumb 110 C3
Branchill Moray 151 F13
Brand Green Glos 36 B4
Branderburgh Moray 152 A2
Brandesburton E Yorks 97 E7
Brandeston Suff 57 C6
Brandhill Shrops 49 B6
Brandis Corner Devon 9 D6
Brandiston Norf 81 E7
Brandon Durham 110 F5
Brandon Lincs 78 E2
Brandon Northumb 117 C6
Brandon Suff 67 F7
Brandon Warks 52 B2
Brandon Bank Cambs 67 F6
Brandon Creek Norf 67 E6
Brandon Parva Norf 68 D3
Brandsby N Yorks 95 B8
Brandy Wharf Lincs 90 E4
Brane Corn 2 D3
Branksome Poole 13 E8
Branksome Park Poole 13 E8
Bransby Lincs 77 B8
Branscombe Devon 11 F6
Bransford Worcs 50 D2
Bransgore Hants 14 E2
Branshill Clack 127 E7
Bransholme Hull 97 F7
Branson's Cross Worcs 51 B5
Branston Leics 64 B5
Branston Lincs 78 C3
Branston Staffs 63 B6
Branston Booths Lincs 78 C3
Branstone IoW 15 F6
Bransty Cumb 98 C1
Brant Broughton Lincs 78 D2
Brantham Suff 56 F5
Branthwaite Cumb 98 B2
Branthwaite Cumb 108 F2
Brantingham E Yorks 90 B3
Branton Northumb 117 C6
Branton S Yorks 89 D7
Branxholm Park Borders 115 C7
Branxholme Borders 115 C7
Branxton Northumb 122 F4
Brassey Green Ches W 74 C2
Brassington Derbys 76 D2
Brasted Kent 29 D5
Brasted Chart Kent 29 D5
Brathens Aberds 141 E5
Bratoft Lincs 79 C7
Brattleby Lincs 90 F3
Bratton Telford 61 C6
Bratton Wilts 24 D4
Bratton Clovelly Devon 9 E6
Bratton Fleming Devon 20 F5
Bratton Seymour Som 12 B4
Braughing Herts 41 B6
Braunston Northants 52 C3
Braunston-in-Rutland Rutland 64 D5
Braunstone Town Leicester 64 D2
Braunton Devon 20 F3
Brawby N Yorks 96 B3
Brawl Highld 157 C11
Brawlbin Highld 158 E2
Bray Windsor 27 B7
Bray Shop Corn 5 B8
Bray Wick Windsor 27 B6
Braybrooke Northants 64 F4
Braye Ald 16
Brayford Devon 21 F5
Braystones Cumb 98 D2
Braythorn N Yorks 94 E5
Brayton N Yorks 95 F9
Brazacott Corn 8 E4
Breach Kent 30 C2
Breachacha Castle Argyll 146 F4
Breachwood Green Herts 40 B4
Breacleit W Isles 154 D6
Breaden Heath Shrops 73 F8
Breadsall Derbys 76 F3
Breadstone Glos 36 D4
Breage Corn 2 D5
Breakachy Highld 150 G7
Bream Glos 36 D3
Breamore Hants 14 C2
Brean Som 22 D4
Breanais W Isles 154 E4
Brearton N Yorks 95 C6
Breascleit W Isles 154 D7
Breaston Derbys 76 F4
Brechfa Carms 46 F4
Brechin Angus 135 C5
Breck of Cruan Orkney 159 G4
Breckan Orkney 159 H3
Breckrey Highld 149 B10
Brecon = Aberhonddu Powys 34 B4
Bredbury Gtr Man 87 E7
Brede E Sus 18 D5
Bredenbury Hereford 49 D8
Bredfield Suff 57 D6
Bredgar Kent 30 C2
Bredhurst Kent 29 C8
Bredicot Worcs 50 D4
Bredon Worcs 50 F4
Bredon's Norton Worcs 50 F4
Bredwardine Hereford 48 E5
Breedon on the Hill Leics 63 B8
Breibhig W Isles 148 J1
Breibhig W Isles 155 D9
Breich W Loth 120 C2
Breightmet Gtr Man 86 D5
Breighton E Yorks 96 F3
Breinton Hereford 49 F6
Breinton Common Hereford 49 E6
Breiwick Shetland 160 J6
Bremhill Wilts 24 B4
Bremirehoull Shetland 160 L6
Brenchley Kent 29 E7
Brendon Devon 21 E6
Brenkley T&W 110 B5
Brent Eleigh Suff 56 E3
Brent Knoll Som 22 D5
Brent Pelham Herts 54 F5
Brentford London 28 B2
Brentingby Leics 64 C4
Brentwood Essex 42 E1
Brenzett Kent 19 C7
Brereton Staffs 62 C4
Brereton Green Ches E 74 C4
Brereton Heath Ches E 74 C5
Bressingham Norf 68 F3
Bretby Derbys 63 B6
Bretford Warks 52 B2
Bretforton Worcs 51 E5
Bretherdale Head Cumb 99 D7
Bretherton Lancs 86 B2
Brettabister Shetland 160 H6
Brettenham Norf 68 F2
Brettenham Suff 56 D3
Bretton Derbys 76 B2
Bretton Flint 73 C7
Brewer Street Sur 28 D4
Brewlands Bridge Angus 134 C1
Brewood Staffs 62 D2
Briach Moray 151 F13
Briants Puddle Dorset 13 E6
Brick End Essex 42 B1
Brickendon Herts 41 D6
Bricket Wood Herts 40 D4
Bricklehampton Worcs 50 E4
Bride IoM 84 B4
Bridekirk Cumb 107 F8
Bridell Pembs 45 E3
Bridestowe Devon 9 F7
Brideswell Aberds 152 E5
Bridford Devon 10 F3
Bridfordmills Devon 10 F3
Bridge Kent 31 D5
Bridge End Lincs 78 F4
Bridge Green Essex 55 F5
Bridge Hewick N Yorks 95 B6
Bridge of Alford Aberds 140 C4
Bridge of Allan Stirling 127 E6
Bridge of Avon Moray 152 E1
Bridge of Awe Argyll 125 C6
Bridge of Balgie Perth 132 E2
Bridge of Cally Perth 133 D8
Bridge of Canny Aberds 141 E5
Bridge of Craigisla Angus 134 D2
Bridge of Dee Dumfries 106 D4
Bridge of Don Aberdeen 141 C8
Bridge of Dun Angus 135 D6
Bridge of Dye Aberds 141 F5
Bridge of Earn Perth 128 C3
Bridge of Ericht Perth 132 D2
Bridge of Feugh Aberds 141 E6
Bridge of Forss Highld 157 C13
Bridge of Gairn Aberds 140 E2
Bridge of Gaur Perth 132 D2
Bridge of Muchalls Aberds 141 E7
Bridge of Oich Highld 137 D6
Bridge of Orchy Argyll 125 B8
Bridge of Waith Orkney 159 G3
Bridge of Walls Shetland 160 H4
Bridge of Weir Renfs 118 C3
Bridge Sollers Hereford 49 E6
Bridge Street Suff 56 E2
Bridge Trafford Ches W 73 B8
Bridge Yate S Glos 23 B8
Bridgefoot Angus 134 F3
Bridgefoot Cumb 98 B2
Bridgehampton Som 12 B3
Bridgehill Durham 110 D3
Bridgemary Hants 15 D6
Bridgemont Derbys 87 F8
Bridgend Aberds 140 C4
Bridgend Aberds 152 E5
Bridgend Angus 135 C5
Bridgend Argyll 142 B4
Bridgend Argyll 143 E8
Bridgend Argyll 145 D7
Bridgend = Pen-Y-Bont Ar Ogwr Bridgend 21 B8
Bridgend Cumb 99 C5
Bridgend Fife 129 C5
Bridgend Moray 152 E3
Bridgend N Lanark 119 B6
Bridgend Pembs 45 E3
Bridgend W Loth 120 B3
Bridgend of Lintrathen Angus 134 D2
Bridgerule Devon 8 D4
Bridges Shrops 60 E3
Bridgeton Glasgow 119 C6
Bridgetown Corn 8 F5
Bridgetown Som 21 F8
Bridgham Norf 68 F2
Bridgnorth Shrops 61 E7
Bridgtown Staffs 62 D3
Bridgwater Som 22 F5
Bridlington E Yorks 97 C7
Bridport Dorset 12 E2
Bridstow Hereford 36 B2
Brierfield Lancs 93 F8
Brierley Glos 36 C3
Brierley Hereford 49 D6
Brierley S Yorks 88 C5
Brierley Hill W Mid 62 F3
Briery Hill Bl Gwent 35 D5
Brig o'Turk Stirling 126 D4
Brigg N Lincs 90 D4
Briggswath N Yorks 103 D6
Brigham Cumb 107 F7
Brigham E Yorks 97 D6
Brighouse W Yorks 88 B2
Brighstone IoW 14 F5
Brightgate Derbys 76 D2
Brighthampton Oxon 38 D3
Brightling E Sus 18 C3
Brightlingsea Essex 43 C6
Brighton Brighton 17 D7
Brighton Corn 4 D4
Brighton Hill Hants 26 E4
Brightons Falk 120 B2
Brightwalton W Berks 26 B2
Brightwell Suff 57 E6
Brightwell Baldwin Oxon 39 E6
Brightwell cum Sotwell Oxon 39 E5
Brignall Durham 101 C5
Brigsley NE Lincs 91 D6
Brigsteer Cumb 99 F6
Brigstock Northants 65 F6
Brill Bucks 39 C6
Brilley Hereford 48 E4
Brimaston Pembs 44 C4
Brimfield Hereford 49 C7
Brimington Derbys 76 B4
Brimley Devon 7 B5
Brimpsfield Glos 37 C6
Brimpton W Berks 26 C3
Brims Orkney 159 K3
Brimscombe Glos 37 D5
Brimstage Mers 85 F4
Brinacory Highld 147 B10
Brind E Yorks 96 F3
Brindister Shetland 160 H4
Brindister Shetland 160 K6
Brindle Lancs 86 B4
Brindley Ford Stoke 75 D5
Brineton Staffs 62 C2
Bringhurst Leics 64 E5
Brington Cambs 53 B8
Brinian Orkney 159 F5
Briningham Norf 81 D6
Brinkhill Lincs 79 B6
Brinkley Cambs 55 D7
Brinklow Warks 52 B2
Brinkworth Wilts 37 F7
Brinmore Highld 138 B2
Brinscall Lancs 86 B4
Brinsea N Som 23 C6
Brinsley Notts 76 E4
Brinsop Hereford 49 E6
Brinsworth S Yorks 88 F5
Brinton Norf 81 D6
Brisco Cumb 108 D4
Brisley Norf 81 E5
Brislington Bristol 23 B8
Bristol Bristol 23 B7
Briston Norf 81 D6
Britannia Lancs 87 B6
Britford Wilts 14 B2
Brithdir Gwyn 58 C4
British Legion Village Kent 29 D8
Briton Ferry Neath 33 E8
Britwell Salome Oxon 39 E6
Brixham Torbay 7 D7
Brixton Devon 6 D3
Brixton London 28 B4
Brixton Deverill Wilts 24 F3
Brixworth Northants 52 B5
Brize Norton Oxon 38 D3
Broad Blunsdon Swindon 38 E1
Broad Campden Glos 51 F6
Broad Chalke Wilts 13 B8
Broad Green C Beds 53 E7
Broad Green Essex 42 B4
Broad Green Worcs 50 D2
Broad Haven Pembs 44 D3
Broad Heath Worcs 49 C8
Broad Hill Cambs 55 B6
Broad Hinton Wilts 25 B6
Broad Laying Hants 26 C2
Broad Marston Worcs 51 E6
Broad Oak Carms 33 B6
Broad Oak Cumb 98 E3
Broad Oak Dorset 12 E2
Broad Oak Dorset 13 C5
Broad Oak E Sus 18 C3
Broad Oak E Sus 18 D5
Broad Oak Hereford 36 B1
Broad Oak Mers 86 E3
Broad Street Kent 30 D2
Broad Street Green Essex 42 D4
Broad Town Wilts 25 B5
Broadbottom Gtr Man 87 E7
Broadbridge W Sus 16 D2
Broadbridge Heath W Sus 28 F2
Broadclyst Devon 10 E4
Broadfield Gtr Man 87 C6
Broadfield Lancs 86 B3
Broadfield Pembs 32 D2
Broadfield W Sus 28 F3
Broadford Highld 149 F11
Broadford Bridge W Sus 16 B4
Broadhaugh Borders 115 D7
Broadhaven Highld 158 E5
Broadheath Gtr Man 87 F5
Broadhembury Devon 11 D6
Broadhempston Devon 7 C6
Broadholme Derbys 76 E3
Broadholme Lincs 77 B8
Broadland Row E Sus 18 D5
Broadlay Carms 32 D4
Broadley Lancs 87 C6
Broadley Moray 152 B3
Broadley Common Essex 41 D7
Broadmayne Dorset 12 F5
Broadmeadows Borders 121 F7
Broadmere Hants 26 E4
Broadmoor Pembs 32 D1
Broadoak Kent 31 C5
Broadrashes Moray 152 C4
Broadsea Aberds 153 B9
Broadstairs Kent 31 C7
Broadstone Poole 13 E8
Broadstone Shrops 60 F5
Broadtown Lane Wilts 25 B5
Broadwas Worcs 50 D2
Broadwater Herts 41 B5
Broadwater W Sus 17 D5
Broadway Carms 32 D3
Broadway Pembs 44 D3
Broadway Som 11 C8
Broadway Suff 57 B7
Broadway Worcs 51 F5
Broadwell Glos 36 C2
Broadwell Glos 38 B2
Broadwell Oxon 38 D2
Broadwell Warks 52 C2
Broadwell House Northumb 110 D2
Broadwey Dorset 12 F4
Broadwindsor Dorset 12 D2
Broadwood Kelly Devon 9 D8
Broadwoodwidger Devon 9 F6
Brobury Hereford 48 E5
Brochel Highld 149 D10
Brochloch Dumfries 113 E5
Brochroy Argyll 125 B6
Brockamin Worcs 50 D2
Brockbridge Hants 15 C7
Brockdam Northumb 117 B7
Brockdish Norf 57 B6
Brockenhurst Hants 14 D4
Brocketsbrae S Lanark 119 F8
Brockford Street Suff 56 C5
Brockhall Northants 52 C4
Brockham Sur 28 E2
Brockhampton Glos 37 B7
Brockhampton Hereford 49 F7
Brockholes W Yorks 88 C2
Brockhurst Derbys 76 C3
Brockhurst Hants 15 D7
Brocklebank Cumb 108 E3
Brocklesby Lincs 90 C5
Brockley N Som 23 C6
Brockley Green Suff 56 D2
Brockleymoor Cumb 108 F4
Brockton Shrops 60 D3
Brockton Shrops 60 F3
Brockton Shrops 61 D7
Brockton Shrops 61 E5
Brockton Telford 61 C7
Brockweir Glos 36 D2
Brockwood Hants 15 B7
Brockworth Glos 37 C5
Brocton Staffs 62 C3
Brodick N Ayrs 143 E11
Brodsworth S Yorks 89 D6
Brogaig Highld 149 B9
Brogborough C Beds 53 F7
Broken Cross Ches E 75 B5
Broken Cross Ches W 74 B3
Brokenborough Wilts 37 F6
Bromborough Mers 85 F4
Brome Suff 56 B5
Brome Street Suff 57 B5
Bromeswell Suff 57 D7
Bromfield Cumb 107 E8
Bromfield Shrops 49 B6
Bromham Bedford 53 D8
Bromham Wilts 24 C4
Bromley London 28 C5
Bromley W Mid 62 F3
Bromley Common London 28 C5
Bromley Green Kent 19 B6
Brompton Medway 29 C8
Brompton N Yorks 102 E1
Brompton N Yorks 103 F7
Brompton-on-Swale N Yorks 101 E7
Brompton Ralph Som 22 F2
Brompton Regis Som 21 F8
Bromsash Hereford 36 B3
Bromsberrow Heath Glos 50 F2
Bromsgrove Worcs 50 B4
Bromyard Hereford 49 D8
Bromyard Downs Hereford 49 D8
Bronaber Gwyn 71 D8
Brongest Ceredig 46 E2
Bronington Wrex 73 F8
Bronllys Powys 48 F3
Bronnant Ceredig 46 C5
Bronwydd Arms Carms 33 B5
Bronydd Powys 48 E4
Bronygarth Shrops 73 F6
Brook Carms 32 D3
Brook Hants 14 B4
Brook Hants 14 C3
Brook IoW 14 F4
Brook Kent 30 E4
Brook Sur 27 E8
Brook Sur 27 F7
Brook End Bedford 53 C8
Brook Hill Hants 14 C3
Brook Street Kent 19 B6
Brook Street Kent 29 E6
Brook Street W Sus 17 B7
Brooke Norf 69 E5
Brooke Rutland 64 D5
Brookenby Lincs 91 E6
Brookend Glos 36 E2
Brookfield Renfs 118 C4
Brookhouse Lancs 92 C5
Brookhouse Green Ches E 74 C5
Brookland Kent 19 C6
Brooklands Dumfries 106 B5
Brooklands Gtr Man 87 E5
Brooklands Shrops 74 E2
Brookmans Park Herts 41 D5
Brooks Powys 59 E8
Brooks Green W Sus 16 B5
Brookthorpe Glos 37 C5
Brookville Norf 67 E7
Brookwood Sur 27 D7
Broom C Beds 54 E2
Broom S Yorks 88 E5
Broom Warks 51 D5
Broom Worcs 50 B4
Broom Green Norf 81 E5
Broom Hill Dorset 13 D8
Broome Norf 69 E6
Broome Shrops 60 F4
Broome Park Northumb 117 C7
Broomedge Warr 86 F5
Broomer's Corner W Sus 16 B5
Broomfield Aberds 153 E9
Broomfield Essex 42 C3
Broomfield Kent 30 D2
Broomfield Kent 31 C5
Broomfield Som 22 F4
Broomfleet E Yorks 90 B2
Broomhall Ches E 74 E3
Broomhall Windsor 27 C7
Broomhaugh Northumb 110 C3
Broomhill Norf 67 D6
Broomhill Northumb 117 D8
Broomhill S Yorks 88 D5
Broomholm Norf 81 D9
Broomley Northumb 110 C3
Broompark Durham 110 E5
Broom's Green Glos 50 F2
Broomy Lodge Hants 14 C3
Brora Highld 157 J12
Broseley Shrops 61 D6
Brotherhouse Bar Lincs 66 C2
Brotherstone Borders 122 F2
Brothertoft Lincs 79 E5
Brotherton N Yorks 89 B5
Brotton Redcar 102 C4
Broubster Highld 157 C13
Brough Cumb 100 C2
Brough Derbys 88 F2
Brough E Yorks 90 B3
Brough Highld 158 C4
Brough Notts 77 D8
Brough Orkney 159 G4
Brough Shetland 160 F6
Brough Shetland 160 F7
Brough Shetland 160 G7
Brough Shetland 160 H6
Brough Shetland 160 J7
Brough Lodge Shetland 160 D7
Brough Sowerby Cumb 100 C2
Broughall Shrops 74 E2
Broughton Borders 120 F4
Broughton Cambs 54 B3
Broughton Flint 73 C7
Broughton Hants 25 F8
Broughton Lancs 92 F5
Broughton M Keynes 53 E6
Broughton N Lincs 90 D3
Broughton N Yorks 94 D2
Broughton N Yorks 96 B3
Broughton Northants 53 B6
Broughton Orkney 159 D5
Broughton Oxon 52 F2
Broughton V Glam 21 B8
Broughton Astley Leics 64 E2
Broughton Beck Cumb 98 F4
Broughton Common Wilts 24 C3
Broughton Gifford Wilts 24 C3
Broughton Hackett Worcs 50 D4
Broughton in Furness Cumb 98 F4
Broughton Mills Cumb 98 E4
Broughton Moor Cumb 107 F7
Broughton Park Gtr Man 87 D6
Broughton Poggs Oxon 38 D2
Broughtown Orkney 159 D7
Broughty Ferry Dundee 134 F4
Browhouses Dumfries 108 C2
Browland Shetland 160 H4
Brown Candover Hants 26 F3
Brown Edge Lancs 85 C4
Brown Edge Staffs 75 D6
Brown Heath Ches W 73 C8
Brownhill Aberds 153 D6
Brownhill Aberds 153 D8
Brownhill Blackburn 93 F6
Brownhill Shrops 60 B4
Brownhills Fife 129 C7
Brownhills W Mid 62 D4
Brownlow Ches E 74 C5
Brownlow Heath Ches E 74 C5
Brownmuir Aberds 135 B7
Brown's End Glos 50 F2
Brownshill Glos 37 D5
Brownston Devon 6 D4
Brownyside Northumb 117 B7
Broxa N Yorks 103 E7
Broxbourne Herts 41 D6
Broxburn E Loth 122 B2
Broxburn W Loth 120 B3
Broxholme Lincs 78 B2
Broxted Essex 42 B1
Broxton Ches W 73 D8
Broxwood Hereford 49 D5
Broyle Side E Sus 17 C8
Brù W Isles 155 C8
Bruairnis W Isles 148 H2
Bruan Highld 158 G5
Bruar Lodge Perth 133 B5
Brucehill W Dunb 118 B3
Bruera Ches W 73 C8
Bruern Abbey Oxon 38 B2
Bruichladdich Argyll 142 B3
Bruisyard Suff 57 C7
Brumby N Lincs 90 D2
Brund Staffs 75 C8
Brundall Norf 69 D6
Brundish Suff 57 C6
Brundish Street Suff 57 B6
Brunery Highld 147 D10
Brunshaw Lancs 93 F8
Brunswick Village T&W 110 B5
Bruntcliffe W Yorks 88 B3
Bruntingthorpe Leics 64 E3
Brunton Fife 128 B5
Brunton Northumb 117 B8
Brunton Wilts 25 D7
Brushford Devon 9 D8
Brushford Som 10 B4
Bruton Som 23 F8
Bryanston Dorset 13 D6
Brydekirk Dumfries 107 B8
Bryher Scilly 2 E3
Brymbo Wrex 73 D6
Brympton Som 12 C3
Bryn Carms 33 D6
Bryn Gtr Man 86 D3
Bryn Neath 34 E2
Bryn Shrops 60 F2
Bryn-coch Neath 33 E8
Bryn Du Anglesey 82 D3
Bryn Gates Gtr Man 86 D3
Bryn-glas Conwy 83 E8
Bryn Golau Rhondda 34 F3
Bryn-Iwan Carms 46 F2
Bryn-mawr Gwyn 70 D3
Bryn-nantllech Conwy 72 C3
Bryn-penarth Powys 59 D8
Bryn Rhyd-yr-Arian Conwy 72 C3
Bryn Saith Marchog Denb 72 D4
Bryn Sion Gwyn 59 C5
Bryn-y-gwenin Mon 35 C7
Bryn-y-maen Conwy 83 D8
Bryn-yr-eryr Gwyn 70 C4
Brynamman Carms 33 C8
Brynberian Pembs 45 F3
Brynbryddan Neath 34 E1
Brynbuga = Usk Mon 35 D7
Bryncae Rhondda 34 F3
Bryncethin Bridgend 34 F3
Bryncir Gwyn 71 C5
Bryncroes Gwyn 70 D3
Bryncrug Gwyn 58 D3
Bryneglwys Denb 72 E5
Brynford Flint 73 B5
Bryngwran Anglesey 82 D3
Bryngwyn Ceredig 45 E4
Bryngwyn Mon 35 D7
Bryngwyn Powys 48 E3
Brynhenllan Pembs 45 F2
Brynhoffnant Ceredig 46 D2
Brynithel Bl Gwent 35 D6
Brynmawr Bl Gwent 35 C5
Brynmenyn Bridgend 34 F3
Brynmill Swansea 33 E7
Brynna Rhondda 34 F3
Brynrefail Anglesey 82 C4
Brynrefail Gwyn 83 E5
Brynsadler Rhondda 34 F4
Brynsiencyn Anglesey 82 E4
Brynteg Anglesey 82 C4
Brynteg Ceredig 46 E3
Buaile nam Bodach W Isles 148 H2
Bualintur Highld 149 F9
Buarthmeini Gwyn 72 F2
Bubbenhall Warks 51 B8
Bubwith E Yorks 96 F3
Buccleuch Borders 115 C6
Buchanhaven Aberds 153 D11
Buchanty Perth 127 B8
Buchlyvie Stirling 126 E4
Buckabank Cumb 108 E3
Buckden Cambs 54 C2
Buckden N Yorks 94 B2
Buckenham Norf 69 D6
Buckerell Devon 11 D6
Buckfast Devon 6 C5
Buckfastleigh Devon 6 C5
Buckhaven Fife 129 E5
Buckholm Borders 121 F7
Buckholt Mon 36 C2
Buckhorn Weston Dorset 13 B5
Buckhurst Hill Essex 41 E7
Buckie Moray 152 B4
Buckies Highld 158 D3
Buckingham Bucks 52 F4
Buckland Bucks 40 C1
Buckland Devon 6 E4
Buckland Glos 51 F5
Buckland Hants 14 E4
Buckland Herts 54 F4
Buckland Kent 31 E7
Buckland Oxon 38 E3
Buckland Sur 28 D3
Buckland Brewer Devon 9 B6
Buckland Common Bucks 40 D2
Buckland Dinham Som 24 D2
Buckland Filleigh Devon 9 D6
Buckland in the Moor Devon 6 B5
Buckland Monachorum Devon 6 C2
Buckland Newton Dorset 12 D4
Buckland St Mary Som 11 C7
Bucklebury W Berks 26 B3
Bucklegate Lincs 79 F6
Bucklerheads Angus 134 F4
Bucklers Hard Hants 14 E5
Bucklesham Suff 57 E6
Buckley = Bwcle Flint 73 C6
Bucklow Hill Ches E 86 F5
Buckminster Leics 65 B5
Bucknall Lincs 78 C4
Bucknall Stoke 75 E6
Bucknell Oxon 39 B5
Bucknell Shrops 49 B5
Buckpool Moray 152 B4
Buck's Cross Devon 8 B5
Bucks Green W Sus 27 F8
Bucks Horn Oak Hants 27 E6
Buck's Mills Devon 9 B5
Bucksburn Aberdeen 141 D7
Buckskin Hants 26 D4
Buckton E Yorks 97 B7
Buckton Hereford 49 B5
Buckton Northumb 123 F6
Buckworth Cambs 54 B2
Budbrooke Warks 51 C7
Budby Notts 77 C6
Budd's Titson Corn 8 D4
Bude Corn 8 D4
Budlake Devon 10 E4
Budle Northumb 123 F7
Budleigh Salterton Devon 11 F5
Budock Water Corn 3 C6
Buerton Ches E 74 E3
Buffler's Holt Bucks 52 F4
Bugbrooke Northants 52 D4
Buglawton Ches E 75 C5
Bugle Corn 4 D5
Bugley Wilts 24 E3
Bugthorpe E Yorks 96 D3
Buildwas Shrops 61 D6
Builth Road Powys 48 D2
Builth Wells = Llanfair-Ym-Muallt Powys 48 D2
Buirgh W Isles 154 H5
Bulby Lincs 65 B7
Bulcote Notts 77 E6
Buldoo Highld 157 C12
Bulford Wilts 25 E6
Bulford Camp Wilts 25 E6
Bulkeley Ches E 74 D2
Bulkington Warks 63 F7
Bulkington Wilts 24 D4
Bulkworthy Devon 9 C5
Bull Hill Hants 14 E4
Bullamoor N Yorks 102 E1
Bullbridge Derbys 76 D3
Bullbrook Brack 27 C6
Bulley Glos 36 C4
Bullgill Cumb 107 F7
Bullington Hants 26 E2
Bullington Lincs 78 B3
Bull's Green Herts 41 C5
Bullwood Argyll 145 F10
Bulmer Essex 56 E2
Bulmer N Yorks 96 C2
Bulmer Tye Essex 56 F2
Bulphan Thurrock 42 F2
Bulverhythe E Sus 18 E4
Bulwark Aberds 153 D9
Bulwell Nottingham 76 E5
Bulwick Northants 65 E6
Bumble's Green Essex 41 D7
Bun a'Mhuillin W Isles 148 G2
Bun Abhainn Eadarra W Isles 154 G6
Bun Loyne Highld 136 D5
Bunacaimb Highld 147 C9
Bunarkaig Highld 136 F4
Bunbury Ches E 74 D2
Bunbury Heath Ches E 74 D2
Bunchrew Highld 151 G9
Bundalloch Highld 149 F13
Buness Shetland 160 C8
Bunessan Argyll 146 J6
Bungay Suff 69 F6
Bunker's Hill Lincs 78 B2
Bunker's Hill Lincs 79 D5
Bunkers Hill Oxon 38 C4
Bunloit Highld 137 B8
Bunnahabhain Argyll 142 A5
Bunny Notts 64 B2
Buntait Highld 150 H6
Buntingford Herts 41 B6
Bunwell Norf 68 E4
Burbage Derbys 75 B7
Burbage Leics 63 E8
Burbage Wilts 25 C7
Burchett's Green Windsor 39 F8
Burcombe Wilts 25 F5
Burcot Oxon 39 E5
Burcott Bucks 40 B1
Burdon T&W 111 D6
Bures Suff 56 F3
Bures Green Suff 56 F3
Burford Ches E 74 D3
Burford Oxon 38 C2
Burford Shrops 49 C7
Burg Argyll 146 G6
Burgar Orkney 159 F4
Burgate Hants 14 C2
Burgate Suff 56 B4
Burgess Hill W Sus 17 C7
Burgh Suff 57 D6
Burgh by Sands Cumb 108 D3
Burgh Castle Norf 69 D7
Burgh Heath Sur 28 D3
Burgh le Marsh Lincs 79 C8
Burgh Muir Aberds 141 B6
Burgh next Aylsham Norf 81 E8
Burgh on Bain Lincs 91 F6
Burgh St Margaret Norf 69 C7
Burgh St Peter Norf 69 E7
Burghclere Hants 26 C2
Burghead Moray 151 E14
Burghfield W Berks 26 C4
Burghfield Common W Berks 26 C4
Burghfield Hill W Berks 26 C4
Burghill Hereford 49 E6
Burghwallis S Yorks 89 C6
Burham Kent 29 C8
Buriton Hants 15 B8
Burland Ches E 74 D3
Burlawn Corn 4 B4
Burleigh Brack 27 C6
Burlescombe Devon 11 C5
Burleston Dorset 13 E5
Burley Hants 14 D3
Burley Rutland 65 C5
Burley W Yorks 95 F5
Burley Gate Hereford 49 E7
Burley in Wharfedale W Yorks 94 E4
Burley Lodge Hants 14 D3
Burley Street Hants 14 D3
Burleydam Ches E 74 E3
Burlingjobb Powys 48 D4
Burlow E Sus 18 D2
Burlton Shrops 60 B4
Burmarsh Kent 19 B7
Burmington Warks 51 F7
Burn N Yorks 89 B6
Burn of Cambus Stirling 127 D6
Burnaston Derbys 76 F2
Burnbank S Lanark 119 D7
Burnby E Yorks 96 E4
Burncross S Yorks 88 E4
Burneside Cumb 99 E7
Burness Orkney 159 D7
Burneston N Yorks 101 F8
Burnett Bath 23 C8
Burnfoot Borders 115 C7
Burnfoot Borders 115 C8
Burnfoot E Ayrs 112 D4
Burnfoot Perth 127 D8
Burnham Bucks 40 F2
Burnham N Lincs 90 C4
Burnham Deepdale Norf 80 C4
Burnham Green Herts 41 C5
Burnham Market Norf 80 C4
Burnham Norton Norf 80 C4
Burnham-on-Crouch Essex 43 E5
Burnham-on-Sea Som 22 E5
Burnham Overy Staithe Norf 80 C4
Burnham Overy Town Norf 80 C4
Burnham Thorpe Norf 80 C4
Burnhead Dumfries 113 E8
Burnhead S Ayrs 112 D2
Burnhervie Aberds 141 C6
Burnhill Green Staffs 61 D7
Burnhope Durham 110 E4
Burnhouse N Ayrs 118 D3
Burniston N Yorks 103 E8
Burnlee W Yorks 88 D2
Burnley Lancs 93 F8
Burnley Lane Lancs 93 F8
Burnmouth Borders 123 C5
Burnopfield Durham 110 D4
Burnsall N Yorks 94 C3
Burnside Angus 135 D5
Burnside E Ayrs 113 C5
Burnside Fife 128 D3
Burnside S Lanark 119 C6
Burnside Shetland 160 F4
Burnside W Loth 120 B3
Burnside of Duntrune Angus 134 F4
Burnswark Dumfries 107 B8
Burnt Heath Derbys 76 B2
Burnt Houses Durham 101 B6
Burnt Yates N Yorks 95 C5
Burntcommon Sur 27 D8
Burnthouse Corn 3 C6
Burntisland Fife 128 F4
Burnton E Ayrs 112 D4
Burntwood Staffs 62 D4
Burnwynd Edin 120 C4
Burpham Sur 27 D8
Burpham W Sus 16 D4
Burradon Northumb 117 D5
Burradon T&W 111 B5
Burrafirth Shetland 160 B8
Burraland Shetland 160 F5
Burraland Shetland 160 J4
Burras Corn 3 C5
Burravoe Shetland 160 F7
Burravoe Shetland 160 G5
Burray Village Orkney 159 J5
Burrells Cumb 100 C1
Burrelton Perth 134 F2
Burridge Devon 20 F4
Burridge Hants 15 C6
Burrill N Yorks 101 F7
Burringham N Lincs 90 D2
Burrington Devon 9 C8
Burrington Hereford 49 B6
Burrington N Som 23 D6
Burrough Green Cambs 55 D7
Burrough on the Hill Leics 64 C4
Burrow-bridge Som 11 B8
Burrowhill Sur 27 C7
Burry Swansea 33 E5
Burry Green Swansea 33 E5
Burry Port = Porth Tywyn Carms 33 D5
Burscough Lancs 86 C2
Burscough Bridge Lancs 86 C2
Bursea E Yorks 96 F4
Burshill E Yorks 97 E6
Bursledon Hants 15 D5
Burslem Stoke 75 E5
Burstall Suff 56 E4
Burstock Dorset 12 D2
Burston Norf 68 F4
Burston Staffs 75 F6
Burstow Sur 28 E4
Burstwick E Yorks 91 B6
Burtersett N Yorks 100 F3
Burtle Som 23 E5
Burton Ches W 73 B7
Burton Ches W 74 C2
Burton Dorset 14 E2
Burton Lincs 78 B2
Burton Northumb 123 F7
Burton Pembs 44 E4
Burton Som 22 E3
Burton Wilts 24 B3
Burton Agnes E Yorks 97 C7
Burton Bradstock Dorset 12 F2
Burton Dassett Warks 51 D8
Burton Fleming E Yorks 97 B6
Burton Green W Mid 51 B7
Burton Green Wrex 73 D7
Burton Hastings Warks 63 E8
Burton-in-Kendal Cumb 92 B5
Burton in Lonsdale N Yorks 93 B6
Burton Joyce Notts 77 E6
Burton Latimer Northants 53 B7
Burton Lazars Leics 64 C4
Burton-le-Coggles Lincs 65 B6
Burton Leonard N Yorks 95 C6
Burton on the Wolds Leics 64 B2
Burton Overy Leics 64 E3
Burton Pedwardine Lincs 78 E4
Burton Pidsea E Yorks 97 F8
Burton Salmon N Yorks 89 B5
Burton Stather N Lincs 90 C2
Burton upon Stather N Lincs 90 C2
Burton upon Trent Staffs 63 B6
Burtonwood Warr 86 E3
Burwardsley Ches W 74 D2
Burwarton Shrops 61 F6
Burwash E Sus 18 C3
Burwash Common E Sus 18 C3
Burwash Weald E Sus 18 C3
Burwell Cambs 55 C6
Burwell Lincs 79 B6
Burwen Anglesey 82 B4
Burwick Orkney 159 K5
Bury Cambs 66 F2
Bury Gtr Man 87 C6
Bury Som 10 B4
Bury W Sus 16 C4
Bury Green Herts 41 B7
Bury St Edmunds Suff 56 C2
Burythorpe N Yorks 96 C3
Busby E Renf 119 D5
Buscot Oxon 38 E2
Bush Bank Hereford 49 D6
Bush Crathie Aberds 139 E8
Bush Green Norf 68 F5
Bushbury W Mid 62 D3
Bushby Leics 64 D3
Bushey Herts 40 E4
Bushey Heath Herts 40 E4
Bushley Worcs 50 F3
Bushton Wilts 25 B5
Buslingthorpe Lincs 90 F4
Busta Shetland 160 G5
Butcher's Cross E Sus 18 C2
Butcher's Pasture Essex 42 B2
Butcombe N Som 23 C7
Butetown Cardiff 22 B3
Butleigh Som 23 F7
Butleigh Wootton Som 23 F7
Butler's Cross Bucks 39 D8
Butler's End Warks 63 F6
Butlers Marston Warks 51 E8
Butley Suff 57 D7
Butley High Corner Suff 57 E7
Butt Green Ches E 74 D3
Butterburn Cumb 109 B6
Buttercrambe N Yorks 96 D3
Butterknowle Durham 101 B6
Butterleigh Devon 10 D4
Buttermere Cumb 98 C3
Buttermere Wilts 25 C8
Buttershaw W Yorks 88 B2
Butterstone Perth 133 E7
Butterton Staffs 75 D7
Butterwick Durham 102 B1
Butterwick Lincs 79 E6
Butterwick N Yorks 96 B3
Butterwick N Yorks 97 B5
Buttington Powys 60 D2
Buttonoak Worcs 50 B2
Butt's Green Hants 14 B4
Buttsash Hants 14 D5
Buxhall Suff 56 D4
Buxhall Fen Street Suff 56 D4
Buxley Borders 122 D4
Buxted E Sus 17 B8
Buxton Derbys 75 B7

Churchtown Mers 85 C4
Churnsike Lodge Northumb 109 B6
Churston Ferrers Torbay 7 D7
Churt Sur 27 F6
Churton Ches W 73 D8
Churwell W Yorks 88 B3
Chute Standen Wilts 25 D8
Chwilog Gwyn 70 D5
Chyandour Corn 2 C3
Cilan Uchaf Gwyn 70 E3
Cilcain Flint 73 C5
Cilcennin Ceredig 46 C4
Cilfor Gwyn 71 D7
Cilfrew Neath 34 D1
Cilfynydd Rhondda 34 E4
Cilgerran Pembs 45 E3
Cilgwyn Carms 33 B8
Cilgwyn Gwyn 82 F4
Cilgwyn Pembs 45 F2
Ciliau Aeron Ceredig 46 D3
Cill Donnain W Isles 148 F2
Cille Bhrighde W Isles 148 G2
Cille Pheadair W Isles 148 G2
Cilmery Powys 48 D2
Cilsan Carms 33 B6
Ciltalgarth Gwyn 72 E2
Cilwendeg Pembs 45 F4
Cilybebyll Neath 33 D8
Cilycwm Carms 47 F6
Cimla Neath 34 E1
Cinderford Glos 36 C3
Cippyn Pembs 45 E3
Circebost W Isles 154 D6
Cirencester Glos 37 D7
Ciribhig W Isles 154 C6
City London 41 F6
City Powys 60 F2
City Dulas Anglesey 82 C4
Clachaig Argyll 145 E10
Clachan Argyll 124 D3
Clachan Argyll 125 D7
Clachan Argyll 130 E2
Clachan Argyll 144 H6
Clachan Highld 149 E10
Clachan W Isles 148 D2
Clachan na Luib W Isles 148 B3
Clachan of Campsie E Dunb 119 B6
Clachan of Glendaruel Argyll 145 E8
Clachan-Seil Argyll 124 D3
Clachan Strachur Argyll 125 E6
Clachaneasy Dumfries 105 B7
Clachanmore Dumfries 104 E4
Clachbreck Argyll 144 F6
Clachnabrain Angus 134 C3
Clachtoll Highld 156 G3
Clackmannan Clack 127 E8
Clacton-on-Sea Essex 43 C7
Cladach Chireboist W Isles 148 B2
Claddach-knockline W Isles 148 B2
Cladich Argyll 125 C6
Claggan Highld 131 B5
Claggan Highld 147 G9
Claigan Highld 148 C7
Claines Worcs 50 D3
Clandown Bath 23 D8
Clanfield Hants 15 C7
Clanfield Oxon 38 D2
Clanville Hants 25 E8
Claonaig Argyll 145 H7
Claonel Highld 157 J8
Clap Hill Kent 19 B7
Clapgate Dorset 13 D8
Clapgate Herts 41 B7
Clapham Bedford 53 D8
Clapham London 28 B3
Clapham N Yorks 93 C7
Clapham W Sus 16 D4
Clappers Borders 122 D5
Clappersgate Cumb 99 D5
Clapton Som 12 D2
Clapton-in-Gordano N Som 23 B6
Clapton-on-the-Hill Glos 38 C1
Clapworthy Devon 9 B8
Clara Vale T&W 110 C4
Clarach Ceredig 58 F3
Clarbeston Pembs 32 B1
Clarbeston Road Pembs 32 B1
Clarborough Notts 89 F8
Clardon Highld 158 D3
Clare Suff 55 E8
Clarebrand Dumfries 106 C4
Clarencefield Dumfries 107 C7
Clarilaw Borders 115 C8
Clark's Green Sur 28 F2
Clarkston E Renf 119 D5
Clashandorran Highld 151 G8
Clashcoig Highld 151 B9
Clashindarroch Aberds 152 E4
Clashmore Highld 151 C10
Clashmore Highld 156 F3
Clashnessie Highld 156 F3
Clashnoir Moray 139 B8
Clate Shetland 160 G7
Clathy Perth 127 C8
Clatt Aberds 140 B4
Clatter Powys 59 E6
Clatterford IoW 15 F5
Clatterin Bridge Aberds 135 B6
Clatworthy Som 22 F2
Claughton Lancs 92 E5
Claughton Lancs 93 C5
Claughton Mers 85 F4
Claverdon Warks 51 C6
Claverham N Som 23 C6
Clavering Essex 55 F5
Claverley Shrops 61 E7
Claverton Bath 24 C2
Clawdd-newydd Denb 72 D4
Clawthorpe Cumb 92 B5
Clawton Devon 9 E5
Claxby Lincs 79 B7
Claxby Lincs 90 E5
Claxton N Yorks 96 C2
Claxton Norf 69 D6
Clay Common Suff 69 F7
Clay Coton Northants 52 B3
Clay Cross Derbys 76 C3
Clay Hill W Berks 26 B3
Clay Lake Lincs 66 B2
Claybokie Aberds 139 E6
Claybrooke Magna Leics 63 F8
Claybrooke Parva Leics 63 F8
Claydon Oxon 52 D2
Claydon Suff 56 D5
Claygate Dumfries 108 B3
Claygate Kent 29 E8
Claygate Sur 28 C2
Claygate Cross Kent 29 D7
Clayhanger Devon 10 B5
Clayhanger W Mid 62 D4
Clayhidon Devon 11 C6
Clayhill E Sus 18 C5
Clayhill Hants 14 D4
Clayock Highld 158 E3
Claypole Lincs 77 E8
Clayton S Yorks 89 D5
Clayton Staffs 75 E5
Clayton W Sus 17 C6
Clayton W Yorks 94 F4
Clayton Green Lancs 86 B3
Clayton-le-Moors Lancs 93 F7
Clayton-le-Woods Lancs 86 B3
Clayton West W Yorks 88 C3
Clayworth Notts 89 F8
Cleadale Highld 146 C7
Cleadon T&W 111 C6
Clearbrook Devon 6 C3
Clearwell Glos 36 D2
Cleasby N Yorks 101 C7
Cleat Orkney 159 K5
Cleatlam Durham 101 C6
Cleator Cumb 98 C2
Cleator Moor Cumb 98 C2
Clebrig Highld 157 F8
Cleckheaton W Yorks 88 B2
Clee St Margaret Shrops 61 F5
Cleedownton Shrops 61 F5
Cleehill Shrops 49 B7
Cleethorpes NE Lincs 91 D7
Cleeton St Mary Shrops 49 B8
Cleeve N Som 23 C6
Cleeve Hill Glos 37 B6
Cleeve Prior Worcs 51 E5
Clegyrnant Powys 59 D6
Clehonger Hereford 49 F6
Cleish Perth 128 E2
Cleland N Lanark 119 D8
Clench Common Wilts 25 C6
Clenchwarton Norf 67 B5
Clent Worcs 50 B4
Cleobury Mortimer Shrops 49 B8
Cleobury North Shrops 61 F6
Cleongart Argyll 143 E7
Clephanton Highld 151 F11
Clerklands Borders 115 B8
Clestrain Orkney 159 H4
Cleuch Head Borders 115 C8
Cleughbrae Dumfries 107 B7
Clevancy Wilts 25 B5
Clevedon N Som 23 B6
Cleveley Oxon 38 B3
Cleveleys Lancs 92 E3
Cleverton Wilts 37 F6
Clevis Bridgend 21 B7
Clewer Som 23 D6
Cley next the Sea Norf 81 C6
Cliaid W Isles 148 H1
Cliasmol W Isles 154 G5
Cliburn Cumb 99 B7
Click Mill Orkney 159 F4
Cliddesden Hants 26 E4
Cliff End E Sus 19 D5
Cliffburn Angus 135 E6
Cliffe Medway 29 B8
Cliffe N Yorks 96 F2
Cliffe Woods Medway 29 B8
Clifford Hereford 48 E4
Clifford W Yorks 95 E7
Clifford Chambers Warks 51 D6
Clifford's Mesne Glos 36 B4
Cliffsend Kent 31 C7
Clifton Bristol 23 B7
Clifton C Beds 54 F2
Clifton Cumb 99 B7
Clifton Derbys 75 E8
Clifton Lancs 92 F4
Clifton N Yorks 94 E4
Clifton Northumb 117 F8
Clifton Nottingham 77 F5
Clifton Oxon 52 F2
Clifton S Yorks 89 E6
Clifton Stirling 131 F7
Clifton Worcs 50 E3
Clifton York 95 D8
Clifton Campville Staffs 63 C6
Clifton Green Gtr Man 87 D5
Clifton Hampden Oxon 39 E5
Clifton Reynes M Keynes 53 D7
Clifton upon Dunsmore Warks 52 B3
Clifton upon Teme Worcs 50 C2
Cliftoncote Borders 116 B4
Cliftonville Kent 31 B7
Climaen gwyn Neath 33 D8
Climping W Sus 16 D4
Climpy S Lanark 120 D2
Clink Som 24 E2
Clint N Yorks 95 D5
Clint Green Norf 68 C3
Clintmains Borders 122 F2
Cliobh W Isles 154 D5
Clippesby Norf 69 C7
Clipsham Rutland 65 C6
Clipston Northants 64 F4
Clipstone Notts 77 C5
Clitheroe Lancs 93 E7
Cliuthar W Isles 154 H6
Clive Shrops 60 B5
Clivocast Shetland 160 C8
Clixby Lincs 90 D5
Clocaenog Denb 72 D4
Clochan Moray 152 B4
Clock Face Mers 86 E3
Clockmill Borders 122 D3
Cloddiau Powys 60 D2
Clodock Hereford 35 B7
Clola Aberds 153 D10
Clophill C Beds 53 F8
Clopton Northants 65 F7
Clopton Suff 57 D6
Clopton Corner Suff 57 D6
Clopton Green Suff 55 D8
Close Clark IoM 84 E2
Closeburn Dumfries 113 E8
Closworth Som 12 C3
Clothall Herts 54 F3
Clotton Ches W 74 C2
Clough Foot W Yorks 87 B7
Cloughton N Yorks 103 E8
Cloughton Newlands N Yorks 103 E8
Clousta Shetland 160 H5
Clouston Orkney 159 G3
Clova Aberds 140 B3
Clova Angus 134 B3
Clove Lodge Durham 100 C4
Clovelly Devon 8 B5
Clovenfords Borders 121 F7
Clovenstone Aberds 141 C6
Clovullin Highld 130 C4
Clow Bridge Lancs 87 B6
Clowne Derbys 76 B4
Clows Top Worcs 50 B2
Cloy Wrex 73 E7
Cluanie Inn Highld 136 C3
Cluanie Lodge Highld 136 C3
Clun Shrops 60 F3
Clunbury Shrops 60 F3
Clunderwen Carms 32 C2
Clune Highld 138 B3
Clunes Highld 136 F5
Clungunford Shrops 49 B5
Clunie Aberds 153 C6
Clunie Perth 133 E8
Clunton Shrops 60 F3
Cluny Fife 128 E4
Cluny Castle Highld 138 E2
Clutton Bath 23 D8
Clutton Ches W 73 D8
Clwt-grugoer Conwy 72 C3
Clwt-y-bont Gwyn 83 E5
Clydach Mon 35 C6
Clydach Swansea 33 D7
Clydach Vale Rhondda 34 E3
Clydebank W Dunb 118 B4
Clydey Pembs 45 F4
Clyffe Pypard Wilts 25 B5
Clynder Argyll 145 E11
Clyne Neath 34 D2
Clynelish Highld 157 J11
Clynnog-fawr Gwyn 82 F4
Clyro Powys 48 E4
Clyst Honiton Devon 10 E4
Clyst Hydon Devon 10 D5
Clyst St George Devon 10 F4
Clyst St Lawrence Devon 10 D5
Clyst St Mary Devon 10 E4
Cnoc Amhlaigh W Isles 155 D10
Cnwch-coch Ceredig 47 B5
Coachford Aberds 152 D4
Coad's Green Corn 5 B7
Coal Aston Derbys 76 B3
Coalbrookdale Telford 61 D6
Coalbrookvale Bl Gwent 35 D5
Coalburn S Lanark 119 F8
Coalburns T&W 110 C4
Coalcleugh Northumb 109 E8
Coaley Glos 36 D4
Coalhall E Ayrs 112 C4
Coalhill Essex 42 E3
Coalpit Heath S Glos 36 F3
Coalport Telford 61 D6
Coalsnaughton Clack 127 E8
Coaltown of Balgonie Fife 128 E4
Coaltown of Wemyss Fife 128 E5
Coalville Leics 63 C8
Coalway Glos 36 C2
Coat Som 12 B2
Coatbridge N Lanark 119 C7
Coatdyke N Lanark 119 C7
Coate Swindon 38 F1
Coate Wilts 24 C5
Coates Cambs 66 E3
Coates Glos 37 D6
Coates Lancs 93 E8
Coates Notts 90 F2
Coates W Sus 16 C3
Coatham Redcar 102 B3
Coatham Mundeville Darl 101 B7
Coatsgate Dumfries 114 D3
Cobbaton Devon 9 B8
Cobbler's Green Norf 69 E5
Coberley Glos 37 C6
Cobham Kent 29 C7
Cobham Sur 28 C2
Cobholm Island Norf 69 D8
Cobleland Stirling 126 E4
Cobnash Hereford 49 C6
Coburty Aberds 153 B9
Cock Bank Wrex 73 E7
Cock Bridge Aberds 139 D8
Cock Clarks Essex 42 D4
Cockayne N Yorks 102 E4
Cockayne Hatley Cambs 54 E3
Cockburnspath Borders 122 B3
Cockenzie and Port Seton E Loth 121 B7
Cockerham Lancs 92 D4
Cockermouth Cumb 107 F8
Cockernhoe Green Herts 40 B4
Cockfield Durham 101 B6
Cockfield Suff 56 D3
Cockfosters London 41 E5
Cocking W Sus 16 C2
Cockington Torbay 7 C6
Cocklake Som 23 E6
Cockley Beck Cumb 98 D4
Cockley Cley Norf 67 D7
Cockshutt Shrops 60 B4
Cockthorpe Norf 81 C5
Cockwood Devon 10 F4
Cockyard Hereford 49 F6
Codda Corn 5 B6
Coddenham Suff 56 D5
Coddington Ches W 73 D8
Coddington Hereford 50 E2
Coddington Notts 77 D8
Codford St Mary Wilts 24 F4
Codford St Peter Wilts 24 F4
Codicote Herts 41 C5
Codmore Hill W Sus 16 B4
Codnor Derbys 76 E4
Codrington S Glos 24 B2
Codsall Staffs 62 D2
Codsall Wood Staffs 62 D2
Coed Duon = Blackwood Caerph 35 E5
Coed Mawr Gwyn 83 D5
Coed Morgan Mon 35 C7
Coed-Talon Flint 73 D6
Coed-y-bryn Ceredig 46 E2
Coed-y-paen Mon 35 E7
Coed-yr-ynys Powys 35 B5
Coed Ystumgwern Gwyn 71 E6
Coedely Rhondda 34 F4
Coedkernew Newport 35 F6
Coedpoeth Wrex 73 D6
Coedway Powys 60 C3
Coelbren Powys 34 C2
Coffinswell Devon 7 C6
Cofton Hackett Worcs 50 B5
Cogan V Glam 22 B3
Cogenhoe Northants 53 C6
Cogges Oxon 38 D3
Coggeshall Essex 42 B4
Coggeshall Hamlet Essex 42 B4
Coggins Mill E Sus 18 C2
Coig Peighinnean W Isles 155 A10
Coig Peighinnean Bhuirgh W Isles 155 B9
Coignafearn Lodge Highld 138 C2
Coilacriech Aberds 140 E2
Coilantogle Stirling 126 D4
Coilleag W Isles 148 G2
Coillore Highld 149 E8
Coity Bridgend 34 F3
Col W Isles 155 C9
Col Uarach W Isles 155 D9
Colaboll Highld 157 H8
Colan Corn 4 C3
Colaton Raleigh Devon 11 F5
Colbost Highld 148 D7
Colburn N Yorks 101 E6
Colby Cumb 100 B1
Colby IoM 84 E2
Colby Norf 81 D8
Colchester Essex 43 B6
Colcot V Glam 22 C3
Cold Ash W Berks 26 C3
Cold Ashby Northants 52 B4
Cold Ashton S Glos 24 B2
Cold Aston Glos 37 C8
Cold Blow Pembs 32 C2
Cold Brayfield M Keynes 53 D7
Cold Hanworth Lincs 90 F4
Cold Harbour Lincs 78 F2
Cold Hatton Telford 61 B6
Cold Hesledon Durham 111 E7
Cold Higham Northants 52 D4
Cold Kirby N Yorks 102 F3
Cold Newton Leics 64 D4
Cold Northcott Corn 8 F4
Cold Norton Essex 42 D4
Cold Overton Leics 64 C5
Coldbackie Highld 157 D9
Coldbeck Cumb 100 D2
Coldblow London 29 B6
Coldean Brighton 17 D7
Coldeast Devon 7 B6
Colden W Yorks 87 B7
Colden Common Hants 15 B5
Coldfair Green Suff 57 C8
Coldham Cambs 66 D4
Coldharbour Glos 36 D2
Coldharbour Kent 29 D6
Coldharbour Sur 28 E2
Coldingham Borders 122 C5
Coldrain Perth 128 D2
Coldred Kent 31 E6
Coldridge Devon 9 D8
Coldstream Angus 134 F3
Coldstream Borders 122 F4
Coldwaltham W Sus 16 C4
Coldwells Aberds 153 D11
Coldwells Croft Aberds 140 B4
Coldyeld Shrops 60 E3
Cole Som 23 F8
Cole Green Herts 41 C5
Cole Henley Hants 26 D2
Colebatch Shrops 60 F3
Colebrook Devon 10 D5
Colebrooke Devon 10 E2
Coleby Lincs 78 C2
Coleby N Lincs 90 C2
Coleford Devon 10 D2
Coleford Glos 36 C2
Coleford Som 23 E8
Colehill Dorset 13 D8
Coleman's Hatch E Sus 29 F5
Colemere Shrops 73 F8
Colemore Hants 26 F5
Coleorton Leics 63 C8
Colerne Wilts 24 B3
Cole's Green Suff 57 C6
Coles Green Suff 56 E4
Colesbourne Glos 37 C6
Colesden Bedford 54 D2
Coleshill Bucks 40 E2
Coleshill Oxon 38 E2
Coleshill Warks 63 F6
Colestocks Devon 11 D5
Colgate W Sus 28 F3
Colgrain Argyll 126 F2
Colinsburgh Fife 129 D6
Colinton Edin 120 C5
Colintraive Argyll 145 F9
Colkirk Norf 80 E5
Collace Perth 134 F2
Collafirth Shetland 160 G6
Collaton St Mary Torbay 7 D6
College Milton S Lanark 119 D6
Collessie Fife 128 C4
Collier Row London 41 E8
Collier Street Kent 29 E8
Collier's End Herts 41 B6
Collier's Green Kent 18 B4
Colliery Row T&W 111 E6
Collieston Aberds 141 B9
Collin Dumfries 107 B7
Collingbourne Ducis Wilts 25 D7
Collingbourne Kingston Wilts 25 D7
Collingham Notts 77 C8
Collingham W Yorks 95 E6
Collington Hereford 49 C8
Collingtree Northants 53 D5
Collins Green Warr 86 E3
Colliston Angus 135 E6
Collycroft Warks 63 F7
Collynie Aberds 153 E8
Collyweston Northants 65 D6
Colmonell S Ayrs 104 A5
Colmworth Bedford 54 D2
Coln Rogers Glos 37 D7
Coln St Aldwyn's Glos 37 D8
Coln St Dennis Glos 37 C7
Colnabaichin Aberds 139 D8
Colnbrook Slough 27 B8
Colne Cambs 54 B4
Colne Lancs 93 E8
Colne Edge Lancs 93 E8
Colne Engaine Essex 56 F2
Colney Norf 68 D4
Colney Heath Herts 41 D5
Colney Street Herts 40 D4
Colpy Aberds 153 E6
Colquhar Borders 121 E6
Colsterdale N Yorks 101 F6
Colsterworth Lincs 65 B6
Colston Bassett Notts 77 F6
Coltfield Moray 151 E14
Colthouse Cumb 99 E5
Coltishall Norf 69 C5
Coltness N Lanark 119 D8
Colton Cumb 99 F5
Colton N Yorks 95 E8
Colton Norf 68 D4
Colton Staffs 62 B4
Colton W Yorks 95 F6
Colva Powys 48 D4
Colvend Dumfries 107 D5
Colvister Shetland 160 D7
Colwall Green Hereford 50 E2
Colwall Stone Hereford 50 E2
Colwell Northumb 110 B2
Colwich Staffs 62 B4
Colwick Notts 77 E6
Colwinston V Glam 21 B8
Colworth W Sus 16 D3
Colwyn Bay = Bae Colwyn Conwy 83 D8
Colyford Devon 11 E7
Colyton Devon 11 E7
Combe Hereford 48 C5
Combe Oxon 38 C4
Combe W Berks 25 C8
Combe Common Sur 27 F7
Combe Down Bath 24 C2
Combe Florey Som 22 F3
Combe Hay Bath 24 D2
Combe Martin Devon 20 E4
Combe Moor Hereford 49 C5
Combe Raleigh Devon 11 D6
Combe St Nicholas Som 11 C8
Combeinteignhead Devon 7 B7
Comberbach Ches W 74 B3
Comberton Cambs 54 D4
Comberton Hereford 49 C6
Combpyne Devon 11 E7
Combridge Staffs 75 F7
Combrook Warks 51 D8
Combs Derbys 75 B7
Combs Suff 56 D4
Combs Ford Suff 56 D4
Combwich Som 22 E4
Comers Aberds 141 D5
Comins Coch Ceredig 58 F3
Commercial End Cambs 55 C6
Commins Capel Betws Ceredig 46 D5
Commins Coch Powys 58 D5
Common Edge Blackpool 92 F3
Common Side Derbys 76 B3
Commondale N Yorks 102 C4
Commonmoor Corn 5 C7
Commonside Ches W 74 B2
Compstall Gtr Man 87 E7
Compton Devon 7 C6
Compton Hants 15 B5
Compton Sur 27 E6
Compton Sur 27 E7
Compton W Berks 26 B3
Compton W Sus 15 C8
Compton Wilts 25 D6
Compton Abbas Dorset 13 C6
Compton Abdale Glos 37 C7
Compton Bassett Wilts 24 B5
Compton Beauchamp Oxon 38 F2
Compton Bishop Som 23 D5
Compton Chamberlayne Wilts 13 B8
Compton Dando Bath 23 C8
Compton Dundon Som 23 F6
Compton Martin Bath 23 D7
Compton Pauncefoot Som 12 B4
Compton Valence Dorset 12 E3
Comrie Fife 128 F2
Comrie Perth 127 B6
Conaglen House Highld 130 C4
Conchra Argyll 145 E9
Concraigie Perth 133 E8
Conder Green Lancs 92 D4
Conderton Worcs 50 F4
Condicote Glos 38 B1
Condorrat N Lanark 119 B7
Condover Shrops 60 D4
Coney Weston Suff 56 B3
Coneyhurst W Sus 16 B5
Coneysthorpe N Yorks 96 B3
Coneythorpe N Yorks 95 D6
Conford Hants 27 F6
Congash Highld 139 B6
Congdon's Shop Corn 5 B7
Congerstone Leics 63 D7
Congham Norf 80 E3
Congl-y-wal Gwyn 71 C8
Congleton Ches E 75 C5
Congresbury N Som 23 C6
Congreve Staffs 62 C3
Conicavel Moray 151 F12
Coningsby Lincs 78 D5
Conington Cambs 54 C4
Conington Cambs 65 F8
Conisbrough S Yorks 89 E6
Conisby Argyll 142 B3
Conisholme Lincs 91 E8
Coniston Cumb 99 E5
Coniston E Yorks 97 F7
Coniston Cold N Yorks 94 D2
Conistone N Yorks 94 C2
Connah's Quay Flint 73 C6
Connel Argyll 124 B5
Connel Park E Ayrs 113 C6
Connor Downs Corn 2 C4
Conon Bridge Highld 151 F8
Conon House Highld 151 F8
Cononley N Yorks 94 E2
Conordan Highld 149 E10
Consall Staffs 75 E6
Consett Durham 110 D4
Constable Burton N Yorks 101 E6
Constantine Corn 3 D6
Constantine Bay Corn 4 B3
Contin Highld 150 F7
Contlaw Aberdeen 141 D7
Conwy Conwy 83 D7
Conyer Kent 30 C3
Conyers Green Suff 56 C2
Cooden E Sus 18 E4
Cooil IoM 84 E3
Cookbury Devon 9 D6
Cookham Windsor 40 F1
Cookham Dean Windsor 40 F1
Cookham Rise Windsor 40 F1
Cookhill Worcs 51 D5
Cookley Suff 57 B7
Cookley Worcs 62 F2
Cookley Green Oxon 39 E6
Cookney Aberds 141 E7
Cookridge W Yorks 95 E5
Cooksbridge E Sus 17 C8
Cooksmill Green Essex 42 D2
Coolham W Sus 16 B5
Cooling Medway 29 B8
Coombe Corn 4 D4
Coombe Corn 8 C4
Coombe Hants 15 B7
Coombe Wilts 25 D6
Coombe Bissett Wilts 14 B2
Coombe Hill Glos 37 B5
Coombe Keynes Dorset 13 F6
Coombes W Sus 17 D5
Coopersale Common Essex 41 D7
Cootham W Sus 16 C4
Copdock Suff 56 E5
Copford Green Essex 43 B5
Copgrove N Yorks 95 C6
Copister Shetland 160 F6
Cople Bedford 54 E2
Copley Durham 101 B5
Coplow Dale Derbys 75 B8
Copmanthorpe York 95 E8
Coppathorne Corn 8 D4
Coppenhall Staffs 62 C3
Coppenhall Moss Ches E 74 D4
Copperhouse Corn 2 C4
Coppingford Cambs 65 F8
Copplestone Devon 10 D2
Coppull Lancs 86 C3
Coppull Moor Lancs 86 C3
Copsale W Sus 17 B5
Copster Green Lancs 93 F6
Copston Magna Warks 63 F8
Copt Heath W Mid 51 B6
Copt Hewick N Yorks 95 B6
Copt Oak Leics 63 C8
Copthorne Shrops 60 C4
Copthorne Sur 28 F4
Copy's Green Norf 80 D5
Copythorne Hants 14 C4
Corbets Tey London 42 F1
Corbridge Northumb 110 C2
Corby Northants 65 F5
Corby Glen Lincs 65 B6
Cordon N Ayrs 143 E11
Coreley Shrops 49 B8
Cores End Bucks 40 F2
Corfe Som 11 C7
Corfe Castle Dorset 13 F7
Corfe Mullen Dorset 13 E7
Corfton Shrops 60 F4
Corgarff Aberds 139 D8
Corhampton Hants 15 B7
Corlae Dumfries 113 E6
Corley Warks 63 F7
Corley Ash Warks 63 F6
Corley Moor Warks 63 F6
Cornaa IoM 84 D4
Cornabus Argyll 142 D4
Cornel Conwy 83 E7
Corner Row Lancs 92 F4
Corney Cumb 98 E3
Cornforth Durham 111 F6
Cornhill Aberds 152 C5
Cornhill-on-Tweed Northumb 122 F4
Cornholme W Yorks 87 B7
Cornish Hall End Essex 55 F7
Cornquoy Orkney 159 J6
Cornsay Durham 110 E4
Cornsay Colliery Durham 110 E4
Corntown Highld 151 F8
Corntown V Glam 21 B8
Cornwell Oxon 38 B2
Cornwood Devon 6 D4
Cornworthy Devon 7 D6
Corpach Highld 130 B4
Corpusty Norf 81 D7
Corran Highld 130 C4
Corran Highld 149 H13
Corranbuie Argyll 145 G7
Corrany IoM 84 D4
Corrie N Ayrs 143 D11
Corrie Common Dumfries 114 F5
Corriecravie N Ayrs 143 F10
Corriemoillie Highld 150 E6
Corriemulzie Lodge Highld 150 B6
Corrievarkie Lodge Perth 132 B2
Corrievorrie Highld 138 B3
Corrimony Highld 150 H6
Corringham Lincs 90 E2
Corringham Thurrock 42 F3
Corris Gwyn 58 D4
Corris Uchaf Gwyn 58 D4
Corrour Shooting Lodge Highld 131 C8
Corrow Argyll 125 E7
Corry Highld 149 F11
Corry of Ardnagrask Highld 151 G8
Corrykinloch Highld 156 G6
Corrymuckloch Perth 133 F5
Corrynachenchy Argyll 147 G9
Cors-y-Gedol Gwyn 71 E6
Corsback Highld 158 C4
Corscombe Dorset 12 D3
Corse Aberds 152 D6
Corse Glos 36 B4
Corse Lawn Worcs 50 F3
Corse of Kinnoir Aberds 152 D5
Corsewall Dumfries 104 C4
Corsham Wilts 24 B3
Corsindae Aberds 141 D5
Corsley Wilts 24 E3
Corsley Heath Wilts 24 E3
Corsock Dumfries 106 B4
Corston Bath 23 C8
Corston Wilts 37 F6
Corstorphine Edin 120 B4
Cortachy Angus 134 D3
Corton Suff 69 E8
Corton Wilts 24 E4
Corton Denham Som 12 B4
Coruanan Lodge Highld 130 C4
Corunna W Isles 148 B3
Corwen Denb 72 E4
Coryton Devon 9 F6
Coryton Thurrock 42 F3
Cosby Leics 64 E2
Coseley W Mid 62 E3
Cosgrove Northants 53 E5
Cosham Ptsmth 15 D7
Cosheston Pembs 32 D1
Cossall Notts 76 E4
Cossington Leics 64 C3
Cossington Som 23 E5
Costa Orkney 159 F4
Costessey Norf 68 C4
Costock Notts 64 B2
Coston Leics 64 B5
Cote Oxon 38 D3
Cotebrook Ches W 74 C2
Cotehill Cumb 108 D4
Cotes Cumb 99 F6
Cotes Leics 64 B2
Cotes Staffs 74 F5
Cotesbach Leics 64 F2
Cotgrave Notts 77 F6
Cothall Aberds 141 C7
Cotham Notts 77 E7
Cothelstone Som 22 F3
Cotherstone Durham 101 C5
Cothill Oxon 38 E4
Cotleigh Devon 11 D7
Cotmanhay Derbys 76 E4
Cotmaton Devon 11 F6
Coton Cambs 54 D5
Coton Northants 52 B4
Coton Staffs 62 B2
Coton Staffs 75 F6
Coton Clanford Staffs 62 B2
Coton Hill Shrops 60 C4
Coton Hill Staffs 75 F6
Coton in the Elms Derbys 63 C6
Cott Devon 7 C5
Cottam E Yorks 97 C5
Cottam Lancs 92 F5
Cottam Notts 77 B8
Cottartown Highld 151 H13
Cottenham Cambs 54 C5
Cotterdale N Yorks 100 E3
Cottered Herts 41 B6
Cotteridge W Mid 50 B5
Cotterstock Northants 65 E7
Cottesbrooke Northants 52 B5
Cottesmore Rutland 65 C6
Cotteylands Devon 10 C4
Cottingham E Yorks 97 F6
Cottingham Northants 64 E5
Cottingley W Yorks 94 F4
Cottisford Oxon 52 F3
Cotton Staffs 75 E7
Cotton Suff 56 C4
Cotton End Bedford 53 E8
Cottown Aberds 140 B4
Cottown Aberds 141 C6
Cottown Aberds 153 D8
Cotwalton Staffs 75 F6
Couch's Mill Corn 5 D6
Coughton Hereford 36 B2
Coughton Warks 51 C5
Coulaghailtro Argyll 144 G6
Coulags Highld 150 G2
Coulby Newham Mbro 102 C3
Coulderton Cumb 98 D1
Coulin Highld 150 F3
Coull Aberds 140 D4
Coull Argyll 142 B3
Coulport Argyll 145 E11
Coulsdon London 28 D3
Coulston Wilts 24 D4
Coulter S Lanark 120 F3
Coulton N Yorks 96 B2
Cound Shrops 61 D5
Coundon Durham 101 B7
Coundon W Mid 63 F7
Coundon Grange Durham 101 B7
Countersett N Yorks 100 F4
Countess Wilts 25 E6
Countess Wear Devon 10 F4
Countesthorpe Leics 64 E2
Countisbury Devon 21 E6
County Oak W Sus 28 F3
Coup Green Lancs 86 B3
Coupar Angus Perth 134 E2
Coupland Northumb 122 F5
Cour Argyll 143 D9
Courance Dumfries 114 E3
Court-at-Street Kent 19 B7
Court Henry Carms 33 B6
Courteenhall Northants 53 D5
Courtsend Essex 43 E6
Courtway Som 22 F4
Cousland Midloth 121 C6
Cousley Wood E Sus 18 B3
Cove Argyll 145 E11
Cove Borders 122 B3
Cove Devon 10 C4
Cove Hants 27 D6
Cove Highld 155 H13
Cove Bay Aberdeen 141 D8
Cove Bottom Suff 57 B8
Covehithe Suff 69 F8
Coven Staffs 62 D3
Coveney Cambs 66 F4
Covenham St Bartholomew Lincs 91 E7
Covenham St Mary Lincs 91 E7
Coventry W Mid 51 B8
Coverack Corn 3 E6
Coverham N Yorks 101 F6
Covesea Moray 152 A1
Covington Cambs 53 B8
Covington S Lanark 120 F2
Cow Ark Lancs 93 E6
Cowan Bridge Lancs 93 B6
Cowbeech E Sus 18 D3
Cowbit Lincs 66 C2
Cowbridge Lincs 79 E6
Cowbridge Som 21 E8
Cowbridge = Y Bont-Faen V Glam 21 B8
Cowdale Derbys 75 B7
Cowden Kent 29 E5
Cowdenbeath Fife 128 E3
Cowdenburn Borders 120 D5
Cowers Lane Derbys 76 E3
Cowes IoW 15 E5
Cowesby N Yorks 102 F2
Cowfold W Sus 17 B6
Cowgill Cumb 100 F2
Cowie Aberds 141 F7
Cowie Stirling 127 F7
Cowley Devon 10 E4
Cowley Glos 37 C6
Cowley London 40 F3
Cowley Oxon 39 D5
Cowleymoor Devon 10 C4
Cowling Lancs 86 C3
Cowling N Yorks 94 E2
Cowling N Yorks 101 F7
Cowlinge Suff 55 D8
Cowpe Lancs 87 B6
Cowpen Northumb 117 F8
Cowpen Bewley Stockton 102 B2
Cowplain Hants 15 C7
Cowshill Durham 109 E8
Cowslip Green N Som 23 C6
Cowstrandburn Fife 128 E2
Cowthorpe N Yorks 95 D7
Cox Common Suff 69 F6
Cox Green Windsor 27 B6
Cox Moor Notts 76 D5
Coxbank Ches E 74 E3
Coxbench Derbys 76 E3
Coxford Norf 80 E4
Coxford Soton 14 C4
Coxheath Kent 29 D8
Coxhill Kent 31 E6
Coxhoe Durham 111 F6
Coxley Som 23 E7
Coxwold N Yorks 95 B8
Coychurch Bridgend 21 B8
Coylton S Ayrs 112 B4
Coylumbridge Highld 138 C5
Coynach Aberds 140 D3
Coynachie Aberds 152 E4
Coytrahen Bridgend 34 F2
Crabadon Devon 7 D5
Crabbs Cross Worcs 50 C5
Crabtree W Sus 17 B6
Crackenthorpe Cumb 100 B1
Crackington Haven Corn 8 E3
Crackley Warks 51 B7
Crackleybank Shrops 61 C7
Crackpot N Yorks 100 E4
Cracoe N Yorks 94 C2
Craddock Devon 11 C5
Cradhlastadh W Isles 154 D5
Cradley Hereford 50 E2
Cradley Heath W Mid 62 F3
Crafthole Corn 5 D8
Cragg Vale W Yorks 87 B8
Craggan Highld 139 B6
Craggie Highld 151 H10
Craggie Highld 157 H11
Craghead Durham 110 D5
Crai Powys 34 B2
Craibstone Moray 152 C4
Craichie Angus 135 E5
Craig Dumfries 106 B3
Craig Dumfries 106 C3
Craig Highld 150 G3
Craig Castle Aberds 140 B3
Craig-cefn-parc Swansea 33 D7
Craig Penllyn V Glam 21 B8
Craig-y-don Conwy 83 C7
Craig-y-nos Powys 34 C2
Craiganor Lodge Perth 132 D3
Craigdam Aberds 153 E8
Craigdarroch Dumfries 113 E7
Craigdarroch Highld 150 F7
Craigdhu Highld 150 G7
Craigearn Aberds 141 C6
Craigellachie Moray 152 D2
Craigencross Dumfries 104 C4
Craigend Perth 128 B3
Craigend Stirling 127 F6
Craigendive Argyll 145 E9
Craigendoran Argyll 126 F2
Craigends Renfs 118 C4
Craigens Argyll 142 B3
Craigens E Ayrs 113 C5
Craighat Stirling 126 F3
Craighead Fife 129 D8
Craighlaw Mains Dumfries 105 C7
Craighouse Argyll 144 G4
Craigie Aberds 141 C8
Craigie Dundee 134 F4
Craigie Perth 128 B3
Craigie Perth 133 E8
Craigie S Ayrs 118 F4
Craigiefield Orkney 159 G5
Craigielaw E Loth 121 B7
Craiglockhart Edin 120 B5
Craigmalloch E Ayrs 112 E4
Craigmaud Aberds 153 C8
Craigmillar Edin 121 B5
Craigmore Argyll 145 G10
Craignant Shrops 73 F6
Craigneuk N Lanark 119 C7
Craigneuk N Lanark 119 D7
Craignure Argyll 124 B3
Craigo Angus 135 C6
Craigow Perth 128 D2
Craigrothie Fife 129 C5
Craigroy Moray 151 F14
Craigruie Stirling 126 B3
Craigston Castle Aberds 153 C7
Craigton Aberdeen 141 D7
Craigton Angus 134 D3
Craigton Angus 135 F5
Craigton Highld 151 B9
Craigtown Highld 157 D11
Craik Borders 115 D6
Crail Fife 129 D8
Crailing Borders 116 B2
Crailinghall Borders 116 B2
Craiselound N Lincs 89 E8
Crakehill N Yorks 95 B7
Crakemarsh Staffs 75 F7
Crambe N Yorks 96 C3
Cramlington Northumb 111 B5
Cramond Edin 120 B4
Cramond Bridge Edin 120 B4
Cranage Ches E 74 C4
Cranberry Staffs 74 F5
Cranborne Dorset 13 C8
Cranbourne Brack 27 B7
Cranbrook Kent 18 B4
Cranbrook Common Kent 18 B4
Crane Moor S Yorks 88 D4
Crane's Corner Norf 68 C2
Cranfield C Beds 53 E7
Cranford London 28 B2
Cranford St Andrew Northants 53 B7
Cranford St John Northants 53 B7
Cranham Glos 37 C5
Cranham London 42 F1
Crank Mers 86 E3
Crank Wood Gtr Man 86 D4
Cranleigh Sur 27 F8
Cranley Suff 57 B5
Cranmer Green Suff 56 B4
Cranmore IoW 14 F4
Cranna Aberds 153 C6
Crannich Argyll 147 G8
Crannoch Moray 152 C4
Cranoe Leics 64 E4
Cransford Suff 57 C7
Cranshaws Borders 122 C2
Cranstal IoM 84 B4
Crantock Corn 4 C2
Cranwell Lincs 78 E3
Cranwich Norf 67 E7
Cranworth Norf 68 D2
Craobh Haven Argyll 124 E3
Crapstone Devon 6 C3
Crarae Argyll 125 F5
Crask Inn Highld 157 G8
Crask of Aigas Highld 150 G7
Craskins Aberds 140 D4
Craster Northumb 117 C8
Craswall Hereford 48 F4
Cratfield Suff 57 B7
Crathes Aberds 141 E6
Crathie Aberds 139 E8
Crathie Highld 137 E8
Crathorne N Yorks 102 D2
Craven Arms Shrops 60 F4
Crawcrook T&W 110 C4
Crawford Lancs 86 D2
Crawford S Lanark 114 B2
Crawfordjohn S Lanark 113 B8
Crawick Dumfries 113 C7
Crawley Hants 26 F2
Crawley Oxon 38 C3
Crawley W Sus 28 F3
Crawley Down W Sus 28 F4
Crawleyside Durham 110 E2
Crawshawbooth Lancs 87 B6
Crawton Aberds 135 B8
Cray N Yorks 94 B2
Cray Perth 133 C8
Crayford London 29 B6
Crayke N Yorks 95 B8
Crays Hill Essex 42 E3
Cray's Pond Oxon 39 F6
Creacombe Devon 10 C3
Creag Ghoraidh W Isles 148 D2
Creagan Argyll 130 E3
Creaguaineach Lodge Highld 131 C7
Creaksea Essex 43 E5
Creaton Northants 52 B5
Creca Dumfries 108 B2
Credenhill Hereford 49 E6
Crediton Devon 10 D3
Creebridge Dumfries 105 C8
Creech Heathfield Som 11 B7
Creech St Michael Som 11 B7
Creed Corn 3 B8
Creekmouth London 41 F7
Creeting Bottoms Suff 56 D5
Creeting St Mary Suff 56 D4
Creeton Lincs 65 B7
Creetown Dumfries 105 D8
Creg-ny-Baa IoM 84 D3
Creggans Argyll 125 E6
Cregneash IoM 84 F1
Cregrina Powys 48 D3
Creich Fife 128 B5
Creigiau Cardiff 34 F4
Cremyll Corn 6 D2
Creslow Bucks 39 B8
Cressage Shrops 61 D5
Cressbrook Derbys 75 B8
Cresselly Pembs 32 D1
Cressing Essex 42 B3
Cresswell Northumb 117 E8
Cresswell Staffs 75 F6
Cresswell Quay Pembs 32 D1
Creswell Derbys 76 B5
Cretingham Suff 57 C6
Cretshengan Argyll 144 G6
Crewe Ches E 74 D4
Crewe Ches W 73 D8
Crewgreen Powys 60 C3
Crewkerne Som 12 D2
Crianlarich Stirling 126 B2
Cribyn Ceredig 46 D4
Criccieth Gwyn 71 D5
Crich Derbys 76 D3
Crichie Aberds 153 D9
Crichton Midloth 121 C6
Crick Mon 36 E1
Crick Northants 52 B3
Crickadarn Powys 48 E2
Cricket Malherbie Som 11 C8
Cricket St Thomas Som 11 D8
Crickheath Shrops 60 B2
Crickhowell Powys 35 C6
Cricklade Wilts 37 E8
Cricklewood London 41 F5
Cridling Stubbs N Yorks 89 B6
Crieff Perth 127 B7
Criggion Powys 60 C2
Crigglestone W Yorks 88 C4
Crimond Aberds 153 C10
Crimonmogate Aberds 153 C10
Crimplesham Norf 67 D6
Crinan Argyll 144 D6
Cringleford Norf 68 D4
Cringles W Yorks 94 E3
Crinow Pembs 32 C2
Cripplesease Corn 2 C4
Cripplestyle Dorset 13 C8
Cripp's Corner E Sus 18 C4
Croasdale Cumb 98 C2
Crock Street Som 11 C8
Crockenhill Kent 29 C6
Crockernwell Devon 10 E2
Crockerton Wilts 24 E3
Crocketford or Ninemile Bar Dumfries 106 B5
Crockey Hill York 96 E2
Crockham Hill Kent 28 D5
Crockleford Heath Essex 43 B6
Crockness Orkney 159 J4
Croes-goch Pembs 44 B3
Croes-lan Ceredig 46 E2
Croes-y-mwyalch Torf 35 E7
Croeserw Neath 34 E2
Croesor Gwyn 71 C7
Croesyceiliog Carms 33 C5
Croesyceiliog Torf 35 E7
Croesywaun Gwyn 82 F5
Croft Leics 64 E2
Croft Lincs 79 C8
Croft Pembs 45 E3
Croft Warr 86 E4
Croft-on-Tees N Yorks 101 D7
Croftamie Stirling 126 F3
Croftmalloch W Loth 120 C2
Crofton W Yorks 88 C4

Crofton Wilts 25 C7
Crofts of Benachielt Highld 158 G3
Crofts of Haddo Aberds 153 E8
Crofts of Inverthernie Aberds 153 D7
Crofts of Meikle Ardo Aberds 153 D8
Crofty Swansea 33 E6
Croggan Argyll 124 C3
Croglin Cumb 109 E5
Croich Highld 150 B7
Crois Dughaill W Isles 148 F2
Cromarty Highld 151 E10
Cromblet Aberds 153 E7
Cromdale Highld 139 B6
Cromer Herts 41 B5
Cromer Norf 81 C8
Cromford Derbys 76 D2
Cromhall S Glos 36 E3
Cromhall Common S Glos 36 F3
Cromor W Isles 155 E9
Cromra Highld 137 E8
Cromwell Notts 77 C7
Cronberry E Ayrs 113 B6
Crondall Hants 27 E5
Cronk-y-Voddy IoM 84 D3
Cronton Mers 86 F2
Crook Cumb 99 E6
Crook Durham 110 F4
Crook of Devon Perth 128 D2
Crookedholm E Ayrs 118 F4
Crookes S Yorks 88 F4
Crookham Northumb 122 F5
Crookham W Berks 26 C3
Crookham Village Hants 27 D5
Crookhaugh Borders 114 B4
Crookhouse Borders 116 B3
Crooklands Cumb 99 F7
Cropredy Oxon 52 E2
Cropston Leics 64 C2
Cropthorne Worcs 50 E4
Cropton N Yorks 103 F5
Cropwell Bishop Notts 77 F6
Cropwell Butler Notts 77 F6
Cros W Isles 155 A10
Crosbost W Isles 155 E8
Crosby Cumb 107 F7
Crosby IoM 84 E3
Crosby N Lincs 90 C2
Crosby Garrett Cumb 100 D2
Crosby Ravensworth Cumb 99 C8
Crosby Villa Cumb 107 F7
Croscombe Som 23 E7
Cross Som 23 D6
Cross Ash Mon 35 C8
Cross-at-Hand Kent 29 E8
Cross Green Devon 9 F5
Cross Green Suff 56 D2
Cross Green Suff 56 D3
Cross Green Warks 51 D8
Cross-hands Carms 32 B2
Cross Hands Carms 33 C6
Cross Hands Pembs 32 C1
Cross Hill Derbys 76 E4
Cross Houses Shrops 60 D5
Cross in Hand E Sus 18 C2
Cross in Hand Leics 64 F2
Cross Inn Ceredig 46 C4
Cross Inn Ceredig 46 D2
Cross Inn Rhondda 34 F4
Cross Keys Kent 29 D6
Cross Lane Head Shrops 61 E7
Cross Lanes Corn 3 D5
Cross Lanes N Yorks 95 C8
Cross Lanes Wrex 73 E7
Cross Oak Powys 35 B5
Cross of Jackston Aberds 153 E7
Cross o'th'hands Derbys 76 E2
Cross Street Suff 57 B5
Crossaig Argyll 143 C9
Crossal Highld 149 E9
Crossapol Argyll 146 G2
Crossburn Falk 119 B8
Crossbush W Sus 16 D4
Crosscanonby Cumb 107 F7
Crossdale Street Norf 81 D8
Crossens Mers 85 C4
Crossflatts W Yorks 94 E4
Crossford Fife 128 F2
Crossford S Lanark 119 E8
Crossgate Lincs 66 B2
Crossgatehall E Loth 121 C6
Crossgates Fife 128 F3
Crossgates Powys 48 C2
Crossgill Lancs 93 C5
Crosshill E Ayrs 112 B4
Crosshill Fife 128 E3
Crosshill S Ayrs 112 D3
Crosshouse E Ayrs 118 F3
Crossings Cumb 108 B5
Crosskeys Caerph 35 E6
Crosskirk Highld 157 B13
Crosslanes Shrops 60 C3
Crosslee Borders 115 C6
Crosslee Renfs 118 C4
Crossmichael Dumfries 106 C4
Crossmoor Lancs 92 F4
Crossroads Aberds 141 E6
Crossroads E Ayrs 118 F4
Crossway Hereford 49 F8
Crossway Mon 35 C8
Crossway Powys 48 D2
Crossway Green Worcs 50 C3
Crossways Dorset 13 F5
Crosswell Pembs 45 F3
Crosswood Ceredig 47 B5
Crosthwaite Cumb 99 E6
Croston Lancs 86 C2
Crostwick Norf 69 C5
Crostwight Norf 69 B6
Crothair W Isles 154 D6
Crouch Kent 29 D7
Crouch Hill Dorset 12 C5
Crouch House Green Kent 28 E5
Croucheston Wilts 13 B8
Croughton Northants 52 F3
Crovie Aberds 153 B8
Crow Edge S Yorks 88 D2
Crow Hill Hereford 36 B3
Crowan Corn 2 C5
Crowborough E Sus 18 B2
Crowcombe Som 22 F3
Crowdecote Derbys 75 C8
Crowden Derbys 87 E8
Crowell Oxon 39 E7
Crowfield Northants 52 E4
Crowfield Suff 56 D5
Crowhurst E Sus 18 D4
Crowhurst Sur 28 E4
Crowhurst Lane End Sur 28 E4
Crowland Lincs 66 C2
Crowlas Corn 2 C4
Crowle N Lincs 89 C8
Crowle Worcs 50 D4
Crowmarsh Gifford Oxon 39 F6
Crown Corner Suff 57 B6
Crownhill Plym 6 D2
Crownland Suff 56 C4
Crownthorpe Norf 68 D3
Crowntown Corn 2 C5
Crows-an-wra Corn 2 D2
Crowshill Norf 68 D2
Crowsnest Shrops 60 D3
Crowthorne Brack 27 C6
Crowton Ches W 74 B2
Croxall Staffs 63 C5
Croxby Lincs 91 E5
Croxdale Durham 111 F5
Croxden Staffs 75 F7
Croxley Green Herts 40 E3
Croxton Cambs 54 C3
Croxton N Lincs 90 C4
Croxton Norf 67 F8
Croxton Staffs 74 F4
Croxton Kerrial Leics 64 B5
Croxtonbank Staffs 74 F4
Croy Highld 151 G10
Croy N Lanark 119 B7
Croyde Devon 20 F3
Croydon Cambs 54 E4
Croydon London 28 C4
Crubenmore Lodge Highld 138 E2
Cruckmeole Shrops 60 D4
Cruckton Shrops 60 C4
Cruden Bay Aberds 153 E10
Crudgington Telford 61 C6
Crudwell Wilts 37 E6
Crug Powys 48 B3
Crugmeer Corn 4 B4
Crugybar Carms 47 F5
Crulabhig W Isles 154 D6
Crumlin = Crymlyn Caerph 35 E6
Crumpsall Gtr Man 87 D6
Crundale Kent 30 E4
Crundale Pembs 44 D4
Cruwys Morchard Devon 10 C3
Crux Easton Hants 26 D2
Crwbin Carms 33 C5
Crya Orkney 159 H4
Cryers Hill Bucks 40 E1
Crymlyn = Crumlin Caerph 35 E6
Crymlyn Gwyn 83 D6
Crymych Pembs 45 F3
Crynant Neath 34 D1
Crynfryn Ceredig 46 C4
Cuaig Highld 149 C12
Cuan Argyll 124 D3
Cubbington Warks 51 C8
Cubeck N Yorks 100 F4
Cubert Corn 4 D2
Cubley S Yorks 88 D3
Cubley Common Derbys 75 F8
Cublington Bucks 39 B8
Cublington Hereford 49 F6
Cuckfield W Sus 17 B7
Cucklington Som 13 B5
Cuckney Notts 77 B5
Cuckoo Hill Notts 89 E8
Cuddesdon Oxon 39 D6
Cuddington Bucks 39 C7
Cuddington Ches W 74 B3
Cuddington Heath Ches W 73 E8
Cuddy Hill Lancs 92 F4
Cudham London 28 D5
Cudliptown Devon 6 B3
Cudworth S Yorks 88 D4
Cudworth Som 11 C8
Cuffley Herts 41 D6
Cuiashader W Isles 155 B10
Cuidhir W Isles 148 H1
Cuidhtinis W Isles 154 J5
Culbo Highld 151 E9
Culbokie Highld 151 F9
Culburnie Highld 150 G7
Culcabock Highld 151 G9
Culcairn Highld 151 E9
Culcharry Highld 151 F11
Culcheth Warr 86 E4
Culdrain Aberds 152 E5
Culduie Highld 149 D12
Culford Suff 56 B2
Culgaith Cumb 99 B8
Culham Oxon 39 E5
Culkein Highld 156 F3
Culkein Drumbeg Highld 156 F4
Culkerton Glos 37 E6
Cullachie Highld 139 B5
Cullen Moray 152 B5
Cullercoats T&W 111 B6
Cullicudden Highld 151 E9
Cullingworth W Yorks 94 F3
Cullipool Argyll 124 D3
Cullivoe Shetland 160 C7
Culloch Perth 127 C6
Culloden Highld 151 G10
Cullompton Devon 10 D5
Culmaily Highld 151 B11
Culmazie Dumfries 105 D7
Culmington Shrops 60 F4
Culmstock Devon 11 C6
Culnacraig Highld 156 J3
Culnaknock Highld 149 B10
Culpho Suff 57 E6
Culrain Highld 151 B8
Culross Fife 127 F8
Culroy S Ayrs 112 C3
Culsh Aberds 140 E2
Culsh Aberds 153 D8
Culshabbin Dumfries 105 D7
Culswick Shetland 160 J4
Cultercullen Aberds 141 B8
Cults Aberdeen 141 D7
Cults Aberds 152 E5
Cults Dumfries 105 E8
Culverstone Green Kent 29 C7
Culverthorpe Lincs 78 E3
Culworth Northants 52 E3
Culzie Lodge Highld 151 D8
Cumbernauld N Lanark 119 B7
Cumbernauld Village N Lanark 119 B7
Cumberworth Lincs 79 B8
Cuminestown Aberds 153 C8
Cumlewick Shetland 160 L6
Cummersdale Cumb 108 D3
Cummertrees Dumfries 107 C8
Cummingston Moray 152 B1
Cumnock E Ayrs 113 B5
Cumnor Oxon 38 D4
Cumrew Cumb 108 D5
Cumwhinton Cumb 108 D4
Cumwhitton Cumb 108 D5
Cundall N Yorks 95 B7
Cunninghamhead N Ayrs 118 E3
Cunnister Shetland 160 D7
Cupar Fife 129 C5
Cupar Muir Fife 129 C5
Cupernham Hants 14 B4
Curbar Derbys 76 B2
Curbridge Hants 15 C6
Curbridge Oxon 38 D3
Curdridge Hants 15 C6
Curdworth Warks 63 E5
Curland Som 11 C7
Curlew Green Suff 57 C7
Currarie S Ayrs 112 E1
Curridge W Berks 26 B2
Currie Edin 120 C4
Curry Mallet Som 11 B8
Curry Rivel Som 11 B8
Curtisden Green Kent 29 E8
Curtisknowle Devon 6 D5
Cury Corn 3 D5
Cushnie Aberds 153 B7
Cushuish Som 22 F3
Cusop Hereford 48 E4
Cutcloy Dumfries 105 F8
Cutcombe Som 21 F8
Cutgate Gtr Man 87 C6
Cutiau Gwyn 58 C3
Cutlers Green Essex 55 F6
Cutnall Green Worcs 50 C3
Cutsdean Glos 51 F5
Cutthorpe Derbys 76 B3
Cutts Shetland 160 K6
Cuxham Oxon 39 E6
Cuxton Medway 29 C8
Cuxwold Lincs 91 D5
Cwm Bl Gwent 35 D5
Cwm Denb 72 B4
Cwm Swansea 33 E7
Cwm-byr Carms 46 F5
Cwm-Cewydd Gwyn 59 C5
Cwm-cou Ceredig 45 E4
Cwm-Dulais Swansea 33 D7
Cwm-felin-fach Caerph 35 E5
Cwm Ffrwd-oer Torf 35 D6
Cwm-hesgen Gwyn 71 E8
Cwm-hwnt Rhondda 34 D3
Cwm Irfon Powys 47 E7
Cwm-Llinau Powys 58 D5
Cwm-mawr Carms 33 C6
Cwm-parc Rhondda 34 E3
Cwm Penmachno Conwy 71 C8
Cwm-y-glo Carms 33 C6
Cwm-y-glo Gwyn 82 E5
Cwmafan Neath 34 E1
Cwmaman Rhondda 34 E4
Cwmann Carms 46 E4
Cwmavon Torf 35 D6
Cwmbâch Rhondda 34 D4
Cwmbach Carms 32 B3
Cwmbach Carms 33 D5
Cwmbach Powys 48 D2
Cwmbach Powys 48 F3
Cwmbelan Powys 59 F6
Cwmbrân = Cwmbran Torf 35 E6
Cwmbran = Cwmbrân Torf 35 E6
Cwmbrwyno Ceredig 58 F4
Cwmcarn Caerph 35 E6
Cwmcarvan Mon 36 D1
Cwmcych Carms 45 F4
Cwmdare Rhondda 34 D3
Cwmderwen Powys 59 D6
Cwmdu Carms 46 F5
Cwmdu Powys 35 B5
Cwmdu Swansea 33 E7
Cwmduad Carms 46 F2
Cwmdwr Carms 47 F6
Cwmfelin Bridgend 34 F2
Cwmfelin M Tydf 34 D4
Cwmfelin Boeth Carms 32 C2
Cwmfelin Mynach Carms 32 B3
Cwmffrwd Carms 33 C5
Cwmgiedd Powys 34 C1
Cwmgors Neath 33 C8
Cwmgwili Carms 33 C6
Cwmgwrach Neath 34 D2
Cwmhiraeth Carms 46 F2
Cwmifor Carms 33 B7
Cwmisfael Carms 33 C5
Cwmllynfell Neath 33 C8
Cwmorgan Pembs 45 F4
Cwmpengraig Carms 46 F2
Cwmrhos Powys 35 B5
Cwmsychpant Ceredig 46 E3
Cwmtillery Bl Gwent 35 D6
Cwmwysg Powys 34 B2
Cwmyoy Mon 35 B6
Cwmystwyth Ceredig 47 B6
Cwrt Gwyn 58 D3
Cwrt-newydd Ceredig 46 E3
Cwrt-y-cadno Carms 47 E5
Cwrt-y-gollen Powys 35 C6
Cydweli = Kidwelly Carms 33 D5
Cyffordd Llandudno = Llandudno Junction Conwy 83 D7
Cyffylliog Denb 72 D4
Cyfronydd Powys 59 D8
Cymer Neath 34 E2
Cyncoed Cardiff 35 F5
Cynghordy Carms 47 E7
Cynheidre Carms 33 D5
Cynwyd Denb 72 E4
Cynwyl Elfed Carms 32 B4
Cywarch Gwyn 59 C5

D

Dacre Cumb 99 B6
Dacre N Yorks 94 C4
Dacre Banks N Yorks 94 C4
Daddry Shield Durham 109 F8
Dadford Bucks 52 F4
Dadlington Leics 63 E8
Dafarn Faig Gwyn 71 C5
Dafen Carms 33 D6
Daffy Green Norf 68 D2
Dagenham London 41 F7
Daglingworth Glos 37 D6
Dagnall Bucks 40 C2
Dail Beag W Isles 154 C7
Dail bho Dheas W Isles 155 A9
Dail bho Thuath W Isles 155 A9
Dail Mor W Isles 154 C7
Daill Argyll 142 B4
Dailly S Ayrs 112 D2
Dairsie or Osnaburgh Fife 129 C6
Daisy Hill Gtr Man 86 D4
Dalabrog W Isles 148 F2
Dalavich Argyll 125 D5
Dalbeattie Dumfries 106 C5
Dalblair E Ayrs 113 C6
Dalbog Angus 135 B5
Dalbury Derbys 76 F2
Dalby IoM 84 E2
Dalby N Yorks 96 B2
Dalchalloch Perth 132 C4
Dalchalm Highld 157 J12
Dalchenna Argyll 125 E6
Dalchirach Moray 152 E1
Dalchork Highld 157 H8
Dalchreichart Highld 137 C5
Dalchruin Perth 127 C6
Dalderby Lincs 78 C5
Dale Pembs 44 E3
Dale Abbey Derbys 76 F4
Dale Head Cumb 99 C6
Dale of Walls Shetland 160 H3
Dalelia Highld 147 E10
Daless Highld 151 H11
Dalfaber Highld 138 C5
Dalgarven N Ayrs 118 E2
Dalgety Bay Fife 128 F3
Dalginross Perth 127 B6
Dalguise Perth 133 E6
Dalhalvaig Highld 157 D11
Dalham Suff 55 C8
Dalinlongart Argyll 145 E10
Dalkeith Midloth 121 C6
Dallam Warr 86 E3
Dallas Moray 151 F14
Dalleagles E Ayrs 113 C5
Dallinghoo Suff 57 D6
Dallington E Sus 18 D3
Dallington Northants 52 C5
Dallow N Yorks 94 B4
Dalmadilly Aberds 141 C6
Dalmally Argyll 125 C7
Dalmarnock Glasgow 119 C6
Dalmary Stirling 126 E4
Dalmellington E Ayrs 112 D4
Dalmeny Edin 120 B4
Dalmigavie Highld 138 C3
Dalmigavie Lodge Highld 138 B3
Dalmore Highld 151 E9
Dalmuir W Dunb 118 B4
Dalnabreck Highld 147 E9
Dalnacardoch Lodge Perth 132 B4
Dalnacroich Highld 150 F6
Dalnaglar Castle Perth 133 C8
Dalnahaitnach Highld 138 B4
Dalnaspidal Lodge Perth 132 B3
Dalnavaid Perth 133 C7
Dalnavie Highld 151 D9
Dalnawillan Lodge Highld 157 E13
Dalness Highld 131 D5
Dalnessie Highld 157 H9
Dalqueich Perth 128 D2
Dalreavoch Highld 157 J10
Dalry N Ayrs 118 E2
Dalrymple E Ayrs 112 C3
Dalserf S Lanark 119 D8
Dalston Cumb 108 D3
Dalswinton Dumfries 114 F2
Dalton Dumfries 107 B8
Dalton Lancs 86 D2
Dalton N Yorks 95 B7
Dalton N Yorks 101 D6
Dalton Northumb 110 B4
Dalton Northumb 110 D2
Dalton S Yorks 89 E5
Dalton-in-Furness Cumb 92 B2
Dalton-le-Dale Durham 111 E7
Dalton-on-Tees N Yorks 101 D7
Dalton Piercy Hrtlpl 111 F7
Dalveich Stirling 126 B5
Dalvina Lodge Highld 157 E9
Dalwhinnie Highld 138 F2
Dalwood Devon 11 D7
Dalwyne S Ayrs 112 E3
Dam Green Norf 68 F3
Dam Side Lancs 92 E4
Damerham Hants 14 C2
Damgate Norf 69 D7
Damnaglaur Dumfries 104 F5
Damside Borders 120 E4
Danbury Essex 42 D3
Danby N Yorks 103 D5
Danby Wiske N Yorks 101 E8
Dandaleith Moray 152 D2
Danderhall Midloth 121 C6
Dane End Herts 41 B6
Danebridge Ches E 75 C6
Danehill E Sus 17 B8
Danemoor Green Norf 68 D3
Danesford Shrops 61 E7
Daneshill Hants 26 D4
Dangerous Corner Lancs 86 C3
Danskine E Loth 121 C8
Darcy Lever Gtr Man 86 D5
Darenth Kent 29 B6
Daresbury Halton 86 F3
Darfield S Yorks 88 D5
Darfoulds Notts 77 B5
Dargate Kent 30 C4
Darite Corn 5 C7
Darlaston W Mid 62 E3
Darley N Yorks 94 D5
Darley Bridge Derbys 76 C2
Darley Head N Yorks 94 D4
Darlingscott Warks 51 E7
Darlington Darl 101 C7
Darliston Shrops 74 F2
Darlton Notts 77 B7
Darnall S Yorks 88 F4
Darnick Borders 121 F8
Darowen Powys 58 D5
Darra Aberds 153 D7
Darracott Devon 20 F3
Darras Hall Northumb 110 B4
Darrington W Yorks 89 B5
Darsham Suff 57 C8
Dartford Kent 29 B6
Dartford Crossing Kent 29 B6
Dartington Devon 7 C5
Dartmeet Devon 6 B4
Dartmouth Devon 7 D6
Darton S Yorks 88 D4
Darvel E Ayrs 119 F5
Darwell Hole E Sus 18 D3
Darwen Blackburn 86 B4
Datchet Windsor 27 B7
Datchworth Herts 41 C5
Datchworth Green Herts 41 C5
Daubhill Gtr Man 86 D5
Daugh of Kinermony Moray 152 D2
Dauntsey Wilts 37 F6
Dava Moray 151 H13
Davenham Ches W 74 B3
Davenport Green Ches E 74 B5
Daventry Northants 52 C3
David's Well Powys 48 B2
Davidson's Mains Edin 120 B5
Davidstow Corn 8 F3
Davington Dumfries 115 D5
Daviot Aberds 141 B6
Daviot Highld 151 H10
Davoch of Grange Moray 152 C4
Davyhulme Gtr Man 87 E5
Daw's House Corn 8 F5
Dawley Telford 61 D6
Dawlish Devon 7 B7
Dawlish Warren Devon 7 B7
Dawn Conwy 83 D8
Daws Heath Essex 42 F4
Daw's House Corn 8 F5
Dawsmere Lincs 79 F7
Dayhills Staffs 75 F6
Daylesford Glos 38 B2
Ddôl-Cownwy Powys 59 C7
Ddrydwy Anglesey 82 D3
Deadwater Northumb 116 E2
Deaf Hill Durham 111 F6
Deal Kent 31 D7
Deal Hall Essex 43 E6
Dean Cumb 98 B2
Dean Devon 6 C5
Dean Devon 20 E4
Dean Dorset 13 C7
Dean Hants 15 C6
Dean Som 23 E8
Dean Prior Devon 6 C5
Dean Row Ches E 87 F6
Deanburnhaugh Borders 115 C6
Deane Gtr Man 86 D4
Deane Hants 26 D3
Deanich Lodge Highld 150 C6
Deanland Dorset 13 C7
Deans W Loth 120 C3
Deanscales Cumb 98 B2
Deanshanger Northants 53 F5
Deanston Stirling 127 D6
Dearham Cumb 107 F7
Debach Suff 57 D6
Debden Essex 41 E7
Debden Essex 55 F6
Debden Cross Essex 55 F6
Debenham Suff 57 C5
Dechmont W Loth 120 B3
Deddington Oxon 52 F2
Dedham Essex 56 F4
Dedham Heath Essex 56 F4
Deebank Aberds 141 E5
Deene Northants 65 E6
Deenethorpe Northants 65 E6
Deepcar S Yorks 88 E3
Deepcut Sur 27 D7
Deepdale Cumb 100 F2
Deeping Gate Lincs 65 D8
Deeping St James Lincs 65 D8
Deeping St Nicholas Lincs 66 C2
Deerhill Moray 152 C4
Deerhurst Glos 37 B5
Deerness Orkney 159 H6
Defford Worcs 50 E4
Defynnog Powys 34 B3
Deganwy Conwy 83 D7
Deighton N Yorks 102 D1
Deighton W Yorks 88 C2
Deighton York 96 E2
Deiniolen Gwyn 83 E5
Delabole Corn 8 F2
Delamere Ches W 74 C2
Delfrigs Aberds 141 B8
Dell Lodge Highld 139 C6
Delliefure Highld 151 H13
Delnabo Moray 139 C7
Delnadamph Aberds 139 D8
Delph Gtr Man 87 D7
Delves Durham 110 E4
Delvine Perth 133 E8
Dembleby Lincs 78 F3
Denaby Main S Yorks 89 E5
Denbigh = Dinbych Denb 72 C4
Denbury Devon 7 C6
Denby Derbys 76 E3
Denby Dale W Yorks 88 D3
Denchworth Oxon 38 E3
Dendron Cumb 92 B2
Denel End C Beds 53 F8
Denend Aberds 152 E6
Denford Northants 53 B7
Dengie Essex 43 D5
Denham Bucks 40 F3
Denham Suff 55 C8
Denham Suff 57 B5
Denham Street Suff 57 B5
Denhead Aberds 153 C9
Denhead Fife 129 C6
Denhead of Arbilot Angus 135 E5
Denhead of Gray Dundee 134 F3
Denholm Borders 115 C8
Denholme W Yorks 94 F3
Denholme Clough W Yorks 94 F3
Denio Gwyn 70 D4
Denmead Hants 15 C7
Denmore Aberdeen 141 C8
Denmoss Aberds 153 D6
Dennington Suff 57 C6
Denny Falk 127 F7
Denny Lodge Hants 14 D4
Dennyloanhead Falk 127 F7
Denshaw Gtr Man 87 C7
Denside Aberds 141 E7
Densole Kent 31 E6
Denston Suff 55 D8
Denstone Staffs 75 E8
Dent Cumb 100 F2
Denton Cambs 65 F8
Denton Darl 101 C7
Denton E Sus 17 D8
Denton Gtr Man 87 E7
Denton Kent 31 E6
Denton Lincs 77 F8
Denton N Yorks 94 E4
Denton Norf 69 F5
Denton Northants 53 D6
Denton Oxon 39 D5
Denton's Green Mers 86 E2
Denver Norf 67 D6
Denwick Northumb 117 C8
Deopham Norf 68 D3
Deopham Green Norf 68 E3
Depden Suff 55 D8
Depden Green Suff 55 D8
Deptford London 28 B4
Deptford Wilts 24 F5
Derby Derby 76 F3
Derbyhaven IoM 84 F2
Dereham Norf 68 C2
Deri Caerph 35 D5
Derril Devon 8 D5
Derringstone Kent 31 E6
Derrington Staffs 62 B2
Derriton Devon 8 D5
Derry Hill Wilts 24 B4
Derryguaig Argyll 146 H7
Derrythorpe N Lincs 90 D2
Dersingham Norf 80 D2
Dervaig Argyll 146 F7
Derwen Denb 72 D4
Derwenlas Powys 58 E4
Desborough Northants 64 F5
Desford Leics 63 D8
Detchant Northumb 123 F6
Detling Kent 29 D8
Deuddwr Powys 60 C2
Devauden Mon 36 E1
Devil's Bridge Ceredig 47 B6
Devizes Wilts 24 C5
Devol Invclyd 118 B3
Devonport Plym 6 D2
Devonside Clack 127 E8
Devoran Corn 3 C6
Dewar Borders 121 E6
Dewlish Dorset 13 E5
Dewsbury W Yorks 88 B3
Dewsbury Moor W Yorks 88 B3
Dewshall Court Hereford 49 F6
Dhoon IoM 84 D4
Dhoor IoM 84 C4
Dhowin IoM 84 B4
Dial Post W Sus 17 C5
Dibden Hants 14 D5
Dibden Purlieu Hants 14 D5
Dickleburgh Norf 68 F4
Didbrook Glos 51 F5
Didcot Oxon 39 F5
Diddington Cambs 54 C2
Diddlebury Shrops 60 F5
Didley Hereford 49 F6
Didling W Sus 16 C2
Didmarton Glos 37 F5
Didsbury Gtr Man 87 E6
Didworthy Devon 6 C4
Digby Lincs 78 D3
Digg Highld 149 B9
Diggle Gtr Man 87 D8
Digmoor Lancs 86 D2
Digswell Park Herts 41 C5
Dihewyd Ceredig 46 D3
Dilham Norf 69 B6
Dilhorne Staffs 75 E6
Dillarburn S Lanark 119 E8
Dillington Cambs 54 C2
Dilston Northumb 110 C2
Dilton Marsh Wilts 24 E3
Dilwyn Hereford 49 D6
Dinas Carms 45 F4
Dinas Gwyn 70 D3
Dinas Cross Pembs 45 F2
Dinas Dinlle Gwyn 82 F4
Dinas-Mawddwy Gwyn 59 C5
Dinas Powys V Glam 22 B3
Dinbych = Denbigh Denb 72 C4
Dinbych-Y-Pysgod = Tenby Pembs 32 D2
Dinder Som 23 E7
Dinedor Hereford 49 F7
Dingestow Mon 36 C1
Dingle Mers 85 F4
Dingleden Kent 18 B5
Dingley Northants 64 F4
Dingwall Highld 151 F8
Dinlabyre Borders 115 E8
Dinmael Conwy 72 E4
Dinnet Aberds 140 E3
Dinnington S Yorks 89 F6
Dinnington Som 12 C2
Dinnington T&W 110 B5
Dinorwic Gwyn 83 E5
Dinton Bucks 39 C7
Dinton Wilts 24 F5
Dinwoodie Mains Dumfries 114 E4
Dinworthy Devon 8 C5
Dippen N Ayrs 143 F11
Dippenhall Sur 27 E6
Dipple Moray 152 C3
Dipple S Ayrs 112 D2
Diptford Devon 6 D5
Dipton Durham 110 D4
Dirdhu Highld 139 B6
Dirleton E Loth 129 F7
Dirt Pot Northumb 109 E8
Discoed Powys 48 C4
Diseworth Leics 63 B8
Dishes Orkney 159 F7
Dishforth N Yorks 95 B6
Disley Ches E 87 F7
Diss Norf 56 B5
Disserth Powys 48 D2
Distington Cumb 98 B2
Ditchampton Wilts 25 F5
Ditcheat Som 23 F8
Ditchingham Norf 69 E6
Ditchling E Sus 17 C7
Ditherington Shrops 60 C5
Dittisham Devon 7 D6
Ditton Halton 86 F2
Ditton Kent 29 D8
Ditton Green Cambs 55 D7
Ditton Priors Shrops 61 F6
Divach Highld 137 B7
Divlyn Carms 47 F6
Dixton Glos 50 F4
Dixton Mon 36 C2
Dobcross Gtr Man 87 D7
Dobwalls Corn 5 C7
Doc Penfro = Pembroke Dock Pembs 44 E4
Doccombe Devon 10 F2
Dochfour Ho. Highld 151 H9
Dochgarroch Highld 151 G9
Docking Norf 80 D3
Docklow Hereford 49 D7
Dockray Cumb 99 B5
Dockroyd W Yorks 94 F3
Dodburn Borders 115 D7
Doddinghurst Essex 42 E1
Doddington Cambs 66 E3
Doddington Kent 30 D3
Doddington Lincs 78 B2
Doddington Northumb 123 F5
Doddington Shrops 49 B8
Doddiscombsleigh Devon 10 F3
Dodford Northants 52 C4
Dodford Worcs 50 B4
Dodington S Glos 24 A2
Dodleston Ches W 73 C7
Dods Leigh Staffs 75 F7
Dodworth S Yorks 88 D4
Doe Green Warr 86 F3
Doe Lea Derbys 76 C4
Dog Village Devon 10 E4
Dogdyke Lincs 78 D5
Dogmersfield Hants 27 D5
Dogridge Wilts 37 F7
Dogsthorpe Pboro 65 D8
Dol-fôr Powys 58 D5
Dôl-y-Bont Ceredig 58 F3
Dol-y-cannau Powys 48 E4
Dolanog Powys 59 C7
Dolau Powys 48 C3
Dolau Rhondda 34 F3
Dolbenmaen Gwyn 71 C6
Dolfach Powys 59 D6
Dolfor Powys 59 F8
Dolgarrog Conwy 83 E7
Dolgellau Gwyn 58 C4
Dolgran Carms 46 F3
Dolhendre Gwyn 72 F2
Doll Highld 157 J11
Dollar Clack 127 E8
Dolley Green Powys 48 C4
Dollwen Ceredig 58 F3
Dolphin Flint 73 B5
Dolphinholme Lancs 92 D5
Dolphinton S Lanark 120 E4
Dolton Devon 9 C7
Dolwen Conwy 83 D8
Dolwen Powys 59 D6
Dolwyd Conwy 83 D8
Dolwyddelan Conwy 83 F7
Dolyhir Powys 48 D4
Doncaster S Yorks 89 D6
Dones Green Ches W 74 B3
Donhead St Andrew Wilts 13 B7
Donhead St Mary Wilts 13 B7
Donibristle Fife 128 F3
Donington Lincs 78 F5
Donington on Bain Lincs 91 F6
Donington South Ing Lincs 78 F5
Donisthorpe Leics 63 C7
Donkey Town Sur 27 C7
Donnington Glos 38 B1
Donnington Hereford 50 F2
Donnington Shrops 61 D5
Donnington Telford 61 C7
Donnington W Berks 26 C2
Donnington W Sus 16 D2
Donnington Wood Telford 61 C7
Donyatt Som 11 C8
Doonfoot S Ayrs 112 C3
Dorback Lodge Highld 139 C6
Dorchester Dorset 12 E4
Dorchester Oxon 39 E5
Dordon Warks 63 D6
Dore S Yorks 88 F4
Dores Highld 151 H8
Dorking Sur 28 E2
Dormansland Sur 28 E5
Dormanstown Redcar 102 B3
Dormington Hereford 49 E7
Dormston Worcs 50 D4
Dornal S Ayrs 105 B6
Dorney Bucks 27 B7
Dornie Highld 149 F13
Dornoch Highld 151 C10
Dornock Dumfries 108 C2
Dorrery Highld 158 E2
Dorridge W Mid 51 B6
Dorrington Lincs 78 D3
Dorrington Shrops 60 D4
Dorsington Warks 51 E6
Dorstone Hereford 48 E5
Dorton Bucks 39 C6
Dorusduain Highld 136 B2
Dosthill Staffs 63 E6
Dottery Dorset 12 E2
Doublebois Corn 5 C6
Dougarie N Ayrs 143 E9
Doughton Glos 37 E5
Douglas IoM 84 E3
Douglas S Lanark 119 F8
Douglas & Angus Dundee 134 F4
Douglas Water S Lanark 119 F8
Douglas West S Lanark 119 F8
Douglastown Angus 134 E4
Doulting Som 23 E8
Dounby Orkney 159 F3
Doune Highld 156 J7
Doune Stirling 127 D6
Doune Park Aberds 153 B7
Douneside Aberds 140 D3
Dounie Highld 151 B8
Dounreay Highld 157 C12
Dousland Devon 6 C3
Dovaston Shrops 60 B3
Dove Holes Derbys 75 B7
Dovenby Cumb 107 F7
Dover Kent 31 E7
Dovercourt Essex 57 F6
Doverdale Worcs 50 C3
Doveridge Derbys 75 F8
Doversgreen Sur 28 E3
Dowally Perth 133 E7
Dowbridge Lancs 92 F4
Dowdeswell Glos 37 C6
Dowlais M Tydf 34 D4
Dowland Devon 9 C7
Dowlish Wake Som 11 C8
Down Ampney Glos 37 E8
Down Hatherley Glos 37 B5
Down St Mary Devon 10 D2
Down Thomas Devon 6 D3
Downcraig Ferry N Ayrs 145 H10
Downderry Corn 5 D8
Downe London 28 C5
Downend IoW 15 F6
Downend S Glos 23 B8
Downend W Berks 26 B2
Downfield Dundee 134 F3
Downgate Corn 5 B8
Downham Essex 42 E3
Downham Lancs 93 E7
Downham Northumb 122 F4
Downham Market Norf 67 D6
Downhead Som 23 E8
Downhill Perth 133 F7
Downhill T&W 111 D6
Downholland Cross Lancs 85 D4
Downholme N Yorks 101 E6
Downies Aberds 141 E8
Downley Bucks 39 E8
Downside Som 23 E8
Downside Sur 28 D2
Downton Hants 14 E3
Downton Wilts 14 B2
Downton on the Rock Hereford 49 B6
Dowsby Lincs 65 B8
Dowsdale Lincs 66 C2
Dowthwaitehead Cumb 99 B5
Doxey Staffs 62 B3
Doxford Northumb 117 B7
Doxford Park T&W 111 D6
Doynton S Glos 24 B2
Draffan S Lanark 119 E7
Dragonby N Lincs 90 C3
Drakeland Corner Devon 6 D3
Drakemyre N Ayrs 118 D2
Drake's Broughton Worcs 50 E4
Drakes Cross Worcs 51 B5
Drakewalls Corn 6 B2
Draughton N Yorks 94 D3
Draughton Northants 53 B5
Drax N Yorks 89 B7
Draycote Warks 52 B2
Draycott Derbys 76 F4
Draycott Glos 51 F6
Draycott Som 23 D6
Draycott in the Clay Staffs 63 B5
Draycott in the Moors Staffs 75 E6
Drayford Devon 10 C2
Drayton Leics 64 E5
Drayton Lincs 78 F5
Drayton Norf 68 C4
Drayton Oxon 38 E4
Drayton Oxon 52 E2
Drayton Ptsmth 15 D7
Drayton Som 12 B2
Drayton Worcs 50 B4
Drayton Bassett Staffs 63 D5
Drayton Beauchamp Bucks 40 C2
Drayton Parslow Bucks 39 B8
Drayton St Leonard Oxon 39 E5
Dre-fach Carms 33 C7
Dre-fach Ceredig 46 E4
Drebley N Yorks 94 D3
Dreemskerry IoM 84 C4
Dreenhill Pembs 44 D4
Drefach Carms 33 C6
Drefach Carms 46 F2
Drefelin Carms 46 F2
Dreghorn N Ayrs 118 F3
Drellingore Kent 31 E6
Drem E Loth 121 B8
Dresden Stoke 75 E6
Dreumasdal W Isles 148 E2
Drewsteignton Devon 10 E2
Driby Lincs 79 B6
Driffield E Yorks 97 D6
Driffield Glos 37 E7
Drigg Cumb 98 E2
Drighlington W Yorks 88 B3
Drimnin Highld 147 F8
Drimpton Dorset 12 D2
Drimsynie Argyll 125 E7
Drinisiadar W Isles 154 H6
Drinkstone Suff 56 C3
Drinkstone Green Suff 56 C3
Drishaig Argyll 125 D7
Drissaig Argyll 124 D5
Drochil Borders 120 E4
Drointon Staffs 62 B4
Droitwich Spa Worcs 50 C3
Droman Highld 156 D4
Dron Perth 128 C3
Dronfield Derbys 76 B3
Dronfield Woodhouse Derbys 76 B3
Drongan E Ayrs 112 C4
Dronley Angus 134 F3
Droxford Hants 15 C7
Droylsden Gtr Man 87 E7
Druid Denb 72 E4
Druidston Pembs 44 D3
Druimarbin Highld 130 B4
Druimavuic Argyll 130 E4
Druimdrishaig Argyll 144 F6
Druimindarroch Highld 147 C9
Druimyeon More Argyll 143 C7
Drum Argyll 145 F8
Drum Perth 128 D2
Drumbeg Highld 156 F4
Drumblade Aberds 152 D5
Drumblair Aberds 153 D6
Drumbuie Dumfries 113 F5
Drumbuie Highld 149 E12
Drumburgh Cumb 108 D2
Drumburn Dumfries 107 C6
Drumchapel Glasgow 118 B5
Drumchardine Highld 151 G8
Drumchork Highld 155 J13
Drumclog S Lanark 119 F6
Drumderfit Highld 151 F9
Drumeldrie Fife 129 D6
Drumelzier Borders 120 F4
Drumfearn Highld 149 G11
Drumgask Highld 138 E2
Drumgley Angus 134 D4
Drumguish Highld 138 E3
Drumin Moray 152 E1
Drumlasie Aberds 140 D5
Drumlemble Argyll 143 G7
Drumligair Aberds 141 C8
Drumlithie Aberds 141 F6
Drummoddie Dumfries 105 E7
Drummond Highld 151 E9
Drummore Dumfries 104 F5
Drummuir Moray 152 D3
Drummuir Castle Moray 152 D3
Drumnadrochit Highld 137 B8
Drumnagorrach Moray 152 C5
Drumoak Aberds 141 E6
Drumpark Dumfries 107 A5
Drumphail Dumfries 105 C6
Drumrash Dumfries 106 B3
Drumrunie Highld 156 J4
Drums Aberds 141 B8
Drumsallie Highld 130 B3
Drumstinchall Dumfries 107 D5
Drumsturdy Angus 134 F4
Drumtochty Castle Aberds 135 B6
Drumtroddan Dumfries 105 E7
Drumuie Highld 149 D9
Drumuillie Highld 138 B5
Drumvaich Stirling 127 D5
Drumwhindle Aberds 153 E9
Drunkendub Angus 135 E6
Drury Flint 73 C6
Drury Square Norf 68 C2
Dry Doddington Lincs 77 E8
Dry Drayton Cambs 54 C4
Drybeck Cumb 100 C1
Drybridge Moray 152 B4
Drybridge N Ayrs 118 F3
Drybrook Glos 36 C3
Dryburgh Borders 121 F8
Dryhope Borders 115 B5
Drylaw Edin 120 B5
Drym Corn 2 C5
Drymen Stirling 126 F3
Drymuir Aberds 153 D9
Drynoch Highld 149 E9
Dryslwyn Carms 33 B6
Dryton Shrops 61 D5
Dubford Aberds 153 B8
Dubton Angus 135 D5
Duchally Highld 156 H6
Duchlage Argyll 126 F2
Duck Corner Suff 57 E7
Duckington Ches W 73 D8
Ducklington Oxon 38 D3
Duckmanton Derbys 76 B4
Duck's Cross Bedford 54 D2
Duddenhoe End Essex 55 F5
Duddingston Edin 121 B5
Duddington Northants 65 D6
Duddleswell E Sus 17 B8
Duddo Northumb 122 E5
Duddon Ches W 74 C2
Duddon Bridge Cumb 98 F4
Dudleston Shrops 73 F7
Dudleston Heath Shrops 73 F7
Dudley T&W 111 B5
Dudley W Mid 62 E3
Dudley Port W Mid 62 E3
Duffield Derbys 76 E3
Duffryn Neath 34 E2
Duffryn Newport 35 F6
Dufftown Moray 152 E3
Duffus Moray 152 B1
Dufton Cumb 100 B1
Duggleby N Yorks 96 C4
Duirinish Highld 149 E12
Duisdalemore Highld 149 G12
Duisky Highld 130 B4
Dukestown Bl Gwent 35 C5
Dukinfield Gtr Man 87 E7
Dulas Anglesey 82 C4
Dulcote Som 23 E7
Dulford Devon 11 D5
Dull Perth 133 E5
Dullatur N Lanark 119 B7
Dullingham Cambs 55 D7
Dulnain Bridge Highld 139 B5
Duloe Bedford 54 C2
Duloe Corn 5 D7
Dulsie Highld 151 G12
Dulverton Som 10 B4
Dulwich London 28 B4
Dumbarton W Dunb 118 B3
Dumbleton Glos 50 F5
Dumcrieff Dumfries 114 D4
Dumfries Dumfries 107 B6
Dumgoyne Stirling 126 F4
Dummer Hants 26 E3
Dumpford W Sus 16 B2
Dumpton Kent 31 C7
Dun Angus 135 D6
Dun Charlabhaigh W Isles 154 C6
Dunain Ho. Highld 151 G9
Dunalastair Perth 132 D4
Dunan Highld 149 F10
Dunans Argyll 145 D9
Dunball Som 22 E5
Dunbar E Loth 122 B2
Dunbeath Highld 158 H3
Dunbeg Argyll 124 B4
Dunblane Stirling 127 D6
Dunbog Fife 128 C4
Duncanston Highld 151 F8
Duncanstone Aberds 140 B4
Dunchurch Warks 52 B2
Duncote Northants 52 D4
Duncow Dumfries 114 F2
Duncraggan Stirling 126 D4
Duncrievie Perth 128 D3
Duncton W Sus 16 C3
Dundas Ho. Orkney 159 K5
Dundee Dundee 134 F4
Dundeugh Dumfries 113 F5
Dundon Som 23 F6
Dundonald S Ayrs 118 F3
Dundonnell Highld 150 C3
Dundonnell Hotel Highld 150 C3
Dundonnell House Highld 150 C4
Dundraw Cumb 108 E2
Dundreggan Highld 137 C6
Dundreggan Lodge Highld 137 C6
Dundrennan Dumfries 106 E4
Dundry N Som 23 C7
Dunecht Aberds 141 D6
Dunfermline Fife 128 F2
Dunfield Glos 37 E8
Dunford Bridge S Yorks 88 D2
Dungworth S Yorks 88 F3
Dunham Notts 77 B8
Dunham-on-the-Hill Ches W 73 B8

Dunham Town Gtr Man 86 F5
Dunhampton Worcs 50 C3
Dunholme Lincs 78 B3
Dunino Fife 129 C7
Dunipace Falk 127 F7
Dunira Perth 127 B6
Dunkeld Perth 133 E7
Dunkerton Bath 24 D2
Dunkeswell Devon 11 D6
Dunkeswick N Yorks 95 E6
Dunkirk Kent 30 D4
Dunkirk Norf 81 E8
Dunk's Green Kent 29 D7
Dunlappie Angus 135 C5
Dunley Hants 26 D2
Dunley Worcs 50 C2
Dunlichity Lodge Highld 151 H9
Dunlop E Ayrs 118 E4
Dunmaglass Lodge Highld 137 B8
Dunmore Argyll 144 G6
Dunmore Falk 127 F7
Dunnet Highld 158 C4
Dunnichen Angus 135 E5
Dunninald Angus 135 D7
Dunning Perth 128 C2
Dunnington E Yorks 97 D7
Dunnington Warks 51 D5
Dunnington York 96 D2
Dunnockshaw Lancs 87 B6
Dunollie Argyll 124 B4
Dunoon Argyll 145 F10
Dunragit Dumfries 105 D5
Dunrostan Argyll 144 E6
Duns Borders 122 D3
Duns Tew Oxon 38 B4
Dunsby Lincs 65 B8
Dunscore Dumfries 113 F8
Dunscroft S Yorks 89 D7
Dunsdale Redcar 102 C4
Dunsden Green Oxon 26 B5
Dunsfold Sur 27 F8
Dunsford Devon 10 F3
Dunshalt Fife 128 C4
Dunshillock Aberds 153 D9
Dunskey Ho. Dumfries 104 D4
Dunsley N Yorks 103 C6
Dunsmore Bucks 40 D1
Dunsop Bridge Lancs 93 D6
Dunstable C Beds 40 B3
Dunstall Staffs 63 B5
Dunstall Common Worcs 50 E3
Dunstall Green Suff 55 C8
Dunstan Northumb 117 C8
Dunstan Steads Northumb 117 B8
Dunster Som 21 E8
Duntson Lincs 78 C3
Dunston Norf 68 D5
Dunston Staffs 62 C3
Dunston T&W 110 C5
Dunsville S Yorks 89 D7
Dunswell E Yorks 97 F6
Dunsyre S Lanark 120 E3
Dunterton Devon 5 B8
Duntisbourne Abbots Glos 37 D6
Duntisbourne Leer Glos 37 D6
Duntisbourne Rouse Glos 37 D6
Duntish Dorset 12 D4
Duntocher W Dunb 118 B4
Dunton Bucks 39 B8
Dunton C Beds 54 E3
Dunton Norf 80 D4
Dunton Bassett Leics 64 E2
Dunton Green Kent 29 D6
Dunton Wayletts Essex 42 E2
Duntulm Highld 149 A9
Dunure S Ayrs 112 C2
Dunvant Swansea 33 E6
Dunvegan Highld 148 D7
Dunwich Suff 57 B8
Dunwood Staffs 75 D6
Dupplin Castle Perth 128 C2
Durdar Cumb 108 D4
Durgates E Sus 18 B3
Durham Durham 111 E5
Durisdeer Dumfries 113 D8
Durisdeermill Dumfries 113 D8
Durkar W Yorks 88 C4
Durleigh Som 22 F4
Durley Hants 15 C6
Durley Wilts 25 C7
Durnamuck Highld 150 B3
Durness Highld 156 C7
Durno Aberds 141 B6
Duror Highld 130 D3
Durran Argyll 125 E5
Durran Highld 158 D3
Durrington W Sus 16 D5
Durrington Wilts 25 E6
Dursley Glos 36 E4
Durston Som 11 B7
Durweston Dorset 13 D6
Dury Shetland 160 G6
Duston Northants 52 C5
Duthil Highld 138 B5
Dutlas Powys 48 B4
Duton Hill Essex 42 B2
Dutson Corn 8 F5
Dutton Ches W 74 B2
Duxford Cambs 55 E5
Duxford Oxon 38 E3
Dwygyfylchi Conwy 83 D7
Dwyran Anglesey 82 E4
Dyce Aberdeen 141 C7
Dye House Northumb 110 D2
Dyffryn Bridgend 34 E2
Dyffryn Carms 32 B4
Dyffryn Pembs 44 B4
Dyffryn Ardudwy Gwyn 71 E6
Dyffryn Castell Ceredig 58 F4
Dyffryn Ceidrych Carms 33 B8
Dyffryn Cellwen Neath 34 D2
Dyke Lincs 65 B8
Dyke Moray 151 F12
Dykehead Angus 134 C3
Dykehead N Lanark 119 D8
Dykehead Stirling 126 E4
Dykelands Aberds 135 C7
Dykends Angus 134 D2
Dykeside Aberds 153 D7
Dykesmains N Ayrs 118 E2
Dylife Powys 59 E5
Dymchurch Kent 19 C7
Dymock Glos 50 F2
Dyrham S Glos 24 B2
Dysart Fife 128 E5
Dyserth Denb 72 B4

E

Eachwick Northumb 110 B4
Eadar Dha Fhadhail W Isles 154 D5
Eagland Hill Lancs 92 E4
Eagle Lincs 77 C8
Eagle Barnsdale Lincs 77 C8
Eagle Moor Lincs 77 C8
Eaglescliffe Stockton 102 C2
Eaglesfield Cumb 98 B2
Eaglesfield Dumfries 108 B2
Eaglesham E Renf 119 D5
Eaglethorpe Northants 65 E7
Eairy IoM 84 E2
Eakley Lanes M Keynes 53 D6
Eakring Notts 77 C6
Ealand N Lincs 89 C8
Ealing London 40 F4
Eals Northumb 109 D6
Eamont Bridge Cumb 99 B7
Earby Lancs 94 E2
Earcroft Blackburn 86 B4
Eardington Shrops 61 E7
Eardisland Hereford 49 D6
Eardisley Hereford 48 E5
Eardiston Shrops 60 B3
Eardiston Worcs 49 C8
Earith Cambs 54 B4
Earl Shilton Leics 63 E8
Earl Soham Suff 57 C6
Earl Sterndale Derbys 75 C7
Earl Stonham Suff 56 D5
Earle Northumb 117 B5
Earley Wokingham 27 B5
Earlham Norf 68 D5
Earlish Highld 149 B8
Earls Barton Northants 53 C6
Earls Colne Essex 42 B4
Earl's Croome Worcs 50 E3
Earl's Green Suff 56 C4
Earlsdon W Mid 51 B8
Earlsferry Fife 129 E6
Earlsfield Lincs 78 F2
Earlsford Aberds 153 E8
Earlsheaton W Yorks 88 B3
Earlsmill Moray 151 F12
Earlston Borders 121 F8
Earlston E Ayrs 118 F4
Earlswood Mon 36 E1
Earlswood Sur 28 E3
Earlswood Warks 51 B6
Earnley W Sus 16 E2
Earsairidh W Isles 148 J2
Earsdon T&W 111 B6
Earsham Norf 69 F6
Earswick York 96 D2
Eartham W Sus 16 D3
Easby N Yorks 101 D6
Easby N Yorks 102 D3
Easdale Argyll 124 D3
Easebourne W Sus 16 B2
Easenhall Warks 52 B2
Eashing Sur 27 E7
Easington Bucks 39 C6
Easington Durham 111 E7
Easington E Yorks 91 C7
Easington Northumb 123 F7
Easington Oxon 39 E6
Easington Oxon 52 F2
Easington Redcar 103 C5
Easington Colliery Durham 111 E7
Easington Lane T&W 111 E6
Easingwold N Yorks 95 C8
Easole Street Kent 31 D6
Eassie Angus 134 E3
East Aberthaw V Glam 22 C2
East Adderbury Oxon 52 F2
East Allington Devon 7 E5
East Anstey Devon 10 B3
East Appleton N Yorks 101 E7
East Ardsley W Yorks 88 B4
East Ashling W Sus 16 D2
East Auchronie Aberds 141 D7
East Ayton N Yorks 103 F7
East Bank Bl Gwent 35 D6
East Barkwith Lincs 91 F5
East Barming Kent 29 D8
East Barnby N Yorks 103 C6
East Barnet London 41 E5
East Barns E Loth 122 B3
East Barsham Norf 80 D5
East Beckham Norf 81 D7
East Bedfont London 27 B8
East Bergholt Suff 56 F4
East Bilney Norf 68 C2
East Blatchington E Sus 17 D8
East Boldre Hants 14 D4
East Brent Som 22 D5
East Bridgford Notts 77 E6
East Buckland Devon 21 F5
East Budleigh Devon 11 F5
East Burrafirth Shetland 160 H5
East Burton Dorset 13 F6
East Butsfield Durham 110 E4
East Butterwick N Lincs 90 D2
East Cairnbeg Aberds 135 B7
East Calder W Loth 120 C3
East Carleton Norf 68 D4
East Carlton Northants 64 F5
East Carlton W Yorks 94 E5
East Chaldon Dorset 13 F5
East Challow Oxon 38 F3
East Chiltington E Sus 17 C7
East Chinnock Som 12 C2
East Chisenbury Wilts 25 D6
East Clandon Sur 27 D8
East Claydon Bucks 39 B7
East Clyne Highld 157 J12
East Coker Som 12 C3
East Combe Som 22 F3
East Common N Yorks 96 F2
East Compton Som 23 E8
East Cottingwith E Yorks 96 E3
East Cowes IoW 15 E6
East Cowick E Yorks 89 B7
East Cowton N Yorks 101 D8
East Cramlington Northumb 111 B5
East Cranmore Som 23 E8
East Creech Dorset 13 F7
East Croachy Highld 138 B2
East Croftmore Highld 139 C5
East Curthwaite Cumb 108 E3
East Dean E Sus 18 F2
East Dean Hants 14 B3
East Dean W Sus 16 C3
East Down Devon 20 E5
East Drayton Notts 77 B7
East Ella Hull 90 B4
East End Dorset 13 E7
East End E Yorks 91 B6
East End Hants 14 E4
East End Hants 26 C2
East End Hants 41 B7
East End Herts 18 B5
East End Kent 18 B5
East End N Som 23 B6
East End Oxon 38 C3
East Farleigh Kent 29 D8
East Farndon Northants 64 F4
East Ferry Lincs 90 E2
East Fortune E Loth 121 B8
East Garston W Berks 25 B8
East Ginge Oxon 38 F4
East Goscote Leics 64 C3
East Grafton Wilts 25 C7
East Grimstead Wilts 14 B3
East Grinstead W Sus 28 F4
East Guldeford E Sus 19 C6
East Haddon Northants 52 C4
East Hagbourne Oxon 39 F5
East Halton N Lincs 90 C5
East Ham London 41 F7
East Hanney Oxon 38 E4
East Hanningfield Essex 42 D3
East Hardwick W Yorks 89 C5
East Harling Norf 68 F2
East Harlsey N Yorks 102 E2
East Harnham Wilts 14 B2
East Harptree Bath 23 D7
East Hartford Northumb 111 B5
East Harting W Sus 15 C8
East Hatley Cambs 54 D3
East Hauxwell N Yorks 101 E6
East Haven Angus 135 F5
East Heckington Lincs 78 E4
East Hedleyhope Durham 110 E4
East Hendred Oxon 38 F4
East Herrington T&W 111 D6
East Heslerton N Yorks 96 B5
East Hoathly E Sus 18 D2
East Horrington Som 23 E7
East Horsley Sur 27 D8
East Horton Northumb 123 F6
East Huntspill Som 22 E5
East Hyde C Beds 40 C4
East Ilkerton Devon 21 E6
East Ilsley W Berks 38 F4
East Keal Lincs 79 C6
East Kennett Wilts 25 C6
East Keswick W Yorks 95 E6
East Kilbride S Lanark 119 D6
East Kirkby Lincs 79 C6
East Knapton N Yorks 96 B4
East Knighton Dorset 13 F6
East Knoyle Wilts 24 F3
East Kyloe Northumb 123 F6
East Lambrook Som 12 C2
East Lamington Highld 151 D10
East Langdon Kent 31 E7
East Langton Leics 64 E4
East Langwell Highld 157 J10
East Lavant W Sus 16 D2
East Lavington W Sus 16 C3
East Layton N Yorks 101 D6
East Leake Notts 64 B2
East Learmouth Northumb 122 F4
East Leigh Devon 9 D8
East Lexham Norf 67 C8
East Lilburn Northumb 117 B6
East Linton E Loth 121 B8
East Liss Hants 15 B8
East Looe Corn 5 D7
East Lound N Lincs 89 E8
East Lulworth Dorset 13 F6
East Lutton N Yorks 96 C5
East Lydford Som 23 F7
East Mains Aberds 141 E5
East Malling Kent 29 D8
East March Angus 134 F4
East Marden W Sus 16 C2
East Markham Notts 77 B7
East Marton N Yorks 94 D2
East Meon Hants 15 B7
East Mere Devon 10 C4
East Mersea Essex 43 C6
East Mey Highld 158 C5
East Molesey Sur 28 C2
East Morden Dorset 13 E7
East Morton W Yorks 94 E3
East Ness N Yorks 96 B2
East Newton E Yorks 97 F8
East Norton Leics 64 D4
East Nynehead Som 11 B6
East Oakley Hants 26 D3
East Ogwell Devon 7 B6
East Orchard Dorset 13 C6
East Ord Northumb 123 D5
East Panson Devon 9 E5
East Peckham Kent 29 E7
East Pennard Som 23 F7
East Perry Cambs 54 C2
East Portlemouth Devon 6 F5
East Prawle Devon 7 F5
East Preston W Sus 16 D4
East Putford Devon 9 C5
East Quantoxhead Som 22 E3
East Rainton T&W 111 E6
East Ravendale NE Lincs 91 E6
East Raynham Norf 80 E4
East Rhidorroch Lodge Highld 150 B5
East Rigton W Yorks 95 E6
East Rounton N Yorks 102 D2
East Row N Yorks 103 C6
East Rudham Norf 80 E4
East Runton Norf 81 C7
East Ruston Norf 69 B6
East Saltoun E Loth 121 C7
East Sleekburn Northumb 117 F8
East Somerton Norf 69 C7
East Stockwith Lincs 89 E8
East Stoke Dorset 13 F6
East Stoke Notts 77 E7
East Stour Dorset 13 B6
East Stourmouth Kent 31 C6
East Stowford Devon 9 B8
East Stratton Hants 26 F3
East Studdal Kent 31 E7
East Suisnish Highld 149 E10
East Taphouse Corn 5 C6
East-the-Water Devon 9 B6
East Thirston Northumb 117 E7
East Tilbury Thurrock 29 B7
East Tisted Hants 26 F5
East Torrington Lincs 90 F5
East Tuddenham Norf 68 C3
East Tytherley Hants 14 B3
East Tytherton Wilts 24 B4
East Village Devon 10 D3
East Wall Shrops 60 E5
East Walton Norf 67 C7
East Wellow Hants 14 B4
East Wemyss Fife 128 E5
East Whitburn W Loth 120 C2
East Williamston Pembs 32 D1
East Winch Norf 67 C6
East Winterslow Wilts 25 F7
East Wittering W Sus 15 E8
East Witton N Yorks 101 F6
East Woodburn Northumb 116 F5
East Woodhay Hants 26 C2
East Worldham Hants 26 F5
East Worlington Devon 10 C2
East Worthing W Sus 17 D5
Eastbourne E Sus 18 F3
Eastbridge Suff 57 C8
Eastburn W Yorks 94 E3
Eastbury London 40 E3
Eastbury W Berks 25 B8
Eastby N Yorks 94 D3
Eastchurch Kent 30 B3
Eastcombe Glos 37 D5
Eastcote London 40 F4
Eastcote Northants 52 D4
Eastcote W Mid 51 B6
Eastcott Corn 8 C4
Eastcott Wilts 24 D5
Eastcourt Wilts 25 C7
Eastcourt Wilts 37 E6
Easter Ardross Highld 151 D9
Easter Balmoral Aberds 139 E8
Easter Boleskine Highld 137 B8
Easter Compton S Glos 36 F2
Easter Cringate Stirling 127 F6
Easter Davoch Aberds 140 D3
Easter Earshaig Dumfries 114 D3
Easter Fearn Highld 151 C9
Easter Galcantray Highld 151 G11
Easter Howgate Midloth 120 C5
Easter Howlaws Borders 122 E3
Easter Kinkell Highld 151 F8
Easter Lednathie Angus 134 C3
Easter Milton Highld 151 F12
Easter Moniack Highld 151 G8
Easter Ord Aberdeen 141 D7
Easter Quarff Shetland 160 K6
Easter Rhynd Perth 128 C3
Easter Row Stirling 127 E6
Easter Silverford Aberds 153 B7
Easter Skeld Shetland 160 J5
Easter Whyntie Aberds 152 B6
Eastergate W Sus 16 D3
Easterhouse Glasgow 119 C6
Eastern Green W Mid 63 F6
Easterton Wilts 24 D5
Eastertown Som 22 D5
Eastertown of Auchleuchries Aberds 153 E10
Eastfield N Lanark 119 C8
Eastfield N Yorks 103 F8
Eastfield Hall Northumb 117 D8
Eastgate Durham 110 F2
Eastgate Norf 81 E7
Eastham Mers 85 F4
Eastham Ferry Mers 85 F4
Easthampstead Brack 27 C6
Eastheath Wokingham 27 C6
Easthope Shrops 61 E5
Easthorpe Essex 43 B5
Easthorpe Leics 77 F8
Easthorpe Notts 77 D7
Easthouses Midloth 121 C6
Eastington Devon 10 D2
Eastington Glos 36 D4
Eastington Glos 37 C8
Eastleach Martin Glos 38 D2
Eastleach Turville Glos 38 D1
Eastleigh Devon 9 B6
Eastleigh Hants 14 C5
Eastling Kent 30 D3
Eastmoor Derbys 76 B3
Eastmoor Norf 67 D7
Eastney Ptsmth 15 E7
Eastnor Hereford 50 F2
Eastoft N Lincs 90 C2
Eastoke Hants 15 E8
Easton Cambs 54 B2
Easton Cumb 108 B4
Easton Cumb 108 D2
Easton Devon 10 F2
Easton Dorset 12 G4
Easton Hants 26 F3
Easton Lincs 65 B6
Easton Norf 68 C4
Easton Som 23 E7
Easton Suff 57 D6
Easton Wilts 24 B3
Easton Grey Wilts 37 F5
Easton-in-Gordano N Som 23 B7
Easton Maudit Northants 53 D6
Easton on the Hill Northants 65 D7
Easton Royal Wilts 25 C7
Eastpark Dumfries 107 C7
Eastrea Cambs 66 E2
Eastriggs Dumfries 108 C2
Eastrington E Yorks 89 B8
Eastry Kent 31 D7
Eastville Bristol 23 B8
Eastville Lincs 79 D7
Eastwell Leics 64 B4
Eastwick Herts 41 C7
Eastwick Shetland 160 F5
Eastwood Notts 76 E4
Eastwood Southend 42 F4
Eastwood W Yorks 87 B7
Eathorpe Warks 51 C8
Eaton Ches E 75 C5
Eaton Ches W 74 C2
Eaton Leics 64 B4
Eaton Norf 68 D5
Eaton Notts 77 B7
Eaton Oxon 38 D4
Eaton Shrops 60 F3
Eaton Shrops 60 F5
Eaton Bishop Hereford 49 F6
Eaton Bray C Beds 40 B2
Eaton Constantine Shrops 61 D5
Eaton Green C Beds 40 B2
Eaton Hastings Oxon 38 E2
Eaton on Tern Shrops 61 B6
Eaton Socon Cambs 54 D2
Eavestone N Yorks 94 C5
Ebberston N Yorks 103 F6
Ebbesbourne Wake Wilts 13 B7
Ebbw Vale = Glyn Ebwy Bl Gwent 35 D5
Ebchester Durham 110 D4
Ebford Devon 10 F4
Ebley Glos 37 D5
Ebnal Ches W 73 E8
Ebrington Glos 51 E6
Ecchinswell Hants 26 D2
Ecclaw Borders 122 C3
Ecclefechan Dumfries 107 B8
Eccles Borders 122 E3
Eccles Gtr Man 87 E5
Eccles Kent 29 C8
Eccles on Sea Norf 69 B7
Eccles Road Norf 68 E3
Ecclesall S Yorks 88 F4
Ecclesfield S Yorks 88 E4
Ecclesgreig Aberds 135 C7
Eccleshall Staffs 62 B2
Eccleshill W Yorks 94 F4
Ecclesmachan W Loth 120 B3
Eccleston Ches W 73 C8
Eccleston Lancs 86 C3
Eccleston Mers 86 E2
Eccleston Park Mers 86 E2
Eccup W Yorks 95 E5
Echt Aberds 141 D6
Eckford Borders 116 B3
Eckington Derbys 76 B4
Eckington Worcs 50 E4
Ecton Northants 53 C6
Edale Derbys 88 F2
Edburton W Sus 17 C6
Edderside Cumb 107 E7
Edderton Highld 151 C10
Eddistone Devon 8 B4
Eddleston Borders 120 E5
Eden Park London 28 C4
Edenbridge Kent 28 E5
Edenfield Lancs 87 C5
Edenhall Cumb 109 F5
Edenham Lincs 65 B7
Edensor Derbys 76 C2
Edentaggart Argyll 126 E2
Edenthorpe S Yorks 89 D7
Edentown Cumb 108 D3
Ederline Argyll 124 E4
Edern Gwyn 70 D3
Edgarley Som 23 F7
Edgbaston W Mid 62 F4
Edgcott Bucks 39 B6
Edgcott Som 21 F7
Edge Shrops 60 D3
Edge End Glos 36 C2
Edge Green Ches W 73 D8
Edge Hill Mers 85 F4
Edgebolton Shrops 61 B5
Edgefield Norf 81 D6
Edgefield Street Norf 81 D6
Edgeside Lancs 87 B6
Edgeworth Glos 37 D6
Edgmond Telford 61 C7
Edgmond Marsh Telford 61 B7
Edgton Shrops 60 F3
Edgware London 40 E4
Edgworth Blackburn 86 C5
Edinample Stirling 126 B4
Edinbane Highld 149 C8
Edinburgh Edin 121 B5
Edingale Staffs 63 C6
Edingight Ho. Moray 152 C5
Edingley Notts 77 D6
Edingthorpe Norf 69 A6
Edingthorpe Green Norf 69 A6
Edington Som 23 F5
Edington Wilts 24 D4
Edintore Moray 152 D4
Edith Weston Rutland 65 D6
Edithmead Som 22 E5
Edlesborough Bucks 40 C2
Edlingham Northumb 117 D7
Edlington Lincs 78 B5
Edmondsham Dorset 13 C8
Edmondsley Durham 110 E5
Edmondthorpe Leics 65 C5
Edmonstone Orkney 159 F6
Edmonton London 41 E6
Edmundbyers Durham 110 D3
Ednam Borders 122 F3
Ednaston Derbys 76 E2
Edradynate Perth 133 D5
Edrom Borders 122 D4
Edstaston Shrops 74 F2
Edstone Warks 51 C6
Edvin Loach Hereford 49 D8
Edwalton Notts 77 F5
Edwardstone Suff 56 E3
Edwinsford Carms 46 F5
Edwinstowe Notts 77 C6
Edworth C Beds 54 E3
Edwyn Ralph Hereford 49 D8
Edzell Angus 135 C5
Efail Isaf Rhondda 34 F4
Efailnewydd Gwyn 70 D4
Efailwen Carms 32 B2
Efenechtyd Denb 72 D5
Effingham Sur 28 D2
Effirth Shetland 160 H5
Efford Devon 10 D3
Egdon Worcs 50 D4
Egerton Gtr Man 86 C5
Egerton Kent 30 E3
Egerton Forstal Kent 30 E2
Eggborough N Yorks 89 B6
Eggbuckland Plym 6 D3
Eggington C Beds 40 B2
Egginton Derbys 63 B6
Egglescliffe Stockton 102 C2
Eggleston Durham 100 B4
Egham Sur 27 B8
Egleton Rutland 65 D5
Eglingham Northumb 117 C7
Egloshayle Corn 4 B5
Egloskerry Corn 8 F4
Eglwys-Brewis V Glam 22 C2
Eglwys Cross Wrex 73 E8
Eglwys Fach Ceredig 58 E3
Eglwysbach Conwy 83 D8
Eglwyswen Pembs 45 F3
Eglwyswrw Pembs 45 F3
Egmanton Notts 77 C7
Egremont Cumb 98 C2
Egremont Mers 85 E4
Egton N Yorks 103 D6
Egton Bridge N Yorks 103 D6
Eight Ash Green Essex 43 B5
Eignaig Highld 130 E1
Eil Highld 138 C4
Eilanreach Highld 149 G13
Eilean Darach Highld 150 C4
Eileanach Lodge Highld 151 E8
Einacleite W Isles 154 E6
Eisgean W Isles 155 F8
Eisingrug Gwyn 71 D7
Elan Village Powys 47 C8
Elberton S Glos 36 F3
Elburton Plym 6 D3
Elcho Perth 128 B3
Elcombe Swindon 37 F8
Eldernell Cambs 66 E3
Eldersfield Worcs 50 F3
Elderslie Renfs 118 C4
Eldon Durham 101 B7
Eldrick S Ayrs 112 F2
Eldroth N Yorks 93 C7
Eldwick W Yorks 94 E4
Elfhowe Cumb 99 E6
Elford Northumb 123 F7
Elford Staffs 63 C5
Elgin Moray 152 B2
Elgol Highld 149 G10
Elham Kent 31 E5
Elie Fife 129 D6
Elim Anglesey 82 C3
Eling Hants 14 C4
Elishader Highld 149 B10
Elishaw Northumb 116 E4
Elkesley Notts 77 B6
Elkstone Glos 37 C6
Ellan Highld 138 B4
Elland W Yorks 88 B2
Ellary Argyll 144 F6
Ellastone Staffs 75 E8
Ellemford Borders 122 C3
Ellenbrook IoM 84 E3
Ellenhall Staffs 62 B2
Ellen's Green Sur 27 F8
Ellerbeck N Yorks 102 E2
Ellerburn N Yorks 103 F6
Ellerby N Yorks 103 C5
Ellerdine Heath Telford 61 B6
Ellerhayes Devon 10 D4
Elleric Argyll 130 E4
Ellerker E Yorks 90 B3
Ellerton E Yorks 96 F3
Ellerton Shrops 61 B7
Ellesborough Bucks 39 D8
Ellesmere Shrops 73 F8
Ellesmere Port Ches W 73 B8
Ellingham Norf 69 E6
Ellingham Northumb 117 B7
Ellingstring N Yorks 101 F6
Ellington Cambs 54 B2
Ellington Northumb 117 E8
Elliot Angus 135 F6
Ellisfield Hants 26 E4
Ellistown Leics 63 C8
Ellon Aberds 153 E9
Ellonby Cumb 108 F4
Ellough Suff 69 F7
Elloughton E Yorks 90 B3
Ellwood Glos 36 D2
Elm Cambs 66 D4
Elm Hill Dorset 13 B6
Elm Park London 41 F8
Elmbridge Worcs 50 C4
Elmdon Essex 55 F5
Elmdon W Mid 63 F5
Elmdon Heath W Mid 63 F5
Elmers End London 28 C4
Elmesthorpe Leics 63 E8
Elmfield IoW 15 E7
Elmhurst Staffs 62 C5
Elmley Castle Worcs 50 E4
Elmley Lovett Worcs 50 C3
Elmore Glos 36 C4
Elmore Back Glos 36 C4
Elmscott Devon 8 B4
Elmsett Suff 56 E4
Elmstead Market Essex 43 B6
Elmsted Kent 30 E5
Elmstone Kent 31 C6
Elmstone Hardwicke Glos 37 B6
Elmswell E Yorks 97 D5
Elmswell Suff 56 C3
Elmton Derbys 76 B5
Elphin Highld 156 H5
Elphinstone E Loth 121 B6
Elrick Aberds 141 D7
Elrig Dumfries 105 E7
Elsdon Northumb 117 E5
Elsecar S Yorks 88 E4
Elsenham Essex 41 B8
Elsfield Oxon 39 C5
Elsham N Lincs 90 C4
Elsing Norf 68 C3
Elslack N Yorks 94 E2
Elson Shrops 73 F7
Elsrickle S Lanark 120 E3
Elstead Sur 27 E7
Elsted W Sus 16 C2
Elsthorpe Lincs 65 B7
Elstob Durham 101 B8
Elston Notts 77 E7
Elston Wilts 25 E5
Elstone Devon 9 C8
Elstow Bedford 53 E8
Elstree Herts 40 E4
Elstronwick E Yorks 97 F8
Elswick Lancs 92 F4
Elsworth Cambs 54 C4
Elterwater Cumb 99 D5
Eltham London 28 B5
Eltisley Cambs 54 D3
Elton Cambs 65 E7
Elton Ches W 73 B8
Elton Derbys 76 C2
Elton Glos 36 C4
Elton Hereford 49 B6
Elton Notts 77 F7
Elton Stockton 102 C2
Elton Green Ches W 73 B8
Elvanfoot S Lanark 114 C2
Elvaston Derbys 76 F4
Elveden Suff 56 B2
Elvingston E Loth 121 B7
Elvington Kent 31 D6
Elvington York 96 E2
Elwick Hrtlpl 111 F7
Elwick Northumb 123 F7
Elworth Ches E 74 C4
Elworthy Som 22 F2
Ely Cambs 66 F5
Ely Cardiff 22 B3
Emberton M Keynes 53 E6
Embleton Cumb 107 F8
Embleton Northumb 117 B8
Embo Highld 151 B11
Embo Street Highld 151 B11
Emborough Som 23 D8
Embsay N Yorks 94 D3
Emery Down Hants 14 D3
Emley W Yorks 88 C3
Emmbrook Wokingham 27 C5
Emmer Green Reading 26 B5
Emmington Oxon 39 D7
Emneth Norf 66 D4
Emneth Hungate Norf 66 D5
Empingham Rutland 65 D6
Empshott Hants 27 F5
Emstrey Shrops 60 C5
Emsworth Hants 15 D8
Enborne W Berks 26 C2
Enchmarsh Shrops 60 E5
Enderby Leics 64 E2
Endmoor Cumb 99 F7
Endon Staffs 75 D6
Endon Bank Staffs 75 D6
Enfield London 41 E6
Enfield Wash London 41 E6
Enford Wilts 25 D6
Engamoor Shetland 160 H4
Engine Common S Glos 36 F3
Englefield W Berks 26 B4
Englefield Green Sur 27 B7
Englesea-brook Ches E 74 D4
English Bicknor Glos 36 C2
English Frankton Shrops 60 B4
Englishcombe Bath 24 C2
Enham Alamein Hants 25 E8
Enmore Som 22 F4
Ennerdale Bridge Cumb 98 C2
Enoch Dumfries 113 D8
Enochdhu Perth 133 C7
Ensay Argyll 146 G6
Ensbury Bmouth 13 E8
Ensdon Shrops 60 C4
Ensis Devon 9 B7
Enstone Oxon 38 B3
Enterkinfoot Dumfries 113 D8
Enterpen N Yorks 102 D2
Enville Staffs 62 F2
Eolaigearraidh W Isles 148 H2
Eorabus Argyll 146 J6
Eòropaidh W Isles 155 A10
Epperstone Notts 77 E6
Epping Essex 41 D7
Epping Green Essex 41 D7
Epping Green Herts 41 D5
Epping Upland Essex 41 D7
Eppleby N Yorks 101 C6
Eppleworth E Yorks 97 F6
Epsom Sur 28 C3
Epwell Oxon 51 E8
Epworth N Lincs 89 D8
Epworth Turbary N Lincs 89 D8
Erbistock Wrex 73 E7
Erbusaig Highld 149 F12
Erchless Castle Highld 150 G7
Erdington W Mid 62 E5
Eredine Argyll 125 E5
Eriboll Highld 156 D7
Ericstane Dumfries 114 C3
Eridge Green E Sus 18 B2
Erines Argyll 145 F7
Eriswell Suff 55 B8
Erith London 29 B6
Erlestoke Wilts 24 D4
Ermine Lincs 78 B2
Ermington Devon 6 D4
Erpingham Norf 81 D7
Errogie Highld 137 B8
Errol Perth 128 B4
Erskine Renfs 118 B4
Erskine Bridge Renfs 118 B4
Ervie Dumfries 104 C4
Erwarton Suff 57 F6
Erwood Powys 48 E2
Eryholme N Yorks 101 D8
Eryrys Denb 73 D6
Escomb Durham 101 B6
Escrick N Yorks 96 E2
Esgairdawe Carms 46 E5
Esgairgeiliog Powys 58 D4
Esh Durham 110 E4
Esh Winning Durham 110 E4
Esher Sur 28 C2
Esholt W Yorks 94 E4
Eshott Northumb 117 E8
Eshton N Yorks 94 D2
Esk Valley N Yorks 103 D6
Eskadale Highld 150 H7
Eskbank Midloth 121 C6
Eskdale Green Cumb 98 D3
Eskdalemuir Dumfries 115 E5
Eske E Yorks 97 E6
Eskham Lincs 91 E7
Esprick Lancs 92 F4
Essendine Rutland 65 C7
Essendon Herts 41 D5
Essich Highld 151 H9
Essington Staffs 62 D3
Esslemont Aberds 141 B8
Eston Redcar 102 C3
Eswick Shetland 160 H6
Etal Northumb 122 F5
Etchilhampton Wilts 24 C5
Etchingham E Sus 18 C4
Etchinghill Kent 19 B8
Etchinghill Staffs 62 C4
Ethie Castle Angus 135 E6
Ethie Mains Angus 135 E6
Etling Green Norf 68 C3
Eton Windsor 27 B7
Eton Wick Windsor 27 B7
Etteridge Highld 138 E2
Ettersgill Durham 100 B3
Ettingshall W Mid 62 E3
Ettington Warks 51 E7
Etton E Yorks 97 E5
Etton Pboro 65 D8
Ettrick Borders 115 C5
Ettrickbridge Borders 115 B6
Ettrickhill Borders 115 C5
Etwall Derbys 76 F2
Euston Suff 56 B2
Euximoor Drove Cambs 66 E4
Euxton Lancs 86 C3
Evanstown Bridgend 34 F3
Evanton Highld 151 E9
Evedon Lincs 78 E3
Evelix Highld 151 B10
Evenjobb Powys 48 C4
Evenley Northants 52 F3
Evenlode Glos 38 B2
Evenwood Durham 101 B6
Evenwood Gate Durham 101 B6
Everbay Orkney 159 F7
Evercreech Som 23 F8
Everdon Northants 52 D3
Everingham E Yorks 96 E4
Everleigh Wilts 25 D7
Everley N Yorks 103 F7
Eversholt C Beds 53 F7
Evershot Dorset 12 D3
Eversley Hants 27 C5
Eversley Cross Hants 27 C5
Everthorpe E Yorks 96 F5
Everton C Beds 54 D3
Everton Hants 14 E3
Everton Mers 85 E4
Everton Notts 89 E7
Evertown Dumfries 108 B3
Evesbatch Hereford 49 E8
Evesham Worcs 50 E5
Evington Leicester 64 D3
Ewden Village S Yorks 88 E3
Ewell Sur 28 C3
Ewell Minnis Kent 31 E6
Ewelme Oxon 39 E6
Ewen Glos 37 E7
Ewenny V Glam 21 B8
Ewerby Lincs 78 E4
Ewerby Thorpe Lincs 78 E4
Ewes Dumfries 115 E6
Ewesley Northumb 117 E6
Ewhurst Sur 27 E8
Ewhurst Green E Sus 18 C4
Ewhurst Green Sur 27 F8
Ewloe Flint 73 C7
Ewloe Green Flint 73 C6
Ewood Blackburn 86 B4
Eworthy Devon 9 E6
Ewshot Hants 27 E6
Ewyas Harold Hereford 35 B7
Exbourne Devon 9 D8
Exbury Hants 14 E5
Exebridge Devon 10 B4
Exelby N Yorks 101 F7
Exeter Devon 10 E4
Exford Som 21 F7
Exhall Warks 51 D6
Exley Head W Yorks 94 F3
Exminster Devon 10 F4
Exmouth Devon 10 F5
Exnaboe Shetland 160 M5
Exning Suff 55 C7
Exton Devon 10 F4
Exton Hants 15 B7
Exton Rutland 65 C6
Exton Som 21 F8
Exwick Devon 10 E4
Eyam Derbys 76 B2
Eydon Northants 52 D3
Eye Hereford 49 C6
Eye Pboro 66 D2
Eye Suff 56 B5
Eye Green Pboro 66 D2
Eyemouth Borders 122 C5
Eyeworth C Beds 54 E3
Eyhorne Street Kent 30 D2
Eyke Suff 57 D7
Eynesbury Cambs 54 D2
Eynort Highld 149 F8
Eynsford Kent 29 C6
Eynsham Oxon 38 D4
Eype Dorset 12 E2
Eyre Highld 149 C9
Eyre Highld 149 E10
Eythorne Kent 31 E6
Eyton Hereford 49 C6
Eyton Shrops 60 F3
Eyton Wrex 73 E7
Eyton upon the Weald Moors Telford 61 C6

F

Faccombe Hants 25 D8
Faceby N Yorks 102 D2
Facit Lancs 87 C6
Faddiley Ches E 74 D2
Fadmoor N Yorks 102 F4
Faerdre Swansea 33 D7
Failand N Som 23 B7
Failford S Ayrs 112 B4
Failsworth Gtr Man 87 D6
Fain Highld 150 D4
Fair Green Norf 67 C6
Fair Hill Cumb 108 F5
Fair Oak Hants 15 C5
Fair Oak Green Hants 26 C4
Fairbourne Gwyn 58 C3
Fairburn N Yorks 89 B5
Fairfield Derbys 75 B7
Fairfield Stockton 102 C2
Fairfield Worcs 50 B4
Fairfield Worcs 50 E5
Fairford Glos 38 D1
Fairhaven Lancs 85 B4
Fairlie N Ayrs 118 D2
Fairlight E Sus 19 D5
Fairlight Cove E Sus 19 D5
Fairmile Devon 11 E5
Fairmilehead Edin 120 C5
Fairoak Staffs 74 F4
Fairseat Kent 29 C7
Fairstead Essex 42 C3
Fairstead Norf 67 C6
Fairwarp E Sus 17 B8
Fairy Cottage IoM 84 D4
Fairy Cross Devon 9 B6
Fakenham Norf 80 E5
Fakenham Magna Suff 56 B3
Fala Midloth 121 C7
Fala Dam Midloth 121 C7
Falahill Borders 121 D6
Falcon Hereford 49 F8
Faldingworth Lincs 90 F4
Falfield S Glos 36 E3
Falkenham Suff 57 F6
Falkirk Falk 119 B8
Falkland Fife 128 D4
Falla Borders 116 C3
Fallgate Derbys 76 C3
Fallin Stirling 127 E7
Fallowfield Gtr Man 87 E6
Fallsidehill Borders 122 E2
Falmer E Sus 17 D7
Falmouth Corn 3 C7
Falsgrave N Yorks 103 F8
Falstone Northumb 116 F3
Fanagmore Highld 156 E4
Fangdale Beck N Yorks 102 E3
Fangfoss E Yorks 96 D3
Fankerton Falk 127 F6
Fanmore Argyll 146 G7
Fannich Lodge Highld 150 E5
Fans Borders 122 E2
Far Bank S Yorks 89 C7
Far Bletchley M Keynes 53 F6
Far Cotton Northants 52 D5
Far Forest Worcs 50 B2
Far Laund Derbys 76 E3
Far Sawrey Cumb 99 E5
Farcet Cambs 66 E2
Farden Shrops 49 B7
Fareham Hants 15 D6
Farewell Staffs 62 C4
Farforth Lincs 79 B6
Faringdon Oxon 38 E2
Farington Lancs 86 B3
Farlam Cumb 109 D5
Farlary Highld 157 J10
Farleigh N Som 23 C6
Farleigh Sur 28 C4
Farleigh Hungerford Som 24 D3
Farleigh Wallop Hants 26 E4
Farlesthorpe Lincs 79 B7
Farleton Cumb 99 F7
Farleton Lancs 93 C5
Farley Shrops 60 D3
Farley Staffs 75 E7
Farley Wilts 14 B3
Farley Green Sur 27 E8
Farley Hill Luton 40 B3
Farley Hill Wokingham 26 C5
Farleys End Glos 36 C4
Farlington N Yorks 96 C2
Farlow Shrops 61 F6
Farmborough Bath 23 C8
Farmcote Glos 37 B7
Farmcote Shrops 61 E7
Farmington Glos 37 C8
Farmoor Oxon 38 D4
Farmtown Moray 152 C5
Farnborough Hants 27 D6
Farnborough London 28 C5
Farnborough W Berks 38 F4
Farnborough Warks 52 E2
Farnborough Green Hants 27 D6
Farncombe Sur 27 E7
Farndish Bedford 53 C7
Farndon Ches W 73 D8
Farndon Notts 77 D7
Farnell Angus 135 D6
Farnham Dorset 13 C7
Farnham Essex 41 B7
Farnham N Yorks 95 C6
Farnham Suff 57 C7
Farnham Sur 27 E6
Farnham Common Bucks 40 F2
Farnham Green Essex 41 B7
Farnham Royal Bucks 40 F2
Farnhill N Yorks 94 E3
Farningham Kent 29 C6
Farnley N Yorks 94 E5
Farnley W Yorks 95 F5
Farnley Tyas W Yorks 88 C2
Farnsfield Notts 77 D6
Farnworth Gtr Man 86 D5
Farnworth Halton 86 F3
Farr Highld 138 D4
Farr Highld 151 H9
Farr Highld 157 C10
Farr House Highld 151 H9
Farringdon Devon 10 E5
Farrington Gurney Bath 23 D8
Farsley W Yorks 94 F5
Farthinghoe Northants 52 F3
Farthingloe Kent 31 E6
Farthingstone Northants 52 D4
Fartown W Yorks 88 C2
Farway Devon 11 E6
Fasag Highld 149 C13
Fascadale Highld 147 D8
Faslane Port Argyll 145 E11
Fasnacloich Argyll 130 E4
Fasnakyle Ho Highld 137 B6
Fassfern Highld 130 B4
Fatfield T&W 111 D6
Fattahead Aberds 153 C6
Faugh Cumb 108 D5
Fauldhouse W Loth 120 C2
Faulkbourne Essex 42 C3
Faulkland Som 24 D2
Fauls Shrops 74 F2
Faversham Kent 30 C4
Favillar Moray 152 E1
Fawdington N Yorks 95 B7
Fawfieldhead Staffs 75 C7
Fawkham Green Kent 29 C6
Fawler Oxon 38 C3
Fawley Bucks 39 F7
Fawley Hants 15 D5
Fawley W Berks 38 F3
Fawley Chapel Hereford 36 B2
Faxfleet E Yorks 90 B2
Faygate W Sus 28 F3
Fazakerley Mers 85 E4
Fazeley Staffs 63 D6
Fearby N Yorks 101 F6
Fearn Highld 151 D11
Fearn Lodge Highld 151 C9
Fearn Station Highld 151 D11
Fearnan Perth 132 E4
Fearnbeg Highld 149 C12
Fearnhead Warr 86 E4
Fearnmore Highld 149 B12
Featherstone Staffs 62 D3
Featherstone W Yorks 88 B5
Featherwood Northumb 116 D4
Feckenham Worcs 50 C5
Feering Essex 42 B4
Feetham N Yorks 100 E4
Feizor N Yorks 93 C7
Felbridge Sur 28 F4
Felbrigg Norf 81 D8
Felcourt Sur 28 E4
Felden Herts 40 D3
Felin-Crai Powys 34 B2
Felindre Carms 33 B6
Felindre Carms 33 B8
Felindre Carms 46 F2
Felindre Carms 47 F5
Felindre Ceredig 46 D4
Felindre Powys 59 F8
Felindre Swansea 33 D7
Felindre Farchog Pembs 45 F3
Felinfach Ceredig 46 D4
Felinfach Powys 48 F2
Felinfoel Carms 33 D6
Felingwm isaf Carms 33 B6

Felingwm uchaf Carms 33 B6
Felinwynt Ceredig 45 D4
Felixkirk N Yorks 102 F2
Felixstowe Suff 57 F6
Felixstowe Ferry Suff 57 F7
Felkington Northumb 122 E5
Felkirk W Yorks 88 C4
Fell Side Cumb 108 F3
Felling T&W 111 C5
Felmersham Bedford 53 D7
Felmingham Norf 81 E8
Felpham W Sus 16 E3
Felsham Suff 56 D3
Felsted Essex 42 B2
Feltham London 28 B2
Felthorpe Norf 68 C4
Felton Hereford 49 E7
Felton N Som 23 C7
Felton Northumb 117 D7
Felton Butler Shrops 60 C3
Feltwell Norf 67 E7
Fen Ditton Cambs 55 C5
Fen Drayton Cambs 54 C4
Fen End W Mid 51 B7
Fen Side Lincs 79 D6
Fenay Bridge W Yorks 88 C2
Fence Lancs 93 F8
Fence Houses T&W 111 D6
Fengate Norf 81 E7
Fengate Pboro 66 E2
Fenham Northumb 123 E6
Fenhouses Lincs 79 E5
Feniscliffe Blackburn 86 B4
Feniscowles Blackburn 86 B4
Feniton Devon 11 E6
Fenlake Bedford 53 E8
Fenny Bentley Derbys 75 D8
Fenny Bridges Devon 11 E6
Fenny Compton Warks 52 D2
Fenny Drayton Leics 63 E7
Fenny Stratford
M Keynes 53 F6
Fenrother Northumb 117 E7
Fenstanton Cambs 54 C4
Fenton Cambs 54 B4
Fenton Lincs 77 B8
Fenton Lincs 77 D8
Fenton Stoke 75 E5
Fenton Barns E Loth 129 F7
Fenton Town Northumb 123 F5
Fenwick E Ayrs 118 E4
Fenwick Northumb 110 B3
Fenwick Northumb 123 E6
Fenwick S Yorks 89 C6
Feochaig Argyll 143 G8
Feock Corn 3 C7
Feolin Ferry Argyll 144 G3
Ferindonald Highld 149 H11
Feriniquarrie Highld 148 C6
Ferlochan Argyll 130 E3
Fern Angus 134 C4
Ferndale Rhondda 34 E4
Ferndown Dorset 13 D8
Ferness Highld 151 G12
Ferney Green Cumb 99 E6
Fernham Oxon 38 E2
Fernhill Heath Worcs 50 D3
Fernhurst W Sus 16 B2
Fernie Fife 128 C5
Ferniegair S Lanark 119 D7
Fernilea Highld 149 E8
Fernilee Derbys 75 B7
Ferrensby N Yorks 95 C6
Ferring W Sus 16 D4
Ferry Hill Cambs 66 F3
Ferry Point Highld 151 C10
Ferrybridge W Yorks 89 B5
Ferryden Angus 135 D7
Ferryhill Aberdeen 141 D8
Ferryhill Durham 111 F5
Ferryhill Station
Durham 111 F6
Ferryside Carms 32 C4
Fersfield Norf 68 F3
Fersit Highld 131 B7
Ferwig Ceredig 45 E3
Feshiebridge Highld 138 D4
Fetcham Sur 28 D2
Fetterangus Aberds 153 C9
Fettercairn Aberds 135 B6
Fettes Highld 151 F8
Fewcott Oxon 39 B5
Fewston N Yorks 94 D4
Ffair-Rhos Ceredig 47 C6
Ffairfach Carms 33 B7
Ffaldybrenin Carms 46 E5
Ffarmers Carms 47 E5
Ffawyddog Powys 35 C6
Fforest Carms 33 D6
Fforest-fâch Swansea 33 E7
Ffos-y-ffin Ceredig 46 C3
Ffostrasol Ceredig 46 E2
Ffridd-Uchaf Gwyn 83 F5
Ffrith Wrex 73 D6
Ffrwd Gwyn 82 F4
Ffynnon ddrain Carms 33 B5
Ffynnon-oer Ceredig 46 D4
Ffynnongroyw Flint 85 F2
Fidden Argyll 146 J6
Fiddes Aberds 141 F7
Fiddington Glos 50 F4
Fiddington Som 22 E4
Fiddleford Dorset 13 C6
Fiddlers Hamlet Essex 41 D7
Field Staffs 75 F7
Field Broughton Cumb 99 F5
Field Dalling Norf 81 D6
Field Head Leics 63 D8
Fifehead Magdalen
Dorset 13 B5
Fifehead Neville
Dorset 13 C5
Fifield Oxon 38 C2
Fifield Wilts 25 D6
Fifield Windsor 27 B7
Fifield Bavant Wilts 13 B8
Figheldean Wilts 25 E6
Filands Wilts 37 F6
Filby Norf 69 C7
Filey N Yorks 97 A7
Filgrave M Keynes 53 E6
Filkins Oxon 38 D2
Filleigh Devon 9 B8
Filleigh Devon 10 C2
Fillingham Lincs 90 F3
Fillongley Warks 63 F6
Filton S Glos 23 B8
Fimber E Yorks 96 C4
Finavon Angus 134 D4
Finchairn Argyll 124 E5
Fincham Norf 67 D6
Finchampstead
Wokingham 27 C5
Finchdean Hants 15 C8
Finchingfield Essex 55 F7
Finchley London 41 E5
Findern Derbys 76 F3
Findhorn Moray 151 E13
Findhorn Bridge
Highld 138 B4
Findo Gask Perth 128 B2
Findochty Moray 152 B4
Findon Aberds 141 E8
Findon W Sus 16 D5
Findon Mains Highld 151 E9
Findrack Ho. Aberds 140 D5
Finedon Northants 53 B7
Fingal Street Suff 57 C6
Fingask Aberds 141 B6
Fingerpost Worcs 50 B2
Fingest Bucks 39 E7
Finghall N Yorks 101 F6
Fingland Cumb 108 D2
Fingland Dumfries 113 C7
Finglesham Kent 31 D7
Fingringhoe Essex 43 B6
Finlarig Stirling 132 F2
Finmere Oxon 52 F4
Finnart Perth 132 D2
Finningham Suff 56 C4
Finningley S Yorks 89 E7
Finnygaud Aberds 152 C5
Finsbury London 41 F6
Finstall Worcs 50 C4
Finsthwaite Cumb 99 F5
Finstock Oxon 38 C3
Finstown Orkney 159 G4
Fintry Aberds 153 C7
Fintry Dundee 134 F4
Fintry Stirling 126 F5
Finzean Aberds 140 E5
Fionnphort Argyll 146 J6
Fionnsbhagh W Isles 154 J5
Fir Tree Durham 110 F4
Firbeck S Yorks 89 F6
Firby N Yorks 96 C3
Firby N Yorks 101 F7
Firgrove Gtr Man 87 C7
Firsby Lincs 79 C7
Firsdown Wilts 25 F7
First Coast Highld 150 B2
Fishbourne IoW 15 E6
Fishbourne W Sus 16 D2
Fishburn Durham 111 F6
Fishcross Clack 127 E7
Fisher Place Cumb 99 C5
Fisherford Aberds 153 E6
Fisher's Pond Hants 15 B5
Fisherstreet W Sus 27 F7
Fisherton Highld 151 F10
Fisherton S Ayrs 112 C2
Fishguard =
Abergwaun Pembs 44 B4
Fishlake S Yorks 89 C7
Fishleigh Barton Devon 9 B7
Fishponds Bristol 23 B8
Fishpool Glos 36 B3
Fishtoft Lincs 79 E6
Fishtoft Drove Lincs 79 E6
Fishtown of Usan
Angus 135 D7
Fishwick Borders 122 D5
Fiskavaig Highld 149 E8
Fiskerton Lincs 78 B3
Fiskerton Notts 77 D7
Fitling E Yorks 97 F8
Fittleton Wilts 25 E6
Fittleworth W Sus 16 C4
Fitton End Cambs 66 C4
Fitz Shrops 60 C4
Fitzhead Som 11 B6
Fitzwilliam W Yorks 88 C5
Fiunary Highld 147 G9
Five Acres Glos 36 C2
Five Ashes E Sus 18 C2
Five Oak Green Kent 29 E7
Five Oaks Jersey 17
Five Oaks W Sus 16 B4
Five Roads Carms 33 D5
Fivecrosses Ches W 74 B2
Fivehead Som 11 B8
Flack's Green Essex 42 C3
Flackwell Heath Bucks 40 F1
Fladbury Worcs 50 E4
Fladdabister Shetland 160 K6
Flagg Derbys 75 C8
Flamborough E Yorks 97 B8
Flamstead Herts 40 C3
Flamstead End Herts 41 D6
Flansham W Sus 16 D3
Flanshaw W Yorks 88 B4
Flasby N Yorks 94 D2
Flash Staffs 75 C7
Flashader Highld 149 C8
Flask Inn N Yorks 103 D7
Flaunden Herts 40 D3
Flawborough Notts 77 E7
Flawith N Yorks 95 C7
Flax Bourton N Som 23 C7
Flaxby N Yorks 95 D6
Flaxholme Derbys 76 E3
Flaxley Glos 36 C3
Flaxpool Som 22 F3
Flaxton N Yorks 96 C2
Fleckney Leics 64 E3
Flecknoe Warks 52 C3
Fledborough Notts 77 B8
Fleet Hants 15 D8
Fleet Hants 27 D6
Fleet Lincs 66 B3
Fleet Hargate Lincs 66 B3
Fleetham Northumb 117 B7
Fleetlands Hants 15 D6
Fleetville Herts 40 D4
Fleetwood Lancs 92 E3
Flemingston V Glam 22 B2
Flemington S Lanark 119 D6
Flempton Suff 56 C2
Fleoideabhagh
W Isles 154 J5
Fletchertown Cumb 108 E2
Fletching E Sus 17 B8
Flexbury Corn 8 D4
Flexford Sur 27 E7
Flimby Cumb 107 F7
Flimwell E Sus 18 B4
Flint = Y Fflint Flint 73 B6
Flint Mountain Flint 73 B6
Flintham Notts 77 E7
Flinton E Yorks 97 F8
Flintsham Hereford 48 D5
Flitcham Norf 80 E3
Flitton C Beds 53 F8
Flitwick C Beds 53 F8
Flixborough N Lincs 90 C2
Flixborough Stather
N Lincs 90 C2
Flixton Gtr Man 86 E5
Flixton N Yorks 97 B6
Flixton Suff 69 F6
Flockton W Yorks 88 C3
Flodaigh W Isles 148 C3
Flodden Northumb 122 F5
Flodigarry Highld 149 A9
Flood's Ferry Cambs 66 E3
Flookburgh Cumb 92 B3
Florden Norf 68 E4
Flore Northants 52 C4
Flotterton Northumb 117 D5
Flowton Suff 56 E4
Flush House W Yorks 88 D2
Flushing Aberds 153 D10
Flushing Corn 3 C7
Flyford Flavell Worcs 50 D4
Foals Green Suff 57 B6
Fobbing Thurrock 42 F3
Fochabers Moray 152 C3
Fochriw Caerph 35 D5
Fockerby N Lincs 90 C2
Fodderletter Moray 139 B7
Fodderty Highld 151 F8
Foel Powys 59 C6
Foel-gastell Carms 33 C6
Foffarty Angus 134 E4
Foggathorpe E Yorks 96 F3
Fogo Borders 122 E3
Fogorig Borders 122 E3
Foindle Highld 156 E4
Folda Angus 134 C1
Fole Staffs 75 F7
Foleshill W Mid 63 F7
Folke Dorset 12 C4
Folkestone Kent 31 F6
Folkingham Lincs 78 F3
Folkington E Sus 18 E2
Folksworth Cambs 65 F8
Folkton N Yorks 97 B6
Folla Rule Aberds 153 E7
Follifoot N Yorks 95 D6
Folly Gate Devon 9 E7
Fonthill Bishop Wilts 24 F4
Fonthill Gifford Wilts 24 F4
Fontmell Magna Dorset 13 C6
Fontwell W Sus 16 D3
Foolow Derbys 75 B8
Foots Cray London 29 B5
Forbestown Aberds 140 C2
Force Mills Cumb 99 E5
Forcett N Yorks 101 C6
Ford Argyll 124 E4
Ford Bucks 39 D7
Ford Devon 9 B6
Ford Glos 37 B7
Ford Northumb 122 F5
Ford Shrops 60 C4
Ford Staffs 75 D7
Ford W Sus 16 D3
Ford Wilts 24 B3
Ford End Essex 42 C2
Ford Street Som 11 C6
Fordcombe Kent 29 E6
Fordell Fife 128 F3
Forden Powys 60 D2
Forder Green Devon 7 C5
Fordham Cambs 55 B7
Fordham Essex 43 B5
Fordham Norf 67 E6
Fordhouses W Mid 62 D3
Fordingbridge Hants 14 C2
Fordon E Yorks 97 B6
Fordoun Aberds 135 B7
Ford's Green Suff 56 C4
Fordstreet Essex 43 B5
Fordwells Oxon 38 C3
Fordwich Kent 31 D5
Fordyce Aberds 152 B5
Forebridge Staffs 62 B3
Forest Durham 109 F8
Forest Becks Lancs 93 D7
Forest Gate London 41 F7
Forest Green Sur 28 E2
Forest Hall Cumb 99 D7
Forest Head Cumb 109 D5
Forest Hill Oxon 39 D5
Forest Lane Head
N Yorks 95 D6
Forest Lodge Argyll 131 E6
Forest Lodge Highld 139 C6
Forest Lodge Perth 133 B6
Forest Mill Clack 127 E8
Forest Row E Sus 28 F5
Forest Town Notts 77 C5
Forestburn Gate
Northumb 117 E6
Foresterseat Moray 152 C1
Forestside W Sus 15 C8
Forfar Angus 134 D4
Forgandenny Perth 128 C2
Forge Powys 58 E4
Forge Side Torf 35 D6
Forgewood N Lanark 119 D7
Forgie Moray 152 C3
Forglen Ho. Aberds 153 C6
Formby Mers 85 D4
Forncett End Norf 68 E4
Forncett St Mary Norf 68 E4
Forncett St Peter
Norf 68 E4
Forneth Perth 133 E7
Fornham All Saints
Suff 56 C2
Fornham St Martin
Suff 56 C2
Forres Moray 151 F13
Forrest Lodge Dumfries 113 F5
Forrestfield N Lanark 119 C8
Forsbrook Staffs 75 E6
Forse Highld 158 G4
Forse Ho. Highld 158 G4
Forsinain Highld 157 E12
Forsinard Highld 157 E11
Forsinard Station
Highld 157 E11
Forston Dorset 12 E4
Fort Augustus Highld 137 D6
Fort George Guern 16
Fort George Highld 151 F10
Fort William Highld 131 B5
Forteviot Perth 128 C2
Forth S Lanark 120 D2
Forth Road Bridge
Edin 120 B4
Forthampton Glos 50 F3
Fortingall Perth 132 E4
Forton Hants 26 E2
Forton Lancs 92 D4
Forton Shrops 60 C4
Forton Som 11 D8
Forton Staffs 61 B7
Forton Heath Shrops 60 C4
Fortrie Aberds 153 D6
Fortrose Highld 151 F10
Fortuneswell Dorset 12 G4
Forty Green Bucks 40 E2
Forty Hill London 41 E6
Forward Green Suff 56 D4
Fosbury Wilts 25 D8
Fosdyke Lincs 79 F6
Foss Perth 132 D4
Foss Cross Glos 37 D7
Fossebridge Glos 37 C7
Foster Street Essex 41 D7
Fosterhouses S Yorks 89 C7
Foston Derbys 75 F8
Foston Lincs 77 E8
Foston N Yorks 96 C2
Foston on the Wolds
E Yorks 97 D7
Fotherby Lincs 91 E7
Fotheringhay Northants 65 E7
Foubister Orkney 159 H6
Foul Mile E Sus 18 D3
Foulby W Yorks 88 C4
Foulden Borders 122 D5
Foulden Norf 67 E7
Foulis Castle Highld 151 E8
Foulridge Lancs 93 E8
Foulsham Norf 81 E6
Fountainhall Borders 121 E7
Four Ashes Staffs 62 F2
Four Ashes Suff 56 B4
Four Crosses Powys 59 D7
Four Crosses Powys 60 C2
Four Crosses Wrex 73 D6
Four Elms Kent 29 E5
Four Forks Som 22 F4
Four Gotes Cambs 66 C4
Four Lane Ends Ches W 74 C2
Four Lanes Corn 3 C5
Four Marks Hants 26 F4
Four Mile Bridge
Anglesey 82 D2
Four Oaks E Sus 19 C5
Four Oaks W Mid 62 E5
Four Oaks W Mid 63 F6
Four Roads Carms 33 D5
Four Roads IoM 84 F2
Four Throws Kent 18 C4
Fourlane Ends Derbys 76 D3
Fourlanes End Ches E 74 D5
Fourpenny Highld 151 B11
Fourstones Northumb 109 C8
Fovant Wilts 13 B8
Foveran Aberds 141 B8
Fowey Corn 5 D6
Fowley Common Warr 86 E4
Fowlis Angus 134 F3
Fowlis Wester Perth 127 B8
Fowlmere Cambs 54 E5
Fownhope Hereford 49 F7
Fox Corner Sur 27 D7
Fox Lane Hants 27 D6
Fox Street Essex 43 B6
Foxbar Renfs 118 C4
Foxcombe Hill Oxon 38 D4
Foxdale IoM 84 E2
Foxearth Essex 56 E2
Foxfield Cumb 98 F4
Foxham Wilts 24 B4
Foxhole Corn 4 D4
Foxhole Swansea 33 E7
Foxholes N Yorks 97 B6
Foxhunt Green E Sus 18 D2
Foxley Norf 81 E6
Foxley Wilts 37 F5
Foxt Staffs 75 E7
Foxton Cambs 54 E5
Foxton Durham 102 B1
Foxton Leics 64 E4
Foxup N Yorks 93 B8
Foxwist Green Ches W 74 C3
Foxwood Shrops 49 B8
Foy Hereford 36 B2
Foyers Highld 137 B7
Fraddam Corn 2 C4
Fraddon Corn 4 D4
Fradley Staffs 63 C5
Fradswell Staffs 75 F6
Fraisthorpe E Yorks 97 C7
Framfield E Sus 17 B8
Framingham Earl Norf 69 D5
Framingham Pigot
Norf 69 D5
Framlingham Suff 57 C6
Frampton Dorset 12 E4
Frampton Lincs 79 F6
Frampton Cotterell
S Glos 36 F3
Frampton Mansell
Glos 37 D6
Frampton on Severn
Glos 36 D4
Frampton West End
Lincs 79 E5
Framsden Suff 57 D5
Framwellgate Moor
Durham 111 E5
Franche Worcs 50 B3
Frankby Mers 85 F3
Frankley Worcs 62 F3
Frank's Bridge Powys 48 D3
Frankton Warks 52 B2
Frant E Sus 18 B2
Fraserburgh Aberds 153 B9
Frating Green Essex 43 B6
Fratton Ptsmth 15 E7
Freathy Corn 5 D8
Freckenham Suff 55 B7
Freckleton Lancs 86 B2
Freeby Leics 64 B5
Freehay Staffs 75 E7
Freeland Oxon 38 C4
Freester Shetland 160 H6
Freethorpe Norf 69 D7
Freiston Lincs 79 E6
Fremington Devon 20 F4
Fremington N Yorks 101 E5
Frenchay S Glos 23 B8
Frenchbeer Devon 9 F8
Frenich Stirling 126 D3
Frensham Sur 27 E6
Fresgoe Highld 157 C12
Freshfield Mers 85 D3
Freshford Bath 24 C2
Freshwater IoW 14 F4
Freshwater Bay IoW 14 F4
Freshwater East Pembs 32 E1
Fressingfield Suff 57 B6
Freston Suff 57 F5
Freswick Highld 158 D5
Fretherne Glos 36 D4
Frettenham Norf 68 C5
Freuchie Fife 128 D4
Freuchies Angus 134 C2
Freystrop Pembs 44 D4
Friar's Gate E Sus 29 F5
Friarton Perth 128 B3
Friday Bridge Cambs 66 D4
Friday Street E Sus 18 E3
Fridaythorpe E Yorks 96 D4
Friern Barnet London 41 E5
Friesland Argyll 146 F4
Friesthorpe Lincs 90 F4
Frieston Lincs 78 E2
Frieth Bucks 39 E7
Frilford Oxon 38 E4
Frilsham W Berks 26 B3
Frimley Sur 27 D6
Frimley Green Sur 27 D6
Frindsbury Medway 29 B8
Fring Norf 80 D3
Fringford Oxon 39 B6
Frinsted Kent 30 D2
Frinton-on-Sea Essex 43 B8
Friockheim Angus 135 E5
Friog Gwyn 58 C3
Frisby on the Wreake
Leics 64 C3
Friskney Lincs 79 D7
Friskney Eaudike Lincs 79 D7
Friskney Tofts Lincs 79 D7
Friston E Sus 18 F2
Friston Suff 57 C8
Fritchley Derbys 76 D3
Frith Bank Lincs 79 E6
Frith Common Worcs 49 C8
Fritham Hants 14 C3
Frithelstock Devon 9 C6
Frithelstock Stone
Devon 9 C6
Frithville Lincs 79 D6
Frittenden Kent 30 E2
Frittiscombe Devon 7 E6
Fritton Norf 68 E5
Fritton Norf 69 D7
Fritwell Oxon 39 B5
Frizinghall W Yorks 94 F4
Frizington Cumb 98 C2
Frocester Glos 36 D4
Frodesley Shrops 60 D5
Frodingham N Lincs 90 C2
Frodsham Ches W 74 B2
Frogden Borders 116 B3
Froggatt Derbys 76 B2
Froghall Staffs 75 E7
Frogmore Devon 7 E5
Frogmore Hants 27 D6
Frognall Lincs 65 C8
Frogshail Norf 81 D8
Frolesworth Leics 64 E2
Frome Som 24 E2
Frome St Quintin
Dorset 12 D3
Fromes Hill Hereford 49 E8
Fron Denb 72 C4
Fron Gwyn 70 D4
Fron Gwyn 82 F5
Fron Powys 48 C2
Fron Powys 59 E8
Fron Powys 60 D2
Froncysyllte Wrex 73 E6
Frongoch Gwyn 72 F3
Frostenden Suff 69 F7
Frosterley Durham 110 F3
Frotoft Orkney 159 F5
Froxfield Wilts 25 C7
Froxfield Green Hants 15 B8
Froyle Hants 27 E5
Fryerning Essex 42 D2
Fryton N Yorks 96 B2
Fulbeck Lincs 78 D2
Fulbourn Cambs 55 D6
Fulbrook Oxon 38 C2
Fulford Som 11 B7
Fulford Staffs 75 F6
Fulford York 96 E2
Fulham London 28 B3
Fulking W Sus 17 C6
Full Sutton E Yorks 96 D3
Fullarton Glasgow 119 C6
Fullarton N Ayrs 118 F3
Fuller Street Essex 42 C3
Fuller's Moor Ches W 73 D8
Fullerton Hants 25 F8
Fulletby Lincs 79 B5
Fullwood E Ayrs 118 D4
Fulmer Bucks 40 F2
Fulmodestone Norf 81 D5
Fulnetby Lincs 78 B3
Fulstow Lincs 91 E7
Fulwell T&W 111 D6
Fulwood Lancs 92 F5
Fulwood S Yorks 88 F4
Fundenhall Norf 68 E4
Fundenhall Street
Norf 68 E4
Funtington W Sus 15 D8
Funtley Hants 15 D6
Funtullich Perth 127 B6
Funzie Shetland 160 D8
Furley Devon 11 D7
Furnace Argyll 125 E6
Furnace Carms 33 D6
Furnace End Warks 63 E6
Furneaux Pelham
Herts 41 B7
Furness Vale Derbys 87 F8
Furze Platt Windsor 40 F1
Furzehill Devon 21 E6
Fyfett Som 11 C7
Fyfield Essex 42 D1
Fyfield Glos 38 D2
Fyfield Hants 25 E7
Fyfield Oxon 38 E4
Fyfield Wilts 25 C6
Fylingthorpe N Yorks 103 D7
Fyvie Aberds 153 E7

G

Gabhsann bho
Dheas W Isles 155 B9
Gabhsann bho
Thuath W Isles 155 B9
Gablon Highld 151 B10
Gabroc Hill E Ayrs 118 D4
Gaddesby Leics 64 C3
Gadebridge Herts 40 D3
Gaer Powys 35 B5
Gaerllwyd Mon 35 E8
Gaerwen Anglesey 82 D4
Gagingwell Oxon 38 B4
Gaick Lodge Highld 138 F3
Gailey Staffs 62 C3
Gainford Durham 101 C6
Gainsborough Lincs 90 E2
Gainsborough Suff 57 E5
Gainsford End Essex 55 F8
Gairloch Highld 149 A13
Gairlochy Highld 136 F4
Gairney Bank Perth 128 E3
Gairnshiel Lodge
Aberds 139 D8
Gaisgill Cumb 99 D8
Gaitsgill Cumb 108 E3
Galashiels Borders 121 F7
Galgate Lancs 92 D4
Galhampton Som 12 B4
Gallaberry Dumfries 114 F2
Gallachoille Argyll 144 E6
Gallanach Argyll 124 C4
Gallanach Argyll 146 E5
Gallantry Bank Ches E 74 D2
Gallatown Fife 128 E4
Galley Common Warks 63 E7
Galley Hill Cambs 54 C4
Galleyend Essex 42 D3
Galleywood Essex 42 D3
Gallin Perth 132 E2
Gallowfauld Angus 134 E4
Gallows Green Staffs 75 E7
Galltair Highld 149 F13
Galmisdale Highld 146 C7
Galmpton Devon 6 E4
Galmpton Torbay 7 D6
Galphay N Yorks 95 B5
Galston E Ayrs 118 F5
Galtrigill Highld 148 C6
Gamblesby Cumb 109 F6
Gamesley Derbys 87 E8
Gamlingay Cambs 54 D3
Gammersgill N Yorks 101 F5
Gamston Notts 77 B7
Ganarew Hereford 36 C2
Ganavan Argyll 124 B4
Gang Corn 5 C8
Ganllwyd Gwyn 71 E8
Gannochy Angus 135 B5
Gannochy Perth 128 B3
Gansclet Highld 158 F5
Ganstead E Yorks 97 F7
Ganthorpe N Yorks 96 B2
Ganton N Yorks 97 B5
Garbat Highld 150 E7
Garbhallt Argyll 125 F6
Garboldisham Norf 68 F3
Garden City Flint 73 C7
Garden Village W Yorks 95 F7
Garden Village Wrex 73 D7
Gardenstown Aberds 153 B7
Garderhouse Shetland 160 J5
Gardham E Yorks 97 E5
Gardin Shetland 160 G6
Gare Hill Som 24 E2
Garelochhead Argyll 145 D11
Garford Oxon 38 E4
Garforth W Yorks 95 F7
Gargrave N Yorks 94 D2
Gargunnock Stirling 127 E6
Garlic Street Norf 68 F5
Garlieston Dumfries 105 E8
Garlinge Green Kent 30 D5
Garlogie Aberds 141 D6
Garmond Aberds 153 C8
Garmony Argyll 147 G9
Garmouth Moray 152 B3
Garn-yr-erw Torf 35 C6
Garnant Carms 33 C7
Garndiffaith Torf 35 D6
Garndolbenmaen
Gwyn 71 C5
Garnedd Conwy 83 F7
Garnett Bridge Cumb 99 E7
Garnfadryn Gwyn 70 D3
Garnkirk N Lanark 119 C6
Garnlydan Bl Gwent 35 C5
Garnswllt Swansea 33 D7
Garrabost W Isles 155 D10
Garraron Argyll 124 E4
Garras Corn 3 D6
Garreg Gwyn 71 C7
Garrick Perth 127 C7
Garrigill Cumb 109 E7
Garriston N Yorks 101 E6
Garroch Dumfries 113 F5
Garrogie Lodge
Highld 137 C8
Garros Highld 149 B9
Garrow Perth 133 E5
Garryhorn Dumfries 113 E5
Garsdale Cumb 100 F2
Garsdale Head Cumb 100 E2
Garsdon Wilts 37 F6
Garshall Green Staffs 75 F6
Garsington Oxon 39 D5
Garstang Lancs 92 E4
Garston Mers 86 F2
Garswood Mers 86 E3
Gartcosh N Lanark 119 C6
Garth Bridgend 34 E2
Garth Gwyn 83 D5
Garth Powys 47 E8
Garth Shetland 160 H4
Garth Wrex 73 E6
Garth Row Cumb 99 E7
Garthamlock Glasgow 119 C6
Garthbrengy Powys 48 F2
Garthdee Aberdeen 141 D8
Gartheli Ceredig 46 D4
Garthmyl Powys 59 E8
Garthorpe Leics 64 B5
Garthorpe N Lincs 90 C2
Gartly Aberds 152 E5
Gartmore Stirling 126 E4
Gartnagrenach Argyll 144 H6
Gartness N Lanark 119 C7
Gartness Stirling 126 F4
Gartocharn W Dunb 126 F3
Garton E Yorks 97 F8
Garton-on-the-
Wolds E Yorks 97 D5
Gartsherrie N Lanark 119 C7
Gartymore Highld 157 H13
Garvald E Loth 121 B8
Garvamore Highld 137 E8
Garvard Argyll 144 D2
Garvault Hotel Highld 157 F10
Garve Highld 150 E6
Garvestone Norf 68 D3
Garvock Aberds 135 B7
Garvock Invclyd 118 B2
Garway Hereford 36 B1
Garway Hill Hereford 35 B8
Gaskan Highld 130 B1
Gastard Wilts 24 C3
Gasthorpe Norf 68 F2
Gatcombe IoW 15 F5
Gate Burton Lincs 90 F2
Gate Helmsley N Yorks 96 D2
Gateacre Mers 86 F2
Gatebeck Cumb 99 F7
Gateford Notts 89 F6
Gateforth N Yorks 89 B6
Gatehead E Ayrs 118 F3
Gatehouse Northumb 116 F3
Gatehouse of
Fleet Dumfries 106 D3
Gatelawbridge
Dumfries 114 E2
Gateley Norf 81 E5
Gatenby N Yorks 101 F8
Gateshead T&W 111 C5
Gatesheath Ches W 73 C8
Gateside Aberds 140 C5
Gateside Angus 134 E4
Gateside E Renf 118 D4
Gateside Fife 128 D3
Gateside N Ayrs 118 D3
Gathurst Gtr Man 86 D3
Gatley Gtr Man 87 F6
Gattonside Borders 121 F8
Gatwick Airport W Sus 28 E3
Gaufron Powys 47 C8
Gaulby Leics 64 D3
Gauldry Fife 129 B5
Gaunt's Common
Dorset 13 D8
Gautby Lincs 78 B4
Gavinton Borders 122 D3
Gawber S Yorks 88 D4
Gawcott Bucks 52 F4
Gawsworth Ches E 75 C5
Gawthorpe W Yorks 88 B3
Gawthrop Cumb 100 F1
Gawthwaite Cumb 98 F4
Gay Street W Sus 16 B4
Gaydon Warks 51 D8
Gayfield Orkney 159 C5
Gayhurst M Keynes 53 E6
Gayle N Yorks 100 F3
Gayles N Yorks 101 D6
Gayton Mers 85 F3
Gayton Norf 67 C7
Gayton Northants 52 D5
Gayton Staffs 62 B3
Gayton le Marsh Lincs 91 F8
Gayton le Wold Lincs 91 F6
Gayton Thorpe Norf 67 C7
Gaywood Norf 67 B6
Gazeley Suff 55 C8
Geanies House
Highld 151 D11
Gearraidh Bhailteas
W Isles 148 F2
Gearraidh Bhaird
W Isles 155 E8
Gearraidh na
h-Aibhne W Isles 154 D7
Gearraidh na
Monadh W Isles 148 G2
Geary Highld 148 B7
Geddes House Highld 151 F11
Gedding Suff 56 D3
Geddington Northants 65 F5
Gedintailor Highld 149 E10
Gedling Notts 77 E6
Gedney Lincs 66 B4
Gedney Broadgate
Lincs 66 B4
Gedney Drove End
Lincs 66 B4
Gedney Dyke Lincs 66 B4
Gedney Hill Lincs 66 C3
Gee Cross Gtr Man 87 E7
Geilston Argyll 118 B3
Geirinis W Isles 148 D2
Geise Highld 158 D3
Geisiadar W Isles 154 D6
Geldeston Norf 69 E6
Gell Conwy 83 E8
Gelli Pembs 32 C1
Gelli Rhondda 34 E3
Gellideg M Tydf 34 D4
Gellifor Denb 72 C5
Gelligaer Caerph 35 E5
Gellilydan Gwyn 71 D7
Gellinudd Neath 33 D8
Gellyburn Perth 133 F7
Gellywen Carms 32 B3
Gelston Dumfries 106 D4
Gelston Lincs 78 E2
Gembling E Yorks 97 D7
Gentleshaw Staffs 62 C4
Geocrab W Isles 154 H6
George Green Bucks 40 F3
George Nympton
Devon 10 B2
Georgefield Dumfries 115 E5
Georgeham Devon 20 F3
Georgetown Bl Gwent 35 D5
Gerlan Gwyn 83 E6
Germansweek Devon 9 E6
Germoe Corn 2 D4
Gerrans Corn 3 C7
Gerrards Cross Bucks 40 F3
Gestingthorpe Essex 56 F2
Geuffordd Powys 60 C2
Gib Hill Ches W 74 B3
Gibbet Hill Warks 64 F2
Gibbshill Dumfries 106 B4
Gidea Park London 41 F8
Gidleigh Devon 9 F8
Giffnock E Renf 119 D5
Gifford E Loth 121 C8
Giffordland N Ayrs 118 E2
Giffordtown Fife 128 C4
Giggleswick N Yorks 93 C8
Gilberdyke E Yorks 90 B2
Gilchriston E Loth 121 C7
Gilcrux Cumb 107 F8
Gildersome W Yorks 88 B3
Gildingwells S Yorks 89 F6
Gileston V Glam 22 C2
Gilfach Caerph 35 E5
Gilfach Goch Rhondda 34 F3
Gilfachrheda Ceredig 46 D3
Gillamoor N Yorks 102 F4
Gillar's Green Mers 86 E2
Gillen Highld 148 C7
Gilling East N Yorks 96 B2
Gilling West N Yorks 101 D6
Gillingham Dorset 13 B6
Gillingham Medway 29 C8
Gillingham Norf 69 E7
Gillock Highld 158 E4
Gillow Heath Staffs 75 D5
Gills Highld 158 C5
Gill's Green Kent 18 B4
Gilmanscleuch
Borders 115 B6
Gilmerton Edin 121 C5
Gilmerton Perth 127 B7
Gilmonby Durham 100 C4
Gilmorton Leics 64 F2
Gilmourton S Lanark 119 E6
Gilsland Northumb 109 C6
Gilsland Spa Cumb 109 C6
Gilston Borders 121 D7
Gilston Herts 41 C7
Gilwern Mon 35 C6
Gimingham Norf 81 D8
Giosla W Isles 154 E6
Gipping Suff 56 C4
Gipsey Bridge Lincs 79 E5
Girdle Toll N Ayrs 118 E3
Girlsta Shetland 160 H6
Girsby N Yorks 102 D1
Girtford C Beds 54 D2
Girthon Dumfries 106 D3
Girton Cambs 54 C5
Girton Notts 77 C8
Girvan S Ayrs 112 E1
Gisburn Lancs 93 E8
Gisleham Suff 69 F8
Gislingham Suff 56 B4
Gissing Norf 68 F4
Gittisham Devon 11 E6
Gladestry Powys 48 D4
Gladsmuir E Loth 121 B7
Glais Swansea 33 D8
Glaisdale N Yorks 103 D5
Glame Highld 149 D10
Glamis Angus 134 E3
Glan Adda Gwyn 83 D5
Glan Conwy Conwy 83 D8
Glan-Conwy Conwy 83 F8
Glan-Duar Carms 46 E4
Glan-Dwyfach Gwyn 71 C5
Glan Gors Anglesey 82 D4
Glan-rhyd Gwyn 82 F4
Glan-traeth Anglesey 82 D2
Glan-y-don Flint 73 B5
Glan-y-nant Powys 59 F6
Glan-y-wern Gwyn 71 D7
Glan-yr-afon Anglesey 83 C6
Glan-yr-afon Gwyn 72 E3
Glan-yr-afon Gwyn 72 E4
Glanaman Carms 33 C7
Glandford Norf 81 C6
Glandwr Pembs 32 B2
Glandy Cross Carms 32 B2
Glandyfi Ceredig 58 E3
Glangrwyney Powys 35 C6
Glanmule Powys 59 E8
Glanrafon Ceredig 58 F3
Glanrhyd Gwyn 70 D3
Glanrhyd Pembs 45 E3
Glanton Northumb 117 C6
Glanton Pike Northumb 117 C6
Glanvilles
Wootton Dorset 12 D4
Glapthorn Northants 65 E7
Glapwell Derbys 76 C4
Glas-allt Shiel Aberds 139 F8
Glasbury Powys 48 F3
Glaschoil Highld 151 H13
Glascoed Denb 72 B3
Glascoed Mon 35 D7
Glascoed Powys 59 C8
Glascorrie Aberds 140 E2
Glascote Staffs 63 D6
Glascwm Powys 48 D3
Glasdrum Argyll 130 E4
Glasfryn Conwy 72 D3
Glasgow Glasgow 119 C5
Glashvin Highld 149 B9
Glasinfryn Gwyn 83 E5
Glasnacardoch
Highld 147 B9
Glasnakille Highld 149 G10
Glasphein Highld 148 D6
Glaspwll Powys 58 E4
Glassburn Highld 150 H6
Glasserton Dumfries 105 F8
Glassford S Lanark 119 E7
Glasshouse Hill Glos 36 B4
Glasshouses N Yorks 94 C4
Glasslie Fife 128 D4
Glasson Cumb 108 C2
Glasson Lancs 92 D4
Glassonby Cumb 109 F5
Glasterlaw Angus 135 D5
Glaston Rutland 65 D5
Glastonbury Som 23 F7
Glatton Cambs 65 F8
Glazebrook Warr 86 E4
Glazebury Warr 86 E4
Glazeley Shrops 61 F7
Gleadless S Yorks 88 F4
Gleadsmoss Ches E 74 C5
Gleann
Tholàstaidh W Isles 155 C10
Gleaston Cumb 92 B2
Gleiniant Powys 59 E6
Glemsford Suff 56 E2
Glen Dumfries 106 B5
Glen Dumfries 106 D2
Glen Auldyn IoM 84 C4
Glen Bernisdale
Highld 149 D9
Glen Ho Borders 121 F5
Glen Mona IoM 84 D4
Glen Nevis House
Highld 131 B5
Glen Parva Leics 64 E2
Glen Sluain Argyll 125 F6
Glen Tanar House
Aberds 140 E3
Glen Trool Lodge
Dumfries 112 F4
Glen Village Falk 119 B8
Glen Vine IoM 84 E3
Glenamachrie Argyll 124 C5
Glenbarr Argyll 143 E7
Glenbeg Highld 139 B6
Glenbeg Highld 147 E8
Glenbervie Aberds 141 F6
Glenboig N Lanark 119 C7
Glenborrodale Highld 147 E9
Glenbranter Argyll 125 F7
Glenbreck Borders 114 B3
Glenbrein Lodge
Highld 137 C7
Glenbrittle House
Highld 149 F9
Glenbuchat Lodge
Aberds 140 C2
Glenbuck E Ayrs 113 B7
Glenburn Renfs 118 C4
Glencalvie Lodge
Highld 150 C7
Glencanisp Lodge
Highld 156 G4
Glencaple Dumfries 107 C6
Glencarron Lodge
Highld 150 F3
Glencarse Perth 128 B3
Glencassley Castle
Highld 156 J7
Glenceitlein Highld 131 E5
Glencoe Highld 130 D4
Glencraig Fife 128 E3
Glencripesdale Highld 147 F9
Glencrosh Dumfries 113 F7
Glendavan Ho. Aberds 140 D3
Glendevon Perth 127 D8
Glendoe Lodge Highld 137 D7
Glendoebeg Highld 137 D7
Glendoick Perth 128 B4
Glendoll Lodge Angus 134 B2
Glendoune S Ayrs 112 E1
Glenduckie Fife 128 C4
Glendye Lodge Aberds 140 F5
Gleneagles Hotel
Perth 127 C8
Gleneagles House
Perth 127 D8
Glenegedale Argyll 142 C4
Glenelg Highld 149 G13
Glenernie Moray 151 G13
Glenfarg Perth 128 C3
Glenfarquhar Lodge
Aberds 141 F6
Glenferness House
Highld 151 G12
Glenfeshie Lodge
Highld 138 E4
Glenfield Leics 64 D2
Glenfinnan Highld 147 C11
Glenfoot Perth 128 C3
Glenfyne Lodge Argyll 125 D8
Glengap Dumfries 106 D3
Glengarnock N Ayrs 118 D3
Glengorm Castle
Argyll 146 F7
Glengrasco Highld 149 D9
Glenhead Farm Angus 134 C2
Glenhoul Dumfries 113 F6
Glenhurich Highld 130 C2
Glenkerry Borders 115 C5
Glenkiln Dumfries 106 B5
Glenkindie Aberds 140 C3
Glenlatterach Moray 152 C1
Glenlee Dumfries 113 F6
Glenlichorn Perth 127 C6
Glenlivet Moray 139 B7
Glenlochsie Perth 133 B7
Glenloig N Ayrs 143 E10
Glenluce Dumfries 105 D6
Glenmallan Argyll 125 F8
Glenmarksie Highld 150 F6
Glenmassan Argyll 145 E10
Glenmavis N Lanark 119 C7
Glenmaye IoM 84 E2
Glenmidge Dumfries 113 F8
Glenmore Argyll 124 D4
Glenmore Highld 149 D9
Glenmore Lodge
Highld 139 D5
Glenmoy Angus 134 C4
Glenogil Angus 134 C4
Glenprosen Lodge
Angus 134 C2
Glenprosen Village
Angus 134 C3
Glenquiech Angus 134 C4
Glenreasdell Mains
Argyll 145 H7
Glenree N Ayrs 143 F10
Glenridding Cumb 99 C5
Glenrossal Highld 156 J7
Glenrothes Fife 128 D4
Glensanda Highld 130 E2
Glensaugh Aberds 135 B6
Glenshero Lodge
Highld 137 E8
Glenstockadale
Dumfries 104 C4
Glenstriven Argyll 145 F9
Glentaggart S Lanark 113 B8
Glentham Lincs 90 E4
Glentirranmuir Stirling 127 E5
Glenton Aberds 140 B5
Glentress Borders 121 F5
Glentromie Lodge
Highld 138 E3
Glentrool Village
Dumfries 105 B7
Glentruan IoM 84 B4
Glentruim House
Highld 138 E2
Glentworth Lincs 90 F3
Glenuig Highld 147 D9
Glenurquhart Highld 151 E10
Glespin S Lanark 113 B8
Gletness Shetland 160 H6
Glewstone Hereford 36 B2
Glinton Pboro 65 D8
Glooston Leics 64 E4
Glororum Northumb 123 F7
Glossop Derbys 87 E8
Gloster Hill Northumb 117 D8
Gloucester Glos 37 C5
Gloup Shetland 160 C7
Glusburn N Yorks 94 E3
Glutt Lodge Highld 157 F12
Glutton Bridge Staffs 75 C7
Glympton Oxon 38 B4
Glyn-Ceiriog Wrex 73 F6
Glyn-cywarch Gwyn 71 D7
Glyn Ebwy = Ebbw
Vale Bl Gwent 35 D5
Glyn-neath =
Glynedd Neath 34 D2
Glynarthen Ceredig 46 E2
Glynbrochan Powys 59 F6
Glyncoch Rhondda 34 E4
Glyncorrwg Neath 34 E2
Glynde E Sus 17 D8
Glyndebourne E Sus 17 C8
Glyndyfrdwy Denb 72 E5
Glynedd = Glyn-
neath Neath 34 D2
Glynogwr Bridgend 34 F3
Glyntaff Rhondda 34 F4
Glyntawe Powys 34 C2
Gnosall Staffs 62 B2
Gnosall Heath Staffs 62 B2
Goadby Leics 64 E4
Goadby Marwood Leics 64 B4
Goat Lees Kent 30 E4
Goatacre Wilts 24 B5
Goathill Dorset 12 C4
Goathland N Yorks 103 D6
Goathurst Som 22 F4
Gobernuisgach
Lodge Highld 156 E7
Gobhaig W Isles 154 G5
Gobowen Shrops 73 F7
Godalming Sur 27 E7
Godley Gtr Man 87 E7
Godmanchester Cambs 54 B3
Godmanstone Dorset 12 E4
Godmersham Kent 30 D4
Godney Som 23 E6
Godolphin Cross Corn 2 C5
Godre'r-graig Neath 34 D1
Godshill Hants 14 C2
Godshill IoW 15 F6
Godstone Sur 28 D4
Godwinscroft Hants 14 E2
Goetre Mon 35 D7
Goferydd Anglesey 82 C2
Goff's Oak Herts 41 D6
Gogar Edin 120 B4
Goginan Ceredig 58 F3
Golan Gwyn 71 C6
Golant Corn 5 D6
Golberdon Corn 5 B8
Golborne Gtr Man 86 E4
Golcar W Yorks 88 C2
Gold Hill Norf 66 E5
Goldcliff Newport 35 F7
Golden Cross E Sus 18 D2
Golden Green Kent 29 E7
Golden Grove Carms 33 C6

Golden Hill Hants 14 E3
Golden Pot Hants 26 E5
Golden Valley Glos 37 B6
Goldenhill Stoke 75 D5
Golders Green London 41 F5
Goldhanger Essex 43 D5
Golding Shrops 60 D5
Goldington Bedford 53 D8
Goldsborough N Yorks 95 D6
Goldsborough N Yorks 103 C6
Goldsithney Corn 2 C4
Goldsworthy Devon 9 B5
Goldthorpe S Yorks 89 D5
Gollanfield Highld 151 F11
Golspie Highld 157 J11
Golval Highld 157 C11
Gomeldon Wilts 25 F6
Gomersal W Yorks 88 B3
Gomshall Sur 27 E8
Gonalston Notts 77 E6
Gonfirth Shetland 160 G5
Good Easter Essex 42 C2
Gooderstone Norf 67 D7
Goodleigh Devon 20 F5
Goodmanham E Yorks 96 E4
Goodnestone Kent 30 C4
Goodnestone Kent 31 D6
Goodrich Hereford 36 C2
Goodrington Torbay 7 D6
Goodshaw Lancs 87 B6
Goodwick = Wdig Pembs 44 B4
Goodworth Clatford Hants 25 E8
Goole E Yorks 89 B8
Goonbell Corn 3 B6
Goonhavern Corn 4 D2
Goose Eye W Yorks 94 E3
Goose Green Gtr Man 86 D3
Goose Green Norf 68 F4
Goose Green W Sus 16 C5
Gooseham Corn 8 C4
Goosey Oxon 38 E3
Goosnargh Lancs 93 F5
Goostrey Ches E 74 B4
Gorcott Hill Warks 51 C5
Gord Shetland 160 L6
Gordon Borders 122 E2
Gordonbush Highld 157 J11
Gordonsburgh Moray 152 B4
Gordonstoun Moray 152 B1
Gordonstown Aberds 152 C5
Gordonstown Aberds 153 E7
Gore Kent 31 D7
Gore Cross Wilts 24 D5
Gore Pit Essex 42 C4
Gorebridge Midloth 121 C6
Gorefield Cambs 66 C4
Gorey Jersey 17
Gorgie Edin 120 B5
Goring Oxon 39 F6
Goring-by-Sea W Sus 16 D5
Goring Heath Oxon 26 B4
Gorleston-on-Sea Norf 69 D8
Gornalwood W Mid 62 E3
Gorrachie Aberds 153 C7
Gorran Churchtown Corn 3 B8
Gorran Haven Corn 3 B9
Gorrenberry Borders 115 E7
Gors Ceredig 46 B5
Gorse Hill Swindon 38 F1
Gorsedd Flint 73 B5
Gorseinon Swansea 33 E6
Gorseness Orkney 159 G5
Gorsgoch Ceredig 46 D3
Gorslas Carms 33 C6
Gorsley Glos 36 B3
Gorstan Highld 150 E6
Gorstanvorran Highld 130 B2
Gorsteyhill Staffs 74 D4
Gorsty Hill Staffs 62 B5
Gortantaoid Argyll 142 A4
Gorton Gtr Man 87 E6
Gosbeck Suff 57 D5
Gosberton Lincs 78 F5
Gosberton Clough Lincs 65 B8
Gosfield Essex 42 B3
Gosford Hereford 49 C7
Gosforth Cumb 98 D2
Gosforth T&W 110 C5
Gosmore Herts 40 B4
Gosport Hants 15 E7
Gossabrough Shetland 160 E7
Gossington Glos 36 D4
Goswick Northumb 123 E6
Gotham Notts 76 F5
Gotherington Glos 37 B6
Gott Shetland 160 J6
Goudhurst Kent 18 B4
Goulceby Lincs 79 B5
Gourdas Aberds 153 D7
Gourdon Aberds 135 B8
Gourock Invclyd 118 B2
Govan Glasgow 119 C5
Govanhill Glasgow 119 C5
Goveton Devon 7 E5
Govilon Mon 35 C6
Gowanhill Aberds 153 B10
Gowdall E Yorks 89 B7
Gowerton Swansea 33 E6
Gowkhall Fife 128 F2
Gowthorpe E Yorks 96 D3
Goxhill E Yorks 97 E7
Goxhill N Lincs 90 B5
Goxhill Haven N Lincs 90 B5
Goybre Neath 34 F1
Grabhair W Isles 155 F8
Graby Lincs 65 B7
Grade Corn 3 E6
Graffham W Sus 16 C3
Grafham Cambs 54 C2
Grafham Sur 27 E8
Grafton Hereford 49 F6
Grafton N Yorks 95 C7
Grafton Oxon 38 D2
Grafton Shrops 60 C4
Grafton Worcs 49 C7
Grafton Flyford Worcs 50 D4
Grafton Regis Northants 53 E5
Grafton Underwood Northants 65 F6
Grafty Green Kent 30 E2
Graianrhyd Denb 73 D6
Graig Conwy 83 D8
Graig Denb 72 B4
Graig-fechan Denb 72 D5
Grain Medway 30 B2
Grainsby Lincs 91 E6
Grainthorpe Lincs 91 E7
Grampound Corn 3 B8
Grampound Road Corn 4 D4
Gramsdal W Isles 148 C3
Granborough Bucks 39 B7
Granby Notts 77 F7
Grandborough Warks 52 C2
Grandtully Perth 133 D6
Grange Cumb 98 C4
Grange E Ayrs 118 F4
Grange Medway 29 C8
Grange Mers 85 F3
Grange Perth 128 B4
Grange Crossroads Moray 152 C4
Grange Hall Moray 151 E13
Grange Hill Essex 41 E7
Grange Moor W Yorks 88 C3
Grange of Lindores Fife 128 C4
Grange-over-Sands Cumb 92 B4
Grange Villa Durham 110 D5
Grangemill Derbys 76 D2
Grangemouth Falk 127 F8
Grangepans Falk 128 F2
Grangetown Cardiff 22 B3
Grangetown Redcar 102 B3
Granish Highld 138 C5
Gransmoor E Yorks 97 D7
Granston Pembs 44 B3
Grantchester Cambs 54 D5
Grantham Lincs 78 F2
Grantley N Yorks 94 C5
Grantlodge Aberds 141 C6
Granton Dumfries 114 D3
Granton Edin 120 B5
Grantown-on-Spey Highld 139 B6
Grantshouse Borders 122 C4
Grappenhall Warr 86 F4
Grasby Lincs 90 D4
Grasmere Cumb 99 D5
Grasscroft Gtr Man 87 D7
Grassendale Mers 85 F4
Grassholme Durham 100 B4
Grassington N Yorks 94 C3
Grassmoor Derbys 76 C4
Grassthorpe Notts 77 C7
Grateley Hants 25 E7
Gratwich Staffs 75 F7
Graveley Cambs 54 C3
Graveley Herts 41 B5
Gravelly Hill W Mid 62 E5
Gravels Shrops 60 D3
Graven Shetland 160 F6
Graveney Kent 30 C4
Gravesend Herts 41 B7
Gravesend Kent 29 B7
Grayingham Lincs 90 E3
Grayrigg Cumb 99 E7
Grays Thurrock 29 B7
Grayshott Hants 27 F6
Grayswood Sur 27 F7
Graythorp Hrtlpl 102 B3
Grazeley Wokingham 26 C4
Greasbrough S Yorks 88 E5
Greasby Mers 85 F3
Great Abington Cambs 55 E6
Great Addington Northants 53 B7
Great Alne Warks 51 D6
Great Altcar Lancs 85 D4
Great Amwell Herts 41 C6
Great Asby Cumb 100 C1
Great Ashfield Suff 56 C3
Great Ayton N Yorks 102 C3
Great Baddow Essex 42 D3
Great Bardfield Essex 55 F7
Great Barford Bedford 54 D2
Great Barr W Mid 62 E4
Great Barrington Glos 38 C2
Great Barrow Ches W 73 C8
Great Barton Suff 56 C2
Great Barugh N Yorks 96 B3
Great Bavington Northumb 117 F5
Great Bealings Suff 57 E6
Great Bedwyn Wilts 25 C7
Great Bentley Essex 43 B7
Great Billing Northants 53 C6
Great Bircham Norf 80 D3
Great Blakenham Suff 56 D5
Great Blencow Cumb 108 F4
Great Bolas Telford 61 B6
Great Bookham Sur 28 D2
Great Bourton Oxon 52 E2
Great Bowden Leics 64 F4
Great Bradley Suff 55 D7
Great Braxted Essex 42 C4
Great Bricett Suff 56 D4
Great Brickhill Bucks 53 F7
Great Bridge W Mid 62 E3
Great Bridgeford Staffs 62 B2
Great Brington Northants 52 C4
Great Bromley Essex 43 B6
Great Broughton Cumb 107 F7
Great Broughton N Yorks 102 D3
Great Budworth Ches W 74 B3
Great Burdon Darl 101 C8
Great Burgh Sur 28 D3
Great Burstead Essex 42 E2
Great Busby N Yorks 102 D3
Great Canfield Essex 42 C1
Great Carlton Lincs 91 F8
Great Casterton Rutland 65 D7
Great Chart Kent 30 E3
Great Chatwell Staffs 61 C7
Great Chesterford Essex 55 E6
Great Cheverell Wilts 24 D4
Great Chishill Cambs 54 F5
Great Clacton Essex 43 C7
Great Cliff W Yorks 88 C4
Great Clifton Cumb 98 B2
Great Coates NE Lincs 91 D6
Great Comberton Worcs 50 E4
Great Corby Cumb 108 D4
Great Cornard Suff 56 E2
Great Cowden E Yorks 97 E8
Great Coxwell Oxon 38 E2
Great Crakehall N Yorks 101 E7
Great Cransley Northants 53 B6
Great Cressingham Norf 67 D8
Great Crosby Mers 85 E4
Great Cubley Derbys 75 F8
Great Dalby Leics 64 C4
Great Denham Bedford 53 E8
Great Doddington Northants 53 C6
Great Dunham Norf 67 C8
Great Dunmow Essex 42 B2
Great Durnford Wilts 25 F6
Great Easton Essex 42 B2
Great Easton Leics 64 E5
Great Eccleston Lancs 92 E4
Great Edstone N Yorks 103 F5
Great Ellingham Norf 68 E3
Great Elm Som 24 E2
Great Eversden Cambs 54 D4
Great Fencote N Yorks 101 E7
Great Finborough Suff 56 D4
Great Fransham Norf 67 C8
Great Gaddesden Herts 40 C3
Great Gidding Cambs 65 F8
Great Givendale E Yorks 96 D4
Great Glemham Suff 57 C7
Great Glen Leics 64 E3
Great Gonerby Lincs 77 F8
Great Gransden Cambs 54 D3
Great Green Norf 69 F5
Great Green Suff 56 D3
Great Habton N Yorks 96 B3
Great Hale Lincs 78 E4
Great Hallingbury Essex 41 C8
Great Hampden Bucks 39 D8
Great Harrowden Northants 53 B6
Great Harwood Lancs 93 F7
Great Haseley Oxon 39 D6
Great Hatfield E Yorks 97 E7
Great Haywood Staffs 62 B4
Great Heath W Mid 63 F7
Great Heck N Yorks 89 B6
Great Henny Essex 56 F2
Great Hinton Wilts 24 D4
Great Hockham Norf 68 E2
Great Holland Essex 43 C8
Great Horkesley Essex 56 F3
Great Hormead Herts 41 B6
Great Horton W Yorks 94 F4
Great Horwood Bucks 53 F5
Great Houghton Northants 53 D5
Great Houghton S Yorks 88 D5
Great Hucklow Derbys 75 B8
Great Kelk E Yorks 97 D7
Great Kimble Bucks 39 D8
Great Kingshill Bucks 40 E1
Great Langton N Yorks 101 E7
Great Leighs Essex 42 C3
Great Lever Gtr Man 86 D5
Great Limber Lincs 90 D5
Great Linford M Keynes 53 E6
Great Livermere Suff 56 B2
Great Longstone Derbys 76 B2
Great Lumley Durham 111 E5
Great Lyth Shrops 60 D4
Great Malvern Worcs 50 E2
Great Maplestead Essex 56 F2
Great Marton Blackpool 92 F3
Great Massingham Norf 80 E3
Great Melton Norf 68 D4
Great Milton Oxon 39 D6
Great Missenden Bucks 40 D1
Great Mitton Lancs 93 F7
Great Mongeham Kent 31 D7
Great Moulton Norf 68 E4
Great Munden Herts 41 B6
Great Musgrave Cumb 100 C2
Great Ness Shrops 60 C3
Great Notley Essex 42 B3
Great Oakley Essex 43 B7
Great Oakley Northants 65 F5
Great Offley Herts 40 B4
Great Ormside Cumb 100 C2
Great Orton Cumb 108 D3
Great Ouseburn N Yorks 95 C7
Great Oxendon Northants 64 F4
Great Oxney Green Essex 42 D2
Great Palgrave Norf 67 C8
Great Parndon Essex 41 D7
Great Paxton Cambs 54 C3
Great Plumpton Lancs 92 F3
Great Plumstead Norf 69 C6
Great Ponton Lincs 78 F2
Great Preston W Yorks 88 B5
Great Raveley Cambs 66 F2
Great Rissington Glos 38 C1
Great Rollright Oxon 51 F8
Great Ryburgh Norf 81 E5
Great Ryle Northumb 117 C6
Great Ryton Shrops 60 D4
Great Saling Essex 42 B3
Great Salkeld Cumb 109 F5
Great Sampford Essex 55 F7
Great Sankey Warr 86 F3
Great Saxham Suff 55 C8
Great Shefford W Berks 25 B8
Great Shelford Cambs 55 D5
Great Smeaton N Yorks 101 D8
Great Snoring Norf 80 D5
Great Somerford Wilts 37 F6
Great Stainton Darl 101 B8
Great Stambridge Essex 42 E4
Great Staughton Cambs 54 C2
Great Steeping Lincs 79 C7
Great Stonar Kent 31 D7
Great Strickland Cumb 99 B7
Great Stukeley Cambs 54 B3
Great Sturton Lincs 78 B5
Great Sutton Ches W 73 B7
Great Sutton Shrops 60 F5
Great Swinburne Northumb 110 B2
Great Tew Oxon 38 B3
Great Tey Essex 42 B4
Great Thurkleby N Yorks 95 B7
Great Thurlow Suff 55 D7
Great Torrington Devon 9 C6
Great Tosson Northumb 117 D6
Great Totham Essex 42 C4
Great Totham Essex 42 C4
Great Tows Lincs 91 E6
Great Urswick Cumb 92 B2
Great Wakering Essex 43 F5
Great Waldingfield Suff 56 E3
Great Walsingham Norf 80 D5
Great Waltham Essex 42 C2
Great Warley Essex 42 E1
Great Washbourne Glos 50 F4
Great Weldon Northants 65 F6
Great Welnetham Suff 56 D2
Great Wenham Suff 56 F4
Great Whittington Northumb 110 B3
Great Wigborough Essex 43 C5
Great Wilbraham Cambs 55 D6
Great Wishford Wilts 25 F5
Great Witcombe Glos 37 C6
Great Witley Worcs 50 C2
Great Wolford Warks 51 F7
Great Wratting Suff 55 E7
Great Wymondley Herts 41 B5
Great Wyrley Staffs 62 D3
Great Wytheford Shrops 61 C5
Great Yarmouth Norf 69 D8
Great Yeldham Essex 55 F8
Greater Doward Hereford 36 C2
Greatford Lincs 65 C7
Greatgate Staffs 75 E7
Greatham Hants 27 F5
Greatham Hrtlpl 102 B2
Greatham W Sus 16 C4
Greatstone on Sea Kent 19 C7
Greatworth Northants 52 E3
Greave Lancs 87 B6
Greeba IoM 84 D3
Green Denb 72 C4
Green End Bedford 54 D2
Green Hammerton N Yorks 95 D7
Green Lane Powys 59 E8
Green Ore Som 23 D7
Green St Green London 29 C5
Green Street Herts 40 E4
Greenbank Shetland 160 C7
Greenburn W Loth 120 C2
Greendikes Northumb 117 B6
Greenfield C Beds 53 F8
Greenfield Flint 73 B6
Greenfield Gtr Man 87 D7
Greenfield Highld 136 D5
Greenfield Oxon 39 E7
Greenford London 40 F4
Greengairs N Lanark 119 B7
Greenham W Berks 26 C2
Greenhaugh Northumb 116 F3
Greenhead Northumb 109 C6
Greenhill Falk 119 B8
Greenhill Kent 31 C5
Greenhill Leics 63 C8
Greenhill London 40 F4
Greenhills N Ayrs 118 D3
Greenhithe Kent 29 B6
Greenholm E Ayrs 118 F5
Greenholme Cumb 99 D7
Greenhouse Borders 115 B8
Greenhow Hill N Yorks 94 C4
Greenigoe Orkney 159 H5
Greenland Highld 158 D4
Greenlands Bucks 39 F7
Greenlaw Aberds 153 C6
Greenlaw Borders 122 E3
Greenlea Dumfries 107 B7
Greenloaning Perth 127 D7
Greenmount Gtr Man 87 C5
Greenmow Shetland 160 L6
Greenock Invclyd 118 B2
Greenock West Invclyd 118 B2
Greenodd Cumb 99 F5
Greenrow Cumb 107 D8
Greens Norton Northants 52 E4
Greenside T&W 110 C4
Greensidehill Northumb 117 C5
Greenstead Green Essex 42 B4
Greensted Essex 41 D8
Greenwich London 28 B4
Greet Glos 50 F5
Greete Shrops 49 B7
Greetham Lincs 79 B6
Greetham Rutland 65 C6
Greetland W Yorks 87 B8
Gregg Hall Cumb 99 E6
Gregson Lane Lancs 86 B3
Greinetobht W Isles 148 A3
Greinton Som 23 F6
Gremista Shetland 160 J6
Grenaby IoM 84 E2
Grendon Northants 53 C6
Grendon Warks 63 D6
Grendon Common Warks 63 E6
Grendon Green Hereford 49 D7
Grendon Underwood Bucks 39 B6
Grenofen Devon 6 B2
Grenoside S Yorks 88 E4
Greosabhagh W Isles 154 H6
Gresford Wrex 73 D7
Gresham Norf 81 D7
Greshornish Highld 149 C8
Gressenhall Norf 68 C2
Gressingham Lancs 93 C5
Gresty Green Ches E 74 D4
Greta Bridge Durham 101 C5
Gretna Dumfries 108 C3
Gretna Green Dumfries 108 C3
Gretton Glos 50 F5
Gretton Northants 65 E5
Gretton Shrops 60 E5
Grewelthorpe N Yorks 94 B5
Grey Green N Lincs 89 D8
Greygarth N Yorks 94 B4
Greynor Carms 33 D6
Greysouthen Cumb 98 B2
Greystoke Cumb 108 F4
Greystone Angus 135 E5
Greystone Dumfries 107 B6
Greywell Hants 26 D5
Griais W Isles 155 C9
Grianan W Isles 155 D9
Gribthorpe E Yorks 96 F3
Gridley Corner Devon 9 E5
Griff Warks 63 F7
Griffithstown Torf 35 E6
Grimbister Orkney 159 G4
Grimblethorpe Lincs 91 F6
Grimeford Village Lancs 86 C4
Grimethorpe S Yorks 88 D5
Griminis W Isles 148 C2
Grimister Shetland 160 D6
Grimley Worcs 50 C3
Grimness Orkney 159 J5
Grimoldby Lincs 91 F7
Grimpo Shrops 60 B3
Grimsargh Lancs 93 F5
Grimsbury Oxon 52 E2
Grimsby NE Lincs 91 C6
Grimscote Northants 52 D4
Grimscott Corn 8 D4
Grimsthorpe Lincs 65 B7
Grimston E Yorks 97 F8
Grimston Leics 64 B3
Grimston Norf 80 E3
Grimston York 96 D2
Grimstone Dorset 12 E4
Grinacombe Moor Devon 9 E6
Grindale E Yorks 97 B7
Grindigar Orkney 159 H6
Grindiscol Shetland 160 K6
Grindle Shrops 61 D7
Grindleford Derbys 76 B2
Grindleton Lancs 93 E7
Grindley Staffs 62 B4
Grindley Brook Shrops 74 E2
Grindlow Derbys 75 B8
Grindon Northumb 122 E5
Grindon Staffs 75 D7
Grindonmoor Gate Staffs 75 D7
Gringley on the Hill Notts 89 E8
Grinsdale Cumb 108 D3
Grinshill Shrops 60 B5
Grinton N Yorks 101 E5
Griomsidar W Isles 155 E8
Grishipoll Argyll 146 F4
Grisling Common E Sus 17 B8
Gristhorpe N Yorks 103 F8
Griston Norf 68 E2
Gritley Orkney 159 H6
Grittenham Wilts 37 F7
Grittleton Wilts 37 F5
Grizebeck Cumb 98 F4
Grizedale Cumb 99 E5
Grobister Orkney 159 F7
Groby Leics 64 D2
Groes Conwy 72 C4
Groes Neath 34 F1
Groes-faen Rhondda 34 F4
Groes-lwyd Powys 60 C2
Groesffordd Marli Denb 72 B4
Groeslon Gwyn 82 E5
Groeslon Gwyn 82 F4
Grogport Argyll 143 D9
Gromford Suff 57 D7
Gronant Flint 72 A4
Groombridge E Sus 18 B2
Grosmont Mon 35 B8
Grosmont N Yorks 103 D6
Groton Suff 56 E3
Grougfoot Falk 120 B3
Grouville Jersey 17
Grove Dorset 12 G5
Grove Kent 31 C6
Grove Notts 77 B7
Grove Oxon 38 E4
Grove Park London 28 B5
Grove Vale W Mid 62 E4
Grovesend Swansea 33 D6
Grudie Highld 150 E6
Gruids Highld 157 J8
Gruinard House Highld 150 B2
Grula Highld 149 F8
Gruline Argyll 147 G8
Grunasound Shetland 160 K5
Grundisburgh Suff 57 D6
Grunsagill Lancs 93 D7
Gruting Shetland 160 J4
Grutness Shetland 160 N6
Gualachulain Highld 131 E5
Gualin Ho. Highld 156 D6
Guardbridge Fife 129 C6
Guarlford Worcs 50 E3
Guay Perth 133 E7
Guestling Green E Sus 19 D5
Guestling Thorn E Sus 18 D5
Guestwick Norf 81 E6
Guestwick Green Norf 81 E6
Guide Blackburn 86 B5
Guide Post Northumb 117 F8
Guilden Morden Cambs 54 E3
Guilden Sutton Ches W 73 C8
Guildford Sur 27 E7
Guildtown Perth 133 F8
Guilsborough Northants 52 B4
Guilsfield Powys 60 C2
Guilton Kent 31 D6
Guineaford Devon 20 F4
Guisborough Redcar 102 C4
Guiseley W Yorks 94 E4
Guist Norf 81 E5
Guith Orkney 159 E6
Guiting Power Glos 37 B7
Gulberwick Shetland 160 K6
Gullane E Loth 129 F6
Gulval Corn 2 C3
Gulworthy Devon 6 B2
Gumfreston Pembs 32 D2
Gumley Leics 64 E3
Gummow's Shop Corn 4 D3
Gun Hill E Sus 18 D2
Gunby E Yorks 96 F3
Gunby Lincs 65 B6
Gundleton Hants 26 F4
Gunn Devon 20 F5
Gunnerside N Yorks 100 E4
Gunnerton Northumb 110 B2
Gunness N Lincs 90 C2
Gunnislake Corn 6 B2
Gunnista Shetland 160 J7
Gunthorpe Norf 81 D6
Gunthorpe Notts 77 E6
Gunthorpe Pboro 65 D8
Gunville IoW 15 F5
Gunwalloe Corn 3 D5
Gurnard IoW 15 E5
Gurnett Ches E 75 B6
Gurney Slade Som 23 E8
Gurnos Powys 34 D1
Gussage All Saints Dorset 13 C8
Gussage St Michael Dorset 13 C7
Guston Kent 31 E7
Gutcher Shetland 160 D7
Guthrie Angus 135 D5
Guyhirn Cambs 66 D3
Guyhirn Gull Cambs 66 D3
Guy's Head Lincs 66 B4
Guy's Marsh Dorset 13 B6
Guyzance Northumb 117 D8
Gwaenysgor Flint 72 A4
Gwalchmai Anglesey 82 D3
Gwaun-Cae-Gurwen Neath 33 C8
Gwaun-Leision Neath 33 C8
Gwbert Ceredig 45 E3
Gweek Corn 3 D6
Gwehelog Mon 35 D7
Gwenddwr Powys 48 E2
Gwennap Corn 3 C6
Gwenter Corn 3 E6
Gwernaffield Flint 73 C6
Gwernesney Mon 35 D8
Gwernogle Carms 46 F4
Gwernymynydd Flint 73 C6
Gwersyllt Wrex 73 D7
Gwespyr Flint 85 F2
Gwithian Corn 2 B4
Gwredog Anglesey 82 C4
Gwyddelwern Denb 72 E4
Gwyddgrug Carms 46 F3
Gwydyr Uchaf Conwy 83 E7
Gwynfryn Wrex 73 D6
Gwystre Powys 48 C2
Gwytherin Conwy 83 E8
Gyfelia Wrex 73 E7
Gyffin Conwy 83 D7
Gyre Orkney 159 H4
Gyrn-goch Gwyn 70 C5

H

Habberley Shrops 60 D3
Habergham Lancs 93 F8
Habrough NE Lincs 90 C5
Haceby Lincs 78 F3
Hacheston Suff 57 D7
Hackbridge London 28 C3
Hackenthorpe S Yorks 88 F5
Hackford Norf 68 D3
Hackforth N Yorks 101 E7
Hackland Orkney 159 F4
Hackleton Northants 53 D6
Hackness N Yorks 103 E7
Hackness Orkney 159 J4
Hackney London 41 F6
Hackthorn Lincs 90 F3
Hackthorpe Cumb 99 B7
Haconby Lincs 65 B8
Hacton London 41 F8
Hadden Borders 122 F3
Haddenham Bucks 39 D7
Haddenham Cambs 55 B5
Haddington E Loth 121 B8
Haddington Lincs 78 C2
Haddiscoe Norf 69 E7
Haddon Cambs 65 E8
Haddon Ches E 75 C6
Hade Edge W Yorks 88 D2
Hademore Staffs 63 D5
Hadfield Derbys 87 E8
Hadham Cross Herts 41 C7
Hadham Ford Herts 41 B7
Hadleigh Essex 42 F4
Hadleigh Suff 56 E4
Hadley Telford 61 C6
Hadley End Staffs 62 B5
Hadlow Kent 29 E7
Hadlow Down E Sus 18 C2
Hadnall Shrops 60 C5
Hadstock Essex 55 E6
Hady Derbys 76 B3
Hadzor Worcs 50 C4
Haffenden Quarter Kent 30 E2
Hafod-Dinbych Conwy 83 F8
Hafod-Iom Conwy 83 D8
Haggate Lancs 93 F8
Haggbeck Cumb 108 B4
Haggerston Northumb 123 E6
Haggrister Shetland 160 F5
Hagley Hereford 49 E7
Hagley Worcs 62 F3
Hagworthingham Lincs 79 C6
Haigh Gtr Man 86 D4
Haigh S Yorks 88 C3
Haigh Moor W Yorks 88 B3
Haighton Green Lancs 93 F5
Hail Weston Cambs 54 C2
Haile Cumb 98 D2
Hailes Glos 50 F5
Hailey Herts 41 C6
Hailey Oxon 38 C3
Hailsham E Sus 18 E2
Haimer Highld 158 D3
Hainault London 41 E7
Hainford Norf 68 C5
Hainton Lincs 91 F5
Hairmyres S Lanark 119 D6
Haisthorpe E Yorks 97 C7
Hakin Pembs 44 E3
Halam Notts 77 D6
Halbeath Fife 128 F3
Halberton Devon 10 C5
Halcro Highld 158 D4
Hale Gtr Man 87 F5
Hale Halton 86 F2
Hale Hants 14 C2
Hale Bank Halton 86 F2
Hale Street Kent 29 E7
Halebarns Gtr Man 87 F5
Hales Norf 69 E6
Hales Staffs 74 F4
Hales Place Kent 30 D5
Halesfield Telford 61 D7
Halesgate Lincs 66 B3
Halesowen W Mid 62 F3
Halesworth Suff 57 B7
Halewood Mers 86 F2
Halford Shrops 60 F4
Halford Warks 51 E7
Halfpenny Furze Carms 32 C3
Halfpenny Green Staffs 62 E2
Halfway Carms 46 F5
Halfway Carms 47 F7
Halfway W Berks 26 C2
Halfway Bridge W Sus 16 B3
Halfway House Shrops 60 C3
Halfway Houses Kent 30 B3
Halifax W Yorks 87 B8
Halket E Ayrs 118 D4
Halkirk Highld 158 E3
Halkyn Flint 73 B6
Hall Dunnerdale Cumb 98 E4
Hall Green W Mid 62 F5
Hall Green W Yorks 88 C4
Hall Grove Herts 41 C5
Hall of Tankerness Orkney 159 H6
Hall of the Forest Shrops 60 F2
Halland E Sus 18 D2
Hallaton Leics 64 E4
Hallatrow Bath 23 D8
Hallbankgate Cumb 109 D5
Hallen S Glos 36 F2
Halliburton Borders 122 E2
Hallin Highld 148 C7
Halling Medway 29 C8
Hallington Lincs 91 F7
Hallington Northumb 110 B2
Halliwell Gtr Man 86 C5
Halloughton Notts 77 D6
Hallow Worcs 50 D3
Hallrule Borders 115 C8
Halls E Loth 122 B2
Hall's Green Herts 41 B5
Hallsands Devon 7 F6
Hallthwaites Cumb 98 F3
Hallworthy Corn 8 F3
Hallyburton House Perth 134 F2
Hallyne Borders 120 E4
Halmer End Staffs 74 E4
Halmore Glos 36 D3
Halmyre Mains Borders 120 E4
Halnaker W Sus 16 D3
Halsall Lancs 85 C4
Halse Northants 52 E3
Halse Som 11 B6
Halsetown Corn 2 C4
Halsham E Yorks 91 B6
Halsinger Devon 20 F4
Halstead Essex 56 F2
Halstead Kent 29 C5
Halstead Leics 64 D4
Halstock Dorset 12 D3
Haltham Lincs 78 C5
Haltoft End Lincs 79 E6
Halton Bucks 40 C1
Halton Halton 86 F3
Halton Lancs 92 C5
Halton Northumb 110 C2
Halton W Yorks 95 F6
Halton Wrex 73 F7
Halton East N Yorks 94 D3
Halton Gill N Yorks 93 B8
Halton Holegate Lincs 79 C7
Halton Lea Gate Northumb 109 D6
Halton West N Yorks 93 D8
Haltwhistle Northumb 109 C7
Halvergate Norf 69 D7
Halwell Devon 7 D5
Halwill Devon 9 E6
Halwill Junction Devon 9 D6
Ham Devon 11 D7
Ham Glos 36 E3
Ham Highld 158 C4
Ham Kent 31 D7
Ham London 28 B2
Ham Shetland 160 K1
Ham Wilts 25 C8
Ham Common Dorset 13 B6
Ham Green Hereford 50 E2
Ham Green Kent 19 C5
Ham Green Kent 30 C2
Ham Green N Som 23 B7
Ham Green Worcs 50 C5
Ham Street Som 23 F7
Hamble-le-Rice Hants 15 D5
Hambleden Bucks 39 F7
Hambledon Hants 15 C7
Hambledon Sur 27 F7
Hambleton Lancs 92 E3
Hambleton N Yorks 95 F8
Hambridge Som 11 B8
Hambrook S Glos 23 B8
Hambrook W Sus 15 D8
Hameringham Lincs 79 C6
Hamerton Cambs 54 B2
Hametoun Shetland 160 K1
Hamilton S Lanark 119 D7
Hammer W Sus 27 F6
Hammerpot W Sus 16 D4
Hammersmith London 28 B3
Hammerwich Staffs 62 D4
Hammerwood E Sus 28 F5
Hammond Street Herts 41 D6
Hammoon Dorset 13 C6
Hamnavoe Shetland 160 E4
Hamnavoe Shetland 160 E6
Hamnavoe Shetland 160 F6
Hamnavoe Shetland 160 K5
Hampden Park E Sus 18 E3
Hamperden End Essex 55 F6
Hampnett Glos 37 C7
Hampole S Yorks 89 C6
Hampreston Dorset 13 E8
Hampstead London 41 F5
Hampstead Norreys W Berks 26 B3
Hampsthwaite N Yorks 95 D5
Hampton London 28 C2
Hampton Shrops 61 F7
Hampton Worcs 50 E5
Hampton Bishop Hereford 49 F7
Hampton Heath Ches W 73 E8
Hampton in Arden W Mid 63 F6
Hampton Loade Shrops 61 F7
Hampton Lovett Worcs 50 C3
Hampton Lucy Warks 51 D7
Hampton on the Hill Warks 51 C7
Hampton Poyle Oxon 39 C5
Hamrow Norf 80 E5
Hamsey E Sus 17 C8
Hamsey Green London 28 D4
Hamstall Ridware Staffs 62 C5
Hamstead IoW 14 E5
Hamstead W Mid 62 E4
Hamstead Marshall W Berks 26 C2
Hamsterley Durham 110 D4
Hamsterley Durham 110 F4
Hamstreet Kent 19 B7
Hamworthy Poole 13 E7
Hanbury Staffs 63 B5
Hanbury Worcs 50 C4
Hanbury Woodend Staffs 63 B5
Hanby Lincs 78 F3
Hanchurch Staffs 74 E5
Handbridge Ches W 73 C8
Handcross W Sus 17 B6
Handforth Ches E 87 F6
Handley Ches W 73 D8
Handsacre Staffs 62 C4
Handsworth S Yorks 88 F5
Handsworth W Mid 62 E4
Handy Cross Devon 9 B6
Hanford Stoke 75 E5
Hanging Langford Wilts 24 F5
Hangleton W Sus 16 D4
Hanham S Glos 23 B8
Hankelow Ches E 74 E3
Hankerton Wilts 37 E6
Hankham E Sus 18 E3
Hanley Stoke 75 E5
Hanley Castle Worcs 50 E3
Hanley Child Worcs 49 C8
Hanley Swan Worcs 50 E3
Hanley William Worcs 49 C8
Hanlith N Yorks 94 C2
Hanmer Wrex 73 F8
Hannah Lincs 79 B8
Hannington Hants 26 D3
Hannington Northants 53 B6
Hannington Swindon 38 E1
Hannington Wick Swindon 38 E1
Hansel Village S Ayrs 118 F3
Hanslope M Keynes 53 E6
Hanthorpe Lincs 65 B7
Hanwell London 40 F4
Hanwell Oxon 52 E2
Hanwood Shrops 60 D4
Hanworth London 28 B2
Hanworth Norf 81 D7
Happendon S Lanark 119 F8
Happisburgh Norf 69 A6
Happisburgh Common Norf 69 B6
Hapsford Ches W 73 B8
Hapton Lancs 93 F7
Hapton Norf 68 E4
Harberton Devon 7 D5
Harbertonford Devon 7 D5
Harbledown Kent 30 D5
Harborne W Mid 62 F4
Harborough Magna Warks 52 B2
Harbottle Northumb 117 D5
Harbury Warks 51 D8
Harby Leics 77 F7
Harby Notts 77 B8
Harcombe Devon 11 E6
Harden W Mid 62 D4
Harden W Yorks 94 F3
Hardenhuish Wilts 24 B4
Hardgate Aberds 141 D6
Hardham W Sus 16 C4
Hardingham Norf 68 D3
Hardingstone Northants 53 D5
Hardington Som 24 D2
Hardington Mandeville Som 12 C3
Hardington Marsh Som 12 D3
Hardley Hants 14 D5
Hardley Street Norf 69 D6
Hardmead M Keynes 53 E7
Hardrow N Yorks 100 E3
Hardstoft Derbys 76 C4
Hardway Hants 15 D7
Hardway Som 24 F2
Hardwick Bucks 39 C8
Hardwick Cambs 54 D4
Hardwick Norf 67 C6
Hardwick Norf 68 F5
Hardwick Northants 53 C6
Hardwick Notts 77 B6
Hardwick Oxon 38 D3
Hardwick Oxon 39 B5
Hardwick W Mid 62 E4
Hardwicke Glos 36 C4
Hardwicke Glos 37 B6
Hardwicke Hereford 48 E4
Hardy's Green Essex 43 B5
Hare Green Essex 43 B6
Hare Hatch Wokingham 27 B6
Hare Street Herts 41 B6
Hareby Lincs 79 C6
Hareden Lancs 93 D6
Harefield London 40 E3
Harehills W Yorks 95 F6
Harehope Northumb 117 B6
Haresceugh Cumb 109 E6
Harescombe Glos 37 C5
Haresfield Glos 37 C5
Hareshaw N Lanark 119 C8
Hareshaw Head Northumb 116 F4
Harewood W Yorks 95 E6
Harewood End Hereford 36 B2
Harford Carms 46 E5
Harford Devon 6 D4
Hargate Norf 68 E4
Hargatewall Derbys 75 B8
Hargrave Ches W 73 C8
Hargrave Northants 53 B8
Hargrave Suff 55 D8
Harker Cumb 108 C3
Harkland Shetland 160 E6
Harkstead Suff 57 F5
Harlaston Staffs 63 C6
Harlaw Ho. Aberds 141 B6
Harlaxton Lincs 77 F8
Harle Syke Lancs 93 F8
Harlech Gwyn 71 D6
Harlequin Notts 77 F6
Harlescott Shrops 60 C5
Harlesden London 41 F5
Harleston Devon 7 E5
Harleston Norf 68 F5
Harleston Suff 56 D4
Harlestone Northants 52 C5
Harley S Yorks 88 E4
Harley Shrops 61 D5
Harleyholm S Lanark 120 F2
Harlington C Beds 53 F8
Harlington London 27 B8
Harlington S Yorks 89 D5
Harlosh Highld 149 D7
Harlow Essex 41 C7
Harlow Hill N Yorks 95 D5
Harlow Hill Northumb 110 C3
Harlthorpe E Yorks 96 F3
Harlton Cambs 54 D4
Harman's Cross Dorset 13 F7
Harmby N Yorks 101 F6
Harmer Green Herts 41 C5
Harmer Hill Shrops 60 B4
Harmondsworth London 27 B8
Harmston Lincs 78 C2
Harnham Northumb 110 B3
Harnhill Glos 37 D7
Harold Hill London 41 E8
Harold Wood London 41 E8
Haroldston West Pembs 44 D3
Haroldswick Shetland 160 B8
Harome N Yorks 102 F4
Harpenden Herts 40 C4
Harpford Devon 11 E5
Harpham E Yorks 97 C6
Harpley Norf 80 E3
Harpley Worcs 49 C8
Harpole Northants 52 C4
Harpsdale Highld 158 E3
Harpsden Oxon 39 F7
Harpswell Lincs 90 F3
Harpur Hill Derbys 75 B7
Harpurhey Gtr Man 87 D6
Harraby Cumb 108 D4
Harrapool Highld 149 F11
Harrier Shetland 160 J1
Harrietfield Perth 127 B8
Harrietsham Kent 30 D2
Harrington Cumb 98 B1
Harrington Lincs 79 B6
Harrington Northants 64 F4
Harringworth Northants 65 E6
Harris Highld 146 B6
Harrogate N Yorks 95 D6
Harrold Bedford 53 D7
Harrow London 40 F4
Harrow on the Hill London 40 F4
Harrow Street Suff 56 F3
Harrow Weald London 40 E4
Harrowbarrow Corn 5 C8
Harrowden Bedford 53 E8
Harrowgate Hill Darl 101 C7
Harston Cambs 54 D5
Harston Leics 77 F8
Harswell E Yorks 96 E4
Hart Hrtlpl 111 F7
Hart Common Gtr Man 86 D4
Hart Hill Luton 40 B4
Hart Station Hrtlpl 111 F7
Hartburn Northumb 117 F6
Hartburn Stockton 102 C2
Hartest Suff 56 D2
Hartfield E Sus 29 F5
Hartford Cambs 54 B3
Hartford Ches W 74 B3
Hartford End Essex 42 C2
Hartfordbridge Hants 27 D5
Hartforth N Yorks 101 D6
Harthill Ches W 74 D2
Harthill N Lanark 120 C2
Harthill S Yorks 89 F5
Hartington Derbys 75 C8
Hartland Devon 8 B4
Hartlebury Worcs 50 B3
Hartlepool Hrtlpl 111 F8
Hartley Cumb 100 D2
Hartley Kent 18 B4
Hartley Kent 29 C7
Hartley Northumb 111 B6
Hartley Westpall Hants 26 D4
Hartley Wintney Hants 27 D5
Hartlip Kent 30 C2
Hartoft End N Yorks 103 E5
Harton N Yorks 96 C3
Harton Shrops 60 F4
Harton T&W 111 C6
Hartpury Glos 36 B4
Hartshead W Yorks 88 B2
Hartshill Warks 63 E7
Hartshorne Derbys 63 B7
Hartsop Cumb 99 C6
Hartwell Northants 53 D5
Hartwood N Lanark 119 D8
Harvieston Stirling 126 F4
Harvington Worcs 51 E5
Harvington Cross Worcs 51 E5
Harwell Oxon 38 F4
Harwich Essex 57 F6
Harwood Durham 109 F8
Harwood Gtr Man 86 C5
Harwood Dale N Yorks 103 E7
Harworth Notts 89 E7
Hasbury W Mid 62 F3
Hascombe Sur 27 E7
Haselbech Northants 52 B5
Haselbury Plucknett Som 12 C2
Haseley Warks 51 C7
Haselor Warks 51 D6
Hasfield Glos 37 B5
Hasguard Pembs 44 E3
Haskayne Lancs 85 D4
Hasketon Suff 57 D6
Hasland Derbys 76 C3
Haslemere Sur 27 F7
Haslingden Lancs 87 B5
Haslingfield Cambs 54 D5
Haslington Ches E 74 D4
Hassall Ches E 74 D4
Hassall Green Ches E 74 D4
Hassell Street Kent 30 E4
Hassendean Borders 115 B8
Hassingham Norf 69 D6
Hassocks W Sus 17 C6
Hassop Derbys 76 B2
Hastigrow Highld 158 D4
Hastingleigh Kent 30 E4
Hastings E Sus 18 E5
Hastingwood Essex 41 D7
Hastoe Herts 40 D2
Haswell Durham 111 E6
Haswell Plough Durham 111 E6
Hatch C Beds 54 E2
Hatch Hants 26 D4
Hatch Wilts 13 B7
Hatch Beauchamp Som 11 B8
Hatch End London 40 E4
Hatch Green Som 11 C8
Hatchet Gate Hants 14 D4
Hatching Green Herts 40 C4
Hatchmere Ches W 74 B2
Hatcliffe NE Lincs 91 D6
Hatfield Hereford 49 D7
Hatfield Herts 41 D5
Hatfield S Yorks 89 C7
Hatfield Worcs 50 D3
Hatfield Broad Oak Essex 41 C8
Hatfield Garden Village Herts 41 D5
Hatfield Heath Essex 41 C8
Hatfield Hyde Herts 41 C5
Hatfield Peverel Essex 42 C3
Hatfield Woodhouse S Yorks 89 D7
Hatford Oxon 38 E3
Hatherden Hants 25 D8
Hatherleigh Devon 9 D7
Hathern Leics 63 B8
Hatherop Glos 38 D1
Hathersage Derbys 88 F3
Hathershaw Gtr Man 87 D7

Hatherton Ches E 74 E3
Hatherton Staffs 62 C3
Hatley St George Cambs 54 D3
Hatt Corn 5 C8
Hattingley Hants 26 F4
Hatton Aberds 153 E10
Hatton Derbys 63 B6
Hatton Lincs 78 B4
Hatton Shrops 60 E4
Hatton Warks 51 C7
Hatton Warr 86 F3
Hatton Castle Aberds 153 D7
Hatton Heath Ches W 73 C8
Hatton of Fintray Aberds 141 C7
Hattoncrook Aberds 141 B7
Haugh E Ayrs 112 B4
Haugh Gtr Man 87 C7
Haugh Lincs 79 B7
Haugh Head Northumb 117 B6
Haugh of Glass Moray 152 E4
Haugh of Urr Dumfries 106 C5
Haugham Lincs 91 F7
Haughley Suff 56 C4
Haughley Green Suff 56 C4
Haughs of Clinterty Aberdeen 141 C7
Haughton Notts 77 B6
Haughton Shrops 60 B3
Haughton Shrops 61 C5
Haughton Shrops 61 D7
Haughton Shrops 61 E6
Haughton Staffs 62 B2
Haughton Castle Northumb 110 B2
Haughton Green Gtr Man 87 E7
Haughton Moss Ches E 74 D2
Haultwick Herts 41 B6
Haunn Argyll 146 G6
Haunn W Isles 148 G2
Haunton Staffs 63 C6
Hauxley Northumb 117 D8
Hauxton Cambs 54 D5
Havant Hants 15 D8
Haven Hereford 49 D6
Haven Bank Lincs 78 D5
Haven Side E Yorks 91 B5
Havenstreet IoW 15 E6
Havercroft W Yorks 88 C4
Haverfordwest = Hwlffordd Pembs 44 D4
Haverhill Suff 55 E7
Haverigg Cumb 92 B1
Havering-atte-Bower London 41 E8
Haveringland Norf 81 E7
Haversham M Keynes 53 E6
Haverthwaite Cumb 99 F5
Haverton Hill Stockton 102 B2
Hawarden = Penarlâg Flint 73 C7
Hawcoat Cumb 92 B2
Hawen Ceredig 46 E2
Hawes N Yorks 100 F3
Hawes' Green Norf 68 E5
Hawes Side Blackpool 92 F3
Hawford Worcs 50 C3
Hawick Borders 115 C8
Hawk Green Gtr Man 87 F7
Hawkchurch Devon 11 D8
Hawkedon Suff 55 D8
Hawkenbury Kent 18 B2
Hawkenbury Kent 30 E2
Hawkeridge Wilts 24 D3
Hawkerland Devon 11 F5
Hawkes End W Mid 63 F7
Hawkesbury S Glos 36 F4
Hawkesbury Warks 63 F7
Hawkesbury Upton S Glos 36 F4
Hawkhill Northumb 117 C8
Hawkhurst Kent 18 B4
Hawkinge Kent 31 F6
Hawkley Hants 15 B8
Hawkridge Som 21 F7
Hawkshead Cumb 99 E5
Hawkshead Hill Cumb 99 E5
Hawksland S Lanark 119 F8
Hawkswick N Yorks 94 B2
Hawksworth Notts 77 E7
Hawksworth W Yorks 94 E4
Hawksworth W Yorks 95 F5
Hawkwell Essex 42 E4
Hawley Hants 27 D6
Hawley Kent 29 B6
Hawling Glos 37 B7
Hawnby N Yorks 102 F3
Haworth W Yorks 94 F3
Hawstead Suff 56 D2
Hawthorn Durham 111 E7
Hawthorn Rhondda 35 F5
Hawthorn Wilts 24 C3
Hawthorn Hill Brack 27 B6
Hawthorn Hill Lincs 78 D5
Hawthorpe Lincs 65 B7
Hawton Notts 77 D7
Haxby York 96 D2
Haxey N Lincs 89 D8
Hay Green Norf 66 C5
Hay-on-Wye = Y Gelli Gandryll Powys 48 E4
Hay Street Herts 41 B6
Haydock Mers 86 E3
Haydon Dorset 12 C4
Haydon Bridge Northumb 109 C8
Haydon Wick Swindon 37 F8
Haye Corn 5 C8
Hayes London 28 C5
Hayes London 40 F4
Hayfield Derbys 87 F8
Hayfield Fife 128 E4
Hayhill E Ayrs 112 C4
Hayhillock Angus 135 E5
Hayle Corn 2 C4
Haynes C Beds 53 E8
Haynes Church End C Beds 53 E8
Hayscastle Pembs 44 C3
Hayscastle Cross Pembs 44 C4
Hayshead Angus 135 E6
Hayton Aberdeen 141 D8
Hayton Cumb 107 E8
Hayton Cumb 108 D5
Hayton E Yorks 96 E4
Hayton Notts 89 F8
Hayton's Bent Shrops 60 F5
Haytor Vale Devon 7 B5
Haywards Heath W Sus 17 B7
Haywood S Yorks 89 C6
Haywood Oaks Notts 77 D6
Hazel Grove Gtr Man 87 F7
Hazel Street Kent 18 B3
Hazelbank S Lanark 119 E8
Hazelbury Bryan Dorset 12 D5
Hazeley Hants 26 D5
Hazelhurst Gtr Man 87 D7
Hazelslade Staffs 62 C4
Hazelton Glos 37 C7
Hazelton Walls Fife 128 B5
Hazelwood Derbys 76 E3
Hazlemere Bucks 40 E1
Hazlerigg T&W 110 B5
Hazlewood N Yorks 94 D3
Hazon Northumb 117 D7
Heacham Norf 80 D2
Head of Muir Falk 127 F7
Headbourne Worthy Hants 26 F2
Headbrook Hereford 48 D5
Headcorn Kent 30 E2
Headingley W Yorks 95 F5
Headington Oxon 39 D5
Headlam Durham 101 C6
Headless Cross Worcs 50 C5
Headley Hants 26 C3
Headley Hants 27 F6
Headley Sur 28 D3
Headon Notts 77 B7
Heads S Lanark 119 E7
Heads Nook Cumb 108 D4
Heage Derbys 76 D3
Healaugh N Yorks 95 E7
Healaugh N Yorks 101 E5
Heald Green Gtr Man 87 F6
Heale Devon 20 E5
Heale Som 23 E8
Healey Gtr Man 87 C6
Healey N Yorks 101 F6
Healey Northumb 110 D3
Healing NE Lincs 91 C6
Heamoor Corn 2 C3
Heanish Argyll 146 G3
Heanor Derbys 76 E4
Heanton Punchardon Devon 20 F4
Heapham Lincs 90 F2
Hearthstane Borders 114 B4
Heasley Mill Devon 21 F6
Heast Highld 149 G11
Heath Cardiff 22 B3
Heath Derbys 76 C4
Heath and Reach C Beds 40 B2
Heath End Hants 26 C3
Heath End Sur 27 E6
Heath End Warks 51 C7
Heath Hayes Staffs 62 C4
Heath Hill Shrops 61 C7
Heath House Som 23 E6
Heath Town W Mid 62 E3
Heathcote Derbys 75 C8
Heather Leics 63 C7
Heatherfield Highld 149 D9
Heathfield Devon 7 B6
Heathfield E Sus 18 C2
Heathfield Som 11 B6
Heathhall Dumfries 107 B6
Heathrow Airport London 27 B8
Heathstock Devon 11 D7
Heathton Shrops 62 E2
Heatley Warr 86 F5
Heaton Lancs 92 C4
Heaton Staffs 75 C6
Heaton T&W 111 C5
Heaton W Yorks 94 F4
Heaton Moor Gtr Man 87 E6
Heaverham Kent 29 D6
Heaviley Gtr Man 87 F7
Heavitree Devon 10 E4
Hebburn T&W 111 C6
Hebden N Yorks 94 C3
Hebden Bridge W Yorks 87 B7
Hebron Anglesey 82 C4
Hebron Carms 32 B2
Hebron Northumb 117 F7
Heck Dumfries 114 F3
Heckfield Hants 26 C5
Heckfield Green Suff 57 B5
Heckfordbridge Essex 43 B5
Heckington Lincs 78 E4
Heckmondwike W Yorks 88 B3
Heddington Wilts 24 C4
Heddle Orkney 159 G4
Heddon-on-the-Wall Northumb 110 C4
Hedenham Norf 69 E6
Hedge End Hants 15 C5
Hedgerley Bucks 40 F2
Hedging Som 11 B8
Hedley on the Hill Northumb 110 D3
Hednesford Staffs 62 C4
Hedon E Yorks 91 B5
Hedsor Bucks 40 F2
Hedworth T&W 111 C6
Hegdon Hill Hereford 49 D7
Heggerscales Cumb 100 C3
Heglibister Shetland 160 H5
Heighington Darl 101 B7
Heighington Lincs 78 C3
Heights of Brae Highld 151 E8
Heights of Kinlochewe Highld 150 E3
Heilam Highld 156 C7
Heiton Borders 122 F3
Hele Devon 10 D4
Hele Devon 20 E4
Helensburgh Argyll 145 E11
Helford Corn 3 D6
Helford Passage Corn 3 D6
Helhoughton Norf 80 E4
Helions Bumpstead Essex 55 E7
Hellaby S Yorks 89 E6
Helland Corn 5 B5
Hellesdon Norf 68 C5
Hellidon Northants 52 D3
Hellifield N Yorks 93 D8
Hellingly E Sus 18 D2
Hellington Norf 69 D6
Hellister Shetland 160 J5
Helm Northumb 117 E7
Helmdon Northants 52 E3
Helmingham Suff 57 D5
Helmington Row Durham 110 F4
Helmsdale Highld 157 H13
Helmshore Lancs 87 B5
Helmsley N Yorks 102 F4
Helperby N Yorks 95 C7
Helperthorpe N Yorks 97 B5
Helpringham Lincs 78 E4
Helpston Pboro 65 D8
Helsby Ches W 73 B8
Helsey Lincs 79 B8
Helston Corn 3 D5
Helstone Corn 8 F2
Helton Cumb 99 B7
Helwith Bridge N Yorks 93 C8
Hemblington Norf 69 C6
Hemel Hempstead Herts 40 D3
Hemingbrough N Yorks 96 F2
Hemingby Lincs 78 B5
Hemingford Abbots Cambs 54 B3
Hemingford Grey Cambs 54 B3
Hemingstone Suff 57 D5
Hemington Leics 63 B8
Hemington Northants 65 F7
Hemington Som 24 D2
Hemley Suff 57 E6
Hemlington Mbro 102 C3
Hemp Green Suff 57 C7
Hempholme E Yorks 97 D6
Hempnall Norf 68 E5
Hempnall Green Norf 68 E5
Hempriggs House Highld 158 F5
Hempstead Essex 55 F7
Hempstead Medway 29 C8
Hempstead Norf 69 B7
Hempstead Norf 81 D7
Hempsted Glos 37 C5
Hempton Norf 80 E5
Hempton Oxon 52 F2
Hemsby Norf 69 C7
Hemswell Lincs 90 E3
Hemswell Cliff Lincs 90 F3
Hemsworth W Yorks 88 C5
Hemyock Devon 11 C6
Hen-feddau fawr Pembs 45 F4
Henbury Bristol 23 B7
Henbury Ches E 75 B5
Hendon London 41 F5
Hendon T&W 111 D7
Hendre Flint 73 C5
Hendre-ddu Conwy 83 E8
Hendreforgan Rhondda 34 F3
Hendy Carms 33 D6
Heneglwys Anglesey 82 D4
Henfield W Sus 17 C6
Henford Devon 9 E5
Henghurst Kent 19 B6
Hengoed Caerph 35 E5
Hengoed Powys 48 D4
Hengoed Shrops 73 F6
Hengrave Suff 56 C2
Henham Essex 41 B8
Heniarth Powys 59 D8
Henlade Som 11 B7
Henley Shrops 49 B7
Henley Som 23 F6
Henley Suff 57 D5
Henley W Sus 16 B2
Henley-in-Arden Warks 51 C6
Henley-on-Thames Oxon 39 F7
Henley's Down E Sus 18 D4
Henllan Ceredig 46 E2
Henllan Denb 72 C4
Henllan Amgoed Carms 32 B2
Henllys Torf 35 E6
Henlow C Beds 54 F2
Hennock Devon 10 F3
Henny Street Essex 56 F2
Henryd Conwy 83 D7
Henry's Moat Pembs 32 B1
Hensall N Yorks 89 B6
Henshaw Northumb 109 C7
Hensingham Cumb 98 C1
Henstead Suff 69 F7
Henstridge Som 12 C5
Henstridge Ash Som 12 B5
Henstridge Marsh Som 12 B5
Henton Oxon 39 D7
Henton Som 23 E6
Henwood Corn 5 B7
Heogan Shetland 160 J6
Heol-las Swansea 33 E7
Heol Senni Powys 34 B3
Heol-y-Cyw Bridgend 34 F3
Hepburn Northumb 117 B6
Hepple Northumb 117 D5
Hepscott Northumb 117 F8
Heptonstall W Yorks 87 B7
Hepworth Suff 56 B3
Hepworth W Yorks 88 D2
Herbrandston Pembs 44 E3
Hereford Hereford 49 E7
Heriot Borders 121 D6
Hermiston Edin 120 B4
Hermitage Borders 115 E8
Hermitage Dorset 12 D4
Hermitage W Berks 26 B3
Hermitage W Sus 15 D8
Hermon Anglesey 82 E3
Hermon Carms 33 B7
Hermon Carms 46 F2
Hermon Pembs 45 F4
Herne Kent 31 C5
Herne Bay Kent 31 C5
Herner Devon 9 B7
Hernhill Kent 30 C4
Herodsfoot Corn 5 C7
Herongate Essex 42 E2
Heronsford S Ayrs 104 A5
Herriard Hants 26 E4
Herringfleet Suff 69 E7
Herringswell Suff 55 B8
Hersden Kent 31 C6
Hersham Corn 8 D4
Hersham Sur 28 C2
Herstmonceux E Sus 18 D3
Herston Orkney 159 J5
Hertford Herts 41 C6
Hertford Heath Herts 41 C6
Hertingfordbury Herts 41 C6
Hesket Newmarket Cumb 108 F3
Hesketh Bank Lancs 86 B2
Hesketh Lane Lancs 93 E6
Heskin Green Lancs 86 C3
Hesleden Durham 111 F7
Hesleyside Northumb 116 F4
Heslington York 96 D2
Hessay York 95 D8
Hessenford Corn 5 D8
Hessett Suff 56 C3
Hessle E Yorks 90 B4
Hest Bank Lancs 92 C4
Heston London 28 B2
Hestwall Orkney 159 G3
Heswall Mers 85 F3
Hethe Oxon 39 B5
Hethersett Norf 68 D4
Hethersgill Cumb 108 C4
Hethpool Northumb 116 B4
Hett Durham 111 F5
Hetton N Yorks 94 D2
Hetton-le-Hole T&W 111 E6
Hetton Steads Northumb 123 F6
Heugh Northumb 110 B3
Heugh-head Aberds 140 C2
Heveningham Suff 57 B7
Hever Kent 29 E5
Heversham Cumb 99 F6
Hevingham Norf 81 E7
Hewas Water Corn 3 B8
Hewelsfield Glos 36 D2
Hewish N Som 23 C6
Hewish Som 12 D2
Heworth York 96 D2
Hexham Northumb 110 C2
Hextable Kent 29 B6
Hexton Herts 54 F2
Hexworthy Devon 6 B4
Hey Lancs 93 E8
Heybridge Essex 42 D4
Heybridge Essex 42 E2
Heybridge Basin Essex 42 D4
Heybrook Bay Devon 6 E3
Heydon Cambs 54 E5
Heydon Norf 81 E7
Heydour Lincs 78 F3
Heylipol Argyll 146 G2
Heylor Shetland 160 E4
Heysham Lancs 92 C4
Heyshott W Sus 16 C2
Heyside Gtr Man 87 D7
Heytesbury Wilts 24 E4
Heythrop Oxon 38 B3
Heywood Gtr Man 87 C6
Heywood Wilts 24 D3
Hibaldstow N Lincs 90 D3
Hickleton S Yorks 89 D5
Hickling Norf 69 B7
Hickling Notts 64 B3
Hickling Green Norf 69 B7
Hickling Heath Norf 69 B7
Hickstead W Sus 17 B6
Hidcote Boyce Glos 51 E6
High Ackworth W Yorks 88 C5
High Angerton Northumb 117 F6
High Bankhill Cumb 109 E5
High Barnes T&W 111 D6
High Beach Essex 41 E7
High Bentham N Yorks 93 C6
High Bickington Devon 9 B8
High Birkwith N Yorks 93 B7
High Blantyre S Lanark 119 D6
High Bonnybridge Falk 119 B8
High Bradfield S Yorks 88 E3
High Bray Devon 21 F5
High Brooms Kent 29 E6
High Bullen Devon 9 B7
High Buston Northumb 117 D8
High Callerton Northumb 110 B4
High Catton E Yorks 96 D3
High Cogges Oxon 38 D3
High Coniscliffe Darl 101 C7
High Cross Hants 15 B8
High Cross Herts 41 C6
High Easter Essex 42 C2
High Eggborough N Yorks 89 B6
High Ellington N Yorks 101 F6
High Ercall Telford 61 C5
High Etherley Durham 101 B6
High Garrett Essex 42 B3
High Grange Durham 110 F4
High Green Norf 68 D4
High Green S Yorks 88 E4
High Green Worcs 50 E3
High Halden Kent 19 B5
High Halstow Medway 29 B8
High Ham Som 23 F6
High Harrington Cumb 98 B2
High Hatton Shrops 61 B6
High Hawsker N Yorks 103 D7
High Hesket Cumb 108 E4
High Hesleden Durham 111 F7
High Hoyland S Yorks 88 C3
High Hunsley E Yorks 97 F5
High Hurstwood E Sus 17 B8
High Hutton N Yorks 96 C3
High Ireby Cumb 108 F2
High Kelling Norf 81 C7
High Kilburn N Yorks 95 B8
High Lands Durham 101 B6
High Lane Gtr Man 87 F7
High Lane Worcs 49 C8
High Laver Essex 41 D8
High Legh Ches E 86 F5
High Leven Stockton 102 C2
High Littleton Bath 23 D8
High Lorton Cumb 98 B3
High Marishes N Yorks 96 B4
High Marnham Notts 77 B8
High Melton S Yorks 89 D6
High Mickley Northumb 110 C3
High Mindork Dumfries 105 D7
High Newton Cumb 99 F6
High Newton-by-the-Sea Northumb 117 B8
High Nibthwaite Cumb 98 F4
High Offley Staffs 61 B7
High Ongar Essex 42 D1
High Onn Staffs 62 C2
High Roding Essex 42 C2
High Row Cumb 108 F3
High Salvington W Sus 16 D5
High Sellafield Cumb 98 D2
High Shaw N Yorks 100 E3
High Spen T&W 110 D4
High Stoop Durham 110 E4
High Street Corn 4 D4
High Street Kent 18 B4
High Street Suff 56 E2
High Street Suff 57 B8
High Street Suff 57 D8
High Street Green Suff 56 D4
High Throston Hrtlpl 111 F7
High Toynton Lincs 79 C5
High Trewhitt Northumb 117 D6
High Valleyfield Fife 128 F2
High Westwood Durham 110 D4
High Wray Cumb 99 E5
High Wych Herts 41 C7
High Wycombe Bucks 40 E1
Higham Derbys 76 D3
Higham Kent 29 B8
Higham Lancs 93 F8
Higham Suff 55 C8
Higham Suff 56 F4
Higham Dykes Northumb 110 B4
Higham Ferrers Northants 53 C7
Higham Gobion C Beds 54 F2
Higham on the Hill Leics 63 E7
Higham Wood Kent 29 E6
Highampton Devon 9 D6
Highbridge Highld 136 F4
Highbridge Som 22 E5
Highbrook W Sus 28 F4
Highburton W Yorks 88 C2
Highbury Som 23 E8
Highclere Hants 26 C2
Highcliffe Dorset 14 E3
Higher Ansty Dorset 13 D5
Higher Ashton Devon 10 F3
Higher Ballam Lancs 92 F3
Higher Bartle Lancs 92 F5
Higher Boscaswell Corn 2 C2
Higher Burwardsley Ches W 74 D2
Higher Clovelly Devon 8 B5
Higher End Gtr Man 86 D3
Higher Kinnerton Flint 73 C7
Higher Penwortham Lancs 86 B3
Higher Town Scilly 2 E4
Higher Walreddon Devon 6 B2
Higher Walton Lancs 86 B3
Higher Walton Warr 86 F3
Higher Wheelton Lancs 86 B4
Higher Whitley Ches W 86 F4
Higher Wincham Ches W 74 B3
Higher Wych Ches W 73 E8
Highfield E Yorks 96 F3
Highfield Gtr Man 86 D5
Highfield N Ayrs 118 D3
Highfield Oxon 39 B5
Highfield S Yorks 88 F4
Highfield T&W 110 D4
Highfields Cambs 54 D4
Highfields Northumb 123 D5
Highgate London 41 F5
Highlane Ches E 75 C5
Highlane Derbys 88 F5
Highlaws Cumb 107 E8
Highleadon Glos 36 B4
Highleigh W Sus 16 E2
Highley Shrops 61 F7
Highmoor Cross Oxon 39 F7
Highmoor Hill Mon 36 F1
Highnam Glos 36 C4
Highnam Green Glos 36 B4
Highsted Kent 30 C3
Highstreet Green Essex 55 F8
Hightae Dumfries 107 B7
Hightown Ches E 75 C5
Hightown Mers 85 D4
Hightown Green Suff 56 D3
Highway Wilts 24 B5
Highweek Devon 7 B6
Highworth Swindon 38 E2
Hilborough Norf 67 D8
Hilcote Derbys 76 D4
Hilcott Wilts 25 D6
Hilden Park Kent 29 E6
Hildenborough Kent 29 E6
Hildersham Cambs 55 E6
Hilderstone Staffs 75 F6
Hilderthorpe E Yorks 97 C7
Hilfield Dorset 12 D4
Hilgay Norf 67 E6
Hill Pembs 32 D2
Hill S Glos 36 E3
Hill W Mid 62 E5
Hill Brow W Sus 15 B8
Hill Dale Lancs 86 C2
Hill Dyke Lincs 79 E6
Hill End Durham 110 F3
Hill End Fife 128 E2
Hill End N Yorks 94 D3
Hill Head Hants 15 D6
Hill Head Northumb 110 C2
Hill Mountain Pembs 44 E4
Hill of Beath Fife 128 E3
Hill of Fearn Highld 151 D11
Hill of Mountblairy Aberds 153 C6
Hill Ridware Staffs 62 C4
Hill Top Durham 100 B4
Hill Top Hants 14 D5
Hill Top W Mid 62 E3
Hill Top W Yorks 88 C4
Hill View Dorset 13 E7
Hillam N Yorks 89 B6
Hillbeck Cumb 100 C2
Hillborough Kent 31 C6
Hillbrae Aberds 141 B6
Hillbrae Aberds 152 D6
Hillbutts Dorset 13 D7
Hillclifflane Derbys 76 E2
Hillcommon Som 11 B6
Hillend Fife 128 F3
Hillerton Devon 10 E2
Hillesden Bucks 39 B6
Hillesley Glos 36 F4
Hillfarance Som 11 B6
Hillhead Aberds 152 E5
Hillhead Devon 7 D7
Hillhead S Ayrs 112 C4
Hillhead of Auchentumb Aberds 153 C9
Hillhead of Cocklaw Aberds 153 D10
Hillhouse Borders 121 D8
Hilliclay Highld 158 D3
Hillingdon London 40 F3
Hillington Glasgow 118 C5
Hillington Norf 80 E3
Hillmorton Warks 52 B3
Hillockhead Aberds 140 C3
Hillockhead Aberds 140 D2
Hillside Aberds 141 E8
Hillside Angus 135 C7
Hillside Mers 85 C4
Hillside Orkney 159 J5
Hillside Shetland 160 G6
Hillswick Shetland 160 F4
Hillway IoW 15 F7
Hillwell Shetland 160 M5
Hilmarton Wilts 24 B5
Hilperton Wilts 24 D3
Hilsea Ptsmth 15 D7
Hilston E Yorks 97 F8
Hilton Aberds 153 E9
Hilton Cambs 54 C3
Hilton Cumb 100 B2
Hilton Derbys 76 F2
Hilton Dorset 13 D5
Hilton Durham 101 B6
Hilton Highld 151 C10
Hilton Shrops 61 E7
Hilton Stockton 102 C2
Hilton of Cadboll Highld 151 D11
Himbleton Worcs 50 D4
Himley Staffs 62 E2
Hincaster Cumb 99 F7
Hinckley Leics 63 E8
Hinderclay Suff 56 B4
Hinderton Ches W 73 B7
Hinderwell N Yorks 103 C5
Hindford Shrops 73 F7
Hindhead Sur 27 F6
Hindley Gtr Man 86 D4
Hindley Green Gtr Man 86 D4
Hindlip Worcs 50 D3
Hindolveston Norf 81 E6
Hindon Wilts 24 F4
Hindringham Norf 81 D5
Hingham Norf 68 D3
Hinstock Shrops 61 B6
Hintlesham Suff 56 E4
Hinton Hants 14 E3
Hinton Hereford 48 F5
Hinton Northants 52 D3
Hinton S Glos 24 B2
Hinton Shrops 60 D4
Hinton Ampner Hants 15 B6
Hinton Blewett Bath 23 D7
Hinton Charterhouse Bath 24 D2
Hinton-in-the-Hedges Northants 52 F3
Hinton Martell Dorset 13 D8
Hinton on the Green Worcs 50 E5
Hinton Parva Swindon 38 F2
Hinton St George Som 12 C2
Hinton St Mary Dorset 13 C5
Hinton Waldrist Oxon 38 E3
Hints Shrops 49 B8
Hints Staffs 63 D5
Hinwick Bedford 53 C7
Hinxhill Kent 30 E4
Hinxton Cambs 55 E5
Hinxworth Herts 54 E3
Hipperholme W Yorks 88 B2
Hipswell N Yorks 101 E6
Hirael Gwyn 83 D5
Hiraeth Carms 32 B2
Hirn Aberds 141 D6
Hirnant Powys 59 B7
Hirst N Lanark 119 C8
Hirst Northumb 117 F8
Hirst Courtney N Yorks 89 B7
Hirwaen Denb 72 C5
Hirwaun Rhondda 34 D3
Hiscott Devon 9 B7
Histon Cambs 54 C5
Hitcham Suff 56 D3
Hitchin Herts 40 B4
Hither Green London 28 B4
Hittisleigh Devon 10 E2
Hive E Yorks 96 F4
Hixon Staffs 62 B4
Hoaden Kent 31 D6
Hoaldalbert Mon 35 B7
Hoar Cross Staffs 62 B5
Hoarwithy Hereford 36 B2
Hoath Kent 31 C6
Hobarris Shrops 48 B5
Hobbister Orkney 159 H4
Hobkirk Borders 115 C8
Hobson Durham 110 D4
Hoby Leics 64 C3
Hockering Norf 68 C3
Hockerton Notts 77 D7
Hockley Essex 42 E4
Hockley Heath W Mid 51 B6
Hockliffe C Beds 40 B2
Hockwold cum Wilton Norf 67 F7
Hockworthy Devon 10 C5
Hoddesdon Herts 41 D6
Hoddlesden Blackburn 86 B5
Hoddom Mains Dumfries 107 B8
Hoddomcross Dumfries 107 B8
Hodgeston Pembs 32 E1
Hodley Powys 59 E8
Hodnet Shrops 61 B6
Hodthorpe Derbys 76 B5
Hoe Hants 15 C6
Hoe Norf 68 C2
Hoe Gate Hants 15 C7
Hoff Cumb 100 C1
Hog Patch Sur 27 E6
Hoggard's Green Suff 56 D2
Hoggeston Bucks 39 B8
Hogha Gearraidh W Isles 148 A2
Hoghton Lancs 86 B4
Hognaston Derbys 76 D2
Hogsthorpe Lincs 79 B8
Holbeach Lincs 66 B3
Holbeach Bank Lincs 66 B3
Holbeach Clough Lincs 66 B3
Holbeach Drove Lincs 66 C3
Holbeach Hurn Lincs 66 B3
Holbeach St Johns Lincs 66 C3
Holbeach St Marks Lincs 79 F6
Holbeach St Matthew Lincs 79 F7
Holbeck Notts 76 B5
Holbeck W Yorks 95 F5
Holbeck Woodhouse Notts 76 B5
Holberrow Green Worcs 50 D5
Holbeton Devon 6 D4
Holborn London 41 F6
Holbrook Derbys 76 E3
Holbrook S Yorks 88 F5
Holbrook Suff 57 F5
Holburn Northumb 123 F6
Holbury Hants 14 D5
Holcombe Devon 7 B7
Holcombe Som 23 E8
Holcombe Rogus Devon 11 C5
Holcot Northants 53 C5
Holden Lancs 93 E7
Holdenby Northants 52 C4
Holdenhurst Bmouth 14 E2
Holdgate Shrops 61 F5
Holdingham Lincs 78 E3
Holditch Dorset 11 D8
Hole-in-the-Wall Hereford 36 B3
Holefield Borders 122 F4
Holehouses Ches E 74 B4
Holemoor Devon 9 D6
Holestane Dumfries 113 E8
Holford Som 22 E3
Holgate York 95 D8
Holker Cumb 92 B3
Holkham Norf 80 C4
Hollacombe Devon 9 D5
Holland Orkney 159 C5
Holland Orkney 159 F7
Holland Fen Lincs 78 E5
Holland-on-Sea Essex 43 C8
Hollandstoun Orkney 159 C8
Hollee Dumfries 108 C2
Hollesley Suff 57 E7
Hollicombe Torbay 7 C6
Hollingbourne Kent 30 D2
Hollington Derbys 76 F2
Hollington E Sus 18 D4
Hollington Staffs 75 F7
Hollington Grove Derbys 76 F2
Hollingworth Gtr Man 87 E8
Hollins Gtr Man 87 D6
Hollins Green Warr 86 E4
Hollins Lane Lancs 92 D4
Hollinsclough Staffs 75 C7
Hollinwood Gtr Man 87 D7
Hollinwood Shrops 74 F2
Hollocombe Devon 9 C8
Hollow Meadows S Yorks 88 F3
Holloway Derbys 76 D3
Hollowell Northants 52 B4
Holly End Norf 66 D4
Holly Green Worcs 50 E3
Hollybush Caerph 35 D5
Hollybush E Ayrs 112 C3
Hollybush Worcs 50 F2
Hollym E Yorks 91 B7
Hollywood Worcs 51 B5
Holmbridge W Yorks 88 D2
Holmbury St Mary Sur 28 E2
Holmbush Corn 4 D5
Holmcroft Staffs 62 B3
Holme Cambs 65 F8
Holme Cumb 92 B5
Holme N Yorks 102 F1
Holme Notts 77 D8
Holme W Yorks 88 D2
Holme Chapel Lancs 87 B6
Holme Green N Yorks 95 E8
Holme Hale Norf 67 D8
Holme Lacy Hereford 49 F7
Holme Marsh Hereford 48 D5
Holme next the Sea Norf 80 C3
Holme-on-Spalding-Moor E Yorks 96 F4
Holme on the Wolds E Yorks 97 E5
Holme Pierrepont Notts 77 F6
Holme St Cuthbert Cumb 107 E8
Holme Wood W Yorks 94 F4
Holmer Hereford 49 E7
Holmer Green Bucks 40 E2
Holmes Chapel Ches E 74 C4
Holmesfield Derbys 76 B3
Holmeswood Lancs 86 C2
Holmewood Derbys 76 C4
Holmfirth W Yorks 88 D2
Holmhead Dumfries 113 F7
Holmhead E Ayrs 113 B5
Holmisdale Highld 148 D6
Holmpton E Yorks 91 B7
Holmrook Cumb 98 E2
Holmsgarth Shetland 160 J6
Holmwrangle Cumb 108 E5
Holne Devon 6 C5
Holnest Dorset 12 D4
Holsworthy Devon 8 D5
Holsworthy Beacon Devon 9 D5
Holt Dorset 13 D8
Holt Norf 81 D6
Holt Wilts 24 C3
Holt Worcs 50 C3
Holt Wrex 73 D8
Holt End Hants 26 F4
Holt End Worcs 51 C5
Holt Fleet Worcs 50 C3
Holt Heath Worcs 50 C3
Holt Park W Yorks 95 E5
Holtby York 96 D2
Holton Oxon 39 D6
Holton Som 12 B4
Holton Suff 57 B7
Holton cum Beckering Lincs 90 F5
Holton Heath Dorset 13 E7
Holton le Clay Lincs 91 D6
Holton le Moor Lincs 90 E4
Holton St Mary Suff 56 F4
Holwell Dorset 12 C5
Holwell Herts 54 F2
Holwell Leics 64 B4
Holwell Oxon 38 D2
Holwick Durham 100 B4
Holworth Dorset 13 F5
Holy Cross Worcs 50 B4
Holy Island Northumb 123 E7
Holybourne Hants 26 E5
Holyhead = Caergybi Anglesey 82 C2
Holymoorside Derbys 76 C3
Holyport Windsor 27 B6
Holystone Northumb 117 D5
Holytown N Lanark 119 C7
Holywell Cambs 54 B4
Holywell Corn 4 D2
Holywell Dorset 12 D3
Holywell E Sus 18 F2
Holywell = Treffynnon Flint 73 B5
Holywell Northumb 111 B6
Holywell Green W Yorks 87 C8
Holywell Lake Som 11 B6
Holywell Row Suff 55 B8
Holywood Dumfries 114 F2
Hom Green Hereford 36 B2
Homer Shrops 61 D6
Homersfield Suff 69 F5
Homington Wilts 14 B2
Honey Hill Kent 30 C5
Honey Street Wilts 25 C6
Honey Tye Suff 56 F3
Honeyborough Pembs 44 E4
Honeybourne Worcs 51 E6
Honeychurch Devon 9 D8
Honiley Warks 51 B7
Honing Norf 69 B6
Honingham Norf 68 C4
Honington Lincs 78 E2
Honington Suff 56 B3
Honington Warks 51 E7
Honiton Devon 11 D6
Honley W Yorks 88 C2
Hoo Green Ches E 86 F5
Hoo St Werburgh Medway 29 B8
Hood Green S Yorks 88 D4
Hooe E Sus 18 E3
Hooe Plym 6 D3
Hooe Common E Sus 18 D3
Hook E Yorks 89 B8
Hook Hants 26 D5
Hook London 28 C2
Hook Pembs 44 D4
Hook Wilts 37 F7
Hook Green Kent 18 B3
Hook Green Kent 29 C7
Hook Norton Oxon 51 F8
Hooke Dorset 12 E3
Hookgate Staffs 74 F4
Hookway Devon 10 E3
Hookwood Sur 28 E3
Hoole Ches W 73 C8
Hooley Sur 28 D3
Hoop Mon 36 D2
Hooton Ches W 73 B7
Hooton Levitt S Yorks 89 E6
Hooton Pagnell S Yorks 89 D5
Hooton Roberts S Yorks 89 E5
Hop Pole Lincs 65 C8
Hope Derbys 88 F2
Hope Devon 6 F4
Hope Highld 156 B7
Hope Powys 60 D2
Hope Shrops 60 D3
Hope Staffs 75 D8
Hope = Yr Hôb Flint 73 D7
Hope Bagot Shrops 49 B7
Hope Bowdler Shrops 60 E4
Hope End Green Essex 42 B1
Hope Green Ches E 87 F7
Hope Mansell Hereford 36 C3
Hope under Dinmore Hereford 49 D7
Hopeman Moray 152 B1
Hope's Green Essex 42 F3
Hopesay Shrops 60 F3
Hopley's Green Hereford 48 D5
Hopperton N Yorks 95 D7
Hopstone Shrops 61 E7
Hopton Shrops 60 B3
Hopton Shrops 61 B5
Hopton Staffs 62 B3
Hopton Suff 56 B3
Hopton Cangeford Shrops 60 F5
Hopton Castle Shrops 49 B5
Hopton on Sea Norf 69 D8
Hopton Wafers Shrops 49 B8
Hoptonheath Shrops 49 B5
Hopwas Staffs 63 D5
Hopwood Gtr Man 87 D6
Hopwood Worcs 50 B5
Horam E Sus 18 D2
Horbling Lincs 78 F4
Horbury W Yorks 88 C3
Horcott Glos 38 D1
Horden Durham 111 E7
Horderley Shrops 60 F4
Hordle Hants 14 E3
Hordley Shrops 73 F7
Horeb Carms 33 B6
Horeb Carms 33 D5
Horeb Ceredig 46 E2
Horfield Bristol 23 B8
Horham Suff 57 B6
Horkesley Heath Essex 43 B5
Horkstow N Lincs 90 C3
Horley Oxon 52 E2
Horley Sur 28 E3
Hornblotton Green Som 23 F7
Hornby Lancs 93 C5
Hornby N Yorks 101 E7
Hornby N Yorks 102 D1
Horncastle Lincs 79 C5
Hornchurch London 41 F8
Horncliffe Northumb 122 E5
Horndean Borders 122 E4
Horndean Hants 15 C8
Horndon Devon 6 B3
Horndon on the Hill Thurrock 42 F2
Horne Sur 28 E4
Horniehaugh Angus 134 C4
Horning Norf 69 C6
Horninghold Leics 64 E5
Horninglow Staffs 63 B6
Horningsea Cambs 55 C5
Horningsham Wilts 24 E3
Horningtoft Norf 80 E5
Hornsby Cumb 108 D5
Horns Corner Kent 18 C4
Horns Cross Devon 9 B5
Horns Cross E Sus 18 C5
Hornsea E Yorks 97 E8
Hornsea Bridge E Yorks 97 E8
Hornsey London 41 F6
Hornton Oxon 51 E8
Horrabridge Devon 6 C3
Horringer Suff 56 C2
Horringford IoW 15 F6
Horse Bridge Staffs 75 D6
Horsebridge Devon 6 B2
Horsebridge Hants 25 F8
Horsebrook Staffs 62 C2
Horsehay Telford 61 D6
Horseheath Cambs 55 E7
Horsehouse N Yorks 101 F5
Horsell Sur 27 D7
Horseman's Green Wrex 73 E8
Horseway Cambs 66 F4
Horsey Norf 69 B7
Horsford Norf 68 C4
Horsforth W Yorks 94 F5
Horsham W Sus 28 F2
Horsham Worcs 50 D2
Horsham St Faith Norf 68 C5
Horsington Lincs 78 C4
Horsington Som 12 B5
Horsley Derbys 76 E3
Horsley Glos 37 E5
Horsley Northumb 110 C3
Horsley Northumb 116 E4
Horsley Cross Essex 43 B7
Horsley Woodhouse Derbys 76 E3
Horsleycross Street Essex 43 B7
Horsleyhill Borders 115 C8
Horsleyhope Durham 110 E3
Horsmonden Kent 29 E7
Horspath Oxon 39 D5
Horstead Norf 69 C5
Horsted Keynes W Sus 17 B7
Horton Bucks 40 C2
Horton Dorset 13 D8
Horton Lancs 93 D8
Horton Northants 53 D6
Horton S Glos 36 F4
Horton Shrops 60 B4
Horton Som 11 C8
Horton Staffs 75 D6
Horton Swansea 33 F5
Horton Wilts 25 C5
Horton Windsor 27 B8
Horton-cum-Studley Oxon 39 C5
Horton Green Ches W 73 E8
Horton Heath Hants 15 C5
Horton in Ribblesdale N Yorks 93 B8
Horton Kirby Kent 29 C6
Hortonlane Shrops 60 C4
Horwich Gtr Man 86 C4
Horwich End Derbys 87 F8
Horwood Devon 9 B7
Hose Leics 64 B4
Hoselaw Borders 122 F4
Hoses Cumb 98 E4
Hosh Perth 127 B7
Hosta W Isles 148 A2
Hoswick Shetland 160 L6
Hotham E Yorks 96 F4
Hothfield Kent 30 E3
Hoton Leics 64 B2
Houbie Shetland 160 D8
Houdston S Ayrs 112 E1
Hough Ches E 74 D4
Hough Ches E 75 B5
Hough Green Halton 86 F2
Hough-on-the-Hill Lincs 78 E2
Hougham Lincs 77 E8
Houghton Cambs 54 B3
Houghton Cumb 108 D4
Houghton Hants 25 F8
Houghton Pembs 44 E4
Houghton W Sus 16 C4
Houghton Conquest C Beds 53 E8
Houghton Green E Sus 19 C6
Houghton Green Warr 86 E4
Houghton-le-Side Darl 101 B7
Houghton-Le-Spring T&W 111 E6
Houghton on the Hill Leics 64 D3
Houghton Regis C Beds 40 B3
Houghton St Giles Norf 80 D5
Houlland Shetland 160 F7
Houlland Shetland 160 H5
Houlsyke N Yorks 103 D5
Hound Hants 15 D5
Hound Green Hants 26 D5
Houndslow Borders 122 E2
Houndwood Borders 122 C4
Hounslow London 28 B2
Hounslow Green Essex 42 C2
Housay Shetland 160 F8
House of Daviot Highld 151 G10
House of Glenmuick Aberds 140 E2
Housetter Shetland 160 E5
Houss Shetland 160 K5
Houston Renfs 118 C4
Houstry Highld 158 G3
Houton Orkney 159 H4
Hove Brighton 17 D6
Hoveringham Notts 77 E6
Hoveton Norf 69 C6
Hovingham N Yorks 96 B2
How Cumb 108 D5
How Caple Hereford 49 F8
How End C Beds 53 E8
How Green Kent 29 E5
Howbrook S Yorks 88 E4
Howden Borders 116 B2
Howden E Yorks 89 B8
Howden-le-Wear Durham 110 F4
Howe Highld 158 D5
Howe N Yorks 101 F8
Howe Norf 69 D5
Howe Bridge Gtr Man 86 D4
Howe Green Essex 42 D3
Howe of Teuchar Aberds 153 D7
Howe Street Essex 42 C2
Howe Street Essex 55 F7
Howell Lincs 78 E4
Howey Powys 48 D2
Howgate Midloth 120 D5
Howick Northumb 117 C8
Howle Durham 101 B5
Howle Telford 61 B6
Howlett End Essex 55 F6
Howley Som 11 D7
Hownam Borders 116 C3
Hownam Mains Borders 116 B3
Howpasley Borders 115 D6
Howsham N Lincs 90 D4
Howsham N Yorks 96 C3
Howslack Dumfries 114 D3
Howtel Northumb 122 F4
Howton Hereford 35 B8
Howtown Cumb 99 C6
Howwood Renfs 118 C3
Hoxne Suff 57 B5
Hoy Orkney 159 H3
Hoylake Mers 85 F3
Hoyland S Yorks 88 D4
Hoylandswaine S Yorks 88 D3
Hubberholme N Yorks 94 B2
Hubbert's Bridge Lincs 79 E5
Huby N Yorks 95 C8
Huby N Yorks 95 E5
Hucclecote Glos 37 C5
Hucking Kent 30 D2
Hucknall Notts 76 E5
Huddersfield W Yorks 88 C2
Huddington Worcs 50 D4
Hudswell N Yorks 101 D6
Huggate E Yorks 96 D4
Hugglescote Leics 63 C8
Hugh Town Scilly 2 E4
Hughenden Valley Bucks 40 E1
Hughley Shrops 61 E5
Huish Devon 9 C7
Huish Wilts 25 C6
Huish Champflower Som 11 B5
Huish Episcopi Som 12 B2
Huisinis W Isles 154 F4
Hulcott Bucks 40 C1
Hulland Derbys 76 E2
Hulland Ward Derbys 76 E2
Hullavington Wilts 37 F5
Hullbridge Essex 42 E4
Hulme Gtr Man 87 E6

Hulme End Staffs 75 D8
Hulme Walfield Ches E 74 C5
Hulver Street Suff 69 F7
Hulverstone IoW 14 F4
Humber Hereford 49 D7
Humber Bridge N Lincs 90 B4
Humberston NE Lincs 91 D7
Humbie E Loth 121 C7
Humbleton E Yorks 97 F8
Humbleton Northumb 117 B5
Humby Lincs 78 F3
Hume Borders 122 E3
Humshaugh Northumb 110 B2
Huna Highld 158 C5
Huncoat Lancs 93 F7
Huncote Leics 64 E2
Hundalee Borders 116 C2
Hunderthwaite Durham 100 B4
Hundle Houses Lincs 79 D5
Hundleby Lincs 79 C6
Hundleton Pembs 44 E4
Hundon Suff 55 E8
Hundred Acres Hants 15 C6
Hundred End Lancs 86 B2
Hundred House Powys 48 D3
Hungarton Leics 64 D3
Hungerford Hants 14 C2
Hungerford W Berks 25 C8
Hungerford Newtown W Berks 25 B8
Hungerton Lincs 65 B5
Hungladder Highld 149 A8
Hunmanby N Yorks 97 B6
Hunmanby Moor N Yorks 97 B7
Hunningham Warks 51 C8
Hunny Hill IoW 15 F5
Hunsdon Herts 41 C7
Hunsingore N Yorks 95 D7
Hunslet W Yorks 95 F6
Hunsonby Cumb 109 F5
Hunspow Highld 158 C4
Hunstanton Norf 80 C2
Hunstanworth Durham 110 E2
Hunsterson Ches E 74 E3
Hunston Suff 56 C3
Hunston W Sus 16 D2
Hunstrete Bath 23 C8
Hunt End Worcs 50 C5
Hunter's Quay Argyll 145 F10
Hunthill Lodge Angus 134 B4
Hunting-tower Perth 128 B2
Huntingdon Cambs 54 B3
Huntingfield Suff 57 B7
Huntingford Dorset 24 F3
Huntington E Loth 121 B7
Huntington Hereford 48 D4
Huntington Staffs 62 C3
Huntington York 96 D2
Huntley Glos 36 C4
Huntly Aberds 152 E5
Huntlywood Borders 122 E2
Hunton Kent 29 E8
Hunton N Yorks 101 E6
Hunt's Corner Norf 68 F3
Hunt's Cross Mers 86 F2
Huntsham Devon 10 B5
Huntspill Som 22 E5
Huntworth Som 22 F5
Hunwick Durham 110 F4
Hunworth Norf 81 D6
Hurdsfield Ches E 75 B6
Hurley Warks 63 E6
Hurley Windsor 39 F8
Hurlford E Ayrs 118 F4
Hurliness Orkney 159 K3
Hurn Dorset 14 E2
Hurn's End Lincs 79 E7
Hursley Hants 14 B5
Hurst N Yorks 101 D5
Hurst Som 12 C2
Hurst Wokingham 27 B5
Hurst Green E Sus 18 C4
Hurst Green Lancs 93 F6
Hurst Wickham W Sus 17 C6
Hurstbourne Priors Hants 26 E2
Hurstbourne Tarrant Hants 25 D8
Hurstpierpoint W Sus 17 C6
Hurstwood Lancs 93 F8
Hurtmore Sur 27 E7
Hurworth Place Darl 101 D7
Hury Durham 100 C4
Husabost Highld 148 C7
Husbands Bosworth Leics 64 F3
Husborne Crawley C Beds 53 F7
Husthwaite N Yorks 95 B8
Hutchwns Bridgend 21 B7
Huthwaite Notts 76 D4
Huttoft Lincs 79 B8
Hutton Borders 122 D5
Hutton Cumb 99 B6
Hutton E Yorks 97 D6
Hutton Essex 42 E2
Hutton Lancs 86 B2
Hutton N Som 22 D5
Hutton Buscel N Yorks 103 F7
Hutton Conyers N Yorks 95 B6
Hutton Cranswick E Yorks 97 D6
Hutton End Cumb 108 F4
Hutton Gate Redcar 102 C3
Hutton Henry Durham 111 F7
Hutton-le-Hole N Yorks 103 E5
Hutton Magna Durham 101 C6
Hutton Roof Cumb 93 B5
Hutton Roof Cumb 108 F3
Hutton Rudby N Yorks 102 D2
Hutton Sessay N Yorks 95 B7
Hutton Village Redcar 102 C3
Hutton Wandesley N Yorks 95 D8
Huxley Ches W 74 C2
Huxter Shetland 160 G7
Huxter Shetland 160 H5
Huxton Borders 122 C4
Huyton Mers 86 E2
Hwlffordd = Haverfordwest Pembs 44 D4
Hycemoor Cumb 98 F2
Hyde Glos 37 D5
Hyde Gtr Man 87 E7
Hyde Hants 14 C2
Hyde Heath Bucks 40 D2
Hyde Park S Yorks 89 D6
Hydestile Sur 27 E7
Hylton Castle T&W 111 D6
Hyndford Bridge S Lanark 120 E2
Hynish Argyll 146 H2
Hyssington Powys 60 E3
Hythe Hants 14 D5
Hythe Kent 19 B8
Hythe End Windsor 27 B8
Hythie Aberds 153 C10

I

Ibberton Dorset 13 D5
Ible Derbys 76 D2
Ibsley Hants 14 D2
Ibstock Leics 63 C8
Ibstone Bucks 39 E7
Ibthorpe Hants 25 D8
Ibworth Hants 26 D3
Ichrachan Argyll 125 B6
Ickburgh Norf 67 E8
Ickenham London 40 F3
Ickford Bucks 39 D6
Ickham Kent 31 D6
Ickleford Herts 54 F2
Icklesham E Sus 19 D5
Ickleton Cambs 55 E5
Icklingham Suff 55 B8
Ickwell Green C Beds 54 E2
Icomb Glos 38 B2
Idbury Oxon 38 C2
Iddesleigh Devon 9 D7
Ide Devon 10 E3
Ide Hill Kent 29 D5
Ideford Devon 7 B6
Iden E Sus 19 C6
Iden Green Kent 18 B4
Iden Green Kent 18 B5
Idle W Yorks 94 F4
Idlicote Warks 51 E7
Idmiston Wilts 25 F6
Idole Carms 33 C5
Idridgehay Derbys 76 E2
Idrigill Highld 149 B8
Idstone Oxon 38 F2
Idvies Angus 135 E5
Iffley Oxon 39 D5
Ifield W Sus 28 F3
Ifold W Sus 27 F8
Iford E Sus 17 D8
Ifton Heath Shrops 73 F7
Ightfield Shrops 74 F2
Ightham Kent 29 D6
Iken Suff 57 D8
Ilam Staffs 75 D8
Ilchester Som 12 B3
Ilderton Northumb 117 B6
Ilford London 41 F7
Ilfracombe Devon 20 E4
Ilkeston Derbys 76 E4
Ilketshall St Andrew Suff 69 F6
Ilketshall St Lawrence Suff 69 F6
Ilketshall St Margaret Suff 69 F6
Ilkley W Yorks 94 E4
Illey W Mid 62 F3
Illingworth W Yorks 87 B8
Illogan Corn 3 B5
Illston on the Hill Leics 64 E4
Ilmer Bucks 39 D7
Ilmington Warks 51 E7
Ilminster Som 11 C8
Ilsington Devon 7 B5
Ilston Swansea 33 E6
Ilton N Yorks 94 B4
Ilton Som 11 C8
Imachar N Ayrs 143 D9
Imeraval Argyll 142 D4
Immingham NE Lincs 91 C5
Impington Cambs 54 C5
Ince Ches W 73 B8
Ince Blundell Mers 85 D4
Ince in Makerfield Gtr Man 86 D3
Inch of Arnhall Aberds 135 B6
Inchbare Angus 135 C6
Inchberry Moray 152 C3
Inchbraoch Angus 135 D7
Incheril Highld 150 E3
Inchgrundle Angus 134 B4
Inchina Highld 150 B2
Inchinnan Renfs 118 C4
Inchkinloch Highld 157 E8
Inchlaggan Highld 136 D4
Inchlumpie Highld 151 D8
Inchmore Highld 150 G6
Inchnacardoch Hotel Highld 137 C6
Inchnadamph Highld 156 G5
Inchree Highld 130 C4
Inchture Perth 128 B4
Inchyra Perth 128 B3
Indian Queens Corn 4 D4
Inerval Argyll 142 D4
Ingatestone Essex 42 E2
Ingbirchworth S Yorks 88 D3
Ingestre Staffs 62 B3
Ingham Lincs 90 F3
Ingham Norf 69 B6
Ingham Suff 56 B2
Ingham Corner Norf 69 B6
Ingleborough Norf 66 C4
Ingleby Derbys 63 B7
Ingleby Lincs 77 B8
Ingleby Arncliffe N Yorks 102 D2
Ingleby Barwick Stockton 102 C2
Ingleby Greenhow N Yorks 102 D3
Inglemire Hull 97 F6
Inglesbatch Bath 24 C2
Inglesham Swindon 38 E2
Ingleton Durham 101 B6
Ingleton N Yorks 93 B6
Inglewhite Lancs 92 E5
Ingliston Edin 120 B4
Ingoe Northumb 110 B3
Ingol Lancs 92 F5
Ingoldisthorpe Norf 80 D2
Ingoldmells Lincs 79 C8
Ingoldsby Lincs 78 F3
Ingon Warks 51 D7
Ingram Northumb 117 C6
Ingrow W Yorks 94 F3
Ings Cumb 99 E6
Ingst S Glos 36 F2
Ingworth Norf 81 E7
Inham's End Cambs 66 E2
Inkberrow Worcs 50 D5
Inkpen W Berks 25 C8
Inkstack Highld 158 C4
Inn Cumb 99 D6
Innellan Argyll 145 F10
Innerleithen Borders 121 F6
Innerleven Fife 129 D5
Innermessan Dumfries 104 C4
Innerwick E Loth 122 B3
Innerwick Perth 132 E2
Innis Chonain Argyll 125 C7
Insch Aberds 140 B5
Insh Highld 138 D4
Inshore Highld 156 C6
Inskip Lancs 92 F4
Instoneville S Yorks 89 C6
Instow Devon 20 F3
Intake S Yorks 89 D6
Inver Aberds 139 E8
Inver Highld 151 C11
Inver Perth 133 E7
Inver Mallie Highld 136 F4
Inverailort Highld 147 C10
Inveraldie Angus 134 F4
Inveralligin Highld 149 C13
Inverallochy Aberds 153 B10
Inveran Highld 151 B8
Inveraray Argyll 125 E6
Inverarish Highld 149 E10
Inverarity Angus 134 E4
Inverarnan Stirling 126 C2
Inverasdale Highld 155 J13
Inverbeg Argyll 126 E2
Inverbervie Aberds 135 B8
Inverboyndie Aberds 153 B6
Inverbroom Highld 150 C4
Invercassley Highld 156 J7
Invercauld House Aberds 139 E7
Inverchaolain Argyll 145 F9
Invercharnan Highld 131 E5
Inverchoran Highld 150 F5
Invercreran Argyll 130 E4
Inverdruie Highld 138 C5
Inverebrie Aberds 153 E9
Invereck Argyll 145 E10
Inverernan Ho. Aberds 140 C2
Invereshie House Highld 138 D4
Inveresk E Loth 121 B6
Inverey Aberds 139 F6
Inverfarigaig Highld 137 B8
Invergarry Highld 137 D6
Invergelder Aberds 139 E8
Invergeldie Perth 127 B6
Invergordon Highld 151 E10
Invergowrie Perth 134 F3
Inverguseran Highld 149 H12
Inverhadden Perth 132 D3
Inverharroch Moray 152 E3
Inverherive Stirling 126 B2
Inverie Highld 147 B10
Inverinan Argyll 125 D5
Inverinate Highld 136 B2
Inverkeilor Angus 135 E6
Inverkeithing Fife 128 F3
Inverkeithny Aberds 153 D6
Inverkip Invclyd 118 B2
Inverkirkaig Highld 156 H3
Inverlael Highld 150 C4
Inverlochlarig Stirling 126 C3
Inverlochy Argyll 125 C7
Inverlochy Highld 131 B5
Inverlussa Argyll 144 E5
Invermark Lodge Angus 140 F3
Invermoidart Highld 147 D9
Invermoriston Highld 137 C7
Invernaver Highld 157 C10
Inverneill Argyll 145 E7
Inverness Highld 151 G9
Invernettie Aberds 153 D11
Invernoaden Argyll 125 F7
Inveroran Hotel Argyll 131 E6
Inverpolly Lodge Highld 156 H3
Inverquharity Angus 134 D4
Inverquhomery Aberds 153 D10
Inverroy Highld 137 F5
Inversanda Highld 130 D3
Invershiel Highld 136 C2
Invershin Highld 151 B8
Inversnaid Hotel Stirling 126 D2
Inverugie Aberds 153 D11
Inveruglas Argyll 126 D2
Inveruglass Highld 138 D4
Inverurie Aberds 141 B6
Invervar Perth 132 E3
Inverythan Aberds 153 D7
Inwardleigh Devon 9 E7
Inworth Essex 42 C4
Iochdar W Isles 148 D2
Iping W Sus 16 B2
Ipplepen Devon 7 C6
Ipsden Oxon 39 F6
Ipsley Worcs 51 C5
Ipstones Staffs 75 D7
Ipswich Suff 57 E5
Irby Mers 85 F3
Irby in the Marsh Lincs 79 C7
Irby upon Humber NE Lincs 91 D5
Irchester Northants 53 C7
Ireby Cumb 108 F2
Ireby Lancs 93 B6
Ireland Orkney 159 H4
Ireland Shetland 160 L5
Ireland's Cross Shrops 74 E4
Ireleth Cumb 92 B2
Ireshopeburn Durham 109 F8
Irlam Gtr Man 86 E5
Irnham Lincs 65 B7
Iron Acton S Glos 36 F3
Iron Cross Warks 51 D5
Ironbridge Telford 61 D6
Irongray Dumfries 107 B6
Ironmacannie Dumfries 106 B3
Ironside Aberds 153 C8
Ironville Derbys 76 D4
Irstead Norf 69 B6
Irthington Cumb 108 C4
Irthlingborough Northants 53 B7
Irton N Yorks 103 F8
Irvine N Ayrs 118 F3
Isauld Highld 157 C12
Isbister Orkney 159 F3
Isbister Orkney 159 G4
Isbister Shetland 160 D5
Isbister Shetland 160 G7
Isfield E Sus 17 C8
Isham Northants 53 B6
Isle Abbotts Som 11 B8
Isle Brewers Som 11 B8
Isle of Whithorn Dumfries 105 F8
Isleham Cambs 55 B7
Isleornsay Highld 149 G12
Islesburgh Shetland 160 G5
Islesteps Dumfries 107 B6
Isleworth London 28 B2
Isley Walton Leics 63 B8
Islibhig W Isles 154 E4
Islington London 41 F6
Islip Northants 53 B7
Islip Oxon 39 C5
Istead Rise Kent 29 C7
Isycoed Wrex 73 D8
Itchen Soton 14 C5
Itchen Abbas Hants 26 F3
Itchen Stoke Hants 26 F3
Itchingfield W Sus 16 B5
Itchington S Glos 36 F3
Itteringham Norf 81 D7
Itton Devon 9 E8
Itton Common Mon 36 E1
Ivegill Cumb 108 E4
Iver Bucks 40 F3
Iver Heath Bucks 40 F3
Iveston Durham 110 D4
Ivinghoe Bucks 40 C2
Ivinghoe Aston Bucks 40 C2
Ivington Hereford 49 D6
Ivington Green Hereford 49 D6
Ivy Chimneys Essex 41 D7
Ivy Cross Dorset 13 B6
Ivy Hatch Kent 29 D6
Ivybridge Devon 6 D4
Ivychurch Kent 19 C7
Iwade Kent 30 C3
Iwerne Courtney or Shroton Dorset 13 C6
Iwerne Minster Dorset 13 C6
Ixworth Suff 56 B3
Ixworth Thorpe Suff 56 B3

J

Jack Hill N Yorks 94 D5
Jack in the Green Devon 10 E5
Jacksdale Notts 76 D4
Jackstown Aberds 153 E7
Jacobstow Corn 8 E3
Jacobstowe Devon 9 D7
Jameston Pembs 32 E1
Jamestown Dumfries 115 E6
Jamestown Highld 150 F7
Jamestown W Dunb 126 F2
Jarrow T&W 111 C6
Jarvis Brook E Sus 18 C2
Jasper's Green Essex 42 B3
Java Argyll 124 B3
Jawcraig Falk 119 B8
Jaywick Essex 43 C7
Jealott's Hill Brack 27 B6
Jedburgh Borders 116 B2
Jeffreyston Pembs 32 D1
Jellyhill E Dunb 119 B6
Jemimaville Highld 151 E10
Jersey Farm Herts 40 D4
Jesmond T&W 111 C5
Jevington E Sus 18 E2
Jockey End Herts 40 C3
John o'Groats Highld 158 C5
Johnby Cumb 108 F4
John's Cross E Sus 18 C4
Johnshaven Aberds 135 C7
Johnston Pembs 44 D4
Johnstone Renfs 118 C4
Johnstonebridge Dumfries 114 E3
Johnstown Carms 33 C5
Johnstown Wrex 73 E7
Joppa Edin 121 B6
Joppa S Ayrs 112 C4
Jordans Bucks 40 E2
Jordanthorpe S Yorks 88 F4
Jump S Yorks 88 D4
Jumpers Green Dorset 14 E2
Juniper Green Edin 120 C4
Jurby East IoM 84 C3
Jurby West IoM 84 C3

K

Kaber Cumb 100 C2
Kaimend S Lanark 120 E2
Kaimes Edin 121 C5
Kalemouth Borders 116 B3
Kames Argyll 124 D4
Kames Argyll 145 F8
Kames E Ayrs 113 B6
Kea Corn 3 B7
Keadby N Lincs 90 C2
Keal Cotes Lincs 79 C6
Kearsley Gtr Man 87 D5
Kearstwick Cumb 99 F8
Kearton N Yorks 100 E4
Kearvaig Highld 156 B5
Keasden N Yorks 93 C7
Keckwick Halton 86 F3
Keddington Lincs 91 F7
Kedington Suff 55 E8
Kedleston Derbys 76 E3
Keelby Lincs 91 C5
Keele Staffs 74 E5
Keeley Green Bedford 53 E8
Keeston Pembs 44 D4
Keevil Wilts 24 D4
Kegworth Leics 63 B8
Kehelland Corn 2 B5
Keig Aberds 140 C5
Keighley W Yorks 94 E3
Keil Highld 130 D3
Keilarsbrae Clack 127 E7
Keilhill Aberds 153 C7
Keillmore Argyll 144 E5
Keillor Perth 134 E2
Keillour Perth 127 B8
Keills Argyll 142 B5
Keils Argyll 144 G4
Keinton Mandeville Som 23 F7
Keir Mill Dumfries 113 E8
Keisby Lincs 65 B7
Keiss Highld 158 D5
Keith Moray 152 C4
Keith Inch Aberds 153 D11
Keithock Angus 135 C6
Kelbrook Lancs 94 E2
Kelby Lincs 78 E3
Keld Cumb 99 C7
Keld N Yorks 100 D3
Keldholme N Yorks 103 F5
Kelfield N Lincs 90 D2
Kelfield N Yorks 95 F8
Kelham Notts 77 D7
Kellan Argyll 147 G8
Kellas Angus 134 F4
Kellas Moray 152 C1
Kellaton Devon 7 F6
Kelleth Cumb 100 D1
Kelleythorpe E Yorks 97 D5
Kelling Norf 81 C6
Kellingley N Yorks 89 B6
Kellington N Yorks 89 B6
Kelloe Durham 111 F6
Kelloholm Dumfries 113 C7
Kelly Devon 9 F5
Kelly Bray Corn 5 B8
Kelmarsh Northants 52 B5
Kelmscot Oxon 38 E2
Kelsale Suff 57 C7
Kelsall Ches W 74 C2
Kelsall Hill Ches W 74 C2
Kelshall Herts 54 F4
Kelsick Cumb 107 D8
Kelso Borders 122 F3
Kelstedge Derbys 76 C3
Kelstern Lincs 91 E6
Kelston Bath 24 C2
Keltneyburn Perth 132 E4
Kelton Dumfries 107 B6
Kelty Fife 128 E3
Kelvedon Essex 42 C4
Kelvedon Hatch Essex 42 E1
Kelvin S Lanark 119 D6
Kelvinside Glasgow 119 C5
Kelynack Corn 2 C2
Kemback Fife 129 C6
Kemberton Shrops 61 D7
Kemble Glos 37 E6
Kemerton Worcs 50 F4
Kemeys Commander Mon 35 D7
Kemnay Aberds 141 C6
Kemp Town Brighton 17 D7
Kempley Glos 36 B3
Kemps Green Warks 51 B6
Kempsey Worcs 50 E3
Kempsford Glos 38 E1
Kempshott Hants 26 D4
Kempston Bedford 53 E8
Kempston Hardwick Bedford 53 E8
Kempton Shrops 60 F3
Kemsing Kent 29 D6
Kemsley Kent 30 C3
Kenardington Kent 19 B6
Kenchester Hereford 49 E6
Kencot Oxon 38 D2
Kendal Cumb 99 E7
Kendoon Dumfries 113 F6
Kendray S Yorks 88 D4
Kenfig Bridgend 34 F2
Kenfig Hill Bridgend 34 F2
Kenilworth Warks 51 B7
Kenknock Stirling 132 F1
Kenley London 28 D4
Kenley Shrops 61 D5
Kenmore Highld 149 C12
Kenmore Perth 132 E4
Kenn Devon 10 F4
Kenn N Som 23 C6
Kennacley W Isles 154 H6
Kennacraig Argyll 145 G7
Kennerleigh Devon 10 D3
Kennet Clack 127 E8
Kennethmont Aberds 140 B4
Kennett Cambs 55 C7
Kennford Devon 10 F4
Kenninghall Norf 68 F3
Kenninghall Heath Norf 68 F3
Kennington Kent 30 E4
Kennington Oxon 39 D5
Kennoway Fife 129 D5
Kenny Hill Suff 55 B7
Kennythorpe N Yorks 96 C3
Kenovay Argyll 146 G2
Kensaleyre Highld 149 C9
Kensington London 28 B3
Kensworth C Beds 40 C3
Kensworth Common C Beds 40 C3
Kent's Oak Hants 14 B4
Kent Street E Sus 18 D4
Kent Street Kent 29 D7
Kent Street W Sus 17 B6
Kentallen Highld 130 D4
Kentchurch Hereford 35 B8
Kentford Suff 55 C8
Kentisbeare Devon 11 D5
Kentisbury Devon 20 E5
Kentisbury Ford Devon 20 E5
Kentmere Cumb 99 D6
Kenton Devon 10 F4
Kenton Suff 57 C5
Kenton T&W 110 C5
Kenton Bankfoot T&W 110 C5
Kentra Highld 147 E9
Kents Bank Cumb 92 B3
Kent's Green Glos 36 B4
Kenwick Shrops 73 F8
Kenwyn Corn 3 B7
Keoldale Highld 156 C6
Keppanach Highld 130 C4
Keppoch Highld 136 B2
Keprigan Argyll 143 G7
Kepwick N Yorks 102 E2
Kerchesters Borders 122 F3
Keresley W Mid 63 F7
Kernborough Devon 7 E5
Kerne Bridge Hereford 36 C2
Kerris Corn 2 D3
Kerry Powys 59 F8
Kerrycroy Argyll 145 G10
Kerry's Gate Hereford 49 F5
Kerrysdale Highld 149 A13
Kersall Notts 77 C7
Kersey Suff 56 E4
Kershopefoot Cumb 115 F7
Kersoe Worcs 50 F4
Kerswell Devon 11 D5
Kerswell Green Worcs 50 E3
Kesgrave Suff 57 E6
Kessingland Suff 69 F8
Kessingland Beach Suff 69 F8
Kessington E Dunb 119 B5
Kestle Corn 3 B8
Kestle Mill Corn 4 D3
Keston London 28 C5
Keswick Cumb 98 B4
Keswick Norf 68 D5
Keswick Norf 81 D9
Ketley Telford 61 C6
Ketley Bank Telford 61 C6
Ketsby Lincs 79 B6
Kettering Northants 53 B6
Ketteringham Norf 68 D4
Kettins Perth 134 F2
Kettlebaston Suff 56 D3
Kettlebridge Fife 128 D5
Kettleburgh Suff 57 C6
Kettlehill Fife 128 D5
Kettleholm Dumfries 107 B8
Kettleness N Yorks 103 C6
Kettleshume Ches E 75 B6
Kettlesing Bottom N Yorks 94 D5
Kettlesing Head N Yorks 94 D5
Kettlestone Norf 81 D5
Kettlethorpe Lincs 77 B8
Kettletoft Orkney 159 E7
Kettlewell N Yorks 94 B2
Ketton Rutland 65 D6
Kew London 28 B2
Kew Br. London 28 B2
Kewstoke N Som 22 C5
Kexbrough S Yorks 88 D4
Kexby Lincs 90 F2
Kexby York 96 D3
Key Green Ches E 75 C5
Keyham Leics 64 D3
Keyhaven Hants 14 E4
Keyingham E Yorks 91 B6
Keymer W Sus 17 C7
Keynsham Bath 23 C8
Keysoe Bedford 53 C8
Keysoe Row Bedford 53 C8
Keyston Cambs 53 B8
Keyworth Notts 77 F6
Kibblesworth T&W 110 D5
Kibworth Beauchamp Leics 64 E3
Kibworth Harcourt Leics 64 E3
Kidbrooke London 28 B5
Kiddemore Green Staffs 62 D2
Kidderminster Worcs 50 B3
Kiddington Oxon 38 B4
Kidlington Oxon 38 C4
Kidmore End Oxon 26 B4
Kidsgrove Staffs 74 D5
Kidstones N Yorks 100 F4
Kidwelly = Cydweli Carms 33 D5
Kiel Crofts Argyll 124 B5
Kielder Northumb 116 E2
Kierfiold Ho Orkney 159 G3
Kilbagie Fife 127 F8
Kilbarchan Renfs 118 C4
Kilbeg Highld 149 H11
Kilberry Argyll 144 G6
Kilbirnie N Ayrs 118 D3
Kilbride Argyll 124 C5
Kilbride Argyll 124 C5
Kilbride Highld 149 F10
Kilburn Angus 134 C3
Kilburn Derbys 76 E3
Kilburn London 41 F5
Kilburn N Yorks 95 B8
Kilby Leics 64 E3
Kilchamaig Argyll 145 G7
Kilchattan Argyll 144 D2
Kilchattan Bay Argyll 145 H10
Kilchenzie Argyll 143 F7
Kilcheran Argyll 124 B4
Kilchiaran Argyll 142 B3
Kilchoan Argyll 124 D3
Kilchoan Highld 146 E7
Kilchoman Argyll 142 B3
Kilchrenan Argyll 125 C6
Kilconquhar Fife 129 D6
Kilcot Glos 36 B3
Kilcoy Highld 151 F8
Kilcreggan Argyll 145 E11
Kildale N Yorks 102 D4
Kildalloig Argyll 143 G8
Kildary Highld 151 D10
Kildermorie Lodge Highld 151 D8
Kildonan N Ayrs 143 F11
Kildonan Lodge Highld 157 G12
Kildonnan Highld 146 C7
Kildrummy Aberds 140 C3
Kildwick N Yorks 94 E3
Kilfinan Argyll 145 F8
Kilfinnan Highld 137 E5
Kilgetty Pembs 32 D2
Kilgwrrwg Common Mon 36 E1
Kilham E Yorks 97 C6
Kilham Northumb 122 F4
Kilkenneth Argyll 146 G2
Kilkerran Argyll 143 G8
Kilkhampton Corn 9 E6
Killamarsh Derbys 89 F5
Killay Swansea 33 E7
Killbeg Argyll 147 G9
Killean Argyll 143 D7
Killearn Stirling 126 F4
Killen Highld 151 F9
Killerby Darl 101 C6
Killichonan Perth 132 D2
Killiechonate Highld 136 F5
Killiechronan Argyll 147 G8
Killiecrankie Perth 133 C6
Killiemor Argyll 146 H7
Killiemore House Argyll 146 J7
Killilan Highld 150 H2
Killimster Highld 158 E5
Killin Stirling 132 F2
Killin Lodge Highld 137 D8
Killinallan Argyll 142 A4
Killinghall N Yorks 95 D5
Killington Cumb 99 F8
Killingworth T&W 111 B5
Killmahumaig Argyll 144 D6
Killochyett Borders 121 E7
Killocraw Argyll 143 E7
Killundine Highld 147 G8
Kilmacolm Invclyd 118 C3
Kilmaha Argyll 124 E5
Kilmahog Stirling 126 D5
Kilmalieu Highld 130 D2
Kilmaluag Highld 149 A9
Kilmany Fife 129 B5
Kilmarie Highld 149 G10
Kilmarnock E Ayrs 118 F4
Kilmaron Castle Fife 129 C5
Kilmartin Argyll 124 F4
Kilmaurs E Ayrs 118 E4
Kilmelford Argyll 124 D4
Kilmeny Argyll 142 B4
Kilmersdon Som 23 D8
Kilmeston Hants 15 B6
Kilmichael Argyll 143 F7
Kilmichael Glassary Argyll 145 D7
Kilmichael of Inverlussa Argyll 144 E6
Kilmington Devon 11 E7
Kilmington Wilts 24 F2
Kilmonivaig Highld 136 F4
Kilmorack Highld 150 G7
Kilmore Argyll 124 C4
Kilmore Highld 149 H11
Kilmory Argyll 144 F6
Kilmory Highld 147 D8
Kilmory Highld 149 H8
Kilmory N Ayrs 143 F10
Kilmuir Highld 148 D7
Kilmuir Highld 149 A8
Kilmuir Highld 151 D10
Kilmuir Highld 151 G9
Kilmun Argyll 124 D5
Kilmun Argyll 145 E10
Kiln Pit Hill Northumb 110 D3
Kilncadzow S Lanark 119 E8
Kilndown Kent 18 B4
Kilnhurst S Yorks 89 E5
Kilninian Argyll 146 G6
Kilninver Argyll 124 C4
Kilnsea E Yorks 91 C8
Kilnsey N Yorks 94 C2
Kilnwick E Yorks 97 E5
Kilnwick Percy E Yorks 96 D4
Kiloran Argyll 144 D2
Kilpatrick N Ayrs 143 F10
Kilpeck Hereford 49 F6
Kilphedir Highld 157 H12
Kilpin E Yorks 89 B8
Kilpin Pike E Yorks 89 B8
Kilrenny Fife 129 D7
Kilsby Northants 52 B3
Kilspindie Perth 128 B4
Kilsyth N Lanark 119 B7
Kiltarlity Highld 151 G8
Kilton Notts 77 B5
Kilton Som 22 E3
Kilton Thorpe Redcar 102 C4
Kilvaxter Highld 149 B8
Kilve Som 22 E3
Kilvington Notts 77 E7
Kilwinning N Ayrs 118 E3
Kimberley Norf 68 D3
Kimberley Notts 76 E5
Kimble Wick Bucks 39 D8
Kimblesworth Durham 111 E5
Kimbolton Cambs 53 C8
Kimbolton Hereford 49 C7
Kimcote Leics 64 F2
Kimmeridge Dorset 13 G7
Kimmerston Northumb 123 F5
Kimpton Hants 25 E7
Kimpton Herts 40 C4
Kinbrace Highld 157 F11
Kinbuck Stirling 127 D6
Kincaple Fife 129 C6
Kincardine Fife 127 F8
Kincardine Highld 151 C9
Kincardine Bridge Falk 127 F8
Kincardine O'Neil Aberds 140 E4
Kinclaven Perth 134 F1
Kincorth Aberdeen 141 D8
Kincorth Ho. Moray 151 E13
Kincraig Highld 138 D4
Kincraigie Perth 133 E6
Kindallachan Perth 133 E6
Kineton Glos 37 B7
Kineton Warks 51 D8
Kinfauns Perth 128 B3
King Edward Aberds 153 C7
King Sterndale Derbys 75 B7
Kingairloch Highld 130 D2
Kingarth Argyll 145 H9
Kingcoed Mon 35 D8
Kingerby Lincs 90 E4
Kingham Oxon 38 B2
Kingholm Quay Dumfries 107 B6
Kinghorn Fife 128 F4
Kingie Highld 136 D4
Kinglassie Fife 128 E4
Kingoodie Perth 128 B5
King's Acre Hereford 49 E6
King's Bromley Staffs 62 C5
King's Caple Hereford 36 B2
King's Cliffe Northants 65 E7
King's Coughton Warks 51 D5
King's Heath W Mid 62 F4
Kings Hedges Cambs 55 C5
Kings Langley Herts 40 D3
King's Hill Kent 29 D7
King's Lynn Norf 67 B6
King's Meaburn Cumb 99 B8
King's Mills Wrex 73 E7
Kings Muir Borders 121 F5
King's Newnham Warks 52 B2
King's Newton Derbys 63 B7
King's Norton Leics 64 D3
King's Norton W Mid 51 B5
King's Nympton Devon 9 C8
King's Pyon Hereford 49 D6
King's Ripton Cambs 54 B3
King's Somborne Hants 25 F8
King's Stag Dorset 12 C5
King's Stanley Glos 37 D5
King's Sutton Northants 52 F2
King's Thorn Hereford 49 F7
King's Walden Herts 40 B4
Kings Worthy Hants 26 F2
Kingsand Corn 6 D2
Kingsbarns Fife 129 C7
Kingsbridge Devon 6 E5
Kingsbridge Som 21 F8
Kingsburgh Highld 149 C8
Kingsbury London 41 F5
Kingsbury Warks 63 E6
Kingsbury Episcopi Som 12 B2
Kingsclere Hants 26 D3
Kingscote Glos 37 E5
Kingscott Devon 9 C7
Kingscross N Ayrs 143 F11
Kingsdon Som 12 B3
Kingsdown Kent 31 E7
Kingseat Fife 128 E3
Kingsey Bucks 39 D7
Kingsfold W Sus 28 F2
Kingsford E Ayrs 118 E4
Kingsford Worcs 62 F2
Kingsforth N Lincs 90 C4
Kingsgate Kent 31 B7
Kingsheanton Devon 20 F4
Kingshouse Hotel Highld 131 D6
Kingside Hill Cumb 107 D8
Kingskerswell Devon 7 C6
Kingskettle Fife 128 D5
Kingsland Anglesey 82 C2
Kingsland Hereford 49 C6
Kingsley Ches W 74 B2
Kingsley Hants 27 F5
Kingsley Staffs 75 E7
Kingsley Green W Sus 27 F6
Kingsley Holt Staffs 75 E7
Kingsley Park Northants 53 C5
Kingsmuir Angus 134 E4
Kingsmuir Fife 129 D7
Kingsnorth Kent 19 B7
Kingstanding W Mid 62 E4
Kingsteignton Devon 7 B6
Kingsthorpe Northants 53 C5
Kingston Cambs 54 D4
Kingston Devon 6 E4
Kingston Dorset 13 D5
Kingston Dorset 13 G7
Kingston E Loth 129 F7
Kingston Hants 14 D2
Kingston IoW 15 F5
Kingston Kent 31 D5
Kingston Moray 152 B3
Kingston Bagpuize Oxon 38 E4
Kingston Blount Oxon 39 E7
Kingston by Sea W Sus 17 D6
Kingston Deverill Wilts 24 F3
Kingston Gorse W Sus 16 D4
Kingston Lisle Oxon 38 F3
Kingston Maurward Dorset 12 E5
Kingston near Lewes E Sus 17 D7
Kingston on Soar Notts 64 B2
Kingston Russell Dorset 12 E3
Kingston Seymour N Som 23 C6
Kingston St Mary Som 11 B7
Kingston Upon Hull Hull 90 B4
Kingston upon Thames London 28 C2
Kingston Vale London 28 B3
Kingstone Hereford 49 F6
Kingstone Som 11 C8
Kingstone Staffs 62 B4
Kingstown Cumb 108 D3
Kingswear Devon 7 D6
Kingswells Aberdeen 141 D7
Kingswinford W Mid 62 F2
Kingswood Bucks 39 C6
Kingswood Glos 36 E4
Kingswood Hereford 48 D4
Kingswood Kent 30 D2
Kingswood Powys 60 D2
Kingswood S Glos 23 B8
Kingswood Sur 28 D3
Kingswood Warks 51 B6
Kingthorpe Lincs 78 B4
Kington Hereford 48 D4
Kington Worcs 50 D4
Kington Langley Wilts 24 B4
Kington Magna Dorset 13 B5
Kington St Michael Wilts 24 B4
Kingussie Highld 138 D3
Kingweston Som 23 F7
Kininvie Ho. Moray 152 D3
Kinkell Bridge Perth 127 C8
Kinknockie Aberds 153 D10
Kinlet Shrops 61 F7
Kinloch Fife 128 C4
Kinloch Highld 146 B6
Kinloch Highld 149 G11
Kinloch Highld 156 F6
Kinloch Perth 133 E8
Kinloch Perth 134 E2
Kinloch Hourn Highld 136 D2
Kinloch Laggan Highld 137 F8
Kinloch Lodge Highld 157 D8
Kinloch Rannoch Perth 132 D3
Kinlochan Highld 130 C2
Kinlochard Stirling 126 D3
Kinlochbeoraid Highld 147 C11
Kinlochbervie Highld 156 D5
Kinlocheil Highld 130 B3
Kinlochewe Highld 150 E3
Kinlochleven Highld 131 C5
Kinlochmoidart Highld 147 D10
Kinlochmorar Highld 147 B11
Kinlochmore Highld 131 C5
Kinlochspelve Argyll 124 C2
Kinloid Highld 147 C9
Kinloss Moray 151 E13
Kinmel Bay Conwy 72 A3
Kinmuck Aberds 141 C7
Kinmundy Aberds 141 C7
Kinnadie Aberds 153 D9
Kinnaird Perth 128 B4
Kinnaird Castle Angus 135 D6
Kinneff Aberds 135 B8
Kinnelhead Dumfries 114 D3
Kinnell Angus 135 D6
Kinnerley Shrops 60 B3
Kinnersley Hereford 48 E5
Kinnersley Worcs 50 E3
Kinnerton Powys 48 C4
Kinnesswood Perth 128 D3
Kinninvie Durham 101 B5
Kinnordy Angus 134 D3
Kinoulton Notts 77 F6
Kinross Perth 128 D3
Kinrossie Perth 134 F1
Kinsbourne Green Herts 40 C4
Kinsey Heath Ches E 74 E3
Kinsham Hereford 49 C5
Kinsham Worcs 50 F4
Kinsley W Yorks 88 C5
Kinson Bmouth 13 E8
Kintbury W Berks 25 C8
Kintessack Moray 151 E12
Kintillo Perth 128 C3
Kintocher Aberds 140 D4
Kinton Hereford 49 B6
Kinton Shrops 60 C3
Kintore Aberds 141 C6
Kintour Argyll 142 C5
Kintra Argyll 142 D4
Kintra Argyll 146 J6
Kintraw Argyll 124 E4
Kinuachdrachd Argyll 124 F3
Kinveachy Highld 138 C5
Kinver Staffs 62 F2
Kippax W Yorks 95 F7
Kippen Stirling 127 E5
Kippford or Scaur Dumfries 106 D5
Kirbister Orkney 159 F7
Kirbister Orkney 159 H4
Kirbuster Orkney 159 F3
Kirby Bedon Norf 69 D5
Kirby Bellars Leics 64 C4
Kirby Cane Norf 69 E6
Kirby Cross Essex 43 B8
Kirby Grindalythe N Yorks 96 C5
Kirby Hill N Yorks 95 C6
Kirby Hill N Yorks 101 D6
Kirby Knowle N Yorks 102 F2
Kirby-le-Soken Essex 43 B8
Kirby Misperton N Yorks 96 B3
Kirby Muxloe Leics 64 D2
Kirby Row Norf 69 E6
Kirby Sigston N Yorks 102 E2
Kirby Underdale E Yorks 96 D4
Kirby Wiske N Yorks 102 F1
Kirdford W Sus 16 B4
Kirk Highld 158 E4
Kirk Bramwith S Yorks 89 C7
Kirk Deighton N Yorks 95 D6
Kirk Ella E Yorks 90 B4
Kirk Hallam Derbys 76 E4
Kirk Hammerton N Yorks 95 D7
Kirk Ireton Derbys 76 D2
Kirk Langley Derbys 76 F2
Kirk Merrington Durham 111 F5
Kirk Michael IoM 84 C3
Kirk of Shotts N Lanark 119 C8
Kirk Sandall S Yorks 89 D7
Kirk Smeaton N Yorks 89 C6
Kirk Yetholm Borders 116 B4
Kirkabister Shetland 160 K6
Kirkandrews Dumfries 106 E3
Kirkandrews upon Eden Cumb 108 D3
Kirkbampton Cumb 108 D3
Kirkbean Dumfries 107 D6
Kirkbride Cumb 108 D2
Kirkbuddo Angus 135 E5
Kirkburn Borders 121 F5
Kirkburn E Yorks 97 D5
Kirkburton W Yorks 88 C2
Kirkby Lincs 90 E4
Kirkby Mers 86 E2
Kirkby N Yorks 102 D3
Kirkby Fleetham N Yorks 101 E7
Kirkby Green Lincs 78 D3
Kirkby in Ashfield Notts 76 D5
Kirkby-in-Furness Cumb 98 F4
Kirkby la Thorpe Lincs 78 E3
Kirkby Lonsdale Cumb 93 B6
Kirkby Malham N Yorks 93 C8
Kirkby Mallory Leics 63 D8
Kirkby Malzeard N Yorks 94 B5
Kirkby Mills N Yorks 103 F5
Kirkby on Bain Lincs 78 C5
Kirkby Overflow N Yorks 95 E6
Kirkby Stephen Cumb 100 D2
Kirkby Thore Cumb 99 B8
Kirkby Underwood Lincs 65 B7
Kirkby Wharfe N Yorks 95 E8
Kirkbymoorside N Yorks 102 F4
Kirkcaldy Fife 128 E4
Kirkcambeck Cumb 108 C5
Kirkcarswell Dumfries 106 E4
Kirkcolm Dumfries 104 C4
Kirkconnel Dumfries 113 C7
Kirkconnell Dumfries 107 C6
Kirkcowan Dumfries 105 C7
Kirkcudbright Dumfries 106 D3
Kirkdale Mers 85 E4
Kirkfieldbank S Lanark 119 E8
Kirkgunzeon Dumfries 107 C5
Kirkham Lancs 92 F4
Kirkham N Yorks 96 C3
Kirkhamgate W Yorks 88 B3
Kirkharle Northumb 117 F6
Kirkheaton Northumb 110 B3
Kirkheaton W Yorks 88 C2
Kirkhill Angus 135 C6
Kirkhill Highld 151 G8
Kirkhill Midloth 120 C5
Kirkhill Moray 152 E2
Kirkhope Borders 115 B6
Kirkhouse Borders 121 F6
Kirkiboll Highld 157 D8
Kirkibost Highld 149 G10
Kirkinch Angus 134 E3
Kirkinner Dumfries 105 D8
Kirkintilloch E Dunb 119 B6
Kirkland Cumb 98 C2
Kirkland Cumb 109 F6
Kirkland Dumfries 113 C7
Kirkland Dumfries 113 E8
Kirkleatham Redcar 102 B3
Kirklevington Stockton 102 D2
Kirkley Suff 69 E8
Kirklington N Yorks 101 F8
Kirklington Notts 77 D6
Kirklinton Cumb 108 C4
Kirkliston Edin 120 B4
Kirkmaiden Dumfries 104 F5
Kirkmichael Perth 133 D8
Kirkmichael S Ayrs 112 D3
Kirkmuirhill S Lanark 119 E7
Kirknewton Northumb 122 F5
Kirknewton W Loth 120 C4
Kirkney Aberds 152 E5
Kirkoswald Cumb 109 E5
Kirkoswald S Ayrs 112 D2
Kirkpatrick Durham Dumfries 106 B4
Kirkpatrick-Fleming Dumfries 108 B2
Kirksanton Cumb 98 F3
Kirkstall W Yorks 95 F5
Kirkstead Lincs 78 C4
Kirkstile Aberds 152 E5
Kirkstyle Highld 158 C5
Kirkton Aberds 140 B5
Kirkton Aberds 153 D6
Kirkton Angus 134 E4
Kirkton Angus 134 F4
Kirkton Borders 115 C8
Kirkton Dumfries 114 F2
Kirkton Fife 129 B5
Kirkton Highld 149 F13
Kirkton Highld 150 G2
Kirkton Highld 151 B10
Kirkton Highld 151 F10
Kirkton Perth 127 C8
Kirkton S Lanark 114 B2
Kirkton Stirling 126 D4
Kirkton Manor Borders 120 F5
Kirkton of Airlie Angus 134 D3

Llanbadarn Fynydd Powys 48 B3
Llanbadarn-y-Garreg Powys 48 E3
Llanbadoc Mon 35 E7
Llanbadrig Anglesey 82 B3
Llanbeder Newport 35 E7
Llanbedr Gwyn 71 E6
Llanbedr Powys 35 B6
Llanbedr Powys 48 E3
Llanbedr-Dyffryn-Clwyd Denb 72 D5
Llanbedr Pont Steffan = Lampeter Ceredig 46 E4
Llanbedr-y-cennin Conwy 83 E7
Llanbedrgoch Anglesey 82 C5
Llanbedrog Gwyn 70 D4
Llanberis Gwyn 83 E5
Llanbethêry V Glam 22 C2
Llanbister Powys 48 B3
Llanblethian V Glam 21 B8
Llanboidy Carms 32 B3
Llanbradach Caerph 35 E5
Llanbrynmair Powys 59 D5
Llancarfan V Glam 22 B2
Llancayo Mon 35 D7
Llancloudy Hereford 36 B1
Llancynfelyn Ceredig 58 E3
Llandaff Cardiff 22 B3
Llandanwg Gwyn 71 E6
Llandarcy Neath 33 E8
Llandawke Carms 32 C3
Llanddaniel Fab Anglesey 82 D4
Llanddarog Carms 33 C6
Llanddeiniol Ceredig 46 B4
Llanddeiniolen Gwyn 82 E5
Llandderfel Gwyn 72 F3
Llanddeusant Anglesey 82 C3
Llanddeusant Carms 34 B1
Llanddew Powys 48 F2
Llanddewi Swansea 33 F5
Llanddewi-Brefi Ceredig 47 D5
Llanddewi Rhydderch Mon 35 C7
Llanddewi Velfrey Pembs 32 C2
Llanddewi'r Cwm Powys 48 E2
Llanddoged Conwy 83 E8
Llanddona Anglesey 83 D5
Llanddowror Carms 32 C3
Llanddulas Conwy 72 B3
Llanddwywe Gwyn 71 E6
Llanddyfynan Anglesey 82 D5
Llandefaelog Fach Powys 48 F2
Llandefaelog-tre'r-graig Powys 35 B5
Llandefalle Powys 48 F3
Llandegai Gwyn 83 D5
Llandegfan Anglesey 83 D5
Llandegla Denb 73 D5
Llandegley Powys 48 C3
Llandegveth Mon 35 E7
Llandegwning Gwyn 70 D3
Llandeilo Carms 33 B7
Llandeilo Graban Powys 48 E2
Llandeilo'r Fan Powys 47 F7
Llandeloy Pembs 44 C3
Llandenny Mon 35 D8
Llandevenny Mon 35 F8
Llandewednock Corn 3 E6
Llandewi Ystradenny Powys 48 C3
Llandinabo Hereford 36 B2
Llandinam Powys 59 F7
Llandissilio Pembs 32 B2
Llandogo Mon 36 D2
Llandough V Glam 21 B8
Llandough V Glam 22 B3
Llandovery = Llanymddyfri Carms 47 F6
Llandow V Glam 21 B8
Llandre Carms 47 E5
Llandre Ceredig 58 F3
Llandrillo Denb 72 F4
Llandrillo-yn-Rhos Conwy 83 C8
Llandrindod = Llandrindod Wells Powys 48 C2
Llandrindod Wells = Llandrindod Powys 48 C2
Llandrinio Powys 60 C2
Llandudno Conwy 83 C7
Llandudno Junction = Cyffordd Llandudno Conwy 83 D7
Llandwrog Gwyn 82 F4
Llandybie Carms 33 C7
Llandyfaelog Carms 33 C5
Llandyfan Carms 33 C7
Llandyfriog Ceredig 46 E2
Llandyfrydog Anglesey 82 C4
Llandygwydd Ceredig 45 E4
Llandynan Denb 73 E5
Llandyrnog Denb 72 C5
Llandysilio Powys 60 C2
Llandyssil Powys 59 E8
Llandysul Ceredig 46 E3
Llanedeyrn Cardiff 35 F6
Llanedi Carms 33 D6
Llaneglwys Powys 48 F2
Llanegryn Gwyn 58 D2
Llanegwad Carms 33 B6
Llaneilian Anglesey 82 B4
Llanelian-yn-Rhos Conwy 83 D8
Llanelidan Denb 72 D5
Llanelieu Powys 48 F3
Llanellen Mon 35 C7
Llanelli Carms 33 E6
Llanelltyd Gwyn 58 C4
Llanelly Mon 35 C6
Llanelly Hill Mon 35 C6
Llanelwedd Powys 48 D2
Llanelwy = St Asaph Denb 72 B4
Llanenddwyn Gwyn 71 E6
Llanengan Gwyn 70 E3
Llanerchymedd Anglesey 82 C4
Llanerfyl Powys 59 D7
Llanfachraeth Anglesey 82 C3
Llanfachreth Gwyn 71 E8
Llanfaelog Anglesey 82 D3
Llanfaelrhys Gwyn 70 E3
Llanfaenor Mon 35 C8
Llanfaes Anglesey 83 D6
Llanfaes Powys 34 B4
Llanfaethlu Anglesey 82 C3
Llanfaglan Gwyn 82 E4
Llanfair Gwyn 71 E6
Llanfair-ar-y-bryn Carms 47 F7
Llanfair Caereinion Powys 59 D8
Llanfair Clydogau Ceredig 46 D5
Llanfair-Dyffryn-Clwyd Denb 72 D5
Llanfair Kilgeddin Mon 35 D7
Llanfair-Nant-Gwyn Pembs 45 F3
Llanfair Talhaiarn Conwy 72 B3
Llanfair Waterdine Shrops 48 B4
Llanfair-Ym-Muallt = Builth Wells Powys 48 D2
Llanfairfechan Conwy 83 D6
Llanfairpwll-gwyngyll Anglesey 82 D5
Llanfairyneubwll Anglesey 82 D3
Llanfairynghornwy Anglesey 82 B3
Llanfallteg Carms 32 C2
Llanfaredd Powys 48 D2
Llanfarian Ceredig 46 B4
Llanfechain Powys 59 B8
Llanfechan Powys 47 D8
Llanfechell Anglesey 82 B3
Llanfendigaid Gwyn 58 D2
Llanferres Denb 73 C5
Llanfflewyn Anglesey 82 C3
Llanfihangel-ar-arth Carms 46 F3
Llanfihangel-Crucorney Mon 35 B7
Llanfihangel Glyn Myfyr Conwy 72 E3
Llanfihangel Nant Bran Powys 47 F8
Llanfihangel-nant-Melan Powys 48 D3
Llanfihangel Rhydithon Powys 48 C3
Llanfihangel Rogiet Mon 35 F8
Llanfihangel Tal-y-llyn Powys 35 B5
Llanfihangel-uwch-Gwili Carms 33 B5
Llanfihangel-y-Creuddyn Ceredig 47 B5
Llanfihangel-y-pennant Gwyn 58 D3
Llanfihangel-y-pennant Gwyn 71 C6
Llanfihangel-y-traethau Gwyn 71 D6
Llanfihangel-yn-Ngwynfa Powys 59 C7
Llanfihangel yn Nhowyn Anglesey 82 D3
Llanfilo Powys 48 F3
Llanfoist Mon 35 C6
Llanfor Gwyn 72 F3
Llanfrechfa Torf 35 E7
Llanfrothen Gwyn 71 C7
Llanfrynach Powys 34 B4
Llanfwrog Anglesey 82 C3
Llanfwrog Denb 72 D5
Llanfyllin Powys 59 C8
Llanfynydd Carms 33 B6
Llanfynydd Flint 73 D6
Llanfyrnach Pembs 45 F4
Llangadfan Powys 59 C7
Llangadog Carms 33 B8
Llangadwaladr Anglesey 82 E3
Llangadwaladr Powys 73 F5
Llangaffo Anglesey 82 E4
Llangain Carms 32 C4
Llangammarch Wells Powys 47 E8
Llangan V Glam 21 B8
Llangarron Hereford 36 B2
Llangasty Talyllyn Powys 35 B5
Llangathen Carms 33 B6
Llangattock Powys 35 C6
Llangattock Lingoed Mon 35 B7
Llangattock nigh Usk Mon 35 D7
Llangattock-Vibon-Avel Mon 36 C1
Llangedwyn Powys 59 B8
Llangefni Anglesey 82 D4
Llangeinor Bridgend 34 F3
Llangeitho Ceredig 46 D5
Llangeler Carms 46 F2
Llangelynin Gwyn 58 D2
Llangendeirne Carms 33 C5
Llangennech Carms 33 D6
Llangennith Swansea 33 E5
Llangenny Powys 35 C6
Llangernyw Conwy 83 E8
Llangian Gwyn 70 E3
Llanglydwen Carms 32 B2
Llangoed Anglesey 83 D6
Llangoedmor Ceredig 45 E3
Llangollen Denb 73 E6
Llangolman Pembs 32 B2
Llangors Powys 35 B5
Llangovan Mon 36 D1
Llangower Gwyn 72 F3
Llangrannog Ceredig 46 D2
Llangristiolus Anglesey 82 D4
Llangrove Hereford 36 C2
Llangua Mon 35 B7
Llangunllo Powys 48 B4
Llangunnor Carms 33 C5
Llangurig Powys 47 B8
Llangwm Conwy 72 E3
Llangwm Mon 35 D8
Llangwm Pembs 44 E4
Llangwnnadl Gwyn 70 D3
Llangwyfan Denb 72 C5
Llangwyfan-isaf Anglesey 82 E3
Llangwyllog Anglesey 82 D4
Llangwyryfon Ceredig 46 B4
Llangybi Ceredig 46 D5
Llangybi Gwyn 70 C5
Llangybi Mon 35 E7
Llangyfelach Swansea 33 E7
Llangynhafal Denb 72 C5
Llangynidr Powys 35 C5
Llangynin Carms 32 C3
Llangynog Carms 32 C4
Llangynog Powys 59 B7
Llangynwyd Bridgend 34 F2
Llanhamlach Powys 34 B4
Llanharan Rhondda 34 F4
Llanharry Rhondda 34 F4
Llanhennock Mon 35 E7
Llanhiledd = Llanhilleth Bl Gwent 35 D6
Llanhilleth = Llanhiledd Bl Gwent 35 D6
Llanidloes Powys 59 F6
Llaniestyn Gwyn 70 D3
Llanifyny Powys 59 F5
Llanigon Powys 48 F4
Llanilar Ceredig 46 B5
Llanilid Rhondda 34 F3
Llanilltud Fawr = Llantwit Major V Glam 21 C8
Llanishen Cardiff 35 F5
Llanishen Mon 36 D1
Llanllawddog Carms 33 B5
Llanllechid Gwyn 83 E6
Llanllowell Mon 35 E7
Llanllugan Powys 59 D7
Llanllwch Carms 32 C4
Llanllwchaiarn Powys 59 E8
Llanllwni Carms 46 F3
Llanllyfni Gwyn 82 F4
Llanmadoc Swansea 33 E5
Llanmaes V Glam 21 C8
Llanmartin Newport 35 F7
Llanmihangel V Glam 21 B8
Llanmorlais Swansea 33 E6
Llannefydd Conwy 72 B3
Llannon Carms 33 D6
Llannor Gwyn 70 D4
Llanon Ceredig 46 C4
Llanover Mon 35 D7
Llanpumsaint Carms 33 B5
Llanreithan Pembs 44 C3
Llanrhaeadr Denb 72 C4
Llanrhaeadr-ym-Mochnant Powys 59 B8
Llanrhian Pembs 44 B3
Llanrhidian Swansea 33 E5
Llanrhos Conwy 83 C7
Llanrhyddlad Anglesey 82 C3
Llanrhystud Ceredig 46 C4
Llanrosser Hereford 48 F4
Llanrothal Hereford 36 C1
Llanrug Gwyn 82 E5
Llanrumsaint Cardiff 35 F6
Llanrwst Conwy 83 E8
Llansadurnen Carms 32 C3
Llansadwrn Anglesey 83 D5
Llansadwrn Carms 47 F5
Llansaint Carms 32 D4
Llansamlet Swansea 33 E7
Llansanffraid-ym-Mechain Powys 60 B2
Llansannan Conwy 72 C3
Llansannor V Glam 21 B8
Llansantffraed Ceredig 46 C4
Llansantffraed Powys 35 B5
Llansantffraed Cwmdeuddwr Powys 47 C8
Llansantffraed-in-Elvel Powys 48 D2
Llansawel Carms 46 F5
Llansilin Powys 60 B2
Llansoy Mon 35 D8
Llanspyddid Powys 34 B4
Llanstadwell Pembs 44 E4
Llansteffan Carms 32 C4
Llanstephan Powys 48 E3
Llantarnam Torf 35 E7
Llanteg Pembs 32 C2
Llanthony Mon 35 B6
Llantilio Crossenny Mon 35 C7
Llantilio Pertholey Mon 35 C7
Llantood Pembs 45 E3
Llantrisant Anglesey 82 C3
Llantrisant Mon 35 E7
Llantrisant Rhondda 34 F4
Llantrithyd V Glam 22 B2
Llantwit Fardre Rhondda 34 F4
Llantwit Major = Llanilltud Fawr V Glam 21 C8
Llanuwchllyn Gwyn 72 F2
Llanvaches Newport 35 E8
Llanvair Discoed Mon 35 E8
Llanvapley Mon 35 C7
Llanvetherine Mon 35 C7
Llanveynoe Hereford 48 F5
Llanvihangel Gobion Mon 35 D7
Llanvihangel-Ystern-Llewern Mon 35 C8
Llanwarne Hereford 36 B2
Llanwddyn Powys 59 C7
Llanwenog Ceredig 46 E3
Llanwern Newport 35 F7
Llanwinio Carms 32 B3
Llanwnda Gwyn 82 F4
Llanwnda Pembs 44 B4
Llanwnnen Ceredig 46 E4
Llanwnog Powys 59 E7
Llanwrda Carms 47 F6
Llanwrin Powys 58 D4
Llanwrthwl Powys 47 C8
Llanwrtud = Llanwrtyd Wells Powys 47 E7
Llanwrtyd Powys 47 E7
Llanwrtyd Wells = Llanwrtud Powys 47 E7
Llanwyddelan Powys 59 D7
Llanyblodwel Shrops 60 B2
Llanybri Carms 32 C4
Llanybydder Carms 46 E4
Llanycefn Pembs 32 B1
Llanychaer Pembs 44 B4
Llanycil Gwyn 72 F3
Llanycrwys Carms 46 E5
Llanymawddwy Gwyn 59 C6
Llanymddyfri = Llandovery Carms 47 F6
Llanymynech Powys 60 B2
Llanynghenedl Anglesey 82 C3
Llanynys Denb 72 C5
Llanyre Powys 48 C2
Llanystumdwy Gwyn 71 D5
Llanywern Powys 35 B5
Llawhaden Pembs 32 C1
Llawnt Shrops 73 F6
Llawr Dref Gwyn 70 E3
Llawryglyn Powys 59 E6
Llay Wrex 73 D7
Llechcynfarwy Anglesey 82 C3
Llecheiddior Gwyn 71 C5
Llechfaen Powys 34 B4
Llechryd Caerph 35 D5
Llechryd Ceredig 45 E4
Llechrydau Powys 73 F6
Lledrod Ceredig 46 B5
Llenmerewig Powys 59 E8
Llethrid Swansea 33 E6
Llidiad Nenog Carms 46 F4
Llidiardau Gwyn 72 F2
Llidiart-y-parc Denb 72 E5
Llithfaen Gwyn 70 C4
Llong Flint 73 C6
Llowes Powys 48 E3
Llundain-fach Ceredig 46 D4
Llwydcoed Rhondda 34 D3
Llwyn Shrops 60 F2
Llwyn-du Mon 35 C6
Llwyn-hendy Carms 33 E6
Llwyn-têg Carms 33 D6
Llwyn-y-brain Carms 32 C2
Llwyn-y-groes Ceredig 46 D4
Llwyncelyn Ceredig 46 D3
Llwyndafydd Ceredig 46 D2
Llwynderw Powys 60 D2
Llwyndyrys Gwyn 70 C4
Llwyngwril Gwyn 58 D2
Llwynmawr Wrex 73 F6
Llwynypia Rhondda 34 E3
Llynclys Shrops 60 B2
Llynfaes Anglesey 82 D4
Llys-y-frân Pembs 32 B1
Llysfaen Conwy 83 D8
Llyswen Powys 48 F3
Llysworney V Glam 21 B8
Llywel Powys 47 F7
Loan Falk 120 B2
Loanend Northumb 122 D5
Loanhead Midloth 121 C5
Loans S Ayrs 118 F3
Loans of Tullich Highld 151 D11
Lobb Devon 20 F3
Loch a Charnain W Isles 148 D3
Loch a' Ghainmhich W Isles 155 E7
Loch Baghasdail = Lochboisdale W Isles 148 G2
Loch Choire Lodge Highld 157 F9
Loch Euphoirt W Isles 148 B3
Loch Head Dumfries 105 E7
Loch Loyal Lodge Highld 157 E9
Loch nam Madadh = Lochmaddy W Isles 148 B4
Loch Sgioport W Isles 148 E3
Lochailort Highld 147 C10
Lochaline Highld 147 G9
Lochanhully Highld 138 B5
Lochans Dumfries 104 D4
Locharbriggs Dumfries 114 F2
Lochassynt Lodge Highld 156 G4
Lochavich Ho Argyll 124 D5
Lochawe Argyll 125 C7
Lochboisdale = Loch Baghasdail W Isles 148 G2
Lochbuie Argyll 124 C2
Lochcarron Highld 149 E13
Lochdhu Highld 157 E13
Lochdochart House Stirling 126 B3
Lochdon Argyll 124 B3
Lochdrum Highld 150 D5
Lochead Argyll 144 F6
Lochearnhead Stirling 126 B4
Lochee Dundee 134 F3
Lochend Highld 151 H8
Lochend Highld 158 D4
Locherben Dumfries 114 E2
Lochfoot Dumfries 107 B5
Lochgair Argyll 145 D8
Lochgarthside Highld 137 C8
Lochgelly Fife 128 E3
Lochgilphead Argyll 145 E7
Lochgoilhead Argyll 125 E8
Lochhill Moray 152 B2
Lochindorb Lodge Highld 151 H12
Lochinver Highld 156 G3
Lochlane Perth 127 B7
Lochluichart Highld 150 E6
Lochmaben Dumfries 114 F3
Lochmaddy = Loch nam Madadh W Isles 148 B4
Lochmore Cottage Highld 158 F2
Lochmore Lodge Highld 156 F5
Lochore Fife 128 E3
Lochportain W Isles 148 A4
Lochranza N Ayrs 143 C10
Lochs Crofts Moray 152 B3
Lochside Aberds 135 C7
Lochside Highld 151 F11
Lochside Highld 156 D7
Lochside Highld 157 F11
Lochslin Highld 151 C11
Lochstack Lodge Highld 156 E5
Lochton Aberds 141 E6
Lochty Angus 135 C5
Lochty Fife 129 D7
Lochty Perth 128 B2
Lochuisge Highld 130 D1
Lochurr Dumfries 113 F7
Lochwinnoch Renfs 118 D3
Lochwood Dumfries 114 E3
Lochyside Highld 131 B5
Lockengate Corn 4 C5
Lockerbie Dumfries 114 F4
Lockeridge Wilts 25 C6
Lockerley Hants 14 B3
Locking N Som 23 D5
Lockinge Oxon 38 F4
Lockington E Yorks 97 E5
Lockington Leics 63 B8
Lockleywood Shrops 61 B6
Locks Heath Hants 15 D6
Lockton N Yorks 103 E6
Lockwood W Yorks 88 C2
Loddington Leics 64 D4
Loddington Northants 53 B6
Loddiswell Devon 6 E5
Loddon Norf 69 E6
Lode Cambs 55 C6
Loders Dorset 12 E2
Lodsworth W Sus 16 B3
Lofthouse N Yorks 94 B4
Lofthouse W Yorks 88 B4
Loftus Redcar 103 C5
Logan E Ayrs 113 B5
Logan Mains Dumfries 104 E4
Loganlea W Loth 120 C2
Loggerheads Staffs 74 F4
Logie Angus 135 C6
Logie Fife 129 B6
Logie Moray 151 F13
Logie Coldstone Aberds 140 D3
Logie Hill Highld 151 D10
Logie Newton Aberds 153 E6
Logie Pert Angus 135 C6
Logiealmond Lodge Perth 133 F6
Logierait Perth 133 D6
Login Carms 32 B2
Lolworth Cambs 54 C4
Lonbain Highld 149 C11
Londesborough E Yorks 96 E4
London Colney Herts 40 D4
Londonderry N Yorks 101 F8
Londonthorpe Lincs 78 F2
Londubh Highld 155 J13
Lonemore Highld 151 C10
Long Ashton N Som 23 B7
Long Bennington Lincs 77 E8
Long Bredy Dorset 12 E3
Long Buckby Northants 52 C4
Long Clawson Leics 64 B4
Long Common Hants 15 C6
Long Compton Staffs 62 B2
Long Compton Warks 51 F7
Long Crendon Bucks 39 D6
Long Crichel Dorset 13 C7
Long Ditton Sur 28 C2
Long Drax N Yorks 89 B7
Long Duckmanton Derbys 76 B4
Long Eaton Derbys 76 F4
Long Green Worcs 50 F3
Long Hanborough Oxon 38 C4
Long Itchington Warks 52 C2
Long Lawford Warks 52 B2
Long Load Som 12 B2
Long Marston Herts 40 C1
Long Marston N Yorks 95 D8
Long Marston Warks 51 E6
Long Marton Cumb 100 B1
Long Melford Suff 56 E2
Long Newnton Glos 37 E6
Long Newton E Loth 121 C8
Long Preston N Yorks 93 D8
Long Riston E Yorks 97 E7
Long Sight Gtr Man 87 D7
Long Stratton Norf 68 E4
Long Street M Keynes 53 E5
Long Sutton Hants 26 E5
Long Sutton Lincs 66 B4
Long Sutton Som 12 B2
Long Thurlow Suff 56 C4
Long Whatton Leics 63 B8
Long Wittenham Oxon 39 E5
Longbar N Ayrs 118 D3
Longbenton T&W 111 C5
Longborough Glos 38 B1
Longbridge W Mid 50 B5
Longbridge Warks 51 C7
Longbridge Deverill Wilts 24 E3
Longburton Dorset 12 C4
Longcliffe Derbys 76 D2
Longcot Oxon 38 E2
Longcroft Falk 119 B7
Longden Shrops 60 D4
Longdon Staffs 62 C4
Longdon Worcs 50 F3
Longdon Green Staffs 62 C4
Longdon on Tern Telford 61 C6
Longdown Devon 10 E3
Longdowns Corn 3 C6
Longfield Kent 29 C7
Longfield Shetland 160 M5
Longford Derbys 76 F2
Longford Glos 37 B5
Longford London 27 B8
Longford Shrops 74 F3
Longford Telford 61 C7
Longford W Mid 63 F7
Longfordlane Derbys 76 F2
Longforgan Perth 128 B5
Longformacus Borders 122 D2
Longframlington Northumb 117 D7
Longham Dorset 13 E8
Longham Norf 68 C2
Longhaven Aberds 153 E11
Longhill Aberds 153 C9
Longhirst Northumb 117 F8
Longhope Glos 36 C3
Longhope Orkney 159 J4
Longhorsley Northumb 117 E7
Longhoughton Northumb 117 C8
Longlane Derbys 76 F2
Longlane W Berks 26 B2
Longlevens Glos 37 B5
Longley W Yorks 88 D2
Longley Green Worcs 50 D2
Longmanhill Aberds 153 B7
Longmoor Camp Hants 27 F5
Longmorn Moray 152 C2
Longnewton Borders 115 B8
Longnewton Stockton 102 C1
Longney Glos 36 C4
Longniddry E Loth 121 B7
Longnor Shrops 60 D4
Longnor Staffs 75 C7
Longparish Hants 26 E2
Longport Stoke 75 E5
Longridge Lancs 93 F6
Longridge Staffs 62 C3
Longridge W Loth 120 C2
Longriggend N Lanark 119 B8
Longsdon Staffs 75 D6
Longshaw Gtr Man 86 D3
Longside Aberds 153 D10
Longstanton Cambs 54 C4
Longstock Hants 25 F8
Longstone Pembs 32 D2
Longstowe Cambs 54 D4
Longthorpe Pboro 65 E8
Longthwaite Cumb 99 B6
Longton Lancs 86 B2
Longton Stoke 75 E6
Longtown Cumb 108 C3
Longtown Hereford 35 B7
Longview Mers 86 E2
Longville in the Dale Shrops 60 E5
Longwick Bucks 39 D7
Longwitton Northumb 117 F6
Longwood Shrops 61 D6
Longworth Oxon 38 E3
Longyester E Loth 121 C8
Lonmay Aberds 153 C10
Lonmore Highld 148 D7
Looe Corn 5 D7
Loose Kent 29 D8
Loosley Row Bucks 39 D8
Lopcombe Corner Wilts 25 F7
Lopen Som 12 C2
Loppington Shrops 60 B4
Lopwell Devon 6 C2
Lorbottle Northumb 117 D6
Lorbottle Hall Northumb 117 D6
Lornty Perth 134 E1
Loscoe Derbys 76 E4
Losgaintir W Isles 154 H5
Lossiemouth Moray 152 A2
Lossit Argyll 142 C2
Lostford Shrops 74 F3
Lostock Gralam Ches W 74 B3
Lostock Green Ches W 74 B3
Lostock Hall Lancs 86 B3
Lostock Junction Gtr Man 86 D4
Lostwithiel Corn 5 D6
Loth Orkney 159 E7
Lothbeg Highld 157 H12
Lothersdale N Yorks 94 E2
Lothmore Highld 157 H12
Loudwater Bucks 40 E2
Loughborough Leics 64 C2
Loughor Swansea 33 E6
Loughton Essex 41 E7
Loughton M Keynes 53 F6
Loughton Shrops 61 F6
Lound Lincs 65 C7
Lound Notts 89 F7
Lound Suff 69 E8
Lount Leics 63 C7
Louth Lincs 91 F7
Love Clough Lancs 87 B6
Lovedean Hants 15 C7
Lover Wilts 14 B3
Loversall S Yorks 89 E6
Loves Green Essex 42 D2
Lovesome Hill N Yorks 102 E1
Loveston Pembs 32 D1
Lovington Som 23 F7
Low Ackworth W Yorks 89 C5
Low Barlings Lincs 78 B3
Low Bentham N Yorks 93 C6
Low Bradfield S Yorks 88 E3
Low Bradley N Yorks 94 E3
Low Braithwaite Cumb 108 E4
Low Brunton Northumb 110 B2
Low Burnham N Lincs 89 D8
Low Burton N Yorks 101 F7
Low Buston Northumb 117 D8
Low Catton E Yorks 96 D3
Low Clanyard Dumfries 104 F5
Low Coniscliffe Darl 101 C7
Low Crosby Cumb 108 D4
Low Dalby N Yorks 103 F6
Low Dinsdale Darl 101 C8
Low Ellington N Yorks 101 F7
Low Etherley Durham 101 B6
Low Fell T&W 111 D5
Low Fulney Lincs 66 B2
Low Garth N Yorks 103 D5
Low Gate Northumb 110 C2
Low Grantley N Yorks 94 B5
Low Habberley Worcs 50 B3
Low Ham Som 12 B2
Low Hesket Cumb 108 E4
Low Hesleyhurst Northumb 117 E6
Low Hutton N Yorks 96 C3
Low Laithe N Yorks 94 C4
Low Leighton Derbys 87 F8
Low Lorton Cumb 98 B3
Low Marishes N Yorks 96 B4
Low Marnham Notts 77 C8
Low Mill N Yorks 102 E4
Low Moor Lancs 93 E7
Low Moor W Yorks 88 B2
Low Moorsley T&W 111 E6
Low Newton Cumb 99 F6
Low Newton-by-the-Sea Northumb 117 B8
Low Row Cumb 108 F3
Low Row Cumb 109 C5
Low Row N Yorks 100 E4
Low Salchrie Dumfries 104 C4
Low Smerby Argyll 143 F8
Low Torry Fife 128 F2
Low Worsall N Yorks 102 D1
Low Wray Cumb 99 D5
Lowbridge House Cumb 99 D7
Lowca Cumb 98 B1
Lowdham Notts 77 E6
Lowe Shrops 74 F2
Lowe Hill Staffs 75 D6
Lower Aisholt Som 22 F4
Lower Arncott Oxon 39 C6
Lower Ashton Devon 10 F3
Lower Assendon Oxon 39 F7
Lower Badcall Highld 156 E4
Lower Bartle Lancs 92 F4
Lower Basildon W Berks 26 B4
Lower Beeding W Sus 17 B6
Lower Benefield Northants 65 F6
Lower Boddington Northants 52 D2
Lower Brailes Warks 51 F8
Lower Breakish Highld 149 F11
Lower Broadheath Worcs 50 D3
Lower Bullingham Hereford 49 F7
Lower Cam Glos 36 D4
Lower Chapel Powys 48 F2
Lower Chute Wilts 25 D8
Lower Cragabus Argyll 142 D4
Lower Crossings Derbys 87 F8
Lower Cumberworth W Yorks 88 D3
Lower Cwm-twrch Powys 34 C1
Lower Darwen Blackburn 86 B4
Lower Dean Bedford 53 C8
Lower Diabaig Highld 149 B12
Lower Dicker E Sus 18 D2
Lower Dinchope Shrops 60 F4
Lower Down Shrops 60 F3
Lower Drift Corn 2 D3
Lower Dunsforth N Yorks 95 C7
Lower Egleton Hereford 49 E8
Lower Elkstone Staffs 75 D7
Lower End C Beds 40 B2
Lower Everleigh Wilts 25 D6
Lower Farringdon Hants 26 F5
Lower Foxdale IoM 84 E2
Lower Frankton Shrops 73 F7
Lower Froyle Hants 27 E5
Lower Gledfield Highld 151 B8
Lower Green Norf 81 D5
Lower Hacheston Suff 57 D7
Lower Halistra Highld 148 C7
Lower Halstow Kent 30 C2
Lower Hardres Kent 31 D5
Lower Hawthwaite Cumb 98 F4
Lower Heath Ches E 75 C5
Lower Hempriggs Moray 151 E14
Lower Hergest Hereford 48 D4
Lower Heyford Oxon 38 B4
Lower Higham Kent 29 B8
Lower Holbrook Suff 57 F5
Lower Hordley Shrops 60 B3
Lower Horsebridge E Sus 18 D2
Lower Killeyan Argyll 142 D3
Lower Kingswood Sur 28 D3
Lower Kinnerton Ches W 73 C7
Lower Langford N Som 23 C6
Lower Largo Fife 129 D6
Lower Leigh Staffs 75 F7
Lower Lemington Glos 51 F7
Lower Lenie Highld 137 B8
Lower Lydbrook Glos 36 C2
Lower Lye Hereford 49 C6
Lower Machen Newport 35 F6
Lower Maes-coed Hereford 48 F5
Lower Mayland Essex 43 D5
Lower Midway Derbys 63 B7
Lower Milovaig Highld 148 C6
Lower Moor Worcs 50 E4
Lower Nazeing Essex 41 D6
Lower Netchwood Shrops 61 E6
Lower Ollach Highld 149 E10
Lower Penarth V Glam 22 B3
Lower Penn Staffs 62 E2
Lower Pennington Hants 14 E4
Lower Peover Ches W 74 B4
Lower Pexhill Ches E 75 B5
Lower Place Gtr Man 87 C7
Lower Quinton Warks 51 E6
Lower Rochford Worcs 49 C8
Lower Seagry Wilts 37 F6
Lower Shelton C Beds 53 E7
Lower Shiplake Oxon 27 B5
Lower Shuckburgh Warks 52 C2
Lower Slaughter Glos 38 B1
Lower Stanton St Quintin Wilts 37 F6
Lower Stoke Medway 30 B2
Lower Stondon C Beds 54 F2
Lower Stow Bedon Norf 68 E2
Lower Street Norf 69 C6
Lower Street Norf 81 D8
Lower Strensham Worcs 50 E4
Lower Stretton Warr 86 F4
Lower Sundon C Beds 40 B3
Lower Swanwick Hants 15 D5
Lower Swell Glos 38 B1
Lower Tean Staffs 75 F7
Lower Thurlton Norf 69 E7
Lower Tote Highld 149 B10
Lower Town Pembs 44 B4
Lower Tysoe Warks 51 E8
Lower Upham Hants 15 C6
Lower Vexford Som 22 F3
Lower Weare Som 23 D6
Lower Welson Hereford 48 D4
Lower Whitley Ches W 74 B3
Lower Wield Hants 26 E4
Lower Winchendon Bucks 39 C7
Lower Withington Ches E 74 C5
Lower Woodend Bucks 39 F8
Lower Woodford Wilts 25 F6
Lower Wyche Worcs 50 E2
Lowesby Leics 64 D4
Lowestoft Suff 69 E8
Loweswater Cumb 98 B3
Lowford Hants 15 C5
Lowgill Cumb 99 E8
Lowgill Lancs 93 C6
Lowick Northants 65 F6
Lowick Northumb 123 F6
Lowick Bridge Cumb 98 F4
Lowick Green Cumb 98 F4
Lowlands Torf 35 E6
Lowmoor Row Cumb 99 B8
Lownie Moor Angus 134 E4
Lowsonford Warks 51 C6
Lowther Cumb 99 B7
Lowthorpe E Yorks 97 C6
Lowton Gtr Man 86 E4
Lowton Common Gtr Man 86 E4
Loxbeare Devon 10 C4
Loxhill Sur 27 F8
Loxhore Devon 20 F5
Loxley Warks 51 D7
Loxton N Som 23 D5
Loxwood W Sus 27 F8
Lubcroy Highld 156 J6
Lubenham Leics 64 F4
Luccombe Som 21 E8
Luccombe Village IoW 15 G6
Lucker Northumb 123 F7
Luckett Corn 5 B8
Luckington Wilts 37 F5
Lucklawhill Fife 129 B6
Luckwell Bridge Som 21 F8
Lucton Hereford 49 C6
Ludag W Isles 148 G2
Ludborough Lincs 91 E6
Ludchurch Pembs 32 C2
Luddenden W Yorks 87 B8
Luddenden Foot W Yorks 87 B8
Luddesdown Kent 29 C7
Luddington N Lincs 90 C2
Luddington Warks 51 D6
Luddington in the Brook Northants 65 F8
Lude House Perth 133 C5
Ludford Lincs 91 F6
Ludford Shrops 49 B7
Ludgershall Bucks 39 C6
Ludgershall Wilts 25 D7
Ludgvan Corn 2 C4
Ludham Norf 69 C6
Ludlow Shrops 49 B7
Ludwell Wilts 13 B7
Ludworth Durham 111 E6
Luffincott Devon 8 E5
Lugar E Ayrs 113 B5
Lugg Green Hereford 49 C6
Luggate Burn E Loth 122 B2
Luggiebank N Lanark 119 B7
Lugton E Ayrs 118 D4
Lugwardine Hereford 49 E7
Luib Highld 149 F10
Lulham Hereford 49 E6
Lullenden Sur 28 E5
Lullington Derbys 63 C6
Lullington Som 24 D2
Lulsgate Bottom N Som 23 C7
Lulsley Worcs 50 D2
Lumb W Yorks 87 B8
Lumby N Yorks 95 F7
Lumloch E Dunb 119 C6
Lumphanan Aberds 140 D4
Lumphinnans Fife 128 E3
Lumsdaine Borders 122 C4
Lumsden Aberds 140 B3
Lunan Angus 135 D6
Lunanhead Angus 134 D4
Luncarty Perth 128 B2
Lund E Yorks 97 E5
Lund N Yorks 96 F2
Lund Shetland 160 C7
Lunderton Aberds 153 D11
Lundie Angus 134 F2
Lundie Highld 136 C4
Lundin Links Fife 129 D6
Lunga Argyll 124 E3
Lunna Shetland 160 G6
Lunning Shetland 160 G7
Lunnon Swansea 33 F6
Lunsford's Cross E Sus 18 D4
Lunt Mers 85 D4
Luntley Hereford 49 D5
Luppitt Devon 11 D6
Lupset W Yorks 88 C4
Lupton Cumb 99 F7
Lurgashall W Sus 16 B3
Lusby Lincs 79 C6
Luson Devon 6 E4
Luss Argyll 126 E2
Lussagiven Argyll 144 E5
Lusta Highld 149 C7
Lustleigh Devon 10 F2
Luston Hereford 49 C6
Luthermuir Aberds 135 C6
Luthrie Fife 128 C5
Luton Devon 7 B7
Luton Luton 40 B3
Luton Medway 29 C8
Lutterworth Leics 64 F2
Lutton Devon 6 D3
Lutton Lincs 66 B4
Lutton Northants 65 F8
Lutworthy Devon 10 C2
Luxborough Som 21 F8
Luxulyan Corn 5 D5
Lybster Highld 158 G4
Lydbury North Shrops 60 F3
Lydcott Devon 21 F5
Lydd Kent 19 C7
Lydd on Sea Kent 19 C7
Lydden Kent 31 E6
Lyddington Rutland 65 E5
Lyde Green Hants 26 D5
Lydeard St Lawrence Som 22 F3
Lydford Devon 9 F7
Lydford-on-Fosse Som 23 F7
Lydgate W Yorks 87 B7
Lydham Shrops 60 E3
Lydiard Green Wilts 37 F7
Lydiard Millicent Wilts 37 F7
Lydiate Mers 85 D4
Lydlinch Dorset 12 C5
Lydney Glos 36 D3
Lydstep Pembs 32 E1
Lye W Mid 62 F3
Lye Green Bucks 40 D2
Lye Green E Sus 18 B2
Lyford Oxon 38 E3
Lymbridge Green Kent 30 E5
Lyme Regis Dorset 11 E8
Lyminge Kent 31 E5
Lymington Hants 14 E4
Lyminster W Sus 16 D4
Lymm Warr 86 F4
Lymore Hants 14 E3
Lympne Kent 19 B8
Lympsham Som 22 D5
Lympstone Devon 10 F4
Lynchat Highld 138 D3
Lyndale Ho. Highld 149 C8
Lyndhurst Hants 14 D4
Lyndon Rutland 65 D6
Lyne Sur 27 C8
Lyne Down Hereford 49 F8
Lyne of Gorthleck Highld 137 B8
Lyne of Skene Aberds 141 C6
Lyneal Shrops 73 F8
Lyneham Oxon 38 B2
Lyneham Wilts 24 B5
Lynemore Highld 139 B6
Lynemouth Northumb 117 E8
Lyness Orkney 159 J4
Lyng Norf 68 C3
Lyng Som 11 B8
Lynmouth Devon 21 E6
Lynsted Kent 30 C3
Lynton Devon 21 E6
Lyon's Gate Dorset 12 D4
Lyonshall Hereford 48 D5
Lytchett Matravers Dorset 13 E7
Lytchett Minster Dorset 13 E7
Lyth Highld 158 D4
Lytham Lancs 85 B4
Lytham St Anne's Lancs 85 B4
Lythe N Yorks 103 C6
Lythes Orkney 159 K5

M

Mabe Burnthouse Corn 3 C6
Mabie Dumfries 107 B6
Mablethorpe Lincs 91 F9
Macclesfield Ches E 75 B6
Macclesfield Forest Ches E 75 B6
Macduff Aberds 153 B7
Mace Green Suff 56 E5
Machariooch Argyll 143 H8
Machen Caerph 35 F6
Machrihanish Argyll 143 F7
Machynlleth Powys 58 D4
Machynys Carms 33 E6
Mackerel's Common W Sus 16 B4
Mackworth Derbys 76 F3
Macmerry E Loth 121 B7
Madderty Perth 127 B8
Maddiston Falk 120 B2
Madehurst W Sus 16 C3
Madeley Staffs 74 E4
Madeley Telford 61 D6
Madeley Heath Staffs 74 E4
Madeley Park Staffs 74 E4
Madingley Cambs 54 C4
Madley Hereford 49 F6
Madresfield Worcs 50 E3
Madron Corn 2 C3
Maen-y-groes Ceredig 46 D2
Maenaddwyn Anglesey 82 C4
Maenclochog Pembs 32 B1
Maendy V Glam 22 B2
Maentwrog Gwyn 71 C7
Maer Staffs 74 F4
Maerdy Conwy 72 E4
Maerdy Rhondda 34 E3
Maes-Treylow Powys 48 C4
Maesbrook Shrops 60 B2
Maesbury Shrops 60 B3
Maesbury Marsh Shrops 60 B3
Maesgwyn-Isaf Powys 59 C8
Maesgwynne Carms 32 B3
Maeshafn Denb 73 C6
Maesllyn Ceredig 46 E2
Maesmynis Powys 48 E2
Maesteg Bridgend 34 E2
Maestir Ceredig 46 E4
Maesy cwmmer Caerph 35 E5
Maesybont Carms 33 C6
Maesycrugiau Carms 46 E3
Maesymeillion Ceredig 46 E3
Magdalen Laver Essex 41 D8
Maggieknockater Moray 152 D3
Magham Down E Sus 18 D3
Maghull Mers 85 D4
Magor Mon 35 F8
Magpie Green Suff 56 B4
Maiden Bradley Wilts 24 F3
Maiden Law Durham 110 E4
Maiden Newton Dorset 12 E3
Maiden Wells Pembs 44 F4
Maidencombe Torbay 7 C7
Maidenhall Suff 57 E5
Maidenhead Windsor 40 F1
Maidens S Ayrs 112 D2
Maiden's Green Brack 27 B6
Maidensgrave Suff 57 E6
Maidenwell Corn 5 B6
Maidenwell Lincs 79 B6
Maidford Northants 52 D4
Maids Moreton Bucks 52 F5
Maidstone Kent 29 D8
Maidwell Northants 52 B5
Mail Shetland 160 L6
Main Powys 59 C8
Maindee Newport 35 F7
Mains of Airies Dumfries 104 C3
Mains of Allardice Aberds 135 B8
Mains of Annochie Aberds 153 D9
Mains of Ardestie Angus 135 F5
Mains of Balhall Angus 135 C5
Mains of Ballindarg Angus 134 D4
Mains of Balnakettle Aberds 135 B6
Mains of Birness Aberds 153 E9
Mains of Burgie Moray 151 F13
Mains of Clunas Highld 151 G11
Mains of Crichie Aberds 153 D9
Mains of Dalvey Highld 151 H1
Mains of Dellavaird Aberds 141 F6
Mains of Drum Aberds 141 E7
Mains of Edingight Moray 152 C5
Mains of Fedderate Aberds 153 D8
Mains of Inkhorn Aberds 153 E9
Mains of Mayen Moray 152 D5
Mains of Melgund Angus 135 D5
Mains of Thornton Aberds 135 B6
Mains of Watten Highld 158 E
Mainsforth Durham 111 F
Mainsriddle Dumfries 107 D
Mainstone Shrops 60 F
Maisemore Glos 37 B
Malacleit W Isles 148 A
Malborough Devon 6 F
Malcoff Derbys 87 F
Maldon Essex 42 D
Malham N Yorks 94 C
Maligar Highld 149 B
Mallaig Highld 147 B
Malleny Mills Edin 120 C
Malling Stirling 126 D
Malltraeth Anglesey 82 E
Mallwyd Gwyn 59 C
Malmesbury Wilts 37 F
Malmsmead Devon 21 E
Malpas Ches W 73 E
Malpas Corn 3 B
Malpas Newport 35 E
Malswick Glos 36 B
Maltby S Yorks 89 E
Maltby Stockton 102 C
Maltby le Marsh Lincs 91 F
Malting Green Essex 43 B
Maltman's Hill Kent 30 E
Malton N Yorks 96 B
Malvern Link Worcs 50 E
Malvern Wells Worcs 50 E
Mamble Worcs 49 B
Man-moel Caerph 35 D
Manaccan Corn 3 D
Manafon Powys 59 D
Manais W Isles 154

226 Mou – Nor

Mountain Water Pembs 44 C4
Mountbenger Borders 115 B6
Mountfield E Sus 18 C4
Mountgerald Highld 151 E8
Mountjoy Corn 4 C3
Mountnessing Essex 42 E2
Mounton Mon 36 E2
Mountsorrel Leics 64 C2
Mousehole Corn 2 D3
Mousen Northumb 123 F7
Mouswald Dumfries 107 B7
Mow Cop Ches E 75 D5
Mowhaugh Borders 116 B4
Mowsley Leics 64 F3
Moxley W Mid 62 E3
Moy Highld 137 F7
Moy Highld 151 H10
Moy Hall Highld 151 H10
Moy Ho. Moray 151 E13
Moy Lodge Highld 137 F7
Moyles Court Hants 14 D2
Moylgrove Pembs 45 E3
Muasdale Argyll 143 D7
Much Birch Hereford 49 F7
Much Cowarne Hereford 49 E8
Much Dewchurch Hereford 49 F6
Much Hadham Herts 41 C7
Much Hoole Lancs 86 B2
Much Marcle Hereford 49 F8
Much Wenlock Shrops 61 D6
Muchalls Aberds 141 E8
Muchelney Som 12 B2
Muchlarnick Corn 5 D7
Muchrachd Highld 150 H5
Muckernich Highld 151 F8
Mucking Thurrock 42 F2
Muckleford Dorset 12 E4
Mucklestone Staffs 74 F4
Muckleton Shrops 61 B5
Muckletown Aberds 140 B4
Muckley Corner Staffs 62 D4
Muckton Lincs 91 F7
Mudale Highld 157 F8
Muddiford Devon 20 F4
Mudeford Dorset 14 E2
Mudford Som 12 C3
Mudgley Som 23 E6
Mugdock Stirling 119 B5
Mugeary Highld 149 E9
Mugginton Derbys 76 E2
Muggleswick Durham 110 E3
Muie Highld 157 J9
Muir Aberds 139 F6
Muir of Fairburn Highld 150 F7
Muir of Fowlis Aberds 140 C4
Muir of Ord Highld 151 F8
Muir of Pert Angus 134 F4
Muirden Aberds 153 C7
Muirdrum Angus 135 F5
Muirhead Angus 134 F3
Muirhead Fife 128 D4
Muirhead N Lanark 119 C6
Muirhead S Ayrs 118 F3
Muirhouselaw Borders 116 B2
Muirhouses Falk 128 F2
Muirkirk E Ayrs 113 B6
Muirmill Stirling 127 F6
Muirshearlich Highld 136 F4
Muirskie Aberds 141 E7
Muirtack Aberds 153 E9
Muirton Highld 151 E10
Muirton Perth 127 C8
Muirton Perth 128 B3
Muirton Mains Highld 150 F7
Muirton of Ardblair Perth 134 E1
Muirton of Ballochy Angus 135 C6
Muiryfold Aberds 153 C7
Muker N Yorks 100 E4
Mulbarton Norf 68 D4
Mulben Moray 152 C3
Mulindry Argyll 142 C4
Mullardoch House Highld 150 H5
Mullion Corn 3 E5
Mullion Cove Corn 3 E5
Mumby Lincs 79 B8
Munderfield Row Hereford 49 D8
Munderfield Stocks Hereford 49 D8
Mundesley Norf 81 D9
Mundford Norf 67 E8
Mundham Norf 69 E6
Mundon Essex 42 D4
Mundurno Aberdeen 141 C8
Munerigie Highld 137 D5
Muness Shetland 160 C8
Mungasdale Highld 150 B2
Mungrisdale Cumb 108 F3
Munlochy Highld 151 F9
Munsley Hereford 49 E8
Munslow Shrops 60 F5
Murchington Devon 9 F8
Murcott Oxon 39 C5
Murkle Highld 158 D3
Murlaggan Highld 136 E3
Murlaggan Highld 137 F6
Murra Orkney 159 H3
Murrayfield Edin 120 B5
Murrow Cambs 66 D3
Mursley Bucks 39 B8
Murthill Angus 134 D4
Murthly Perth 133 F7
Murton Cumb 100 B2
Murton Durham 111 E6
Murton Northumb 123 E5
Murton York 96 D2
Musbury Devon 11 E7
Muscoates N Yorks 102 F4
Musdale Argyll 124 C5
Musselburgh E Loth 121 B6
Muston Leics 77 F8
Muston N Yorks 97 B6
Mustow Green Worcs 50 B3
Mutehill Dumfries 106 E3
Mutford Suff 69 F7
Muthill Perth 127 C7
Mutterton Devon 10 D5
Muxton Telford 61 C7
Mybster Highld 158 E3
Myddfai Carms 34 B1
Myddle Shrops 60 B4
Mydroilyn Ceredig 46 D3
Myerscough Lancs 92 F4
Mylor Bridge Corn 3 C7
Mynachlog-ddu Pembs 45 F3
Myndtown Shrops 60 F3
Mynydd Bach Ceredig 47 B6
Mynydd-bach Mon 36 E1
Mynydd Bodafon Anglesey 82 C4
Mynydd-isa Flint 73 C6
Mynyddygarreg Carms 33 D5
Mynytho Gwyn 70 D4
Myrebird Aberds 141 E6
Myrelandhorn Highld 158 E4
Myreside Perth 128 B4
Myrtle Hill Carms 47 F6
Mytchett Sur 27 D6
Mytholm W Yorks 87 B7
Mytholmroyd W Yorks 87 B8
Myton-on-Swale N Yorks 95 C7
Mytton Shrops 60 C4

N

Na Gearrannan W Isles 154 C6
Naast Highld 155 J13
Naburn York 95 E8
Nackington Kent 31 D5
Nacton Suff 57 E6
Nafferton E Yorks 97 D6
Nailbridge Glos 36 C3
Nailsbourne Som 11 B7
Nailsea N Som 23 B6
Nailstone Leics 63 D8
Nailsworth Glos 37 E5
Nairn Highld 151 F11
Nalderswood Sur 28 E3
Nancegollan Corn 2 C5
Nancledra Corn 2 C3
Nanhoron Gwyn 70 D3
Nannau Gwyn 71 E8
Nannerch Flint 73 C5
Nanpantan Leics 64 C2
Nanpean Corn 4 D4
Nanstallon Corn 4 C5
Nant-ddu Powys 34 C4
Nant-glas Powys 47 C8
Nant Peris Gwyn 83 F6
Nant Uchaf Denb 72 D4
Nant-y-Bai Carms 47 E6
Nant-y-cafn Neath 34 D2
Nant-y-derry Mon 35 D7
Nant-y-ffin Carms 46 F4
Nant-y-moel Bridgend 34 E3
Nant-y-pandy Conwy 83 D6
Nanternis Ceredig 46 D2
Nantgaredig Carms 33 B5
Nantgarw Rhondda 35 F5
Nantglyn Denb 72 C4
Nantgwyn Powys 47 B8
Nantlle Gwyn 82 F5
Nantmawr Shrops 60 B2
Nantmel Powys 48 C2
Nantmor Gwyn 71 C7
Nantwich Ches E 74 D3
Nantycaws Carms 33 C5
Nantyffyllon Bridgend 34 E2
Nantyglo Bl Gwent 35 C5
Naphill Bucks 39 E8
Nappa N Yorks 93 D8
Napton on the Hill Warks 52 C2
Narberth = Arberth Pembs 32 C2
Narborough Leics 64 E2
Narborough Norf 67 C7
Nasareth Gwyn 82 F4
Naseby Northants 52 B4
Nash Bucks 53 F5
Nash Hereford 48 C5
Nash Newport 35 F7
Nash Shrops 49 B8
Nash Lee Bucks 39 D8
Nassington Northants 65 E7
Nasty Herts 41 B6
Nateby Cumb 100 D2
Nateby Lancs 92 E4
Natland Cumb 99 F7
Naughton Suff 56 E4
Naunton Glos 37 B8
Naunton Worcs 50 F3
Naunton Beauchamp Worcs 50 D4
Navenby Lincs 78 D2
Navestock Heath Essex 41 E8
Navestock Side Essex 42 E1
Navidale Highld 157 H13
Nawton N Yorks 102 F4
Nayland Suff 56 F3
Nazeing Essex 41 D7
Neacroft Hants 14 E2
Neal's Green Warks 63 F7
Neap Shetland 160 H7
Near Sawrey Cumb 99 E5
Neasham Darl 101 C8
Neath = Castell-Nedd Neath 33 E8
Neath Abbey Neath 33 E8
Neatishead Norf 69 B6
Nebo Anglesey 82 B4
Nebo Ceredig 46 C4
Nebo Conwy 83 F8
Nebo Gwyn 82 F4
Necton Norf 67 D8
Nedd Highld 156 F4
Nedderton Northumb 117 F8
Nedging Tye Suff 56 E4
Needham Norf 68 F5
Needham Market Suff 56 D4
Needingworth Cambs 54 B4
Needwood Staffs 63 B5
Neen Savage Shrops 49 B8
Neen Sollars Shrops 49 B8
Neenton Shrops 61 F6
Nefyn Gwyn 70 C4
Neilston E Renf 118 D4
Neinthirion Powys 59 D6
Neithrop Oxon 52 E2
Nelly Andrews Green Powys 60 D2
Nelson Caerph 35 E5
Nelson Lancs 93 F8
Nelson Village Northumb 111 B5
Nemphlar S Lanark 119 E8
Nempnett Thrubwell N Som 23 C7
Nene Terrace Lincs 66 D2
Nenthall Cumb 109 E7
Nenthead Cumb 109 E7
Nenthorn Borders 122 F2
Nerabus Argyll 142 C3
Nercwys Flint 73 C6
Nerston S Lanark 119 D6
Nesbit Northumb 123 F5
Ness Ches W 73 B7
Nesscliffe Shrops 60 C3
Neston Ches W 73 B6
Neston Wilts 24 C3
Nether Alderley Ches E 74 B5
Nether Blainslie Borders 121 E8
Nether Booth Derbys 88 F2
Nether Broughton Leics 64 B3
Nether Burrow Lancs 93 B6
Nether Cerne Dorset 12 E4
Nether Compton Dorset 12 C3
Nether Crimond Aberds 141 B7
Nether Dalgliesh Borders 115 D5
Nether Dallachy Moray 152 B3
Nether Exe Devon 10 D4
Nether Glasslaw Aberds 153 C8
Nether Handwick Angus 134 E3
Nether Haugh S Yorks 88 E5
Nether Heage Derbys 76 D3
Nether Heyford Northants 52 D4
Nether Hindhope Borders 116 C3
Nether Howecleuch S Lanark 114 C3
Nether Kellet Lancs 92 C5
Nether Kinmundy Aberds 153 D10
Nether Langwith Notts 76 B5
Nether Leask Aberds 153 E10
Nether Lenshie Aberds 153 D6
Nether Monynut Borders 122 C3
Nether Padley Derbys 76 B2
Nether Park Aberds 153 C10
Nether Poppleton York 95 D8
Nether Silton N Yorks 102 E2
Nether Stowey Som 22 F3
Nether Urquhart Fife 128 D3
Nether Wallop Hants 25 F8
Nether Wasdale Cumb 98 D3
Nether Whitacre Warks 63 E6
Nether Worton Oxon 52 F2
Netheravon Wilts 25 E6
Netherbrae Aberds 153 C7
Netherbrough Orkney 159 G4
Netherburn S Lanark 119 E8
Netherbury Dorset 12 E2
Netherby Cumb 108 B3
Netherby N Yorks 95 E6
Nethercote Warks 52 C3
Nethercott Devon 20 F3
Netherend Glos 36 D2
Netherfield E Sus 18 D4
Netherhampton Wilts 14 B2
Netherlaw Dumfries 106 E4
Netherley Aberds 141 E7
Netherley Mers 86 F2
Nethermill Dumfries 114 F3
Nethermuir Aberds 153 D9
Netherplace E Renf 118 D5
Netherseal Derbys 63 C6
Netherthird E Ayrs 113 C5
Netherthong W Yorks 88 D2
Netherthorpe S Yorks 89 F6
Netherton Angus 135 D5
Netherton Devon 7 B6
Netherton Hants 25 D8
Netherton Mers 85 D4
Netherton Northumb 117 D5
Netherton Oxon 38 E4
Netherton Perth 133 D8
Netherton Stirling 119 B5
Netherton W Mid 62 F3
Netherton W Yorks 88 C2
Netherton W Yorks 88 C3
Netherton Worcs 50 E4
Nethertown Cumb 98 D1
Nethertown Highld 158 C5
Netherwitton Northumb 117 E7
Netherwood E Ayrs 113 B6
Nethy Bridge Highld 139 B6
Netley Hants 15 D5
Netley Marsh Hants 14 C4
Netteswell Essex 41 C7
Nettlebed Oxon 39 F7
Nettlebridge Som 23 E8
Nettlecombe Dorset 12 E3
Nettleden Herts 40 C3
Nettleham Lincs 78 B3
Nettlestead Kent 29 D7
Nettlestead Green Kent 29 D7
Nettlestone IoW 15 E7
Nettlesworth Durham 111 E5
Nettleton Lincs 90 D5
Nettleton Wilts 24 B3
Neuadd Carms 33 B7
Nevendon Essex 42 E3
Nevern Pembs 45 E2
New Abbey Dumfries 107 C6
New Aberdour Aberds 153 B8
New Addington London 28 C4
New Alresford Hants 26 F3
New Alyth Perth 134 E2
New Arley Warks 63 F6
New Ash Green Kent 29 C7
New Barn Kent 29 C7
New Barnetby N Lincs 90 C4
New Barton Northants 53 C6
New Bewick Northumb 117 B6
New-bigging Angus 134 E2
New Bilton Warks 52 B2
New Bolingbroke Lincs 79 D6
New Boultham Lincs 78 B2
New Bradwell M Keynes 53 E6
New Brancepeth Durham 110 E5
New Bridge Wrex 73 E6
New Brighton Flint 73 C6
New Brighton Mers 85 E4
New Brinsley Notts 76 D4
New Broughton Wrex 73 D7
New Buckenham Norf 68 E3
New Byth Aberds 153 C8
New Catton Norf 68 C5
New Cheriton Hants 15 B6
New Costessey Norf 68 C4
New Cowper Cumb 107 E8
New Cross Ceredig 46 B5
New Cross London 28 B4
New Cumnock E Ayrs 113 C6
New Deer Aberds 153 D8
New Delaval Northumb 111 B5
New Duston Northants 52 C5
New Earswick York 96 D2
New Edlington S Yorks 89 E6
New Elgin Moray 152 B2
New Ellerby E Yorks 97 F7
New Eltham London 28 B5
New End Worcs 51 D5
New Farnley W Yorks 94 F5
New Ferry Mers 85 F4
New Fryston W Yorks 89 B5
New Galloway Dumfries 106 B3
New Gilston Fife 129 D6
New Grimsby Scilly 2 E3
New Hainford Norf 68 C5
New Hartley Northumb 111 B6
New Haw Sur 27 C8
New Hedges Pembs 32 D2
New Herrington T&W 111 D6
New Hinksey Oxon 39 D5
New Holkham Norf 80 D4
New Holland N Lincs 90 B4
New Houghton Derbys 76 C4
New Houghton Norf 80 E3
New Houses N Yorks 93 B8
New Humberstone Leicester 64 D3
New Hutton Cumb 99 E7
New Hythe Kent 29 D8
New Inn Carms 46 F3
New Inn Mon 36 D1
New Inn Pembs 45 F2
New Inn Torf 35 E7
New Invention Shrops 48 B4
New Invention W Mid 62 D3
New Kelso Highld 150 G2
New Kingston Notts 64 B2
New Lanark S Lanark 119 E8
New Lane Lancs 86 C2
New Lane End Warr 86 E4
New Leake Lincs 79 D7
New Leeds Aberds 153 C9
New Longton Lancs 86 B3
New Luce Dumfries 105 C5
New Malden London 28 C3
New Marske Redcar 102 B4
New Marton Shrops 73 F7
New Micklefield W Yorks 95 F7
New Mill Aberds 141 F6
New Mill Herts 40 C2
New Mill W Yorks 88 D2
New Mill Wilts 25 C6
New Mills Ches E 87 F5
New Mills Corn 4 D3
New Mills Derbys 87 F7
New Mills Powys 59 D7
New Milton Hants 14 E3
New Moat Pembs 32 B1
New Ollerton Notts 77 C6
New Oscott W Mid 62 E4
New Park N Yorks 95 D5
New Pitsligo Aberds 153 C8
New Polzeath Corn 4 B4
New Quay = Ceinewydd Ceredig 46 D2
New Rackheath Norf 69 C5
New Radnor Powys 48 C4
New Rent Cumb 108 F4
New Ridley Northumb 110 D3
New Road Side N Yorks 94 E2
New Romney Kent 19 C7
New Rossington S Yorks 89 E7
New Row Ceredig 47 B6
New Row Lancs 93 F6
New Row N Yorks 102 C4
New Sarum Wilts 25 F6
New Silksworth T&W 111 D6
New Stevenston N Lanark 119 D7
New Street Staffs 75 D7
New Street Lane Shrops 74 F3
New Swanage Dorset 13 F8
New Totley S Yorks 76 B3
New Town E Loth 121 B7
New Tredegar = Tredegar Newydd Caerph 35 D5
New Trows S Lanark 119 F8
New Ulva Argyll 144 E6
New Walsoken Cambs 66 D4
New Waltham NE Lincs 91 D6
New Whittington Derbys 76 B3
New Wimpole Cambs 54 E4
New Winton E Loth 121 B7
New Yatt Oxon 38 C3
New York Lincs 78 D5
New York N Yorks 94 C4
Newall W Yorks 94 E4
Newark Orkney 159 D8
Newark Pboro 66 D2
Newark-on-Trent Notts 77 D7
Newarthill N Lanark 119 D7
Newbarns Cumb 92 B2
Newbattle Midloth 121 C6
Newbiggin Cumb 92 C2
Newbiggin Cumb 98 E2
Newbiggin Cumb 99 B6
Newbiggin Cumb 99 B8
Newbiggin Cumb 109 E5
Newbiggin Durham 100 B4
Newbiggin N Yorks 100 E4
Newbiggin N Yorks 100 F4
Newbiggin-by-the-Sea Northumb 117 F9
Newbiggin-on-Lune Cumb 100 D2
Newbigging Angus 134 F4
Newbigging Angus 134 F4
Newbigging S Lanark 120 E3
Newbold Derbys 76 B3
Newbold Leics 63 C8
Newbold on Avon Warks 52 B2
Newbold on Stour Warks 51 E7
Newbold Pacey Warks 51 D7
Newbold Verdon Leics 63 D8
Newborough Anglesey 82 E4
Newborough Pboro 66 D2
Newborough Staffs 62 B5
Newbottle Northants 52 F3
Newbottle T&W 111 D6
Newbourne Suff 57 E6
Newbridge Caerph 35 E6
Newbridge Ceredig 46 D4
Newbridge Corn 2 C3
Newbridge Corn 5 C8
Newbridge Dumfries 107 B6
Newbridge Edin 120 B4
Newbridge Hants 14 C3
Newbridge IoW 14 F5
Newbridge Pembs 44 B4
Newbridge Green Worcs 50 F3
Newbridge-on-Usk Mon 35 E7
Newbridge on Wye Powys 48 D2
Newbrough Northumb 109 C8
Newbuildings Devon 10 D2
Newburgh Aberds 141 B8
Newburgh Aberds 153 C9
Newburgh Borders 115 C6
Newburgh Fife 128 C4
Newburgh Lancs 86 C2
Newburn T&W 110 C4
Newbury W Berks 26 C2
Newbury Park London 41 F7
Newby Cumb 99 B7
Newby Lancs 93 E8
Newby N Yorks 93 B7
Newby N Yorks 102 C3
Newby N Yorks 103 E8
Newby Bridge Cumb 99 F5
Newby East Cumb 108 D4
Newby West Cumb 108 D3
Newby Wiske N Yorks 102 F1
Newcastle Mon 35 C8
Newcastle Shrops 60 F2
Newcastle Emlyn = Castell Newydd Emlyn Carms 46 E2
Newcastle-under-Lyme Staffs 74 E5
Newcastle Upon Tyne T&W 110 C5
Newcastleton or Copshaw Holm Borders 115 F7
Newchapel Pembs 45 F4
Newchapel Powys 59 F6
Newchapel Staffs 75 D5
Newchapel Sur 28 E4
Newchurch Carms 32 B4
Newchurch IoW 15 F6
Newchurch Kent 19 B7
Newchurch Lancs 93 F8
Newchurch Mon 36 E1
Newchurch Powys 48 D4
Newchurch Staffs 62 B5
Newcott Devon 11 D7
Newcraighall Edin 121 B6
Newdigate Sur 28 E2
Newell Green Brack 27 B6
Newenden Kent 18 C5
Newent Glos 36 B4
Newerne Glos 36 D3
Newfield Durham 110 F5
Newfield Highld 151 D10
Newford Scilly 2 E4
Newfound Hants 26 D3
Newgale Pembs 44 C3
Newgate Norf 81 C6
Newgate Street Herts 41 D6
Newhall Ches E 74 E3
Newhall Derbys 63 B6
Newhall House Highld 151 E9
Newhall Point Highld 151 E10
Newham Northumb 117 B7
Newham Hall Northumb 117 B7
Newhaven Derbys 75 D8
Newhaven E Sus 17 D8
Newhaven Edin 121 B5
Newhey Gtr Man 87 C7
Newholm N Yorks 103 C6
Newhouse N Lanark 119 C7
Newick E Sus 17 B8
Newingreen Kent 19 B8
Newington Kent 19 B8
Newington Kent 30 C2
Newington Kent 31 C7
Newington Notts 89 E7
Newington Oxon 39 E6
Newington Shrops 60 F4
Newland Glos 36 D2
Newland Hull 97 F6
Newland N Yorks 89 B7
Newland Worcs 50 E2
Newlandrig Midloth 121 C6
Newlands Borders 115 E8
Newlands Highld 151 G10
Newlands Moray 152 C3
Newlands Northumb 110 D3
Newland's Corner Sur 27 E8
Newlands of Geise Highld 158 D2
Newlands of Tynet Moray 152 B3
Newlands Park Anglesey 82 C2
Newlandsmuir S Lanark 119 D6
Newlot Orkney 159 G6
Newlyn Corn 2 D3
Newmachar Aberds 141 C7
Newmains N Lanark 119 D8
Newmarket Suff 55 C7
Newmarket W Isles 155 D9
Newmill Borders 115 C7
Newmill Corn 2 C3
Newmill Moray 152 C4
Newmill of Inshewan Angus 134 C4
Newmills of Boyne Aberds 152 C5
Newmiln Perth 133 F8
Newmilns E Ayrs 118 F5
Newnham Cambs 54 D5
Newnham Glos 36 C3
Newnham Hants 26 D5
Newnham Herts 54 F3
Newnham Kent 30 D3
Newnham Northants 52 D3
Newnham Bridge Worcs 49 C8
Newpark Fife 129 C6
Newport Devon 20 F4
Newport E Yorks 96 F4
Newport Essex 55 F6
Newport Highld 158 H3
Newport IoW 15 F6
Newport = Casnewydd Newport 35 F7
Newport Norf 69 C8
Newport = Trefdraeth Pembs 45 F2
Newport Telford 61 C7
Newport-on-Tay Fife 129 B6
Newport Pagnell M Keynes 53 E6
Newpound Common W Sus 16 B4
Newquay Corn 4 C3
Newsbank Ches E 74 C5
Newseat Aberds 153 D10
Newseat Aberds 153 E7
Newsham N Yorks 101 C6
Newsham N Yorks 102 F1
Newsham Northumb 111 B6
Newsholme E Yorks 89 B8
Newsholme Lancs 93 D8
Newsome W Yorks 88 C2
Newstead Borders 121 F8
Newstead Northumb 117 B7
Newstead Notts 76 D5
Newthorpe N Yorks 95 F7
Newton Argyll 125 F6
Newton Borders 116 B2
Newton Bridgend 21 B7
Newton Cambs 54 E5
Newton Cambs 66 C4
Newton Cardiff 22 B4
Newton Ches W 73 C8
Newton Ches W 74 B2
Newton Ches W 74 D2
Newton Cumb 92 B2
Newton Derbys 76 D4
Newton Dorset 13 C5
Newton Dumfries 108 B2
Newton Dumfries 114 E4
Newton Gtr Man 87 E7
Newton Hereford 48 F5
Newton Hereford 49 D7
Newton Highld 151 E10
Newton Highld 151 G10
Newton Highld 156 F5
Newton Highld 158 F5
Newton Lancs 92 F4
Newton Lancs 93 B5
Newton Lancs 93 D6
Newton Lincs 78 F3
Newton Moray 152 B1
Newton Norf 67 C8
Newton Northants 65 F5
Newton Northumb 110 C3
Newton Notts 77 E6
Newton Perth 133 F5
Newton S Lanark 119 C6
Newton S Lanark 120 F2
Newton S Yorks 89 D6
Newton Staffs 62 B4
Newton Suff 56 E3
Newton Swansea 33 F7
Newton W Loth 120 B3
Newton Warks 52 B3
Newton Wilts 14 B3
Newton Abbot Devon 7 B6
Newton Arlosh Cumb 107 D8
Newton Aycliffe Durham 101 B7
Newton Bewley Hrtlpl 102 B2
Newton Blossomville M Keynes 53 D7
Newton Bromswold Northants 53 C7
Newton Burgoland Leics 63 D7
Newton by Toft Lincs 90 F4
Newton Ferrers Devon 6 E3
Newton Flotman Norf 68 E5
Newton Hall Northumb 110 C3
Newton Harcourt Leics 64 E3
Newton Heath Gtr Man 87 D6
Newton Ho. Aberds 141 B5
Newton Kyme N Yorks 95 E7
Newton-le-Willows Mers 86 E3
Newton-le-Willows N Yorks 101 F7
Newton Longville Bucks 53 F6
Newton Mearns E Renf 118 D5
Newton Morrell N Yorks 101 D7
Newton Mulgrave N Yorks 103 C5
Newton of Ardtoe Highld 147 D9
Newton of Balcanquhal Perth 128 C3
Newton of Falkland Fife 128 D4
Newton on Ayr S Ayrs 112 B3
Newton on Ouse N Yorks 95 D8
Newton-on-Rawcliffe N Yorks 103 E6
Newton-on-the-Moor Northumb 117 D7
Newton on Trent Lincs 77 B8
Newton Park Argyll 145 G10
Newton Poppleford Devon 11 F5
Newton Purcell Oxon 52 F4
Newton Regis Warks 63 D6
Newton Reigny Cumb 108 F4
Newton Solney Derbys 63 B6
Newton St Cyres Devon 10 E3
Newton St Faith Norf 68 C5
Newton St Loe Bath 24 C2
Newton St Petrock Devon 9 C6
Newton Stacey Hants 26 E2
Newton Stewart Dumfries 105 C8
Newton Tony Wilts 25 E7
Newton Tracey Devon 9 B7
Newton under Roseberry Redcar 102 C3
Newton upon Derwent E Yorks 96 E3
Newton Valence Hants 26 F5
Newtonairds Dumfries 113 F8
Newtongrange Midloth 121 C6
Newtonhill Aberds 141 E8
Newtonhill Highld 151 G8
Newtonmill Angus 135 C6
Newtonmore Highld 138 E3
Newtown Argyll 125 E6
Newtown Ches W 74 B2
Newtown Corn 3 D6
Newtown Cumb 107 E7
Newtown Cumb 108 C5
Newtown Derbys 87 F7
Newtown Devon 10 B2
Newtown Glos 36 D3
Newtown Glos 50 F4
Newtown Hants 14 B4
Newtown Hants 14 C3
Newtown Hants 15 C6
Newtown Hants 15 C7
Newtown Hants 15 D5
Newtown Hants 26 C2
Newtown Hereford 49 E8
Newtown Highld 137 D6
Newtown IoM 84 E3
Newtown IoW 14 E5
Newtown Northumb 117 B6
Newtown Northumb 117 D6
Newtown Northumb 123 F5
Newtown Poole 13 E8
Newtown = Y Drenewydd Powys 59 E8
Newtown Shrops 73 F8
Newtown Staffs 75 C6
Newtown Staffs 75 C7
Newtown Wilts 13 B7
Newtown Linford Leics 64 D2
Newtown St Boswells Borders 121 F8
Newtown Unthank Leics 63 D8
Newtyle Angus 134 E2
Neyland Pembs 44 E4
Niarbyl IoM 84 E2
Nibley S Glos 36 F3
Nibley Green Glos 36 E4
Nibon Shetland 160 F5
Nicholashayne Devon 11 C6
Nicholaston Swansea 33 F6
Nidd N Yorks 95 C6
Nigg Aberdeen 141 D8
Nigg Highld 151 D11
Nigg Ferry Highld 151 E10
Nightcott Som 10 B3
Nilig Denb 72 D4
Nine Ashes Essex 42 D1
Nine Mile Burn Midloth 120 D4
Nine Wells Pembs 44 C2
Ninebanks Northumb 109 D7
Ninfield E Sus 18 D4
Ningwood IoW 14 F4
Nisbet Borders 116 B2
Nisthouse Orkney 159 G4
Nisthouse Shetland 160 G7
Niton IoW 15 G6
Nitshill Glasgow 118 C5
No Man's Heath Ches W 74 E2
No Man's Heath Warks 63 D6
Noak Hill London 41 E8
Noblethorpe S Yorks 88 D3
Nobottle Northants 52 C4
Nocton Lincs 78 C3
Noke Oxon 39 C5
Nolton Pembs 44 D3
Nolton Haven Pembs 44 D3
Nomansland Devon 10 C3
Nomansland Wilts 14 C3
Noneley Shrops 60 B4
Nonikiln Highld 151 D9
Nonington Kent 31 D6
Noonsbrough Shetland 160 H4
Norbreck Blackpool 92 E3
Norbridge Hereford 50 E2
Norbury Ches E 74 E2
Norbury Derbys 75 E8
Norbury Shrops 60 E3
Norbury Staffs 61 B7
Nordelph Norf 67 D5
Norden Gtr Man 87 C6
Norden Heath Dorset 13 F7
Nordley Shrops 61 E6
Norham Northumb 122 E5
Norley Ches W 74 B2
Norleywood Hants 14 E4
Norman Cross Cambs 65 E8
Normanby N Lincs 90 C2
Normanby N Yorks 103 F5
Normanby Redcar 102 C3
Normanby-by-Spital Lincs 90 F4
Normanby by Stow Lincs 90 F2
Normanby le Wold Lincs 90 E5
Normandy Sur 27 D7
Norman's Bay E Sus 18 E3
Norman's Green Devon 11 D5
Normanstone Suff 69 E8
Normanton Derby 76 F3
Normanton Leics 77 E8
Normanton Lincs 78 E2
Normanton Notts 77 D7
Normanton Rutland 65 D6
Normanton W Yorks 88 B4
Normanton le Heath Leics 63 C7
Normanton on Soar Notts 64 B2
Normanton-on-the-Wolds Notts 77 F6
Normanton on Trent Notts 77 C7
Normoss Lancs 92 F3
Norney Sur 27 E7
Norrington Common Wilts 24 C3
Norris Green Mers 85 E4
Norris Hill Leics 63 C7
North Anston S Yorks 89 F6
North Aston Oxon 38 B4
North Baddesley Hants 14 C4
North Ballachulish Highld 130 C4
North Barrow Som 12 B4
North Barsham Norf 80 D5
North Benfleet Essex 42 F3
North Bersted W Sus 16 D3
North Berwick E Loth 129 F7
North Boarhunt Hants 15 C7
North Bovey Devon 10 F2
North Bradley Wilts 24 D3
North Brentor Devon 9 F6
North Brewham Som 24 F2
North Buckland Devon 20 E3
North Burlingham Norf 69 C6
North Cadbury Som 12 B4
North Cairn Dumfries 104 B3
North Carlton Lincs 78 B2
North Carrine Argyll 143 H7
North Cave E Yorks 96 F4
North Cerney Glos 37 D7
North Charford Wilts 14 C2
North Charlton Northumb 117 B7
North Cheriton Som 12 B4
North Cliff E Yorks 97 E8
North Cliffe E Yorks 96 F4
North Clifton Notts 77 B8
North Cockerington Lincs 91 E7
North Coker Som 12 C3
North Collafirth Shetland 160 E5
North Common E Sus 17 B7
North Connel Argyll 124 B5
North Cornelly Bridgend 34 F2
North Cotes Lincs 91 D7
North Cove Suff 69 F7
North Cowton N Yorks 101 D7
North Crawley M Keynes 53 E7
North Cray London 29 B5
North Creake Norf 80 D4
North Curry Som 11 B8
North Dalton E Yorks 96 D5
North Dawn Orkney 159 H5
North Deighton N Yorks 95 D6
North Duffield N Yorks 96 F2
North Elkington Lincs 91 E6
North Elmham Norf 81 E5
North Elmshall W Yorks 89 C5
North End Bucks 39 B8
North End E Yorks 97 F8
North End Essex 42 C2
North End Hants 26 C2
North End Lincs 78 E5
North End N Som 23 C6
North End Ptsmth 15 D7
North End Som 11 B7
North End W Sus 16 D5
North Erradale Highld 155 J12
North Fambridge Essex 42 E4
North Fearns Highld 149 E10
North Featherstone W Yorks 88 B5
North Ferriby E Yorks 90 B3
North Frodingham E Yorks 97 D7
North Gluss Shetland 160 F5
North Gorley Hants 14 C2
North Green Norf 68 F5
North Green Suff 57 C7
North Greetwell Lincs 78 B3
North Grimston N Yorks 96 C4
North Halley Orkney 159 H6
North Halling Medway 29 C8
North Hayling Hants 15 D8
North Hazelrigg Northumb 123 F6
North Heasley Devon 21 F6
North Heath W Sus 16 B4
North Hill Cambs 55 B5
North Hill Corn 5 B7
North Hinksey Oxon 38 D4
North Holmwood Sur 28 E2
North Howden E Yorks 96 F3
North Huish Devon 6 D5
North Hykeham Lincs 78 C2
North Johnston Pembs 44 D4
North Kelsey Lincs 90 D4
North Kelsey Moor Lincs 90 D4
North Kessock Highld 151 G9
North Killingholme N Lincs 90 C5
North Kilvington N Yorks 102 F2
North Kilworth Leics 64 F3
North Kirkton Aberds 153 C11
North Kiscadale N Ayrs 143 F11
North Kyme Lincs 78 D4
North Lancing W Sus 17 D5
North Lee Bucks 39 D8
North Leigh Oxon 38 C3
North Leverton with Habblesthorpe Notts 89 F8
North Littleton Worcs 51 E5
North Lopham Norf 68 F3
North Luffenham Rutland 65 D6
North Marden W Sus 16 C2
North Marston Bucks 39 B7
North Middleton Midloth 121 D6
North Middleton Northumb 117 B6
North Molton Devon 10 B2
North Moreton Oxon 39 F5
North Mundham W Sus 16 D2
North Muskham Notts 77 D7
North Newbald E Yorks 96 F5
North Newington Oxon 52 F2
North Newnton Wilts 25 D6
North Newton Som 22 F4
North Nibley Glos 36 E4
North Oakley Hants 26 D3
North Ockendon London 42 F1
North Ormesby Mbro 102 B3
North Ormsby Lincs 91 E6
North Otterington N Yorks 102 F1
North Owersby Lincs 90 E4
North Perrott Som 12 D2
North Petherton Som 22 F4
North Petherwin Corn 8 F4
North Pickenham Norf 67 D8
North Piddle Worcs 50 D4
North Poorton Dorset 12 E3
North Port Argyll 125 C6
North Queensferry Fife 128 F3
North Radworthy Devon 21 F6
North Rauceby Lincs 78 E3
North Reston Lincs 91 F7
North Rigton N Yorks 95 E5
North Rode Ches E 75 C5
North Roe Shetland 160 E5
North Runcton Norf 67 C6
North Sandwick Shetland 160 D7
North Scale Cumb 92 C1
North Scarle Lincs 77 C8
North Seaton Northumb 117 F8
North Shian Argyll 130 E3
North Shields T&W 111 C6
North Shoebury Southend 43 F5
North Shore Blackpool 92 F3
North Side Cumb 98 B2
North Side Pboro 66 E2
North Skelton Redcar 102 C4
North Somercotes Lincs 91 E8
North Stainley N Yorks 95 B5
North Stainmore Cumb 100 C3
North Stifford Thurrock 42 F2
North Stoke Bath 24 C2
North Stoke Oxon 39 F6
North Stoke W Sus 16 C4
North Street Hants 26 F4
North Street Kent 30 D4
North Street Medway 30 B2
North Street W Berks 26 B4
North Sunderland Northumb 123 F8
North Tamerton Corn 8 E5
North Tawton Devon 9 D8
North Thoresby Lincs 91 E6
North Tidworth Wilts 25 E7
North Togston Northumb 117 D8
North Tuddenham Norf 68 C3
North Walbottle T&W 110 C4
North Walsham Norf 81 D8
North Waltham Hants 26 E3
North Warnborough Hants 26 D5
North Water Bridge Angus 135 C6
North Watten Highld 158 E4
North Weald Bassett Essex 41 D7
North Wheatley Notts 89 F8
North Whilborough Devon 7 C6
North Wick Bath 23 C7
North Willingham Lincs 91 F5
North Wingfield Derbys 76 C4
North Witham Lincs 65 B6
North Woolwich London 28 B5
North Wootton Dorset 12 C4
North Wootton Norf 67 B6
North Wootton Som 23 E7
North Wraxall Wilts 24 B3
North Wroughton Swindon 38 F1
Northacre Norf 68 E2
Northallerton N Yorks 102 E1
Northam Devon 9 B6
Northam Soton 14 C5
Northampton Northants 53 C5
Northaw Herts 41 D5
Northbeck Lincs 78 E3
Northborough Pboro 65 D8
Northbourne Kent 31 D7
Northbridge Street E Sus 18 C4
Northchapel W Sus 16 B3
Northchurch Herts 40 D2
Northcott Devon 8 E5
Northdown Kent 31 B7
Northdyke Orkney 159 F3
Northend Bath 24 C2
Northend Bucks 39 E7
Northend Warks 51 D8
Northenden Gtr Man 87 E6
Northfield Aberdeen 141 D8
Northfield Borders 122 C5
Northfield E Yorks 90 B4
Northfield W Mid 50 B5
Northfields Lincs 65 D7
Northfleet Kent 29 B7
Northgate Lincs 65 B8
Northhouse Borders 115 D7
Northiam E Sus 18 C5
Northill C Beds 54 E2
Northington Hants 26 F3
Northlands Lincs 79 D6
Northlea Durham 111 D7
Northleach Glos 37 C8
Northleigh Devon 11 E6
Northlew Devon 9 E7
Northmoor Oxon 38 D4
Northmoor Green or Moorland Som 22 F5
Northmuir Angus 134 D3
Northney Hants 15 D8
Northolt London 40 F4
Northop Flint 73 C6
Northop Hall Flint 73 C6
Northorpe Lincs 65 C7
Northorpe Lincs 78 F5
Northorpe Lincs 90 E2
Northover Som 12 B3
Northover Som 23 F6
Northowram W Yorks 88 B2
Northport Dorset 13 F7
Northpunds Shetland 160 L6
Northrepps Norf 81 D8
Northtown Orkney 159 J5
Northway Glos 50 F4
Northwich Ches W 74 B3
Northwick S Glos 36 F2
Northwold Norf 67 E7
Northwood Derbys 76 C2
Northwood IoW 15 E5
Northwood Kent 31 C7
Northwood London 40 E3
Northwood Shrops 73 F8
Northwood Green Glos 36 C4
Norton E Sus 17 D8
Norton Glos 37 B5
Norton Halton 86 F3
Norton Herts 54 F3
Norton IoW 14 F4
Norton Mon 35 C8
Norton Northants 52 C4
Norton Notts 77 B5
Norton Powys 48 C5
Norton S Yorks 89 C6
Norton Shrops 60 F4
Norton Shrops 61 D5
Norton Shrops 61 D7
Norton Stockton 102 B2
Norton Suff 56 C3
Norton W Sus 16 D3
Norton W Sus 16 E2
Norton Wilts 37 F5
Norton Worcs 50 D3
Norton Worcs 50 E5
Norton Bavant Wilts 24 E4
Norton Bridge Staffs 75 F5
Norton Canes Staffs 62 D4
Norton Canon Hereford 49 E5
Norton Corner Norf 81 E6
Norton Disney Lincs 77 D8
Norton East Staffs 62 D4
Norton Ferris Wilts 24 F2
Norton Fitzwarren Som 11 B6
Norton Green IoW 14 F4
Norton Hawkfield Bath 23 C7
Norton Heath Essex 42 D1
Norton in Hales Shrops 74 F4
Norton-in-the-Moors Stoke 75 D5
Norton-Juxta-Twycross Leics 63 D7
Norton-le-Clay N Yorks 95 B7
Norton Lindsey Warks 51 C7
Norton Malreward Bath 23 C8
Norton Mandeville Essex 42 D1
Norton-on-Derwent N Yorks 96 B3
Norton St Philip Som 24 D2
Norton sub Hamdon Som 12 C2
Norton Woodseats S Yorks 88 F4

Plymstock Plym 6 D3
Plymtree Devon 11 D5
Pockley N Yorks 102 F4
Pocklington E Yorks 96 E4
Pode Hole Lincs 66 B2
Podimore Som 12 B3
Podington Bedford 53 C7
Podmore Staffs 74 F4
Point Clear Essex 43 C6
Pointon Lincs 78 F4
Pokesdown Bmouth 14 E2
Pol a Charra W Isles 148 G2
Polbae Dumfries 105 B6
Polbain Highld 156 H2
Polbathic Corn 5 D8
Polbeth W Loth 120 C3
Polchar Highld 138 D4
Pole Elm Worcs 50 E3
Polebrook Northants 65 F7
Polegate E Sus 18 E2
Poles Highld 151 B10
Polesworth Warks 63 D6
Polgigga Corn 2 D2
Polglass Highld 156 J3
Polgooth Corn 4 D4
Poling W Sus 16 D4
Polkerris Corn 5 D5
Polla Highld 156 D6
Pollington E Yorks 89 C7
Polloch Highld 130 C1
Pollok Glasgow 118 C5
Pollokshields Glasgow 119 C5
Polmassick Corn 3 B8
Polmont Falk 120 B2
Polnessan E Ayrs 112 C4
Polnish Highld 147 C10
Polperro Corn 5 D7
Polruan Corn 5 D6
Polsham Som 23 E7
Polstead Suff 56 F3
Poltalloch Argyll 124 F4
Poltimore Devon 10 E4
Polton Midloth 121 C5
Polwarth Borders 122 D3
Polyphant Corn 8 F4
Polzeath Corn 4 B4
Ponders End London 41 E6
Pondersbridge Cambs 66 E2
Pondtail Hants 27 D6
Ponsanooth Corn 3 C6
Ponsworthy Devon 6 B5
Pont Aber Carms 33 B8
Pont Aber-Geirw Gwyn 71 E8
Pont-ar-gothi Carms 33 B6
Pont ar Hydfer Powys 34 B2
Pont-ar-llechau Carms 33 B8
Pont Cwm Pydew Denb 72 F4
Pont Cyfyng Conwy 83 F7
Pont Cysyllte Wrex 73 E6
Pont Dolydd Prysor Gwyn 71 D8
Pont-faen Powys 47 F8
Pont Fronwydd Gwyn 58 B5
Pont-gareg Pembs 45 E3
Pont-Henri Carms 33 D5
Pont-Llogel Powys 59 C7
Pont Pen-y-benglog Gwyn 83 E6
Pont Rhyd-goch Conwy 83 E6
Pont-Rhyd-sarn Gwyn 59 B5
Pont Rhyd-y-cyff Bridgend 34 F2
Pont-rhyd-y-groes Ceredig 47 B6
Pont-rug Gwyn 82 E5
Pont Senni = Sennybridge Powys 34 B3
Pont-siân Ceredig 46 E3
Pont-y-gwaith Rhondda 34 E4
Pont-Y-Pŵl = Pontypool Torf 35 D6
Pont-y-pant Conwy 83 F7
Pont y Pennant Gwyn 59 B6
Pont yr Afon-Gam Gwyn 71 C8
Pont-yr-hafod Pembs 44 C4
Pontamman Carms 33 C7
Pontantwn Carms 33 C5
Pontardawe Neath 33 D8
Pontarddulais Swansea 33 D6
Pontarsais Carms 33 B5
Pontblyddyn Flint 73 C6
Pontbren Araeth Carms 33 B7
Pontbren Llwyd Rhondda 34 D3
Pontefract W Yorks 89 B5
Ponteland Northumb 110 B4
Ponterwyd Ceredig 58 F4
Pontesbury Shrops 60 D3
Pontfadog Wrex 73 F6
Pontfaen Pembs 45 F2
Pontgarreg Ceredig 46 D2
Ponthir Torf 35 E7
Ponthirwaun Ceredig 45 E4
Pontllanfraith Caerph 35 E5
Pontlliw Swansea 33 D7
Pontllyfni Gwyn 82 F4
Pontlottyn Caerph 35 D5
Pontneddfechan Powys 34 D3
Pontnewydd Torf 35 E6
Pontrhydfendigaid Ceredig 47 C6
Pontrhydyfen Neath 34 E1
Pontrilas Hereford 35 B7
Pontrobert Powys 59 C8
Ponts Green E Sus 18 D3
Pontshill Hereford 36 B3
Pontsticill M Tydf 34 C4
Pontwgan Conwy 83 D7
Pontyates Carms 33 D5
Pontyberem Carms 33 C6
Pontyclun Rhondda 34 F4
Pontycymer Bridgend 34 E3
Pontyglasier Pembs 45 F3
Pontypool = Pont-Y-Pŵl Torf 35 D6
Pontypridd Rhondda 34 F4
Pontywaun Caerph 35 E6
Pooksgreen Hants 14 C4
Pool Corn 3 B5
Pool W Yorks 94 E5
Pool o'Muckhart Clack 128 D2
Pool Quay Powys 60 C2
Poole Poole 13 E8
Poole Keynes Glos 37 E6
Poolend Staffs 75 D6
Poolewe Highld 155 J13
Pooley Bridge Cumb 99 B6
Poolfold Staffs 75 D5
Poolhill Glos 36 B4
Poolsbrook Derbys 76 B4
Pootings Kent 29 E5
Pope Hill Pembs 44 D4
Popeswood Brack 27 C6
Popham Hants 26 E3
Poplar London 41 F6
Popley Hants 26 D4
Porchester Nottingham 77 E5
Porchfield IoW 14 E5
Porin Highld 150 F6
Poringland Norf 69 D5
Porkellis Corn 3 C5
Porlock Som 21 E7
Porlock Weir Som 21 E7
Port Ann Argyll 145 E8
Port Appin Argyll 130 E3
Port Arthur Shetland 160 K5
Port Askaig Argyll 142 B5
Port Bannatyne Argyll 145 G9
Port Carlisle Cumb 108 C2
Port Charlotte Argyll 142 C3
Port Clarence Stockton 102 B2
Port Driseach Argyll 145 F8
Port e Vullen IoM 84 C4
Port Ellen Argyll 142 D4
Port Elphinstone Aberds 141 C6
Port Erin IoM 84 F1
Port Erroll Aberds 153 E10
Port-Eynon Swansea 33 F5
Port Gaverne Corn 8 F2
Port Glasgow Invclyd 118 B3
Port Henderson Highld 149 A12
Port Isaac Corn 4 A4
Port Lamont Argyll 145 F9
Port Lion Pembs 44 E4
Port Logan Dumfries 104 E4
Port Mholair W Isles 155 D10
Port Mor Highld 146 D7
Port Mulgrave N Yorks 103 C5
Port Nan Giùran W Isles 155 D10
Port nan Long W Isles 148 A3
Port Nis W Isles 155 A10
Port of Menteith Stirling 126 D4
Port Quin Corn 4 A4
Port Ramsay Argyll 130 E2
Port St Mary IoM 84 F2
Port Sunlight Mers 85 F4
Port Talbot Neath 34 E1
Port Tennant Swansea 33 E7
Port Wemyss Argyll 142 C2
Port William Dumfries 105 E7
Portachoillan Argyll 144 H6
Portavadie Argyll 145 G8
Portbury N Som 23 B7
Portchester Hants 15 D7
Portclair Highld 137 C7
Portencalzie Dumfries 104 B4
Portencross N Ayrs 118 E1
Portesham Dorset 12 F4
Portessie Moray 152 B4
Portfield Gate Pembs 44 D4
Portgate Devon 9 F6
Portgordon Moray 152 B3
Portgower Highld 157 H13
Porth Corn 4 C3
Porth Rhondda 34 E4
Porth Navas Corn 3 D6
Porth Tywyn = Burry Port Carms 33 D5
Porth-y-waen Shrops 60 B2
Porthaethwy = Menai Bridge Anglesey 83 D5
Porthallow Corn 3 D6
Porthallow Corn 5 D7
Porthcawl Bridgend 21 B7
Porthcothan Corn 4 B3
Porthcurno Corn 2 D2
Porthgain Pembs 44 B3
Porthill Shrops 60 C4
Porthkerry V Glam 22 C2
Porthleven Corn 2 D5
Porthllechog Anglesey 82 B4
Porthmadog Gwyn 71 D6
Porthmeor Corn 2 C3
Portholland Corn 3 B8
Porthoustock Corn 3 D7
Porthpean Corn 4 D5
Porthtowan Corn 3 B5
Porthyrhyd Carms 33 C6
Porthyrhyd Carms 47 F6
Portincaple Argyll 145 D11
Portington E Yorks 96 F3
Portinnisherrich Argyll 125 D5
Portinscale Cumb 98 B4
Portishead N Som 23 B6
Portkil Argyll 145 E11
Portknockie Moray 152 B4
Portlethen Aberds 141 E8
Portling Dumfries 107 D5
Portloe Corn 3 C8
Portmahomack Highld 151 C12
Portmeirion Gwyn 71 D6
Portmellon Corn 3 B9
Portmore Hants 14 E4
Portnacroish Argyll 130 E3
Portnahaven Argyll 142 C2
Portnalong Highld 149 E8
Portnaluchaig Highld 147 C9
Portnancon Highld 156 C7
Portnellan Stirling 126 B3
Portobello Edin 121 B6
Porton Wilts 25 F6
Portpatrick Dumfries 104 D4
Portreath Corn 3 B5
Portree Highld 149 D9
Portscatho Corn 3 C7
Portsea Ptsmth 15 D7
Portskerra Highld 157 C11
Portskewett Mon 36 F2
Portslade Brighton 17 D6
Portslade-by-Sea Brighton 17 D6
Portsmouth Ptsmth 15 D7
Portsmouth W Yorks 87 B7
Portsonachan Argyll 125 C6
Portsoy Aberds 152 B5
Portswood Soton 14 C5
Porttanachy Moray 152 B3
Portuairk Highld 146 E7
Portway Hereford 49 F6
Portway Worcs 51 B5
Portwrinkle Corn 5 D8
Poslingford Suff 55 E8
Postbridge Devon 6 B4
Postcombe Oxon 39 E7
Postling Kent 19 B8
Postwick Norf 69 D5
Potholm Dumfries 115 F6
Potsgrove C Beds 40 B2
Pott Row Norf 80 E3
Pott Shrigley Ches E 75 B6
Potten End Herts 40 D3
Potter Brompton N Yorks 97 B5
Potter Heigham Norf 69 C7
Potter Street Essex 41 D7
Potterhanworth Lincs 78 C3
Potterhanworth Booths Lincs 78 C3
Potterne Wilts 24 D4
Potterne Wick Wilts 24 D5
Potternewton W Yorks 95 F6
Potters Bar Herts 41 D5
Potter's Cross Staffs 62 F2
Potterspury Northants 53 E5
Potterton Aberds 141 C8
Potterton W Yorks 95 F7
Potto N Yorks 102 D2
Potton C Beds 54 E3
Poughill Corn 8 D4
Poughill Devon 10 D3
Poulshot Wilts 24 D4
Poulton Glos 37 D8
Poulton Mers 85 E4
Poulton-le-Fylde Lancs 92 F3
Pound Bank Worcs 50 B2
Pound Green E Sus 18 C2
Pound Green IoW 14 F4
Pound Green Worcs 50 B2
Pound Hill W Sus 28 F3
Poundfield E Sus 18 B2
Poundland S Ayrs 112 F1
Poundon Bucks 39 B6
Poundsgate Devon 6 B5
Poundstock Corn 8 E4
Powburn Northumb 117 C6
Powderham Devon 10 F4
Powerstock Dorset 12 E3
Powfoot Dumfries 107 C8
Powick Worcs 50 D3
Powmill Perth 128 E2
Poxwell Dorset 12 F5
Poyle Slough 27 B8
Poynings W Sus 17 C6
Poyntington Dorset 12 C4
Poynton Ches E 87 F7
Poynton Green Telford 61 C5
Poystreet Green Suff 56 D3
Praa Sands Corn 2 D4
Pratt's Bottom London 29 C5
Praze Corn 2 C4
Praze-an-Beeble Corn 2 C5
Predannack Wollas Corn 3 E5
Prees Shrops 74 F2
Prees Green Shrops 74 F2
Prees Heath Shrops 74 F2
Prees Higher Heath Shrops 74 F2
Prees Lower Heath Shrops 74 F2
Preesall Lancs 92 E3
Preesgweene Shrops 73 F6
Prenderguest Borders 122 D5
Prendwick Northumb 117 C6
Prengwyn Ceredig 46 E3
Prenteg Gwyn 71 C6
Prenton Mers 85 F4
Prescot Mers 86 E2
Prescott Shrops 60 B4
Pressen Northumb 122 F4
Prestatyn Denb 72 A4
Prestbury Ches E 75 B6
Prestbury Glos 37 B6
Presteigne = Llanandras Powys 48 C5
Presthope Shrops 61 E5
Prestleigh Som 23 E8
Preston Borders 122 D3
Preston Brighton 17 D7
Preston Devon 7 B6
Preston Dorset 12 F5
Preston E Loth 121 B8
Preston E Yorks 97 F7
Preston Glos 37 D7
Preston Glos 49 F8
Preston Herts 40 B4
Preston Kent 30 C4
Preston Kent 31 C6
Preston Lancs 86 B3
Preston Northumb 117 B7
Preston Rutland 65 D5
Preston Shrops 60 C5
Preston Wilts 24 B5
Preston Wilts 25 B7
Preston Bagot Warks 51 C6
Preston Bissett Bucks 39 B6
Preston Bowyer Som 11 B6
Preston Brockhurst Shrops 60 B5
Preston Brook Halton 86 F3
Preston Candover Hants 26 E4
Preston Capes Northants 52 D3
Preston Crowmarsh Oxon 39 E6
Preston Gubbals Shrops 60 C4
Preston on Stour Warks 51 E7
Preston on the Hill Halton 86 F3
Preston on Wye Hereford 49 E5
Preston Plucknett Som 12 C3
Preston St Mary Suff 56 D3
Preston-under-Scar N Yorks 101 E5
Preston upon the Weald Moors Telford 61 C6
Preston Wynne Hereford 49 E7
Prestonmill Dumfries 107 D6
Prestonpans E Loth 121 B6
Prestwich Gtr Man 87 D6
Prestwick Northumb 110 B4
Prestwick S Ayrs 112 B3
Prestwood Bucks 40 D1
Price Town Bridgend 34 E3
Prickwillow Cambs 67 F5
Priddy Som 23 D7
Priest Hutton Lancs 92 B5
Priest Weston Shrops 60 E2
Priesthaugh Borders 115 D7
Primethorpe Leics 64 E2
Primrose Green Norf 68 C3
Primrose Valley N Yorks 97 B7
Primrosehill Herts 40 D3
Princes Gate Pembs 32 C2
Princes Risborough Bucks 39 D8
Princethorpe Warks 52 B2
Princetown Caerph 35 C5
Princetown Devon 6 B3
Prion Denb 72 C4
Prior Muir Fife 129 C7
Prior Park Northumb 123 D5
Priors Frome Hereford 49 F7
Priors Hardwick Warks 52 D2
Priors Marston Warks 52 D2
Priorslee Telford 61 C7
Priory Wood Hereford 48 E4
Priston Bath 23 C8
Pristow Green Norf 68 F4
Prittlewell Southend 42 F4
Privett Hants 15 B7
Prixford Devon 20 F4
Probus Corn 3 B7
Proncy Highld 151 B10
Prospect Cumb 107 E8
Prudhoe Northumb 110 C3
Ptarmigan Lodge Stirling 126 D2
Pubil Perth 132 E1
Puckeridge Herts 41 B6
Puckington Som 11 C8
Pucklechurch S Glos 23 B8
Pucknall Hants 14 B4
Puckrup Glos 50 F3
Puddinglake Ches W 74 C4
Puddington Ches W 73 B7
Puddington Devon 10 C3
Puddledock Norf 68 E3
Puddletown Dorset 13 E5
Pudleston Hereford 49 D7
Pudsey W Yorks 94 F5
Pulborough W Sus 16 C4
Puleston Telford 61 B7
Pulford Ches W 73 D7
Pulham Dorset 12 D5
Pulham Market Norf 68 F4
Pulham St Mary Norf 68 F5
Pulloxhill C Beds 53 F8
Pumpherston W Loth 120 C3
Pumsaint Carms 47 E5
Puncheston Pembs 32 B1
Puncknowle Dorset 12 F3
Punnett's Town E Sus 18 C3
Purbrook Hants 15 D7
Purewell Dorset 14 E2
Purfleet Thurrock 29 B6
Puriton Som 22 E5
Purleigh Essex 42 D4
Purley London 28 C4
Purley W Berks 26 B4
Purlogue Shrops 48 B4
Purls Bridge Cambs 66 F4
Purse Caundle Dorset 12 C4
Purslow Shrops 60 F3
Purston Jaglin W Yorks 88 C5
Purton Glos 36 D3
Purton Glos 36 D3
Purton Wilts 37 F7
Purton Stoke Wilts 37 E7
Pury End Northants 52 E5
Pusey Oxon 38 E3
Putley Hereford 49 F8
Putney London 28 B3
Putsborough Devon 20 E3
Puttenham Herts 40 C1
Puttenham Sur 27 E7
Puxton N Som 23 C6
Pwll Carms 33 D5
Pwll-glas Denb 72 D5
Pwll-trap Carms 32 C3
Pwll-y-glaw Neath 34 E1
Pwllcrochan Pembs 44 E4
Pwllgloyw Powys 48 F2
Pwllheli Gwyn 70 D4
Pwllmeyric Mon 36 E2
Pye Corner Newport 35 F7
Pye Green Staffs 62 C3
Pyecombe W Sus 17 C6
Pyewipe NE Lincs 91 C6
Pyle = Y Pîl Bridgend 34 F2
Pyle IoW 15 G5
Pylle Som 23 F8
Pymoor Cambs 66 F4
Pyrford Sur 27 D8
Pyrton Oxon 39 E6
Pytchley Northants 53 B6
Pyworthy Devon 8 D5

Q

Quabbs Shrops 60 F2
Quadring Lincs 78 F5
Quainton Bucks 39 C7
Quarley Hants 25 E7
Quarndon Derbys 76 E3
Quarrier's Homes Invclyd 118 C3
Quarrington Lincs 78 E3
Quarrington Hill Durham 111 F6
Quarry Bank W Mid 62 F3
Quarryford E Loth 121 C8
Quarryhill Highld 151 C10
Quarrywood Moray 152 B1
Quarter S Lanark 119 D7
Quatford Shrops 61 E7
Quatt Shrops 61 F7
Quebec Durham 110 E4
Quedgeley Glos 37 C5
Queen Adelaide Cambs 67 F5
Queen Camel Som 12 B3
Queen Charlton Bath 23 C8
Queen Dart Devon 10 C3
Queen Oak Dorset 24 F2
Queen Street Kent 29 E7
Queen Street Wilts 37 F7
Queenborough Kent 30 B3
Queenhill Worcs 50 F3
Queen's Head Shrops 60 B3
Queen's Park Bedford 53 E8
Queen's Park Northants 53 C5
Queensbury W Yorks 94 F4
Queensferry Edin 120 B4
Queensferry Flint 73 C7
Queenstown Blackpool 92 F3
Queenzieburn N Lanark 119 B6
Quemerford Wilts 24 C5
Quendale Shetland 160 M5
Quendon Essex 55 F6
Queniborough Leics 64 C3
Quenington Glos 37 D8
Quernmore Lancs 92 D5
Quethiock Corn 5 C8
Quholm Orkney 159 G3
Quicks Green W Berks 26 B3
Quidenham Norf 68 F3
Quidhampton Hants 26 D3
Quidhampton Wilts 25 F6
Quilquox Aberds 153 E9
Quina Brook Shrops 74 F2
Quindry Orkney 159 J5
Quinton Northants 53 D5
Quinton W Mid 62 F3
Quintrell Downs Corn 4 C3
Quixhill Staffs 75 E8
Quoditch Devon 9 E6
Quoig Perth 127 B7
Quorndon Leics 64 C2
Quothquan S Lanark 120 F2
Quoyloo Orkney 159 F3
Quoyness Orkney 159 H3
Quoys Shetland 160 B8
Quoys Shetland 160 G6

R

Raasay Ho. Highld 149 E10
Rabbit's Cross Kent 29 E8
Raby Mers 73 B7
Rachan Mill Borders 120 F4
Rachub Gwyn 83 E6
Rackenford Devon 10 C3
Rackham W Sus 16 C4
Rackheath Norf 69 C5
Racks Dumfries 107 B7
Rackwick Orkney 159 D5
Rackwick Orkney 159 J3
Radbourne Derbys 76 F2
Radcliffe Gtr Man 87 D5
Radcliffe Northumb 117 D8
Radcliffe on Trent Notts 77 F6
Radclive Bucks 52 F4
Radcot Oxon 38 E2
Raddery Highld 151 F10
Radernie Fife 129 D6
Radford Semele Warks 51 C8
Radipole Dorset 12 F4
Radlett Herts 40 E4
Radley Oxon 39 E5
Radmanthwaite Notts 76 C5
Radmoor Shrops 61 B6
Radmore Green Ches E 74 D2
Radnage Bucks 39 E7
Radstock Bath 23 D8
Radstone Northants 52 E3
Radway Warks 51 E8
Radway Green Ches E 74 D4
Radwell Bedford 53 D8
Radwell Herts 54 F3
Radwinter Essex 55 F7
Radyr Cardiff 35 F5
Rafford Moray 151 F13
Ragdale Leics 64 C3
Raglan Mon 35 D8
Ragnall Notts 77 B8
Rahane Argyll 145 E11
Rainford Mers 86 D2
Rainford Junction Mers 86 D2
Rainham London 41 F8
Rainham Medway 30 C2
Rainhill Mers 86 E2
Rainhill Stoops Mers 86 E3
Rainow Ches E 75 B6
Rainton N Yorks 95 B6
Rainworth Notts 77 D5
Raisbeck Cumb 99 D8
Raise Cumb 109 E7
Rait Perth 128 B4
Raithby Lincs 79 C6
Raithby Lincs 91 F7
Rake W Sus 16 B2
Rakewood Gtr Man 87 C7
Ram Carms 46 E4
Ram Lane Kent 30 E3
Ramasaig Highld 148 D6
Rame Corn 3 C6
Rame Corn 6 E2
Rameldry Mill Bank Fife 128 D5
Ramnageo Shetland 160 C8
Rampisham Dorset 12 D3
Rampside Cumb 92 C2
Rampton Cambs 54 C5
Rampton Notts 77 B7
Ramsbottom Gtr Man 87 C5
Ramsbury Wilts 25 B7
Ramscraigs Highld 158 H3
Ramsdean Hants 15 B8
Ramsdell Hants 26 D3
Ramsden Oxon 38 C3
Ramsden Bellhouse Essex 42 E3
Ramsden Heath Essex 42 E3
Ramsey Cambs 66 F2
Ramsey Essex 57 F6
Ramsey IoM 84 C4
Ramsey Forty Foot Cambs 66 F3
Ramsey Heights Cambs 66 F2
Ramsey Island Essex 43 D5
Ramsey Mereside Cambs 66 F2
Ramsey St Mary's Cambs 66 F2
Ramseycleuch Borders 115 C5
Ramsgate Kent 31 C7
Ramsgill N Yorks 94 B4
Ramshorn Staffs 75 E7
Ramsnest Common Sur 27 F7
Ranais W Isles 155 E9
Ranby Lincs 78 B5
Ranby Notts 89 F7
Rand Lincs 78 B4
Randwick Glos 37 D5
Ranfurly Renfs 118 C3
Rangag Highld 158 F3
Rangemore Staffs 63 B5
Rangeworthy S Glos 36 F3
Rankinston E Ayrs 112 C4
Ranmoor S Yorks 88 F4
Ranmore Common Sur 28 D2
Rannerdale Cumb 98 C3
Rannoch Station Perth 131 D8
Ranochan Highld 147 C11
Ranskill Notts 89 F7
Ranton Staffs 62 B2
Ranworth Norf 69 C6
Raploch Stirling 127 E6
Rapness Orkney 159 D6
Rascal Moor E Yorks 96 F4
Rascarrel Dumfries 106 E4
Rashiereive Aberds 141 B8
Raskelf N Yorks 95 B7
Rassau Bl Gwent 35 C5
Rastrick W Yorks 88 B2
Ratagan Highld 136 C2
Ratby Leics 64 D2
Ratcliffe Culey Leics 63 E7
Ratcliffe on Soar Leics 63 B8
Ratcliffe on the Wreake Leics 64 C3
Rathen Aberds 153 B10
Rathillet Fife 129 B5
Rathmell N Yorks 93 D8
Ratho Edin 120 B4
Ratho Station Edin 120 B4
Rathven Moray 152 B4
Ratley Warks 51 E8
Ratlinghope Shrops 60 E4
Rattar Highld 158 C4
Ratten Row Lancs 92 E4
Rattery Devon 6 C5
Rattlesden Suff 56 D3
Rattray Perth 134 E1
Raughton Head Cumb 108 E3
Raunds Northants 53 B7
Ravenfield S Yorks 89 E5
Ravenglass Cumb 98 E2
Raveningham Norf 69 E6
Ravenscar N Yorks 103 D7
Ravenscraig Invclyd 118 B2
Ravensdale IoM 84 C3
Ravensden Bedford 53 D8
Ravenseat N Yorks 100 D3
Ravenshead Notts 77 D5
Ravensmoor Ches E 74 D3
Ravensthorpe Northants 52 B4
Ravensthorpe W Yorks 88 B3
Ravenstone Leics 63 C8
Ravenstone M Keynes 53 D6
Ravenstonedale Cumb 100 D2
Ravenstown Cumb 92 B3
Ravenstruther S Lanark 120 E2
Ravensworth N Yorks 101 D6
Raw N Yorks 103 D7
Rawcliffe E Yorks 89 B7
Rawcliffe York 95 D8
Rawcliffe Bridge E Yorks 89 B7
Rawdon W Yorks 94 F5
Rawmarsh S Yorks 88 E5
Rawreth Essex 42 E3
Rawridge Devon 11 D7
Rawtenstall Lancs 87 B6
Raxton Aberds 153 E8
Raydon Suff 56 F4
Raylees Northumb 117 E5
Rayleigh Essex 42 E4
Rayne Essex 42 B3
Rayners Lane London 40 F4
Raynes Park London 28 C3
Reach Cambs 55 C6
Read Lancs 93 F7
Reading Reading 26 B5
Reading Street Kent 19 B6
Reagill Cumb 99 C8
Rearquhar Highld 151 B10
Rearsby Leics 64 C3
Reaster Highld 158 D4
Reawick Shetland 160 J5
Reay Highld 157 C12
Rechullin Highld 149 C13
Reculver Kent 31 C6
Red Dial Cumb 108 E2
Red Hill Worcs 50 D3
Red Houses Jersey 17
Red Lodge Suff 55 B7
Red Rail Hereford 36 B2
Red Rock Gtr Man 86 D3
Red Roses Carms 32 C3
Red Row Northumb 117 E8
Red Street Staffs 74 D5
Red Wharf Bay Anglesey 82 C5
Redberth Pembs 32 D1
Redbourn Herts 40 C4
Redbourne N Lincs 90 E3
Redbrook Mon 36 C2
Redbrook Wrex 74 E2
Redburn Highld 151 E8
Redburn Highld 151 G12
Redburn Northumb 109 C7
Redcar Redcar 102 B4
Redcastle Angus 135 D6
Redcastle Highld 151 G8
Redcliff Bay N Som 23 B6
Redding Falk 120 B2
Reddingmuirhead Falk 120 B2
Reddish Gtr Man 87 E6
Redditch Worcs 50 C5
Rede Suff 56 D2
Redenhall Norf 69 F5
Redesdale Camp Northumb 116 E4
Redesmouth Northumb 116 F4
Redford Aberds 135 B7
Redford Angus 135 E5
Redford Durham 110 F3
Redfordgreen Borders 115 C6
Redgorton Perth 128 B2
Redgrave Suff 56 B4
Redhill Aberds 141 D6
Redhill Aberds 153 E6
Redhill N Som 23 C7
Redhill Sur 28 D3
Redhouse Argyll 145 G7
Redhouses Argyll 142 B4
Redisham Suff 69 F7
Redland Bristol 23 B7
Redland Orkney 159 F4
Redlingfield Suff 57 B5
Redlynch Som 23 F9
Redlynch Wilts 14 B3
Redmarley D'Abitot Glos 50 F2
Redmarshall Stockton 102 B1
Redmile Leics 77 F7
Redmire N Yorks 101 E5
Redmoor Corn 5 C5
Rednal Shrops 60 B3
Redpath Borders 121 F8
Redpoint Highld 149 B12
Redruth Corn 3 B5
Redvales Gtr Man 87 D6
Redwick Newport 35 F8
Redwick S Glos 36 F2
Redworth Darl 101 B7
Reed Herts 54 F4
Reedham Norf 69 D7
Reedness E Yorks 89 B8
Reeds Beck Lincs 78 C5
Reepham Lincs 78 B3
Reepham Norf 81 E6
Reeth N Yorks 101 E5
Regaby IoM 84 C4
Regoul Highld 151 F11
Reiff Highld 156 H2
Reigate Sur 28 D3
Reighton N Yorks 97 B7
Reighton Gap N Yorks 97 B7
Reinigeadal W Isles 154 G7
Reiss Highld 158 E5
Rejerrah Corn 4 D2
Releath Corn 3 C5
Relubbus Corn 2 C4
Relugas Moray 151 G12
Remenham Wokingham 39 F7
Remenham Hill Wokingham 39 F7
Remony Perth 132 E4
Rempstone Notts 64 B2
Rendcomb Glos 37 D7
Rendham Suff 57 C7
Rendlesham Suff 57 D7
Renfrew Renfs 118 C5
Renhold Bedford 53 D8
Renishaw Derbys 76 B4
Rennington Northumb 117 C8
Renton W Dunb 118 B3
Renwick Cumb 109 E5
Repps Norf 69 C7
Repton Derbys 63 B7
Reraig Highld 149 F13
Rescobie Angus 135 D5
Resipole Highld 147 E10
Resolis Highld 151 E9
Resolven Neath 34 D2
Reston Borders 122 C4
Reswallie Angus 135 D5
Retew Corn 4 D4
Retford Notts 89 F8
Rettendon Essex 42 E3
Rettendon Place Essex 42 E3
Revesby Lincs 79 C5
Revesby Bridge Lincs 79 C6
Rew Street IoW 15 E5
Rewe Devon 10 E4
Reydon Suff 57 B8
Reydon Smear Suff 57 B8
Reymerston Norf 68 D3
Reynalton Pembs 32 D1
Reynoldston Swansea 33 E5
Rezare Corn 5 B8
Rhaeadr Gwy = Rhayader Powys 47 C8
Rhandirmwyn Carms 47 E6
Rhayader = Rhaeadr Gwy Powys 47 C8
Rhedyn Gwyn 70 D3
Rhemore Highld 147 F8
Rhencullen IoM 84 C3
Rhes-y-cae Flint 73 B5
Rhewl Denb 72 C5
Rhewl Denb 73 E5
Rhian Highld 157 H8
Rhicarn Highld 156 G3
Rhiconich Highld 156 D5
Rhicullen Highld 151 D9
Rhidorroch Ho. Highld 150 B4
Rhifail Highld 157 E10
Rhigos Rhondda 34 D3
Rhilochan Highld 157 J10
Rhiroy Highld 150 C4
Rhisga = Risca Caerph 35 E6
Rhiw Gwyn 70 E3
Rhiwabon = Ruabon Wrex 73 E7
Rhiwbina Cardiff 35 F5
Rhiwbryfdir Gwyn 71 C7
Rhiwderin Newport 35 F6
Rhiwlas Gwyn 72 F3
Rhiwlas Gwyn 83 E5
Rhiwlas Powys 73 F5
Rhodes Gtr Man 87 D6
Rhodes Minnis Kent 31 E5
Rhodesia Notts 77 B5
Rhodiad Pembs 44 C2
Rhondda Rhondda 34 E3
Rhonehouse or Kelton Hill Dumfries 106 D4
Rhoose = Y Rhws V Glam 22 C2
Rhôs Carms 46 F2
Rhôs Neath 33 D8
Rhos-fawr Gwyn 70 D4
Rhos-goch Powys 48 E3
Rhos-hill Pembs 45 E3
Rhos-on-Sea Conwy 83 C8
Rhos-y-brithdir Powys 59 B8
Rhos-y-garth Ceredig 46 B5
Rhos-y-gwaliau Gwyn 72 F3
Rhos-y-llan Gwyn 70 D3
Rhos-y-Madoc Wrex 73 E7
Rhos-y-meirch Powys 48 C4
Rhosaman Carms 33 C8
Rhosbeirio Anglesey 82 B3
Rhoscefnhir Anglesey 82 D5
Rhoscolyn Anglesey 82 D2
Rhoscrowther Pembs 44 E4
Rhosesmor Flint 73 C6
Rhosgadfan Gwyn 82 F5
Rhosgoch Anglesey 82 C4
Rhoshirwaun Gwyn 70 E2
Rhoslan Gwyn 71 C5
Rhoslefain Gwyn 58 D2
Rhosllanerchrugog Wrex 73 E6
Rhosmaen Carms 33 B7
Rhosmeirch Anglesey 82 D4
Rhosneigr Anglesey 82 D3
Rhosnesni Wrex 73 D7
Rhosrobin Wrex 73 D7
Rhossili Swansea 33 F5
Rhosson Pembs 44 C2
Rhostryfan Gwyn 82 F4
Rhostyllen Wrex 73 E7
Rhosybol Anglesey 82 C4
Rhu Argyll 145 E11
Rhu Argyll 145 G7
Rhuallt Denb 72 B4
Rhuddall Heath Ches W 74 C2
Rhuddlan Ceredig 46 E3
Rhuddlan Denb 72 B4
Rhue Highld 150 B3
Rhulen Powys 48 E3
Rhunahaorine Argyll 143 D8
Rhuthun = Ruthin Denb 72 D5
Rhyd Gwyn 71 C7
Rhyd Powys 59 D6
Rhyd-Ddu Gwyn 83 F5
Rhyd-moel-ddu Powys 48 B2
Rhyd-Rosser Ceredig 46 C4
Rhyd-uchaf Gwyn 72 F3
Rhyd-wen Gwyn 58 C4
Rhyd-y-clafdy Gwyn 70 D4
Rhyd-y-foel Conwy 72 B3
Rhyd-y-fro Neath 33 D8
Rhyd-y-gwin Swansea 33 D7
Rhyd-y-meirch Mon 35 D7
Rhyd-y-meudwy Denb 72 D5
Rhyd-y-pandy Swansea 33 D7
Rhyd-y-sarn Gwyn 71 C7
Rhyd-yr-onen Gwyn 58 D3
Rhydaman = Ammanford Carms 33 C7
Rhydargaeau Carms 33 B5
Rhydcymerau Carms 46 F4
Rhydd Worcs 50 E3
Rhydding Neath 33 E8
Rhydfudr Ceredig 46 C4
Rhydlewis Ceredig 46 E2
Rhydlios Gwyn 70 D2
Rhydlydan Conwy 83 F8
Rhydness Powys 48 E3
Rhydowen Ceredig 46 E3
Rhydspence Hereford 48 E4
Rhydtalog Flint 73 D6
Rhydwyn Anglesey 82 C3
Rhydycroesau Powys 73 F6
Rhydyfelin Ceredig 46 B4
Rhydyfelin Rhondda 34 F4
Rhydymain Gwyn 58 B5
Rhydymwyn Flint 73 C6
Rhyl = Y Rhyl Denb 72 A4
Rhymney = Rhymni Caerph 35 D5
Rhymni = Rhymney Caerph 35 D5
Rhynd Fife 129 B6
Rhynd Perth 128 B3
Rhynie Aberds 140 B3
Rhynie Highld 151 D11
Ribbesford Worcs 50 B2
Ribblehead N Yorks 93 B7
Ribbleton Lancs 93 F5
Ribchester Lancs 93 F6
Ribigill Highld 157 D8
Riby Lincs 91 D5
Riby Cross Roads Lincs 91 D5
Riccall N Yorks 96 F2
Riccarton E Ayrs 118 F4
Richards Castle Hereford 49 C6
Richings Park Bucks 27 B8
Richmond London 28 B2
Richmond N Yorks 101 D6
Rickarton Aberds 141 F7
Rickinghall Suff 56 B4
Rickleton T&W 111 D5
Rickling Essex 55 F5
Rickmansworth Herts 40 E3
Riddings Cumb 108 B4
Riddings Derbys 76 D4
Riddlecombe Devon 9 C8
Riddlesden W Yorks 94 E3
Riddrie Glasgow 119 C6
Ridge Dorset 13 F7
Ridge Hants 14 C4
Ridge Wilts 24 F4
Ridge Green Sur 28 E4
Ridge Lane Warks 63 E6
Ridgebourne Powys 48 C2
Ridgehill N Som 23 C7
Ridgeway Cross Hereford 50 E2
Ridgewell Essex 55 E8
Ridgewood E Sus 17 C8
Ridgmont C Beds 53 F7
Riding Mill Northumb 110 C3
Ridleywood Wrex 73 D8
Ridlington Norf 69 A6
Ridlington Rutland 64 D5
Ridsdale Northumb 116 F5
Riechip Perth 133 E7
Riemore Perth 133 E7
Rienachait Highld 156 F3
Rievaulx N Yorks 102 F3
Rift House Hrtlpl 111 F7
Rigg Dumfries 108 C2
Riggend N Lanark 119 B7
Rigsby Lincs 79 B7
Rigside S Lanark 119 F8
Riley Green Lancs 86 B4
Rileyhill Staffs 62 C5
Rilla Mill Corn 5 B7
Rillington N Yorks 96 B4
Rimington Lancs 93 E8
Rimpton Som 12 B4
Rimswell E Yorks 91 B7
Rinaston Pembs 44 C4
Ringasta Shetland 160 M5
Ringford Dumfries 106 D3
Ringinglow S Yorks 88 F3
Ringland Norf 68 C4
Ringles Cross E Sus 17 B8
Ringmer E Sus 17 C8
Ringmore Devon 6 E4
Ringorm Moray 152 D2
Ring's End Cambs 66 D3
Ringsfield Suff 69 F7
Ringsfield Corner Suff 69 F7
Ringshall Herts 40 C2
Ringshall Suff 56 D4
Ringshall Stocks Suff 56 D4
Ringstead Norf 80 C3
Ringstead Northants 53 B7
Ringwood Hants 14 D2
Ringwould Kent 31 E7
Rinmore Aberds 140 C3
Rinnigill Orkney 159 J4
Rinsey Corn 2 D4
Riof W Isles 154 D6
Ripe E Sus 18 D2
Ripley Derbys 76 D3
Ripley Hants 14 E2
Ripley N Yorks 95 C5
Ripley Sur 27 D8
Riplingham E Yorks 97 F5
Ripon N Yorks 95 B6
Rippingale Lincs 65 B7
Ripple Kent 31 E7
Ripple Worcs 50 F3
Ripponden W Yorks 87 C8
Rireavach Highld 150 B3
Risabus Argyll 142 D4
Risbury Hereford 49 D7
Risby Suff 55 C8
Risca = Rhisga Caerph 35 E6
Rise E Yorks 97 E7
Riseden E Sus 18 B3
Risegate Lincs 66 B2
Riseholme Lincs 78 B2
Riseley Bedford 53 C8
Riseley Wokingham 26 C5
Rishangles Suff 57 C5
Rishton Lancs 93 F7
Rishworth W Yorks 87 C8
Rising Bridge Lancs 87 B5
Risley Derbys 76 F4
Risley Warr 86 E4
Risplith N Yorks 94 C5
Rispond Highld 156 C7
Rivar Wilts 25 C8
Rivenhall End Essex 42 C4
River Bank Cambs 55 C6
Riverhead Kent 29 D6
Rivington Lancs 86 C4
Roa Island Cumb 92 C2
Roachill Devon 10 B3
Road Green Norf 69 E5
Roade Northants 53 D5
Roadhead Cumb 108 B5
Roadmeetings S Lanark 119 E8
Roadside Highld 158 D3
Roadside of Catterline Aberds 135 B8
Roadside of Kinneff Aberds 135 B8
Roadwater Som 22 F2
Roag Highld 149 D7
Roath Cardiff 22 B3
Roberton Borders 115 C7
Roberton S Lanark 114 B2
Robertsbridge E Sus 18 C4
Roberttown W Yorks 88 B2
Robeston Cross Pembs 44 E3
Robeston Wathen Pembs 32 C1
Robin Hood W Yorks 88 B4
Robin Hood's Bay N Yorks 103 D7
Roborough Devon 6 C3
Roborough Devon 9 C7
Roby Mers 86 E2
Roby Mill Lancs 86 D3
Rocester Staffs 75 F8
Roch Pembs 44 C3
Roch Gate Pembs 44 C3
Rochdale Gtr Man 87 C6
Roche Corn 4 C4
Rochester Medway 29 C8
Rochester Northumb 116 E4
Rochford Essex 42 E4
Rock Corn 4 B4
Rock Northumb 117 B8
Rock W Sus 16 C5
Rock Worcs 50 B2
Rock Ferry Mers 85 F4
Rockbeare Devon 10 E5
Rockbourne Hants 14 C2
Rockcliffe Cumb 108 C3
Rockcliffe Dumfries 107 D5
Rockfield Highld 151 C12
Rockfield Mon 36 C1
Rockford Hants 14 D2
Rockhampton S Glos 36 E3
Rockingham Northants 65 E5
Rockland All Saints Norf 68 E2
Rockland St Mary Norf 69 D6
Rockland St Peter Norf 68 E2
Rockley Wilts 25 B6
Rockwell End Bucks 39 F7
Rockwell Green Som 11 B6
Rodborough Glos 37 D5
Rodbourne Swindon 37 F8
Rodbourne Wilts 37 F6
Rodbourne Cheney Swindon 37 F8
Rodd Hereford 48 C5
Roddam Northumb 117 B6
Rodden Dorset 12 F4
Rode Som 24 D3
Rode Heath Ches E 74 D5
Rodeheath Ches E 75 C5
Roden Telford 61 C5
Rodhuish Som 22 F2
Rodington Telford 61 C5
Rodley Glos 36 C4
Rodley W Yorks 94 F5
Rodmarton Glos 37 E6
Rodmell E Sus 17 D8
Rodmersham Kent 30 C3
Rodney Stoke Som 23 D6
Rodsley Derbys 76 E2
Rodway Som 22 E4
Rodwell Dorset 12 G4
Roe Green Herts 54 F4
Roecliffe N Yorks 95 C6
Roehampton London 28 B3
Roesound Shetland 160 G5
Roffey W Sus 28 F2
Rogart Highld 157 J10
Rogart Station Highld 157 J10
Rogate W Sus 16 B2
Rogerstone Newport 35 F6
Roghadal W Isles 154 J5
Rogiet Mon 36 F1
Rogue's Alley Cambs 66 D3
Roke Oxon 39 E6
Roker T&W 111 D7
Rollesby Norf 69 C7
Rolleston Leics 64 D4
Rolleston Notts 77 D7
Rolleston-on-Dove Staffs 63 B6
Rolston E Yorks 97 E8
Rolvenden Kent 18 B5
Rolvenden Layne Kent 19 B5
Romaldkirk Durham 100 B4
Romanby N Yorks 102 E1
Romannobridge Borders 120 E4
Romansleigh Devon 10 C2
Romford London 41 F8
Romiley Gtr Man 87 E7
Romsey Hants 14 B4
Romsey Town Cambs 55 D5
Romsley Shrops 61 F7
Romsley Worcs 50 B4
Ronague IoM 84 E2
Rookhope Durham 110 E2
Rookley IoW 15 F6
Rooks Bridge Som 23 D5
Roos E Yorks 97 F8
Roosebeck Cumb 92 C2
Rootham's Green Bedford 54 D2
Rootpark S Lanark 120 D2
Ropley Hants 26 F4
Ropley Dean Hants 26 F4
Ropsley Lincs 78 F2
Rora Aberds 153 C10
Rorandle Aberds 141 C5
Rorrington Shrops 60 D3
Roscroggan Corn 3 B5
Rose Corn 4 D2
Rose Ash Devon 10 B2
Rose Green W Sus 16 E3
Rose Grove Lancs 93 F8
Rose Hill E Sus 17 C8
Rose Hill Lancs 93 F8
Rose Hill Suff 57 E5
Roseacre Kent 29 D8
Roseacre Lancs 92 F4
Rosebank S Lanark 119 E8
Rosebrough Northumb 117 B7
Rosebush Pembs 32 B1
Rosecare Corn 8 E3
Rosedale Abbey N Yorks 103 E5
Roseden Northumb 117 B6
Rosefield Highld 151 F11

Ros – Shi 229

Rosehall Highld 156 J7
Rosehaugh Mains Highld 151 F9
Rosehearty Aberds 153 B9
Rosehill Shrops 74 F3
Roseisle Moray 152 B1
Roselands E Sus 18 E3
Rosemarket Pembs 44 E4
Rosemarkie Highld 151 F10
Rosemary Lane Devon 11 C6
Rosemount Perth 134 E1
Rosenannon Corn 4 C4
Rosewell Midloth 121 C5
Roseworth Stockton 102 B2
Roseworthy Corn 2 C5
Rosgill Cumb 99 C7
Roshven Highld 147 D10
Roskhill Highld 149 D7
Roskill House Highld 151 F9
Rosley Cumb 108 E3
Roslin Midloth 121 C5
Rosliston Derbys 63 C6
Rosneath Argyll 145 E11
Ross Dumfries 106 E3
Ross Northumb 123 F7
Ross Perth 127 B6
Ross-on-Wye Hereford 36 B3
Rossett Wrex 73 D7
Rossett Green N Yorks 95 D6
Rossie Ochill Perth 128 C2
Rossie Priory Perth 134 F2
Rossington S Yorks 89 E7
Rosskeen Highld 151 E9
Rossland Renfs 118 B4
Roster Highld 158 G4
Rostherne Ches E 86 F5
Rosthwaite Cumb 98 C4
Roston Derbys 75 E8
Rosyth Fife 128 F3
Rothbury Northumb 117 D6
Rotherby Leics 64 C3
Rotherfield E Sus 18 C2
Rotherfield Greys Oxon 39 F7
Rotherfield Peppard Oxon 39 F7
Rotherham S Yorks 88 E5
Rothersthorpe Northants 52 D5
Rotherwick Hants 26 D5
Rothes Moray 152 D2
Rothesay Argyll 145 G9
Rothiebrisbane Aberds 153 E7
Rothienorman Aberds 153 E7
Rothiesholm Orkney 159 F7
Rothley Leics 64 C2
Rothley Northumb 117 F6
Rothley Shield East Northumb 117 E6
Rothmaise Aberds 153 E6
Rothwell Lincs 91 E5
Rothwell Northants 64 F5
Rothwell W Yorks 88 B4
Rothwell Haigh W Yorks 88 B4
Rotsea E Yorks 97 D6
Rottal Angus 134 C3
Rotten End Suff 57 C7
Rottingdean Brighton 17 D7
Rottington Cumb 98 C1
Roud IoW 15 F6
Rough Close Staffs 75 F6
Rough Common Kent 30 D5
Rougham Norf 80 E4
Rougham Suff 56 C3
Rougham Green Suff 56 C3
Roughburn Highld 137 F6
Roughlee Lancs 93 E8
Roughley W Mid 62 E5
Roughsike Cumb 108 B5
Roughton Lincs 78 C5
Roughton Norf 81 D8
Roughton Shrops 61 E7
Roughton Moor Lincs 78 C5
Roundhay W Yorks 95 F6
Roundstonefoot Dumfries 114 D4
Roundstreet Common W Sus 16 B4
Roundway Wilts 24 C5
Rous Lench Worcs 50 D5
Rousdon Devon 11 E7
Routenburn N Ayrs 118 C1
Routh E Yorks 97 E6
Row Corn 5 B5
Row Cumb 99 F6
Row Heath Essex 43 C7
Rowanburn Dumfries 108 B4
Rowardennan Stirling 126 E2
Rowde Wilts 24 C4
Rowen Conwy 83 D7
Rowfoot Northumb 109 C6
Rowhedge Essex 43 B6
Rowhook W Sus 28 F2
Rowington Warks 51 C7
Rowland Derbys 76 B2
Rowlands Castle Hants 15 C8
Rowlands Gill T&W 110 D4
Rowledge Sur 27 E6
Rowlestone Hereford 35 B7
Rowley E Yorks 97 F5
Rowley Shrops 60 D3
Rowley Hill W Yorks 88 C2
Rowley Regis W Mid 62 F3
Rowly Sur 27 E8
Rowney Green Worcs 50 B5
Rownhams Hants 14 C4
Rowrah Cumb 98 C2
Rowsham Bucks 39 C8
Rowsley Derbys 76 C2
Rowstock Oxon 38 F4
Rowston Lincs 78 D3
Rowton Ches W 73 C8
Rowton Shrops 60 C3
Rowton Telford 61 C6
Roxburgh Borders 122 F3
Roxby N Lincs 90 C3
Roxby N Yorks 103 C5
Roxton Bedford 54 D2
Roxwell Essex 42 D2
Royal Leamington Spa Warks 51 C8
Royal Oak Darl 101 B7
Royal Oak Lancs 86 D2
Royal Tunbridge Wells Kent 18 B2
Roybridge Highld 137 F5
Roydhouse W Yorks 88 C3
Roydon Essex 41 D7
Roydon Norf 68 F3
Roydon Norf 80 E3
Roydon Hamlet Essex 41 D7
Royston Herts 54 E4
Royston S Yorks 88 C4
Royton Gtr Man 87 D7
Rozel Jersey 17
Ruabon = Rhiwabon Wrex 73 E7
Ruaig Argyll 146 G3
Ruan Lanihorne Corn 3 B7
Ruan Minor Corn 3 E6
Ruarach Highld 136 B2
Ruardean Glos 36 C3
Ruardean Woodside Glos 36 C3
Rubery Worcs 50 B4
Ruckcroft Cumb 108 E5
Ruckhall Hereford 49 F6
Ruckinge Kent 19 B7
Ruckland Lincs 79 B6
Ruckley Shrops 60 D5
Rudbaxton Pembs 44 C4
Rudby N Yorks 102 D2
Ruddington Notts 77 F5
Rudford Glos 36 B4
Rudge Shrops 62 E2
Rudge Som 24 D3
Rudgeway S Glos 36 F3
Rudgwick W Sus 27 F8
Rudhall Hereford 36 B3
Rudheath Ches W 74 B3
Rudley Green Essex 42 D4
Rudry Caerph 35 F5
Rudston E Yorks 97 C6
Rudyard Staffs 75 D6
Rufford Lancs 86 C2
Rufforth York 95 D8
Rugby Warks 52 B3
Rugeley Staffs 62 C4
Ruglen S Ayrs 112 D2
Ruilick Highld 151 G8
Ruishton Som 11 B7
Ruisigearraidh W Isles 154 J4
Ruislip London 40 F3
Ruislip Common London 40 F3
Rumbling Bridge Perth 128 E2
Rumburgh Suff 69 F6
Rumford Corn 4 B3
Rumney Cardiff 22 B4
Runcorn Halton 86 F3
Runcton W Sus 16 D2
Runcton Holme Norf 67 D6
Rundlestone Devon 6 B3
Runfold Sur 27 E6
Runhall Norf 68 D3
Runham Norf 69 C7
Runham Norf 69 D8
Runnington Som 11 B6
Runsell Green Essex 42 D3
Runswick Bay N Yorks 103 C6
Runwell Essex 42 E3
Ruscombe Wokingham 27 B5
Rush Green London 41 F8
Rush-head Aberds 153 D8
Rushall Hereford 49 F8
Rushall Norf 68 F4
Rushall W Mid 62 D4
Rushall Wilts 25 D6
Rushbrooke Suff 56 C2
Rushbury Shrops 60 E5
Rushden Herts 54 F4
Rushden Northants 53 C7
Rushenden Kent 30 B3
Rushford Norf 68 F2
Rushlake Green E Sus 18 D3
Rushmere Suff 69 F7
Rushmere St Andrew Suff 57 E6
Rushmoor Sur 27 E6
Rushock Worcs 50 B3
Rusholme Gtr Man 87 E6
Rushton Ches W 74 C2
Rushton Northants 64 F5
Rushton Shrops 61 D6
Rushton Spencer Staffs 75 C6
Rushwick Worcs 50 D3
Rushyford Durham 101 B7
Ruskie Stirling 126 D5
Ruskington Lincs 78 D3
Rusland Cumb 99 F5
Rusper W Sus 28 F3
Ruspidge Glos 36 C3
Russell's Water Oxon 39 F7
Russel's Green Suff 57 B6
Rusthall Kent 18 B2
Rustington W Sus 16 D4
Ruston N Yorks 103 F7
Ruston Parva E Yorks 97 C6
Ruswarp N Yorks 103 D6
Rutherford Borders 122 F2
Rutherglen S Lanark 119 C6
Ruthernbridge Corn 4 C5
Ruthin = Rhuthun Denb 72 D5
Ruthrieston Aberdeen 141 D8
Ruthven Aberds 152 D5
Ruthven Angus 134 E2
Ruthven Highld 138 E3
Ruthven Highld 151 H11
Ruthven House Angus 134 E3
Ruthvoes Corn 4 C4
Ruthwell Dumfries 107 C7
Ruyton-XI-Towns Shrops 60 B3
Ryal Northumb 110 B3
Ryal Fold Blackburn 86 B4
Ryall Dorset 12 E2
Ryarsh Kent 29 D7
Rydal Cumb 99 D5
Ryde IoW 15 E6
Rye E Sus 19 C6
Rye Foreign E Sus 19 C5
Rye Harbour E Sus 19 D6
Rye Park Herts 41 C6
Rye Street Worcs 50 F2
Ryecroft Gate Staffs 75 C6
Ryehill E Yorks 91 B6
Ryhall Rutland 65 C7
Ryhill W Yorks 88 C4
Ryhope T&W 111 D7
Rylstone N Yorks 94 D2
Ryme Intrinseca Dorset 12 C3
Ryther N Yorks 95 F8
Ryton Glos 50 F2
Ryton N Yorks 96 B3
Ryton Shrops 61 D7
Ryton T&W 110 C4
Ryton-on-Dunsmore Warks 51 B8

S

Sabden Lancs 93 F7
Sacombe Herts 41 C6
Sacriston Durham 110 E5
Sadberge Darl 101 C8
Saddell Argyll 143 E8
Saddington Leics 64 E3
Saddle Bow Norf 67 C6
Saddlescombe W Sus 17 C6
Sadgill Cumb 99 D6
Saffron Walden Essex 55 F6
Sageston Pembs 32 D1
Saham Hills Norf 68 D2
Saham Toney Norf 68 D2
Saighdinis W Isles 148 B3
Saighton Ches W 73 C8
St Abbs Borders 122 C5
St Abb's Haven Borders 122 C5
St Agnes Corn 4 D2
St Agnes Scilly 2 F3
St Albans Herts 40 D4
St Allen Corn 4 D3
St Andrews Fife 129 C7
St Andrew's Major V Glam 22 B3
St Anne Ald 16
St Annes Lancs 85 B4
St Ann's Dumfries 114 E3
St Ann's Chapel Corn 6 B2
St Ann's Chapel Devon 6 E4
St Anthony-in-Meneage Corn 3 D6
St Anthony's Hill E Sus 18 E3
St Arvans Mon 36 E2
St Asaph = Llanelwy Denb 72 B4
St Athan V Glam 22 C2
St Aubin Jersey 17
St Austell Corn 4 D5
St Bees Cumb 98 C1
St Blazey Corn 5 D5
St Boswells Borders 121 F8
St Brelade Jersey 17
St Breock Corn 4 B4
St Breward Corn 5 B5
St Briavels Glos 36 D2
St Bride's Pembs 44 D3
St Brides Major V Glam 21 B7
St Bride's Netherwent Mon 35 F8
St Brides super Ely V Glam 22 B2
St Brides Wentlooge Newport 35 F6
St Budeaux Plym 6 D2
St Buryan Corn 2 D3
St Catherine Bath 24 B2
St Catherine's Argyll 125 E7
St Clears = Sanclêr Carms 32 C3
St Cleer Corn 5 C7
St Clement Corn 3 B7
St Clements Jersey 17
St Clether Corn 8 F4
St Colmac Argyll 145 G9
St Columb Major Corn 4 C4
St Columb Minor Corn 4 C3
St Columb Road Corn 4 D4
St Combs Aberds 153 B10
St Cross South Elmham Suff 69 F5
St Cyrus Aberds 135 C7
St David's Perth 127 B8
St David's = Tyddewi Pembs 44 C2
St Day Corn 3 B6
St Dennis Corn 4 D4
St Devereux Hereford 49 F6
St Dogmaels Pembs 45 E3
St Dogwells Pembs 44 C4
St Dominick Corn 6 C2
St Donat's V Glam 21 C8
St Edith's Wilts 24 C4
St Endellion Corn 4 B4
St Enoder Corn 4 D3
St Erme Corn 4 D3
St Erney Corn 5 D8
St Erth Corn 2 C4
St Ervan Corn 4 B3
St Eval Corn 4 C3
St Ewe Corn 3 B8
St Fagans Cardiff 22 B3
St Fergus Aberds 153 C10
St Fillans Perth 127 B5
St Florence Pembs 32 D1
St Genny's Corn 8 E3
St George Conwy 72 B3
St George's V Glam 22 B2
St Germans Corn 5 D8
St Giles Lincs 78 B2
St Giles in the Wood Devon 9 C7
St Giles on the Heath Devon 9 E5
St Harmon Powys 47 B8
St Helen Auckland Durham 101 B6
St Helena Warks 63 D6
St Helen's E Sus 18 D5
St Helens IoW 15 F7
St Helens Mers 86 E3
St Helier Jersey 17
St Helier London 28 C3
St Hilary Corn 2 C4
St Hilary V Glam 22 B2
Saint Hill W Sus 28 F4
St Illtyd Bl Gwent 35 D6
St Ippollytts Herts 40 B4
St Ishmael's Pembs 44 E3
St Issey Corn 4 B4
St Ive Corn 5 C8
St Ives Cambs 54 B4
St Ives Corn 2 B4
St Ives Dorset 14 D2
St James South Elmham Suff 69 F6
St Jidgey Corn 4 C4
St John Corn 6 D2
St John's IoM 84 D2
St John's Jersey 17
St John's Sur 27 D7
St John's Worcs 50 D3
St John's Chapel Durham 109 F8
St John's Fen End Norf 66 C5
St John's Highway Norf 66 C5
St John's Town of Dalry Dumfries 113 F6
St Judes IoM 84 C3
St Just Corn 2 C2
St Just in Roseland Corn 3 C7
St Katherine's Aberds 153 E7
St Keverne Corn 3 D6
St Kew Corn 4 B5
St Kew Highway Corn 4 B5
St Keyne Corn 5 C7
St Lawrence Corn 4 C5
St Lawrence Essex 43 D5
St Lawrence IoW 15 G6
St Leonard's Bucks 40 D2
St Leonards Dorset 14 D2
St Leonards E Sus 18 E4
Saint Leonards S Lanark 119 D6
St Levan Corn 2 D2
St Lythans V Glam 22 B3
St Mabyn Corn 4 B5
St Madoes Perth 128 B3
St Margaret's Hereford 49 F5
St Margarets Herts 41 C6
St Margaret's at Cliffe Kent 31 E7
St Margaret's Hope Orkney 159 J5
St Margaret South Elmham Suff 69 F6
St Mark's IoM 84 E2
St Martin Corn 5 D7
St Martins Corn 3 D6
St Martin's Jersey 17
St Martins Perth 134 F1
St Martin's Shrops 73 F7
St Mary Bourne Hants 26 D2
St Mary Church V Glam 22 B2
St Mary Cray London 29 C5
St Mary Hill V Glam 21 B8
St Mary Hoo Medway 30 B2
St Mary in the Marsh Kent 19 C7
St Mary's Jersey 17
St Mary's Orkney 159 H5
St Mary's Bay Kent 19 C7
St Maughans Mon 36 C1
St Mawes Corn 3 C7
St Mawgan Corn 4 C3
St Mellion Corn 5 C8
St Mellons Cardiff 35 F6
St Merryn Corn 4 B3
St Mewan Corn 4 D4
St Michael Caerhays Corn 3 B8
St Michael Penkivel Corn 3 B7
St Michael South Elmham Suff 69 F6
St Michael's Kent 19 B5
St Michaels Worcs 49 C7
St Michael's on Wyre Lancs 92 E4
St Minver Corn 4 B4
St Monans Fife 129 D7
St Neot Corn 5 C6
St Neots Cambs 54 C2
St Newlyn East Corn 4 D3
St Nicholas Pembs 44 B3
St Nicholas V Glam 22 B2
St Nicholas at Wade Kent 31 C6
St Ninians Stirling 127 E6
St Osyth Essex 43 C7
St Osyth Heath Essex 43 C7
St Ouens Jersey 17
St Owens Cross Hereford 36 B2
St Paul's Cray London 29 C5
St Paul's Walden Herts 40 B4
St Peter Port Guern 16
St Peter's Jersey 17
St Peter's Kent 31 C7
St Petrox Pembs 44 F4
St Pinnock Corn 5 C7
St Quivox S Ayrs 112 B3
St Ruan Corn 3 E6
St Sampson Guern 16
St Stephen Corn 4 D4
St Stephen's Corn 8 F5
St Stephens Corn 6 D2
St Stephens Herts 40 D4
St Teath Corn 8 F2
St Thomas Devon 10 E4
St Tudy Corn 5 B5
St Twynnells Pembs 44 F4
St Veep Corn 5 D6
St Vigeans Angus 135 E6
St Wenn Corn 4 C4
St Weonards Hereford 36 B1
Saintbury Glos 51 F6
Salcombe Devon 6 F5
Salcombe Regis Devon 11 F6
Salcott Essex 43 C5
Sale Gtr Man 87 E5
Sale Green Worcs 50 D4
Saleby Lincs 79 B7
Salehurst E Sus 18 C4
Salem Carms 33 B7
Salem Ceredig 58 F3
Salen Argyll 147 G8
Salen Highld 147 E9
Salesbury Lancs 93 F6
Salford C Beds 53 F7
Salford Gtr Man 87 E6
Salford Oxon 38 B2
Salford Priors Warks 51 D5
Salfords Sur 28 E3
Salhouse Norf 69 C6
Saline Fife 128 E2
Salisbury Wilts 14 B2
Sallachan Highld 130 C3
Sallachy Highld 150 H2
Sallachy Highld 157 J8
Salle Norf 81 E7
Salmonby Lincs 79 B6
Salmond's Muir Angus 135 F5
Salperton Glos 37 B7
Salph End Bedford 53 D8
Salsburgh N Lanark 119 C8
Salt Staffs 62 B3
Salt End E Yorks 91 B5
Saltaire W Yorks 94 F4
Saltash Corn 6 D2
Saltburn Highld 151 E10
Saltburn-by-the-Sea Redcar 102 B4
Saltby Leics 65 B5
Saltcoats Cumb 98 E2
Saltcoats N Ayrs 118 E2
Saltdean Brighton 17 D7
Salter Lancs 93 C6
Salterforth Lancs 93 E8
Salterswall Ches W 74 C3
Saltfleet Lincs 91 E8
Saltfleetby All Saints Lincs 91 E8
Saltfleetby St Clements Lincs 91 E8
Saltfleetby St Peter Lincs 91 F8
Saltford Bath 23 C8
Salthouse Norf 81 C6
Saltmarshe E Yorks 89 B8
Saltney Flint 73 C7
Salton N Yorks 96 B3
Saltwick Northumb 110 B4
Saltwood Kent 19 B8
Salum Argyll 146 G3
Salvington W Sus 16 D5
Salwarpe Worcs 50 C3
Salwayash Dorset 12 E2
Sambourne Warks 51 C5
Sambrook Telford 61 B7
Samhla W Isles 148 B2
Samlesbury Lancs 93 F5
Samlesbury Bottoms Lancs 86 B4
Sampford Arundel Som 11 C6
Sampford Brett Som 22 E2
Sampford Courtenay Devon 9 D8
Sampford Peverell Devon 10 C5
Sampford Spiney Devon 6 B3
Sampool Bridge Cumb 99 F6
Samuelston E Loth 121 B7
Sanachan Highld 149 D13
Sanaigmore Argyll 142 A3
Sanclêr = St Clears Carms 32 C3
Sancreed Corn 2 D3
Sancton E Yorks 96 F5
Sand Highld 150 B2
Sand Shetland 160 J5
Sand Hole E Yorks 96 F4
Sand Hutton N Yorks 96 D2
Sandaig Highld 149 H12
Sandal Magna W Yorks 88 C4
Sandale Cumb 108 E2
Sandbach Ches E 74 C4
Sandbank Argyll 145 E10
Sandbanks Poole 13 F8
Sandend Aberds 152 B5
Sanderstead London 28 C4
Sandfields Glos 37 B6
Sandford Cumb 100 C2
Sandford Devon 10 D3
Sandford Dorset 13 F7
Sandford IoW 15 F6
Sandford N Som 23 D6
Sandford S Lanark 119 E7
Sandford Shrops 74 F2
Sandford on Thames Oxon 39 D5
Sandford Orcas Dorset 12 B4
Sandford St Martin Oxon 38 B4
Sandfordhill Aberds 153 D11
Sandgate Kent 19 B8
Sandgreen Dumfries 106 D2
Sandhaven Aberds 153 B9
Sandhead Dumfries 104 E4
Sandhills Sur 27 F7
Sandhoe Northumb 110 C2
Sandholme E Yorks 96 F4
Sandholme Lincs 79 F6
Sandhurst Brack 27 C6
Sandhurst Glos 37 B5
Sandhurst Kent 18 C4
Sandhurst Cross Kent 18 C4
Sandhutton N Yorks 102 F1
Sandiacre Derbys 76 F4
Sandilands Lincs 91 F9
Sandilands S Lanark 119 F8
Sandiway Ches W 74 B3
Sandleheath Hants 14 C2
Sandling Kent 29 D8
Sandlow Green Ches E 74 C4
Sandness Shetland 160 H3
Sandon Essex 42 D3
Sandon Herts 54 F4
Sandon Staffs 75 F6
Sandown IoW 15 F6
Sandplace Corn 5 D7
Sandridge Herts 40 C4
Sandridge Wilts 24 C4
Sandringham Norf 67 B6
Sandsend N Yorks 103 C6
Sandside Ho. Highld 157 C12
Sandsound Shetland 160 J5
Sandtoft N Lincs 89 D8
Sandway Kent 30 D2
Sandwell W Mid 62 F4
Sandwich Kent 31 D7
Sandwick Cumb 99 C6
Sandwick Orkney 159 K5
Sandwick Shetland 160 L6
Sandwith Cumb 98 C1
Sandy C Beds 54 E2
Sandy Carms 33 D5
Sandy Bank Lincs 79 D5
Sandy Haven Pembs 44 E3
Sandy Lane Wilts 24 C4
Sandy Lane Wrex 73 E7
Sandycroft Flint 73 C7
Sandyford Dumfries 114 E5
Sandyford Stoke 75 D5
Sandygate IoM 84 C3
Sandyhills Dumfries 107 D5
Sandylands Lancs 92 C4
Sandypark Devon 10 F2
Sandysike Cumb 108 C3
Sangobeg Highld 156 C7
Sangomore Highld 156 C7
Sanna Highld 146 E7
Sanndabhaig W Isles 148 D3
Sanndabhaig W Isles 155 D9
Sannox N Ayrs 143 D11
Sanquhar Dumfries 113 D7
Santon N Lincs 90 C3
Santon Bridge Cumb 98 D3
Santon Downham Suff 67 F8
Sapcote Leics 63 E8
Sapey Common Hereford 50 C2
Sapiston Suff 56 B3
Sapley Cambs 54 B3
Sapperton Glos 37 D6
Sapperton Lincs 78 F3
Saracen's Head Lincs 66 B3
Sarclet Highld 158 F5
Sardis Carms 33 D6
Sarn Bridgend 34 F3
Sarn Powys 60 E2
Sarn Bach Gwyn 70 E4
Sarn Meyllteyrn Gwyn 70 D3
Sarnau Carms 32 C4
Sarnau Ceredig 46 D2
Sarnau Gwyn 72 F3
Sarnau Powys 48 F2
Sarnau Powys 60 C2
Sarnesfield Hereford 49 D5
Saron Carms 33 C7
Saron Carms 46 F2
Saron Denb 72 C4
Saron Gwyn 82 E5
Saron Gwyn 82 F4
Sarratt Herts 40 E3
Sarre Kent 31 C6
Sarsden Oxon 38 B2
Sarsgrum Highld 156 C6
Satley Durham 110 E4
Satron N Yorks 100 E4
Satterleigh Devon 9 B8
Satterthwaite Cumb 99 E5
Satwell Oxon 39 F7
Sauchen Aberds 141 C5
Saucher Perth 134 F1
Sauchie Clack 127 E7
Sauchieburn Aberds 135 C6
Saughall Ches W 73 B7
Saughtree Borders 115 E8
Saul Glos 36 D4
Saundby Notts 89 F8
Saundersfoot Pembs 32 D2
Saunderton Bucks 39 D7
Saunton Devon 20 F3
Sausthorpe Lincs 79 C6
Saval Highld 157 J8
Savary Highld 147 G9
Savile Park W Yorks 87 B8
Sawbridge Warks 52 C3
Sawbridgeworth Herts 41 C7
Sawdon N Yorks 103 F7
Sawley Derbys 76 F4
Sawley Lancs 93 E7
Sawley N Yorks 94 C5
Sawston Cambs 55 E5
Sawtry Cambs 65 F8
Saxby Leics 64 C5
Saxby Lincs 90 F4
Saxby All Saints N Lincs 90 C3
Saxelbye Leics 64 B4
Saxham Street Suff 56 C4
Saxilby Lincs 77 B8
Saxlingham Norf 81 D6
Saxlingham Green Norf 68 E5
Saxlingham Nethergate Norf 68 E5
Saxlingham Thorpe Norf 68 E5
Saxmundham Suff 57 C7
Saxon Street Cambs 55 D7
Saxondale Notts 77 F6
Saxtead Suff 57 C6
Saxtead Green Suff 57 C6
Saxthorpe Norf 81 D7
Saxton N Yorks 95 F7
Sayers Common W Sus 17 C6
Scackleton N Yorks 96 B2
Scadabhagh W Isles 154 H6
Scaftworth Notts 89 E7
Scagglethorpe N Yorks 96 B4
Scaitcliffe Lancs 87 B5
Scalasaig Argyll 144 D2
Scalby E Yorks 90 B2
Scalby N Yorks 103 E8
Scaldwell Northants 53 B5
Scale Houses Cumb 109 E5
Scaleby Cumb 108 C4
Scaleby Hill Cumb 108 C4
Scales Cumb 92 B2
Scales Cumb 99 B5
Scales Lancs 92 F4
Scalford Leics 64 B4
Scaling Redcar 103 C5
Scallastle Argyll 124 B2
Scalloway Shetland 160 K6
Scalpay W Isles 154 H7
Scalpay Ho. Highld 149 F11
Scalpsie Argyll 145 H9
Scamadale Highld 147 B10
Scamblesby Lincs 79 B5
Scamodale Highld 130 B2
Scampston N Yorks 96 B4
Scampton Lincs 78 B2
Scapa Orkney 159 H5
Scapegoat Hill W Yorks 87 C8
Scar Orkney 159 D7
Scarborough N Yorks 103 F8
Scarcliffe Derbys 76 C4
Scarcroft W Yorks 95 E6
Scarcroft Hill W Yorks 95 E6
Scardroy Highld 150 F5
Scarff Shetland 160 E4
Scarfskerry Highld 158 C4
Scargill Durham 101 C5
Scarinish Argyll 146 G3
Scarisbrick Lancs 85 C4
Scarning Norf 68 C2
Scarrington Notts 77 E7
Scartho NE Lincs 91 D6
Scarwell Orkney 159 F3
Scatness Shetland 160 M5
Scatraig Highld 151 H10
Scawby N Lincs 90 D3
Scawsby S Yorks 89 D6
Scawton N Yorks 102 F3
Scayne's Hill W Sus 17 B7
Scethrog Powys 35 B5
Scholar Green Ches E 74 D5
Scholes W Yorks 88 B2
Scholes W Yorks 88 D2
Scholes W Yorks 95 F6
School Green Ches W 74 C3
Scleddau Pembs 44 B4
Sco Ruston Norf 81 E8
Scofton Notts 89 F7
Scole Norf 56 B5
Scolpaig W Isles 148 A2
Scone Perth 128 B3
Sconser Highld 149 E10
Scoonie Fife 129 D5
Scoor Argyll 146 K7
Scopwick Lincs 78 D3
Scoraig Highld 150 B3
Scorborough E Yorks 97 E6
Scorrier Corn 3 B6
Scorton Lancs 92 E5
Scorton N Yorks 101 D7
Scotbheinn W Isles 148 C3
Scotby Cumb 108 D4
Scotch Corner N Yorks 101 D7
Scotforth Lancs 92 D4
Scothern Lincs 78 B3
Scotland Gate Northumb 117 F8
Scotlandwell Perth 128 D3
Scotsburn Highld 151 D10
Scotscalder Station Highld 158 E2
Scotscraig Fife 129 B6
Scots' Gap Northumb 117 F6
Scotston Aberds 135 B7
Scotston Perth 133 E6
Scotstoun Glasgow 118 C5
Scotstown Highld 130 C2
Scotswood T&W 110 C4
Scottas Highld 149 H12
Scotter Lincs 90 D2
Scotterthorpe Lincs 90 D2
Scottlethorpe Lincs 65 B7
Scotton Lincs 90 E2
Scotton N Yorks 95 D6
Scotton N Yorks 101 E6
Scottow Norf 81 E8
Scoughall E Loth 129 F8
Scoulag Argyll 145 H10
Scoulton Norf 68 D2
Scourie Highld 156 E4
Scourie More Highld 156 E4
Scousburgh Shetland 160 M5
Scrabster Highld 158 C2
Scrafield Lincs 79 C6
Scrainwood Northumb 117 D5
Scrane End Lincs 79 E6
Scraptoft Leics 64 D3
Scratby Norf 69 C8
Scrayingham N Yorks 96 C3
Scredington Lincs 78 E3
Scremby Lincs 79 C7
Scremerston Northumb 123 E6
Screveton Notts 77 E7
Scrivelsby Lincs 79 C5
Scriven N Yorks 95 D6
Scrooby Notts 89 E7
Scropton Derbys 75 F8
Scrub Hill Lincs 78 D5
Scruton N Yorks 101 E7
Sculcoates Hull 97 F6
Sculthorpe Norf 80 D4
Scunthorpe N Lincs 90 C2
Scurlage Swansea 33 F5
Sea Palling Norf 69 B7
Seaborough Dorset 12 D2
Seacombe Mers 85 E4
Seacroft Lincs 79 C8
Seacroft W Yorks 95 F6
Seadyke Lincs 79 F6
Seafield S Ayrs 112 B3
Seafield W Loth 120 C3
Seaford E Sus 17 E8
Seaforth Mers 85 E4
Seagrave Leics 64 C3
Seaham Durham 111 E7
Seahouses Northumb 123 F8
Seal Kent 29 D6
Sealand Flint 73 C7
Seale Sur 27 E6
Seamer N Yorks 102 C2
Seamer N Yorks 103 F8
Seamill N Ayrs 118 E2
Searby Lincs 90 D4
Seasalter Kent 30 C4
Seascale Cumb 98 D2
Seathorne Lincs 79 C8
Seathwaite Cumb 98 C4
Seathwaite Cumb 98 E4
Seatoller Cumb 98 C4
Seaton Corn 5 D8
Seaton Cumb 107 F7
Seaton Devon 11 F7
Seaton Durham 111 D6
Seaton E Yorks 97 E7
Seaton Northumb 111 B6
Seaton Rutland 65 E6
Seaton Burn T&W 110 B5
Seaton Carew Hrtlpl 102 B3
Seaton Delaval Northumb 111 B6
Seaton Ross E Yorks 96 E3
Seaton Sluice Northumb 111 B6
Seatown Aberds 152 B5
Seatown Dorset 12 E2
Seave Green N Yorks 102 D3
Seaview IoW 15 E7
Seaville Cumb 107 D8
Seavington St Mary Som 12 C2
Seavington St Michael Som 12 C2
Sebergham Cumb 108 E3
Seckington Warks 63 D6
Second Coast Highld 150 B2
Sedbergh Cumb 100 E1
Sedbury Glos 36 E2
Sedbusk N Yorks 100 E3
Sedgeberrow Worcs 50 F5
Sedgebrook Lincs 77 F8
Sedgefield Durham 102 B1
Sedgeford Norf 80 D3
Sedgehill Wilts 13 B6
Sedgley W Mid 62 E3
Sedgwick Cumb 99 F7
Sedlescombe E Sus 18 D4
Sedlescombe Street E Sus 18 D4
Seend Wilts 24 C4
Seend Cleeve Wilts 24 C4
Seer Green Bucks 40 E2
Seething Norf 69 E6
Sefton Mers 85 D4
Seghill Northumb 111 B5
Seifton Shrops 60 F4
Seighford Staffs 62 B2
Seilebost W Isles 154 H5
Seion Gwyn 82 E5
Seisdon Staffs 62 E2
Seisiadar W Isles 155 D10
Selattyn Shrops 73 F6
Selborne Hants 26 F5
Selby N Yorks 96 F2
Selham W Sus 16 B3
Selhurst London 28 C4
Selkirk Borders 115 B7
Sellack Hereford 36 B2
Sellafirth Shetland 160 D7
Sellibister Orkney 159 D8
Sellindge Kent 19 B7
Sellindge Lees Kent 19 B8
Selling Kent 30 D4
Sells Green Wilts 24 C4
Selly Oak W Mid 62 F4
Selmeston E Sus 18 E2
Selsdon London 28 C4
Selsey W Sus 16 E2
Selsfield Common W Sus 28 F4
Selsted Kent 31 E6
Selston Notts 76 D4
Selworthy Som 21 E8
Semblister Shetland 160 H5
Semer Suff 56 E3
Semington Wilts 24 C3
Semley Wilts 13 B6
Send Sur 27 D8
Send Marsh Sur 27 D8
Senghenydd Caerph 35 E5
Sennen Corn 2 D2
Sennen Cove Corn 2 D2
Sennybridge = Pont Senni Powys 34 B3
Serlby Notts 89 F7
Sessay N Yorks 95 B7
Setchey Norf 67 C6
Setley Hants 14 D4
Setter Shetland 160 E6
Setter Shetland 160 H5
Setter Shetland 160 J7
Settiscarth Orkney 159 G4
Settle N Yorks 93 C8
Settrington N Yorks 96 B4
Seven Kings London 41 F7
Seven Sisters Neath 34 D2
Sevenhampton Glos 37 B7
Sevenoaks Kent 29 D6
Sevenoaks Weald Kent 29 D6
Severn Beach S Glos 36 F2
Severn Stoke Worcs 50 E3
Severnhampton Swindon 38 E2
Sevington Kent 30 E4
Sewards End Essex 55 F6
Sewardstone Essex 41 E6
Sewardstonebury Essex 41 E6
Sewerby E Yorks 97 C7
Seworgan Corn 3 C6
Sewstern Leics 65 B5
Sezincote Glos 51 F6
Sgarasta Mhor W Isles 154 H5
Sgiogarstaigh W Isles 155 A10
Shabbington Bucks 39 D6
Shackerstone Leics 63 D7
Shackleford Sur 27 E7
Shade W Yorks 87 B7
Shadforth Durham 111 E6
Shadingfield Suff 69 F7
Shadoxhurst Kent 19 B6
Shadsworth Blackburn 86 B5
Shadwell Norf 68 F2
Shadwell W Yorks 95 F6
Shaftesbury Dorset 13 B6
Shafton S Yorks 88 C4
Shalbourne Wilts 25 C8
Shalcombe IoW 14 F4
Shalden Hants 26 E4
Shaldon Devon 7 B7
Shalfleet IoW 14 F5
Shalford Essex 42 B3
Shalford Sur 27 E8
Shalford Green Essex 42 B3
Shallowford Devon 21 E6
Shalmsford Street Kent 30 D4
Shalstone Bucks 52 F4
Shamley Green Sur 27 E8
Shandon Argyll 145 E11
Shandwick Highld 151 D11
Shangton Leics 64 E4
Shankhouse Northumb 111 B5
Shanklin IoW 15 F6
Shanquhar Aberds 152 E5
Shanzie Perth 134 D2
Shap Cumb 99 C7
Shapwick Dorset 13 D7
Shapwick Som 23 F6
Shardlow Derbys 76 F4
Shareshill Staffs 62 D3
Sharlston W Yorks 88 C4
Sharlston Common W Yorks 88 C4
Sharnbrook Bedford 53 D7
Sharnford Leics 63 E8
Sharoe Green Lancs 92 F5
Sharow N Yorks 95 B6
Sharp Street Norf 69 B6
Sharpenhoe C Beds 53 F8
Sharperton Northumb 117 D5
Sharpness Glos 36 D3
Sharpthorne W Sus 28 F4
Sharrington Norf 81 D6
Shatterford Worcs 61 F7
Shaugh Prior Devon 6 C3
Shavington Ches E 74 D4
Shaw Gtr Man 87 D7
Shaw W Berks 26 C2
Shaw Wilts 24 C3
Shaw Green Lancs 86 C3
Shaw Mills N Yorks 95 C5
Shawbury Shrops 61 B5
Shawdon Hall Northumb 117 C6
Shawell Leics 64 F2
Shawford Hants 15 B5
Shawforth Lancs 87 B6
Shawhead Dumfries 107 B5
Shawhill Dumfries 108 C2
Shawton S Lanark 119 E6
Shawtonhill S Lanark 119 E6
Shear Cross Wilts 24 E3
Shearington Dumfries 107 C7
Shearsby Leics 64 E3
Shebbear Devon 9 D6
Shebdon Staffs 61 B7
Shebster Highld 157 C13
Sheddens E Renf 119 D5
Shedfield Hants 15 C6
Sheen Staffs 75 C8
Sheepscar W Yorks 95 F6
Sheepscombe Glos 37 C5
Sheepstor Devon 6 C3
Sheepwash Devon 9 D6
Sheepway N Som 23 B6
Sheepy Magna Leics 63 D7
Sheepy Parva Leics 63 D7
Sheering Essex 41 C8
Sheerness Kent 30 B3
Sheet Hants 15 B8
Sheffield S Yorks 88 F4
Sheffield Bottom W Berks 26 C4
Sheffield Green E Sus 17 B8
Shefford C Beds 54 F2
Shefford Woodlands W Berks 25 B8
Sheigra Highld 156 C4
Sheinton Shrops 61 D6
Shelderton Shrops 49 B6
Sheldon Derbys 75 C8
Sheldon Devon 11 D6
Sheldon W Mid 63 F5
Sheldwich Kent 30 D4
Shelf W Yorks 88 B2
Shelfanger Norf 68 F4
Shelfield W Mid 62 D4
Shelfield Warks 51 C6
Shelford Notts 77 E6
Shellacres Northumb 122 E4
Shelley Essex 42 D1
Shelley Suff 56 F4
Shelley W Yorks 88 C3
Shellingford Oxon 38 E3
Shellow Bowells Essex 42 D2
Shelsley Beauchamp Worcs 50 C2
Shelsley Walsh Worcs 50 C2
Shelthorpe Leics 64 C2
Shelton Bedford 53 C8
Shelton Norf 68 E5
Shelton Notts 77 E7
Shelton Shrops 60 C4
Shelton Green Norf 68 E5
Shelve Shrops 60 E3
Shelwick Hereford 49 E7
Shenfield Essex 42 E2
Shenington Oxon 51 E8
Shenley Herts 40 D4
Shenley Brook End M Keynes 53 F6
Shenley Church End M Keynes 53 F6
Shenleybury Herts 40 D4
Shenmore Hereford 49 F5
Shennanton Dumfries 105 C7
Shenstone Staffs 62 D5
Shenstone Worcs 50 B3
Shenton Leics 63 D7
Shenval Highld 137 B7
Shenval Moray 139 B8
Shepeau Stow Lincs 66 C3
Shephall Herts 41 B5
Shepherd's Green Oxon 39 F7
Shepherd's Port Norf 80 D2
Shepherdswell Kent 31 E6
Shepley W Yorks 88 D2
Shepperdine S Glos 36 E3
Shepperton Sur 27 C8
Shepreth Cambs 54 E4
Shepshed Leics 63 C8
Shepton Beauchamp Som 12 C2
Shepton Mallet Som 23 E8
Shepton Montague Som 23 F8
Shepway Kent 29 D8
Sheraton Durham 111 F7
Sherborne Dorset 12 C4
Sherborne Glos 38 C1
Sherborne St John Hants 26 D4
Sherbourne Warks 51 C7
Sherburn Durham 111 E6
Sherburn N Yorks 97 B5
Sherburn Hill Durham 111 E6
Sherburn in Elmet N Yorks 95 F7
Shere Sur 27 E8
Shereford Norf 80 E4
Sherfield English Hants 14 B3
Sherfield on Loddon Hants 26 D4
Sherford Devon 7 E5
Sheriff Hutton N Yorks 96 C2
Sheriffhales Shrops 61 C7
Sheringham Norf 81 C7
Sherington M Keynes 53 E6
Shernal Green Worcs 50 C4
Shernborne Norf 80 D3
Sherrington Wilts 24 F4
Sherston Wilts 37 F5
Sherwood Green Devon 9 B7
Shettleston Glasgow 119 C6
Shevington Gtr Man 86 D3
Shevington Moor Gtr Man 86 C3
Shevington Vale Gtr Man 86 D3
Sheviock Corn 5 D8
Shide IoW 15 F5
Shiel Bridge Highld 136 C2
Shieldaig Highld 149 A13
Shieldaig Highld 149 C13
Shieldhill Dumfries 114 F3
Shieldhill Falk 119 B8
Shieldhill S Lanark 120 E3
Shielfoot Highld 147 E9
Shielhill Angus 134 D4
Shielhill Invclyd 118 B2
Shifford Oxon 38 D3
Shifnal Shrops 61 D7
Shilbottle Northumb 117 D7
Shildon Durham 101 B7
Shillingford Devon 10 B4
Shillingford Oxon 39 E5
Shillingford St George Devon 10 F4
Shillingstone Dorset 13 C6
Shillington C Beds 54 F2
Shillmoor Northumb 116 D4
Shilton Oxon 38 D2
Shilton Warks 63 F8
Shilvington Northumb 117 F7
Shimpling Norf 68 F4
Shimpling Suff 56 D2
Shimpling Street Suff 56 D2
Shincliffe Durham 111 E5
Shiney Row T&W 111 D6
Shinfield Wokingham 26 C5
Shingham Norf 67 D7
Shingle Street Suff 57 E7
Shinner's Bridge Devon 7 C5
Shinness Highld 157 H8
Shipbourne Kent 29 D6
Shipdham Norf 68 D2
Shipham Som 23 D6
Shiphay Torbay 7 C6
Shiplake Oxon 27 B5
Shipley Derbys 76 E4
Shipley Northumb 117 C7
Shipley Shrops 62 E2
Shipley W Sus 16 B5
Shipley W Yorks 94 F4
Shipley Shiels Northumb 116 E3
Shipmeadow Suff 69 F6
Shippea Hill Station Cambs 67 F6
Shippon Oxon 38 E4
Shipston-on-Stour Warks 51 E7
Shipton Glos 37 C7
Shipton N Yorks 95 D8
Shipton Shrops 61 E5
Shipton Bellinger Hants 25 E7
Shipton Gorge Dorset 12 E2
Shipton Green W Sus 16 E2
Shipton Moyne Glos 37 F5
Shipton on Cherwell Oxon 38 C4
Shipton Solers Glos 37 C7
Shipton-under-Wychwood Oxon 38 C2
Shiptonthorpe E Yorks 96 E4
Shirburn Oxon 39 E6
Shirdley Hill Lancs 85 C4
Shirebrook Derbys 76 C5

Stoke sub Hamdon Som 12 C2
Stoke Talmage Oxon 39 E6
Stoke Trister Som 12 B5
Stoke Wake Dorset 13 D5
Stokeford Dorset 13 F6
Stokeham Notts 77 B7
Stokeinteignhead Devon 7 B7
Stokenchurch Bucks 39 E7
Stokenham Devon 7 E6
Stokesay Shrops 60 F4
Stokesby Norf 69 C7
Stokesley N Yorks 102 D3
Stolford Som 22 E4
Ston Easton Som 23 D8
Stondon Massey Essex 42 D1
Stone Bucks 39 C7
Stone Glos 36 E3
Stone Kent 19 C6
Stone Kent 29 B6
Stone S Yorks 89 F6
Stone Staffs 75 F6
Stone Worcs 50 B3
Stone Allerton Som 23 D6
Stone Bridge Corner Pboro 66 D2
Stone Chair W Yorks 88 B2
Stone Cross E Sus 18 E3
Stone Cross Kent 31 D7
Stone-edge Batch N Som 23 B6
Stone House Cumb 100 F2
Stone Street Kent 29 D6
Stone Street Suff 56 F3
Stone Street Suff 69 F6
Stonebroom Derbys 76 D4
Stoneferry Hull 97 F7
Stonefield S Lanark 119 D6
Stonegate E Sus 18 C3
Stonegate N Yorks 103 D5
Stonegrave N Yorks 96 B2
Stonehaugh Northumb 109 B7
Stonehaven Aberds 141 F7
Stonehouse Glos 37 D5
Stonehouse Northumb 109 D6
Stonehouse S Lanark 119 E7
Stoneleigh Warks 51 B8
Stonely Cambs 54 C2
Stoner Hill Hants 15 B8
Stone's Green Essex 43 B7
Stonesby Leics 64 B5
Stonesfield Oxon 38 C3
Stonethwaite Cumb 98 C4
Stoney Cross Hants 14 C3
Stoney Middleton Derbys 76 B2
Stoney Stanton Leics 63 E8
Stoney Stoke Som 24 F2
Stoney Stratton Som 23 F8
Stoney Stretton Shrops 60 D3
Stoneybreck Shetland 160 N8
Stoneyburn W Loth 120 C2
Stoneygate Aberds 153 E10
Stoneygate Leicester 64 D3
Stoneyhills Essex 43 E5
Stoneykirk Dumfries 104 D4
Stoneywood Aberdeen 141 C7
Stoneywood Falk 127 F6
Stonganess Shetland 160 C7
Stonham Aspal Suff 56 D5
Stonnall Staffs 62 D4
Stonor Oxon 39 F7
Stonton Wyville Leics 64 E4
Stony Cross Hereford 50 E2
Stony Stratford M Keynes 53 E5
Stonyfield Highld 151 D9
Stoodleigh Devon 10 C4
Stopes S Yorks 88 F3
Stopham W Sus 16 C4
Stopsley Luton 40 B4
Stores Corner Suff 57 E7
Storeton Mers 85 F4
Stornoway W Isles 155 D9
Storridge Hereford 50 E2
Storrington W Sus 16 C4
Storrs Cumb 99 E5
Storth Cumb 99 F6
Storwood E Yorks 96 E3
Stotfield Moray 152 A2
Stotfold C Beds 54 F3
Stottesdon Shrops 61 F6
Stoughton Leics 64 D3
Stoughton Sur 27 D7
Stoughton W Sus 16 C2
Stoul Highld 147 B10
Stoulton Worcs 50 E4
Stour Provost Dorset 13 B5
Stour Row Dorset 13 B6
Stourbridge W Mid 62 F3
Stourpaine Dorset 13 D6
Stourport on Severn Worcs 50 B3
Stourton Staffs 62 F2
Stourton Warks 51 F7
Stourton Wilts 24 F2
Stourton Caundle Dorset 12 C5
Stove Orkney 159 E7
Stove Shetland 160 L6
Stoven Suff 69 F7
Stow Borders 121 E7
Stow Lincs 78 F3
Stow Lincs 90 F2
Stow Bardolph Norf 67 D6
Stow Bedon Norf 68 E2
Stow cum Quy Cambs 55 C6
Stow Longa Cambs 54 B2
Stow Maries Essex 42 E4
Stow-on-the-Wold Glos 38 B1
Stowbridge Norf 67 D6
Stowe Shrops 48 B5
Stowe-by-Chartley Staffs 62 B4
Stowe Green Glos 36 D2
Stowell Som 12 B4
Stowford Devon 9 F6
Stowlangtoft Suff 56 C3
Stowmarket Suff 56 D4
Stowting Kent 30 E5
Stowupland Suff 56 D4
Straad Argyll 145 G9
Strachan Aberds 141 E5
Stradbroke Suff 57 B6
Stradishall Suff 55 D8
Stradsett Norf 67 D6
Stragglethorpe Lincs 78 D2
Straid S Ayrs 112 E1
Straith Dumfries 113 F8
Straiton Edin 121 C5
Straiton S Ayrs 112 D3
Straloch Aberds 141 B7
Straloch Perth 133 C7
Stramshall Staffs 75 F7
Strang IoM 84 E3
Stranraer Dumfries 104 C4
Stratfield Mortimer W Berks 26 C4
Stratfield Saye Hants 26 C4
Stratfield Turgis Hants 26 D4
Stratford London 41 F6
Stratford St Andrew Suff 57 C7
Stratford St Mary Suff 56 F4
Stratford Sub Castle Wilts 25 F6
Stratford Tony Wilts 13 B8
Stratford-upon-Avon Warks 51 D6
Strath Highld 149 A12
Strath Highld 158 E4
Strathan Highld 136 E2
Strathan Highld 156 G3
Strathan Highld 157 C8
Strathaven S Lanark 119 E7
Strathblane Stirling 119 B5
Strathcanaird Highld 156 J4
Strathcarron Highld 150 G2
Strathcoil Argyll 124 B2
Strathdon Aberds 140 C2
Strathellie Aberds 153 B10
Strathkinness Fife 129 C6
Strathmashie House Highld 137 E8
Strathmiglo Fife 128 C4
Strathmore Lodge Highld 158 F3
Strathpeffer Highld 150 F7
Strathrannoch Highld 150 D6
Strathtay Perth 133 D6
Strathvaich Lodge Highld 150 D6
Strathwhillan N Ayrs 143 E11
Strathy Highld 157 C11
Strathyre Stirling 126 C4
Stratton Corn 8 D4
Stratton Dorset 12 E4
Stratton Glos 37 D7
Stratton Audley Oxon 39 B6
Stratton on the Fosse Som 23 D8
Stratton St Margaret Swindon 38 F1
Stratton St Michael Norf 68 E5
Stratton Strawless Norf 81 E8
Stravithie Fife 129 C7
Streat E Sus 17 C7
Streatham London 28 B4
Streatley C Beds 40 B3
Streatley W Berks 39 F5
Street Lancs 92 D5
Street N Yorks 103 D5
Street Som 23 F6
Street Dinas Shrops 73 F7
Street End Kent 30 D5
Street End W Sus 16 E2
Street Gate T&W 110 D5
Street Lydan Wrex 73 F8
Streethay Staffs 62 C5
Streetlam N Yorks 101 E8
Streetly W Mid 62 E4
Streetly End Cambs 55 E7
Strefford Shrops 60 F4
Strelley Notts 76 E5
Strensall York 96 C2
Stretcholt Som 22 E4
Strete Devon 7 E6
Stretford Gtr Man 87 E6
Strethall Essex 55 F5
Stretham Cambs 55 B6
Strettington W Sus 16 D2
Stretton Ches W 73 D8
Stretton Derbys 76 C3
Stretton Rutland 65 C6
Stretton Staffs 62 C2
Stretton Staffs 63 B6
Stretton Warr 86 F4
Stretton Grandison Hereford 49 E8
Stretton-on-Dunsmore Warks 52 B2
Stretton-on-Fosse Warks 51 F7
Stretton Sugwas Hereford 49 E6
Stretton under Fosse Warks 63 F8
Stretton Westwood Shrops 61 E5
Strichen Aberds 153 C9
Strines Gtr Man 87 F7
Stringston Som 22 E3
Strixton Northants 53 C7
Stroat Glos 36 E2
Stromeferry Highld 149 E13
Stromemore Highld 149 E13
Stromness Orkney 159 H3
Stronaba Highld 136 F5
Stronachlachar Stirling 126 C3
Stronchreggan Highld 130 B4
Stronchrubie Highld 156 H5
Strone Argyll 145 E10
Strone Highld 136 F4
Strone Highld 137 B8
Strone Involyd 118 B2
Stronmilchan Argyll 125 C7
Strontian Highld 130 C2
Strood Medway 29 C8
Strood Green Sur 28 E3
Strood Green W Sus 16 B4
Strood Green W Sus 28 F2
Stroud Glos 37 D5
Stroud Hants 15 B8
Stroud Green Essex 42 E4
Stroxton Lincs 78 F2
Struan Highld 149 E8
Struan Perth 133 C5
Strubby Lincs 91 F8
Strumpshaw Norf 69 D6
Strutherhill S Lanark 119 E7
Struy Highld 150 H6
Stryt-issa Wrex 73 E6
Stuartfield Aberds 153 D9
Stub Place Cumb 98 E2
Stubbington Hants 15 D6
Stubbins Lancs 87 C5
Stubbs Cross Kent 19 B6
Stubb's Green Norf 69 E5
Stubbs Green Norf 69 E6
Stubhampton Dorset 13 C7
Stubton Lincs 77 E8
Stuckgowan Argyll 126 D2
Stuckton Hants 14 C2
Stud Green Windsor 27 B6
Studham C Beds 40 C3
Studland Dorset 13 F8
Studley Warks 51 C5
Studley Wilts 24 B4
Studley Roger N Yorks 95 B5
Stump Cross Essex 55 E6
Stuntney Cambs 55 B6
Sturbridge Staffs 74 F5
Sturmer Essex 55 E7
Sturminster Marshall Dorset 13 D7
Sturminster Newton Dorset 13 C5
Sturry Kent 31 C5
Sturton N Lincs 90 D3
Sturton by Stow Lincs 90 F2
Sturton le Steeple Notts 89 F8
Stuston Suff 56 B5
Stutton N Yorks 95 E7
Stutton Suff 57 F5
Styal Ches E 87 F6
Styrrup Notts 89 E7
Suainebost W Isles 155 A10
Suardail W Isles 155 D9
Succoth Aberds 152 E4
Succoth Argyll 125 E8
Suckley Worcs 50 D2
Suckquoy Orkney 159 K5
Sudborough Northants 65 F6
Sudbourne Suff 57 D8
Sudbrook Lincs 78 E2
Sudbrook Mon 36 F2
Sudbrooke Lincs 78 B3
Sudbury Derbys 75 F8
Sudbury London 40 F4
Sudbury Suff 56 E2
Suddie Highld 151 F9
Sudgrove Glos 37 D6
Suffield N Yorks 103 E7
Suffield Norf 81 D8
Sugnall Staffs 74 F4
Suladale Highld 149 C8
Sulaisiadar W Isles 155 D10
Sulby IoM 84 C3
Sulgrave Northants 52 E3
Sulham W Berks 26 B4
Sulhamstead W Berks 26 C4
Sulland Orkney 159 D6
Sullington W Sus 16 C4
Sullom Shetland 160 F5
Sullom Voe Oil Terminal Shetland 160 F5
Sully V Glam 22 C3
Sumburgh Shetland 160 N6
Summer Bridge N Yorks 94 C5
Summer-house Darl 101 C7
Summercourt Corn 4 D3
Summerfield Norf 80 D3
Summergangs Hull 97 F7
Summerleaze Mon 35 F8
Summersdale W Sus 16 D2
Summerseat Gtr Man 87 C5
Summertown Oxon 39 D5
Summit Gtr Man 87 D7
Sunbury-on-Thames Sur 28 C2
Sundaywell Dumfries 113 F8
Sunderland Argyll 142 B3
Sunderland Cumb 107 F8
Sunderland T&W 111 D6
Sunderland Bridge Durham 111 F5
Sundhope Borders 115 B6
Sundon Park Luton 40 B3
Sundridge Kent 29 D5
Sunipol Argyll 146 F6
Sunk Island E Yorks 91 C6
Sunningdale Windsor 27 C7
Sunninghill Windsor 27 C7
Sunningwell Oxon 38 D4
Sunniside Durham 110 F4
Sunniside T&W 110 D5
Sunnyhurst Blackburn 86 B4
Sunnylaw Stirling 127 E6
Sunnyside W Sus 28 F4
Sunton Wilts 25 D7
Surbiton London 28 C2
Surby IoM 84 E2
Surfleet Lincs 66 B2
Surfleet Seas End Lincs 66 B2
Surlingham Norf 69 D6
Sustead Norf 81 D7
Susworth Lincs 90 D2
Sutcombe Devon 8 C5
Suton Norf 68 E3
Sutors of Cromarty Highld 151 E11
Sutterby Lincs 79 B6
Sutterton Lincs 79 F5
Sutton C Beds 54 E3
Sutton Cambs 54 B5
Sutton Kent 31 E7
Sutton London 28 C3
Sutton Mers 86 E3
Sutton N Yorks 89 B5
Sutton Norf 69 B6
Sutton Notts 77 F7
Sutton Notts 89 F7
Sutton Oxon 38 D4
Sutton Pboro 65 E7
Sutton S Yorks 89 C6
Sutton Shrops 61 F7
Sutton Shrops 74 F3
Sutton Som 23 F8
Sutton Staffs 61 B7
Sutton Suff 57 E7
Sutton Sur 27 E8
Sutton W Sus 16 C3
Sutton at Hone Kent 29 B6
Sutton Bassett Northants 64 E4
Sutton Benger Wilts 24 B4
Sutton Bonington Notts 64 B2
Sutton Bridge Lincs 66 B4
Sutton Cheney Leics 63 D8
Sutton Coldfield W Mid 62 E5
Sutton Courtenay Oxon 39 E5
Sutton Crosses Lincs 66 B4
Sutton Grange N Yorks 95 B5
Sutton Green Sur 27 D8
Sutton Howgrave N Yorks 95 B6
Sutton In Ashfield Notts 76 D4
Sutton-in-Craven N Yorks 94 E3
Sutton in the Elms Leics 64 E2
Sutton Ings Hull 97 F7
Sutton Lane Ends Ches E 75 B6
Sutton Leach Mers 86 E3
Sutton Maddock Shrops 61 D7
Sutton Mallet Som 23 F5
Sutton Mandeville Wilts 13 B7
Sutton Manor Mers 86 E3
Sutton Montis Som 12 B4
Sutton on Hull Hull 97 F7
Sutton on Sea Lincs 91 F9
Sutton-on-the-Forest N Yorks 95 C8
Sutton on the Hill Derbys 76 F2
Sutton on Trent Notts 77 C7
Sutton Scarsdale Derbys 76 C4
Sutton Scotney Hants 26 F2
Sutton St Edmund Lincs 66 C3
Sutton St James Lincs 66 C3
Sutton St Nicholas Hereford 49 E7
Sutton under Brailes Warks 51 F8
Sutton-under-Whitestonecliffe N Yorks 102 F2
Sutton upon Derwent E Yorks 96 E3
Sutton Valence Kent 30 E2
Sutton Veny Wilts 24 E3
Sutton Waldron Dorset 13 C6
Sutton Weaver Ches W 74 B2
Sutton Wick Bath 23 D7
Swaby Lincs 79 B6
Swadlincote Derbys 63 C7
Swaffham Norf 67 D8
Swaffham Bulbeck Cambs 55 C6
Swaffham Prior Cambs 55 C6
Swafield Norf 81 D8
Swainby N Yorks 102 D2
Swainshill Hereford 49 E6
Swainsthorpe Norf 68 D5
Swainswick Bath 24 C2
Swalcliffe Oxon 51 F8
Swalecliffe Kent 30 C5
Swallow Lincs 91 D5
Swallowcliffe Wilts 13 B7
Swallowfield Wokingham 26 C5
Swallownest S Yorks 89 F5
Swallows Cross Essex 42 E2
Swan Green Ches W 74 B4
Swan Green Suff 57 B6
Swanage Dorset 13 G8
Swanbister Orkney 159 H4
Swanbourne Bucks 39 B8
Swanland E Yorks 90 B3
Swanley Kent 29 C6
Swanley Village Kent 29 C6
Swanmore Hants 15 C6
Swannington Leics 63 C8
Swannington Norf 68 C4
Swanscombe Kent 29 B7
Swansea = Abertawe Swansea 33 E7
Swanton Abbott Norf 81 E8
Swanton Morley Norf 68 C3
Swanton Novers Norf 81 D6
Swanton Street Kent 30 D2
Swanwick Derbys 76 D4
Swanwick Hants 15 D6
Swarby Lincs 78 E3
Swardeston Norf 68 D5
Swarister Shetland 160 E7
Swarkestone Derbys 63 B7
Swarland Northumb 117 D7
Swarland Estate Northumb 117 D7
Swarthmoor Cumb 92 B2
Swathwick Derbys 76 C3
Swaton Lincs 78 F4
Swavesey Cambs 54 C4
Sway Hants 14 E3
Swayfield Lincs 65 B6
Swaythling Soton 14 C5
Sweet Green Worcs 49 C8
Sweetham Devon 10 E3
Sweethouse Corn 5 C5
Sweffling Suff 57 C7
Swepstone Leics 63 C7
Swerford Oxon 51 F8
Swettenham Ches E 74 C5
Swetton N Yorks 94 B4
Swffryd Caerph 35 E6
Swiftsden E Sus 18 C4
Swilland Suff 57 D5
Swillington W Yorks 95 F6
Swimbridge Devon 9 B8
Swimbridge Newland Devon 20 F5
Swinbrook Oxon 38 C2
Swinderby Lincs 77 C8
Swindon Glos 37 B6
Swindon Staffs 62 E2
Swindon Swindon 38 F1
Swine E Yorks 97 F7
Swinefleet E Yorks 89 B8
Swineshead Bedford 53 C8
Swineshead Lincs 78 E5
Swineshead Bridge Lincs 78 E5
Swiney Highld 158 G4
Swinford Leics 52 B3
Swinford Oxon 38 D4
Swingate Notts 76 E5
Swingfield Minnis Kent 31 E6
Swingfield Street Kent 31 E6
Swinhoe Northumb 117 B8
Swinhope Lincs 91 E6
Swining Shetland 160 G6
Swinithwaite N Yorks 101 F5
Swinnow Moor W Yorks 94 F5
Swinscoe Staffs 75 E8
Swinside Hall Borders 116 C3
Swinstead Lincs 65 B7
Swinton Borders 122 E4
Swinton Gtr Man 87 D5
Swinton N Yorks 94 B5
Swinton N Yorks 96 B3
Swinton S Yorks 88 E5
Swintonmill Borders 122 E4
Swithland Leics 64 C2
Swordale Highld 151 E8
Swordland Highld 147 B10
Swordly Highld 157 C10
Sworton Heath Ches E 86 F4
Swydd-ffynnon Ceredig 47 C5
Swynnerton Staffs 75 F5
Swyre Dorset 12 F3
Sychtyn Powys 59 D6
Syde Glos 37 C6
Sydenham London 28 B4
Sydenham Oxon 39 D7
Sydenham Damerel Devon 6 B2
Syderstone Norf 80 D4
Sydling St Nicholas Dorset 12 E4
Sydmonton Hants 26 D2
Syerston Notts 77 E7
Syke Gtr Man 87 C6
Sykehouse S Yorks 89 C7
Sykes Lancs 93 D6
Syleham Suff 57 B6
Sylen Carms 33 D6
Symbister Shetland 160 G7
Symington S Ayrs 118 F3
Symington S Lanark 120 F2
Symonds Yat Hereford 36 C2
Symondsbury Dorset 12 E2
Synod Inn Ceredig 46 D3
Syre Highld 157 E9
Syreford Glos 37 B7
Syresham Northants 52 E4
Syston Leics 64 C3
Syston Lincs 78 E2
Sytchampton Worcs 50 C3
Sywell Northants 53 C6

T

Taagan Highld 150 E3
Tàbost W Isles 155 A10
Tabost W Isles 155 F8
Tackley Oxon 38 B4
Tacleit W Isles 154 D6
Tacolneston Norf 68 E4
Tadcaster N Yorks 95 E7
Taddington Derbys 75 B8
Taddiport Devon 9 C6
Tadley Hants 26 C4
Tadlow C Beds 54 E3
Tadmarton Oxon 51 F8
Tadworth Sur 28 D3
Tafarn-y-gelyn Denb 73 C5
Tafarnau-bach BI Gwent 35 C5
Taff's Well Rhondda 35 F5
Tafolwern Powys 59 D5
Tai Conwy 83 E7
Tai-bach Powys 59 B8
Tai-mawr Conwy 72 E3
Tai-Ucha Denb 72 D4
Taibach Neath 34 F1
Taigh a Ghearraidh W Isles 148 A2
Tain Highld 151 C10
Tain Highld 158 D4
Tainant Wrex 73 E6
Tainlon Gwyn 82 F4
Tairbeart = Tarbert W Isles 154 G6
Tai'r-Bull Powys 34 B3
Tairgwaith Neath 33 C8
Takeley Essex 42 B1
Takeley Street Essex 41 B8
Tal-sarn Ceredig 46 D4
Tal-y-bont Ceredig 58 F3
Tal-y-Bont Conwy 83 E7
Tal-y-bont Gwyn 71 E6
Tal-y-bont Gwyn 83 D6
Tal-y-cafn Conwy 83 D7
Tal-y-llyn Gwyn 58 D4
Tal-y-wern Powys 58 D5
Talachddu Powys 48 F2
Talacre Flint 85 F2
Talardd Gwyn 59 B5
Talaton Devon 11 E5
Talbenny Pembs 44 D3
Talbot Green Rhondda 34 F4
Talbot Village Poole 13 E8
Tale Devon 11 D5
Talerddig Powys 59 D6
Talgarreg Ceredig 46 D3
Talgarth Powys 48 F3
Talisker Highld 149 E8
Talke Staffs 74 D5
Talkin Cumb 109 D5
Talla Linnfoots Borders 114 B4
Talladale Highld 150 D2
Tallarn Green Wrex 73 E8
Tallentire Cumb 107 F8
Talley Carms 46 F5
Tallington Lincs 65 D7
Talmine Highld 157 C8
Talog Carms 32 B4
Talsarn Carms 34 B1
Talsarnau Gwyn 71 D7
Talskiddy Corn 4 C4
Talwrn Anglesey 82 D4
Talwrn Wrex 73 E6
Talybont-on-Usk Powys 35 B5
Talygarn Rhondda 34 F4
Talyllyn Powys 35 B5
Talysarn Gwyn 82 F4
Talywain Torf 35 D6
Tame Bridge N Yorks 102 D3
Tamerton Foliot Plym 6 C2
Tamworth Staffs 63 D6
Tan Hinon Powys 59 F5
Tan-lan Conwy 83 E7
Tan-lan Gwyn 71 C7
Tan-y-bwlch Gwyn 71 C7
Tan-y-fron Conwy 72 C3
Tan-y-graig Anglesey 82 D5
Tan-y-graig Gwyn 70 D4
Tan-y-groes Ceredig 45 E4
Tan-y-pistyll Powys 59 B7
Tan-yr-allt Gwyn 82 F4
Tandem W Yorks 88 C2
Tanden Kent 19 B6
Tandridge Sur 28 D4
Tanerdy Carms 33 B5
Tanfield Durham 110 D4
Tanfield Lea Durham 110 D4
Tangasdal W Isles 148 J1
Tangiers Pembs 44 D4
Tangley Hants 25 D8
Tanglwst Carms 46 F2
Tangmere W Sus 16 D3
Tangwick Shetland 160 F4
Tankersley S Yorks 88 D4
Tankerton Kent 30 C5
Tannach Highld 158 F5
Tannachie Aberds 141 F6
Tannadice Angus 134 D4
Tannington Suff 57 C6
Tansley Derbys 76 D3
Tansley Knoll Derbys 76 C3
Tansor Northants 65 E7
Tantobie Durham 110 D4
Tanton N Yorks 102 C3
Tanworth-in-Arden Warks 51 B6
Tanygrisiau Gwyn 71 C7
Tanyrhydiau Ceredig 47 C6
Taobh a Chaolais W Isles 148 G2
Taobh a Thuath Loch Aineort W Isles 148 F2
Taobh a Tuath Loch Baghasdail W Isles 148 F2
Taobh a'Ghlinne W Isles 155 F8
Taobh Tuath W Isles 154 J4
Taplow Bucks 40 F2
Tapton Derbys 76 B3
Tarbat Ho. Highld 151 D10
Tarbert Argyll 143 C7
Tarbert Argyll 144 E5
Tarbert Argyll 145 G7
Tarbert = Tairbeart W Isles 154 G6
Tarbet Argyll 126 D2
Tarbet Highld 147 B10
Tarbet Highld 156 E4
Tarbock Green Mers 86 F2
Tarbolton S Ayrs 112 B4
Tarbrax S Lanark 120 D3
Tardebigge Worcs 50 C5
Tarfside Angus 134 B4
Tarland Aberds 140 D3
Tarleton Lancs 86 B2
Tarlogie Highld 151 C10
Tarlscough Lancs 86 C2
Tarlton Glos 37 E6
Tarnbrook Lancs 93 D5
Tarporley Ches W 74 C2
Tarr Som 22 F3
Tarrant Crawford Dorset 13 D7
Tarrant Gunville Dorset 13 C7
Tarrant Hinton Dorset 13 C7
Tarrant Keyneston Dorset 13 D7
Tarrant Launceston Dorset 13 D7
Tarrant Monkton Dorset 13 D7
Tarrant Rawston Dorset 13 D7
Tarrant Rushton Dorset 13 D7
Tarrel Highld 151 C11
Tarring Neville E Sus 17 D8
Tarrington Hereford 49 E8
Tarsappie Perth 128 B3
Tarskavaig Highld 149 H10
Tarves Aberds 153 E8
Tarvie Highld 150 F7
Tarvie Perth 133 C7
Tarvin Ches W 73 C8
Tasburgh Norf 68 E5
Tasley Shrops 61 E6
Taston Oxon 38 B3
Tatenhill Staffs 63 B6
Tathall End M Keynes 53 E6
Tatham Lancs 93 C6
Tathwell Lincs 91 F7
Tatling End Bucks 40 F3
Tatsfield Sur 28 D5
Tattenhall Ches W 73 D8
Tattenhoe M Keynes 53 F6
Tatterford Norf 80 E4
Tattersett Norf 80 D4
Tattershall Lincs 78 D5
Tattershall Bridge Lincs 78 D4
Tattershall Thorpe Lincs 78 D5
Tattingstone Suff 56 F5
Tatworth Som 11 D8
Taunton Som 11 B7
Taverham Norf 68 C4
Tavernspite Pembs 32 C2
Tavistock Devon 6 B2
Taw Green Devon 9 E8
Tawstock Devon 9 B7
Taxal Derbys 75 B7
Tay Bridge Dundee 129 B6
Tayinloan Argyll 143 D7
Taymouth Castle Perth 132 E4
Taynish Argyll 144 E6
Taynton Glos 36 B4
Taynton Oxon 38 C2
Taynuilt Argyll 125 B6
Tayport Fife 129 B6
Tayvallich Argyll 144 E6
Tealby Lincs 91 E5
Tealing Angus 134 F4
Teangue Highld 149 H11
Teanna Mhachair W Isles 148 B2
Tebay Cumb 99 D8
Tebworth C Beds 40 B2
Tedburn St Mary Devon 10 E3
Teddington Glos 50 F4
Teddington London 28 B2
Tedstone Delamere Hereford 49 D8
Tedstone Wafre Hereford 49 D8
Teeton Northants 52 B4
Teffont Evias Wilts 24 F4
Teffont Magna Wilts 24 F4
Tegryn Pembs 45 F4
Teigh Rutland 65 C5
Teigncombe Devon 9 F8
Teigngrace Devon 7 B6
Teignmouth Devon 7 B7
Telford Telford 61 D6
Telham E Sus 18 D4
Tellisford Som 24 D3
Telscombe E Sus 17 D8
Telscombe Cliffs E Sus 17 D7
Templand Dumfries 114 F3
Temple Corn 5 B6
Temple Glasgow 118 C5
Temple Midloth 121 D6
Temple Balsall W Mid 51 B7
Temple Bar Carms 33 C6
Temple Bar Ceredig 46 D4
Temple Cloud Bath 23 D8
Temple Combe Som 12 B5
Temple Ewell Kent 31 E6
Temple Grafton Warks 51 D6
Temple Guiting Glos 37 B7
Temple Herdewyke Warks 51 D8
Temple Hirst N Yorks 89 B7
Temple Normanton Derbys 76 C4
Temple Sowerby Cumb 99 B8
Templehall Fife 128 E4
Templeton Devon 10 C3
Templeton Pembs 32 C2
Templeton Bridge Devon 10 C3
Templetown Durham 110 D4
Tempsford C Beds 54 D2
Ten Mile Bank Norf 67 E6
Tenbury Wells Worcs 49 C7
Tenby = Dinbych-Y-Pysgod Pembs 32 D2
Tendring Essex 43 B7
Tendring Green Essex 43 B7
Tenston Orkney 159 G3
Tenterden Kent 19 B5
Terling Essex 42 C3
Ternhill Shrops 74 F3
Terregles Banks Dumfries 107 B6
Terrick Bucks 39 D8
Terrington N Yorks 96 B2
Terrington St Clement Norf 66 C5
Terrington St John Norf 66 C5
Teston Kent 29 D8
Testwood Hants 14 C4
Tetbury Glos 37 E5
Tetbury Upton Glos 37 E5
Tetchill Shrops 73 F7
Tetcott Devon 8 E5
Tetford Lincs 79 B6
Tetney Lincs 91 D7
Tetney Lock Lincs 91 D7
Tetsworth Oxon 39 D6
Tettenhall W Mid 62 E2
Teuchan Aberds 153 E10
Teversal Notts 76 C4
Teversham Cambs 55 D5
Teviothead Borders 115 D7
Tewel Aberds 141 F7
Tewin Herts 41 C5
Tewkesbury Glos 50 F3
Teynham Kent 30 C3
Thackthwaite Cumb 98 B3
Thainston Aberds 135 B6
Thakeham W Sus 16 C5
Thame Oxon 39 D7
Thames Ditton Sur 28 C2
Thames Haven Thurrock 42 F3
Thamesmead London 41 F7
Thanington Kent 30 D5
Thankerton S Lanark 120 F2
Tharston Norf 68 E4
Thatcham W Berks 26 C3
Thatto Heath Mers 86 E3
Thaxted Essex 55 F7
The Aird Highld 149 C9
The Arms Norf 67 E8
The Bage Hereford 48 E4
The Balloch Perth 127 C7
The Barony Orkney 159 F3
The Bog Shrops 60 E3
The Bourne Sur 27 E6
The Braes Highld 149 E10
The Broad Hereford 49 C6
The Butts Som 24 E2
The Camp Glos 37 D6
The Camp Herts 40 D4
The Chequer Wrex 73 E8
The City Bucks 39 E7
The Common Wilts 25 F7
The Craigs Highld 150 B7
The Cronk IoM 84 C3
The Dell Suff 69 E7
The Den N Ayrs 118 D3
The Eals Northumb 116 F3
The Eaves Glos 36 D3
The Flatt Cumb 109 B5
The Four Alls Shrops 74 F3
The Garths Shetland 160 B8
The Green Cumb 98 F3
The Green Wilts 24 F3
The Grove Dumfries 107 B6
The Hall Shetland 160 D8
The Haven W Sus 27 F8
The Heath Norf 81 E7
The Heath Suff 56 F5
The Hill Cumb 98 F3
The Howe Cumb 99 F6
The Howe IoM 84 F1
The Hundred Hereford 49 C7
The Lee Bucks 40 D2
The Lhen IoM 84 B3
The Marsh Powys 60 E3
The Marsh Wilts 37 F7
The Middles Durham 110 D5
The Moor Kent 18 C4
The Mumbles = Y Mwmbwls Swansea 33 F7
The Murray S Lanark 119 D6
The Neuk Aberds 141 E6
The Oval Bath 24 C2
The Pole of Itlaw Aberds 153 C6
The Quarry Glos 36 E4
The Rhos Pembs 32 C1
The Rock Telford 61 D6
The Ryde Herts 41 D5
The Sands Sur 27 E6
The Stocks Kent 19 C6
The Throat Wokingham 27 C6
The Vauld Hereford 49 E7
The Wyke Shrops 61 D7
Theakston N Yorks 101 F8
Thealby N Lincs 90 C2
Theale Som 23 E6
Theale W Berks 26 B4
Thearne E Yorks 97 F6
Theberton Suff 57 C8
Theddingworth Leics 64 F3
Theddlethorpe All Saints Lincs 91 F8
Theddlethorpe St Helen Lincs 91 F8
Thelbridge Barton Devon 10 C2
Thelnetham Suff 56 B4
Thelveton Norf 68 F4
Thelwall Warr 86 F4
Themelthorpe Norf 81 E6
Thenford Northants 52 E3
Therfield Herts 54 F4
Thetford Lincs 65 C8
Thetford Norf 67 F8
Theydon Bois Essex 41 E7
Thickwood Wilts 24 B3
Thimbleby Lincs 78 C5
Thimbleby N Yorks 102 E2
Thingwall Mers 85 F3
Thirdpart N Ayrs 118 E1
Thirlby N Yorks 102 F2
Thirlestane Borders 121 E8
Thirn N Yorks 101 F7
Thirsk N Yorks 102 F2
Thirtleby E Yorks 97 F7
Thistleton Lancs 92 F4
Thistleton Rutland 65 C6
Thistley Green Suff 55 B7
Thixendale N Yorks 96 C4
Thockrington Northumb 110 B2
Tholomas Drove Cambs 66 D3
Tholthorpe N Yorks 95 C7
Thomas Chapel Pembs 32 D2
Thomas Close Cumb 108 E4
Thomastown Aberds 152 E5
Thompson Norf 68 E2
Thomshill Moray 152 C2
Thong Kent 29 B7
Thongsbridge W Yorks 88 D2
Thoralby N Yorks 101 F5
Thoresway Lincs 91 E5
Thorganby Lincs 91 E6
Thorganby N Yorks 96 E2
Thorgill N Yorks 103 E5
Thorington Suff 57 B8
Thorington Street Suff 56 F4
Thorlby N Yorks 94 D2
Thorley Herts 41 C7
Thorley Street Herts 41 C7
Thorley Street IoW 14 F4
Thormanby N Yorks 95 B7
Thornaby-on-Tees Stockton 102 C2
Thornage Norf 81 D6
Thornborough Bucks 52 F5
Thornborough N Yorks 95 B5
Thornbury Devon 9 D6
Thornbury Hereford 49 D8
Thornbury S Glos 36 E3
Thornbury W Yorks 94 F4
Thornby Northants 52 B4
Thorncliffe Staffs 75 D7
Thorncombe Dorset 11 D8
Thorncombe Dorset 13 D6
Thorncombe Street Sur 27 E8
Thorncote Green C Beds 54 E2
Thorncross IoW 14 F5
Thorndon Suff 56 C5
Thorndon Cross Devon 9 E7
Thorne S Yorks 89 C7
Thorne St Margaret Som 11 B5
Thorner W Yorks 95 E6
Thorney Notts 77 B8
Thorney Pboro 66 D2
Thorney Crofts E Yorks 91 B6
Thorney Green Suff 56 C4
Thorney Hill Hants 14 E2
Thorney Toll Pboro 66 D3
Thornfalcon Som 11 B7
Thornford Dorset 12 C4
Thorngumbald E Yorks 91 B6
Thornham Norf 80 C3
Thornham Magna Suff 56 B5
Thornham Parva Suff 56 B5
Thornhaugh Pboro 65 D7
Thornhill Cardiff 35 F5
Thornhill Cumb 98 D2
Thornhill Derbys 88 F2
Thornhill Dumfries 113 E8
Thornhill Soton 15 C5
Thornhill Stirling 127 E5
Thornhill W Yorks 88 C3
Thornhill Edge W Yorks 88 C3
Thornhill Lees W Yorks 88 C3
Thornholme E Yorks 97 C7
Thornley Durham 110 F4
Thornley Durham 111 F6
Thornliebank E Renf 118 D5
Thorns Suff 55 D8
Thorns Green Ches E 87 F5
Thornsett Derbys 87 F8
Thornthwaite Cumb 98 B4
Thornthwaite N Yorks 94 D4
Thornton Angus 134 E3
Thornton Bucks 53 F5
Thornton E Yorks 96 E3
Thornton Fife 128 E4
Thornton Lancs 92 E3
Thornton Leics 63 D8
Thornton Lincs 78 C5
Thornton Mbro 102 C2
Thornton Mers 85 D4
Thornton Northumb 123 E5
Thornton Pembs 44 E4
Thornton W Yorks 94 F4
Thornton Curtis N Lincs 90 C4
Thornton Heath London 28 C4
Thornton Hough Mers 85 F4
Thornton in Craven N Yorks 94 E2
Thornton-le-Beans N Yorks 102 E1
Thornton-le-Clay N Yorks 96 C2
Thornton-le-Dale N Yorks 103 F6
Thornton le Moor Lincs 90 E4
Thornton-le-Moor N Yorks 102 F1
Thornton-le-Moors Ches W 73 B8
Thornton-le-Street N Yorks 102 F2
Thornton Rust N Yorks 100 F4
Thornton Steward N Yorks 101 F6
Thornton Watlass N Yorks 101 F7
Thorntonhall S Lanark 119 D5
Thorntonloch E Loth 122 B3
Thorntonpark Northumb 122 E5
Thornwood Common Essex 41 D7
Thornydykes Borders 122 E2
Thoroton Notts 77 E7
Thorp Arch W Yorks 95 E7
Thorpe Derbys 75 D8
Thorpe E Yorks 97 E5
Thorpe Lincs 91 F8
Thorpe N Yorks 94 C3
Thorpe Norf 69 E7
Thorpe Notts 77 E7
Thorpe Sur 27 C8
Thorpe Abbotts Norf 57 B5
Thorpe Acre Leics 64 B2
Thorpe Arnold Leics 64 B4
Thorpe Audlin W Yorks 89 C5
Thorpe Bassett N Yorks 96 B4
Thorpe Bay Southend 43 F5
Thorpe by Water Rutland 65 E5
Thorpe Common Suff 57 F6
Thorpe Constantine Staffs 63 D6
Thorpe Culvert Lincs 79 C7
Thorpe End Norf 69 C5
Thorpe Fendykes Lincs 79 C7
Thorpe Green Essex 43 B7
Thorpe Green Suff 56 D3
Thorpe Hesley S Yorks 88 E4
Thorpe in Balne S Yorks 89 C6
Thorpe in the Fallows Lincs 90 F3
Thorpe Langton Leics 64 E4
Thorpe Larches Durham 102 B1
Thorpe-le-Soken Essex 43 B7
Thorpe le Street E Yorks 96 E4
Thorpe Malsor Northants 53 B6
Thorpe Mandeville Northants 52 E3
Thorpe Market Norf 81 D8
Thorpe Marriot Norf 68 C4
Thorpe Morieux Suff 56 D3
Thorpe on the Hill Lincs 78 C2
Thorpe Salvin S Yorks 89 F6
Thorpe Satchville Leics 64 C4
Thorpe St Andrew Norf 69 D5
Thorpe St Peter Lincs 79 C7
Thorpe Thewles Stockton 102 B2
Thorpe Tilney Lincs 78 D4
Thorpe Underwood N Yorks 95 D7
Thorpe Waterville Northants 65 F7
Thorpe Willoughby N Yorks 95 F8
Thorpeness Suff 57 D8
Thorrington Essex 43 C6
Thorverton Devon 10 D4
Thrandeston Suff 56 B5
Thrapston Northants 53 B7
Thrashbush N Lanark 119 C7
Threapland Cumb 107 F8
Threapland N Yorks 94 C2
Threapwood Ches W 73 E8
Threapwood Staffs 75 E7
Three Ashes Hereford 36 B2
Three Bridges W Sus 28 F3
Three Burrows Corn 3 B6
Three Chimneys Kent 18 B5
Three Cocks Powys 48 F3
Three Crosses Swansea 33 E6
Three Cups Corner E Sus 18 C3
Three Holes Norf 66 D5
Three Leg Cross E Sus 18 B3
Three Legged Cross Dorset 13 D8
Three Oaks E Sus 18 D5
Threehammer Common Norf 69 C6
Threekingham Lincs 78 F3
Threemile Cross Wokingham 26 C5
Threemilestone Corn 3 B6
Threemiletown W Loth 120 B3
Threlkeld Cumb 99 B5
Threshfield N Yorks 94 C2
Thrigby Norf 69 C7
Thringarth Durham 100 B4
Thringstone Leics 63 C8
Thrintoft N Yorks 101 E8
Thriplow Cambs 54 E5
Throckenholt Lincs 66 D3
Throcking Herts 54 F4
Throckley T&W 110 C4
Throckmorton Worcs 50 E4
Throphill Northumb 117 F7
Thropton Northumb 117 D6
Throsk Stirling 127 E7
Throwleigh Devon 9 E8
Throwley Kent 30 D3
Thrumpton Notts 76 F5
Thrumster Highld 158 F5
Thrunton Northumb 117 C6
Thrupp Glos 37 D5
Thrupp Oxon 38 C4
Thrushelton Devon 9 F6
Thrussington Leics 64 C3
Thruxton Hants 25 E7
Thruxton Hereford 49 F6
Thrybergh S Yorks 89 E5
Thulston Derbys 76 F4
Thundergay N Ayrs 143 D9
Thundersley Essex 42 F3
Thundridge Herts 41 C6
Thurcaston Leics 64 C2
Thurcroft S Yorks 89 F5
Thurgarton Norf 81 D7
Thurgarton Notts 77 E6
Thurgoland S Yorks 88 D3
Thurlaston Leics 64 E2
Thurlaston Warks 52 B2
Thurlbear Som 11 B7
Thurlby Lincs 65 C8
Thurlby Lincs 78 C2
Thurleigh Bedford 53 D8
Thurlestone Devon 6 E4
Thurloxton Som 22 F4
Thurlstone S Yorks 88 D3
Thurlton Norf 69 E7
Thurlwood Ches E 74 D5
Thurmaston Leics 64 D3
Thurnby Leics 64 D3
Thurne Norf 69 C7
Thurnham Kent 30 D2
Thurnham Lancs 92 D4
Thurning Norf 81 E6
Thurning Northants 65 F7
Thurnscoe S Yorks 89 D5
Thurnscoe East S Yorks 89 D5
Thursby Cumb 108 D3
Thursford Norf 81 D5
Thursley Sur 27 F7
Thurso Highld 158 D3
Thurso East Highld 158 D3
Thurstaston Mers 85 F3
Thurston Suff 56 C3
Thurstonfield Cumb 108 D3
Thurstonland W Yorks 88 C2
Thurton Norf 69 D6
Thurvaston Derbys 76 F2
Thuxton Norf 68 D3
Thwaite N Yorks 100 E3

Thwaite Suff 56 C5
Thwaite St Mary Norf 69 E6
Thwaites W Yorks 94 E3
Thwaites Brow W Yorks 94 E3
Thwing E Yorks 97 B6
Tibbermore Perth 128 B2
Tibberton Glos 36 B4
Tibberton Telford 61 B6
Tibberton Worcs 50 D4
Tibenham Norf 68 F4
Tibshelf Derbys 76 C4
Tibthorpe E Yorks 97 D5
Ticehurst E Sus 18 B3
Tichborne Hants 26 F3
Tickencote Rutland 65 D6
Tickenham N Som 23 B6
Tickhill S Yorks 89 E6
Ticklerton Shrops 60 E4
Ticknall Derbys 63 B7
Tickton E Yorks 97 E6
Tidcombe Wilts 25 D7
Tiddington Oxon 39 D6
Tiddington Warks 51 D7
Tidebrook E Sus 18 C3
Tideford Corn 5 D8
Tideford Cross Corn 5 C8
Tidenham Glos 36 E2
Tideswell Derbys 75 B8
Tidmarsh W Berks 26 B4
Tidmington Warks 51 F7
Tidpit Hants 13 C8
Tidworth Wilts 25 E7
Tiers Cross Pembs 44 D4
Tiffield Northants 52 D4
Tifty Aberds 153 D7
Tigerton Angus 135 C5
Tigh-na-Blair Perth 127 C6
Tighnabruaich Argyll 145 F8
Tighnafiline Highld 155 J13
Tigley Devon 7 C5
Tilbrook Cambs 53 C8
Tilbury Thurrock 29 B7
Tilbury Juxta Clare Essex 55 E8
Tile Cross W Mid 63 F5
Tile Hill W Mid 51 B7
Tilehurst Reading 26 B4
Tilford Sur 27 E6
Tilgate W Sus 28 F3
Tilgate Forest Row W Sus 28 F3
Tillathrowie Aberds 152 E4
Tilley Shrops 60 B5
Tillicoultry Clack 127 E8
Tillingham Essex 43 D5
Tillington Hereford 49 E6
Tillington W Sus 16 B3
Tillington Common Hereford 49 E6
Tillyarblet Angus 135 C5
Tillybirloch Aberds 141 D5
Tillycorthie Aberds 141 B8
Tillydrine Aberds 140 E5
Tillyfour Aberds 140 C4
Tillyfourie Aberds 140 C5
Tillygarmond Aberds 140 E5
Tillygreig Aberds 141 B7
Tillykerrie Aberds 141 B7
Tilmanstone Kent 31 D7
Tilney All Saints Norf 67 C5
Tilney High End Norf 67 C5
Tilney St Lawrence Norf 66 C5
Tilshead Wilts 24 E5
Tilstock Shrops 74 F2
Tilston Ches W 73 D8
Tilstone Fearnall Ches W 74 C2
Tilsworth C Beds 40 B2
Tilton on the Hill Leics 64 D4
Timberland Lincs 78 D4
Timbersbrook Ches E 75 C5
Timberscombe Som 21 E8
Timble N Yorks 94 D4
Timperley Gtr Man 87 F5
Timsbury Bath 23 D8
Timsbury Hants 14 B4
Timsgearraidh W Isles 154 D5
Timworth Green Suff 56 C2
Tincleton Dorset 13 E5
Tindale Cumb 109 D6
Tingewick Bucks 52 F4
Tingley W Yorks 88 B3
Tingrith C Beds 53 F8
Tingwall Orkney 159 F4
Tinhay Devon 9 F5
Tinshill W Yorks 95 F5
Tinsley S Yorks 88 E5
Tintagel Corn 8 F2
Tintern Parva Mon 36 D2
Tintinhull Som 12 C3
Tintwistle Derbys 87 E8
Tinwald Dumfries 114 F3
Tinwell Rutland 65 D7
Tipperty Aberds 141 B8
Tipsend Norf 66 E5
Tipton W Mid 62 E3
Tipton St John Devon 11 E5
Tiptree Essex 42 C4
Tir-y-dail Carms 33 C7
Tirabad Powys 47 E7
Tiraghoil Argyll 146 J6
Tirley Glos 37 B5
Tirphil Caerph 35 D5
Tirril Cumb 99 B7
Tisbury Wilts 13 B7
Tisman's Common W Sus 27 F8
Tissington Derbys 75 D8
Titchberry Devon 8 B4
Titchfield Hants 15 D6
Titchmarsh Northants 53 B8
Titchwell Norf 80 C3
Tithby Notts 77 F6
Titley Hereford 48 C5
Titlington Northumb 117 C7
Titsey Sur 28 D5
Tittensor Staffs 75 F5
Tittleshall Norf 80 E4
Tiverton Ches W 74 C2
Tiverton Devon 10 C4
Tivetshall St Margaret Norf 68 F4
Tivetshall St Mary Norf 68 F4
Tividale W Mid 62 E3
Tivy Dale S Yorks 88 D3
Tixall Staffs 62 B3
Tixover Rutland 65 D6
Toab Orkney 159 H6
Toab Shetland 160 M5
Toadmoor Derbys 76 D3
Tobermory Argyll 147 F8
Toberonochy Argyll 124 E3
Tobha Mor W Isles 148 E2
Tobhtarol W Isles 154 D6
Tobson W Isles 154 D6
Tocher Aberds 153 E6
Tockenham Wilts 24 B5
Tockenham Wick Wilts 37 F7
Tockholes Blackburn 86 B4
Tockington S Glos 36 F3
Tockwith N Yorks 95 D7
Todber Dorset 13 B6
Todding Hereford 49 B6
Toddington C Beds 40 B3
Toddington Glos 50 F5
Todenham Glos 51 F7
Todhills Cumb 108 C3
Todlachie Aberds 141 C5
Todmorden W Yorks 87 B7
Todrig Borders 115 C7
Todwick S Yorks 89 F5
Toft Cambs 54 D4
Toft Lincs 65 C7
Toft Hill Durham 101 B6
Toft Hill Lincs 78 C5
Toft Monks Norf 69 E7
Toft next Newton Lincs 90 F4
Toftrees Norf 80 E4
Tofts Highld 158 D5
Toftwood Norf 68 C2
Togston Northumb 117 D8
Tokavaig Highld 149 G11
Tokers Green Oxon 26 B5
Tolastadh a Chaolais W Isles 154 D6
Tolastadh bho Thuath W Isles 155 C10
Toll Bar S Yorks 89 D6
Toll End W Mid 62 E3
Toll of Birness Aberds 153 E10
Tolland Som 22 F3
Tollard Royal Wilts 13 C7
Tollbar End W Mid 51 B8
Toller Fratrum Dorset 12 E3
Toller Porcorum Dorset 12 E3
Tollerton N Yorks 95 C8
Tollerton Notts 77 F6
Tollesbury Essex 43 C5
Tolleshunt D'Arcy Essex 43 C5
Tolleshunt Major Essex 43 C5
Tolm W Isles 155 D9
Tolpuddle Dorset 13 E5
Tolvah Highld 138 E4
Tolworth London 28 C2
Tomatin Highld 138 B4
Tombreck Highld 151 H9
Tomchrasky Highld 137 C5
Tomdoun Highld 136 D4
Tomich Highld 137 B6
Tomich Highld 151 D9
Tomich House Highld 151 G8
Tomintoul Aberds 139 E7
Tomintoul Moray 139 C7
Tomnaven Moray 152 E4
Tomnavoulin Moray 139 B8
Ton-Pentre Rhondda 34 E3
Tonbridge Kent 29 E6
Tondu Bridgend 34 F2
Tonfanau Gwyn 58 D2
Tong Shrops 61 D7
Tong W Yorks 94 F5
Tong Norton Shrops 61 D7
Tonge Leics 63 B8
Tongham Sur 27 E6
Tongland Dumfries 106 D3
Tongue Highld 157 D8
Tongue End Lincs 65 C8
Tongwynlais Cardiff 35 F5
Tonna Neath 34 E1
Tonwell Herts 41 C6
Tonypandy Rhondda 34 E3
Tonyrefail Rhondda 34 F4
Toot Baldon Oxon 39 D5
Toot Hill Essex 41 D8
Toothill Hants 14 C4
Top of Hebers Gtr Man 87 D6
Topcliffe N Yorks 95 B7
Topcroft Norf 69 E5
Topcroft Street Norf 69 E5
Toppesfield Essex 55 F8
Toppings Gtr Man 86 C5
Topsham Devon 10 F4
Torbay Torbay 7 D7
Torbeg N Ayrs 143 F10
Torboll Farm Highld 151 B10
Torbrex Stirling 127 E6
Torbryan Devon 7 C6
Torcross Devon 7 E6
Tore Highld 151 F9
Torinturk Argyll 145 G7
Torksey Lincs 77 B8
Torlum W Isles 148 C2
Torlundy Highld 131 B5
Tormarton S Glos 24 B2
Tormisdale Argyll 142 C2
Tormitchell S Ayrs 112 E2
Tormore N Ayrs 143 E9
Tornagrain Highld 151 G10
Tornahaish Aberds 139 D8
Tornaveen Aberds 140 D5
Torness Highld 137 B8
Toronto Durham 110 F4
Torpenhow Cumb 108 F2
Torphichen W Loth 120 B2
Torphins Aberds 140 D5
Torpoint Corn 6 D2
Torquay Torbay 7 C7
Torquhan Borders 121 E7
Torran Argyll 124 E4
Torran Highld 149 D10
Torran Highld 151 D10
Torrance E Dunb 119 B6
Torrans Argyll 146 J7
Torranyard N Ayrs 118 E3
Torre Torbay 7 C7
Torridon Highld 150 F2
Torridon Ho. Highld 149 C13
Torrin Highld 149 F10
Torrisdale Highld 157 C9
Torrisdale-Square Argyll 143 E8
Torrish Highld 157 H12
Torrisholme Lancs 92 C4
Torroble Highld 157 J8
Torry Aberdeen 141 D8
Torry Aberds 152 E4
Torryburn Fife 128 F2
Torterston Aberds 153 D10
Torthorwald Dumfries 107 B7
Tortington W Sus 16 D4
Tortworth S Glos 36 E4
Torvaig Highld 149 D9
Torver Cumb 98 E4
Torwood Falk 127 F7
Torworth Notts 89 F7
Tosberry Devon 8 B4
Toscaig Highld 149 E12
Toseland Cambs 54 C3
Tosside N Yorks 93 D7
Tostock Suff 56 C3
Totaig Highld 148 C7
Totaig Highld 149 F13
Tote Highld 149 D9
Totegan Highld 157 C11
Tothill Lincs 91 F8
Totland IoW 14 F4
Totnes Devon 7 C6
Toton Notts 76 F5
Totronald Argyll 146 F4
Totscore Highld 149 B8
Tottenham London 41 E6
Tottenhill Norf 67 C6
Tottenhill Row Norf 67 C6
Totteridge London 41 E5
Totternhoe C Beds 40 B2
Tottington Gtr Man 87 C5
Totton Hants 14 C4
Touchen End Windsor 27 B6
Tournaig Highld 155 J13
Toux Aberds 153 C9
Tovil Kent 29 D8
Tow Law Durham 110 F4
Toward Argyll 145 G10
Towcester Northants 52 E4
Towednack Corn 2 C3
Tower End Norf 67 C6
Towersey Oxon 39 D7
Towie Aberds 140 C3
Towie Aberds 153 B8
Towiemore Moray 152 D3
Town End Cambs 66 E4
Town End Cumb 99 F6
Town Row E Sus 18 B2
Town Yetholm Borders 116 B4
Townend W Dunb 118 B4
Towngate Lincs 65 C8
Townhead Cumb 108 F5
Townhead Dumfries 106 E3
Townhead S Ayrs 112 D2
Townhead S Yorks 88 D2
Townhead of Greenlaw Dumfries 106 C4
Townhill Fife 128 F3
Townsend Bucks 39 D7
Townsend Herts 40 D4
Townshend Corn 2 C4
Towthorpe York 96 D2
Towton N Yorks 95 F7
Towyn Conwy 72 B3
Toxteth Mers 85 F4
Toynton All Saints Lincs 79 C6
Toynton Fen Side Lincs 79 C6
Toynton St Peter Lincs 79 C7
Toy's Hill Kent 29 D5
Trabboch E Ayrs 112 B4
Traboe Corn 3 D6
Tradespark Highld 151 F11
Tradespark Orkney 159 H5
Trafford Park Gtr Man 87 E5
Trallong Powys 34 B3
Tranent E Loth 121 B7
Tranmere Mers 85 F4
Trantlebeg Highld 157 D11
Trantlemore Highld 157 D11
Tranwell Northumb 117 F7
Trapp Carms 33 C7
Traprain E Loth 121 B8
Traquair Borders 121 F6
Trawden Lancs 94 F2
Trawsfynydd Gwyn 71 D8
Tre-Gibbon Rhondda 34 D3
Tre-Taliesin Ceredig 58 E3
Tre-vaughan Carms 32 B4
Tre-wyn Mon 35 B7
Trealaw Rhondda 34 E4
Treales Lancs 92 F4
Trearddur Anglesey 82 D2
Treaslane Highld 149 C8
Trebanog Rhondda 34 E4
Trebanos Neath 33 D8
Trebartha Corn 5 B7
Trebarwith Corn 8 F2
Trebetherick Corn 4 B4
Treborough Som 22 F2
Trebudannon Corn 4 C3
Trebullett Corn 5 B8
Treburley Corn 5 B8
Trebyan Corn 5 C5
Trecastle Powys 34 B2
Trecenydd Caerph 35 F5
Trecwn Pembs 44 B4
Trecynon Rhondda 34 D3
Tredavoe Corn 2 D3
Treddiog Pembs 44 C3
Tredegar Bl Gwent 35 D5
Tredegar = Newydd New Tredegar Caerph 35 D5
Tredington Glos 37 B6
Tredington Warks 51 E7
Tredinnick Corn 4 B4
Tredomen Powys 48 F3
Tredunnock Mon 35 E7
Tredustan Powys 48 F3
Treen Corn 2 D2
Treeton S Yorks 88 F5
Tref-Y-Clawdd = Knighton Powys 48 B4
Trefaldwyn = Montgomery Powys 60 E2
Trefasser Pembs 44 B3
Trefdraeth Anglesey 82 D4
Trefdraeth = Newport Pembs 45 F2
Trefecca Powys 48 F3
Trefechan Ceredig 58 F2
Trefeglwys Powys 59 E6
Trefenter Ceredig 46 C5
Treffgarne Pembs 44 C4
Treffynnon = Holywell Flint 73 B5
Treffynnon Pembs 44 C3
Trefgarn Owen Pembs 44 C3
Trefil Bl Gwent 35 C5
Trefilan Ceredig 46 D4
Trefin Pembs 44 B3
Treflach Shrops 60 B2
Trefnanney Powys 60 C2
Trefnant Denb 72 B4
Trefonen Shrops 60 B2
Trefor Anglesey 82 C3
Trefor Gwyn 70 C4
Treforest Rhondda 34 F4
Trefriw Conwy 83 E7
Trefynwy = Monmouth Mon 36 C2
Tregadillett Corn 8 F4
Tregaian Anglesey 82 D4
Tregare Mon 35 C8
Tregaron Ceredig 47 D5
Tregarth Gwyn 83 E6
Tregeare Corn 8 F4
Tregeiriog Wrex 73 F5
Tregele Anglesey 82 B3
Tregidden Corn 3 D6
Treglemais Pembs 44 C3
Tregole Corn 8 E3
Tregonetha Corn 4 C4
Tregony Corn 3 B8
Tregoss Corn 4 C4
Tregoyd Powys 48 F4
Tregroes Ceredig 46 E3
Tregurrian Corn 4 C3
Tregynon Powys 59 E7
Trehafod Rhondda 34 E4
Treharris M Tydf 34 E4
Treherbert Rhondda 34 E3
Trekenner Corn 5 B8
Treknow Corn 8 F2
Trelan Corn 3 E6
Trelash Corn 8 E3
Trelassick Corn 4 D3
Trelawnyd Flint 72 B4
Trelech Carms 45 F4
Treleddyd-fawr Pembs 44 C2
Trelewis M Tydf 35 E5
Treligga Corn 8 F2
Trelights Corn 4 B4
Trelill Corn 4 B5
Trelissick Corn 3 C7
Trellech Mon 36 D2
Trelleck Grange Mon 36 D1
Trelogan Flint 85 F2
Trelystan Powys 60 D2
Tremadog Gwyn 71 C6
Tremail Corn 8 F3
Tremain Ceredig 45 E4
Tremaine Corn 8 F4
Tremar Corn 5 C7
Trematon Corn 5 D8
Tremeirchion Denb 72 B4
Trenance Corn 4 C3
Trenarren Corn 3 B9
Trench Telford 61 C6
Treneglos Corn 8 F4
Trenewan Corn 5 D6
Trent Dorset 12 C3
Trent Vale Stoke 75 E5
Trentham Stoke 75 E5
Trentishoe Devon 20 E5
Treoes V Glam 21 B8
Treorchy = Treorci Rhondda 34 E3
Treorci = Treorchy Rhondda 34 E3
Tre'r-ddôl Ceredig 58 E3
Trerule Foot Corn 5 D8
Tresaith Ceredig 45 D4
Tresawle Corn 3 B7
Trescott Staffs 62 E2
Trescowe Corn 2 C4
Tresham Glos 36 E4
Tresillian Corn 3 B7
Tresinwen Pembs 44 A4
Treskinnick Cross Corn 8 E4
Tresmeer Corn 8 F4
Tresparrett Corn 8 E3
Tresparrett Posts Corn 8 E3
Tressait Perth 133 C5
Tresta Shetland 160 D8
Tresta Shetland 160 H5
Treswell Notts 77 B7
Trethosa Corn 4 D4
Trethurgy Corn 4 D5
Tretio Pembs 44 C2
Tretire Hereford 36 B2
Tretower Powys 35 B5
Treuddyn Flint 73 D6
Trevalga Corn 8 F2
Trevalyn Wrex 73 D7
Trevanson Corn 4 B4
Trevarren Corn 4 C4
Trevarrian Corn 4 C3
Trevarrick Corn 3 B8
Trevaughan Carms 32 C2
Treveighan Corn 5 B5
Trevellas Corn 4 D2
Treverva Corn 3 C6
Trevethin Torf 35 D6
Trevigro Corn 5 C8
Treviscoe Corn 4 D4
Trevone Corn 4 B3
Trewarmett Corn 8 F2
Trewassa Corn 8 F3
Trewellard Corn 2 C2
Trewen Corn 8 F4
Trewennack Corn 3 D5
Trewern Powys 60 C2
Trewethern Corn 4 B5
Trewidland Corn 5 D7
Trewint Corn 8 E3
Trewint Corn 8 F4
Trewithian Corn 3 C7
Trewoofe Corn 2 D3
Trewoon Corn 4 D4
Treworga Corn 3 B7
Treworlas Corn 3 C7
Treyarnon Corn 4 B3
Treyford W Sus 16 C2
Trezaise Corn 4 D4
Triangle W Yorks 87 B8
Trickett's Cross Dorset 13 D8
Triffleton Pembs 44 C4
Trimdon Durham 111 F6
Trimdon Colliery Durham 111 F6
Trimdon Grange Durham 111 F6
Trimingham Norf 81 D8
Trimley Lower Street Suff 57 F6
Trimley St Martin Suff 57 F6
Trimley St Mary Suff 57 F6
Trimpley Worcs 50 B2
Trimsaran Carms 33 D5
Trimstone Devon 20 E3
Trinafour Perth 132 C4
Trinant Caerph 35 D6
Tring Herts 40 C2
Tring Wharf Herts 40 C2
Trinity Angus 135 C6
Trinity Jersey 17
Trisant Ceredig 47 B6
Trislaig Highld 130 B4
Trispen Corn 4 D3
Tritlington Northumb 117 E8
Trochry Perth 133 E6
Trodigal Argyll 143 F7
Troed-rhiwdalar Powys 47 D8
Troedyraur Ceredig 46 E2
Troedyrhiw M Tydf 34 D4
Tromode IoM 84 E3
Trondavoe Shetland 160 F5
Troon Corn 3 C5
Troon S Ayrs 118 F3
Trosaraidh W Isles 148 G2
Trossachs Hotel Stirling 126 D4
Troston Suff 56 B2
Trottiscliffe Kent 29 C7
Trotton W Sus 16 B2
Troutbeck Cumb 99 B5
Troutbeck Cumb 99 D6
Troutbeck Bridge Cumb 99 D6
Trow Green Glos 36 D2
Trowbridge Wilts 24 D3
Trowell Notts 76 F4
Trowle Common Wilts 24 D3
Trowley Bottom Herts 40 C3
Trows Borders 122 F2
Trowse Newton Norf 68 D5
Trudoxhill Som 24 E2
Trull Som 11 B7
Trumaisgearraidh W Isles 148 A3
Trumpan Highld 148 B7
Trumpet Hereford 49 F8
Trumpington Cambs 54 D5
Trunch Norf 81 D8
Trunnah Lancs 92 E3
Truro Corn 3 B7
Trusham Devon 10 F3
Trusley Derbys 76 F2
Trusthorpe Lincs 91 F9
Trysull Staffs 62 E2
Tubney Oxon 38 E4
Tuckenhay Devon 7 D6
Tuckhill Shrops 61 F7
Tuckingmill Corn 3 B5
Tuddenham Suff 55 B8
Tuddenham St Martin Suff 57 E5
Tudeley Kent 29 E7
Tudhoe Durham 111 F5
Tudorville Hereford 36 B2
Tudweiliog Gwyn 70 D3
Tuesley Sur 27 E7
Tuffley Glos 37 C5
Tufton Hants 26 E2
Tufton Pembs 32 B1
Tugby Leics 64 D4
Tugford Shrops 61 F5
Tullibardine Perth 127 C8
Tullibody Clack 127 E7
Tullich Argyll 125 D6
Tullich Highld 138 B2
Tullich Muir Highld 151 D10
Tulliemet Perth 133 D6
Tulloch Aberds 135 B7
Tulloch Aberds 153 E8
Tulloch Perth 128 B2
Tulloch Castle Highld 151 F8
Tullochgorm Argyll 125 F5
Tulloes Angus 135 E5
Tullybannocher Perth 127 B6
Tullybelton Perth 133 F7
Tullyfergus Perth 134 E2
Tullymurdoch Perth 134 D1
Tullynessle Aberds 140 C4
Tumble Carms 33 C6
Tumby Woodside Lincs 79 D5
Tummel Bridge Perth 132 D4
Tunga W Isles 155 D9
Tunstall E Yorks 97 F9
Tunstall Kent 30 C2
Tunstall Lancs 93 B6
Tunstall N Yorks 101 E7
Tunstall Norf 69 D7
Tunstall Stoke 75 D5
Tunstall Suff 57 D7
Tunstall T&W 111 D6
Tunstead Derbys 75 B8
Tunstead Gtr Man 87 D8
Tunstead Norf 81 E8
Tunworth Hants 26 E4
Tupsley Hereford 49 E7
Tupton Derbys 76 C3
Tur Langton Leics 64 E4
Turgis Green Hants 26 D4
Turin Angus 135 D5
Turkdean Glos 37 C8
Turleigh Wilts 24 C3
Turn Lancs 87 C6
Turnastone Hereford 49 F5
Turnberry S Ayrs 112 D2
Turnditch Derbys 76 E2
Turners Hill W Sus 28 F4
Turners Puddle Dorset 13 E6
Turnford Herts 41 D6
Turnhouse Edin 120 B4
Turnworth Dorset 13 D6
Turriff Aberds 153 C7
Turton Bottoms Blackburn 86 C5
Turves Cambs 66 E3
Turvey Bedford 53 D7
Turville Bucks 39 E7
Turville Heath Bucks 39 E7
Turweston Bucks 52 F4
Tushielaw Borders 115 C6
Tutbury Staffs 63 B6
Tutnall Worcs 50 B4
Tutshill Glos 36 E2
Tuttington Norf 81 E8
Tutts Clump W Berks 26 B3
Tuxford Notts 77 B7
Twatt Orkney 159 F3
Twatt Shetland 160 H5
Twechar E Dunb 119 B7
Tweedmouth Northumb 123 D5
Tweedsmuir Borders 114 B3
Twelve Heads Corn 3 B6
Twemlow Green Ches E 74 C4
Twenty Lincs 65 B8
Twerton Bath 24 C2
Twickenham London 28 B2
Twigworth Glos 37 B5
Twineham W Sus 17 C6
Twinhoe Bath 24 D2
Twinstead Essex 56 F2
Twinstead Green Essex 56 F2
Twiss Green Warr 86 E4
Twiston Lancs 93 E8
Twitchen Devon 21 F6
Twitchen Shrops 49 B5
Two Bridges Devon 6 B4
Two Dales Derbys 76 C2
Two Mills Ches W 73 B7
Twycross Leics 63 D7
Twyford Bucks 39 B6
Twyford Derbys 63 B7
Twyford Hants 15 B5
Twyford Leics 64 C4
Twyford Lincs 65 B6
Twyford Norf 81 E6
Twyford Wokingham 27 B5
Twyford Common Hereford 49 F7
Twyn-y-Sheriff Mon 35 D8
Twynholm Dumfries 106 D3
Twyning Glos 50 F3
Twyning Green Glos 50 F4
Twynllanan Carms 34 B1
Twynmynydd Carms 33 C7
Twywell Northants 53 B7
Ty-draw Conwy 83 F8
Ty-hen Carms 32 B4
Ty-hen Gwyn 70 D2
Ty-mawr Anglesey 82 C4
Ty Mawr Carms 46 E4
Ty Mawr Cwm Conwy 72 E3
Ty-nant Conwy 72 E3
Ty-nant Gwyn 59 B6
Ty-uchaf Powys 59 B7
Tyberton Hereford 49 F5
Tyburn W Mid 62 E5
Tycroes Carms 33 C7
Tycrwyn Powys 59 C8
Tydd Gote Lincs 66 C4
Tydd St Giles Cambs 66 C4
Tydd St Mary Lincs 66 C4
Tyddewi = St David's Pembs 44 C2
Tyddyn-mawr Gwyn 71 C6
Tye Green Essex 41 D7
Tye Green Essex 42 B3
Tye Green Essex 55 F6
Tyldesley Gtr Man 86 D4
Tyler Hill Kent 30 C5
Tylers Green Bucks 40 E2
Tylorstown Rhondda 34 E4
Tylwch Powys 59 F6
Tyn-y-celyn Wrex 73 F5
Tyn-y-coed Shrops 60 B2
Tyn-y-fedwen Powys 72 F5
Tyn-y-ffridd Powys 72 F5
Tyn-y-graig Powys 48 D2
Ty'n-y-groes Conwy 83 D7
Ty'n-y-maes Gwyn 83 E6
Tyn-y-pwll Anglesey 82 C4
Ty'n-yr-eithin Ceredig 47 C5
Tyncelyn Ceredig 46 C5
Tyndrum Stirling 131 F7
Tyne Tunnel T&W 111 C6
Tyneham Dorset 13 F6
Tynehead Midloth 121 D6
Tynemouth T&W 111 C6
Tynewydd Rhondda 34 E3
Tyninghame E Loth 122 B2
Tynron Dumfries 113 E8
Tynygongl Anglesey 82 C5
Tynygraig Ceredig 47 C5
Tŷ'r-felin-isaf Conwy 83 E8
Tyrie Aberds 153 B9
Tyringham M Keynes 53 E6
Tythecott Devon 9 C6
Tythegston Bridgend 21 B7
Tytherington Ches E 75 B6
Tytherington S Glos 36 F3
Tytherington Som 24 E2
Tytherington Wilts 24 E4
Tytherleigh Devon 11 D8
Tywardreath Corn 5 D5
Tywyn Conwy 83 D7
Tywyn Gwyn 58 D2

U

Uachdar W Isles 148 C2
Uags Highld 149 E12
Ubbeston Green Suff 57 B7
Ubley Bath 23 D7
Uckerby N Yorks 101 D7
Uckfield E Sus 17 B8
Uckington Glos 37 B6
Uddingston S Lanark 119 C6
Uddington S Lanark 119 F8
Udimore E Sus 19 D5
Udny Green Aberds 141 B7
Udny Station Aberds 141 B8
Udston S Lanark 119 D6
Udstonhead S Lanark 119 E7
Uffcott Wilts 25 B6
Uffculme Devon 11 C5
Uffington Lincs 65 D7
Uffington Oxon 38 F3
Uffington Shrops 60 C5
Ufford Pboro 65 D7
Ufford Suff 57 D6
Ufton Warks 51 C8
Ufton Nervet W Berks 26 C4
Ugadale Argyll 143 F8
Ugborough Devon 6 D4
Uggeshall Suff 69 F7
Ugglebarnby N Yorks 103 D6
Ughill S Yorks 88 E3
Ugley Essex 41 B8
Ugley Green Essex 41 B8
Ugthorpe N Yorks 103 C5
Uidh W Isles 148 J1
Uig Argyll 145 E10
Uig Highld 148 C6
Uig Highld 149 B8
Uigen W Isles 154 D5
Uigshader Highld 149 D9
Uisken Argyll 146 K6
Ulbster Highld 158 F5
Ulceby Lincs 79 B7
Ulceby N Lincs 90 C5
Ulceby Skitter N Lincs 90 C5
Ulcombe Kent 30 E2
Uldale Cumb 108 F2
Uley Glos 36 E4
Ulgham Northumb 117 E8
Ullapool Highld 150 B4
Ullenhall Warks 51 C6
Ullenwood Glos 37 C6
Ulleskelf N Yorks 95 E8
Ullesthorpe Leics 64 F2
Ulley S Yorks 89 F5
Ullingswick Hereford 49 E7
Ullinish Highld 149 E8
Ullock Cumb 98 B2
Ulnes Walton Lancs 86 C3
Ulpha Cumb 98 E3
Ulrome E Yorks 97 D7
Ulsta Shetland 160 E6
Ulva House Argyll 146 H7
Ulverston Cumb 92 B2
Ulwell Dorset 13 F8
Umberleigh Devon 9 B8
Unapool Highld 156 F5
Unasary W Isles 148 F2
Underbarrow Cumb 99 E6
Undercliffe W Yorks 94 F4
Underhoull Shetland 160 C7
Underriver Kent 29 D6
Underwood Notts 76 D4
Undy Mon 35 F8
Unifirth Shetland 160 H4
Union Cottage Aberds 141 E7
Union Mills IoM 84 E3
Union Street E Sus 18 B4
Unstone Derbys 76 B3
Unstone Green Derbys 76 B3
Unthank Cumb 108 F4
Unthank Cumb 109 E6
Unthank End Cumb 108 F4
Up Cerne Dorset 12 D4
Up Exe Devon 10 D4
Up Hatherley Glos 37 B6
Up Holland Lancs 86 D3
Up Marden W Sus 15 C8
Up Nately Hants 26 D4
Up Somborne Hants 25 F8
Up Sydling Dorset 12 D4
Upavon Wilts 25 D6
Upchurch Kent 30 C2
Upcott Hereford 48 D5
Upend Cambs 55 D7
Upgate Norf 68 C4
Uphall W Loth 120 B3
Uphall Station W Loth 120 B3
Upham Devon 10 D3
Upham Hants 15 B6
Uphampton Worcs 50 C3
Uphill N Som 22 D5
Uplawmoor E Renf 118 D4
Upleadon Glos 36 B4
Upleatham Redcar 102 C4
Uplees Kent 30 C3
Uploders Dorset 12 E3
Uplowman Devon 10 C5
Uplyme Devon 11 E8
Upminster London 42 F1
Upnor Medway 29 B8
Upottery Devon 11 D7
Upper Affcot Shrops 60 F4
Upper Ardchronie Highld 151 C9
Upper Arley Worcs 61 F7
Upper Arncott Oxon 39 C6
Upper Astrop Northants 52 F3
Upper Badcall Highld 156 E4
Upper Basildon W Berks 26 B3
Upper Beeding W Sus 17 C5
Upper Benefield Northants 65 F6
Upper Bighouse Highld 157 D11
Upper Boddington Northants 52 D2
Upper Borth Ceredig 58 F3
Upper Boyndlie Aberds 153 B9
Upper Brailes Warks 51 F8
Upper Breakish Highld 149 F11
Upper Breinton Hereford 49 E6
Upper Broadheath Worcs 50 D3
Upper Broughton Notts 64 B3
Upper Bucklebury W Berks 26 C3
Upper Burnhaugh Aberds 141 E7
Upper Caldecote C Beds 54 E2
Upper Catesby Northants 52 D3
Upper Chapel Powys 48 E2
Upper Church Village Rhondda 34 F4
Upper Chute Wilts 25 D7
Upper Clatford Hants 25 E8
Upper Clynnog Gwyn 71 C5
Upper Cumberworth W Yorks 88 D3
Upper Cwm-twrch Powys 34 C1
Upper Cwmbran Torf 35 E6
Upper Dallachy Moray 152 B3
Upper Dean Bedford 53 C8
Upper Denby W Yorks 88 D3
Upper Denton Cumb 109 C6
Upper Derraid Highld 151 H13
Upper Dicker E Sus 18 E2
Upper Dovercourt Essex 57 F6
Upper Druimfin Argyll 147 F8
Upper Dunsforth N Yorks 95 C7
Upper Eathie Highld 151 E10
Upper Elkstone Staffs 75 D7
Upper End Derbys 75 B7
Upper Farringdon Hants 26 F5
Upper Framilode Glos 36 C4
Upper Glenfintaig Highld 137 F5
Upper Gornal W Mid 62 E3
Upper Gravenhurst C Beds 54 F2
Upper Green Mon 35 C7
Upper Green W Berks 25 C8
Upper Grove Common Hereford 36 B2
Upper Hackney Derbys 76 C2
Upper Hale Sur 27 E6
Upper Halistra Highld 148 C7
Upper Halling Medway 29 C7
Upper Hambleton Rutland 65 D6
Upper Hardres Court Kent 31 D5
Upper Hartfield E Sus 29 F5
Upper Haugh S Yorks 88 E5
Upper Heath Shrops 61 F5
Upper Hellesdon Norf 68 C5
Upper Helmsley N Yorks 96 D2
Upper Hergest Hereford 48 D4
Upper Heyford Northants 52 D4
Upper Heyford Oxon 38 B4
Upper Hill Hereford 49 D6
Upper Hopton W Yorks 88 C2
Upper Horsebridge E Sus 18 D2
Upper Hulme Staffs 75 C7
Upper Inglesham Swindon 38 E2
Upper Inverbrough Highld 151 H11
Upper Killay Swansea 33 E6
Upper Knockando Moray 152 D1
Upper Lambourn W Berks 38 F3
Upper Leigh Staffs 75 F7
Upper Lenie Highld 137 B8
Upper Lochton Aberds 141 E5
Upper Longdon Staffs 62 C4
Upper Lybster Highld 158 G4
Upper Lydbrook Glos 36 C3
Upper Maes-coed Hereford 48 F5
Upper Midway Derbys 63 B6
Upper Milovaig Highld 148 D6
Upper Minety Wilts 37 E7
Upper Mitton Worcs 50 B3
Upper North Dean Bucks 39 E8
Upper Obney Perth 133 F7
Upper Ollach Highld 149 E10
Upper Padley Derbys 76 B2
Upper Pollicott Bucks 39 C7
Upper Poppleton York 95 D8
Upper Quinton Warks 51 E6
Upper Ratley Hants 14 B4
Upper Rissington Glos 38 C2
Upper Rochford Worcs 49 C8
Upper Sandaig Highld 149 G12
Upper Sanday Orkney 159 H6
Upper Sapey Hereford 49 C8
Upper Saxondale Notts 77 F6
Upper Seagry Wilts 37 F6
Upper Shelton C Beds 53 E7
Upper Sheringham Norf 81 C7
Upper Skelmorlie N Ayrs 118 C2
Upper Slaughter Glos 38 B1
Upper Soudley Glos 36 C3
Upper Stondon C Beds 54 F2
Upper Stowe Northants 52 D4
Upper Stratton Swindon 38 F1
Upper Street Hants 14 C2
Upper Street Norf 69 C6
Upper Street Norf 69 C6
Upper Street Suff 56 F5
Upper Strensham Worcs 50 F4
Upper Sundon C Beds 40 B3
Upper Swell Glos 38 B1
Upper Tean Staffs 75 F7
Upper Tillyrie Perth 128 D3
Upper Tooting London 28 B3
Upper Tote Highld 149 C10
Upper Town N Som 23 C7
Upper Treverward Shrops 48 B4
Upper Tysoe Warks 51 E8
Upper Upham Wilts 25 B7
Upper Wardington Oxon 52 E2
Upper Weald M Keynes 53 F5
Upper Weedon Northants 52 D4
Upper Wield Hants 26 F4
Upper Winchendon Bucks 39 C7
Upper Witton W Mid 62 E4
Upper Woodend Aberds 141 C5
Upper Woodford Wilts 25 F6
Upper Wootton Hants 26 D3
Upper Wyche Hereford 50 E2
Upperby Cumb 108 D4
Uppermill Gtr Man 87 D7
Uppersound Shetland 160 J6
Upperthong W Yorks 88 D2
Upperthorpe N Lincs 89 D8
Upperton W Sus 16 B3
Uppertown Derbys 76 C3
Uppertown Highld 158 C5
Uppertown Orkney 159 J5
Uppingham Rutland 65 E5
Uppington Shrops 61 D6
Upsall N Yorks 102 F2
Upshire Essex 41 D7
Upstreet Kent 31 C6
Upthorpe Suff 56 B3
Upton Cambs 54 B2
Upton Ches W 73 C8
Upton Corn 8 D4
Upton Dorset 12 F5
Upton Dorset 13 E7
Upton Hants 14 C4
Upton Hants 25 D8
Upton Leics 63 E7
Upton Lincs 90 F2
Upton Mers 85 F3
Upton Norf 69 C6
Upton Northants 52 C5
Upton Notts 77 B7
Upton Notts 77 D7
Upton Oxon 39 F5
Upton Pboro 65 D8
Upton Slough 27 B7
Upton Som 10 B4
Upton W Yorks 89 C5
Upton Bishop Hereford 36 B3
Upton Cheyney S Glos 23 C8
Upton Cressett Shrops 61 E6
Upton Cross Corn 5 B7
Upton Grey Hants 26 E4
Upton Hellions Devon 10 D3
Upton Lovell Wilts 24 E4
Upton Magna Shrops 61 C5
Upton Noble Som 24 F2
Upton Pyne Devon 10 E4
Upton Scudamore Wilts 24 E3
Upton St Leonard's Glos 37 C5
Upton Snodsbury Worcs 50 D4
Upton upon Severn Worcs 50 E3
Upton Warren Worcs 50 C4
Upwaltham W Sus 16 C3
Upware Cambs 55 B6
Upwell Norf 66 D4
Upwey Dorset 12 F4
Upwood Cambs 66 F2
Uradale Shetland 160 K6
Urafirth Shetland 160 F5
Urchfont Wilts 24 D5
Urdimarsh Hereford 49 E7
Ure Shetland 160 F4
Ure Bank N Yorks 95 B6
Urgha W Isles 154 H6
Urishay Common Hereford 48 F5
Urlay Nook Stockton 102 C1
Urmston Gtr Man 87 E5
Urpeth Durham 110 D5
Urquhart Highld 151 F8
Urquhart Moray 152 B2
Urra N Yorks 102 D3
Urray Highld 151 F8
Ushaw Moor Durham 110 E5
Usk = Brynbuga Mon 35 D7
Usselby Lincs 90 E4
Usworth T&W 111 D6
Utkinton Ches W 74 C2
Utley W Yorks 94 E3
Uton Devon 10 E3
Utterby Lincs 91 E7
Uttoxeter Staffs 75 F7
Uwchmynydd Gwyn 70 E2
Uxbridge London 40 F3
Uyeasound Shetland 160 C7
Uzmaston Pembs 44 D4

V

Valley Anglesey 82 D2
Valley Truckle Corn 8 F2
Valleyfield Dumfries 106 D3
Valsgarth Shetland 160 B8
Valtos Highld 149 B10
Van Powys 59 F6
Vange Essex 42 F3
Varteg Torf 35 D6
Vatten Highld 149 D7
Vaul Argyll 146 G3
Vaynor M Tydf 34 C4
Veensgarth Shetland 160 J6
Velindre Powys 48 F3
Vellow Som 22 F2
Veness Orkney 159 F6
Venn Green Devon 9 C5
Venn Ottery Devon 11 E5
Vennington Shrops 60 D3
Venny Tedburn Devon 10 E3
Ventnor IoW 15 G6
Vernham Dean Hants 25 D8
Vernham Street Hants 25 D8
Vernolds Common Shrops 60 F4
Verwood Dorset 13 D8
Veryan Corn 3 C8
Vicarage Devon 11 F7
Vickerstown Cumb 92 C1
Victoria Corn 4 C4
Victoria S Yorks 88 D2
Vidlin Shetland 160 G6
Viewpark N Lanark 119 C7
Vigo Village Kent 29 C7
Vinehall Street E Sus 18 C4
Vine's Cross E Sus 18 D2
Viney Hill Glos 36 D3
Virginia Water Sur 27 C8
Virginstow Devon 9 E5
Vobster Som 24 E2
Voe Shetland 160 E5
Voe Shetland 160 G6
Vowchurch Hereford 49 F5
Voxter Shetland 160 F5
Voy Orkney 159 G3

W

Wackerfield Durham 101 B6
Wacton Norf 68 E4
Wadbister Shetland 160 J6
Wadborough Worcs 50 E4
Waddesdon Bucks 39 C7
Waddingham Lincs 90 E3
Waddington Lancs 93 E7
Waddington Lincs 78 C2
Wadebridge Corn 4 B4
Wadeford Som 11 C8
Wadenhoe Northants 65 F7
Wadesmill Herts 41 C6
Wadhurst E Sus 18 B3
Wadshelf Derbys 76 B3
Wadsley S Yorks 88 E4
Wadsley Bridge S Yorks 88 E4
Wadworth S Yorks 89 E6
Waen Denb 72 C3
Waen Denb 72 C5
Waen Fach Powys 60 C2
Waen Goleugoed Denb 72 B4
Wag Highld 157 G13
Wainfleet All Saints Lincs 79 D7
Wainfleet Bank Lincs 79 D7
Wainfleet St Mary Lincs 79 D8
Wainfleet Tofts Lincs 79 D7
Wainhouse Corner Corn 8 E3
Wainscott Medway 29 B8
Wainstalls W Yorks 87 B8
Waitby Cumb 100 D2
Waithe Lincs 91 D6
Wake Lady Green N Yorks 102 E4
Wakefield W Yorks 88 B4
Wakerley Northants 65 E6
Wakes Colne Essex 42 B4
Walberswick Suff 57 B8
Walberton W Sus 16 D3
Walbottle T&W 110 C4
Walcot Lincs 78 F3
Walcot N Lincs 90 B2
Walcot Shrops 60 F3
Walcot Swindon 38 F1
Walcot Telford 61 C5
Walcot Green Norf 68 F4
Walcote Leics 64 F2
Walcote Warks 51 D6
Walcott Lincs 78 D4
Walcott Norf 69 A6
Walden N Yorks 101 F5
Walden Head N Yorks 100 F4
Walden Stubbs N Yorks 89 C6
Waldersey Cambs 66 D4
Walderslade Medway 29 C8
Walderton W Sus 15 C8
Walditch Dorset 12 E2
Waldley Derbys 75 F8
Waldridge Durham 111 D5
Waldringfield Suff 57 E6
Waldringfield Heath Suff 57 E6
Waldron E Sus 18 D2
Wales S Yorks 89 F5
Walesby Lincs 90 E5
Walesby Notts 77 B6
Walford Hereford 36 B2
Walford Hereford 49 B5
Walford Shrops 60 B4

County and unitary authority boundaries

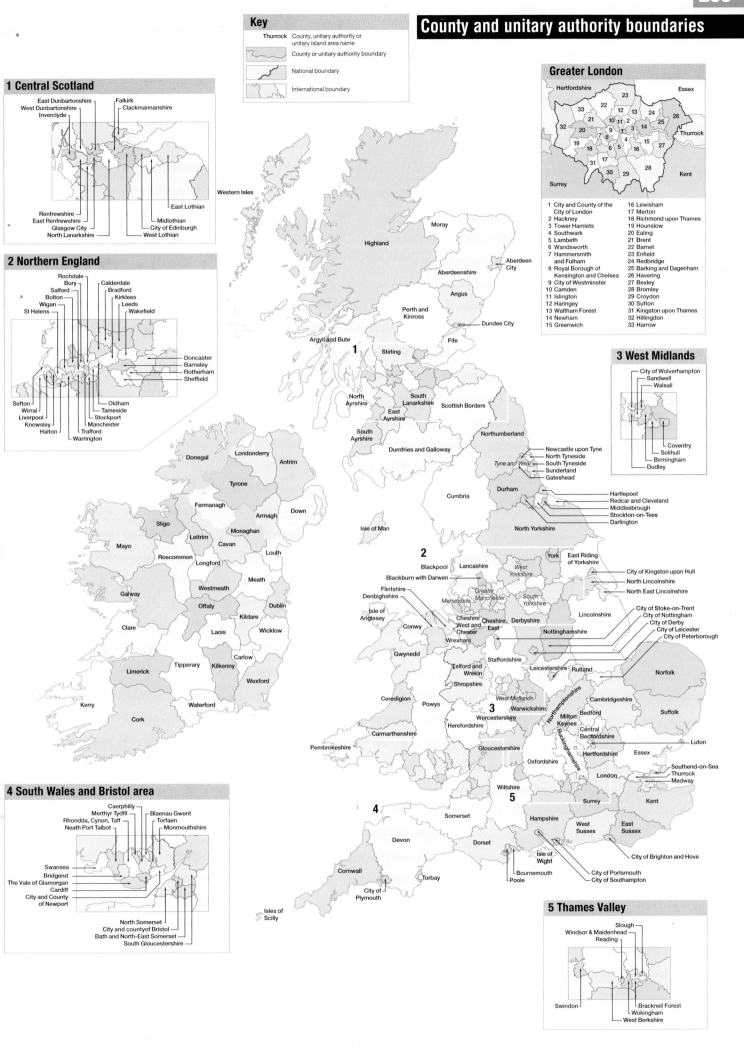

Key

Thurrock — County, unitary authority or unitary island area name

County or unitary authority boundary

National boundary

International boundary

1 Central Scotland

- East Dunbartonshire
- West Dunbartonshire
- Inverclyde
- Falkirk
- Clackmannanshire
- Renfrewshire
- East Renfrewshire
- Glasgow City
- North Lanarkshire
- East Lothian
- Midlothian
- City of Edinburgh
- West Lothian

2 Northern England

- Rochdale
- Bury
- Salford
- Bolton
- Wigan
- St Helens
- Calderdale
- Bradford
- Kirklees
- Leeds
- Wakefield
- Doncaster
- Barnsley
- Rotherham
- Sheffield
- Sefton
- Wirral
- Liverpool
- Knowsley
- Halton
- Oldham
- Tameside
- Stockport
- Manchester
- Trafford
- Warrington

3 West Midlands

- City of Wolverhampton
- Sandwell
- Walsall
- Coventry
- Solihull
- Birmingham
- Dudley

4 South Wales and Bristol area

- Caerphilly
- Merthyr Tydfil
- Rhondda, Cynon, Taff
- Neath Port Talbot
- Blaenau Gwent
- Torfaen
- Monmouthshire
- Swansea
- Bridgend
- The Vale of Glamorgan
- Cardiff
- City and County of Newport
- North Somerset
- City and county of Bristol
- Bath and North-East Somerset
- South Gloucestershire

Greater London

- Hertfordshire
- Essex
- Thurrock
- Surrey
- Kent

1 City and County of the City of London
2 Hackney
3 Tower Hamlets
4 Southwark
5 Lambeth
6 Wandsworth
7 Hammersmith and Fulham
8 Royal Borough of Kensington and Chelsea
9 City of Westminster
10 Camden
11 Islington
12 Haringey
13 Waltham Forest
14 Newham
15 Greenwich
16 Lewisham
17 Merton
18 Richmond upon Thames
19 Hounslow
20 Ealing
21 Brent
22 Barnet
23 Enfield
24 Redbridge
25 Barking and Dagenham
26 Havering
27 Bexley
28 Bromley
29 Croydon
30 Sutton
31 Kingston upon Thames
32 Hillingdon
33 Harrow

5 Thames Valley

- Slough
- Windsor & Maidenhead
- Reading
- Swindon
- Bracknell Forest
- Wokingham
- West Berkshire

Map labels

Western Isles

Highland
Moray
Aberdeenshire
Aberdeen City
Angus
Perth and Kinross
Dundee City
Argyll and Bute
Stirling
Fife
North Ayrshire
South Lanarkshire
East Ayrshire
Scottish Borders
South Ayrshire
Dumfries and Galloway
Northumberland

Newcastle upon Tyne
North Tyneside
South Tyneside
Sunderland
Gateshead
Tyne and Wear

Cumbria
Durham
Hartlepool
Redcar and Cleveland
Middlesbrough
Stockton-on-Tees
Darlington

Isle of Man
North Yorkshire

Donegal
Londonderry
Antrim
Tyrone
Fermanagh
Armagh
Down
Sligo
Monaghan
Leitrim
Cavan
Louth
Mayo
Roscommon
Longford
Westmeath
Meath
Galway
Offaly
Dublin
Kildare
Clare
Laois
Wicklow
Limerick
Tipperary
Carlow
Kilkenny
Wexford
Kerry
Waterford
Cork

Blackpool
Lancashire
York
East Riding of Yorkshire
Blackburn with Darwen
West Yorkshire
City of Kingston upon Hull
North Lincolnshire
North East Lincolnshire
Flintshire
Denbighshire
Greater Manchester
Merseyside
South Yorkshire
Isle of Anglesey
Conwy
Cheshire West and Chester
Cheshire East
Derbyshire
City of Stoke-on-Trent
City of Nottingham
City of Derby
City of Leicester
City of Peterborough
Wrexham
Nottinghamshire
Gwynedd
Staffordshire
Telford and Wrekin
Leicestershire
Rutland
Norfolk
Shropshire
Ceredigion
Powys
West Midlands
Warwickshire
Northamptonshire
Cambridgeshire
Worcestershire
Milton Keynes
Bedford
Suffolk
Herefordshire
Central Bedfordshire
Carmarthenshire
Buckinghamshire
Hertfordshire
Essex
Luton
Pembrokeshire
Gloucestershire
Oxfordshire
London
Southend-on-Sea
Thurrock
Medway
Wiltshire
Surrey
Kent
Somerset
Hampshire
West Sussex
East Sussex
Devon
Dorset
Isle of Wight
City of Brighton and Hove
Cornwall
Torbay
Bournemouth
Poole
City of Portsmouth
City of Southampton
City of Plymouth
Isles of Scilly